Australian taxation

SECOND EDITION

John Bevacqua

Stephen Marsden

Elizabeth Morton

Ken Devos

Annette Morgan

Luke Xu

Second edition published 2023 by
John Wiley & Sons Australia, Ltd
42 McDougall Street, Milton Qld 4064

Typeset in Times LT Std Roman 10/12pt

Wiley acknowledges the Traditional Custodians of the land on which we operate, live and gather as employees, and recognise their continuing connection to land, water and community. We pay respect to Elders past, present and emerging.

Creators
John Bevacqua (author), Stephen Marsden (author), Elizabeth Morton (author), Ken Devos (author), Annette Morgan (author), Luke Xu (author), Robert Whait (author)

Wiley
Mark Levings (Executive Publisher), Simone Bella (Product Manager), Kylie Challenor (Director, Content Management), Jess Carr (Manager, Higher Education Content Management), Rebecca Campbell (Senior Production Editor), Emily Brain (Production Editor), Laura Brinums (Publishing Coordinator), Liam Gallagher (Publishing Assistant), Ines Yap (Copyright & Image Research), Delia Sala (Cover Design)

Cover image: © Nico Soro / Getty Images

Typeset in India by diacriTech

Printed in Singapore
M120783_070622

BRIEF CONTENTS

CONTENTS

CHAPTER 4

Capital gains tax 103

CHAPTER 5

Fringe benefits tax 141

CHAPTER 9

Tax accounting and trading stock 307

Overview 308

CHAPTER 13

Goods and services tax   471

PREFACE

Wiley's *Australian Taxation* is the final instalment in Wiley's collection of texts for accounting majors. Most Australian taxation texts are written from a predominantly legalistic perspective, whereas *Australian Taxation* is written with accounting students in mind. The text is concise, to the point, easy to digest and applied rather than legalistic. *Australian Taxation* aims to demystify legal jargon and legal technicality without sacrificing essential core legal knowledge and meaning. Importantly, the text provides the requisite foundation for business students who intend to later undertake the professional programs of either the CPA Australia or the Chartered Accountants Australia and New Zealand (CA ANZ).

Australian Taxation second edition builds on the strengths of the first edition and has been fully updated to reflect the changes to the 2021–2022 tax rates (including changes to the March 2022 budget). New to this edition are stronger links to case law and an enhanced discussion of ethics with the inclusion of 'Ethics in practice' boxes. This edition will also expand its coverage of technology with the inclusion of 'Technology in action' boxes that focus on cryptocurrency/blockchain examples in every chapter. *Australian Taxation* second edition will also align to TPB standards to ensure that the content covers this accreditation.

This edition includes a list of cases and legislations, and a case map, where relevant links to legislation and case law will be included in the interactive eBook.

The interactive eBook for *Australian Taxation* is available via the code on the inside cover. The eBook features a range of instructional media, including brand new practitioner interview videos, animated worked problems, and questions with immediate feedback, to provide students with an engaging learning experience. This media can also form the basis of a blended learning solution for lecturers.

Special thanks to Donovan Castelyn, Curtin University, for his work preparing the PowerPoint slides and video development, to John Tretola, University of Notre Dame, for his work as technical editor on the project, to Lisa Greig, Principal Perigee Advisers Pty Ltd, and to Jeff Ham, Director, Mosaic Chartered Accountants, for sharing their knowledge, as well as sharing their time, to create the practitioner videos.

Executive summary — key changes in each chapter

Chapter	Key changes
Chapter 1 The Australian taxation system and the tax formula	• Tax administration content has been moved to chapter 14 • Includes an introductory discussion on ethics • Increased discussion of other organisations involved in the tax system of Australia
Chapter 2 Residency and source of income	• Addition of *Harding's* case, as well as cases regarding 183-day rule; working holiday/temporary/partial residency examples and details; the reform on residency • A significant rewrite to include the residency rule reforms • Increased number and depth of cases
Chapter 3 Assessable income/income tax	• Revised and expanded discussion on isolated and extraordinary transactions • Increased number and depth of cases • Increased depth of the compensation principles topic
Chapter 4 Capital gains tax	• Included more capital gains tax (CGT) events; new section on modification rules; increased depth on PUA, collectables, exemptions • Included a discussion of cryptocurrencies/cryptoassets • Addition of critical CGT advanced discussion and different cost bases, and included a brief mention of roll-over reliefs • Increased discussion of capital proceeds • Included greater discussions on CGT for SEB (e.g. SI and CS 80% test on shares etc.) • Included more on small business CGT rollover restructures • Expanded coverage of trust and CGT events • Inclusion of individual capital gains

(continued)

Chapter	Key changes
Chapter 5 Fringe benefits tax	• A deeper dive into the definition of a fringe benefit • Greater analysis on the interrelationship between FBT, income tax and GST • More examples illustrating the calculation of fringe benefits • Greater discussion on the most common exempt fringe benefits • Extracts of the FBT return included • More detail on effective salary sacrifice arrangements • Further detail/examples when/why salary sacrifice arrangement is beneficial to the employer and when it would not be (e.g. tax rate, cost to employer, exempt versus non-exempt/concessional treated benefits)
Chapter 6 General deductions	• Expansion of cases with respect to various categories of expenses • Additional discussion of specific expense categories
Chapter 7 Specific deductions and applications of deductibility	• Updated regarding cents per km rate change • Addition of listing of guidance with respect to TR 2020/1 • Expansion of cases with respect to various categories of expenses • Expansion of considerations specific to COVID-19
Chapter 8 Capital allowances	• Increased discussion where an asset is partly used for business and private purposes, bringing in CGT event K7 • Increased depth of detail of a depreciable asset, with greater clarity and examples on the difference between Division 40 and Division 43 • Updated full temporary expensing rules • Included more extracts from tax returns showing the depreciation labels • Updated on the tax bill proposing certain intangible assets to be self-assessed
Chapter 9 Tax accounting and trading stock	• Included cases on what constitutes 'on hand' for trading stock • Increased depth of (and examples of) stock lost or destroyed, ceasing or becoming trading stock, non-arm's length etc. • Expanded detail on the latest Taxation Determination relating to stock taken for personal consumption
Chapter 10 Taxation of individuals	• Addition of an example on withholding tax • Expanded content on taxing and crowd funding • Expanded treatment of franchising • Updated discussion of ETP for employees
Chapter 11 Taxation of companies	• Addition of BRE concept/company tax rates • Inclusion of company losses • Increased discussion of loss carry back
Chapter 12 Taxation of partnerships, joint ventures, trusts and superannuation entities	• Inclusion of examples for whether a partnership exists/does not exist • Addition of superannuation and termination payments • Addition of a discussion of SBE concessions and treats for SBE turnovers, SBE discount • Inclusion of a discussion of minors • Inclusion of a discussion of Subdivision 7E for trusts, looking at asset protection, income and CGT minimisation, and ease of administration • Inclusion of superannuation discussion
Chapter 13 Goods and services tax	• Updated statistics on GST collections • Increased content on some of the GST-free and input taxed supplies • Inclusion of more diagrams showing the four supplies: taxable, GST-free, input taxed and out-of-scope • Inclusion of extracts from a BAS showing how the labels reflect the GST calculations • Inclusion of a sample BAS in the appendix • Inclusion of a section on GST anti-avoidance • Inclusion of important GST cases

Chapter 14 Tax administration, tax avoidance and tax evasion	• Inclusion of tax administration discussion and expanded with more detail • More detail added to the outline of TASA code of conduct • Increased number and depth of cases • Inclusion of a discussion of cryptocurrencies • Expanded the discussion on technology • Inclusion of ethical and legal consequences of tax evasion and avoidance for tax practitioners • Inclusion of income tax returns • Inclusion of assessment, payment and recovery methods, objections and appeals • Inclusion of role and powers of Australian Taxation Office • Addition of penalties and ATO rulings

ABOUT THE AUTHORS

John Bevacqua

Dr John Bevacqua, lLB, BCom, PhD, is a Senior Lecturer in the Department of Business Law and Taxation at Monash University. His prior roles include positions as Academic Director of La Trobe Online and Director of Teaching and Learning for the School of Law at La Trobe University. During these roles, John has developed a significant expertise in developing innovative and engaging curriculum for business students studying law subjects. During his academic career, he has been responsible for business law and taxation-related curriculum development, quality assurance and delivery at both undergraduate and postgraduate levels. John is an active researcher in tax administration and taxpayer rights, and is published regularly in leading Australian and international tax journals. John is also a qualified lawyer admitted to practice in multiple jurisdictions and had a ten-year career as a commercial and tax lawyer, working at top tier commercial law firms prior to becoming a full-time academic.

Stephen Marsden

Stephen Marsden is a full-time lecturer employed in the Business School at the Queensland University of Technology (QUT), Brisbane. In this role, he is responsible for lecturing and tutoring a wide range of undergraduate and postgraduate financial accounting and taxation law subjects. Prior to that, he worked at KPMG for eight years in their business advisory and management consultancy divisions. Stephen has a Master of Business (Accountancy) and is a member of the Chartered Accountants Australia and New Zealand, CPA Australia, the Australian Institute of Company Directors and the National Tax and Accountants Association. He is also a Chartered Tax Advisor of the Taxation Institute of Australia. Stephen has presented numerous professional development seminars and workshops over the past 30 years in the areas of financial accounting, taxation, GST and FBT for a range of professional associations, accounting firms, listed companies, non-profit organisations and government departments. Stephen is also a registered tax agent, where he provides tax advice and attends to the taxation affairs of a variety of clients in the public and private sectors.

Elizabeth Morton

Dr Elizabeth Morton, BCom (Hons), PhD, FTI, CA, is the coordinator and lecturer of the undergraduate taxation course in the School of Accounting, Information Systems and Supply Chain at RMIT University, as well as being seconded to the RMIT Blockchain Innovation Hub as Research Fellow. During her academic career, Elizabeth has taught across the commerce discipline, and has been involved in the development of undergraduate courses and online learning resources, including the production of a tax podcast series. Her research is currently underpinned by three core themes: tax compliance, crypto-related activities and practitioner competencies. Elizabeth regularly publishes in peer-reviewed academic and professional tax journals and engages with industry through discussion groups, policy submissions, articles, blogs, seminars, podcasts, and more. Previous to academia, Elizabeth worked as an accountant in small business taxation in regional Victoria. Her professional experience includes various aspects of accounting and taxation services for all entity types, including matters in relation to capital gains tax and investments, GST and FBT compliance, as well as superannuation.

Ken Devos

Dr Ken Devos, BBus, Grad Dip Tax, MTax, PhD, CPA, is an Associate Professor of Accounting/Tax at Swinburne Business School. Ken is the Unit Chair in Tax and teaches in both undergraduate and graduate tax courses. He has conducted tax training courses for the Australian Taxation Office, CPA Australia and accounting firms, and is a co-author of the CPA Tax Program. Ken has also published several books and articles (both national and international) and presented numerous conference papers on taxation issues. Ken's particular research areas include taxpayer compliance, administration, evasion and tax policy. His doctorate, 'Factors influencing individual taxpayer compliance behaviour', was supported by funding from Taxpayers Australia and was published by *Springer* in 2014. Ken is also a member of the Australasian Tax Teachers Association, is represented on the editorial board for *The New Zealand Journal of Taxation Law and Policy* and is the Australian correspondent for the *International Tax Law Review*.

Annette Morgan

Annette is an experienced lecturer and Clinical Professional at Curtin University, is the Course Lead of Taxation within the Curtin Law School, and is the Director of her own SME accounting practice in Perth. Her substantial practical experience is supported by qualifications in commerce, accounting and taxation, including a Master of Taxation. Professional accreditations include being a Certified Practising Accountant (FCPA) and a Chartered Tax Adviser (CTA). Annette's principal clinical activities are centred around the Curtin Tax Clinic (CTC). As co-founder, Clinic Director, and the registered Tax Agent, she is directly responsible for the continued performance of the CTC as both an educational tool and niche tax practice. This is supplemented by her role as the Study Tour Director for the successful national and international tax study tours operating at Curtin University. Annette is a current State Councillor of the WA Taxation Institute and the Chair of the Women in Tax in WA. Annette is also a member of the Legal Costs Committee of WA appointed by the WA Government in 2022.

HOW TO USE THIS TEXT

The structure of *Australian Taxation* is aligned to the typical taxation course taught in Australian universities. Each chapter features the following.

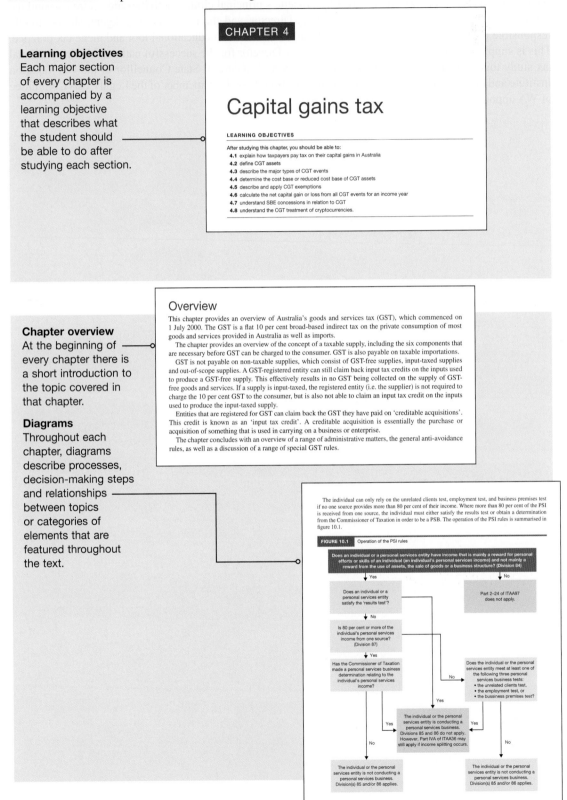

Learning objectives
Each major section of every chapter is accompanied by a learning objective that describes what the student should be able to do after studying each section.

CHAPTER 4

Capital gains tax

LEARNING OBJECTIVES

After studying this chapter, you should be able to:
- **4.1** explain how taxpayers pay tax on their capital gains in Australia
- **4.2** define CGT assets
- **4.3** describe the major types of CGT events
- **4.4** determine the cost base or reduced cost base of CGT assets
- **4.5** describe and apply CGT exemptions
- **4.6** calculate the net capital gain or loss from all CGT events for an income year
- **4.7** understand SBE concessions in relation to CGT
- **4.8** understand the CGT treatment of cryptocurrencies.

Chapter overview
At the beginning of every chapter there is a short introduction to the topic covered in that chapter.

Diagrams
Throughout each chapter, diagrams describe processes, decision-making steps and relationships between topics or categories of elements that are featured throughout the text.

Overview

This chapter provides an overview of Australia's goods and services tax (GST), which commenced on 1 July 2000. The GST is a flat 10 per cent broad-based indirect tax on the private consumption of most goods and services provided in Australia as well as imports.

The chapter provides an overview of the concept of a taxable supply, including the six components that are necessary before GST can be charged to the consumer. GST is also payable on taxable importations.

GST is not payable on non-taxable supplies, which consist of GST-free supplies, input-taxed supplies and out-of-scope supplies. A GST-registered entity can still claim back input tax credits on the inputs used to produce a GST-free supply. This effectively results in no GST being collected on the supply of GST-free goods and services. If a supply is input-taxed, the registered entity (i.e. the supplier) is not required to charge the 10 per cent GST to the consumer, but is also not able to claim an input tax credit on the inputs used to produce the input-taxed supply.

Entities that are registered for GST can claim back the GST they have paid on 'creditable acquisitions'. This credit is known as an 'input tax credit'. A creditable acquisition is essentially the purchase or acquisition of something that is used in carrying on a business or enterprise.

The chapter concludes with an overview of a range of administrative matters, the general anti-avoidance rules, as well as a discussion of a range of special GST rules.

The individual can only rely on the unrelated clients test, employment test, and business premises test if no one source provides more than 80 per cent of their income. Where more than 80 per cent of the PSI is received from one source, the individual must either satisfy the results test or obtain a determination from the Commissioner of Taxation in order to be a PSB. The operation of the PSI rules is summarised in figure 10.1.

FIGURE 10.1 Operation of the PSI rules

Examples

Conceptual and mathematical examples of the application of taxation law and principles appear throughout each chapter.

EXAMPLE 4.18

Main residence exemption

In January 2003, Mark acquired a house in Sydney and lived in it immediately. He rented it out in May 2006 because he was transferred overseas for a business project until April 2010 (4 years of absence). Mark then moved back into this house upon his return to Sydney in 2010. In 2015, he was again posted overseas for another project for 4 years and he rented the house out again during this period. When he returned in 2021, Mark sold the house. During this whole period from 2003 to 2021, Mark did not have any other main residence.

What is the CGT treatment of the sale of the house?

In this case, Mark is entitled to the full main residence exemption and the capital gain that he earned from this transaction is fully disregarded because each of his absences was shorter than 6 years.

EXAMPLE 4.19

Partial main residence exemption

In August 2009, Tanya bought a 5-bedroom house to live in. She rented it out in August 2012 as she got a job in another city. The house was sold in August 2021 and Tanya made a capital gain of $12 000. In this case, Tanya's total ownership period includes 12 years from August 2009 to August 2021. During this period, she rented the house out for 9 years from August 2012 to August 2021.

What is the CGT treatment of the sale?

According to section 118-145, Tanya can choose to treat this house as her main residence for the first 6 years in the total rental period of 9 years, for which she receives the partial main residence exemption. Therefore, Tanya is considered to have made a capital gain for the 3 years when the house is not her main residence and the calculation is as follows.[35]

$$\text{Capital gain} = \$12\,000 \times \frac{365 \times 3}{365 \times 12}$$
$$= \$3000$$

Ethics in practice

Feature boxes in each chapter use the tacit code of conduct as a guide to address practical scenarios, highlighting elements of the code.

ETHICS IN PRACTICE

Possible manipulation of the GST system

In advising your client Francesco with regards to the tax implications on purchasing the table, you note that he is not forthcoming with any additional information. In trying to provide creditable evidence to support the reason behind the purchase, Francesco insists that the table was for his own private use. Francesco is very pleased with the outcome in that he obtained the best resale value for the table once its true value was realised. However, you have your doubts and want to establish Francesco's true motives.

What would be your reaction in solving this ethical dilemma? Consider the following options.

(a) You would direct Francesco to the matters the Commissioner will consider under section 165-15 and gather that information.

(b) As Francesco has a very sound argument, and due to your time pressures, you are prepared to take his word.

(c) You would be able to charge Francesco an additional fee if you were to accept his position.

(d) You can advise Francesco of the possible outcomes of accepting his position and ifincorrect, the possible tax and penalties that may apply.

Technology in action

Feature boxes in each chapter highlight how technology is being used in taxation law, with a focus on crytpocurrency and blockchain examples.

TECHNOLOGY IN ACTION

Cryptoactivities, CGT complexities and tax reform

According to the Final Report of the Australia as a Technology and Financial Centre Committee (hereafter the 'Bragg Report'),[52] there are as many as 25 per cent of Australians who have held (whether currently or previously) cryptoassets. Cryptoassets are not limited to Bitcoin or other more traditional forms of cryptocurrencies. In recent years, there has been an explosion of activity in what is described as the 'metaverse'. For example, non-fungible tokens (NFTs) can represent anything from artwork, gaming or other unique property, or bundles of rights. Unlike Bitcoin, each NFT is unique and, through scarcity and verifiability, they yield intrinsic value, like that of a piece of artwork.[53]

Where taxpayers hold cryptoassets for investment purposes, cryptoassets are considered CGT assets and their disposals as CGT events.[54] Tax practitioners need to appreciate what crypto-related activities their clients may have undertaken to appropriately determine whether the specific categories of CGT asset apply (personal use asset or collectable) and therefore any relevant special rules or exemptions. Many taxpayers have been perhaps disappointed to learn that the $10 000 threshold for personal use assets will not apply unless, for example, they have acquired Bitcoin to simply buy a pizza! In contrast, could an NFT that represents a digital piece of artwork meet the definition of a collectable?[55]

Determining a taxpayer's CGT consequences can become challenging due to a number of factors, including the frequency in which a taxpayer can transact, the varying characterisation of activities possible, as well as the types of arrangements entered into that can lead to a multitude of CGT events. For example, to acquire a CGT asset such as an NFT, the taxpayer generally needs another cryptoasset to do so (e.g. ETH on the Ethereum blockchain). The acquisition of the NFT triggers a disposal of the ETH, as ETH is not money or currency. Taxpayers may be operating layers and layers away from dollars and never 'cash in'. Due to this use of cryptoassets as a means of payment, this invokes the principles of barter transactions,[56] requiring market values to be used[56] (which can be challenging to determine for many cryptoassets). Third-party tax crypto-calculators can assist both taxpayers and tax practitioners.[57]

The Committee agreed that the number of taxable events (i.e. CGT events A1) created by blockchain protocols is problematic and not all should result in taxable events.[58] In response to the growing challenges faced within the crypto-economy and its metaverse, the Bragg Report recommended that the CGT regime be amended to ensure that digital asset transactions only create a CGT event when they 'genuinely result in a clearly definable capital gain or loss'.[59] This could be achieved via a new kind of CGT asset or new kind of CGT event.[60] The Report also highlighted the need for Treasury and the ATO to be proactive and keep pace with the developments in this space.[61]

··

REFLECTION

What progress has been made, if any, on reforming the CGT regime with respect to digital asset transactions? If none, what do you think a possible CGT event or CGT asset category could look like for cryptoassets to balance simplicity for taxpayers whilst ensuring government objectives are met?

Case law summaries
Brief case law summaries are included throughout the text. Each summary has been structured to present the facts and the decision of each case, as well as provide an explanation and commentary about the case.

Chapter summaries
At the end of each chapter there is a summary, where each learning objective is concisely summarised.

End-of-chapter questions
There are ten short answer questions and five applied problems at the end of each chapter. The short answer questions test basic recall and students' understanding of key concepts. The applied problems require students to make decisions based on a scenario.

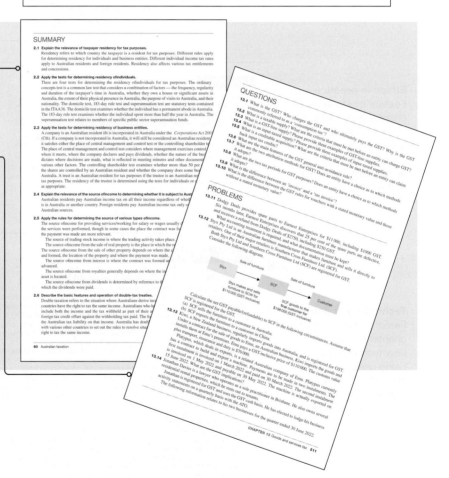

Herald and Weekly Times Ltd v FCT (1932) 48 CLR 113

Facts: The publisher of a newspaper claimed a deduction for damages paid arising from defamatory matter it had published. The Commissioner denied the deduction on the basis that the expenditure was not wholly and exclusively incurred in producing assessable income.
Held: The deduction was allowed pursuant to the former section 51(1) of the ITAA36.
Comment: The Court concluded that there was a sufficient nexus between the expenditure and the production of assessable income. As per Gavan Duffy CJ and Dixon J:

> None of the libels or supposed libels was published with any other object in view than the sale of the newspaper. The liability to damages was incurred, or the claim was encountered, because of the very act of publishing the newspaper. The thing which produced the assessable income was the thing which exposed the taxpayer to the liability or claim discharged by the expenditure. It is true that when the sums were paid the taxpayer was actuated in paying them, not by any desire to produce income, but, in the case of damages or compensation, by the necessity of satisfying a claim or liability to which it had become subject, and, in the case of law costs, by the desirability or urgency of defeating or diminishing such a claim. But this expenditure flows as a necessary or a natural consequence from the inclusion of the alleged defamatory matter in the newspaper and its publication. Expenditure in which the taxpayer is repeatedly or recurrently involved in an enterprise or exertion undertaken in order to gain assessable income cannot be excluded … simply because the obligation to make it is an unintended consequence which the taxpayer desired to avoid. No point is made of the fact that the publication took place in a former year, and properly so. The continuity of the enterprise requires that the expenditure should be attributed to the year in which it was actually defrayed.[17]

CASES

The Australian taxation system and the tax formula

LEARNING OBJECTIVES

After studying this chapter, you should be able to:

1.1 describe the basic legal structure of the Australian tax system

1.2 explain the key sources of Australian tax law

1.3 describe the key ethical responsibilities of tax professionals

1.4 describe different types of taxes

1.5 describe different types of taxpayers

1.6 explain the fundamental income tax formula for calculating income tax liability.

Overview

This chapter introduces the basic structure of Australia's taxation system. The discussion will include an outline of the background and purpose of the Australian taxation system and describe the sources of tax law. Key bodies involved in Australia's tax system and its administration are also introduced, together with an introduction to the ethical responsibilities of tax practitioners.

The chapter will also set the foundation for the chapters that follow by introducing the main types of Australian taxes, different types of taxpayers and the fundamental income tax formula which underpins income tax liability calculations.

1.1 The Australian taxation system

LEARNING OBJECTIVE 1.1 Describe the basic legal structure of the Australian tax system.

The Australian tax system is complex. When Commonwealth, State and Local government taxes are taken into account, Australia has well in excess of 100 different taxes. Table 1.1 shows the revenue collected from various Commonwealth, State and Local government taxes and gives a sense of the breadth and quantum of taxes collected in Australia.

TABLE 1.1 Total tax revenue by level of government and category

	2014–15 $m	2015–16 $m	2016–17 $m	2017–18 $m	2018–19 $m	2019–20 $m
Commonwealth Government						
Taxes on income	258 610	265 116	281 157	312 474	338 667	328 580
Employers' payroll taxes	735	670	605	1 107	1 069	1 034
Taxes on property	—	—	—	—	—	—
Taxes on provision of goods and services	92 225	97 181	99 913	104 965	107 114	109 149
Taxes on use of goods and performance of activities	3 661	6 289	6 900	8 898	8 922	8 845
Total taxation revenue	**355 232**	**369 257**	**388 576**	**427 444**	**455 773**	**447 608**
State Government						
Taxes on income	—	—	—	—	—	—
Employers' payroll taxes	22 041	22 684	23 194	24 413	25 854	24 993
Taxes on property	9 283	10 029	11 346	12 222	13 790	14 225
Taxes on provision of goods and services	31 625	34 416	35 373	35 055	33 896	33 176
Taxes on use of goods and performance of activities	10 824	11 523	11 875	12 570	12 873	13 566
Total taxation revenue	**73 773**	**78 652**	**81 787**	**84 260**	**86 414**	**85 960**
Local Government						
Taxes on income	—	—	—	—	—	—
Employers' payroll taxes	—	—	—	—	—	—
Taxes on property	15 779	16 620	17 399	18 083	18 904	19 578
Taxes on provision of goods and services	—	—	—	—	—	—

Taxes on use of goods and performance of activities	–	–	–	–	–	–
Total taxation revenue	**15 779**	**16 620**	**17 399**	**18 083**	**18 904**	**19 578**
All levels of government						
Taxes on income	258 605	265 111	281 140	312 474	338 656	328 570
Employers' payroll taxes	22 032	22 590	23 003	24 680	26 034	25 105
Taxes on property	25 016	26 602	28 693	30 249	32 632	33 743
Taxes on provision of goods and services	123 850	131 596	135 286	140 020	141 007	142 324
Taxes on use of goods and performance of activities	14 420	17 736	18 666	21 332	21 677	22 291
Total taxation revenue	**443 923**	**463 635**	**486 788**	**528 755**	**560 006**	**552 033**

Source: Australian Bureau of Statistics, *Taxation Revenue, Australia, 2019–20* (Catalogue no 5506.0, 27 April 2021) www.abs.gov.au/ausstats/abs@.nsf/mf/5506.0.

The four main Commonwealth Government taxes are:
- **income tax**
- **capital gains tax (CGT)**
- **fringe benefits tax (FBT)**
- **goods and services tax (GST)**.

It is important to recognise, however, that there are many other Commonwealth Government taxes including customs duties, fuel excises and resource taxes and that these other taxes may be relevant to the individual circumstances of a taxpayer. Figure 1.1 shows the contribution of the various Commonwealth Government taxes to the total Commonwealth Government revenue. There are also many State and Territory taxes that apply to taxpayers depending on their circumstances. These include various stamp duties, payroll taxes, motor vehicle taxes, gambling taxes and land taxes.

There are a number of different regulatory and professional bodies engaged in various aspects of administering the taxation system and regulating tax professionals. The **Commissioner of Taxation** is the official with the primary tax administration and Federal revenue collection powers and responsibilities. The Commissioner oversees the **Australian Taxation Office (ATO)** to exercise these powers and responsibilities on his or her behalf.[1] The tax administration system and the ATO are overseen by the independent Office of the Inspector-General of Taxation and Taxation Ombudsman (IGTO).[2] We discuss the powers and responsibilities of the ATO and the function of IGTO in some detail in a later chapter on tax administration; however, a brief introduction to both (along with the other key bodies involved in aspects of our tax system) follows. The ATO website states the following.

> Our role is to effectively manage and shape the tax and superannuation systems that support and fund services for Australians, including:
> - collecting revenue
> - administering the goods and services tax (GST) on behalf of the Australian states and territories
> - administering a range of programs that provide transfers and benefits to the community
> - administering the major aspects of Australia's superannuation system
> - being custodian of the Australian Business Register.[3]

A good source of information about the ATO are the Annual Reports prepared by the Commissioner and presented to Parliament. The ATO also publishes tax statistics which provide a range of useful information.[4]

---

1 References to the Commissioner of Taxation and the ATO are interchangeable.
2 The link to the Inspector-General of Taxation website is at: www.igt.gov.au.
3 Australian Taxation Office, *Who we are* (Web Page, 2019) www.ato.gov.au/about-ato/who-we-are.
4 The Annual Reports and tax statistics are available from the ATO website: www.ato.gov.au.

FIGURE 1.1   Commonwealth government tax revenue (2021–22)

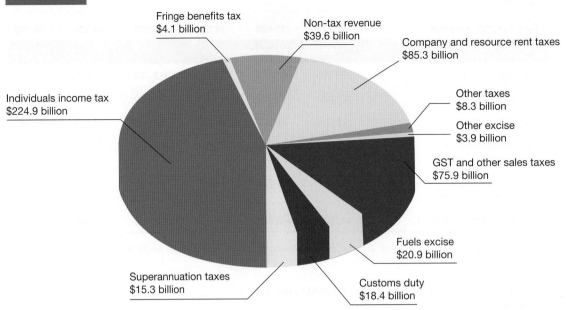

Source: Australian Government, *Budget 2021–22* (Appendix B: Revenue and spending, 2021) https://budget.gov.au/2021-22/content/overview.htm#three.

Familiarity with the ATO website is important, both in your studies and in your careers, as tax professionals and as taxpayers. The site divides information into categories for individuals, businesses, not-for-profit organisations, tax advisers and those seeking information about superannuation.

The site also serves as a portal for online services and, given the ATO has committed itself to a 'digital by default' approach to interacting with taxpayers, these online services are increasingly becoming the primary avenue for tax information and ATO service provision. These are discussed further in a later section.

The ATO website hosts a range of tax forms and background information sheets that can be quite helpful in providing a basic understanding of various tax laws. There are also a number of calculators. These can assist in providing estimates of tax liability or the applicability of various tax provisions.[5]

The ATO website is also an invaluable resource for finding tax law. It has a legal database which contains relevant Australian and international tax cases, legislation, and ATO rulings and determinations as well as information containing the ATO official interpretation and stance on the full gamut of controversial and complex tax matters.[6] It is advisable to become familiar with how to use the ATO legal database.

The **Inspector-General of Taxation (IGTO)** is an independent officer appointed by the Commonwealth Governor-General. The services of the IGTO are free for taxpayers and the IGTO makes recommendations to the ATO following its investigations or reviews. These recommendations are not binding on the Commissioner of Taxation but will usually be followed. Figure 1.2 provides an overview of the IGTO's functions.

The Board of Taxation is another body involved in our tax system. The Board is a non-statutory advisory body charged with contributing a business and broader community perspective to improve the design of taxation laws and their operation.[7] Among the activities of the Board is the task of reviewing and reporting on specific issues if requested by the Federal Treasurer and providing other tax policy advice to the government on various tax, economic and budgetary initiatives. A good example of the work of the Board is in the next chapter, where we consider the recommended changes to Australia's tax residency rules resulting from a self-initiated review of those rules by the Board. The Board of Taxation also administers a collaborative space, 'Sounding Board', which allows users to submit and prioritise ideas to improve the tax system. Further information can be found at Sounding Board.

---

5 The link to the ATO's simple income tax calculator is at: www.ato.gov.au/calculators-and-tools/simple-tax-calculator.
6 The link to the ATO Legal Database portal is at: www.ato.gov.au/Law/#Law.
7 The website for the Board of Taxation is at: https://taxboard.gov.au.

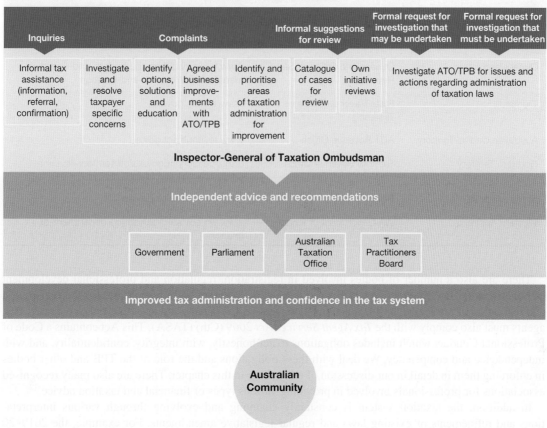

FIGURE 1.2 Overview of the Inspector-General of Taxation

Overview of the IGTO's function

Inquiries		Complaints			Informal suggestions for review		Formal request for investigation that may be undertaken	Formal request for investigation that must be undertaken
Informal tax assistance (information, referral, confirmation)	Investigate and resolve taxpayer specific concerns	Identify options, solutions and education	Agreed business improvements with ATO/TPB	Identify and prioritise areas of taxation administration for improvement	Catalogue of cases for review	Own initiative reviews	Investigate ATO/TPB for issues and actions regarding administration of taxation laws	

Inspector-General of Taxation Ombudsman

Independent advice and recommendations

Government	Parliament	Australian Taxation Office	Tax Practitioners Board

Improved tax administration and confidence in the tax system

Australian Community

Source: Australian Government, *Inspector-General of Taxation* (Web Page, as at 2022) www.igt.gov.au/about-us.

The Australian Government Treasury also plays a significant role in our tax system. The Treasury describes its role on its website as follows.

> It is the role of the Treasury to provide advice on effective tax and retirement income arrangements that contribute to the overall fiscal outcome, influence strong sustainable economic growth for the good of the Australian people. The Treasury is responsible for assessing and advising on the general design of the tax system and its components, and retirement income policy, in relation to economic efficiency, equity, income distribution, budgetary requirements and economic feasibility.[8]

It is good practice to be familiar with various initiatives being considered by Treasury. For example, at the time of writing, Treasury is seeking consultation on a proposal to extend the powers of the Administrative Appeals Tribunal to pause or modify ATO debt recovery actions against taxpayers. Tax advisers need to be aware of such proposals when advising their clients as to their rights and obligations.

The Australian National Audit Office (ANAO) has a long-standing role in auditing the performance of the ATO in carrying out its duties. Its performance audits have focused on identifying areas where the ATO could improve its own performance within the existing environment. Further information about the role and current activities of the ANAO insofar as taxation is concerned is available on their website.[9] The ANAO will focus its work program on key aspects of tax administration. For example, one of the 2020–21 initiatives is to examine the ATO's data governance practices. This is especially significant given the increasing use of technology by the ATO to carry out its duties.[10]

The State regulators include State-based revenue authorities, which are listed in table 1.2. In some States, this function forms part of the relevant Finance or Treasury Department.

---

8 The website for the Australian Government Treasury is at: https://treasury.gov.au/policy-topics/taxation.

9 The website for the ANAO is at: https://www.anao.gov.au.

10 For more information on this review, see: https://www.anao.gov.au/work/performance-audit/data-governance-the-australian-taxation-office.

TABLE 1.2 State and Territory revenue authorities

State	Authority	Website
Victoria	State Revenue Office Victoria	www.sro.vic.gov.au
New South Wales	Revenue NSW	www.revenue.nsw.gov.au
Queensland	Queensland Office of State Revenue	www.treasury.qld.gov.au/budget-and-financial-management/revenue-and-taxation
Tasmania	State Revenue Office of Tasmania	www.sro.tas.gov.au
Australian Capital Territory	ACT Revenue Office	www.revenue.act.gov.au
Northern Territory	Territory Revenue Office	http://treasury.nt.gov.au/dtf/territory-revenue-office
South Australia	Revenue SA	www.revenuesa.sa.gov.au
Western Australia	WA Department of Finance	www.wa.gov.au/organisation/department-of-finance

There are also a number of bodies involved in registration, regulation and professional development of tax advisers. The Tax Practitioners Board (TPB) is the national body responsible for the registration and regulation of tax agents, business activity statement (BAS), agents and tax (financial) advisers.[11] Tax agents must also comply with the *Tax Agent Services Act 2009* (Cth) (TASA). This Act contains a Code of Professional Conduct which includes obligations to act honestly, with integrity, confidentiality, and with independence and competency. We deal with these obligations and the role of the TPB and other bodies in enforcing them in detail in our discussion of ethics later in this chapter. There are also many recognised associations for professionals involved in providing various types of financial and taxation advice.[12]

In addition, the taxation system is constantly changing and evolving through various interpretations and refinements of existing laws and regular legislative amendments. For example, the 2019–20 Commonwealth Budget alone contained 28 separate measures involving various changes to the tax and superannuation system.

To stay abreast of these amendments, a good practice is to refer to the Tax Practitioners Board updates.[13] As a tax professional, it is vital to keep up-to-date with changes such as these and it is useful when studying tax to understand the ever-changing nature of tax law.

When tax laws are introduced into Parliament, they are accompanied by an Explanatory Memorandum. The Explanatory Memorandum usually sets out the background and purpose of the proposed tax law. Explanatory Memoranda are an excellent source for understanding both the intent and purpose of a tax and the intended meaning of particular tax provisions.[14]

1.1.1 Purposes of taxes

Different taxes have different purposes. For example, customs and excises, when originally introduced, were aimed at addressing 'sins' or vices such as smoking and alcohol consumption. To some extent, the large excise duties which continue to be imposed on cigarettes and alcohol retain this social goal of discouraging use of these harmful products.

Specific-purpose taxes aside, the goals of taxation are generally to fund the important functions of government. For example, taxes are used to fund governmental welfare programs, to fund the military and protection of our national borders, to establish and fund important regulators such as environmental authorities, and to fund important community services such as State schools and hospitals, and the criminal justice system. Figure 1.3 shows the projected distribution of Commonwealth Government taxes in the 2021–22 financial year.

---

11 Tax Practitioners Board, 'Overview' (Web Page, 31 March 2022) www.tpb.gov.au/tpb-overview.

12 For a comprehensive list of these, see: www.tpb.gov.au/recognised-professional-associations.

13 Tax Practitioners Board, 'Latest news on tax law and policy' (Web Page, 31 March 2022) www.ato.gov.au/general/new-legislation/latest-news-on-tax-law-and-policy.

14 The link to the Explanatory Memoranda is at: http://classic.austlii.edu.au/au/legis/cth/bill_em.

FIGURE 1.3 Distribution of Commonwealth Government taxes

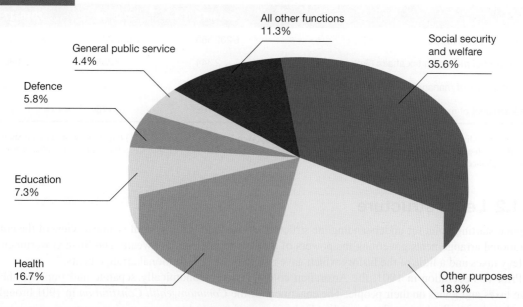

Source: Australian Government, *Budget 2021–22* (Appendix B: Revenue and spending, 27 April 2021) www.budget.gov.au/2021-22/content/overview.htm.

Taxes and their administration can have significant effects on economic activity, such as business investment and consumer spending. Hence, tax laws are an important tool for economic policy. Taxes also play an important social policy role. For example, taxes play an important role in equitably redistributing income and reducing social inequality, as well as funding aid for those in need.

Similarly, the system of tax administration is designed according to a number of features to ensure taxes do not impose unintended or unacceptable burdens. Celebrated economist Adam Smith set out four core features ('canons') of a well-designed tax system in his seminal economic text — *An Inquiry into the Nature and Causes of the Wealth of Nations* — in 1776: equality, certainty, convenience and economy.[15]

Equality is essentially the idea that taxes should be imposed relative to an individual's capacity to pay. **Certainty** was described by Adam Smith in the following terms.

> The tax which each individual is bound to pay ought to be certain, and not arbitrary. The time of payment, the manner of payment, the quantity to be paid ought all to be clear and plain to the contributor, and to every other person.[16]

Convenience is the idea that a tax should only be imposed at a time and in a manner which minimises inconvenience. According to Smith, **economy** means:

> Every tax ought to be so contrived as both to take out and keep out of the pockets of the people as little as possible over and above what it brings into the public treasury of the state.[17]

Building upon these four basic canons, significant modern-day attention is paid to the aim of ensuring taxes do not impose any unnecessary compliance costs. In large part, this and the other fundamental canons of a desirable tax system have driven a significant recent focus on tax simplification and the elimination of tax complexity. In terms of complexity, a 2016 Treasury White Paper found that:

> The complexity of the Australian tax system reduces integrity and transparency, and imposes unnecessary compliance costs on taxpayers, as well as other costs on the Australian economy.[18]

The ATO publishes tax compliance cost data in its Annual Statistics publications. Table 1.3 presents the latest available data at the time of writing.

---

15 Adam Smith, *An Inquiry into the Nature and Causes of the Wealth of Nations* (1776) 825.
16 Ibid.
17 Ibid 826.
18 The link to the White Paper is at: https://treasury.gov.au/review/tax-white-paper/at-a-glance.

TABLE 1.3 Cost of managing tax affairs — individuals

	2014–15	2015–16	2016–17
Number of individuals	6 202 558	6 087 224	6 102 730
Total cost of managing tax affairs ($m)	2 344	2 256	2 286
Average cost of managing tax affairs ($)	378	371	375
Median cost of managing tax affairs ($)	165	170	171

Source: Australian Tax Office, 'Cost of tax compliance statistics' (Web Page, 14 December 2021) https://www.ato.gov.au/About-ATO/Research-and-statistics/In-detail/Taxation-statistics/Taxation-statistics-2018-19/?anchor=Costoftaxcompliancestatistics#Cost oftaxcompliancestatistics.

1.1.2 Legal structure

A good starting point for understanding the structure of Australia's tax system is an overview of the constitutional arrangements governing the powers of the Australian Commonwealth and State Governments to levy taxes and a little of the history which gave rise to those constitutional arrangements.[19]

Prior to Federation in 1901, the Australian colonies were economically separate and imposed their own taxes and levies on their people. The enactment of the *Commonwealth Constitution* in 1901 brought together those colonies into the Australian Federation we know today.

This bringing together involved the colonies agreeing to share their powers with the new Commonwealth Parliament. Hence, the *Constitution* sets out the agreements reached on how law-making powers and responsibilities are shared between the States and Territories and the Commonwealth Parliament.[20] In general terms, these power-sharing arrangements set out in the *Constitution* divide law-making powers into three categories: exclusive powers, concurrent powers and residual powers.

- **Exclusive powers.** Powers entirely transferred by the colonies to the Commonwealth Parliament. These include inherently logical national responsibilities such as customs and duties (*Constitution* section 90) and military powers (section 114). This is why we have a single army and single customs rules for entry and exit from the country.
- **Concurrent powers.** Powers shared by the States and Territories and the Australian Parliament. These are listed in the *Constitution*, but are not expressed as powers which exclusively belong to the Commonwealth Parliament. Examples include taxation, marriage and postal services. In situations where both the Commonwealth Parliament and State and Territories make inconsistent laws on the same subject matter, section 109 of the *Constitution* says Commonwealth law will take priority to the extent of any inconsistency.
- **Residual powers.** Powers remaining exclusively the responsibility of the States and Territories. Anything that isn't expressly mentioned in the *Constitution* is a residual power. This extends to education, transport and public health. This is why it is possible to have different road rules, different education systems and different hospital systems in each State and Territory.

As noted, the power to levy taxes falls into the concurrent power category; that is, both the States and Territories and the Commonwealth Parliament can make laws with respect to taxes. The power is contained in section 51(ii) of the *Constitution*. It specifically provides that the Commonwealth Parliament has power to make laws with respect to taxation, but not so as to discriminate between States or parts of States. This means that theoretically we could, for example, have both Commonwealth and State income taxes. Indeed, for a time after Federation, we did!

The first Commonwealth Government income tax was introduced in 1915. However, it was not until an agreement with the States in 1942 that the States agreed not to exercise their powers to make laws with respect to taxes insofar as income tax was concerned. Initially, the proposal was intended to transfer powers to the Commonwealth Parliament to aid in funding the World War II war effort. The proposal was the subject of a constitutional challenge in the High Court by Victoria, South Australia, Queensland and

---

19 For an excellent summary of the history of the Australian tax system, see this link: https://treasury.gov.au/publication/economic-roundup-winter-2006/a-brief-history-of-australias-tax-system.

20 For a summary of the *Constitution* see: www.aph.gov.au/About_Parliament/House_of_Representatives/Powers_practice_and_procedure/00---Infosheets/Infosheet_13---The_Constitution.

Western Australia. There were two High Court challenges which have become known as the 'Uniform Tax Cases'.[21] The applicant States claimed the proposed new arrangements were in breach of section 51(ii) of the *Constitution*. Although the High Court affirmed the ability of the States to levy their own income taxes, the High Court upheld the overall validity of the uniform tax arrangements. Since then we have had a single Australia-wide Commonwealth income tax.

Arrangements with respect to other taxes have resulted in the States eventually assuming sole responsibility for levying those taxes. Examples include payroll taxes and land taxes which for a time after Federation (up until 1971 in the case of payroll tax, and 1952 in the case of land tax) were levied both at national and State levels, but are today only levied by the States and Territories.

Much of the debate between the Commonwealth and State and Territory governments continues to concern the sharing of tax revenue collected by the Commonwealth Government for distribution to the States and Territories. For example, the *Intergovernmental Agreement on Federal Financial Relations*, the *Federal Financial Relations Act 2009* (Cth) and the *COAG Reform Fund Act 2008* (Cth), which collectively deal with various aspects of the equitable sharing of Commonwealth revenue and support between the States and Territories, are a constant source of political tension and debate.[22]

Table 1.4 presents a timeline of key events in Australia's tax history.

TABLE 1.4   **A timeline of key events in Australian tax history**

Tax history timeline		
Date	Tax event	Background information
Prior to 1901	Taxes imposed by each colony	Each colony (later State and Territory) had its own tax system. Most of their revenue was gained from customs and excise duty. There was no free trade between the colonies. Income tax in various forms was introduced to Tasmania in 1880, South Australia 1884, New South Wales and Victoria in 1895 and Queensland in 1902.
1901	Federation	Under the *Commonwealth of Australia Constitution Act 1900* (UK), the States and Territories gave up the right to levy customs and excise duties. This meant a removal of all duties on goods traded between the States and Territories. The States and Territories gave up a number of other powers to the Commonwealth Government.
1915	World War I	The Commonwealth Government introduced a personal income tax and a tax on retained company profits to help pay for war expenses. The States were also still collecting income taxes. By 1918, income tax revenue provided one-third of Commonwealth tax revenue and half of state tax revenue. The name of the Land Tax Office, established in 1910, was changed to the Taxation Office to reflect its wider tax administration and collection roles.
1942	World War II	The Committee on Uniform Taxation recommended that the Commonwealth Government become the single income taxing body for the period of World War II. Much of the tax collected was then distributed to the states for their use.
1942	PAYE tax	The pay as you earn (PAYE) tax system where employees had their tax deducted periodically by their employer was introduced for wage and salary earners. A provisional tax system was introduced for non-wages and salary income.
1983	Contractor payments	The Prescribed Payments System was introduced to cover taxpayers paid by contract in certain industries such as building and construction.

(continued)

---

21 *South Australia v Commonwealth* (1942) 65 CLR 373 (First Uniform Tax Case) www.austlii.edu.au/au/cases/cth/HCA/1942/14.pdf; *Victoria v Commonwealth* (1957) 99 CLR 575 http://www8.austlii.edu.au/cgi-bin/viewdoc/au/cases/cth/HCA/1957/54.html.

22 For further information about the income-sharing arrangements between the Commonwealth and State and Territory Governments, see the website for the Council on Federal Financial Relations: www.federalfinancialrelations.gov.au/Default.aspx.

TABLE 1.4 *(continued)*

	Tax history timeline	
Date	**Tax event**	**Background information**
1984	Medicare levy	The Medicare levy was introduced.
1985	Capital gains tax	The capital gains tax (CGT) is a tax on the profits made on the sale of certain assets.
1986	Fringe benefits tax	The fringe benefits tax (FBT) taxes businesses that pay employees in fringe benefits such as cars and shares. The CGT and FBT were introduced to widen the tax base and are designed to stop tax avoidance.
1997	Simplifying the Income Tax Act	The Commonwealth Government tried to simplify the *Income Tax Assessment Act 1997* (Cth) by introducing a new Act and rewriting the provisions.
2000	GST	A New Tax System (ANTS) introduced major changes to the Australian taxation system. The changes included a 10 per cent goods and services tax (GST) on the sale of most goods and services, changes in tax rates for individualsand introduction of the Business Activity Statement (BAS).
2006	Closing of tax havens	Project Wickenby, a multi-agency taskforce, was established with the aim of protecting the integrity of Australian financial and regulatory systems. It aimed to prevent taxpayers from participating in the use of secret tax havens.
2008	Proposed reform of tax system	The Review Panel on Australia's Future Tax System, known as the 'Henry Review', looked into a comprehensive review of the tax system.

Source: Australian Tax Office, 'History of tax in Australia' (Web Page) www.taxsuperandyou.gov.au/node/133/take.

1.2 Australian tax law

LEARNING OBJECTIVE 1.2 Explain the key sources of Australian tax law.

This section of the chapter will discuss the sources of tax law, including legislation and case law, as well as avenues of appeal that taxpayers may pursue if they disagree with the way in which the law has been interpreted or applied.

1.2.1 Sources of tax law

The main source of Australian tax law is **legislation**. Our income tax legislation alone runs to more than 6000 pages. There are two primary pieces of legislation covering income tax. These are the *Income Tax Assessment Act 1936* (Cth) (ITAA36) and the *Income Tax Assessment Act 1997* (Cth) (ITAA97). The key provisions referred to are included in the commentary and/or the appendix. However, the AUSTLII website and the Federal Register of Legislation website are good sources for finding the full legislation.[23]

The main reason there are two Income Tax Assessment Acts is that the ITAA97 arose from the Tax Law Improvement Project established in 1993 to renumber and rewrite the ITAA36 into plain English. The aim of the project was 'to reduce compliance costs, and improve compliance, by making the law easier to use and understand'.[24] Unfortunately this process has not yet resulted in completely enabling the repeal of the ITAA36, hence some important provisions still remain in the ITAA36. However, new tax provisions when introduced are added to the ITAA97. In addition, significant parts of the ITAA36 that were renowned for their complexity, such as the CGT provisions, have been completely rewritten in a much more easily understandable form and are now entirely contained in the ITAA97.

It is important to note that among the plain English simplifications introduced in the ITAA97 was a new way of stating section numbers using dashes — for example, section 5-1. In contrast, the ITAA36 would describe the same section number using brackets — that is, section 5(1). This difference can be

---

23 AUSTLII website: www.austlii.edu.au; Federal Register of Legislation website: www.legislation.gov.au/Home.
24 The link to the Explanatory Memorandum for the ITAA97 is at: http://classic.austlii.edu.au/au/legis/cth/bill_em/itab1996250/memo_1.html.

very helpful for identifying whether you are looking at a section from the ITAA97 and the ITAA36. Keep this in mind when navigating through later chapters.

A number of important primary tax administration rules are contained in the *Taxation Administration Act 1953* (Cth). This Act establishes the office of the Commissioner of Taxation. The Commissioner of Taxation is entrusted with the general administration of Australia's Federal tax laws (e.g. section 1-17 of the ITAA97 and section 8 of the ITAA36). The *Taxation Administration Act* also contains rules concerning tax objections, reviews and appeals, general interest charges, penalties, tax prosecutions and offences. Some of these rules are discussed further later in this chapter.

Other key laws we will be examining are the *Fringe Benefits Tax Assessment Act 1986* (Cth) (FBTAA86) and the *A New Tax System (Goods and Services Tax) Act 1999* (Cth) (GST Act). It bears repeating that, unlike the GST and FBT, the CGT is not contained in separate legislation; it is contained in a later chapter of the ITAA97.

1.2.2 Doctrine of precedent

Courts play a key role in the law-making process. They do this through interpreting and clarifying laws in deciding cases before them. This is true in all fields of law, including taxation. To understand how this works it is important to understand the **doctrine of precedent**. At the heart of the doctrine of precedent is the legal convention that judges will decide cases that are factually similar in the same way judges before them have decided those cases. There is good logic behind this convention. Imagine the uncertainty and mayhem if courts decided to apply laws in factually identical cases in opposing ways?

However, the doctrine of precedent also includes sensible constraints to ensure that the law can evolve and change with the times without undue compromise of certainty and consistency. The first such constraint is that judges only need to follow the reasoning of judges in more senior courts. Figure 1.4 outlines the court hierarchy in Australia.

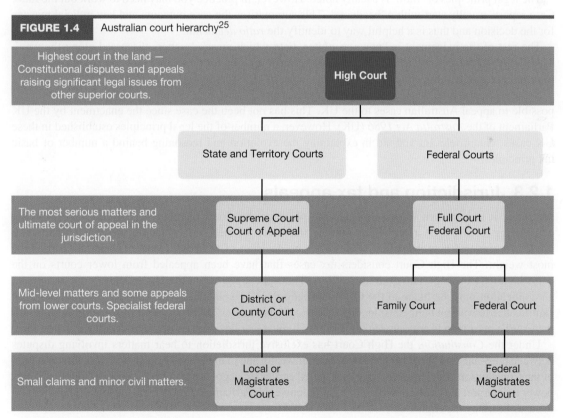

FIGURE 1.4 Australian court hierarchy[25]

At the top of the court hierarchy sits the High Court of Australia. Its interpretations of the law are binding (i.e. they must be followed) on judges in all the other courts across the whole country. In addition, State and Territory court judges are bound to follow the interpretations of the law of courts above them on the

---

25 For a starting point for further information about each of the courts on the hierarchy, as well as links to the various court websites, see the Federal Attorney-General's Department website: www.ag.gov.au/LegalSystem/Courts/Pages/default.aspx.

court hierarchy in their particular State or Territory. Typically, the top court on the hierarchy of the various States and Territories is known as the 'Supreme Court' or 'Court of Appeal'. When dealing with State-level court decisions it is important to check the level on the court hierarchy in that State or Territory of the particular court.[26]

It is important when considering judicial determinations in tax cases to bear in mind the level of the court hierarchy on the decision-making court, as this will determine the extent to which the legal reasoning can be considered legally binding and, consequently, as an authoritative statement of legal principle.

Sometimes, judges will choose to follow decisions of superior courts in other jurisdictions (e.g. from Supreme Courts in other States or Territories or decisions in other Commonwealth countries, such as Canada or the United Kingdom). Judges are free to do this, but are not bound to do so by the doctrine of precedent. The doctrine only requires judges to follow the reasoning of courts higher on the same court hierarchy.

It is also important to bear in mind that superior court decisions typically involve a panel of judges. For instance, the full bench of the High Court consists of all seven of the High Court justices. This means that often decisions will be decided on a majority rather than an unanimous basis (e.g. 4:3). The binding part of such a decision is the reasoning of the majority rather than the minority dissenting judges.

A further logical constraint is that only parts of the judgement are considered statements of legal principle which are binding on other courts. Judgements will often run to over a hundred pages. Many of these pages will contain judicial discussion of the particular facts of the case, various submissions of the parties made during the case, various evidentiary statements made by witnesses, and summaries of legal principle from previous cases mentioned by the parties. Most of this cannot be considered 'law' even if made by a judge of a court higher on the same court hierarchy. The only part that is binding is known as the *ratio decidendi* of the case. This means the reason for the decision. Often this might be a sentence or two.

The legal principles or 'ratio' is usually noted. However, in practice you may need to work out the ratio. Case reports usually start with a 'headnote'. This summarises the case outcome and key judicial reasons for the decision and thus is a helpful way to identify the *ratio decidendi*.

The rest of the judgement is known as *obiter dicta* which means 'matters discussed along the way'. This can be useful for understanding the ratio or, in some cases for predicting how the law might evolve in future cases (e.g. if the obiter was comments made by a dissenting judge in the case).

Some references to older United Kingdom cases are cited. These cases stem from the time when it was possible to appeal Australian cases to the UK. This has not been the case since the enactment by the UK Parliament of the *Australia Act 1986* (UK). However, a number of the legal principles established in these UK cases remain relevant and aid in explaining the evolution and reasoning behind a number of basic tax principles.

1.2.3 Jurisdiction and tax appeals

As noted, it is important to bear in mind the place on the Court hierarchy of any tax cases you are considering relying upon as providing binding statements of the Court which decided what a particular tax law means and how it applies. Obviously, any decision of the High Court of Australia carries the most weight. The High Court considers tax cases that have been appealed from lower courts on the court hierarchy on important questions of law. The right to appeal to the High Court is not automatic; an application must be made to the Court and they must be convinced it is a matter of sufficient legal significance to warrant their consideration. Hence, if a tax matter has been determined by the High Court, the Court's reasoning is not only legally binding; it must involve a matter of significant legal importance.

Under the *Constitution*, the High Court has exclusive jurisdiction to hear matters involving disputes between the States and Territories and the Commonwealth and matters involving questions of interpretation of the Constitution. The Uniform Tax Cases, noted earlier, are a good example of the High Court using this power to interpret the taxing powers of the Commonwealth Parliament. You should pay particular attention to cases heard by the High Court.

The vast majority of tax cases do not get to the High Court. They are determined either in the **Administrative Appeals Tribunal (AAT)**,[27] the Federal Court[28] or the State or Territory Supreme Courts.

---

26 The Federal Attorney General's Department contains links to the various State and Territory Supreme Court websites: www.ag. gov.au/LegalSystem/Courts/Pages/default.aspx.
27 The website for the AAT is at: www.aat.gov.au.
28 The website for the Federal Court is at: www.fedcourt.gov.au.

The AAT is responsible for reviewing administrative decisions of Commonwealth agencies, such as the Commissioner of Taxation.[29] It is divided into a number of specialist divisions. The 2 divisions pertaining to tax decisions are the Taxation and Commercial Decisions Division and the Small Business Taxation Division.[30] The *Taxation Administration Act 1953* (Cth) (TAA53) empowers the AAT to review most tax decisions of the Commissioner of Taxation such as decisions concerning taxpayer objections to tax assessments and applications for extensions of time to pay their taxes.[31]

1.2.3.1 Administrative Appeals Tribunal

The AAT is the only review body with the jurisdiction to 'stand in the shoes of the ATO' and effectively reconsider the entire case, including all the legal issues and the original facts presented by the taxpayer, and substituting its own factual and legal findings in the place of the ATO as the original decision-maker. In contrast, court appeals are limited to questions of law. For this reason, the distinction between a question of law and fact is an important one. An example of an appeal based on an error of law would be an allegation that the ATO applied the wrong legal test to determine the deductibility of expenses claimed by a taxpayer. In contrast, an appeal on the grounds that the ATO should have believed the taxpayer's account of the facts raises no legal question — simply questions of fact or the 'merits' of the taxpayer's case.

1.2.3.2 Federal Court

The Federal Court of Australia has jurisdiction to hear disputes concerning a range of matters involving Commonwealth legislation.[32] The Court is organised into 9 'practice areas', including Commonwealth crimes, employment and industrial relations, intellectual property and native title. One of the 9 practice areas is taxation, and tax cases can come before the Court in a number of ways.

First, the TAA53 allows taxpayers to appeal against objection decisions of the Commissioner of Taxation directly to the Federal Court instead of the AAT.[33] As with appeals to the AAT, appeals against ATO objection decisions must be lodged within 60 days of the handing down of the decision being appealed. There are some modifications to usual appeal rules that apply in the tax context. In particular, the ATO is not prevented from recovering tax assessed or otherwise implementing their decision while the matter is subject to appeal.[34] In other words, the decision of the ATO applies unless and until the court ultimately overturns the decision. Similarly, there is a presumption that the amount of tax assessed as owing is correct, such that if a taxpayer alleges that a tax assessment is excessive, they also bear the burden of proof of proving this is the case.[35]

Second, the Federal Court also hears appeals on questions of law from the AAT. It also hears applications for judicial review under the *Administrative Decisions (Judicial Review) Act 1977* (Cth) (ADJR Act).[36] Section 5(1) of the ADJR Act allows for appeals for breaches by statutory decision-makers of 'natural justice', improper legal processes, lack of jurisdiction, improper exercises of power, unauthorised decisions, errors of law, fraud, lack of evidence or otherwise contrary to the law.

However, this jurisdiction is quite restricted in the tax context as the ADJR Act prohibits appeals against tax assessment decisions. Specifically, Schedule 1(e) of the ADJR Act prohibits judicial review of decisions concerning assessments or calculations of tax, decisions disallowing objections to tax assessments or calculations and decisions amending, or refusing to amend assessments or calculations of tax. This significantly restricts the Court's jurisdiction and affirms the relatively narrow scope of any appeals beyond the AAT.

Most Federal Court appeals are heard in the first instance by a single judge. These decisions can be appealed to the Full Court of the Federal Court. The Full Court means a panel of Federal Court judges consisting of 3 judges.

---

29 The AAT was established by the *Administrative Appeals Tribunal Act 1975* (Cth).
30 Administrative Appeals Tribunal, *A Guide to the Small Business Tax Division* (Web Page, 1 July 2021) www.aat.gov.au/AAT /media/AAT/Files/Directions%20and%20guides/Guide-to-the-Small-Business-Taxation-Division.pdf.
31 TAA Part IVC Division 4.
32 The Federal Court of Australia was established by the *Federal Court of Australia Act 1976* (Cth).
33 TAA Part IVC Division 5.
34 TAA section 14ZZR.
35 TA section 14ZZO.
36 The link to the ADJR Act is at: www.legislation.gov.au/Details/C2019C00309.

1.2.3.3 State Courts

State Courts share jurisdiction with the Federal Court to hear some tax matters. State Supreme Courts can hear cases that raise substantial issues concerning tax, including disputes regarding GST. They also hear disputes concerning State taxes from the relevant State. Figure 1.5 shows the typical appeal jurisdiction options available to taxpayers who want to appeal against an objection or other decision of the ATO.

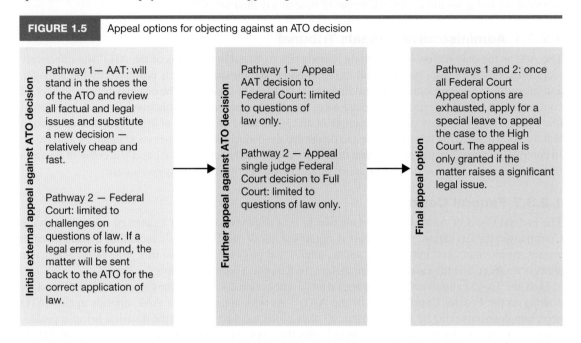

FIGURE 1.5   Appeal options for objecting against an ATO decision

Initial external appeal against ATO decision

Pathway 1— AAT: will stand in the shoes the of the ATO and review all factual and legal issues and substitute a new decision — relatively cheap and fast.

Pathway 2 — Federal Court: limited to challenges on questions of law. If a legal error is found, the matter will be sent back to the ATO for the correct application of law.

Further appeal against ATO decision

Pathway 1— Appeal AAT decision to Federal Court: limited to questions of law only.

Pathway 2 — Appeal single judge Federal Court decision to Full Court: limited to questions of law only.

Final appeal option

Pathways 1 and 2: once all Federal Court Appeal options are exhausted, apply for a special leave to appeal the case to the High Court. The appeal is only granted if the matter raises a significant legal issue.

1.3 Ethics and the tax professional

LEARNING OBJECTIVE 1.3 Describe key ethical responsibilities of tax professionals.

1.3.1 Introduction to ethics

Ethics has been contemplated, discussed and written about for many centuries and has been mainly concerned with the appropriate conduct of individuals. More recently, the conduct of corporations (as groups of individuals in an organised structure) has also entered the discussion.

Law and ethics are not necessarily the same thing. Behaviour may be legal, but unethical and vice versa. This is because ethics is an aspect of philosophy rather than law. Ethics and the law are related in the sense that they may both regulate or control behaviour, although neither are necessarily restricted solely to that concern. With respect to tax-paying behaviour and decisions, for example, decisions about whether to engage in tax evasion and avoidance, the law prescribes a systematic and detailed set of rules for determining the tax that ought to be paid, whereas ethical theories provide guiding principles only. Since tax laws are binding on citizens, noncompliance with tax laws may lead to fines and punishment, but ethical theories are guides only with no necessary punishment for not adhering to them. As we have noted earlier in this chapter, the purpose of tax laws is to raise revenue for governments, to provide goods and services for society, redistribute income from the wealthy to the poor and manage the economy. In contrast, the purpose of ethics is to help people to decide how to behave or live appropriately or to determine courses of action in uncertain contexts.

Despite these differences, laws and ethics are linked in that ethical principles can be used to guide behaviour when the law is ambiguous, as is often the case where tax law is involved. Indeed, ethical principles can guide our attitudes and behaviour with respect to the entire tax system including the tax legislation. Furthermore, professional codes of conduct contain expectations regarding ethical conduct as well as other principles such as acting in the client's best interest and avoiding conflicts of interest. The focus of the balance of this part is on elaborating these core professional ethical conduct principles. It is important to understand these from the outset and also to consider ethical dimensions that arise in the context of making tax decisions and providing tax advice. This book contains ethical problems and discussions in a range of different contexts in each of the later chapters. The material that follows will provide the necessary background information and ethical frameworks which apply to tax professionals to enable you to understand and solve those applied ethical problems and many others that you will inevitably encounter in future as a tax professional.

1.3.2 General professional ethical codes and standards

Tax practitioners may come from a range of different professional backgrounds. In particular, tax practitioners may be lawyers or they may be accountants or financial advisers. Hence, these individuals will be subject to ethical standards and practising requirements set out by their relevant professional bodies and industry regulators. These are in addition to tax-specific legal and ethical responsibilities.

In the case of accountants, the Accounting Professional and Ethical Standards Board (APESB)[37] is the national body that sets the code of ethics and professional standards with which accounting professionals must comply, irrespective of whether they are engaged in providing tax advice. These standards are mandatory for members of Chartered Accountants Australia and New Zealand (CA ANZ), CPA Australia and the Institute of Public Accountants (IPA). The APESB standards, therefore, apply to all accountants, whether or not they work in accounting firms, government or the private sector.

The APESB core ethical standards are set out in APES 110 *Code of Ethics for Professional Accountants (including Independence Standards)* (the APESB Code).[38] The 5 fundamental principles set out in the APESB Code are integrity, objectivity, professional competence and due care, confidentiality and professional behaviour Section 110.1 A1 of the APESB Code summarises each of these key principles as follows.

(a) Integrity — to be straightforward and honest in all professional and business relationships.
(b) Objectivity — not to compromise professional or business judgements because of bias, conflict of interest or undue influence of others.
(c) Professional competence and due care — to: (i) attain and maintain professional knowledge and skill at the level required to ensure that a client or employing organisation receives competent professional activities, based on current technical and professional standards and relevant legislation; and (ii) act diligently and in accordance with applicable technical and professional standards.
(d) Confidentiality — to respect the confidentiality of information acquired as a result of professional and business relationships.
(e) Professional behaviour — to comply with relevant laws and regulations and avoid any conduct that the Member knows or should know might discredit the profession.[39]

Each of the principles is elaborated in subsequent parts of the Code (integrity in section 111, objectivity in section 112, professional competence and due care in section 113, confidentiality in section 114 and professional behaviour in section 115). In cases of a risk of potential breach of the fundamental principles, the Code requires practitioners to apply a conceptual framework to assess the risk. This framework requires practitioners to: '(a) identify threats to compliance with the fundamental principles; (b) evaluate the threats identified; and (c) address the threats by eliminating or reducing them to an acceptable level'.[40] APESB has also issued a series of standards and guidance notes to assist members to understand and apply the Code in relation to the professional activities they perform.

All of the fundamental principles are subject to an overarching expectation that 'a distinguishing mark of the accountancy profession is its acceptance of the responsibility to act in the public interest. A Member's responsibility is not exclusively to satisfy the needs of an individual client or employing organisation'.[41] This can be an issue for those engaged in tax practice who may feel pressured to provide clients or employers with favourable tax advice in complex situations where they have some reservations or doubts.

In addition to these core requirements, accountants engaged in the provision of taxation services must also comply with further standards set out in APES 220.[42] Taxation services is defined in APES 220 as including:

> … any Professional Activities performed by a Member relating to ascertaining a Client's or Employer's tax liabilities or entitlements or satisfying their obligations under a Taxation Law,

---

37 The link to the APESB website is at: www.apesb.org.au.
38 The Code is based on a similar international code issued by the International Ethics Standards Board for Accountants.
39 The link to the Code is at: https://apesb.org.au/wp-content/uploads/2020/09/APES_110_Restructured_Code_Nov_2018.pdf.
40 See section 120.2 of the Code.
41 Section 100.1 A1 of the Code.
42 A copy of these standards is at: https://apesb.org.au/standards-guidance/taxation-services.

provided under circumstances where they can reasonably expect to rely on the Professional Activities. This includes: (a) preparation of a return, notice, statement, application or other document for lodgement with a Revenue Authority, and responding on behalf of a Client or Employer to the Revenue Authority's requests for further information; (b) preparation of tax calculations to be used as the basis for the accounting entries in the financial statements; (c) provision of tax planning and other tax advisory services; and (d) assisting a Client or Employer in the resolution of tax disputes.[43]

APES 220 sets out tax-specific applications of the fundamental principles set out in the APESB Code. It also sets out particular ethical obligations and considerations in particular circumstances such as situations involving preparation of tax returns and involvement in tax schemes or arrangements. Insofar as the latter is concerned, section 5 sets out a number of obligations including the following requirements.

> 5.3 A Member shall not knowingly or recklessly be associated with any arrangement which involves documents or accounting entries that are intended to misrepresent a transaction or which depend upon lack of disclosure for its effectiveness.
>
> 5.4 A Member shall not promote, or assist in the promotion of, or otherwise encourage any tax schemes or arrangements where the dominant purpose is to derive a tax benefit, and it is not reasonably arguable that the tax benefit is available under Taxation Law.[44]

Enforcement of the APESB pronouncements and disciplinary action in the event of breaches rests with the relevant professional bodies: CPA Australia, CA ANZ and the IPA. Each of these bodies has disciplinary procedures and structures in place, including a disciplinary tribunal. For example, CA ANZ has a professional conduct committee and a disciplinary tribunal and maintains a public register of disciplinary proceedings decisions as well as forthcoming hearings.[45] A range of sanctions can be imposed on CA ANZ members found to have breached the APESB standards. These can include cancelling or suspending the membership of a member, imposing monetary penalties, requiring the member to complete professional development, cancelling a member's certificate of public practice and reprimanding or severely reprimanding the member.[46]

Lawyers are required to comply with the Australian Solicitors Conduct Rules (ASCR). This set of rules was developed collaboratively by respective State and Territory legal professional bodies and comprise a statement of professional and ethical obligations as derived from legislation, common law and equity.[47] The paramount duty of lawyers is to the court and to the administration of justice, even if this is inconsistent with other duties such as acting in the best interests of a client. This can often see lawyers faced with difficult ethical dilemmas similar to those faced by accountants in complying with their overarching responsibility to act in the public interest as noted previously.

1.3.3 The *Tax Agent Services Act 2009* (Cth) (TASA) and the TASA Code of Conduct

1.3.3.1 TASA registration requirements

Since the introduction of the TASA in 2009, individuals wishing to provide tax agent services for a fee or to engage in other conduct connected with providing such services must also register as tax or BAS agents or tax (financial) advisers. In order to qualify for registration, individuals must be 'fit and proper' persons. This means they must be of good fame, integrity and character, and must not have been an undischarged bankrupt or in prison at any time in the previous 5 years. Registration will also be denied to individuals who have been convicted of a serious tax offence, an offence involving fraud or dishonesty, or who have been penalised for promoting a tax exploitation scheme.[48] Accompanying TASA are a set

---

43 Definition of 'Taxation Services' is contained in section 2 of APES 220.
44 Paragraphs 5.3 and 5.4 of APES 220.
45 The link to the CA ANZ disciplinary decisions register is at: https://www.charteredaccountantsanz.com/about-us/complaints/decisions-register.
46 CPA Australia also have a disciplinary tribunal capable of imposing a similar range of sanctions on members found to have breached the APES standards. For further information, see: https://www.cpaaustralia.com.au/about-cpa-australia/governance/member-conduct-and-discipline/member-guide-to-disciplinary-process#:~:text=The%20Disciplinary%20Tribunal%20is%20made,the%20purposes%20of%20a%20transcript. For further information about the IPA disciplinary procedures and structures, see: https://www.publicaccountants.org.au/about/complaint-investigation/tribunal-hearings-decisions.
47 The ASCR is available via the Australian Law Council website: https://www.lawcouncil.asn.au/files/web-pdf/Aus_Solicitors_Conduct_Rules.
48 TASA section 20-15.

---

of Regulations (*Tax Agent Services Regulations 2009*) which contain the qualifications and experience requirements for registration as a tax agent, BAS agent or tax (financial) adviser.

'Tax agent services' are defined in section 90-5 of the TASA:

(1) A tax agent service is any service:
　　(a) that relates to:
　　　　(i) ascertaining liabilities, obligations or entitlements of an entity that arise, or could arise, under a taxation law; or
　　　　(ii) advising an entity about liabilities, obligations or entitlements of the entity or another entity that arise, or could arise, under a taxation law; or
　　　　(iii) representing an entity in their dealings with the Commissioner; and
　　(b) that is provided in circumstances where the entity can reasonably be expected to rely on the service for either or both of the following purposes:
　　　　(i) to satisfy liabilities or obligations that arise, or could arise, under a taxation law;
　　　　(ii) to claim entitlements that arise, or could arise, under a taxation law.

The TPB website lists the following services as a non-exhaustive list of the types of services that it considers to be tax agent services.

- Preparing returns, notices, statements, applications or other documents about your client's liabilities, obligations or entitlements under a taxation law.
- Lodging returns, notices, statements, applications or other documents about your client's liabilities, obligations or entitlements under a taxation law.
- Assisting clients with tax concessions for expenditure incurred on research and development activities where the service involves the application of taxation laws.
- Preparing depreciation schedules on the deductibility of capital expenditure.
- Preparing or lodging objections on behalf of a taxpayer under Part IVC of the *Taxation Administration Act 1953* (TAA) against an assessment, determination, notice or decision under a taxation law.
- Giving clients advice about a taxation law that they can reasonably be expected to rely on to satisfy their taxation obligations.
- Dealing with the Commissioner on behalf of clients.
- Applying to the Commissioner or the Administrative Appeals Tribunal (AAT) for a review of, or instituting an appeal against, a decision on an objection under Part IVC of the TAA.
- Reconciling BAS provision data entry to ascertain the figures to be included on a client's activity statement.
- Filling in an activity statement on behalf of a client or instructing them which figures to include.
- Ascertaining the withholding obligations for employees of your clients, including preparing income statements.
- Coding transactions, particularly in circumstances where it requires the interpretation or application of a taxation law.
- Providing a payroll service which involves interpreting and applying a taxation law, including reporting of employee payroll information through the use of single touch payroll (STP) enabled software.
- Undertaking a payroll compliance review, providing an assessment and/or opinion as to whether the client is compliant with their taxation obligations under one or more taxation laws.
- Providing tax related advice specific to client's circumstances regarding: PAYG withholding liability, Superannuation Guarantee obligations, fringe benefits tax laws, and termination and redundancy payments.[49]

There are some exemptions from the registration requirements. Prime among these is an exemption for legal practitioners, provided the practitioner is not prohibited from providing tax agent services under a State or Territory law regulating legal practice and the provision of legal services, and does not prepare and lodge tax returns or similar statement except in the course of acting for a trust or deceased estate as a trustee or legal personal representative.

For those who are required to be registered, unregistered conduct can result in severe penalties under the TASA. Prohibited conduct includes providing tax agent services for fee or reward without being registered, advertising tax agent services without being registered or representing yourself as a tax agent despite not being registered. These offences and the applicable penalties are dealt with in Subdivision 50A of the TASA. For the most serious offences, the TPB can apply to the Federal Court to have civil penalties applied

---

49 Tax Practitioners Board, 'Tax agent services' https://www.tpb.gov.au/tax-agent-services.

of up to 250 penalty units for an individual and 1250 penalty units for a body corporate.[50] The TPB can also apply to the Federal Court for an injunction preventing the continuation of the prohibited conduct.

1.3.3.2 The TASA Code of Conduct

The TASA introduced a legislative Code of Conduct (TASA Code). The TASA Code requirements are enforced by the Tax Practitioners Board (TPB) (which we introduced earlier in this chapter).

Similar to the APESB Code, the TASA Code contains five core categories of professional responsibilities:

1. honesty and integrity
2. independence
3. confidentiality
4. confidence
5. other responsibilities.

The TASA Code is contained in section 30-10 of the TASA which is reproduced in full as follows.

The Code of Professional Conduct

Honesty and integrity

(1) You must act honestly and with integrity.
(2) You must comply with the taxation laws in the conduct of your personal affairs.
(3) If:
    (a) you receive money or other property from or on behalf of a client; and
    (b) you hold the money or other property on trust;
    you must account to your client for the money or other property.

Independence

(4) You must act lawfully in the best interests of your client.[51]
(5) You must have in place adequate arrangements for the management of conflicts of interest that may arise in relation to the activities that you undertake in the capacity of a registered tax agent, BAS agent or tax (financial) adviser.

Confidentiality

(6) Unless you have a legal duty to do so, you must not disclose any information relating to a client's affairs to a third party without your client's permission.

Competence

(7) You must ensure that a tax agent service that you provide, or that is provided on your behalf, is provided competently.
(8) You must maintain knowledge and skills relevant to the tax agent services that you provide.
(9) You must take reasonable care in ascertaining a client's state of affairs, to the extent that ascertaining the state of those affairs is relevant to a statement you are making or a thing you are doing on behalf of the client.
(10) You must take reasonable care to ensure that taxation laws are applied correctly to the circumstances in relation to which you are providing advice to a client.

Other responsibilities

(11) You must not knowingly obstruct the proper administration of the taxation laws.
(12) You must advise your client of the client's rights and obligations under the taxation laws that are materially related to the tax agent services you provide.
(13) You must maintain professional indemnity insurance that meets the Board's requirements.
(14) You must respond to requests and directions from the Board in a timely, responsible and reasonable manner.

---

50 A penalty unit is currently (since 1 July 2020) equal to $222.
51 The Explanatory Paper is here: TPB(EP) 01/2010: *Code of Professional Conduct*: https://www.tpb.gov.au/explanatory-paper-tpbep-012010-code-professional-conduct.

The TPB has issued an explanatory paper which provides a detailed explanation of each of these categories of ethical responsibilities. Subdivision 30-B of the TASA sets out the penalties for breaching the TASA Code of Practice. These include a written caution, orders that you complete a course of education or training, restriction to providing tax agent services only under supervision of another registered tax agent, restrictions on the types of tax agent services you are permitted to provide, suspension of registration or termination of registration.

1.3.4 Technology, ethics and tax professionals

Technology is playing an increasingly important role in tax administration and the ATO uses technology in many ways to carry out its tax administration functions. We outline the various uses of technology in tax administration in a later chapter. For tax professionals, the digitalisation of tax administration means that the primary avenue for interacting with the ATO is increasingly via online channels. For example,[52] the ATO 'Online services for agents' system portal provides registered tax agents access to a range of services and information for their clients. Key features include the following.

1. Login service
2. Search communication history — to search and retrieve tax agent communications with the ATO
3. View communication history — to view a piece of correspondence found in the search function
4. Access practice and client reports
5. Access Single Touch Payroll (STP) reports
6. View client accounts
7. Create or view mail messages
8. File transfer — displays the availability of the file transfer facility to upload approved files
9. Access super clearing house — availability of the small business super clearing house (SBSCH)
10. Add or remove clients
11. Update client details
12. View/lodge activity statements
13. Prefill
14. On Demand reports

Figure 1.6 shows the portal home page interface.

To access 'Online services for agents', two identity verification and authorisation systems need to be used: myGovID, an app that lets you prove who you are when logging into government online services, and Relationship Authorisation Manager (RAM). RAM is an authorisation service that allows you to act on behalf of a practice online when linked with your myGovID. myGovID is used to log in to RAM.[53]

The ATO also increasingly interacts with individual taxpayers electronically, via their myGov account. This is different to myGovID outlined earlier — it is a single secure access point used by individuals for accessing a range of government services including the ATO with one login and one password. Where a taxpayer links their ATO details to their myGov account, any ATO mail will be sent to the linked myGov account inbox instead of by mail. This extends to notices of assessment, reminders and confirmation notices, business activity statements and instalment notices.[54]

The ATO is also increasingly using artificial intelligence via machine-learning algorithms using the data banks of information held by the ATO. According to the ATO: 'Machine learning means that a process which could take months, if done manually, can be done in days, saving time and resources.'[55]

Increasing reliance is also being placed on digital approaches to collection and validation of taxpayer information by the ATO such as through the expansion of electronic activities of data-matching, tax return pre-filling and industry benchmarking. We provide more detail on these and other uses of technology in tax administration in a later chapter.

---

52 Australian Taxation Office, *Annual Report 2018–19* www.ato.gov.au/uploadedFiles/Content/CR/Downloads/Annual_report _2018-19/n0995_2018-19_Annual_Report.pdf 24.

53 See the ATO website for further information about mGovID and RAM at: https://www.ato.gov.au/General/Online-services/Tax-agents/myGovID-and-RAM-for-tax-professionals.

54 The online ATO services available to individuals and sole traders via the myGov interface are detailed at: https://www.ato.gov.au/General/Online-services/Using-ATO-online-services/?anchor=Whatyoucandoonline&anchor=Whatyou candoonline.

55 Australian Taxation Office, *How we use data and analytics* www.ato.gov.au/about-ato/managing-the-tax-and-super-system/ insight--building-trust-and-confidence/how-we-use-data-and-analytics.

FIGURE 1.6 The ATO tax agent portal user guide

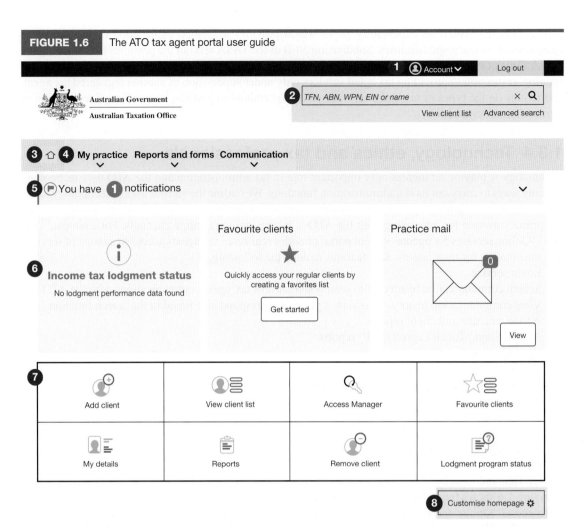

Source: Australian Taxation Office, 'Online Services for Agents User Guide' (Web Page, 8 December 2021) https://www.ato.gov.au/Tax-professionals/Digital-services/In-detail/Online-services-for-agents-user-guide/?page=3#:~:text=The%20agent%20home%20page%20is,functions%20that%20best%20suit%20you.

These types of technological advancements have dramatically changed tax practice and have, in many respects, enabled more timely and accurate information collection and communication with clients. However, technology also raises some new issues and potential ethical challenges for tax practitioners, particularly where new and emerging investments such as cryptocurrency transactions are concerned. The following technology think box an example to get you thinking about these types of challenges. Throughout the subsequent chapters of this text, you will encounter similar scenarios encouraging you to consider both technological and ethical dimensions of tax law and tax practice.

TECHNOLOGY IN ACTION

Blockchain technology and the evolving role of the tax practitioner

As the next generation of tax practitioners, you will examine a variety of tax issues beyond what we envisage today. With the digitalisation of activities within the economy continuing to accelerate, you will see more and more technological impacts on everyday life. We continue to see the developments in artificial intelligence, automation, big data and cloud technologies, for example. The connectivity of applications across platforms are changing the face of tax practice. Tax practitioners have access to a multitude of digital platforms and services, such as client prefilling, reporting and lodgement activities, thereby connecting tax and business services.

Not only is the day-to-day practice of the tax practitioner shifting, but so too is that of their clients. Take, for example, blockchain technology. Although there are numerous definitions, IBM describes blockchain as:

a shared, immutable ledger that facilitates the process of recording transactions and tracking assets in a business network. An asset can be tangible ([such as] a house) or intangible ([such as] intellectual property). Virtually anything of value can be tracked and traded on a blockchain network, reducing risk and cutting costs for all involved.[56]

Although relatively young, it is becoming increasingly important that tax practitioners have a sound understanding of the implications of this technology for tax practice. Blockchain technology has received substantial attention (and notoriety) as a result of the introduction of Bitcoin, a peer-to-peer system of payment. However, the capabilities of blockchain technology go much further. Not only does it offer alternative forms of digital 'currency', but the technology also offers solutions across supply chain provenance, credentialing, ownership and more.

As clients increasingly transact and do business 'on chain', there is an increasing need for tax practitioners to be able to understand and interpret the tax consequences of such activities. Importantly, this will not always be straightforward as the regulatory frameworks race to catch up.

For the tax system, experimentation that results in new forms of assets, new forms of business and new forms of financing, create practical challenges for taxpayers, tax practitioners and the regulatory frameworks that compliance relies upon.

The Australian Tax Office (ATO) released a set of Tax Determinations in 2014 to deal with the various tax treatments of cryptoassets and related issues; however, the continued evolution of crypto-activities has resulted in several updates on the ATO website to guide tax compliance to attempt to keep up with the technology. In many cases, the tax position remains challenging and unresolved. As at the time of writing, the Board of Taxation has been tasked with advising Treasury by the end of 2022 on a policy framework for the taxation of digital transactions and assets.

REFLECTION

With a lag between regulatory uncertainty and reflecting on the TASA Code of Conduct, why may it be important for tax practitioners to develop an understanding of the tax implications of blockchain technology? Consider the ethical challenges and responsibilities for tax advisers in ensuring their clients understand and correctly report any cryptocurrency transactions.

1.4 Types of taxes

LEARNING OBJECTIVE 1.4 Describe different types of taxes.

The main taxes imposed by the Commonwealth Government include income tax, capital gains tax (CGT), fringe benefits tax (FBT) and goods and services tax (GST). As noted earlier, these taxes are a core focus.

1.4.1 Income tax

Income tax is governed by the ITAA36 and the ITAA97. It is discussed in some detail throughout the chapter and we will look at it again in a later section. Briefly, income tax is charged against taxable income (which reflects income and various deductions) less offsets. Australian income tax is progressive, so the rate charged increases as taxable income increases. These concepts will be discussed in more detail in a later section.

1.4.2 Capital gains tax

Capital gains tax (CGT) came into force in 1985. It is a tax on 'CGT events' — various types of transactions involving 'CGT assets'. A typical example of a CGT event is the sale of a capital asset such as property. The tax is payable on capital gains (taxable increases in value of the asset) that realised as a result of the CGT event. Part of the reason for introducing the CGT was to ensure that capital transactions were subject to tax in appropriate circumstances.

There has been a long-standing controversy in tax concerning how to distinguish between a capital and income transaction. Prior to the introduction of the CGT, the categorisation could have meant the difference between whether a transaction was subject to tax (if it was classed as income) or whether it was classed as a capital transaction. The distinction between capital and income remains significant (and is discussed in

---

56 IBM, 'What is blockchain technology?' (Web Page) https://www.ibm.com/topics/what-is-blockchain#:~:text=Blockchain%20defined%3A%20Blockchain%20is%20a,assets%20in%20a%2.

detail in a later chapter), but in the wake of CGT the issue is more commonly one of whether the transaction is subject to CGT or taxable under other provisions of the Income Tax Acts rather than whether it is taxable at all. You will learn more about CGT in a later chapter.

1.4.3 Fringe benefits tax

Fringe benefits tax (FBT) came into force in 1986. The tax is contained in the *Fringe Benefits Tax Assessment Act 1986* (Cth). FBT is a tax on certain 'fringe benefits' paid by an employer to an employee. The genesis of the tax was to address the disparity between benefits paid to employees in the form of a salary or wage (which were subject to income tax) and benefits in other forms, such as vehicles or payment of expenses on behalf of employees by their employer — which were much less likely to be subject to tax. Different fringe benefits are subject to different tax arrangements and there are a number of exemptions and concessions under the FBT. You will learn more about FBT in a later chapter.

1.4.4 Goods and services tax

The goods and services tax (GST) came into force on 1 July 2000. The GST is contained in the GST Act. The GST is a 'consumption' tax (such taxes are also sometimes described as 'value added taxes' or 'VAT'). This means it is levied on purchases of goods and services rather than income. The tax is levied at the rate of 10 per cent of the value of most sales of goods and services sold in Australia. Businesses with a GST turnover in excess of $75 000 must register for the GST. This means they must levy GST on their sales, collect the GST and remit it via a Business Activity Statement (BAS). Taxpayers are entitled to claim GST 'tax credits' for GST which they paid on purchases and there are a number of exemptions and concessions. You will learn more about the GST in a later chapter.

Part of the impetus for introducing the GST was to broaden the 'tax base' of the Commonwealth Government. The introduction of the GST corresponded with the abolition of a range of State and Territory-based sales taxes. The trade-off for the States and Territories was that the GST collected by the Commonwealth Government would be distributed to the States and Territories according to a formula. This distribution formula has been a bone of contention in the wake of the introduction of the GST.

There are also calls to further broaden the range of goods and services to which the GST applies and also to increase the rate. Figure 1.7 compares the levels of consumption taxes in Australia to other OECD countries. It is clear that Australia's GST rate is relatively low compared to many other countries with only Japan, Canada and Switzerland having lower rates.

Others argue that taxes such as the GST are regressive in that lower-income individuals tend to spend a greater proportion of their income on consumption (and are thus subject to paying GST on that spending) than higher-income individuals who are more likely to save or invest a proportion of their income and thus, not have to expose that income to GST. The rules and operation of GST are discussed in a later chapter.

1.4.5 Other taxes

There are many other Commonwealth Government taxes that will not be examined in detail. However, tax advisers and taxpayers need to be aware of the existence of these other taxes as they may be relevant to their circumstances. These include taxes on various types of goods known as **excise duties**. Excise duties include taxes on alcohol, petroleum and tobacco. There are also **resources taxes** payable on profits from sales of petroleum commodities. At various times, Australia has also had a number of other Commonwealth taxes which have now been abolished including inheritance taxes and, more recently, taxes on carbon emissions and on mining super-profits.

Similarly, State and Territory-based taxes will not be examined in detail. These include various stamp duties on transfers of assets including motor vehicles, land, shares and certain business assets. These taxes are often very significant and advisors need to be alert to when and how these taxes apply. States and Territories also levy payroll taxes and land taxes. The websites for the various State revenue authorities are excellent sources for the latest information concerning these taxes and these were listed in table 1.2.

Figure 1.8 graphs State Government revenues and the various taxes from which those revenues are derived.

Local governments levy local rates on land owners and occupiers within their municipalities. These are typically levied based on a percentage of the value of the land and buildings owned by ratepayers. They help fund services provided by local municipalities such as garbage collection and recycling services, street and public space upkeep, sewerage treatment and community amenities. In 2019–20, local government collected almost $19.6 billion in rates.[57]

FIGURE 1.7   Consumption tax — country comparison

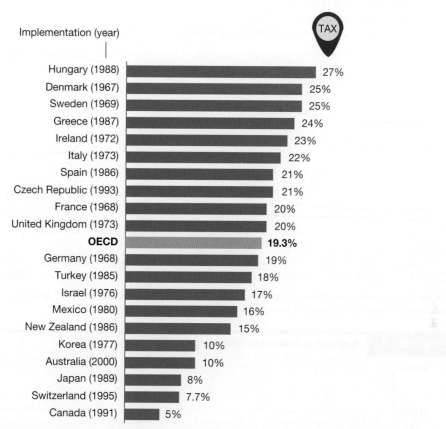

Source: OECD, *OECD Consumption Tax Trends 2020* (Web Page, 2020) https://www.oecd.org/tax/consumption/infographic-standard-vat-rates.png.

Business and individuals can be affected by a range of these various Commonwealth, State and Local taxes.[58] It is important to think broadly and ensure you are aware of this potential.

1.5 Types of taxpayers

LEARNING OBJECTIVE 1.5   Describe different types of taxpayers.

In Australia's tax system, different types of taxpayers are treated in different ways. For example, business and individual taxpayers are treated differently in terms of calculating and assessing their income and in terms of any tax deductions which they can claim. Different taxpayers are also entitled to different types of tax concessions. We will be discussing these differential treatments in later chapters.

For example, there are differences in the treatment of Australian resident taxpayers and non-resident taxpayers. These differences extend to different rates of tax (see the next section) and the sources of income upon which they are taxed. You will learn about the other differences in a later chapter.

Tax treatment also varies depending on the type of organisational structure and form. The figure 1.9 shows the number of businesses in Australia in each of the different forms of legal organisation — sole traders, partnerships, trusts and companies. Figure 1.9 demonstrates the importance for any business adviser to understand how the various structures operate. This extends to understanding and being able to advise on the different tax rules which apply to each type of legal entity.

Sole traders are not legally different from individuals, so their income simply forms part of the individual's income. Sole traders may have obligations in relation to other taxes though, including GST.

---

57 A summary of local rates and expenditures is at: https://alga.asn.au/facts-and-figures.
58 A summary of the types of taxes affecting businesses is at: www.business.gov.au/Finance/Taxation.

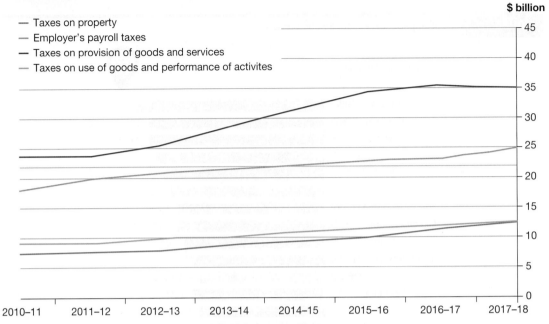

FIGURE 1.8 State Government taxation revenue

$ billion

— Taxes on property
— Employer's payroll taxes
— Taxes on provision of goods and services
— Taxes on use of goods and performance of activites

Source: Australian Bureau of Statistics, *Taxation Revenue, Australia* (Catalogue no. 5506.0, 27 April 2021) https://www.abs.gov.au/statistics/economy/government/taxation-revenue-australia/latest-release.

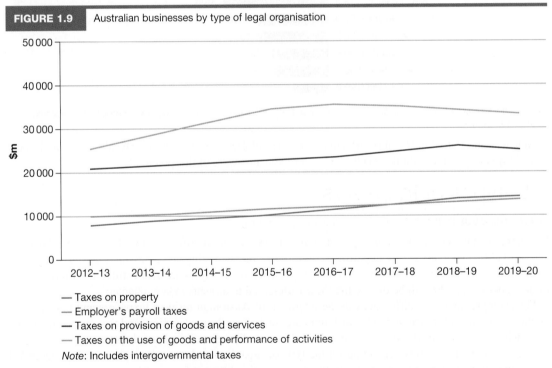

FIGURE 1.9 Australian businesses by type of legal organisation

$m

— Taxes on property
— Employer's payroll taxes
— Taxes on provision of goods and services
— Taxes on the use of goods and performance of activities
Note: Includes intergovernmental taxes

Source: Australian Bureau of Statistics, *Counts of Australian businesses including entries and exits, June 2014 to June 2018* (Catalogue No 8165.0, 21 February 2019) www.abs.gov.au/ausstats/abs@.nsf/Previousproducts/8165.0Main%20Features 1June%202014%20to%20June%202018?opendocument&tabname=Summary&prodno=8165.0&issue=June%202014%20 to%20June%202018&num=&view=.

Although partnerships are the least common business structure in terms of numbers, partnerships are very important and are very common in particular industries, including professions such as legal, accounting and medical services. Partnerships are effectively treated as a conduit for tax purposes. In other words, a partnership is not a taxable entity separate to the owners of the business (the partners). This means that, although partnership net income is calculated in aggregate at the partnership level, tax is not paid by the partnership. Instead the income is then distributed to the partners in accordance with their legal share of the partnership income according to the Partnership Act of the State in which the partnership is established and any contractual agreement between the parties. In this way, the partners are those who pay tax on the taxable income of the partnership rather than the partnership. The main rules governing the taxation of partnerships are contained in Division 5 of Part III of the ITAA36. You will learn about these rules in a later chapter.

Trusts are taxed according to the income tax rules contained in Division 6 of Part III of the ITAA36. As figure 1.9 shows, trusts are the third most common vehicle for the conduct of business and investment in Australia in terms of numbers. As with partnerships, a trust is also not treated as a separate taxpayer — simply a conduit through which income flows to those associated with a trust — the beneficiaries (the beneficial owners of the trust assets and those for whose benefit the trust is established and run) and the trustee (the legal owner of the trust assets and the person or persons charged with the responsibility of managing the trust assets for the benefit of the beneficiaries). Essentially, the net income generated by the trust is assessed either in the hands of the beneficiaries of the trust or the trustees of the trust. The rules for determining in whose hands the income of the trust is taxed are complex and depend on an understanding of important definitions, such as whether a beneficiary has a 'present entitlement' to a share of the income of the trust. You will learn about these in a later chapter.

In contrast to trusts and partnerships, companies are treated as a separate entity to their directors and shareholders — in other words, companies are taxpayers for income tax purposes.

The base company tax rate is 30 per cent. However, small companies pay a lower rate of 26 per cent. Further rate changes have been legislated for future tax years. Table 1.5 shows the rates and when they apply.

TABLE 1.5 **Progressive changes to the company tax rate**

Income year	Aggregated turnover threshold	Tax rate for base rate entities under the threshold	Tax rate for all other companies
2017–18	$25m	27.5%	30.0%
2018–19 to 2019–20	$50m	27.5%	30.0%
2020–21	$50m	26.0%	30.0%
2021–22	$50m	25.0%	30.0%

Source: Australian Taxation Office, 'Changes to company tax rates' (Web Page, 28 October 2021) www.ato.gov.au/Rates/Changes-to-company-tax-rates.

The company receives tax credits (known as 'franking credits') for tax paid by the company. Income distributed to the shareholders of the company (dividends) is then assessed at the relevant marginal rate of the shareholder. Most shareholders get a discount on the tax payable equal to the amount of tax on the dividends already paid by the company. This system is known as a 'dividend imputation' system. You will learn about this system and how companies and shareholders are taxed in a later chapter.

There are also particular rules that apply to superannuation funds, insurance companies, banks and other structures under various taxes. For example, banks and institutions offering financial services are subject to special rules under the GST. You will learn more about these rules in a later chapter. There are also various differences in the application of FBT and CGT rules depending on the legal structure of the taxpayer. You will be introduced to the most important of these in the chapters dealing with the FBT and CGT.

1.6 The income tax formula

LEARNING OBJECTIVE 1.6 Explain the fundamental income tax formula for calculating income tax liability.

At the heart of Australia's income tax is the deceptively simple **income tax formula**:

$$\text{Income Tax Payable} = (\text{Taxable Income} \times \text{Tax Rate}) - \text{Tax Offsets}$$

This formula is set out in subsection 4-10(3) of the ITAA97. This subsection also contains the following 'method statement' elaborating on how the formula works.

$$\text{Taxable Income} = \text{Assessable Income} - \text{Deductions}$$

Step 1: Work out your taxable income for the income year. To do this, see section 4-15.

Step 2: Work out your basic income tax liability on your taxable income using:
(a) the income tax rate or rates that apply to you for the income year; and
(b) any special provisions that apply to working out that liability.

See the *Income Tax Rates Act 1986* and section 4-25.

Step 3: Work out your tax offsets for the income year. A tax offset reduces the amount of income tax you have to pay. For the list of tax offsets, see section 13-1.

Step 4: Subtract your tax offsets from your basic income tax liability. The result is how much income tax you owe for the financial year.

There is also a simple-looking formula for working out 'Taxable Income' in section 4-15.

$$\text{Taxable Income} = \text{Assessable Income} - \text{Deductions}$$

Again, the ITAA97 provides a method statement for applying this formula.

Step 1: Add up all your assessable income for the income year. To find out about your assessable income, see Division 6.

Step 2: Add up your deductions for the income year. To find out what you can deduct, see Division 8.

Step 3: Subtract your deductions from your assessable income (unless they exceed it). The result is your taxable income. (If the deductions equal or exceed the assessable income, you don't have a taxable income.)

Later chapters will deal at length with the concepts of 'assessable income' and 'deductions'. A detailed understanding of these concepts is essential to a fundamental understanding of the operation of the Australian income tax system. The core provisions for assessable income and deductions are section 6-5 and section 8-1 of the ITAA97 respectively.

Assessable income includes 'income according to ordinary concepts' and 'statutory income.' Essentially, income according to ordinary concepts is the concept of income as it has been developed and refined through the application of various indicators of income in tax cases over many years. In contrast, statutory income is income which is deemed to be income by virtue of the operation of particular statutory provisions — even if that income might not otherwise satisfy the various tests for income according to ordinary concepts.

Section 6-1 of the ITAA97 contains figure 1.10, showing the relationship between income according to ordinary concepts and statutory income.

Figure 1.10 also shows two additional terms which will also be elaborated and discussed further in later chapters but are worth noting from the outset — 'exempt income' and 'non-assessable non-exempt income'. Exempt income is defined in section 6-20 of the *ITAA97* as income that is deemed exempt from being taxed by a provision of the tax law. Lists of types of exempt income are contained in sections 11-5 and 11-15. Essentially exempt income is any income derived from tax exempt organisations, such as charities and religious institutions, or specific types of income earned by others who are not tax exempt — for example, certain allowances to defence force personnel.

Section 6-23 defines 'non-assessable, non-exempt' income. As the name suggests, this is income that is neither expressly assessable nor exempt. This means it is income-tax-free income. It also means you cannot claim tax deductions for expenses you incurred in earning that income. However, it may be assessable under other taxes such as non-cash fringe benefits assessable under the FBT. Section 11-55 of the ITAA97 lists provisions that make certain types of income non-exempt and non-assessable.

A deduction reduces your assessable income to arrive at your 'taxable income' before tax is levied at the applicable tax rate. Similar to assessable income, a 'deduction' can be a 'general deduction' as a result of satisfying the basic indicators of deductibility which have been developed over many years of cases considering disputes concerning deductibility (and which are codified in section 8-1 of the ITAA97) or because particular expenditure is expressly classified as a deduction in a specific statutory provision. General deductibility applies to losses or outgoings incurred in earning your assessable income or 'necessarily incurred' in carrying on a business to produce assessable income. You will learn about general and specific deductions in later chapters.

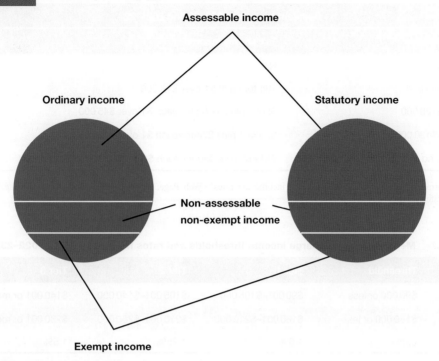

Source: ITAA97 section 6-1.

1.6.1 Tax rates, levies and offsets

Australia's income tax system is known as a 'progressive' tax system.[59] This means that the rate of tax that taxpayers pay varies depending on their level of income — the higher the income, the higher the 'marginal tax rate' which applies. The applicable rates also vary depending on the type of taxpayer. Table 1.6 shows the income tax rates applicable to resident Australian taxpayers for income earned during the 2020–21 financial year and the 2021–22 financial year. The income tax financial year runs from 1 July to 30 June.

As table 1.6 shows, resident taxpayers do not pay any income tax on their first $18 200 of income earned during the financial year and the marginal tax rate gradually increases as more income is earned. Taxpayers who earn more than $180 000 dollars will pay the top marginal rate of 45 per cent of all additional income earned.[60] In addition to the marginal rates set out in table 1.6, most Australian resident taxpayers are also required to pay a Medicare levy of 2 per cent. Be careful when calculating taxable liability to ensure you don't forget to add the Medicare levy!

In order to encourage higher-income taxpayers to take out and retain private health cover, these taxpayers must also pay a Medicare levy surcharge. Specifically, higher income resident taxpayers who do not hold private health cover are liable to pay the Medicare levy surcharge in addition to the usual 2 per cent Medicare levy at the rates shown in table 1.7.

Conversely, low-income taxpayers do not have to pay any Medicare levy — this applies if taxable income is equal to or below $23 226 (for 2020–21). Seniors and pensioners entitled to the seniors' and pensioners' tax offset do not pay the levy if their income is $36 056 or less. A reduced levy is payable if taxable income is between $23 226 and $29 033 ($36 705 and $45 881 for seniors and pensioners entitled to the seniors' and pensioners' tax offset) — within these ranges, the Medicare levy is calculated at 10 per cent of the excess over the bottom of the range. For example, if your income is $25 000, you will pay 10 per cent of the amount by which your income exceeds $23 226. Please note that above these ranges, the levy is payable on every dollar of income earned.

---

59 An interesting Treasury discussion paper on progressivity trends in Australia is at: https://treasury.gov.au/publication/p2019 -t396438.

60 Income tax rates can be found in the Schedules of the *Tax Rates Act 1986* (Cth). This Act can be found at: www.austlii. edu.au/cgibin/viewdb/au/legis/cth/consol_act/itra1986174.

TABLE 1.6   **Resident tax rates, 2020–21 and 2021–22**

Resident tax rates 2020–21 and 2021–22	
Taxable income	**Tax on this income**
$0–$18 200	Nil
$18 201–$45 000	19c for each $1 over $18 200
$45 001–$120 000	$5092 plus 32.5c for each $1 over $45 000
$120 001–$180 000	$29 467 plus 37c for each $1 over $120 000
$180 001 and over	$51 667 plus 45c for each $1 over $180 000

Source: Australian Taxation Office, 'Individual income tax rates' (Web Page, 1 July 2021) www.ato.gov.au/Rates/Individual-income-tax-rates.

TABLE 1.7   **Medicare levy surcharge income thresholds and rates from 2014–15 to 2022–23**

	Threshold	Tier 1	Tier 2	Tier 3
Singles	$90 000 or less	$90 001–$105 000	$105 001–$140 000	$140 001 or more
Families	$180 000 or less	$180 001–$210 000	$210 001–$280 000	$280 001 or more
Rates	0.0%	1.0%	1.25%	1.5%

Source: Australian Taxation Office, 'Income thresholds and rates for the Medicare levy surcharge' (Web Page, 5 July 2021) https://www.ato.gov.au/Individuals/Medicare-and-private-health-insurance/Medicare-levy-surcharge/Income-thresholds-and-rates-for-the-Medicare-levy-surcharge/#Incomethresholdandratesfrom201415to20181.

EXAMPLE 1.1

Calculating total tax liability

Jolene is an Australian resident who earned $45 000 of taxable income for the 2020–21 financial year. She pays no income tax on the first $18 200 of that income. On the remaining $26 800, she pays 19 per cent tax (i.e. $5092). In addition, she must pay the 2 per cent Medicare levy on the entire $45 000 (i.e. an additional $900). Her total tax liability including the Medicare levy is $5992.

For taxpayers who are overseas residents the income tax rates are different. As you can see from table 1.8, these taxpayers do not enjoy the same $18 200 tax-free threshold as resident taxpayers. Instead these taxpayers pay a minimum of 32.5 per cent tax on every dollar of income earned from Australian sources. Foreign residents are exempt from paying the Medicare levy. Taxation of overseas taxpayers is discussed in detail in a later chapter, as are the rules for determining the source of various types of taxable income.

TABLE 1.8   **Foreign resident tax rates, 2020–21 and 2021–22**

Taxable income	Tax on this income
$0–$120 000	32.5c for each $1
$120 001–$180 000	$39 000 plus 37c for each $1 over $120 000
$180 001 and over	$61 200 plus 45c for each $1 over $180 000

Source: Australian Taxation Office, 'Individual income tax rates' (Web Page, 1 July 2021) www.ato.gov.au/Rates/Individual-income-tax-rates.

A further important concept to be able to accurately calculate income tax payable is a tax offset. Tax offsets reduce the amount of tax otherwise payable. So, in other words, using the example of Jolene, if Jolene is entitled to a tax offset of $1000 then, once you have calculated her tax liability as $5992, the tax offset reduces her tax liability by $1000 to $4992.

Section 13-1 of the ITAA97 lists the dozens of income tax offsets that exist. Some of these are very specific and limited in their applicability and we won't be covering most of them. However, you do need to know some of the more commonly arising offsets. Most of these will be covered in later chapters where they are relevant. Among these is the foreign income tax offset. This offset operates as a reduction in tax payable by an amount equal to tax already paid overseas on the same income. Offsets are also discussed further in the context of the taxation of individuals in a later chapter.

It is important to be clear on the difference between an 'offset' and a 'deduction'. A deduction reduces assessable income to work out taxable income before tax payable is worked out. An offset is applied to reduce income tax liability and reduces the tax payable by the full amount of the offset.

SUMMARY

1.1 Describe the basic legal structure of the Australian tax system.

The legal powers of the Commonwealth and State Governments are set out in the Commonwealth *Constitution*. The main Commonwealth Government taxes are income tax, capital gains tax, fringe benefits tax and goods and services tax. State- and Territory-based revenue authorities are responsible for administering a wide range of taxes, including stamp duties, payroll taxes and gambling taxes. The overarching purpose of most taxes is to fund the functions of government. Taxes are designed to avoid imposing an unreasonable burden and the tax system aims to make compliance as simple as possible.

1.2 Explain the key sources of Australian tax law.

The main source of Australian tax law is legislation. The key income tax legislation is the *Income Tax Assessment Act 1936* (Cth) and the *Income Tax Assessment Act 1997* (Cth). The *Taxation Administration Act 1953* (Cth) establishes the Commissioner of Taxation, who is responsible for the administration of the Commonwealth tax laws. Fringe benefits tax and goods and service tax are each legislated in their own Acts. Capital gains tax is covered by the ITAA97. Courts also play a role in Australian tax law by interpreting and clarifying laws when deciding on cases that come before them. The doctrine of precedent obliges judges to follow the reasoning of higher courts. In addition to the courts, the Administrative Appeals Tribunal can reconsider ATO decisions if a taxpayer wishes to appeal them.

1.3 Describe the key ethical responsibilities of tax professionals.

Tax professionals must adhere to the ethical requirements of their industry associations and regulators. For example, accountants must comply with ethical obligations set out in the APESB Code. The APESB Code requires them to act professionally, with integrity, objectivity, with professional competence and due care and in a manner that respects confidentiality. In addition, registered tax agents must comply with the TASA Code of Conduct which imposes similar obligations on professionals engaged in providing taxation agent services. Severe penalties can apply to those who breach the TASA Code.

1.4 Describe different types of taxes.

Income tax is governed by the ITAA37 and the ITAA97. It is charged against taxable income (income less deductions) less offsets. Income tax in Australia is progressive so that higher income earners pay proportionately more tax. Capital gains tax is payable on increases in value realised when a transaction takes place involving a relevant asset. Fringe benefits tax is charged on benefits paid by employers to employees when those benefits are not subject to income tax. The goods and services tax is a consumption tax and is charged at 10 per cent on most of the goods and services sold in Australia. Businesses registered for GST are obliged to collect it on their sales and can claim it back on their purchases. A variety of other Commonwealth and State/Territory taxes also exist.

1.5 Describe different types of taxpayers.

Taxpayers in Australia are differentiated based on their legal structure (e.g. individuals and various business structures) and residency status. Sole traders are generally taxed in the same way as individuals. Partnerships and trusts distribute their income to partners or beneficiaries, respectively, who are then taxed as individuals. Companies are a legal entity and pay income tax. When companies distribute profits to shareholders, shareholders receive a credit for the tax the company has already paid.

1.6 Explain the fundamental income tax formula for calculating income tax liability.

The income tax formula is:

$$\text{Income Tax Payable} = (\text{Taxable Income} \times \text{Tax Rate}) - \text{Tax Offsets}$$

The basic application of the formula involves:

Step 1. Add up all your assessable income for the income year. To find out about your assessable income, see Division 6.

Step 2. Add up your deductions for the income year. To find out what you can deduct, see Division 8.

Step 3. Subtract your deductions from your assessable income (unless they exceed it). The result is your taxable income. (If the deductions equal or exceed the assessable income, you don't have a taxable income.)

KEY TERMS

Administrative Appeals Tribunal (AAT) A body empowered by the *Taxation Administration Act 1953* (Cth) to review the decisions of Commonwealth agencies, including the Commissioner of Taxation.

Australian Taxation Office (ATO) The agency that exercises the Commissioner of Taxation's powers.

capital gains tax A part of income tax, paid on a capital gain (the extent to which the proceeds of the sale of a capital asset exceed the cost of acquiring it).

certainty The idea that the tax which each individual is bound to pay, the time of payment and the manner of payment should be clear.

Commissioner of Taxation The official with primary tax administration and Commonwealth Government revenue collection powers and responsibilities.

concurrent powers Powers not expressly belonging to the Commonwealth or State/Territory governments, including taxation powers, under the Commonwealth *Constitution*.

convenience The idea that a tax should only be imposed at a time and in a manner that minimises inconvenience.

doctrine of precedent The legal convention that judges will find similarly in cases that are similar to previous cases heard in higher courts.

economy The idea that a tax should impose as little costs on taxpayers as possible beyond what it contributes to government revenue.

equality The idea that taxes should be imposed relative to an individual's capacity to pay.

excise duties Taxes charged on specific products such as tobacco and alcohol.

exclusive powers Powers that rest entirely with the Commonwealth Government under the Commonwealth *Constitution*.

fringe benefits tax (FBT) A tax charged on benefits paid by employers to employees when those benefits are not subject to income tax.

goods and services tax (GST) GST is a broad-based tax of 10 per cent on the supply of most of the goods, services and anything else consumed in Australia, and the importation of goods into Australia.

income tax A tax charged on taxable income (income less deductions) less offsets.

income tax formula Income Tax Payable = (Taxable Income × Tax Rate) – Tax Offsets.

Inspector-General of Taxation (IGTO) An independent officer who can review or investigate ATO decisions and make non-binding recommendations to the Commissioner of Taxation.

legislation Laws established as an Act of Parliament.

obiter dicta Matters discussed during a judgement that are not part of the *ratio decidendi*.

ratio decidendi The binding part of a judgement.

residual powers Powers that rest entirely with the State/Territory governments under the Commonwealth *Constitution*.

resources taxes Taxes payable on profits from sales of petroleum commodities.

QUESTIONS

1.1 Other than income tax, what other forms of taxation are present in Australia?

1.2 What is the doctrine of precedent? How does it help you in working out the legal significance of a tax case?

1.3 Under the Commonwealth *Constitution,* what type of power is the power to make laws with respect to taxation?

1.4 What was the legal significance of the Uniform Tax Cases?

1.5 What are the main ethical obligations on tax agents under the TASA Code of Conduct? What are the potential consequences of breaching those ethical obligations?

1.6 Is acting in the best interests of your client or your employer sufficient to satisfy your ethical responsibilities as a tax professional?

1.7 What is the basic income tax formula? In what provision of the *Income Tax Assessment Act* is it set out?

1.8 What is the difference between assessable income and taxable income?

1.9 What is the difference between a tax deduction and a tax offset? Give some examples of tax offsets.

1.10 What is exempt income? Give examples.

PROBLEMS

1.11 Simeon is a young accountant employed by an accounting firm to prepare tax and BAS returns for clients of the firm. In preparing a tax return for a particular client based on the client's tax receipts, Simeon comes across some diary notes recording a list of amounts on a page titled 'off the books cash from customers'. Simeon approaches his boss, asking him what to do. His boss advises him to disregard the notes as the client is very important to the firm and obviously didn't intend to send in the diary notes with his other records. What ethical obligations of tax practitioners might Simeon breach if he does as his boss instructs and what might be the consequences?

1.12 Laura is single and has no dependents. For the 2020–21 financial year she earned $105 000 in taxable income. She did not hold any private health insurance at any time during the financial year.
   (a) Calculate the Medicare levy and any applicable Medicare levy surcharge payable by Laura for the 2020–21 financial year.
   (b) Repeat the calculations, but this time assume Laura's taxable income was $27 000.

1.13 Amna is an Australian resident. She is a full-time postgraduate business student and part-time tax tutor. For the 2020–21 financial year she has received the following amounts:
   • $20 000 in rental income from overseas investment properties she owns
   • $50 000 from her part-time private tutoring job
   • $5000 university scholarship for her excellent grades last year.
   (a) What is Amna's assessable income? What is Amna's assessable income if she was a foreign resident for Australian tax purposes?
   (b) What is the income tax payable by Amna for the 2020–21 financial year? What is the income tax payable if she was a foreign tax resident?

1.14 For the 2020–21 financial year Li-You has earned $75 000 of assessable income and has deductions of $2000. She also has a foreign tax offset of $3000. Her employer has already withheld PAYG tax instalments of $4000 from her salary. Calculate the income tax payable by Li-You.

1.15 Superstar Tax Pty Ltd is an Australian company with a $1million dollar turnover. For the 2020–21 financial year, the company earns $100 000 in taxable income. Calculate the tax payable by Superstar Tax. How would your answer be different if the annual turnover of the company for the 2020–21 financial year was $60 million dollars?

ACKNOWLEDGEMENTS

Figures 1.1, 1.3: © Australian Government. Licensed under CC BY 3.0.
Figure 1.2: © Inspector-General of Taxation. Licensed under CC BY 3.0.
Figure 1.6: © Australian Taxation Office
Figure 1.7: © OECD
Figures 1.8, 1.9: © Australian Bureau of Statistics. Licensed under CC BY 4.0.
Figure 1.10: © Federal Register of Legislation. Licensed under CC BY 4.0.
Table 1.1: © Australian Bureau of Statistics. Licensed under CC BY 4.0.
Tables 1.3–1.8: © Australian Taxation Office
Extract: © Australian Taxation Office
Extract: © The Treasury. Licensed under CC BY 3.0.
Extracts: © Accounting Professional & Ethical Standards Board (APESB)
Extracts: © Federal Register of Legislation. Licensed under CC BY 4.0.
Extract: © Commonwealth of Australia. Licensed under CC BY 3.0.
Extract: © IBM

CHAPTER 2

Residency and source of income

LEARNING OBJECTIVES

After studying this chapter, you should be able to:

2.1 explain the relevance of taxpayer residency for tax purposes

2.2 apply the tests for determining residency of individuals

2.3 apply the tests for determining residency of business entities

2.4 explain the relevance of the source of income to determining whether it is subject to Australian tax

2.5 apply the rules for determining the source of various types of income

2.6 describe the basic features and operation of double tax treaties

2.7 describe how the challenges of taxing multinational corporations are addressed in the tax law

2.8 explain the implications of residency for the GST

2.9 explain the main features of the planned individual tax residency rules overhaul.

Overview

In this chapter you will learn about how a taxpayer's residency (i.e. the country in which they live) and the source of their income (in which country it is earned) affects how and how much they are taxed in Australia. The topic is especially significant in the context of:

- increasing transnational business operation and transactions
- increasing geographic mobility of individuals
- online transactions and complex multinational business structures that sometimes make it difficult to apply the traditional rules for determining source of income and residency of the parties to the transaction.

We will start by discussing the relevance of taxpayer residency and the rules to help determine residency for tax purposes. Then we will cover the various tests which have been developed to determine the residency of individuals and business entities (companies and trusts in particular).

We will then look at the rules for determining the source of income and the relevance of source to whether that income is subject to Australian tax.

Focus will then shift to discussing the various mechanisms for dealing with situations where income is taxable according to more than one country's tax rules and eliminating the risk of 'double-taxation' — the income being subject to tax in both countries.

This chapter concludes by flagging major changes to the individual tax residency rules announced by the Australian Government in the 2021 Federal Budget.

2.1 Residency

LEARNING OBJECTIVE 2.1 Explain the relevance of taxpayer residency for tax purposes.

In the Australian tax system, the main unit of taxation is the individual. When considering the tax treatment to be applied and the tax advice to be provided, the first question to answer is: 'Who is the taxpayer?' For example, in a company context, the tax treatment will vary significantly depending on whether the taxpayer is a shareholder taxpayer or whether the company is a taxpayer in its own right.

Once the taxpayer is identified, the next question is: 'What is this taxpayer's country of residence for tax purposes?' The answer to this **residency** question is critical to being able to work out the taxpayer's tax liability and providing accurate and appropriate advice to that taxpayer.

The previous chapter flagged one of the basic differences between the tax treatment of Australian residents and foreign residents — the income tax rates that apply. Table 2.1 presents the 2021–22 individual income tax rates for Australian residents and foreign residents side-by-side for easy comparison. Note that there are different rates that apply to income earned by working-holiday visa holders (set out in Part III of Schedule 7 of the *Income Tax Rates Act 1986* (Cth)), irrespective of their residency status, and these are explained and discussed later in th chapter in the context of discussion of a November 2021 High Court decision on the tax treatment of these individuals: *Addy v Commissioner of Taxation* [2021] HCA 34.

TABLE 2.1 Individual income tax rates for Australian residents and foreign residents

Australian residents		Foreign residents	
Taxable income	**Tax on this income**	**Taxable income**	**Tax on this income**
0–$18 200	Nil		
$18 201–$45 000	19c for each $1 over $18 200	$0–$120 000	32.5c for each $1
$45 001–$120 000	$5092 plus 32.5c for each $1 over $45 000		
$120 001–$180 000	$29 467 plus 37c for each $1 over $120 000	$120 001–$180 000	$39 000 plus 37c for each $1 over $120 000
$180 001 and over	$51 667 plus 45c for each $1 over $180 000	$180 001 and over	$61 200 plus 45c for each $1 over $180 000

Source: Australian Taxation Office, *Individual income tax rates* (Web Page, 1 July 2021) https://www.ato.gov.au/Rates/Individual-income-tax-rates.

Table 2.1 exhibits three key differences.

1. Foreign residents have no tax-free threshold. They pay tax on every dollar of income subject to Australian income tax.
2. The minimum tax rate foreign residents pay is 32.5%, whereas even above the tax-free threshold, residents only start paying 32.5% tax once their income exceeds $45 000 for the financial year.
3. At all income levels, foreign residents in Australia pay a greater proportion of their income as tax than Australian residents.

Unlike Australian residents, however, foreign residents do not pay the Medicare levy. Recall that the Medicare levy of 2 per cent applies as a flat rate on every dollar of taxable income of most Australian residents (see the previous chapter to refresh your memory on how the Medicare levy works).

Example 2.1 provides a simple illustration of the differences.

EXAMPLE 2.1

Comparison of Australian resident and foreign resident tax liability

Mohammed earns $100 000 of taxable income from Australian sources during the 2021–22 financial year. What is his tax liability if (a) Mohammed is an Australian resident for tax purposes and (b) Mohammed is a foreign resident for tax purposes?

(a) Australian resident: Mohammed pays $22 967. In addition, Mohammed must pay a further 2 per cent of the whole $100 000 in Medicare levy. The total tax payable is: $22 967 + $2000 Medicare levy = $24 967.

(b) Foreign resident: Mohammed pays $32 500. He pays no Medicare levy. The total tax payable is: $32 500.

Of course, the examples encountered in practice are unlikely to be as simple as example 2.1. For example, a person may be a resident of Australia for part of the year and a foreign resident for part of the year. In these situations, the tax-free threshold that Australian residents enjoy is reduced by the number of months that the taxpayer resided overseas. Specifically, in this situation, the tax-free threshold is $13 464 and the remaining $4736 of the resident threshold of $18 200 is pro-rated to reflect the number of months the taxpayer resided in Australia. Example 2.2 illustrates the calculation of a part-year tax-free threshold.

EXAMPLE 2.2

Calculating a part-year tax-free threshold

Mohammed is an Australian resident, but only resided in Australia for 7 months of the 2021–22 financial year.

Mohammed's tax-free threshold will be $13 464 + ($4736 × 7/12) = $16 226. Mohammad will pay no tax on the first $16 226 of his income.

Australian residents are taxed on income from *all* sources (sections 6-5(2) and 6-10(4) of the ITAA97) whereas foreign residents are taxed only on income sources in Australia (sections 6-5(3) and 6-10(5)). A later section explains how to work out the source of different types of income — this can be complicated.

Another challenge when working out the Australian income tax payable by a foreign resident or by an Australian resident on income sourced from overseas is resolving those situations in which the income is taxable according to more than one country's tax rules. These situations raise the potential for 'double-taxation' — the income being subject to tax in both countries. There are several rules to assist in resolving these situations.

The primary mechanism is the **foreign tax credit offset** which taxpayers can claim to reduce the Australian tax payable in situations where tax has been paid to another country on that income. The application of these rules is described in a later section. There are also **double taxation agreements (DTAs)** which Australia has with several other countries that contain 'tie-breaker' arrangements for helping resolve situations where both countries would otherwise have priority under their domestic tax laws to tax the same income of the taxpayer.

Residency is also important for working out various tax entitlements and concessions as many of these concessions and entitlements are restricted to Australian residents. For example, residents do not normally pay capital gains tax (CGT) on the proceeds of selling their principal place of residence. This exemption does not apply to non-residents at the time of the sale. You will learn about the CGT principal residence exemption rules in a later chapter.

Of course, the starting point for resolving all these complexities is working out whether a taxpayer is a resident for Australian income tax purposes. A few tests have been developed to assist here. Some of these apply to working out whether an *individual* is an Australian resident for tax purposes, and a different set of tests apply for working out whether a *business entity* is an Australian resident for tax purposes. We will now look at these tests in detail, starting with the individual taxpayer residency tests.

2.2 Individual residency tests

LEARNING OBJECTIVE 2.2 Apply the tests for determining residency of individuals.

There are four different tests that can be applied to work out whether an individual taxpayer is an Australian resident for tax purposes. These are:
1. the **ordinary concepts** (ordinary meaning of the word 'resident') test
2. the domicile test
3. the 183-day rule
4. the superannuation test.

If a taxpayer satisfies the ordinary concepts test, the outcomes of the other three tests are irrelevant. The other three tests are used to work out whether a person can be considered a resident *even though their circumstances might not meet the ordinary meaning of the word 'residency'*. A taxpayer only needs to satisfy *one* of these tests to qualify as an Australian resident for tax purposes (although, in many situations, an individual may satisfy more than one of the tests). If the individual does not satisfy any of the tests, then they will be taxed as a foreign resident.

Subsection 6(1) of the ITAA36 lists these tests. Additionally, according to subsection 6(1), a resident of Australia is:

> (a) a person, other than a company, who resides in Australia and includes a person:
>> (i) whose domicile is in Australia, unless the Commissioner is satisfied that the person's permanent place of abode is outside Australia;
>> (ii) who has actually been in Australia, continuously or intermittently, during more than one half of the year of income, unless the Commissioner is satisfied that the person's usual place of abode is outside Australia and that the person does not intend to take up residence in Australia; or
>> (iii) who is:
>>> (A) a member of the superannuation scheme established by deed under the *Superannuation Act 1990*; or
>>> (B) an eligible employee for the purposes of the *Superannuation Act 1976*; or
>>> (C) the spouse, or a child under 16.[1]

We will now discuss each of the four tests in turn.

2.2.1 Ordinary concepts test

The **ordinary concepts test** is a 'common law' test. This simply means the test has been developed by judges deciding cases. Essentially the test is a set of factors to help work out where a taxpayer lives and, therefore, give practical meaning to the term 'resident'.

The ordinary concepts test is *usually* used to work out whether an overseas person visiting Australia is an Australian resident for tax purposes.

The courts have developed these factors in deciding complex cases — cases where a person travels in and out of the country and may have homes or connections to other countries at the same time. Therefore, it makes sense that the factors the courts have developed are based on residency being a question of degree — in other words, a person does not have to permanently live in Australia according to the ordinary concepts test to be classed as an Australian resident for tax purposes.

---

1 ITAA36 section 6(1).

With this logic in mind, courts will look at a combination of the following issues.

1. Frequency, regularity and duration of the taxpayer's visits to Australia.
2. Whether the taxpayer owns or maintains a house or owns other significant assets in Australia. Owning a house in Australia can be a good indicator of residency, but there can be situations where a person owns a house in Australia but is not a resident or does not own a house but can be considered a resident.
3. Extent of physical presence in the country (you need to be physically here at least some of the time to be a resident under this test). If you live in Australia for more than half the year, this is a very good indicator that you are a resident (and the Commissioner of Taxation will assume you are a resident unless you can demonstrate otherwise). There are situations where people live in Australia for more than half of the year and can still prove they are not residents because of the nature of why they are in Australia, how they spend their time in Australia and the nature of their connections in the country. An obvious example is someone who is in Australia for a long holiday spanning more than 6 months. The converse situation (less than half a year and still considered a resident under ordinary concepts) also applies; for an example, see the discussion of *Levene v IRC*.
4. Purpose of visits — in particular, whether they are family or social visits indicating social and family connections to Australia, or simply business visits.
5. The nationality of the individual (e.g. as stated in their passport).

Courts tend to look at clusters of factors rather than any individual issue to help work out residency. Courts will give different weights to different factors depending on the facts of the case.

Several leading cases on this issue are old United Kingdom cases. Two leading examples are *Levene v IRC* [1928] 13 UKHL TC 486 and *IRC v Lysaght* [1928] AC 234. Australian judges have accepted that the reasoning in those cases applies with equal force in Australia.

Levene v IRC [1928] 13 UKHL TC 486

Facts: Mr Levene was a UK resident who had always lived in the UK. In 1918, he gave up his lease and spent a number of years living in various hotels in Monaco and France on medical advice. He spent 5 months per year intermittently visiting the UK to visit family and medical specialists and attend to various business, personal and religious interests.

The dispute was whether in these circumstances Mr Levene could still be considered a UK resident during the years in which he lived intermittently abroad.

Held: The Court decided Mr Levene was a UK resident for tax purposes given he retained his family and social ties with England, the lack of permanency of his overseas living arrangements, and his general 'habits of life'.

IRC v Lysaght [1928] AC 234

Facts: Until 1919, Mr Lysaght lived in England. In that year, he semi-retired from his role as a company director that involved conducting business in the UK. He remained an advisor for the company but sold his English house and permanently relocated with his family to Ireland. He continued in his advisory role for the company and travelled to Australia for a period. When he returned, he rented a house in England and spent time going to and from England, including to attend company meetings, and for a number of years spent between 48 and 101 days per year in England. He continued to own land in England and had no business interests outside of England.

The legal dispute was whether during the years in which Mr Lysaght was travelling to and from his home in Ireland he remained an English resident for tax purposes.

Held: That Mr Lysaght was a resident of England for tax purposes. Lawrence LJ observed: 'Whether a person is resident in the United Kingdom … is no doubt a question of degree and depends on a due consideration of all the facts, but in my opinion a person who regularly comes to, and stays for a substantial period in, the United Kingdom is prima facie resident therein … although he may not have any fixed place of abode therein'.

Note that the Court in *Lysaght* deemed that Mr Lysaght was a resident of England for tax purposes even though, unlike in *Levene*, it was clear here that Mr Lysaght permanently resided in Ireland during the period of his regular business visits to England. Hence, the fact that a person has a permanent residence elsewhere does not preclude the possibility of that person still being considered a resident of a second country for tax purposes.

More recent Australian cases have continued to refine and illustrate the application of the ordinary concepts test in various contexts and its complexities. Two recent examples are the cases of *Harding v Commissioner of Taxation* [2019] FCAFC 29 and *Commissioner of Taxation v Pike* [2020] FCAFC 158.

Harding v Commissioner of Taxation [2019] FCAFC 29

Facts: Mr Harding was an Australian citizen and aircraft engineer. In 2009, Mr Harding took a job in Saudi Arabia and moved to Bahrain so he could fulfil his work duties. The plan was that his family would join him there in 2011. During the time he was apart from his family, he took all his personal belongings with him, made plans for the relocation of his family including making school arrangements for his youngest child. He purchased a car in Bahrain and lived in various leased furnished apartments during this time. He also visited his family in Australia regularly, spending 91 days in Australia in 2011 in the family home he owned and retained during this time. However, Mr Harding's relationship with his wife broke down during this time, as he was unable to convince her to relocate overseas, with the couple separating in October 2011 and ultimately divorcing in 2014.

The legal dispute was whether during 2011 Mr Harding was an Australian tax resident either under the ordinary concepts or under the domicile test.

Held: The Full Federal Court held that he was NOT an Australian resident under either test on the facts. Despite Mr Harding retaining a number of connections with Australia during the relevant time including his numerous visits, maintaining ownership of an Australian family home and retaining financial connections in Australia, he was not deemed as satisfying the ordinary concepts test. This is because, on balance, the Court was satisfied that Mr Harding always maintained an intention to permanently or indefinitely relocate overseas and that his actions at all times were consistent with that intention. During the relevant period, the connections with Australia were simply 'remnants' of his previous residency rather than indicating an intention to reside in Australia. The reasoning of the Court on the domicile test is discussed section 2.2.2.

This case illustrates the complexities that can arise in applying the current residency tests in unusual factual circumstances such as those of Mr Harding. The Australian Taxation Office (ATO) has issued a Decision Impact Statement setting out its response to the decision. Cases such as this one have also led to support for calls for simplification of the law. The reforms announced in the 2021 Federal Budget to address these concerns are outlined in section 2.9.

The Commissioner of Taxation has published a public ruling on his interpretation of the ordinary concepts test — TR 98/17.[2] Figure 2.1 shows the front page of the ruling.

The ruling contains many pages of case examples illustrating how the ordinary concepts test will be applied by the Commissioner of Taxation in various more complicated situations. Complications can arise when, for example, a person comes to Australia not intending to become a resident, but at some stage changes their intentions or stays longer or shorter than the time they had intended.

Examples 2.3 and 2.4 are adapted from examples in TR 98/17 — one is an example of a situation in which the foreign visitor is a resident, and one in which the foreign visitor is not a resident applying the ordinary concepts test.

EXAMPLE 2.3

Ordinary concepts test

Ralph, an American Football player is offered a 2-year contract to play for an Australian Rules Football club. The club provides a house for Ralph and his family to live in while in Australia. He leases his home in the United States, sells his car, redirects his email to Australia and has his furniture shipped to Australia. He enrols his children in an Australian school and they attend that school.

Unfortunately, however, Ralph has difficulty adjusting to life in Australia. Eventually his performance suffers, and he loses his football employment contract. He and his family return to the United States after only 4 months.

Was Ralph an Australian resident according to ordinary concepts during the 4 months he was here?

---

2 See Australian Taxation Office, *Income tax: residency status of individuals entering Australia* (TR 98/17, 1998).

The answer is 'yes'. Even though he returned home early, his actions in selling his house and relocating his family and other possessions all indicated a clear intention to live in Australia. He is taxable as an Australian resident on the income he earned during the 4 months he resided in Australia.

Source: Adapted from Australian Taxation Office, *Income tax: residency status of individuals entering Australia* (TR 98/17, 1998) https://www.ato.gov.au/law/view/pdf/pbr/tr1998-017.pdf.

FIGURE 2.1   TR 98/17 — page 1

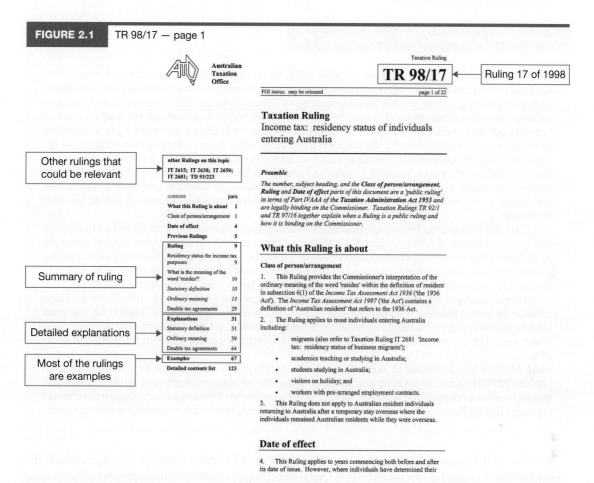

Source: Australian Taxation Office, *Income tax: residency status of individuals entering Australia* (TR 98/17, 1998) https://www.ato.gov.au/law/view/document?Docid=TXR/TR9817/NAT/ATO/00001.

EXAMPLE 2.4

Ordinary concepts test

Michelle is a French wine expert who comes to Australia to do some research for 5 months. The research takes longer than she envisaged, and she ends up staying in Australia for 8 months.

Michelle's family do not travel with her to Australia. She continues to help to run the family wine business in France from Australia. She stays in a backpacker hostel while she is in Australia. She uses credit cards to meet day-to-day expenses rather than opening a bank account. At one stage she needs to go back to France for a week to sort out some problems with the business there.

Is Michelle an Australian resident according to ordinary concepts during her stay?

The answer is 'no'. Even though Michelle was in Australia for a relatively long time and was not here for pleasure, all of the other factors relating to her presence in Australia suggest that the quality and character of her stay reflect that of a visitor who is temporarily in Australia rather than residing here. This includes the continuing significant business activity she is involved with in France while she is here, the fact that her family did not accompany her, the temporary nature of her accommodation and financial arrangements, and the lack of any other arrangements indicating any permanency in her Australian plans.

Source: Adapted from Australian Taxation Office, *Income tax: residency status of individuals entering Australia* (TR 98/17, 1998) https://www.ato.gov.au/law/view/pdf/pbr/tr1998-017.pdf.

As previously mentioned, a further recent case that has considered the ordinary concepts test is *Commissioner of Taxation v Pike* [2020] FCAFC 158. The case demonstrates the factual complexities that can arise in determining both domicile and ordinary residency and provides a contemporary confirmation that an individual can be a resident of more than one country at the same time. The case also considered the domicile test and the tie-breaker provisions for determining residence under Australia's double tax agreement with Thailand. We discuss double tax agreements later in this chapter but we will not consider those aspects for present purposes.

Commissioner of Taxation v Pike [2020] FCAFC 158

Facts: Mr Pike was born in Zimbabwe. In early 2005, he accepted a job in Australia and relocated to Australia with his de facto spouse and children. He rented a home for himself and his family, and purchased a car and furnishings. Later, in 2005, Mr Pike returned to Zimbabwe to dispose of his assets and complete his employment contract there. However, he did not sell his home in Zimbabwe. He then returned to Australia but was unable to find further Australian work and, in 2006, he accepted a job in Thailand. Mr Pike then worked in Thailand for the following 8 years until 2014, living in rental accommodation for the entire time. His family remained in rental accommodation in Australia throughout this time as his spouse did not want to relocate to Thailand. During his time in Thailand, Mr Pike formed close sporting and social connections there, although he regularly visited his family in Australia whenever possible. The percentage of his time he spent in Australia during these years fluctuated between 8 and 42 per cent of the year.

In 2009, Mr Pike and his family were granted permanent Australian residency. In August 2010, his wife and children became Australian citizens. Mr Pike also became an Australian citizen, but not until April 2014. During this time, the family had purchased vacant land in Australia (in 2010) with a view to building a home; however, this did not eventuate and the block was sold in 2013. In 2014, Mr Pike relocated to Tanzania for work, and in 2016 relocated again to Dubai. His family continued to reside in Australia.

The legal issue was whether Mr Pike was a resident of Australia from 2009 to 2016. There was also an issue of application of the tie-breaker test in the DTA between Australia and Thailand for the years Mr Pike was working in Thailand. However, for present purposes, we will focus on the residency issue which required the Court to consider the application of the ordinary concepts test to this complicated set of facts.

Held: Mr Pike was a resident of Australia under the ordinary concepts test for the entire period from 2009 to 2016. He was also an Australian resident under the domicile test from April 2014 (when he was granted Australian citizenship). Note that, having determined that Mr Pike was a resident under the ordinary concepts test for the entire period, the Court was not technically required to examine the domicile test.

In terms of the ordinary concepts test, the Full Court of the Federal Court in *Pike* agreed with the determination of Logan J at first instance. In his judgement, Logan J confirmed that a person can be resident in more than one country at the same time. His Honour observed: 'A person's preference might be to reside in one place but the exigencies of business might require that they reside in another. And, where a person has a close family, the exigencies of business might require that they reside in two places, the one where work is available; the other where their family is located, dividing their time as best they can between the two. That is this case.'[3]

Logan J elaborated as follows: 'The combined exigencies of Mr Pike's existing skill and experience and the absence of relevant work in Australia meant that the earning potential of that skill and experience could only be realised by living and working abroad. … But no less enduring and, as a matter of personal character, no less compelling for him, has been his devotion to his family. The evidence discloses that, over the relevant years, there is a pattern or habit on Mr Pike's part of living and working abroad and also of returning here to live with his family as often and for as long as possible'.[4] And further: 'The reality on the whole of the evidence is that Mr Pike has led and continues to lead two lives, a working life abroad with an attendant social life and a family life in Australia. The two lives are inter-connected not just by the financial support that Mr Pike provides from the fruits of his working life but also by enduring ties of love and affection for his wife and sons and physical presence when possible.'[5]

---

3 *Pike v Commissioner of Taxation* [2019] FCA 2185, [59].
4 Ibid [61].
5 Ibid [62].

The Full Court also accepted Logan J's reasoning that rental of accommodation rather than purchasing a home did not preclude Mr Pike being treated as a resident for tax purposes. Further, citizenship is not determinative of the question of whether someone is a resident under the ordinary concepts test. It is not a requirement of the ordinary concepts test, but did support the conclusion in this case, combined with the other facts of the case, that Mr Pike was a resident according to the ordinary concepts test throughout the relevant years.

2.2.2 Domicile test

The **domicile test** is one of the three statutory tests for determining residency where the ordinary concepts test is not satisfied. **Domicile** essentially means a person's country of origin (like citizenship) or later country chosen by a person as the country in which they intend to permanently live. This is consistent with the *Domicile Act 1982* (Cth) section 10, which states: 'The intention that a person must have in order to acquire a domicile of choice in a country is the intention to make his home indefinitely in that country.'[6]

Most of the cases in which this test is applied are to taxpayers who were born with an Australian domicile but who now live overseas. So, the question is usually whether their domicile has changed to that country.

Essentially, under the domicile test, a taxpayer will be considered a resident if 'domiciled' in Australia unless the Commissioner of Taxation is satisfied the taxpayer has a 'permanent abode' somewhere else. Hence, the key issue is working out the taxpayer's 'permanent abode'. Taxation Ruling IT 2650 sets out the Commissioner's views on how the domicile test applies.[7]

IT 2650 specifies that the Commissioner will consider:

(a) the intended and actual length of the taxpayer's stay in the overseas country
(b) whether the taxpayer intended to stay in the overseas country only temporarily and then to move on to another country or to return to Australia at some definite point in time
(c) whether the taxpayer has established a home (in the sense of dwelling place; a house or other shelter that is the fixed residence of a person, a family or a household), outside Australia
(d) whether any residence or place of abode exists in Australia or has been abandoned because of the overseas absence
(e) the duration and continuity of the taxpayer's presence in the overseas country
(f) the durability of association that the person has with a particular place in Australia; that is, maintaining bank accounts in Australia, informing government departments such as the Department of Social Security that he or she is leaving permanently and that family allowance payments should be stopped, place of education of the taxpayer's children, family ties and so on.[8]

This list of factors reflects the approach taken by judges in several cases. Most of the cases concern Australians who have worked overseas for some time and the question of their *permanent* residency intentions. Two leading examples are *FCT v Applegate* [1979] FCA 37[9] and *FCT v Jenkins* (1982) 12 ATR 745. Although, as flagged earlier in the chapter, recent leading cases such as *Harding* and *Pike* have also considered the question of domicile.

FCT v Applegate [1979] FCA 37

Facts: Mr Applegate was an Australian lawyer sent to work in Vanuatu at the Vanuatu branch of the Australian law firm by which he was employed. There was no time limit set for his return although, when he left, he did intend to return to Australia at some point in the distant future. The taxpayer and his wife sold all their Australian assets and moved to Vanuatu. They stayed for 2 years before he got ill and had to return to Australia.

The issue was whether the income he earned while in Vanuatu was assessable in Australia as income earned by an Australian resident overseas.

---

6 See the *Domicile Act 1982* (Cth) section 10, which states: 'The intention that a person must have in order to acquire a domicile of choice in a country is the intention to make his home indefinitely in that country'.
7 This link to this Ruling is at: www.ato.gov.au/law/view/pdf/pbr/it2650.pdf.
8 Taxation Ruling IT 2650, [23].
9 The link to the case is at: www.austlii.edu.au/cgi-bin/viewdoc/au/cases/cth/FCA/1979/37.html?context=1;query=applegate; mask_path=.

The Commissioner of Taxation argued that because the taxpayer intended to return to Australia at some point in the future, he never ceased being 'domiciled' in Australia.

Held: The Federal Court disagreed with the Commissioner and found in favour of the taxpayer. In particular, the Court said intention to return is just one factor to be considered in working out a person's 'permanent abode' to satisfy the domicile test. The nature and quality of the taxpayer's connection with the overseas country is more important. Fisher J said:

Material factors for consideration will be the continuity or otherwise of the taxpayer's presence, the duration of his presence and the durability of his association with the particular place.[10]

FCT v Jenkins (1982) 59 FLR 467

Facts: This case involved a transfer of a bank officer to Vanuatu for 3 years. The taxpayer became ill and returned to Australia early (after 18 months). The taxpayer had tried to sell his Australian house before leaving and leased it out when he couldn't find a buyer. He also retained an Australian bank account while he was away.

Held: The Queensland Supreme Court found in favour of the taxpayer, even though the taxpayer had no intention to 'indefinitely' live overseas. Essentially, in the circumstances, the intention to live overseas for 3 years was considered sufficient to show the taxpayer had a 'permanent place of abode' outside Australia while he was working in Vanuatu and therefore was not an Australian resident for tax purposes during that time.

You may be wondering why these cases both happen to be about individuals working in Vanuatu. Vanuatu has no general income taxes. Hence, income earned in Vanuatu is tax free! Vanuatu has historically been known as a 'tax haven'.

While at first glance *Levene* and *Jenkins* may seem inconsistent, applied in an Australian context they both confirm that intention to return to Australia at some point in future does not preclude a finding that a taxpayer can have a permanent place of abode overseas. *Levene* illustrates that a taxpayer can have a permanent abode overseas, even if there was always an intention to return to Australia at some indeterminate time in future.

Jenkins confirms this also applies if the intention to live and work overseas is only for a fixed period of as little as 3 years. This is because the issue of permanent abode will ultimately be determined by a number of factors indicating the overall nature and quality of connection with the overseas country while the taxpayer is living there — not simply the nature or timing of the taxpayer's intentions to return to Australia.

As previously mentioned, the *Harding* case also considered the domicile test and, in particular, considered the question of whether the taxpayer in that case had a 'permanent place of abode' in Australia. The Full Federal Court determined that Mr Harding did not have a permanent place of abode in Australia, despite maintaining an Australian family home and only leasing an apartment while residing overseas. The key principle from the case is the Court's determination that 'place' of abode does not simply mean a specific house or dwelling, but also refers to a town or country. And it was clear on the facts that, despite maintaining an Australian house for his family, Mr Harding's permanent *place* of abode was at all relevant times overseas. This interpretation of permanent place of abode as being a place and not necessarily a specific house or dwelling was recently applied by the Administrative Appeals Tribunal in *Handsley v Commissioner of Taxation* [2019] AATA 917.

As also outlined earlier, domicile was considered in the *Pike* case, although not strictly required, as the taxpayer was deemed to be a resident under the ordinary concepts test for the entire relevant period. It will be recalled from our earlier discussion of that case that the Court confirmed the possibility of being resident in more than one country at the same time. However, the Court in *Pike* also confirmed that it is NOT possible to be domiciled in more than one country at once. In the case of Mr Pike, the Court considered it uncontroversial that Mr Pike's domicile of origin was Zimbabwe. The Commissioner had submitted that Mr Pike acquired a domicile of choice in Australia in 2005 and has retained that ever since. Mr Pike contested that, maintaining that he did not acquire a domicile of choice until living in

---

10 (1979) FCA 37, [18].

Thailand, retaining that until he left there in 2014 with Tanzania and the UAE successively becoming his domicile of choice. The key issue was whether and when Mr Pike formed any intention to make his home in Australia indefinitely. The complexities were described by Logan J at first instance as follows:

> ... [T]he evidence discloses that Mr Pike contemplated cutting but did not fully cut his ties with Zimbabwe in 2010. That was when he and Ms Thornicroft sold the Harare home and bought the Brookwater land, intending to build a home on it, when she and their sons acquired Australian citizenship and when he made inquiries about Australian citizenship. But as late as 2012 Mr Pike renewed his Zimbabwean passport. He had also used his Zimbabwean driver's licence in Thailand. In relation both to Thailand and Tanzania (and now the UAE), he contemplated, in discussion with Ms Thornicroft, her joining him to live there. In terms of physical presence in Australia ... it has been as short as 32 days in one year and yet as long as 155 days in another. There was both genuine commitment but also an element of expediency in Mr Pike's acquisition of Australian citizenship in 2014. Truly, there are mixed signals, in terms of the acquisition of a domicile of choice, sent by Mr Pike's conduct since his arrival in Australia in 2005. Yet there is a consistent pattern of his returning to live in Australia in what he so very clearly regards as his family home, year after year, on and from his first departure for Thailand in 2006.[11]

In light of the 'mixed signals' noted by Logan J, his Honour ultimately concluded that it was only clear that Mr Pike intended to make his home in Australia indefinitely from 2014 when he finally acquired Australian citizenship.

Pike is a good example of the challenges that can arise in determining whether there has been a change of domicile. There are a number of further examples in IT 2650. Example 2.5 is adapted from one of the examples in Taxation Ruling IT 2650. Note that this Ruling is currently being reviewed to take into account the *Harding* decision. Nevertheless, this Ruling remains useful as a tool to test your understanding of how the domicile test applies. Many of the examples in IT 2650 are based on real cases, and hence, are worth looking at to further enhance your understanding.

EXAMPLE 2.5

The domicile test

An architect secures a position with a US firm and undertakes to work in New York for 30 months. She sells her home in Australia and purchases a home in New York. She closes her Australian bank account. She enrols her two children in a secondary school near the new home which they attend for 2 years. With no other close family ties in Australia, she does not return to visit during her stay in the United States. At the end of the 30 months, she decides to extend her stay for a further year.

Where is her permanent place of abode? What factors are relevant to your decision?

On these facts, the taxpayer's permanent place of abode is the United States. She will be a foreign resident for Australian tax purposes. This is because of the permanent nature of her connection with the United States. The purchase of a home in New York and the sale of her home in Australia are significant indicators. So is her absence of family ties in Australia, and the fact that her children travelled with her and attended school in the United States. In these circumstances, the fact that the appointment overseas was for 30 months (42 months with the extension) *might* indicate an intention to return to Australia at some stage does not outweigh those factors and indicate any permanent abode in Australia.

Source: Adapted from Australian Taxation Office, *Income tax: residency status of individuals entering Australia* (IT 2650, 1991) https://www.ato.gov.au/law/view/document?locid=ITR/IT2650/NAT/ATO.

2.2.3 183-day rule

As the name suggests, the **183-day rule** simply provides that an individual will be considered a resident for tax purposes if they have had a physical presence in Australia for more than half the year (i.e. at least 183 days). Bear in mind that this test is currently only relevant where a person is not considered a resident under the ordinary concepts test. Physical presence in the country for more than half the year is an important factor in favour of a person being considered a resident under that test as discussed.

However, it should be noted that physical presence in Australia will be of increased significance for determining residency under the simplified residency rules announced in the 2021 Federal Budget and slated for commence on 1 July 2022. The broad nature of these proposed reforms is set out in section 2.9.

---

11 Ibid [77].

A couple of things to note about the current 183-day rule — the 183 days doesn't have to be a continuous period. So, if a person lived in Australia for several shorter stays which in total add to 183 days or more, then that is enough to satisfy the rule.

However, an important exception exists: the Commissioner of Taxation has discretion *not* to apply the rule even when a taxpayer has been in Australia for more than 183 days in a year. The Commissioner will apply this discretion when they are satisfied that both of the following apply.

1. The taxpayer's 'usual' place of abode is outside Australia (note that 'usual' abode is less strict than 'permanent' abode, which is the standard applied in the domicile test).
2. The taxpayer doesn't intend to take up residence in Australia. The Commissioner considers ordinary concepts test factors to determine whether the taxpayer has any intention to take up residence in Australia.

A recent example considering the application of the 183-day test is the case of *Stockton v Commissioner of Taxation* [2019] FCA 1679.

Stockton v Commissioner of Taxation [2019] FCA 1679

Facts: Ms Stockton was an 18-year-old United States citizen who decided to travel to Australia on a working holiday. She was in Australia from September 2016, returning to the USA in June 2017. During her time in Australia she travelled extensively, living in various short-term forms of accommodation such as youth hostels and other accommodation sourced mainly on Airbnb. Her room in her family home in the USA where she lived prior to her travels was retained for her during her visit to Australia and she left behind all of her belongings other than those she needed for her Australian trip. She bought a car while in Australia, but sold it before departing back to the USA. The question was whether she was an Australian resident for the 2017 financial year. The Court also considered the question of whether, if deemed to be a resident, she would be a resident from the first day of the month in which she arrived in Australia until the last day of the month in which she departed from Australia (i.e. for the period from 1 September 2016 until 30 June 2017) or for the entire financial year.

Held: The Court considered both the ordinary concepts test and the 183-day test and determined that Ms Stockton was not a resident under either test. Further, had she been deemed to be a resident under the 183-day test, she would only be considered a resident for the months in which she was present in Australia, not the entire financial year.

Insofar as the 183-day test was concerned, Ms Stockton was clearly present in Australia for more than half of the 2017 income year (295 days in all). Hence, the question was whether, notwithstanding her physical presence in Australia for more than 183 days in the year, her usual place of abode remained in the USA during that period. The Court held that at no point was Australia Ms Stockton's usual place of abode. The following extract from the judgement of Logan J identifies the facts supporting this conclusion:

> On the whole of the evidence, there is just no doubt that the Commissioner ought to have been satisfied that Ms Stockton's usual place of abode was certainly the USA and, as it happened, her family home in Florida. That is where she had usually lived for her whole life before coming to Australia. That is to where she returned to live for an extended period after she visited here. And that is where, during her visit here, she intentionally, and permissively, retained her residential base. None of this was coincidental. That her room at the family home remained reserved for her with such of her belongings as she did not consider necessary to take to Australia tells against any conclusion that her coming to Australia marked a departure from the hitherto residential habit of a lifetime. … Each of these facts is eloquent as to where her usual place of abode was located in the 2017 income year. Ms Stockton was a welcome guest entrant to Australia but always a self-supporting, unsettled itinerant, not just of finite but of uncertain duration of presence. Her usual 'place of abode' was in the USA.[12]

2.2.4 Superannuation test

The **superannuation test** is only relevant to Commonwealth public servants working overseas. Essentially, if a person is an Australian public servant (defined by reference to membership of certain Commonwealth superannuation funds[13]) that individual will be considered a resident, even if they would not be considered

---

12 Ibid [44].

13 The superannuation funds this applies to are now closed to new members, so over time this test is becoming less relevant.

---

a resident under any of the other tests. This test is designed to ensure diplomats and other Australian Government employees posted overseas continue to be treated as Australian residents during their overseas posting.

Note that it is currently proposed to replace the superannuation test with a new test — an 'overseas government officials test' which will simply deem any Australian overnment official to be an Australian tax resident during the term of any deployment overseas. The proposed reforms are discussed furterher in section 2.9.

Note also that the superannuation test and all the other preceding tests can be overridden by international tax treaties and DTAs made pursuant to those treaties. These are explained later in this chapter.

2.3 Business entity residency tests

LEARNING OBJECTIVE 2.3 Apply the tests for determining residency of business entities.

In this section, we will describe the residency tests for two types of business entities: companies and trusts.

2.3.1 Residency tests for companies

As noted earlier, companies are considered a taxpayer in their own right — separate from the individuals who own and run the company. To determine whether a company is an Australian resident for tax purposes, the tests are different to those applying to individuals.

Specifically, there are three different tests and, provided a company satisfies at least one of these three tests, it will be considered an Australian resident for tax purposes. The three tests are:

1. place of incorporation
2. place of central management and control
3. controlling shareholder.

A useful way to approach decisions about company residency is:

1. a company is an Australian resident if it is incorporated in Australia
2. if a company is not incorporated in Australia, it will still be considered an Australian resident if it satisfies either:
   (a) the place of central management and control test, or
   (b) the controlling shareholder test.

2.3.1.1 Place of incorporation test

A company comes into legal existence as a **person** when it is 'incorporated'. The **place of incorporation test** simply means that if a company is incorporated in Australia under Australian Corporations Law (the *Corporations Act 2001* (Cth)), the company will be considered an Australian resident for tax purposes. A company's Certificate of Incorporation will usually state the place where the company was registered or incorporated. The Certificate of Incorporation is considered conclusive evidence of the place of incorporation of a company.

2.3.1.2 Place of central management and control test

The **place of central management and control test** is more complicated than the place of incorporation test. The test applies in situations where, even if the company is not incorporated in Australia, it can be shown that the central management and control of the company is based in Australia and the company carries on some business in Australia. The complexity arises in trying to work out where a company has its central management and control. Case law helps to give us some guidelines. *Malayan Shipping Co v FCT* [1946] FCA 7[14] considered the concept of central management and control.

Malayan Shipping Co v FCT [1946] FCA 7

Facts: In this case, Malayan Shipping Co was a charter ship company incorporated in Singapore and the only trading contracts of the company were made in Singapore. However, the controlling shareholder and managing director, Mr Sleigh, was an Australian resident. No company decisions could be made ▶

---

14 The link to the case is at: www.austlii.edu.au/au/cases/cth/HCA/1946/7.pdf.

without the approval of Mr Sleigh. He also negotiated all company contracts and the company constitution specified that no resolution of the company could be legally effective without his approval.

The legal issue was whether the company was taxable as an Australian resident.

Held: The High Court ruled the company was an Australian resident for tax purposes. Williams J reasoned that to determine residency for tax purposes you must look at where the *real* control of the company is located. This means looking at where high-level decision-making and monitoring occurs and where decisions are made. This is the key consideration, irrespective of whether contracts or other paperwork are made in other countries. Hence, even though the only trading contracts of the company were made in Singapore, the company was still an Australian resident for tax purposes.

In order to understand how the place of central management and control test works, it is helpful to know how companies work and, in particular the role of directors and shareholders respectively in a company. Usually, the board of directors of a company are responsible for making the company's management decisions.

For this reason, where company directors reside and meet to make management decisions can be a useful indicator for determining the place of central management and control of a company. However, increasingly decisions are made via email, video-conferencing or other use of technology so it can be difficult to determine exactly where the management decisions are actually made.

The shareholders or members of a company are principally the owners of the company rather than those who make the management decisions. Via their voting rights attached to their shares they can exercise control over the composition and overall management direction of the board of directors but cannot directly intervene in the board's management decisions.

Again, there is a Taxation Ruling that sets out the Commissioner's views on how the central management and control test works — TR 2018/5.[15] Example 2.6 is derived from one of the examples in TR 2018/5 to help you understand the types of decisions indicating exercises of central management and control.

EXAMPLE 2.6

Place of central management and control test

Pattisons Limited makes shoelace aglets (the little metal or plastic pieces at the ends of shoelaces). It sells aglets direct to customers and wholesale around the world. Three types of decisions are commonly made in operating the business.

1. Setting of sales and trading policies, including what markets to sell in, whether to operate physical and online stores and pricing policies.
2. Decisions concerning outsourcing of production and where to set up and run its own factories.
3. Sales and production management decisions, such as hiring and firing of low and middle-level staff, inventory management and distribution and marketing and pricing decisions.

Which of these are decisions amounting to exercises of central management and control?

The answer is both 1 and 2. These are the types of management decisions typically made by the board of directors. In contrast, the types of decisions described in 3 are day-to-day sales and production management decisions made by Pattisons Ltd employees following and implementing high-level trading and production policies set by the board of directors.[16]

Paragraphs 36 and 37 of the ruling set out the following list of factors that courts have considered in applying the test (the relevance and weight given to each factor will vary from case-to-case but the first five are the most important):

1. where those who exercise central management control do so, rather than where they live
2. where the governing body of the company meets
3. where the company declares and pays dividends
4. the nature of the business and whether it dictates where control and management decisions are made in practice

---

15 This link to this Ruling is at: www.ato.gov.au/law/view/document?docid=TXR/TR20185/NAT/ATO/00001. The ATO has also issued a Practical Compliance Guideline (PCG 2018/9) to assist in interpreting the Ruling: www.ato.gov.au/law/view/document?DocID=COG/PCG20189/NAT/ATO/00001.

16 Derived from the example at paragraph 24 of the Guideline accompanying Ruling 2018/5 — Practical Compliance Guideline PCG 2019/9. See Ibid.

5. minutes or other documents recording where high-level decisions are made
6. where those who control and direct the company's operations live
7. where the company's books are kept
8. where its registered office is located
9. where the company's register of shareholders is kept
10. where shareholder meetings are held
11. where shareholders live.

The ATO approach does not depend on any actual trading operations of the company being conducted in Australia. A company can be considered an Australian resident for tax purposes if its central management and control is in Australia, even if it does not conduct any other activities in Australia.

At paragraph 8 of TR 2018/5, the ATO explains:

> It is not necessary for any part of the actual trading or investment operations of the business of the company to take place in Australia. This is because the central management and control of a business is factually part of carrying on that business. A company carrying on business does so both where its trading and investment activities take place, and where the central management and control of those activities occurs.

This is controversial, and deviates from the historic approach taken by the ATO.

The leading recent High Court case considering the question of what constitutes 'central management and control' is *Bywater Investments Ltd & Ors v Commissioner of Taxation* [2016] HCA 45.

Bywater Investments Ltd & Ors v Commissioner of Taxation [2016] HCA 45

Facts: An Australian accountant set up a series of companies incorporated in several foreign (mostly low-income tax) jurisdictions. The companies were used to invest in the Australian stock market. Mr Gould appointed foreign resident directors to each company. However, these directors in effect simply acted on the instructions of Mr Gould, the Australian resident controller of the companies.

The issue was whether, in these circumstances, the central management and control of the company was located in Australia or abroad.

Held: The companies were Australian residents as the foreign directors were 'mere puppets' of the Australian resident controller. The Court explained, at paragraph 41 of the decision:

> Ordinarily, the board of directors of a company makes the higher-level decisions which set the policy and determine the direction of operations and transactions of the company. Ordinarily, therefore, it will be found that a company is resident where the meetings of its board are conducted. But ... it does not follow that the result should be the same where a board of directors abrogates its decision-making power in favour of an outsider and operates as a puppet or cypher, effectively doing no more than noting and implementing decisions made by the outsider as if they were in truth decisions of the board.

Consider example 2.7 to help understand the effect of the *Bywater* case and how the central management and control test applies.

EXAMPLE 2.7

Place of central management and control test

Underwater Ltd is a company incorporated in the Bahamas. All the shares in Underwater Ltd are owned by its Australian parent company — Downunderwater Ltd. The business of Underwater Ltd is investing in stock exchanges around the world. Its directors are residents of the Bahamas. The directors regularly receive investment proposals from Downunderwater Ltd.

Where is the management and control of Underwater Ltd being exercised — Australia or the Bahamas?

It depends. If the directors of Underwater Ltd, despite meeting and making their decisions in the Bahamas, always simply 'rubber stamp' the investment decisions of the Australian parent company, they will be considered merely puppets and in accordance with *Bywater*, the central management and control of the company will be deemed to be Australia. However, if the directors actively consider investment proposals from the Australian parent company before implementing them, and seek independent advice where necessary prior to doing so rather than blindly following the instructions from the Australian parent company, the central management and control of the company would be considered to be the Bahamas.

2.3.1.3 Controlling shareholder (voting power) test

The **controlling shareholder (voting power) test** looks at whether the voting power in the company is controlled by Australian residents and does some business in Australia (i.e. to satisfy the test, the company must carry on business in Australia and have its shareholder voting power controlled by Australian residents). The relevant threshold for control for the purpose of this test is legal ownership of more than 50 per cent of the shares in the company.

Note that the company residency tests may be overridden by the provisions in international tax treaties between Australia and other countries. Hence, where a company has dual residency, double tax treaty provisions will help determine the tax situation. Usually these provide that a company is considered resident where its central or 'effective' management and control is located.

2.3.2 Residency tests for trusts

We will examine the taxation of trusts in detail in a later chapter. However, given the popularity of trusts as a vehicle for conducting business and investment in Australia, it is important to have a basic understanding of when a trust will be considered an Australian resident for tax purposes.

A trust is essentially a business structure that separates ownership and control of property or assets. Specifically, a **trust** separates the legal ownership from the beneficial ownership of the assets in the trust. The legal owner of the assets is known as the **trustee**. For example, if the trust holds land, the Certificate of Title recording the ownership of the land will show the name of the Trustee as the legal owner of the land. The trustee holds and manages the assets of the trust for the benefit of the **beneficiaries** of the trust. Trustees of a trust can be natural persons or entities (e.g. companies). The beneficiaries have a 'beneficial' interest in the income and assets of the trust. Beneficiaries can be individuals or entities such as companies.

A trust will be considered an Australian resident trust for tax purposes if the trustee of the trust is an Australian resident for income tax purposes. Just like any other Australian resident, an Australian resident trust will be liable to pay Australian income tax on all its income, irrespective of whether that income has an Australian or overseas source.

Therefore, to determine the residency of a trust, work out whether the trustee of the trust is an Australian resident. If the trustee is a natural person, the tests for determining residency of individuals outlined earlier will apply. If the trustee is a company, the tests for determining whether a company is an Australian resident outlined in the previous section will be relevant.

This is consistent with section 95 of the ITAA36 which says the 'net income' of a trust means the total assessable income of the trust calculated as if the trustee was a taxpayer in respect of that income and was a resident. The operation of section 95 will be discussed in a later chapter. Consider example 2.8.

EXAMPLE 2.8

Residency tests for trusts

A company, Wandin Pty Ltd, is trustee of the Wandin Family Trust. The beneficiaries of the Wandin family trust are the members of the Wandin family — Mr and Mrs Wandin and their four adult children. All the members of the Wandin family currently live in New Zealand. However, the trust was set up years ago when the family was living in Australia. As such, Wandin Pty Ltd is a company incorporated in Australia. The only assets of the trust are shares in companies listed on the United States stock exchange.

Is the Wandin Family Trust an Australian resident trust for income tax purposes?

Yes. This is because the trustee, Wandin Pty Ltd, is a company incorporated in Australia. Remember from subsection 2.3.1 that a company incorporated in Australia will be considered an Australian resident for tax purposes. Hence, the trust is an Australian resident, even though the beneficiaries reside overseas and the income earning assets of the trust are shares in foreign companies.

Residency of trusts for capital gains tax purposes is a little more complicated and depends on the type of trust involved. For trusts that are *not* unit trusts, section 995-1 of the ITAA97 defines a 'resident trust for CGT purposes' as a trust that at any time during the relevant income year either had a trustee that was an Australian resident or the central management and control of the trust was in Australia.

A **unit trust** is a trust in which the beneficiaries have a fixed entitlement in the income of the trust (usually corresponding to the number of units the beneficiary holds in the trust, like a shareholder entitlement to company dividends). For example, if a beneficiary owns 6 of the 10 issued units in a unit trust, they would normally be entitled to 60 per cent of the income and assets of the trust.

This is different to the other common form of trust — a discretionary trust. In **discretionary trusts** the beneficiaries have a 'mere expectancy' in the trust — their entitlement to share in the income of the trust is subject to the exercise of discretion of the trustee which can vary from year to year. For example, if a person is one of 10 beneficiaries of a discretionary trust, this does *not* mean that they own 10 per cent of the assets of the trust or are entitled to 10 per cent of the income of the trust. The trustee has the discretion to decide from year to year whether, and in what proportions, to distribute the income of the trust to the beneficiaries. The differences between unit trusts and discretionary trusts will be discussed further in a later chapter.

A unit trust will be an Australian resident for CGT purposes where it satisfies at least *one* of the requirements in each column of table 2.2. This is applied in example 2.9.

TABLE 2.2 **Residency test for unit trusts**

At least one of:	and	At least one of:
Any property of the trust located in Australia		Central management and control of the trust is in Australia
The trust carries on a business in Australia		Australian residents held more than 50 per cent of the beneficial interests in the trust income or property

EXAMPLE 2.9

Residency test for unit trusts

The Wandin Investments Unit Trust is a trust in which there are 10 issued units. The ownership of units in the trust are held by the beneficiaries of the trust as follows.
- Mr Wandin: 3 units.
- Mrs Wandin: 3 units.
- Each of the four Wandin children: 1 unit each.

The trust also owns some residential unit blocks. Most of these are located overseas, but the trust does own a small block of residential units in Sydney. Mr and Mrs Wandin live in Sydney. The four Wandin children live overseas. The Trustee of the trust is Wandin Investments Pty Ltd, a foreign company managed by the four Wandin children from overseas, where they make all the management decisions.

Is the Wandin Investments Unit Trust an Australian resident trust?

Yes. This is because it satisfies at least one of the conditions in each column of table 2.2. Column 1 is satisfied because some of the property of the trust is located in Australia (i.e. the Sydney units). Column 2 is satisfied because Australian residents hold more than 50 per cent of the beneficial interests in the trust. Remember that the beneficiaries are the beneficial owners of a trust. In this case, Mr and Mrs Wandin are Australian residents and between them they hold 6 of the 10 units in the trust (i.e. 60 per cent of the beneficial ownership of the trust).

ETHICS IN PRACTICE

Ethics in residency and source of income

A close personal friend approaches you for tax advice in your capacity as an accountant and registered tax agent. She operates a successful business designing virtual reality equipment and apps which she distributes across the world. The business is conducted via a company incorporated in Singapore.

She has always been the managing director, majority shareholder and overall decision-maker and controller of the company. Accordingly, her move to Australia resulted in central management and control of the company also changing to Australia.

She says she is sick of paying tax in Australia. She tells you: 'I have no intention of surrendering effective control of my company or moving back to Singapore, but I need you to do whatever is necessary so that on paper it looks like the central management and control of my company has changed back to Singapore. Because you are my friend, I will pay you a fee equal to 50 per cent of the tax I save each year for doing this for me.'

What are the potential ethical problems with this proposal you face as an accountant and registered tax agent?

Setting aside the potential serious legal implications of being involved in facilitating what appears to be an arrangement clearly designed to avoid or evade tax (which we deal with in a later chapter), there are a number of ethical principles of both the TASA Code of Conduct and APES Code that are likely to be breached by acting in this situation. These principles include the requirement to act with integrity, particularly insofar as there is a clear element of dishonesty in the course of action proposed by your client/friend. Proceeding also risk a loss of objectivity, including a potential conflict of interest through the proposed commission payment arrangement in this situation. If you provide advice to the client that the proposed arrangements would be legal in accordance with the principles for determining tax residency of companies, then this would also indicate a lack of professional competence and due care given this is patently not correct. The proposed behaviour would breach the ethical requirement to behave professionally in terms of complying with relevant laws and regulations. There is also a risk that the proposed arrangement would be considered a breach of the APES Code by constituting involvement in conduct that the adviser knows or should know might discredit the profession. Similar obligations contained in the TASA Code are also likely to have been breached here.

2.4 Source of income

LEARNING OBJECTIVE 2.4 Explain the relevance of the source of income to determining whether it is subject to Australian tax.

The preceding tests for working out Australian residency for tax purposes are necessary for several reasons including — fundamentally — whether an individual or company is subject to Australian tax laws. However, it will be recalled that one of the key differences between the tax treatment of Australian residents and non-residents is that the former are liable to pay Australian income tax on all their income — irrespective of whether the source of that income is Australia or some other country.

In contrast, a foreign resident is still liable to pay Australian tax, but *only* on income from Australian sources. For this reason, working out the source of income is very important for tax purposes. Unfortunately, there is no precise meaning to the term 'source'. In fact, the High Court has stated:

> The Legislature in using the word 'source' meant, not a legal concept, but something which a practical man would regard as a real source of income. Legal concepts must, of course, enter into the question when we have to consider to whom a given source belongs. But the ascertainment of the actual source of a given income is a practical, hard matter of fact.[17]

As such, over time, courts have developed different rules for determining the source of income, depending on the type of income being considered. The next section will describe these different rules.

2.5 Source for each class of income

LEARNING OBJECTIVE 2.5 Apply the rules for determining the source of various types of income.

As noted, different rules concerning the source of income apply depending on the type of income being considered. So, the first step is to work out the type of income — once that is done, the source of income can be determined by applying the rules described. In the balance of this part, we will consider the rules for determining the source of various types of income. We will also, however, at the end of this part of the chapter, also consider the practical challenges that transactions using modern technologies such as blockchain pose for determining source of various types of income derived from activities utilising these technologies.

2.5.1 Services/salary and wages

The source of income from providing services usually depends on identifying the place where the services were performed. The following two cases illustrate how the court works this out: *FCT v French* [1957] HCA 73 and *FCT v Efstathakis* [1979] FCA 28.[18]

---

17 *Nathan v Federal Commissioner of Taxation* (1918) 25 CLR 183, 189 (Isaacs J).
18 The link to the case is at: www.austlii.edu.au/cgi-bin/viewdoc/au/cases/cth/FCA/1979/28.html.

FCT v French [1957] HCA 73

Facts: The taxpayer was an Australian engineer who for a short period earned income from engineering services he carried out for his Australian employer in New Zealand. The income was paid monthly into a Sydney bank account.

Was the income Australian source income?

Held: The High Court decided this was income from an overseas (New Zealand) source because this was where the work was performed, even though the income was paid in Australia and into an Australian bank account.

FCT v Efstathakis [1979] FCA 28

Facts: The taxpayer was a Greek citizen, paid a salary by the Greek Government for work conducted in Sydney at the Greek Press and Information service.

Was the salary taxable as Australian source income?

Held: The Federal Court held that because the services were performed in Australia the income was Australian source income. In this case, Bowen CJ observed that source of income is to be determined according to a '... weighing of the relative importance of the various factors which the cases have shown to be relevant'.

The matter is more complex when the place where the services were performed is relatively unimportant. In these cases, consideration must also be given to the place where the contract for the provision of the services was formed, and where the payment for the services was made — for example, *FCT v Mitchum* [1965] HCA 23.[19]

FCT v Mitchum [1965] HCA 23

Facts: The United States film actor, Robert Mitchum, entered into an agreement in Switzerland to act in a movie called *The Sundowners* which was partly filmed in Australia. He was in Australia for about 3 months. His remuneration was paid to him in the United States.

The issue was whether this income was taxable as Australian source income.

Held: The High Court held that in this case the income was not Australian source income, despite the source of salary and wage payments usually considered to be where the work is performed. The Court reasoned that in this case Mr Mitchum was using his creative powers or special knowledge to such a high degree that the place where those powers or knowledge was utilised was relatively unimportant. In these situations, other factors such as where the contract is made (Switzerland in this case) and the place where the income was paid (USA in this case) can determine the source.

2.5.2 Trading stock

Trading stock is anything a business buys, produces or manufactures for the purpose of selling to its customers in the ordinary course of business. For example, the trading stock of a shoe store will be the stock of shoes the business sells to its customers. In the case of farms, trading stock includes the farm livestock, but does not include crops growing in the field — these only become trading stock when they are harvested.

The formal definition of trading stock is contained in section 70-10(1) of the ITAA97. You will learn about the tax treatment of trading stock in a later chapter. For the purpose of determining the source of trading stock income, the income source is where the trading activity takes place.

---

19 The link to the case is at: www8.austlii.edu.au/cgi-bin/viewdoc/au/cases/cth/HCA/1957/73.html.

2.5.3 Sale of property

The source depends on the type of property involved — in particular, whether it is 'real' property or not.

Real property is land, or a building permanently affixed to land. Because of the immobile nature of real property, the source of income from the sale of real property is where the real property is located.

It is more complicated where other property (which includes intellectual property, goods and other items of personal property) is concerned. The source of income from these other types of property depends on a number of factors — the place where the contract was formed, the location of the property, the place where the contract was negotiated, and where the payment for the transfer of the property was made.

2.5.4 Interest

The source of interest payments is the place of the loan or other contract under which the interest is payable was formed and where the funds were advanced. A relevant case is *Spotless Services v FCT* [1993] FCA 276.

Spotless Services v FCT [1993] FCA 276

Facts: In this case, Spotless Services deposited $40 million with European Pacific Banking Company Limited, a bank incorporated in the Cook Islands and which carried on its business there. It did not carry out any business in Australia. Spotless deposited the $40 million under a contract formed in the Cook Islands.

The issue was whether the interest earned by Spotless Services on the $40 million deposit was assessable as Australian source income.

Held: The Federal Court determined the interest was derived from a source outside of Australia. Key factors leading to this decision was the fact that the borrower was incorporated in the Cook Islands and carried on no Australian business and the fact that the contract was formed in the Cook Islands. In addition, the deposit was repaid together with interest less withholding tax from the Cook Islands.

Where the interest is paid under a loan secured by a mortgage of Australian property, the source of the interest payment will be deemed to be Australia — see section 25(2) of the ITAA36.

2.5.5 Royalties

Royalties are a payment made in return for being able to use the asset of another. For example, royalties may be paid to use particular intellectual property assets (e.g. a trade mark such as Coca-Cola or a Beatles song featured in a movie) or to a land-owner (e.g. for extracting minerals from their land). To work out the source of royalties you should work out where the intellectual property or other asset from which the royalties are derived are located. There is an important exception though: where royalties are paid by an Australian firm to an overseas firm, the royalties are deemed to be Australian source income — see section 6C of the ITAA36.

2.5.6 Dividends

Under section 44(1) of the ITAA36, Australian resident shareholders are assessed on all dividends from whatever their source. Non-resident shareholders are only assessed on dividend income where that income is paid out of profits derived from a source in Australia. Therefore, working out the source in these cases requires working out the source of the company profits out of which the dividends were paid — this could mean applying any of the rules for the other categories of income.

2.5.7 Technological challenges to source-based taxation

As flagged earlier, before moving on from source it is worth noting that transactions utilising new technologies such as blockchain are posing practical challenges to the traditional application of source-based rules for determining taxing jurisdiction. Consider the following.

Global reach of blockchain-related activities and the digital economy

It is important to appreciate that the Australian tax system relies on the 'world-wide' income approach, which considers both taxpayer residency and income source. For the growing digital economy, including blockchain-related activities, these considerations are creating a multitude of challenges.[20]

In late 2021, the Australian Taxation Office updated their guidance to highlight the issue around taxpayers utilising foreign cryptocurrency exchanges[21] to undertake cryptoasset transactions.[22] The key message: using these exchanges creates the potential for tax obligations in other tax jurisdictions[23] (i.e. the taxpayer may have an obligation to tax not only in Australia, but in the respective overseas jurisdiction).

Similarly, where the taxpayer is a foreign resident for tax purposes, could there be tax obligations in Australia for their blockchain-related activities? This would come down to an examination of the income being derived. It is important to remember here the diversity in activities occurring on-chain: Do you think you could easily establish the source of blockchain activities?

The global reach of blockchain — and other digital activities — leads onto issues of double taxation, double tax agreements, as well as withholding tax and foreign tax credit considerations. The more we delve into the variety of activities occurring on-chain, the more complex the legal and tax implications become. Currently, there is substantial uncertainty in this space.

According to the Final Report of the Australia as a Technology and Financial Centre Committee (hereafter the 'Bragg Report'),[24] there is a recognition of a need for robustness in policy and regulatory frameworks when it comes to digital assets to ensure protection for consumers, promotion of investment and market competition.

> Governments and regulators the world over are grappling with the best way to bring digital assets within a suitable regulatory framework. While there is a need for regulation to ensure trust in the industry and protect consumers, the global nature of digital businesses means that overly burdensome requirements in a jurisdiction such as Australia will simply drive companies elsewhere. As such, there must be a balance between bringing digital assets into the regulated world while preserving their dynamism.[25]

More broadly, particularly with respect to multinational enterprises (MNEs), there is, in general, a push towards global solutions to taxation to address digitalisation of the economy, including the OECD/G20 BEPS two-pillar solution for (1) taxing rights for jurisdictions and (2) a global minimum tax.[26]

REFLECTION

Do you think source-based taxation makes sense for digital-economic activity, such as that found on blockchain?

2.6 Double taxation

LEARNING OBJECTIVE 2.6 Describe the basic features and operation of double tax treaties.

Residency and tax rules are not the same in every country. Hence, there are situations when an individual or company might be considered a resident of more than one country at the same time for tax purposes. This means they might be liable to pay tax on the same income in more than one country. In these situations, DTAs between Australia and other countries can help work out which country has the right to tax the income.

---

20 See, eg, the discussion in this chapter on the reform to the residency tests as well as issues regarding multinationals and the 'Google tax'.

21 A digital currency exchange provider is an individual, business or organisation that exchanges either money (Australian or foreign currency) for digital currency or vice versa: see AUSTRAC, 'Digital currency exchange providers' (Web Page, 20 August 2021) https://www.austrac.gov.au/business/industry-specific-guidance/digital-currency-exchange-providers.

22 Australian Taxation Office, *Cryptocurrency and tax* (Web Page, 8 December 2021) https://www.ato.gov.au/General/Other-languages/In-detail/Information-in-other-languages/Cryptocurrency-and-tax.

23 Ibid.

24 The Senate, *Select Committee on Australia as a Technology and Financial Centre* (Final Report, October 2021) 133 ('Bragg Report').

25 Ibid.

26 OECD, *Statement on a Two-Pillar Solution to Address the Tax Challenges Arising from the Digitalisation of the Economy* (Web Page, 8 October 2021) https://www.oecd.org/tax/beps/statement-on-a-two-pillar-solution-to-address-the-tax-challenges-arising-from-the-digitalisation-of-the-economy-october-2021.pdf.

2.6.1 Withholding taxes and foreign tax credit offsets

In circumstances where an Australian resident has been taxed on overseas income (e.g. dividend payments from overseas companies of which the taxpayer is a shareholder or interest payments from overseas investments), 'withholding tax' arrangements apply. The rules are contained in Division 770 of the ITAA97 and require the taxpayer to do two things:

1. include both the income and the **withholding tax** in their assessable income
2. claim the withholding tax paid as a **foreign tax credit offset**.

The maximum a taxpayer can claim as a foreign tax credit offset is the Australian tax payable on that income. For example, if $600 of overseas tax has been paid on $1000 of overseas source income but the amount of Australian tax payable on that income is only $400, the maximum that can be claimed as a foreign tax credit offset is $400.

The operation of foreign tax credit offsets is demonstrated in example 2.10.

EXAMPLE 2.10

Foreign tax credit offset calculations

Mohammed is an Australian resident. During the 2021–22 financial year, he earned $80 000 of assessable income from Australian sources and $60 000 of income from investments in the United States. He has already paid $20 000 in US tax on the $60 000 investment income. The same investments were only liable to $10 000 tax if taxed in Australia.

What is his Australian income tax liability?

	$
Assessable income	140 000[1]
Taxable income (assuming no deductions)	140 000
Tax payable before any offsets	39 667[2]
Less: Foreign tax credit offset	10 000[3]
Tax payable	**29 667**

1. $80 000 + $40 000, *plus* overseas tax withheld of $20 000.
2. $29 467 plus 37c for each $1 over $120 000 = $36 867, *plus* Medicare levy (2% of $140 000) of $2800.
3. *Note:* This is the maximum he can claim equal to the Australian tax which would have been payable on his US income.

Where payments are made by Australians to overseas persons (such as Australian company dividends to overseas shareholders, interest payments or royalties to overseas persons), Australian tax is generally required to be withheld from those payments. The amount and requirement to withhold will depend on the existence and terms of any tax treaty between Australia and the country of residence of the person to whom the payment is made. For example, a withholding tax of 15 per cent usually applies to payments of unfranked dividends paid to overseas shareholders in tax treaty countries and a rate of 30 per cent applies to payments to residents of non-treaty countries.

2.6.2 Tax treaties

Tax treaties or **DTAs** are agreements that Australia has with other countries to address possible double taxation and resolve taxation rights over income flows between various countries. Australia has separate agreements with more than 40 countries.[27] Where the terms of a DTA conflict with provisions of Australia's domestic tax law, the provisions of the DTA prevail.[28] The DTAs contain 'tie-breaker' clauses for determining tax arrangements where both countries have a right to tax according to their domestic laws.

---

27 The list of countries with whom Australia has signed DTAs and the DTAs themselves are at: www.treasury.gov.au/tax-treaties/income-tax-treaties.
28 *International Tax Agreements Act 1953* (Cth) section 4.

For example, Article 4 of Australia's DTA with the United States[29] contains a good example of a tie-breaker provision in circumstances where a person is considered a resident of both countries for tax purposes. Specifically, Article 4(2) says:

> (2) Where by application of paragraph (1) an individual is a resident of both Contracting States, he shall be deemed to be a resident of the State:
>
> (a) in which he maintains his permanent home;
>
> (b) if the provisions of sub-paragraph (a) do not apply, in which he has an habitual abode if he has his permanent home in both Contracting States or in neither of the Contracting States; or
>
> (c) if the provisions of sub-paragraphs (a) and (b) do not apply, with which his personal and economic relations are closer if he has an habitual abode in both Contracting States or in neither of the Contracting States.
>
> For the purposes of this paragraph, in determining an individual's permanent home, regard shall be given to the place where the individual dwells with his family, and in determining the Contracting State with which an individual's personal and economic relations are closer, regard shall be given to his citizenship (if he is a citizen of one of the Contracting States).

The DTAs contain specific rules for dealing with different types of income including royalties, interest, pensions, proceeds from the sale of property and personal service income. Table 2.3 sets out some of these rules.

TABLE 2.3   DTA rules for different types of income

Type of income	Rule
Personal service income	Taxed in the country of residence unless the services are performed in another country
Dividends	Taxable in the country of residence unless paid by the other country
Interest	Taxable in the country of residence unless paid by the other country
Royalties	Taxable in the country of residence unless paid by the other country
Real property	Taxable in the country of residence unless the real property is in the other country

Australia's DTAs also use the concept of permanent establishment to aid in determining taxation treatment of business profits of entities conducting business both in Australia and in the foreign jurisdiction. Where an enterprise from a country that has a tax treaty with Australia and has a permanent establishment in Australia, Australian source business income of that enterprise is taxable in Australia. Where there is no permanent establishment, business profits will be taxable in the country of residence.

A **permanent establishment** includes a fixed place of business where the business of an enterprise is wholly or partly carried out. This could mean one or more of a factory, office, workshop, farm or other property or other place of management. The existence of a warehouse or similar stock-holding facility is not enough on its own to constitute a permanent establishment nor is carrying on business through an agent or broker.

There are also DTA provisions dealing with specific types of taxpayers, such as students or entertainers and government employees.

As noted earlier, the DTAs aim to minimise and resolve situations of double taxation — the same income being subject to tax in two countries. If an Australian taxpayer finds themselves in a double taxation situation involving a country with which Australia has no DTA, there may still be relief available. The taxpayer may still be able to claim a foreign tax credit offset for the overseas tax paid on the Australian assessable income.

---

29 The link to the DTA is at: www.austlii.edu.au/au/other/dfat/treaties/1983/16.html.

2.6.3 Recent development — tax treaties and working-holiday visa holders

As noted in section 2.2.3, pursuant to Part III of Schedule 7 to the *Income Tax Rates Act 1986* (Cth), working-holiday visa holders pay tax at rates different to other visitors to Australia. This is irrespective of their residency status. Broadly speaking, these changes, effective from 1 January 2017, mean that working-holiday-makers pay more tax than Australian resident taxpayers on the equivalent amount of income, but less than other non-residents. Specifically, under Part III of Schedule 7, working-holiday-makers pay a flat rate of tax of 15 per cent on the first $37 000 of their 'working holiday taxable income' for 2019–20 and earlier years (15 per cent on the first $45 000 of working holiday taxable income for 2020-21 and later income years).[30] In contrast, the tax payable by an Australian resident deriving taxable income from the same source as an individual earning working-holiday-maker taxable income during the same period would be less with no tax being payable on the first $18 200 earned.

EXAMPLE 2.11

Working-holiday visas and taxable income

Adele earns $45 000 taxable income for the 2021–22 financial year. How much tax will Adele pay if she (1) is an Australian resident who is not a workingholidaymaker; (2) is in Australia as a working–holiday-maker (irrespective of her residency status); or (3) is a non-resident who is not a working-holiday-maker?

Adele would pay the following in tax in each situation.

1. Adele pays no tax on the first $18 200 of income and pays 19% tax on the balance.
2. Adele pays tax of 15% on the entire amount.
3. Adele pays tax of 32.5% on the entire amount.

However, these arrangements have recently been tested in the High Court in *Addy v Commonwealth of Australia* [2021] HCA 34. This case considered the interaction of these rules with Australia's existing DTA treaty obligations with the United Kingdom. The case provides a good example of the impact of DTAs on Australia's domestic tax laws.

Addy v Commonwealth of Australia [2021] HCA 34

Facts: Catherine Addy was a United Kingdom resident who came to Australia under a working-holiday temporary visa in 2015. Between August 2015 and May 2017 she lived and worked in Australia in the hospitality industry as permitted under her visa. During 2017, she earned approximately $26 000. The Commissioner assessed Ms Addy pursuant to the working-holiday visa holder rates, despite Ms Addy otherwise qualifying as an Australian resident. Ms Addy challenged the assessment, arguing that this breached article 25(1) of Australia's DTA with the United Kingdom which provides that UK nationals will not be subjected in Australia to 'other or more burdensome' taxation than is imposed on Australian nationals 'in the same circumstances, in particular with respect to residence'.

After a series of hearings in lower courts, the matter ultimately reached the High Court.

Held: The High Court unanimously ruled in favour of the taxpayer, concluding that more burdensome taxation was imposed on Ms Addy owing to her nationality. The Court held that: 'Ms Addy's circumstances in the 2017 income year including that of her residency in Australia for taxation purposes were relevantly the same as an Australian national. She did the same kind of work and earned the same amount of income from the same source; yet an Australian national was subject to Pt I of Sch 7 to the *Rates Act* to pay less tax.'[31] This constituted a contravention of article 25(1) of Australia's DTA with the United Kingdom, which prevails over Australian law imposing taxation, to the extent of any inconsistency.

As at November 2021, the ATO is still considering its position in response to the *Addy* case. However, the decision will have immediate impact upon foreign nationals from other nations with which Australia has a DTA containing similar non-discrimination provisions. Presently there are 11 such countries in addition to the United Kingdom: Norway, Finland, Japan, South Africa, New Zealand, Chile, Turkey, India, Switzerland, Germany and Israel.

---

30 Amounts in excess of $37 000 ($45 000 for the 2020–21 financial year and later) are taxed at the normal rates depending on the residency status of the taxpayer.

31 *Addy v Commonwealth of Australia* [2021] HCA 34, [8].

2.7 Multinationals and the 'Google tax'

LEARNING OBJECTIVE 2.7 Describe how the challenges of taxing multinational corporations are addressed in the tax law.

In December 2015, changes to the ITAA36 came into force to ensure that multinational companies do not structure their affairs in such a way as to exploit domestic tax residency and international tax treaty permanent establishment rules to avoid paying Australian tax on income earned in Australia. This 'diverted profits tax' has also been referred to as the 'Google tax'.

In announcing the tax,[32] the Commissioner noted that the new rules are part of a global effort to help prevent multinational businesses from 'exploiting loopholes' and taking advantage of different taxing arrangements in different countries by structuring their affairs so as to shift their profits to no-tax or low-tax countries, rather than the countries in which they are earning the profits.

The global efforts include a series of 15 actions developed by the OECD as part of a project known as 'BEPS' (base erosion and profit shifting). The aim of the BEPS project is to 'equip governments with domestic and international rules and instruments to address tax avoidance, ensuring that profits are taxed where economic activities are performed and where value is created'.[33] The OECD has provided a further summary of the issues that BEPS (and new provisions such as Australia's 'Google tax') aim to address and why they are important:

> BEPS refers to tax planning strategies that exploit gaps and mismatches in tax rules to artificially shift profits to low or no-tax locations where there is little or no economic activity or to erode tax bases through deductible payments such as interest or royalties. Although some of the schemes used are illegal, most are not. This undermines the fairness and integrity of tax systems because businesses that operate across borders can use BEPS to gain a competitive advantage over enterprises that operate at a domestic level. Moreover, when taxpayers see multinational corporations legally avoiding income tax, it undermines voluntary compliance by all taxpayers.[34]

The new Australian rules will result in Australia's tax anti-avoidance rules applying to schemes by 'significant global entities' deriving income from supplies to Australian consumers where that entity has an Australian permanent establishment as well as a foreign entity and some or all of the Australian income is not attributed to the permanent establishment in Australia.

A 'significant global entity' is an entity or consolidated group of entities with an annual global income of $1 billion or more.

Where the arrangements are made in order to obtain a tax benefit, the Commissioner of Taxation has the power to undo that tax benefit; for example, by treating relevant supplies as being made through an Australian resident permanent establishment.

Specifically, a new section 177DA of the ITAA36 was introduced. This section applies to a significant global entity who has engaged in a scheme involving the avoidance of the attribution of income to an Australian permanent establishment where the principle purpose of the scheme included obtaining a tax benefit.

The ATO has issued a Taxation Ruling — LCR 2015/2 — detailing how it considers the new rules will apply.[35] In it, the ATO discusses the 'principal purpose' requirement under section 177DA which differs from the 'sole or dominant' purpose test that normally applies for determining whether there has been tax avoidance. This test will be discussed at length in a later chapter.

These rules are an extension of existing rules dealing with **transfer pricing**. These rules are contained in Division 815 of the ITAA97 (formerly Division 13 of the ITAA36). If a multinational business has international transactions with a related party — such as a loan from a foreign **subsidiary** to a parent company — the amount of Australian tax can be adjusted if the amounts for the transaction don't comply with the 'arm's length' principle under the transfer pricing rules. In other words, if a multinational business attempts to shift profits to a low-tax jurisdiction by setting an unrealistic price for their commercial or financial dealings with their related parties, the rules allow for the possibility of audit by the ATO and

---

32 For more information see: www.smh.com.au/business/the-economy/australia-now-officially-has-a-google-tax-diverted-profits-tax-laws-pass-parliament-20170328-gv83va.html.

33 For more information about the BEPS project and each of the 15 BEPS actions see: www.oecd.org/tax/beps/beps-actions.

34 OECD, *What is BEPS* (Web Page, 2019) www.oecd.org/tax/beps/about/#mission-impact.

35 The link to the Ruling is at: www.ato.gov.au/law/view/document?DocID=COG/LCR20152/NAT/ATO/00001&PiT=201802190 00001.

the imposition of pricing adjustments and penalties. The Commissioner has issued a Taxation Ruling — TR 97/20 — explaining the arm's length principle for the purpose of the transfer pricing rules.[36]

2.8 GST and overseas goods and services

LEARNING OBJECTIVE 2.8 Explain the implications of residency for the GST.

The GST is a 10 per cent consumption tax charged on the sale of most goods and services. We will be examining the GST in detail in a later chapter. However, it is important to note that the source of goods and services and the residency of the consumer to whom they are sold can also be relevant to the application of the GST. In particular, you should note that the GST applies to sales of imported goods and services 'connected with Australia'. Connection with Australia means that the goods or services are sold to an Australian resident consumer.

Overseas businesses must levy and collect GST where they sell more than $75 000 (in Australian dollars) of goods and services to Australian consumers. These businesses must register for GST, charge GST on sales of imported services and digital products to Australian consumers, and pay the GST collected to the ATO.

Overseas suppliers must work out if their customer is an Australian consumer by using information about the purchaser from their business systems and/or taking reasonable steps to obtain residency information about the purchaser. GST is payable irrespective of whether the supply of the overseas goods or services is made by an Australian business or by a business located overseas.

Example 2.12 illustrates how this works.

EXAMPLE 2.12

GST payable

Nina purchases a new pair of trousers from a major online clothing supplier located in China. The Chinese supplier sold $200 000 worth of clothing to Australian consumers in the last year. If the trousers are on sale for $100, the supplier must also charge GST on the sale calculated at an additional 10 per cent of the purchase price. In other words, Nina will pay $110 for the trousers. The Chinese business must report the GST collected to the ATO in its GST return.

On 1 July 2018, GST was extended to apply to 'low value' overseas imports (i.e. under $1000). In these cases, the business that charges GST on sales of overseas goods to Australian consumers can be the merchant who sells the imported goods or digital services or products or an 'electronic distribution platform operator' (e.g. an app store or an online marketplace such as eBay or Alibaba).

If the sale is made through an electronic distribution platform operator, it is that operator who is generally responsible for registering, reporting and paying the GST. The new rules and who is responsible for paying the GST are explained by the ATO in a Law Companion Ruling — LCR 2018/2.[37]

2.9 Pending overhaul of individual tax residency rules

LEARNING OBJECTIVE 2.9 Explain the main features of the planned individual tax residency rules overhaul.

As flagged earlier in this chapter, in the 2021 Federal Budget, the Australian Government announced its intention to overhaul Australia's individual tax residency rules. The proposed new laws are intended to take effect from the commencement of the 2022–23 financial year. As at November 2021, the Government is yet to release draft legislation. However, it is possible to set out a generalbroad outline of the proposed changes. Broadly speaking the genesis of the proposed reforms was a 2016 Australian Government Board of Taxation review of the individual tax residency rules. That review found that the existing individual tax residency rules needed modernising and simplifying. The final Report of the Board handed down in 2019 recommended a new simplified residency test based on a 'two-step' model – a simple bright-line test followed by a more detailed analysis applicable only in more complex cases.[38]

---

36 The link to TR 97/20 is at: www.ato.gov.au/law/view/pdf/pbr/tr1997-020.pdf.
37 The link to LCR 2018/2 is at: www.ato.gov.au/law/view/document?DocID=COG/LCR20182/NAT/ATO/00001.
38 The link to the final report is at: https://taxboard.gov.au/sites/taxboard.gov.au/files/migrated/2019/12/Tax-Residency-Report.pdf.

This is the model the Federal Government proposes to become law in Australia in place of the existing residency rules. The bright-line test proposed to be adopted to determine residency of all individuals will be the 183-day test. In essence, where an individual spends 183 days or more in Australia in the relevant tax year, they will be deemed to be an Australian tax resident. You will recall that this is a significant shift from the current rules which only require application of the 183-day test where the ordinary residency test cannot resolve the matter.

Under the proposed new rules, where an individual is in Australia for fewer than 183 days in an income year a secondary set of rules is intended to be applied. Specifically, in these circumstances, consideration will be given to the number of days the individual spent in Australia together with a new 'factor test'. The factor test considers four separate factors aimed at demonstrating an individual's connection to Australia and applies in situations where an individual may have commenced residency during the relevant period or ceased residency during the relevant period. A commencing residency situation is where an individual was not a resident in the previous income year but spent between 45 and 182 days (inclusive) in Australia during the relevant year. A ceasing residency situation arises where an individual was previously a short-term resident (a resident for up to two consecutive income years) but spent less than 45 days in Australia during the relevant year. In either of these situations, the following four factors will determine whether the individual will be considered a tax resident for the relevant year: (1) the right to reside in Australia (e.g. citizenship or permanent residency); (2) Australian accommodation; (3) Australian family; and (4) Australian economic connections.

Where the individual is physically present in Australia for the requisite time period and two or more of these factors are satisfied, the individual will be considered an Australian resident. Significantly, these four factors will replace existing tests such the ordinary concepts test and eliminate subjective elements such as residency intentions that are inherent in permanent place of abode considerations for the existing residency tests.

EXAMPLE 2.13

Pending overhaul of individual tax residency rules

Although the legislation is yet to be released, consider the situation of Mr Harding from the *Harding* case discussed in section 2.2.1. You will recall that, in the facts of that case, under the current individual residency rules Mr Harding was not considered a tax resident. Go back and read the outline of the facts of that case to refresh your memory.

Would Mr Harding be more or less likely to be considered a tax resident under the proposed new rules?

Mr Harding would be ore likely to be considered a tax resident. Mr Harding was only in Australia for 91 days during the relevant tax year so would not satisfy the 183-day test. Under the new rules, therefore, the issue would come down to whether Mr Harding commenced residency in the relevant year. Mr Harding appears to satisfy two or more or the four factors applicable in this situation. He was an Australian citizen with a right to reside in Australia at the time, had family in Australia (his wife and children), had Australian accommodation in the form of the family home he owned, and he had economic connections in Australia in the form of his Australian assets. Note the fact that his intention was to permanently reside overseas during the relevant period would not be relevant under the proposed new rules.

The superannuation test is also proposed to be replaced with an 'overseas government officials test' as part of the individual tax residency rules overhaul. This test would simply provided that federal, state and territory government officials deployed overseas in service of the Australian Government would be considered Australian tax residents for the term of their deployment.

SUMMARY

2.1 Explain the relevance of taxpayer residency for tax purposes.

Residency refers to which country the taxpayer is a resident for tax purposes. Different rules apply for determining residency for individuals and business entities. Different individual income tax rates apply to Australian residents and foreign residents. Residency also affects various tax entitlements and concessions.

2.2 Apply the tests for determining residency of individuals.

There are four tests for determining the residency of individuals for tax purposes. The ordinary concepts test is a common law test that considers a combination of factors — the frequency, regularity and duration of the taxpayer's time in Australia, whether they own a house or significant assets in Australia, the extent of their physical presence in Australia, the purpose of visits to Australia, and their nationality. The domicile test, 183-day rule test and superannuation test are statutory tests contained in the ITAA36. The domicile test examines whether the individual has a permanent abode in Australia. The 183-day rule test examines whether the individual spent more than half the year in Australia. The superannuation test relates to members of specific public sector superannuation funds.

2.3 Apply the tests for determining residency of business entities.

A company is an Australian resident if it is incorporated in Australia under the *Corporations Act 2001* (Cth). If a company is not incorporated in Australia, it will still be considered an Australian resident if it satisfies either the place of central management and control test or the controlling shareholder test. The place of central management and control test considers where management exercises control and where it meets, where the company declares and pays dividends, whether the nature of the business dictates where decisions are made, what is reflected in meeting minutes and other documents, and various other factors. The controlling shareholder test examines whether more than 50 per cent of the shares are controlled by an Australian resident and whether the company does some business in Australia. A trust is an Australian resident for tax purposes if the trustee is an Australian resident for tax purposes. The residency of the trustee is determined using the tests for individuals or companies as appropriate.

2.4 Explain the relevance of the source of income to determining whether it is subject to Australian tax.

Australian residents pay Australian income tax on all their income regardless of whether the source is in Australia or another country. Foreign residents pay Australian income tax only on income from Australian sources.

2.5 Apply the rules for determining the source of various types of income.

The source of income for providing services/working for salary or wages usually depends on where the services were performed, though in some cases the place the contract was formed and the place the payment was made are more relevant.

The source of trading stock income is where the trading activity takes place.

The source of income from the sale of real property is the place in which the real property is located. The source of income from the sale of other property depends on where the contract was negotiated and formed, the location of the property and where the payment was made.

The source of income from interest is where the contract was formed and where the funds were advanced.

The source of income from royalties generally depends on where the intellectual property or other asset is located.

The source of income from dividends is determined by reference to the source of the income from which the dividends were paid.

2.6 Describe the basic features and operation of double-tax treaties.

Double taxation refers to the situation where Australians derive income from two countries, and both countries have the right to tax the same income. Australians who have been taxed on overseas income include both the income and the tax withheld as part of their assessable income and then claim a foreign tax credit offset against the withholding tax paid. The foreign tax credit offset cannot exceed the Australian tax liability on that income. Australia has double-taxation agreements or tax treaties with various other countries to set out the rules to resolve situations in which both countries have the right to tax the same income.

2.7 Describe how the challenges of taxing multinational corporations are addressed in the tax law.

The ITAA36 was amended in 2015 to prevent multinationals from structuring their affairs to avoid paying tax in Australia on income earned in Australia. Multinationals often attempt to structure their constituent companies to shift profits to jurisdictions with low tax rates. The OECD has developed a series of actions under its base erosion and profit-sharing project to help countries tackle the problem. The new rules supplement established rules on transfer pricing — intended to govern transactions within a corporate group to prevent profits being shifted to low-tax countries.

2.8 Explain the implications of residency for the GST.

Imported goods and services sold to an Australian resident consumer are subject to GST. Overseas businesses must collect GST if they sell more than $75 000 (in Australian dollars) of goods and services a year to Australian consumers. They are responsible for determining whether the consumer is an Australian resident. The rules also apply to electronic distribution platform operators acting as a marketplace, such as eBay.

2.9 Explain the main features of the planned individual tax residency rules overhaul.

The essence of the proposal is to replace the current individual tax residency rules with a simplified 'two-step' model. In this model, the 183-day test will operate as a 'bright line' determinant of residency for tax purposes. In complex cases involving questions of whether or not residency has commenced or ceased during the relevant income tax year, attention will turn to a new 4 'factor test' which involves considering, in addition to any period of physical presence in Australia, any right to reside in Australia, family in Australia, accommodation in Australia, and financial connection to Australia.

KEY TERMS

183-day rule A statutory test for determining residency that simply provides that an individual will be considered a resident for tax purposes if they have had a physical presence in Australia for more than half the year (i.e. at least 183 days).

beneficiaries In the case of a trust, the parties in a trust relationship that are entitled to benefits, including income, arising from trust property.

controlling shareholder (voting power) test A test of company residency that looks at whether the voting power in the company is controlled by Australian residents and does some business in Australia. The relevant threshold for control for the purpose of this test is legal ownership of more than 50 per cent of the shares in the company.

discretionary trust A trust in which the beneficiaries have a 'mere expectancy' in the trust — their entitlement to share in the income of the trust is subject to the exercise of discretion of the trustee which can vary from year to year.

domicile A person's country of origin or later country chosen by a person as the country in which they intend to permanently live.

domicile test A statutory test for determining residency based on a person's domicile, where the ordinary concepts test is not satisfied.

double taxation agreements (DTAs) Agreements between countries to help resolve situations where both countries would otherwise have priority under their domestic tax laws to tax the same income of the taxpayer.

foreign tax credit offset A tax offset in which an Australian resident can claim tax paid overseas to reduce their Australian tax liability.

ordinary concepts test A common law test that relies on a set of factors to work out where a taxpayer lives and, therefore, give practical meaning to the term 'resident'. It is usually used to work out whether an overseas person visiting Australia is an Australian resident for tax purposes.

permanent establishment A fixed place of business where the business of the enterprise is carried out

person A company is an example of an 'artificial person'. However, a company on incorporation enjoys most of the legal powers of a 'natural person'. A natural person is the term sometimes used to describe an individual and to distinguish a human from an artificial legal person such as a company.

place of central management and control test A test of company residency that applies in situations where, even if the company is not incorporated in Australia, it can be shown that the central management and control of the company is based in Australia and the company carries on some business in Australia.

place of incorporation test If a company is incorporated in Australia under the *Corporations Act 2001* (Cth), the company will be considered an Australian resident for tax purposes.

real property Land or a building permanently affixed to land.

residency A taxpayer's country of residence for tax purposes.

royalties Payments made by one person for the use of rights or patents owned by another person.

subsidiary A company owned and controlled by the parent entity as part of a corporate group. In the company context, subsidiary is defined in section 46 of the *Corporations Act 2001* (Cth).

superannuation test A statutory test for determining residency that specifies a person who is an Australian public servant (defined by reference to being a member of certain Commonwealth superannuation funds) will be considered a resident, even if they would not be considered a resident under any of the other tests. This test is designed to ensure diplomats and other Australian government employees posted overseas continue to be treated as Australian residents during their overseas posting.

tax treaty See double-taxation agreement.

trading stock For taxation purposes, trading stock is defined as including anything produced, manufactured or acquired that is held for the purpose of manufacture, sale or exchange in the ordinary course of a business or livestock. Referred to as 'inventory' for accounting purposes.

transfer pricing Transactions between related parties across tax jurisdictions, which are governed by tax rules to prevent multinationals from shifting profits to lower tax jurisdictions.

trust An obligation imposed on a person or other entity to hold property for the benefit of beneficiaries. A trust is a relationship rather than a legal entity, but trusts are treated as entities for tax purposes.

trustee The party in a trust relationship that holds the trust property for the benefit of the beneficiaries.

unit trust A trust in which the beneficiaries have a fixed entitlement in the income of the trust (usually based upon the number of units the beneficiary holds in the trust, similar to a shareholder entitlement to company dividends).

withholding tax Tax paid to the tax authority by the payer of income rather than the receiver of income.

QUESTIONS

2.1 Why is it important to determine whether a person is a resident for tax purposes?

2.2 What is the ordinary concepts test? What factors will help you determine whether a person is a resident for ordinary purposes?

2.3 What is the domicile test? When does the domicile test apply? Can a person be domiciled in more than one country at the same time?

2.4 Will a person who owns a family home in Australia but lives in rented accommodation while working overseas, away from her family for most of the year, be considered an Australian resident or overseas resident according to the ordinary concepts test? Explain your answer with reference to relevant case law.

2.5 Andrea, a United States citizen, has been in Australia on a working holiday for 277 days in the last financial year. During this time, she lived in a variety of short-term accommodation sourced on Airbnb as she travelled and worked her way around Australia. At the end of her time in Australia, she returned to the United States and resumed living in her parent's home where she resided before she left. She only brought with her the essential items she needed for her working holiday in Australia, leaving all her other things in the United States. Is she an Australian resident for tax purposes according to the 183-day rule?

2.6 What is the shareholder test? When does it apply?

2.7 What are the relevant factors for determining the source of income from personal services? What will usually be considered the determinative factor?

2.8 How might technological developments like blockchain make it more difficult to determine the source of income derived from activities utilising these technologies?

2.9 What is a foreign tax credit offset? When does it apply?

2.10 What is a double-tax agreement and how are they relevant to determining questions of residency and source for income tax purposes?

2.11 How was Australia's double tax agreement with the United Kingdom relevant to the case of *Addy v Commissioner of Taxation*?

PROBLEMS

2.12 Which of the following would satisfy the ordinary principles test and be classified as an Australian resident?

(a) Jonte, a South African company manager, is in Australia for a 9-month advanced management course at an Australian University. She does not bring her husband or children with her. She lives on campus and, when she is not studying, she is writing company reports for her South African company. She returns home as soon as she finishes her studies.

(b) Giuseppe is an Italian man with Australian relatives and several Australian property investments. He visits Australia every year to visit his relatives and check on his investments. As a result of a serious illness, Guiseppe's doctor advises that he give up work. He decides to live with his sister in Sydney to recover from his illness; stays for 9 months, and leases his home in Rome. While in Australia, he opens an Australian bank account, joins some social clubs and leases a car.

(c) Aisling is a wealthy Irish businesswoman. She owns several properties in Australia. Each year she comes to Australia to inspect the properties and have a holiday at the beach. Her stays vary in length from 1 to 2 months. This year she decides she needs a longer break and stays for 9 months, living at various holiday resorts in Queensland.

2.13 Would the following persons be considered 'domiciled' in Australia?

(a) A bank manager was posted to Vanuatu for 2 years. During that time, he and his family lived in a furnished house provided by the bank. The taxpayer's home in Australia was leased and he closed his Australian bank accounts.

(b) An Australian accountant has just accepted a dream job at a London accounting firm for an initial contract term of 2 years with an option to remain permanently employed with the firm at the end of the 2 years. She and her husband relocated to London, renting a furnished apartment. They kept their Australian home and other Australian investments and, during the first year after relocating, returned to Australia for a cumulative total of 2 months, during which they lived in the family home and visited friends and their parents. Unfortunately, after a year, the taxpayer and her husband separated, with her husband deciding to return to Australia and the taxpayer moving into a smaller rented apartment. After another year, the taxpayer and her husband divorced and the taxpayer decided to extend her employment with the London firm with a view to settling in London permanently.

(c) An airline pilot took a 2-year posting to Japan expecting to return to Australia at the end of that period. She was accompanied by her husband and children and purchased a home in Japan while renting out the family home in Australia. At the end of the 2 years she and her family returned to Australia as planned.

2.14 Ajax Ltd is a company incorporated in Canada, where the company conducts its business of holiday tours of Canadian ski fields. The company has 3 directors. One director lives in Australia and two live in Canada. Due to the pandemic, board meetings are presently conducted by Zoom video conference with directors participating equally from where they are based. However, prior to the pandemic, they would meet in Toronto, Canada. No single director controls the decision-making to the exclusion of the others.

(a) Where is the central management and control of the company located?

(b) Would your answer be any different if the Australian director is also the majority shareholder of the company and the Canadian directors are accustomed to usually acting in accordance with her instructions on all major decisions?

(c) If Ajax Ltd were the trustee of a trust, would the trust be considered an Australian resident in the situations described in (a) or (b)?

2.15 Which of the following amounts would be assessable income? Why?

(a) Binh is an Australian resident. He receives rental income from a property he owns in Sydney. Would your answer be different if Binh was an Australian resident?

(b) Mo permanently resides in Australia. He still has a bank account in Scotland, where he used to live. He receives $1000 each year in interest on the funds held in the Scottish bank account.

(c) Mikala, a Ukranian resident, receives a $5000 royalty from a patent located in Canberra and $10 000 in company dividends from a company located in Ukraine.

(d) Pierre is a visiting French researcher in Australia to interview French students living in Australia. He is paid by his French University into a French bank account, pursuant to an employment contract was formed in Australia.

2.16 On 1 January 2022, Annette, a lawyer for a large Australian commercial law firm, was transferred to the Dubai office of the firm for a period of 2 years. As a result, Annette leased out her house in Melbourne and her furniture was stored at her employer's cost. Because of an illness in the family, Annette returned to Australia for a month. During this time, she worked in the Melbourne office of the firm, but her salary continued to be paid in Dubai. For the year ended 30 June 2022, Annette received a salary equivalent to $80 000 from the Dubai office from which UAE taxes had been deducted. As well, she received $50 000 from the Melbourne office for the 6 months to 31 December 2021. She also earned $15 000 from renting her house in Melbourne. Ignoring any double-tax treaties, advise Annette as to whether any of the amounts are assessable income in Australia, and, if so, why.

ACKNOWLEDGEMENTS

Figure 2.1: © Australian Taxation Office
Table 2.1: © Australian Taxation Office
Examples 2.3, 2.4, 2.5: © Australian Taxation Office
Extract: © Federal Register of Legislation. Licensed under CC BY 4.0.
Extracts: © AustLII
Extracts: © Australian Taxation Office
Extracts: © High Court of Australia
Extract: © Department of Foreign Affairs and Trade. Licensed under CC BY 4.0.
Extract: © OECD

CHAPTER 3

Assessable income/income tax

LEARNING OBJECTIVES

After studying this chapter, you should be able to:

3.1 explain the importance of the concept of assessable income to the income taxation system

3.2 apply the tests for determining whether an amount is ordinary income

3.3 apply the tests for determining whether an amount is statutory income

3.4 differentiate between income and capital

3.5 describe the assessability of personal services and employment income

3.6 describe the assessability of business income

3.7 describe the assessability of property income

3.8 explain the tax treatment of isolated transactions and compensation payments.

Overview

This chapter introduces the important concept of assessable income. A working understanding of this concept is essential to understanding income tax. The concept is multifaceted and we will be covering the key aspects in turn in each part of the chapter. You will learn about the distinction and characteristics of 'ordinary' and 'statutory' income. In addition, we will introduce the important distinction between income and capital.

The discussion will extend to different categories of income including personal service and employment income, business income and income from property. You will also learn when isolated transactions and compensation payments can be considered assessable income.

3.1 Characterising income

LEARNING OBJECTIVE 3.1 Explain the importance of the concept of assessable income to the income taxation system.

Characterising income is central to the Australian income tax system and calculating income tax payable. Recall from the chapter on the Australian taxation system and the formula in section 4-15 of the ITAA97 for basic income tax calculation:

$$\text{Taxable income} = \text{assessable income} - \text{deductions}$$

Hence, one of the primary tasks for determining taxable income is to characterise each receipt against a legal test of whether the receipt is **assessable income**.[1] The first step is to ask whether the receipt is **ordinary income**. This step is reflected in section 6-5(1) of the ITAA97: 'Your assessable income includes income according to ordinary concepts which is called ordinary income'.

Unfortunately, there is no more precise statutory definition of 'ordinary income' other than the confirmation that the term 'ordinary income' is simply an abbreviation of 'income according to ordinary concepts' and, hence, is intended to reflect common usage and common, everyday meaning.

It is also important not to confuse 'ordinary income' for tax purposes with accounting definitions of income. The two are not the same (aspects of accounting treatment of income and expenses will be dealt with further in a later chapter and several specific differences will be highlighted throughout the chapters of this text).

The second step in determining taxable income is working out whether an amount is **statutory income** — this is reflected in sections 6-10(1) and (2) of the ITAA97.

Section 6-10(1) confirms that assessable income includes items that are not ordinary income. Section 6-10(2) confirms that items which are not ordinary income but are included in your assessable income by provisions about assessable income are called 'statutory income'.

Most items of assessable income are assessable because they are 'ordinary income'. Some receipts qualify both as ordinary income and statutory income. In these cases, section 6-25(2) says that unless a contrary intention appears from a particular statutory provision, the statutory income provision will prevail over the ordinary income rules. This means that such amounts will usually be included in assessable income as items of statutory income. Working out whether an item is ordinary or statutory income is important, irrespective of the type of income involved — income from personal services, from business, from property or otherwise. This is because the tax treatment may be different depending on the characterisation, including the calculation of the taxable amount and potentially the applicable tax rate. The characterisation of the income can also have significant flow-on consequences for the deductions that can be claimed for expenses necessarily incurred in deriving the income. These differences will be discussed in later chapters in the context of considering general deductions and specific deductions and capital allowances respectively.

3.2 Ordinary income

LEARNING OBJECTIVE 3.2 Apply the tests for determining whether an amount is ordinary income.

As noted, ordinary income has no precise statutory definition and each item must be considered in light of the common usage and meaning of the term. This has been considered and clarified in many tax cases,

---

1 Refer to an earlier chapter for a discussion of the relationships between the various components of assessable income, exempt income and non-assessable and non-exempt income.

resulting in broad themes related to the source of the payment, and the purpose and inherent characteristics of the receipt. These can be broken down into a series of 'general indicators' of ordinary income that can help to determine whether an amount has the essential character of ordinary income or not.

Figure 3.1 is a simple checklist setting out these general indicators, each of which will be introduced and explained in this chapter. However, before considering each indicator it is important to appreciate that all these indicators do not necessarily need to be present for an item to be considered 'ordinary income'. In addition, no single factor is determinative and the determinative factor may vary depending on the factual issue involved in a particular case.

FIGURE 3.1 Ordinary income — general indicators

1. Derived: Ordinary income must be 'derived' or realised by the taxpayer.
2. Sufficient nexus: Ordinary income must have a sufficient nexus with an earning activity.
3. Cash: Receipt is either cash or convertible to cash.
4. Mutuality principle satisfied: Receipt cannot be a payment to oneself.
5. Capital receipts are not usually considered ordinary income.
6. Substitution principle: Compensation received in lieu of ordinary income is ordinary income.
7. Undissected payments for capital and income are capital receipts *not* ordinary income.
8. Repetition and regularity are strong indicators that payments are ordinary income.
9. Refunds of previously deductible amounts are not automatically considered ordinary income.
10. Ordinary income must generally result in some gain to the taxpayer.
11. Ordinary income from personal services cannot usually be alienated or split.
12. Receipts from illegal or immoral activities can still constitute assessable ordinary income.

In the rest of this section we will examine the first four key indicators from figure 3.1 in detail.

3.2.1 Ordinary income must be 'derived' by the taxpayer

Section 6-5(4) of the ITAA97 states:

> In working out whether you have derived an amount of ordinary income, and (if so) when you derived it, you are taken to have received the amount as soon as it is applied or dealt with in any way on your behalf or as you direct.

Although this falls short of a comprehensive definition of what 'derived' means, one thing should immediately be obvious from this definition — there is no requirement that the taxpayer actually personally receives the income in order for it to be considered derived by that taxpayer. Income is considered derived when it is applied or dealt with in any way on behalf of the taxpayer or as the taxpayer directs. This means, for example, if you direct your employer to pay income owed to you to somebody to whom you owe money, the income will be considered derived by you, even though you have not physically received the income or had the income physically pass through your hands. The fact that it has been directed to be paid by you to somebody else is enough for it to be assessable as ordinary income derived by you.

The character of an amount — whether it is ordinary income — must also be considered at the time that it is derived by the taxpayer. For example, a payment to a former employee may not have the same character as if the same payment was derived at an earlier time while the recipient was still an employee. *FCT v Rowe* [1997] HCA 16 illustrates this principle.

FCT v Rowe [1997] HCA 16

Facts: This case involved a local council engineer who was suspended and investigated due to a series of complaints made against him. The taxpayer was successful in defending the complaints, but only after incurring substantial legal costs in defending himself. Almost 3 years later (long after the employee ceased being an employee of the council) he received an *ex gratia* payment from the government as reimbursement for these legal costs.

The Commissioner of Taxation argued this payment was assessable as ordinary income.

Held: The High Court found in favour of the taxpayer because the payment could not be characterised as a payment for employment services of the taxpayer (which had been rendered years earlier).

> **Comment:** Had the payment been made while the taxpayer was an employee, the payment is more likely to have been characterised as ordinary income.

The fact that 'derived' is not the same as 'received' also has implications for which tax period you must report an amount as assessable. It is in the context of arguments over this issue that many of the cases considering whether and when income has been derived have arisen.

Judges have developed several rules to assist in determining whether and when income is derived in different circumstances. Different rules have been developed based on the type of taxpayer involved and the type of transaction giving rise to the amount received. Where there is a conflict between the derivation rules applying to the type of taxpayer and the type of income involved, the rules for type of income apply.

3.2.1.1 Type of taxpayer

In terms of type of taxpayer, whether and when a receipt is derived depends on if the taxpayer is required to report their income on a 'cash' (receipts) basis or an 'accruals' (right to receive) basis. The general principle is that the correct reporting method is the one which is 'calculated to give a substantially correct reflex' (i.e. most accurate reflection) of the taxpayer's 'true income'. This terminology is from a case known as '*Carden's* case'.[2] We will discuss *Carden's* case in further detail in a later chapter.

Hence, the correct method depends on the facts of the case. Generally, a cash/receipts basis is used to determine when an individual derives assessable income A cash basis is also considered an appropriate basis for determining when income is derived where the receipt relates to the rendering of personal services by an individual. This is demonstrated in *FCT v Firstenberg*.

FCT v Firstenberg [1977] VicRp 1

Facts: The taxpayer was a solicitor who was a sole practitioner but employed a secretary to assist with administrative tasks. The taxpayer had always reported his income on a cash basis; that is, when received from the client.

The Commissioner sought to assess the taxpayer on an accruals (right to receive) basis.

Held: A cash basis was the appropriate accounting method for recording derivation of income in these circumstances. McInerny J observed: 'I have come to the conclusion that in the case of a one-man professional practitioner the essential feature of income "derived" is receipt'.

Conversely, an accruals/earnings basis is generally accepted as being appropriate for determining when income has been derived in contexts involving trading businesses or professional activities run like a business. Larger professional practices would normally be considered to have derived their income on an accrual basis. This was exemplified in *Henderson v FCT*.[3]

Henderson v FCT [1970] HCA 62

Facts: A large accounting firm with 19 partners and which employed another 150 employed accountants decided to switch from a cash accounting method to an accruals accounting method.

The Commissioner of Taxation did not accept the change and continued to assess the firm's income as derived on a cash basis (i.e. upon receipt).

Held: The Court agreed with the taxpayer that the size, structure and method of operating the business meant an accruals basis was appropriate for determining when income was derived for tax purposes.

The chapter on tax accounting and trading stock will examine cash accounting and accrual accounting in more detail.

---

2 *Commissioner of Taxes (South Australia) v The Executor Trustee and Agency Co of South Australia Ltd* [1938] HCA 69 ('*Carden's* case'). This case is discussed in greater detail in a later chapter.

3 The link to the case is at: http://www.austlii.edu.au/cgi-bin/sinodisp/au/cases/cth/HCA/1970/62.html?query=.

3.2.1.2 Type of transaction

In terms of the type of transaction involved, there are different tests for determining whether and when an amount is derived.

Table 3.1 sets out the rules of thumb that have emerged from the cases. Each of these will also be examined in further detail in a later chapter.

TABLE 3.1 Derivation of ordinary income

Income	Description
Rent	Derived when received.
Dividends	Derived when paid, *not* when declared by directors.
Cheques	Derived when received, *not* when presented.
Interest	Derived when received (except in the case of banks or financial institutions, which derive their income on an accruals basis).
Salary/Wages	Derived when received or directed by the taxpayer to be received by someone else.
Work in progress	Derived only when a right to recover from customer arises (typically once the work in progress has been billed and enforceable as a debt due by the client).

3.2.2 Nexus with earning activity

A core test for determining whether an item is ordinary income is whether the item is sufficiently connected to an earning activity or a product of employment. This is often described as a requirement that the item has a **sufficient nexus** with this earning activity. Again, case law is the best guide on the range of circumstances in which a sufficient nexus will exist and when it will not. For example:

- *Sufficient nexus.* Generally speaking, receipts which are 'products' of personal exertion, property or employment or services will usually be ordinary income. This extends to payments which are properly characterised as products of personal exertion even if they are:
  - voluntary or gratuitous (e.g. a waiter's tips)
  - for past or future services
  - from a third party
  - isolated (i.e. irregular).
- *Insufficient nexus.* Gains of the following types will not usually be considered to have a sufficient nexus to income-earning activity to be considered ordinary income:
  - lottery wins
  - 'windfall gains'
  - gifts
  - tips and gratuities.

3.2.2.1 Lottery wins and prizes

Let's look first at lottery wins and prizes. Such receipts are merely windfall gains for the recipient — not a product or reward for any income-earning activity. In the case of lottery and gambling winnings and prizes, such receipts are the product of luck or chance. While this might seem a straightforward proposition, gambling winnings and prizes can sometimes give rise to complexities. There can be cases where such receipts can be properly characterised as a product or incident of employment or a reward for services rendered, such that they will be considered assessable as ordinary income from services. There can also be situations where such activities might constitute a business. For example, we will deal with gambling later in the chapter in the context of discussion of when gambling activities might constitute a business. We will also look at prizes received by professional sportspersons as part of their business activities later in the chapter.

For now, to illustrate the potential complexities, consider the following example of a reality show contestant.

Lottery wins and prizes

Frank is a contestant on a reality TV show *Big Sister*. Consider the two following scenarios.

Scenario 1: Frank appears for a few nights before being voted out of the show by fellow contestants, taking away a consolation prize.

Scenario 2: Frank's appearance is just one of many successful previous appearances on reality TV and game shows and he was invited to appear on the show as a 'celebrity contestant'.

Would Frank's winnings be assessable income in either scenario?

In scenario 1, it is highly unlikely that the winnings would be assessable. They are most likely to be considered a once-off windfall gain, the result of chance rather than skill.

However, in scenario 2, given the regularity of Frank's appearances on reality TV and game shows, an argument could be made that the winnings are assessable. This is particularly true if his regular appearances and celebrity status means he has been paid appearance fees for being on the show. According to the Commissioner in Taxation Ruling IT 167, this would be the case, whether the award for appearing is paid directly in the form of a fee or indirectly through the opportunity to win valuable prizes, either in cash or in kind.

3.2.2.2 Windfall gains

Example 3.1 above is a simple example of the practical importance of looking closely at the facts to determine whether or not a prize or other windfall gain is assessable as ordinary income. Where windfall gains are concerned, many of the cases have involved determining whether an amount is properly characterised as a **mere gift** or not. There are good reasons why mere gifts are not considered ordinary income. A gift, though made in a voluntary manner, if nevertheless related to employment or services rendered will be assessable as income in the hands of the recipient on that basis. On the other hand, a mere gift made in a voluntary manner that is unrelated to services or employment would not be assessable as income in the hands of the recipient.

Courts have developed a series of considerations for determining whether or not a receipt is a mere gift or has a sufficient nexus with employment or services rendered to be considered assessable as ordinary income.

Key among these are the following.

1. Consider the nature of the payment in the hands of the recipient rather than the motivation of the gift-giver in making the payment.
2. Look at whether the gift was expected or unexpected by the recipient. If expected, it is more likely to be considered assessable income.
3. Determine whether the gift was deserved in a moral sense given the work performed by the recipient of the gift. If deserved in a moral sense, it is more likely to be considered assessable income.
4. Consider whether the gift is a regular, recurrent, or periodical type of receipt commonplace in the recipient's industry. If it is, it is more likely to be considered assessable income.

None of these is individually determinative of whether there is a sufficient nexus between the payment and provision of work or service. They are simply considerations to help determine the key issue of whether the payments are really an incident or a product of employment rather than a mere gift. Two cases which illustrate the application of some of these principles are *Scott v FCT* [1966] HCA 48 and *Hayes v FCT* [1956] HCA 21.

Facts: Mr Scott was a solicitor who for many years had been engaged to do legal work for Mr and Mrs Freestone, for which he had always been paid. However, the relationship between the Freestones and Mr Scott also extended to other business activities. When Mr Freestone died, Mrs Freestone engaged Mr Scott do to the legal work on the estate which included acting on the sale of properties owned by Mr Scott including a property known as 'Greenacres'. Mrs Freestone decided to make a substantial gift (£10 000) to Mr Scott from the sale of Greenacres. The key issue for the High Court was whether this gift was assessable income in the hands of Mr Scott or a mere gift.

---

4 The link to the case is at: https://www.ato.gov.au/law/view/document?docid=JUD/*1966*HCA48/00001.

Held: The gift was not assessable income. Key factors included the acceptance by the Court that there was no expectation of any gift by the recipient, and that, in making the gift, the donor was motivated by the longstanding personal relationship between the taxpayer and her and her late husband. However, Windeyer J noted the factual and legal complexities in determining the question of whether a gift is assessable income:

> Whether or not a particular receipt is income depends upon its quality in the hands of the recipient. It does not depend upon whether it was a payment or provision that the payer or provider was lawfully obliged to make. The ordinary illustrations of this are gratuities regularly received as an incident of a particular employment. On the other hand, gifts of an exceptional kind, not such as are a common incident of a man's calling or occupation, do not ordinarily form part of his income. Whether or not a gratuitous payment is income in the hands of the recipient is thus a question of mixed law and fact. The motives of the donor do not determine the answer. They are, however, a relevant circumstance.

A further example is the case of *Hayes v FCT* [1956] HCA 21.

Hayes v FCT [1956] HCA 21

Facts: The taxpayer, Mr Hayes, was an accountant employed by Mr Richardson as an accountant and general financial adviser to his business for which he received a salary. The business subsequently was incorporated as a company in which Mr Hayes held shares and was a director and secretary. He was paid from the company for his services. Mr Richardson subsequently purchased the shares held by Mr Hayes in order to retain exclusive control of the business. Mr Hayes remained secretary of the company and was paid for that work. Ultimately, the business was a success and Mr Richardson decided to gift shares in his successful company to a number of people and organisations, including Mr Hayes. There was evidence that the relationship between Mr Hayes and Mr Richardson was one of personal friendship as described by the Court as follows.

> ... it may be truly said that there was a close business relationship between the two men, and he [Hayes] and his wife and Richardson and his wife were on terms of personal friendship. Richardson often discussed business matters with him, and asked and received his advice in an informal way on matters connected with the business of the companies and as to his own private investments and affairs. One gathers that the advice was generally accepted, and the result seldom, if ever, regretted. There can be no doubt, I think, that in 1950, when the public company was formed and Richardson felt that he had 'made a success of things', he was disposed to give a real measure of credit for that success to advice and assistance received over the years from his business associate and personal friend.[5]

As such, the key issue for the High Court was whether the transfer of the shares to Mr Hayes, although voluntary and a 'gift' in the sense that there was no obligation on the part of Mr Richardson to make it, was income in the hands of Mr Hayes.

Held: The shares were a non-assessable gift rather than ordinary income. Relevant factors included the motive of the donor which the Court described as 'a general feeling of goodwill arising from a close relationship which had both a business aspect and a personal aspect'.[6]

However, the decisive factor for the Court was the character of the receipt in the hands of the recipient which the Court described as follows: '... it is impossible to relate the receipt of the shares by Hayes to any income-producing activity on his part. It is impossible to point to any employment or "personal exertion", of which the receipt of the shares was in any real sense an incident, or which can fairly be said to have produced that receipt'.[7]

3.2.2.3 Gifts and prizes

The question of whether an amount received is a mere gift or prize or income with a sufficient nexus to income-earning activity arises regularly in situations involving athletes and those who receive gifts, prizes or rewards regularly as part of their jobs (such as restaurant waitstaff). Both of these factual scenarios are discussed in turn next.

---

5 *Hayes v FCT* [1956] HCA 21, [10].
6 Ibid [19].
7 Ibid [18].

As noted, prizes and gifts are usually (but not always) assessable as ordinary income. In a sporting context, where it can be demonstrated that the receipts are made on a once-off basis, do not relate to the performance of the athlete, are promotional and provided after any sporting services were provided by the taxpayer, the nexus requirement will not be satisfied. *Kelly v FCT* examined this issue.

Kelly v FCT 85 ATC 4283

Facts: An Australian footballer received $20 000 as the prize for winning the league's best and fairest player award.

The Commissioner treated the payment as income, considering it a bonus or benefit with a sufficient nexus to the employment and services provided by the taxpayer as a professional footballer. The taxpayer appealed.

Held: The payment was ordinary income. The payment had a sufficient nexus to his professional pursuit in playing football to the best of his abilities. The fact that the payment was unexpected was irrelevant. The payment was 'caused' by his employment as a footballer. The Court also affirmed that the motivation of the donor when a gift is involved should not be considered the determinative factor in working out whether the payment has a sufficient nexus to the employment or personal services provided by the taxpayer.

The reasoning in *Kelly v FCT* applies with the same force to cases involving amateur athletes (such as those who compete in the Olympic Games). This is illustrated in the case of *Commissioner of Taxation v Stone* [2005] HCA 21.[8]

Commissioner of Taxation v Stone [2005] HCA 21

Facts: The taxpayer's full-time occupation was as a police officer. However, she was also a highly skilled amateur javelin thrower. In fact, in 1996 she had been a member of the Australian Olympic team, competing in the women's javelin event. She also competed at a number of other national and international athletics events. As a result of her sporting achievements, the taxpayer received sums as prize money, as grants by the Australian Olympic Committee and Queensland Academy of Sport, as appearance fees at some events, and as cash or other items (including clothing and a car) from sponsors. The Commissioner sought to assess all the receipts as assessable income of the taxpayer. Although the taxpayer accepted that the receipts from sponsors were assessable, the taxpayer objected to the other receipts being treated as assessable income, essentially arguing that she was a career police officer. Although she received reward for her success as an athlete, she was not engaged in a business activity to exploit her sporting talents for financial gain. Her only motivation was her desire to excel, to represent her country and win medals, not to make money.

Held: All the receipts were assessable income. The majority judges observed that:

> Taken as a whole, the athletic activities of the taxpayer ... constituted the conduct of a business. She wanted to compete at the highest level. To do that cost money — for equipment, training, travel, accommodation. She sought sponsorship to help defray those costs. She agreed to accept grants that were made to her and agreed to the commercial inhibitions that came with those grants so that she might meet the costs that she incurred in pursuing her goals. Although she did not seek to maximise her receipts from prize money, preferring to seek out the best rather than the most lucrative competitions, her pursuit of excellence, if successful, necessarily entailed the receipt of prizes, increased grants, and the opportunity to obtain more generous sponsorship arrangements. That other sports and other athletes may have attracted larger rewards is irrelevant.[9]

Insofar as the lack of a subjective profit-making motive was concerned, the Court observed: 'If a taxpayer has a view to profit, the conclusion that the taxpayer is engaged in business may easily be reached. If a taxpayer's motives are idealistic rather than mercenary, the conclusion that the taxpayer is engaged in a business may still be reached'.[10]

---

8 See *Commissioner of Taxation v Stone* [2005] HCA 21.
9 Ibid [54].
10 Ibid [55].

3.2.2.4 Tips and gratuities

The customary receipt of 'tips' by hospitality employees or others as part of their employment is assessable both as ordinary income and as statutory income under section 15-2 of the ITAA97. This is the case irrespective of whether the payment was made by the employer of the taxpayer, by a customer or by any other third party. The key issue remains the question of whether the payment was incidental to the employment or work of the taxpayer. In *FCT v Dixon*,[11] Dixon CJ and Williams J surmised:

> It is clear that if payments are really incidental to an employment, it is unimportant whether they come from the employer or from somebody else and are obtained as a right of work or merely as a recognised incident of the employment or work.[12]

Example 3.2 explores this issue.

EXAMPLE 3.2

Tips and gratuities

Wayne is a chauffeur. His contract provides for payment of a weekly wage by his employer but makes no reference to tips. However, it is custom for Wayne's wealthy passengers to pay him tips. Are those tips assessable?

Yes, the tips are assessable. Just because the payments are voluntary does not make them any less assessable. The central issue is whether they are made as a reward for services or as a gift on personal grounds. Wayne's tips from his rich customers are clearly in the former category.

This example is similar to the UK case of *Calvert v Wainwright* [1947] 1 All ER 282. In this case, a taxi driver who was employed under a fixed wage contract would regularly receive tips from customers. He argued these were mere gifts and not assessable income. The Court disagreed, with Atkinson J observing: 'Tips received by a man as a reward for services rendered, although voluntary gifts made by people other than his employers, are assessable to tax as part of the profits for services, but, on the other hand, personal gifts which are gifts to a man on personal grounds, irrespective of and without regard to the question whether services have been rendered or not, are not assessable.'[13]

The Commissioner of Taxation has issued a public ruling touching upon the issue: TR 95/11. Note that that even if not assessable as ordinary income, tips would normally be caught as assessable under section 15-2 of the ITAA97 as this section includes as assessable: allowances, gratuities, compensation, benefits, bonuses or premiums provided to the taxpayer in respect of or in relation directly or indirectly to any employment or services provided by the taxpayer. We discuss section 15-2 in section 3.3 in the context of our discussion of statutory income.[14]

3.2.3 Benefit must be cash or convertible to cash

The leading case establishing the principle that the benefit must be in cash or convertible to cash is *FCT v Cooke & Sherden* [1980] FCA 37. In this case, the taxpayers had a door-to-door soft drink sales business. As a sales incentive, the soft drink manufacturer provided the taxpayers with free holidays when certain sales quotas were met. The Commissioner argued the value of the holidays was assessable as ordinary income. The Federal Court determined the holidays were not assessable as ordinary income, because they were not convertible to money or money's worth.

Similar reasoning has more recently been applied in cases involving 'Frequent Flyer' and similar airline loyalty program benefits. The leading case here is *Payne v FCT* (1996) 66 FCR 299.

---

11 *FCT v Dixon* [1952] HCA 65.
12 Dixon CJ and William J at [5].
13 *Calvert v Wainwright* [1947] 1 All ER 282, 282.
14 Australian Taxation Office, *Income tax: hospitality industry employees – allowances, reimbursements and work-related deductions* (TR 95/11, 1 June 1995) https://www.ato.gov.au/law/view/document?DocID=TXR/TR9511/NAT/ATO/00001.

Facts: The taxpayer, an employee of a chartered accounting firm, was required to do a lot of travel as part of her job. The employer would pay for flight costs and other travel costs for these business trips. The taxpayer would travel Qantas, as Qantas was a client of her employer (although employees were not required to travel Qantas). She joined the Qantas frequent flyer program without her employer's knowledge. As a result, she earned frequent flyer points which she could not convert to cash but could claim as flight rewards for herself or family members. She used these points to buy airfares for her parents. The reward points she accrued were from a combination of employer-paid and privately-paid travel (although most points were from the work-related travel). The Commissioner claimed the value of the flight tickets from points accrued from employer-paid travel were assessable as ordinary income.

Held: The Federal Court disagreed with the Commissioner. The Court applied similar reasoning as in *FCT v Cooke and Sherden* — namely, that the flight reward was not money or money's worth and not convertible into cash.[15]

Foster J drew a close analogy with the *Cooke and Sherden* case, observing that: 'The reward tickets available because of the accrual of the required number of points could be used only by the Program member or his or her permitted nominee. They were not transferable and, if sold, were subject to cancellation. They were not money and, in my view, could not be turned to pecuniary account. They could not therefore be regarded as "income" within the meaning of s25(1)'.

We will return to the *Payne* case again in the context of our discussion of statutory income and section 15-2 of the ITAA97.

It is important to avoid making the mistake of thinking non-cash benefits can never be treated as ordinary income. They can — provided they are convertible to cash. Non-cash benefits (sometimes called 'benefits in kind'), which are convertible to cash, are valued at their realisable value and an amount of income equal to that realisable value can constitute assessable income according to ordinary income. An example of a benefit clearly convertible to cash is payment in the form of a parcel of shares in a company.

Also, the convertibility to cash requirement does not apply to non-cash *business* benefits. Section 21A of the ITAA36 says that 'in determining the income derived by a taxpayer, a "non-cash business benefit" [a benefit arising directly or indirectly from a business relationship] that is not convertible to cash shall be treated as if it were convertible to cash'.

3.2.4 Mutuality: receipt cannot be a payment to oneself

A payment to oneself is not ordinary income. This principle is sometimes referred to as the principle of **mutuality**. At its heart, this principle means income must derive from a source other than the taxpayer to be considered ordinary income in the hands of that taxpayer. The issue most commonly arises in cases involving entities and transactions between those entities and their members or owners. For example, in *Bohemians Club v Acting FCT* [1918] HCA 16, the Commissioner sought to assess the taxpayer (an unincorporated social club) on a surplus of membership funds received from its members. The High Court determined the surplus essentially represented savings in the form of contributions paid by the body of members and to be applied solely for the benefit of the members; that is, essentially payments made by members for spending on themselves. Hence the surplus was not assessable as income.[16]

3.3 Statutory income

LEARNING OBJECTIVE 3.3 Apply the tests for determining whether an amount is statutory income.

Statutory income is defined in section 6-10(2) of the ITAA97 as: 'Amounts that are not ordinary income but are included in your assessable income by provisions about assessable income, are called statutory income'.

These provisions can be found throughout the Income Tax Assessment Acts but a good starting point for a list of items included as assessable income as forms of 'statutory income' is Division 15 of the ITAA97.

---

15 The Commissioner of Taxation has issued a Taxation Ruling dealing with *Payne's* case and frequent flyer programs generally (see TR 1999/6).

16 Other case examples applying similar reasoning include *Lambe v IRC* (1934) 1 KB 178; *Royal Automobile Club of Victoria v FCT* [1974] VicRp 80; *Sydney Water Board Employees' Credit Union v FCT* [1973] HCA 47.

This Division contains a broad range of items spanning from various employment-related items such as allowances, return to work payments, and accrued leave entitlements (these will be dealt with in the context of taxation of individuals discussed in the chapter on taxation of individuals). The Division also includes royalties (section 15-20), profits from profit-making schemes (section 15-15, discussed further in section 3.6.3) and insurance payments for losses of assessable income (section 15-30).

In addition to these, a key form of statutory income is capital gains falling within the capital gains tax provisions contained in Chapter 3 of the ITAA97. These provisions are the main type of statutory income considered and are dealt with in a later chapter.

Aside from the capital gains tax provisions, one of the most frequently litigated and important provisions dealing with statutory income is section 15-2 of the ITAA97. Section 15-2 includes as assessable income in the hands of the taxpayer all 'allowances, gratuities, compensation, benefits, bonuses and premiums' provided either 'directly or indirectly' by virtue of any employment or services rendered by the taxpayer.[17]

This provision is broader than the ordinary conception of income from employment or from personal service provision. This is because the provision is centred on capturing items associated with the employment relationship itself rather than the provision of services stemming from that relationship.

The provision reflects longstanding legal reasoning that gifts made in employment contexts are assessable income. This extends to items such as Christmas gifts provided by an employer to employees.[18]

For example, in the UK case of *Laidler v Perry* [1965] 2 All ER 121, a Christmas bonus paid to employees in the form of a voucher redeemable for a fixed value of goods was deemed to be income. All staff received the same value voucher irrespective of their level of experience or seniority, provided they had been employed for at least 10 months. The vouchers were sent with a letter of thanks from management for each employee's service throughout the year. Despite the voluntary nature of the payment, the Court took the view that the payments were not a mere personal gift as they were made with a view to obtaining beneficial results for the company in the future.

However, section 15-2 is also broad enough to capture situations where a payment is made by a third party rather than the employer, provided the third party is aware of the employment relationship. This was discussed in the case of *FCT v Payne* (1996) 66 FCR 299 (which we introduced in section 3.2.3). You should note that *Payne*, as well as many other older cases, will refer to the predecessor to section 15-2 of the ITAA97 which was section 26(e) of the ITAA36.

Specifically, in *Payne*, Foster J observed that:

> The [frequent flyer] benefit was received under a scheme instituted by Qantas for its benefit [not because of any employment arrangement between the taxpayer and her employer]. The employer had no part in the scheme as such. The employer did not arrange for the employee to participate in the scheme. It did not pay for the employee's participation in the scheme. It did not even, so far as the facts show, encourage its employees to participate in the scheme. It did nothing to provide the benefit alleged to be taxable in the employee's hand.

All of this meant that, on the facts, the benefits received by the taxpayer in *Payne* could not be considered to be directly or indirectly provided by virtue of any employment arrangement or service provision by the taxpayer as required in order to be assessable under section 15-2.

It is important to note that where an item is caught as statutory income under section 15-2 and is also assessable as ordinary income, section 15-2(d) says the amount is to be assessed as ordinary income.

A further complexity arises in that many of the items potentially within the scope of section 15-2 may also be caught under the provisions of the fringe benefits tax. In such situations, section 23L of the ITAA36 provides that the amount will be exempt for income tax purposes. Fringe benefits tax will be discussed in a later chapter.

Figure 3.2 illustrates an approach to dealing with payments arising out of an employment relationship and the relationship between statutory and ordinary income in that context.

---

17 Prior to being rewritten as part of the ITAA97, this provision was contained in section 26(e) of the ITAA36. Many of the cases relevant to considering the provision refer to the predecessor section 26(e) but apply with equal force to the rewritten provision.
18 *Laidler v Perry* [1965] UKHL TC_42_351.

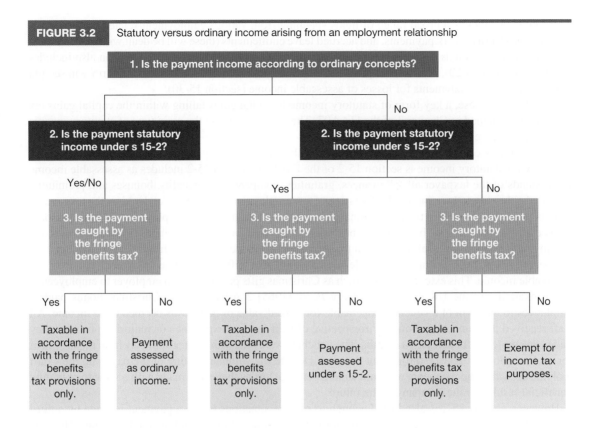

FIGURE 3.2 Statutory versus ordinary income arising from an employment relationship

3.4 The income/capital distinction

LEARNING OBJECTIVE 3.4 Differentiate between income and capital.

Ordinary income excludes **capital receipts**. A common analogy which is sometimes called upon to illustrate the distinction between income and capital receipts is the analogy of a fruit tree. The tree itself can be considered the 'capital asset'. Hence, proceeds from the sale of the tree would normally be considered a capital receipt. However, proceeds from the sale of the fruit from the tree can be considered equivalent to the income derived from a capital asset.[19]

The distinction between income and capital has been the focus of countless cases. The issue was especially common prior to the enactment of the capital gains tax in 1985. Before the enactment of this legislation, capital receipts were generally not taxable unless they could be characterised as ordinary income. Hence, whether a payment was properly characterised as an income or capital receipt often meant the difference between whether the payment would be taxed or tax free.

Since 1985, capital gains have been brought to tax under the capital gains tax provisions (now in Chapter 3 of the ITAA97). In other words, these amounts are now potentially assessable as a form of statutory income. However, the issue is still significant as the taxing of capital gains under the capital gains tax provisions differs to the tax treatment of other forms of income. We cover capital gains tax in detail in a later chapter.

The issue is also relevant to the question of deductibility of expenses. This is because the general definition of deductibility of expenses in section 8-1 of the ITAA97 expressly states that losses or outgoings of a capital nature are not generally deductible. Hence, we will examine the distinction again in that context in later chapters.

In the income context, the distinction continues to cause difficulties mainly in the following categories.
1. Payments in return for giving up a valuable right/restrictive covenants.
2. Payments in compensation for injury or wrong to the person, reputation or for loss of income-earning capacity.
3. Compensation for loss of business contracts, franchise rights or agency agreement.

---

19 This analogy has origins in the United States' case of *Eisner v Macomber* (1920) 252 US 189. This case involved the issue of bonus shares in a company which was considered a capital receipt in the hands of the taxpayer rather than income.

We will now look at some cases falling within category 1, and then consider cases concerning compensation payments and whether they are capital or income in section 3.8.

A **restrictive covenant** is a contractual commitment to either do or not do something in return for a payment. Typical examples arise in the employment context (e.g. agreement restricting your right to work in some way) and in the business context (e.g. an agreement to restrict your right to compete with a business competitor in some way). Three case examples are discussed next.

FCT v Woite (1982) 31 SASR 223

Facts: A footballer, Peter Woite, entered into a contract with a Victorian football club from which he received a $10 000 payment in return for which he agreed not to play for any other football club in Victoria. He was not bound to play for the club and was free to play for any other club outside Victoria. In fact, the taxpayer chose not to play football in Victoria.

The Commissioner sought to assess the $10 000 as income from the taxpayer's professional football activities. The taxpayer argued that the $10 000 was a capital receipt.

Held: Payment was not income. The Court concluded that in these circumstances the payment was not sufficiently related to the provision of any footballing services as it did not require the taxpayer to play for the Victorian club and was simply an agreement in return for giving up the right to play for any other Victorian club.

Higgs v Olivier [1951] Ch 899

Facts: Actor Laurence Olivier and a film company entered a contractual arrangement for a movie — *Henry V*. The film was made and was not particularly popular. Hence, the parties agreed to boost the popularity of the film through Mr Olivier agreeing not to appear in any other film for 18 months in return for a lump sum payment of £15 000.

The UK Inspector of Taxes sought to assess the payment as income as a profit from his professional acting career. The taxpayer argued it was a capital payment for agreeing to the restrictive covenant.

Held: The Court agreed with the taxpayer. Key to this finding was the fact that the agreement was entered into after the film was completed. The payment was made under a new later separate agreement. Hence, the payment was not for any agreement from his vocation as an actor but simply for his agreement to forgo opportunities to profit from his film-acting vocation. Also relevant was the fact that such arrangements were not common in the film industry at the time with the Court observing: 'Had there been evidence that it was a regular practice with actors to accept sums as a condition of not exercising their art, it would not be right to come to the conclusion that it was not an incident of the vocation of such persons'.

Brent v FCT [1971] HCA 48

Facts: The taxpayer was the wife of a criminal involved in a heist known as 'The Great Train Robbery'. She entered into an agreement with a TV station to sell her story. The sum was paid in three parts — part upon signing the agreement, the bulk upon signing a copy of the manuscript of her story and the balance was payable 30 days after expiry of the agreement.

The taxpayer argued the payment was not income but rather a capital payment for disposing of an asset — namely, the exclusive rights to her story.

Held: The payment was income. The High Court characterised the payment as income for services in the form of agreeing to be interviewed and to disclose the story of her life with her criminal husband. The payment was not a capital payment for disposing of an asset as she possessed no exclusive right to her story, assigned no copyright in her story to the journalist as part of her agreement, nor was it the disposal of an asset acquired as part of a business.

3.5 Personal services and employment income

LEARNING OBJECTIVE 3.5 Describe the assessability of personal services and employment income.

As the name suggests, **personal service income** is income generally considered personal to the individual who performed the service. As such, one of the general rules concerning the tax treatment of personal service income is that this income is taxable in the hands of the person who carried out the service — it cannot be redirected to be taxable in the hands of somebody else. This general rule is elaborated on next and is one of the reasons why it is important to consider whether income is properly characterised as personal services income or as a different category of income, such as income from business or property.

The key factor to determining whether an amount is personal services income is to work out whether the amount is a product or incident of employment. By the end of this part of the chapter you should also understand how to apply that test. Personal services income is addressed in detail in the chapter on taxation of individuals.

3.5.1 The general test of assessability — a product or incident of employment

The key test for determining whether a payment is income from personal services is whether the payment can be considered a 'product' or 'incident' of the employment. Courts have considered several factors to help them apply this test including the following.

- Considering whether the payment is a lump sum payment or one of a series of regular or periodical payments. Periodical or regular payments are more likely to be viewed as a product or incident of employment.
- The motive of the donor in making the payment (although this is not usually considered determinative).
- Considering who made the payment. A payment from an employer to an employee will usually be considered a product or incident of employment. However, payments from third parties can also be a product or incident of employment in the hands of the recipient.

Two leading cases, *FCT v Harris* [1980] FLR 36 and *FCT v Dixon* [1952] HCA 65, illustrate and further describe how these considerations are applied.

FCT v Harris [1980] FLR 36

Facts: Once-off lump sum payments were made to an employee by an employer on retirement. The taxpayer was a former bank employee. He was paid a lump sum on retirement (just like everybody else who retired from the bank). The amounts paid to each retiring employee were not identical, but the amount was not specifically calculated based on previous length of service, quality of work or former position held. The payments were primarily made to compensate the employees for the effects of inflation on the pensions they would receive on retirement from the bank, which had eroded the real value of those pensions over time.

Held: In characterising the payment as a non-assessable capital payment, Bowen CJ provided an excellent summary of the principles which informed this conclusion. He pointed out that the key test is whether the payment can be considered 'a product' of the employment. Other factors such as recurrence of the payments and motive of the donor are relevant, but not decisive:

> It may be said that a gift by one person to another will not ordinarily be regarded as income in the hands of the recipient. Thus, a present given by a father to his son out of natural love and affection is not income in the hands of the son. On the other hand, a tip given to a waiter or a taxi driver is income in the hands of the donor. It is considered to be the product of the services which have been rendered … whether or not a particular receipt is income depends upon its quality in the hands of the recipient … The motives of the donor may be relevant but are seldom, if ever, decisive … The regularity and periodicity of the payment will be a relevant though generally not decisive consideration … A generally decisive consideration is whether the receipt is the product in a real sense of any employment of, or services rendered by the recipient, or of any business, or, indeed, any revenue producing activity carried on by him …[20]

FCT v Dixon [1952] HCA 65

Facts: In this case, an employer paid employees a 'top up salary' to encourage military service.

The payment was calculated to make up the difference between the salary payable to employees and the lower salary payable to enlisted soldiers, thus ensuring employees who enlisted in the army continued to enjoy the same level of income as if they had remained employees of the employer. The taxpayer argued

---

20 *FCT v Harris* [1980] FLR 36, 39–40.

the payments were essentially a recurrent gift from a former employer (because once an employee joined the army they naturally ceased being employed in their prior job) which the former employer was under no legal obligation to make or continue to make and to which the employee had no legally enforceable right. As such, the payments were not properly characterised as ordinary income.

Conversely, the Commissioner argued the payments were taxable as ordinary income[21] because they formed part of the regular receipts of the taxpayer that he depended on and arose as a consequence of the employment of the taxpayer.

Held: Chief Justice Dixon and Williams J considered the payments as clearly 'incidental' to the taxpayer's employment and as such concluded:

> It is clear that if payments are really incidental to an employment, it is unimportant whether they come from the employer or from somebody else and are obtained as a right of work or merely as a recognised incident of the employment or work.[22]

As such, the High Court affirmed that it does not matter whether the payment is made by an employer, a former employer or another third party — the test of assessability of personal service income remains whether the payment can properly be considered a 'product' or 'incident' of the employment.

3.5.2 Redirection of personal service income and personal service businesses

A further key principle of assessability of personal services income/income from personal exertion is that generally this income is taxable in the hands of the person who carried out the service or personal exertion. In other words, such income cannot be redirected or **alienated** to make it taxable in the hands of somebody else.[23]

This general principle is reflected in section 6-5(4) of the ITAA97. You will recall from earlier in this chapter that this section provides:

> (4) In working out whether you have derived an amount of ordinary income, and (if so) when you derived it, you are taken to have received the amount as soon as it is applied or dealt with in any way on your behalf or as you direct.

The implication is that, even if you direct income earned as a result of personal exertion to be paid to somebody else, for example, another member of your family, you will still be considered the person who derived the income and that redirected income will be assessable in your hands as ordinary income.

In addition, however, Divisions 84–87 of the ITAA97 expressly deal with the issue of individuals attempting to redirect personal service income (PSI). The specific aims of this legislation are captured in sections 85-5 and 85-10. The former specifies that the aim of the legislation is to stop individuals (and more particularly employees) alienating their personal service income (where that income is gained mainly as a reward for the personal efforts or skills of an individual), to an associated company, partnership trust or individual. Section 85-10 adds an additional objective of denying certain business deductions not normally available to employees.

The PSI provisions do not apply if the income is:

1. not 'personal service income'
2. derived as part of a 'personal service business'.

Where an individual has attempted to redirect personal service income but is unable to establish they are operating a 'personal services business' they will be personally assessable on that income at their applicable tax rate, and they will be denied certain deductions normally not available to employees; for example, certain travel expenses, rent, mortgage interest, rates or land tax in relation to your premises.[24]

There are a number of tests for working out if you are carrying on a **personal services business (PSB)** (section 87-15). These tests are set out in a later chapter.

---

21 They also argued they were assessable as statutory income under section 26(e) (the predecessor to section 15-2 of the ITAA97) — an argument that was ultimately rejected by the Court.

22 [1952] HCA 65, [5].

23 When we look at entities in a later chapter — partnerships and trusts in particular — we will explore some of the subtleties of this general rule.

24 The ATO has issued TR 2003/10, which deals with deductions that relate to personal service income (www.ato.gov.au/law/view /pdf/pbr/tr2003-010.pdf).

3.6 Business income

LEARNING OBJECTIVE 3.6 Describe the assessability of business income.

Determining the assessability of business income depends on answering three key questions.

1. Is the taxpayer carrying on a business?
2. Is the sum received by the taxpayer within the scope of the taxpayer's business?
3. If the sum received is for activities outside the scope of the taxpayer's business, did the sum received result from a 'profit-making scheme'?

Figure 3.3 illustrates how the answers to these three questions affect the determination of whether a receipt is assessable as business income for income tax purposes.

FIGURE 3.3 Determining whether a receipt is assessable as business income

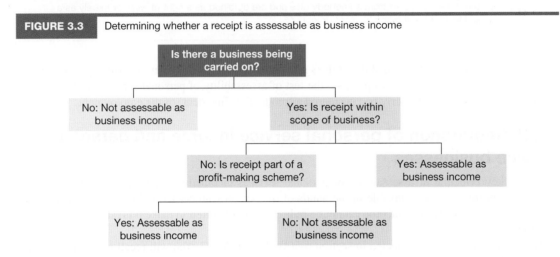

3.6.1 Is a business being carried on?

There are several reasons why it is important to determine whether a business is being carried on. First, for income tax purposes, generally income from a business is assessable and expenditure incurred in deriving that income is deductible. In addition, the tax treatment of particular income can be different depending on whether the income is business income or income from property or personal service employment. There are also a number of particular tax rules that only apply where a business is being carried on. These include various concessions only available to businesses. You will learn about a number of these in later chapters.

There are some issues you need to consider in order to work out whether a business is being carried on. One situation that can raise some interesting issues is when a business is in the process of being started. It might sound surprising, but it can be difficult in some cases to work out precisely when a business has actually commenced. The case of *Softwood Pulp & Paper Ltd v FCT* (1976) 7 ATR 101 provides a good example. In that case, the issue was whether the expenses a company incurred in conducting a feasibility study before a decision to start-up the business was made were deductible expenses. The Court determined that the expenses were not deductible as at the time the expenditure was incurred no business was actually being carried on.

It gets trickier where a business operation clearly exists, but it is unclear whether certain new activities engaged in by the business entity constitute a new business or simply a change to the scope of the existing business. For example, a fast food store introducing a new range of burgers would typically be considered merely an expansion or change to the scope of an existing business. On the other hand, a fast food business deciding to branch out into electronics would be far more likely to be considered the establishment of a new business. In this case, the question of when the electronics business had commenced and the scope of the new business would be relevant to determining tax treatment of income and expenditure of the electronics business.

Beyond the question of whether a business has actually commenced, a further complication arises by virtue of there being no statutory definition of what 'carrying on a business' means. In effect, the issue is treated in a similar manner to the definition of 'ordinary income' — that is, the issue is determined by looking for the presence or absence of a number of 'indicators'. To understand these, we need to look at the case law.

Key questions the courts have asked to help them decide whether there is a business include the following.

1. Is there a profit motive for the activity (even if there is no objective evidence that a profit will ever actually be made)?
2. What is the scale of the activity? Is it run on commercial principles characteristic of that sort of business venture?
3. Are the activities repetitive and do they have a permanent character?
4. Is there continuity in the activities?
5. Is there a systematic approach to how the activity is being conducted?

None of the 'indicators' are determinative on their own. You need to look at whether there is an overall 'commercial flavour' to the enterprise. Equally, not all these questions need to be answered with a 'yes' for the activity to qualify as a business. It is a question of fact and degree.

Even if a business is *not* being carried on, there may still be tax consequences. For example, the activity may be considered a 'hobby'. Hobby income can be assessable where it relates to service provision — see sections 6-5 and 15-2 of the ITAA97.

Some activities pose particular challenges – examples include farming and gambling. These cases are worth looking at because they illustrate how courts approach working out whether an activity is a business or merely a hobby and the application of the indicators of business. Increasingly also, the sharing economy and technological advances facilitating the expansion of activities such as cryptocurrency investment (which we discuss later in the chapter in the context of income from property) are also posing new challenges and applications of the principles for determining whether a business is being carried on. The sharing economy will be discussed later in this part of the chapter.

3.6.1.1 Farming: business or hobby?

In farming cases, the issue arises where taxpayers engage in relatively small-scale enterprises and the question is whether those enterprises are just a hobby or a farming business. Whether these small-scale enterprises are businesses depends on whether they are being conducted in a 'commercial' or 'business-like' manner. To work this out, courts will consider factors such as the degree of organisation and repetition to the business activities, whether the taxpayer is actively involved in the business, and the presence of profit-making intentions.

Ferguson v FCT is a leading example illustrating how courts approach these types of cases.

Ferguson v FCT [1979] FCA 29[1]

Facts: The taxpayer was a member of the Navy. In anticipation of his retirement in 3 years, he leased five cows and entered into an agreement with a management company to agist, breed from, and otherwise care for and manage the cows. The taxpayer intended, on his retirement, to buy a farm and raise beef cattle, so the five cows were leased with the aim of building his herd. The taxpayer took a keen interest in the development of the herd, received monthly reports from the management company as to their progress, and maintained a card index system for his leased cows and their offspring.

The taxpayer claimed deductions for expenses associated with the cows. The Commissioner denied the deductions, arguing the taxpayer was not carrying on a business.

Held: The taxpayer was carrying on a business. The activities were being conducted on a commercial basis. Evidence of this was the regular reporting, the card ledger system, the appointment of a manager, and regular reading by the taxpayer of industry literature. Even though the business was running at a loss, was of low volume and relatively small investment, these did not alter the fundamental commercial nature of the activity.

Example 3.3 demonstrates a further application of the reasoning in the *Ferguson* case.

EXAMPLE 3.3

Farming: business or hobby?

Anika was a real estate agent. In anticipation of her retirement in a few years, she purchased an angora breeding goat for $3000. She intended to breed the goat and hoped the offspring would be sold for

▶

$3000 each. Anika actively involved herself in seeking out expert advice, reading industry literature and kept detailed accounts. Unfortunately, things went badly — despite several breeding cycles over a few years, most of the offspring died and the others sold for low prices. She ultimately sold her breeding goat for $100. If she is running a business, she can claim a deduction for her losses. Is she running a business?

Yes, the taxpayer had a profit-making purpose and there was repetition and regularity to the activities. She was actively involved in the business and kept detailed accounts. In these circumstances, the small scale of the activity does not alter the commercial nature of the activity. In fact, this example broadly mirrors the facts in a real case — *FCT v Walker* (1985) 85 ATC 179 — in which the taxpayer was also found to be running a business.

Thomas v FCT (1972) 3 ATR 165

Facts: This case was another example of a small-scale agricultural activity that was held to be a business. In this case, a solicitor purchased a small parcel of land where he resided and also planted crops of trees such as macadamias and avocados together with some trees for timber production. He also invested in irrigation infrastructure for the trees. However, he never made a profit, particularly after some of his trees were destroyed in a bushfire and had to be replanted. The Commissioner contended that the activities of the taxpayer in many respects were not conducted in a business-like manner and that there was little if any prospect that a profit would ever be derived from the taxpayer's activities which were more akin to a hobby than a business.

Held: The High Court held that the taxpayer was conducting a primary production business during the relevant year of income, notwithstanding the fact that no income was derived during the relevant year and the fact that the business was not conducted with the maximum of efficiency.

3.6.1.2 Gambling: business or hobby?

Gambling will usually be considered a hobby rather than a business. Courts usually consider 'sport, excitement and amusement' as being the primary motivation for the activity.

Evans v FCT [1989] FCA 205[25]

Facts: The taxpayer was a frequent gambler on both horse and greyhound racing. He was relatively successful in his gambling, winning enough to fund his lifestyle. However, he was not particularly systematic in his approach. For example, he kept no records, had no system to his betting, engaged no administrative support or invested in any research into the industry that might better inform his gambling endeavours. His gambling activities were described as intuitive and high risk. The Commissioner sought to characterise the taxpayer's activities as a business, treating his winnings as assessable income.

Held: The Federal Court held that the taxpayer's activities were more akin to a hobby than a business, due in large part to the lack of system or organisation involved. Hence, the proceeds were not assessable as ordinary income from a business. The Court characterised the taxpayer simply as being a person heavily addicted to gambling.

Cases such as *Evans* illustrate that, to be considered a business, the taxpayer will have to prove their gambling is more than just a hobby or addiction. There must be evidence that the activities are:
- systematic, organised and business-like
- for the primary objective purpose of profit-making rather than pleasure
- based on a system reliant on judgement or skill rather than just chance
- considered by the taxpayer to be a business rather than a mere hobby or pastime.[26]

Usually, successful cases have also involved taxpayers whose betting activities are related to other similar business activities (e.g. breeding of racehorses). This was the case in *Trautwein v FCT* [1936] HCA 46, in which the taxpayer, a hotelier, also raced his own horses and horses under lease, and devoted a substantial amount of time to the activity. He bet frequently and systematically using valuable racing

---

25 The link to the case is at: http://www8.austlii.edu.au/cgi-bin/viewdoc/au/cases/cth/FCA/1989/205.html?query=.
26 See *Brajkovich v FCT* 89 ATC 5227.

information which he acquired from trainers and others and used agents to place bets for him. He was not a mere punter. It was found that Mr Trautwein's betting was neither dominated by enjoyment and amusement of the sport, nor was such enjoyment or amusement the main factor in it. However, it should be noted that being involved in the industry by, for example, owning racehorses, is not enough on its own to constitute a business. A good example illustrating this point is *Martin v FCT* [1953] HCA 100.[27]

Martin v FCT [1953] HCA 100

Facts: Mr Martin was a hotelier and a keen gambler. He also owned a number of racehorses and contended he was carrying on a gambling business.

Held: Mr Martin did not satisfy the High Court that his gambling activities amounted to a systematic or substantial enough enterprise to be considered a business. The Court described his gambling pursuits as follows.

So it appears that the taxpayer, like many other persons who find pleasure in betting and even more pleasure in winning, used a system which he believed would bring him out on the credit side in the long run, that he sometimes got a friend who accompanied him to the races to lay his bets for him when he was himself occupied in the saddling paddock, and that he engaged trainers from time to time to train his racehorses. But we do not consider this evidence to be symptomatic of a business of betting or racing. It illustrates the normal and usual activities and nothing more of persons who derive pleasure from betting on the racecourse and racing under their own colours.

Example 3.4 demonstrates the principles established by the High Court in the *Martin* case.

EXAMPLE 3.4

Gambling: business or hobby?

Rodney is a retired property investor and a keen horse and greyhound racing gambler. There is no method or pattern to his gambling, he has no office from which he conducts his gambling activities, no staff, does not study prior to placing bets and does not analyse race results or trends. He describes his betting as based on 'a mixture of intuition and judgement'. Apart from his gambling, he is not involved in the horseracing or greyhound racing industries. Is he running a gambling business?

No. Rodney's lack of system and organisation to his betting, his lack of exercise of skill and study to inform his betting and his lack of involvement in the industry more generally lead to a strong conclusion that his activities are purely for 'sport, excitement and amusement' rather than business. In fact, even if Rodney owned some greyhounds or racehorses or was otherwise involved in the industry, the lack of system and organisation to his betting would still likely result in his gambling not being considered a business.

3.6.1.3 Sharing economy

The term 'sharing economy' has become a somewhat ubiquitous term to describe a range of potential income-earning activities conducted through a digital platform for some sort of fee or reward. The sharing economy is also sometimes referred to as the 'gig economy', 'mesh economy' and the 'peer-to-peer market'. The range of activities continues to expand and these various differing contexts can raise a range of different challenges concerning the appropriate tax treatment of taxpayer receipts resulting from engagement in them. Examples include ride-sharing services such as Uber, short-term accommodation services such as Airbnb, and a range of platforms facilitating the provision of various types of personal services such as Airtasker.

There is no special tax regime that applies to the sharing economy. Generally speaking, the same rules that apply to the general economy apply equally to sharing economy activities. Potential tax implications of engaging in the peer economy include capital gains tax and GST implications. For example, those using their principal residences to supply Airbnb accommodation services may need to consider the implications for their ability to claim main residence CGT concessions in future. Those with turnover that exceed the GST registration threshold will need to levy GST on their services and register for GST.

---

27 The link to this case is at: http://www.austlii.edu.au/cgi-bin/viewdoc/au/cases/cth/HCA/1953/100.html?context=1;query=martin; mask_path=au/cases/cth/HCA.

In addition, taxpayers involved in the sharing economy will need to be conscious of the tax record-keeping requirements and ensure they register for an Australian Business Number as required. There will also be implications for the tax deductions able to be claimed, including expense apportionment complexities arising in situations were assets used by the taxpayer for sharing economy income earning purposes (such as an Uber driver's car) are also used for private non-income earning purposes.

In the present context of considering the assessability of receipts from sharing economy activities, broadly speaking, the ATO takes the view that income earned from sharing economy activities will be assessable income even where the level of engagement and income earned is relatively small. Receipts are likely to be considered receipts from business rather than receipts from a hobby in the vast majority of cases. There have been some recent determinations by the Australian Fair Work Commission in which gig workers have been deemed to be employees rather than independent contractors;[28] however, it remains the case that usually income from sharing economy activities will be considered business income.

The reasons for this were concisely set out by the Board of Taxation in their 2017 report titled *Tax and the Sharing Economy* (the Report):

> In the majority of cases, sharing economy participants were:
> - looking to generate income or profit from their activities;
> - using commercial platforms (and paying platform fees) to access customers;
> - were providing their services (or access to their assets) to third parties; and
> - were undertaking regular activities (for example, transporting people in their car, performing house maintenance or removalist services) that could not be plausibly described as a hobby or pastime.
>
> Typically sharing economy participants would not go through the compliance burden of registering with a platform for a hobby activity.[29]

The Board of Taxation highlighted in the Report that there is still a high degree of confusion among taxpayers engaged in the sharing economy as to their tax obligations. To explain why this is the case, the Board pointed to factors such as 'the relatively unique nature of participation in the sharing economy, that is, intermittent provision of services, use of private property, receipts usually supplementing other sources of income, etc'.[30] As such, key recommendations in the Report centre on ensuring greater tax compliance and better understanding by participants in the sharing economy of their tax obligations.

There has also been some international research indicating that 'the sharing economy inherently lends itself to dishonest reporting of taxable income'.

ETHICS IN PRACTICE

Ethics in assessable income tax

Jacqueline comes to you to prepare her tax return. She is a new client who is a full-time mechanic but in her spare time in the evenings and on weekends for the last couple of years has done occasional car restoration work for clients who access her services via 'MechanicsAnon' — an online personal services sharing economy website for connecting mechanics with potential customers. She encourages her clients to pay her in cash and does not keep records of her earnings which she estimates totalled approximately $20 000 last financial year. She asks you not to include any of her MechanicsAnon earnings in her tax return, claiming it's just a side hobby anyway. She says her previous accountant treated these proceeds in this way in her previous year's tax return and expects you will do the same.

What do you think your response should be to Jacqueline's demands?

1. Do as she asks — the client is always right! And ultimately, she will be the one in trouble if she has underreported her assessable income, so it's not my problem.
2. I really can't afford to upset a new client, even if treating the proceeds as hobby earnings in this situation is probably not reasonably arguable, it is not a well-understood area of the law so it is worth the risk to keep the client.
3. Not including the proceeds as assessable income is legally incorrect and I would need to inform her of this and that my responsibilities under the Code of Conduct for tax advisers extend to taking reasonable care to ensure the tax law is applied correctly.

---

28 See, eg, *Diego France v Deliveroo Australia Pty Ltd* [2021] FWC 2818; *Joshua Klooger v Foodora Australia Pty Ltd* [2018] FWC 6836.

29 Australian Government Board of Taxation, *Tax and the Sharing Economy* (Final Report, July 2017), [4.4].

30 Ibid [4.15].

3.6.2 What is the scope of the business?

As noted in figure 3.3, once you have worked out whether there is a business being carried on, the next question is what is the 'scope' of the business. This can also be tricky and is another issue where case law provides guidance. Particular difficulties arise where isolated transactions and sales of capital assets are involved. Each of these difficulties are explained next.

3.6.2.1 Normal proceeds of business

The **normal proceeds** of a business are assessable as ordinary income. However, sometimes it is difficult to identify the true nature of a business in order to identify what are the 'normal proceeds' of the business.

To work out whether an activity is within the scope of the business, courts ask whether the activity is a 'regular, ordinary and expected incident of the taxpayer's business activities'. Courts in Australia tend to take a broader view of activities properly considered a regular, ordinary and expected incident of the business, but it is very important to closely consider the facts as subtle differences can affect the result as the following cases (all of which involve taxpayers engaged in various forms of equipment hire business) illustrate.

GKN Kwikform (1991) 21 ATR 1532[31]

Facts: The taxpayer ran a scaffolding hire business. The standard hire contract entered into with customers included a large fee for failure to return some or all of the scaffolding at the end of the hire period. This was a regular occurrence of the business and the issue for the Federal Court was whether the profits from the non-return fees were assessable income which, in turn, required the Court to determine whether the profits derived were a regular expected and ordinary incident of the carrying on of the business.

Held: There was a regular 'leakage' or 'short return' of items of scaffolding from the amounts ordered by customers for hire for particular jobs. As such, the profits from the charging of the non-return fees were assessable income because the receipts were a regular, ordinary and expected incident of the taxpayer's business.

FCT v Cyclone Scaffolding Pty Ltd [1987] FCA 455

Facts: The taxpayer was also in the scaffolding hire business. As in the *Kwikform* case, equipment was also occasionally sold (usually when equipment was damaged or not returned) but this was the *exception* rather than the rule, with approximately 80 per cent of the taxpayer's revenue being derived from its hiring activities.

Held: The taxpayer's dominant or substantial business was the hiring out of scaffolding equipment. Although there was in contemplation the possibility that some of the equipment could be sold in the future if required, the incidence of such sales was rare. As such, the scope of the business was confined to the hire of scaffolding equipment. Hence, the profit made on the sales of the equipment was not assessable as ordinary income.

It should be noted that in both of the previous cases, the scaffolding equipment was not deemed to be trading stock of the business. Sales of trading stock are ordinary income of a business. In contrast, proceeds from sales of fixed capital assets are not usually considered ordinary income.

Repetition and regularity are key factors that courts will often use to determine whether a receipt should be treated as a capital receipt from sale of a business asset or income within the scope of the business. This was one of the key differences between the two scaffolding cases discussed. The point is further highlighted in two further equipment hire business cases: *Memorex v FCT* (1987) 77 ALR 299 and *Hyteco Hiring Pty Ltd* [1992] FCA 515.

Both cases involved asset lease businesses and the proceeds of sales of assets to customers at the end of their lease.

---

31 The link to this case is at: https://jade.io/article/151587

Facts: The taxpayer was primary engaged in selling computer equipment to businesses. However, it would also lease equipment to customers. Occasionally, it would ultimately sell this leased equipment to the customers. This sale of leased equipment generated profits and the key issue was whether these profits should be considered assessable as ordinary proceeds of the business. The Commissioner took the view that sale of ex-lease equipment was within the ordinary scope of the taxpayer's business. The taxpayer contended that the sale proceeds were capital receipts because the hiring activities were outside the scope of the taxpayer's equipment hire business.

Held: Because the sales of the business equipment happened regularly, the Court deemed the taxpayer was effectively operating a 'computer distribution' business, including both leasing and sales of computers in the normal course of the business. Hence, the profits from the sales of the ex-lease equipment were assessable income.

Facts: The taxpayer's primary business activity was hiring of forklifts. The forklifts would usually be returned to the taxpayer for their residual value at the end of the lease. When the forklifts reached the end of their effective lives and could no longer be leased, they would be sold by a related company of the taxpayer. The Commissioner contended that any profits from these sales constituted assessable income, as sales of forklifts was an ordinary incident of the business.

Held: The occasional sales of ex-hire forklifts was not deemed to be an ordinary incident of the taxpayer's forklift hire business. Neither the scale nor regularity of the earning of profits from these sales supported a conclusion that these activities were an ordinary incident of the business. The Court also noted that, although regularity of receipt is an indicator of income, it is insufficient on its own.

If the activity is entirely outside the scope of the business — that is, it is not a transaction which is either clearly within the usual daily activities of the business or a transaction that although unusual is still objectively capable of being viewed as a *regular, ordinary and expected incident of the taxpayer's business* — then the proceeds from the transaction can only constitute assessable business income if the transaction is part of a 'profit-making scheme'. This possibility was considered in a number of the previous cases. For example, had the Court in *Hyteco Hiring* determined that the forklifts were purchased by the taxpayer with the dominant or primary intention of making profit from resale of those forklifts, then the proceeds from those sales, although extraordinary transactions, could have been considered assessable income from a profit-making scheme.

Profit-making schemes are discussed in our discussion of income from isolated transactions in section 3.6.3.

3.6.2.2 Illegal business activities

Before moving on, it should also be noted that there is no restriction on receipts from illegal or immoral business activities being considered ordinary income. Proceeds of illegal business activities (e.g. drug dealing) are assessable. This was confirmed in Australia in *La Rosa v FCT* (2003) 53 ATR 1.[32] In this case, the taxpayer conducted an illegal heroin drug dealing business. He had not filed tax returns, and the Commissioner issued default tax assessments based on estimates of the illegal income earned by the taxpayer as ordinary income from the taxpayer's illegal drug dealing business. The Federal Court confirmed that whether a business is legal or illegal does not affect whether income generated from the business is assessable as ordinary income or not. Accordingly, in this case, income from the illegal drug dealing business was assessable as ordinary income.[33]

---

32 English authority for this proposition was established in *Partridge v Mallandaine* (1886) 18 QBD 27, a case involving illegal horse race betting business activities.

33 However, the Court also ruled that as a result, a substantial deduction for losses incurred by the taxpayer due to a robbery during an attempted drug deal was also allowable. This outcome is discussed further in a later chapter. The case ultimately brought about the enactment of section 26-54 to expressly deny claims for tax deductions for expenses incurred in conducting a completely illegal business.

3.6.3 Extraordinary and isolated transactions

There are some situations where extraordinary or isolated transactions can be assessable as business income. The situations that raise the possibility of this occurring are cases involving the once-off realisations of assets (e.g. sales of land) or other transactions which, although not necessarily once-off transactions, still fall outside normal business activities (extraordinary transactions).

Section 15-15 of the ITAA97 deals with the assessability of income from profit-making undertakings or plans. Section 15-15(1) states that: 'assessable income includes profit arising from the carrying on or carrying out of a profit-making undertaking or plan'.

Subsection 2 makes it clear, however, that this does not include profit that would otherwise be assessable as ordinary income or 'arises in respect of the sale of property acquired on or after 20 September 1985' (the date the capital gains tax (CGT) provisions came into effect).

The net effect of this provision is that where profits from profit-making schemes are *not* assessable as ordinary income or assessable under the CGT provisions, they will be considered assessable as statutory income under section 15-15(1).

Whether these transactions are assessable as ordinary income (section 6-5) or statutory income (section 15-15) depends on the particular facts of the case and the transactions involved. It also depends on whether the transactions can be considered as being extraordinary or isolated, but still in the ordinary course of business, or transactions outside the scope of the business (or not part of a business at all), but part of a 'profit-making scheme' (explained in the rest of this part of the chapter).

3.6.3.1 Isolated transaction proceeds as 'ordinary income'

Isolated transactions can give rise to assessable income which is ordinary income (within the meaning of section 6-5) where, even though the transaction was not part of the usual daily business activities of the business, there was a profit-making motive for entering the transaction.

In TR 92/3,[34] the Commissioner takes the view that a gain from an **isolated transaction** is generally assessable as a profit-making scheme if the:

1. intention or purpose of the taxpayer in entering into the transaction was to make a profit or gain, and
2. transaction was entered into and the profit made in the course of carrying on a business *or* in carrying out a business operation or commercial transaction.

Several cases have provided further clarification to assist in working out whether there is a profit-making scheme.

1. Profit doesn't have to be the only motive for a transaction to be a 'profit-making scheme'. It just needs to be a dominant motivation.
2. The scheme by which the profit is made must be the same as the scheme contemplated at the outset — that is, a general profit motive is not enough.

Taxation Ruling TR 92/3 was issued in response to the High Court decision in *FCT v Myer Emporium* [1987] HCA 18.

FCT v Myer Emporium [1987] HCA 18

Facts: A taxpayer had a business running department stores. It entered into a loan agreement with a subsidiary company, Myer Finance Limited, in which it loaned the subsidiary $80 million in return for a right to 12.5 per cent interest payable per annum on the loan. Three days later (as was always the plan) it assigned the right to these interest payments to a finance company, Citicorp, in return for a lump sum payment of $45.37 million.

The question was whether this payment was assessable, despite the transaction being clearly an isolated transaction outside the normal scope of the taxpayer's business. The Commissioner sought to assess the receipt either as ordinary income or as profit from a profit-making undertaking or scheme. The taxpayer contended that the receipt was simply a capital receipt for realising a capital asset (the right to receive the interest payments) as a result of an isolated transaction outside of its ordinary business activities, and that the payment was not assessable.

Held: The payment was assessable as proceeds from a 'profit-making scheme' entered into in the course of the taxpayer's business.

---

34 The ruling can be found at: https://www.ato.gov.au/law/view/pdf/pbr/tr1992-003.pdf.

The Court rejected the taxpayer's argument that the assignment of the loan to Citicorp was a mere realisation of a capital asset. The Court noted that the assignment could not be separated from the initial loan given that the loan would not have occurred if the assignment to Citicorp had not been pre-arranged to occur shortly after the loan was made. In effect, the two transactions were to be view as part of a single profit-making scheme.

The characterisation of both the loan and the assignment as part of a single profit-making scheme meant the Court could conclude that the profit-making intention existed from when the loan was made and was realised in the manner contemplated upon assignment to Citicorp of the right to the interest payments pursuant to the loan a few days later.

> Because a business is carried on with a view to profit, a gain made in the ordinary course of carrying on the business is invested with the profit-making purpose, thereby stamping the profit with the character of income. But a gain made otherwise than in the ordinary course of carrying on the business which nevertheless arises from a transaction entered into by the taxpayer with the intention or purpose of making a profit or gain may well constitute income. Whether it does depends very much on the circumstances of the case. Generally speaking, however, it may be said that if the circumstances are such as to give rise to the inference that the taxpayer's intention or purpose in entering into the transaction was to make a profit or gain, the profit or gain will be income, notwithstanding that the transaction was extraordinary judged by reference to the ordinary course of the taxpayer's business. Nor does the fact that a profit or gain is made as the result of an isolated venture or a 'one-off' transaction preclude it from being properly characterized as income … The authorities establish that a profit or gain so made will constitute income if the property generating the profit or gain was acquired in a business operation or commercial transaction for the purpose of profit-making by the means giving rise to the profit.

The second strand of the reasoning in the *Myer* case is also important, but more limited in its application. It relates to the Court's additional conclusion that in factual situations involving the conversion of a future right to interest into a lump sum, the lump sum will be considered of an income nature. In broad terms, this is a manifestation of the 'replacement principle' that we will discuss further later in the chapter as part of our discussion of the tax treatment of compensation payments. In the specific context of the transaction in *Myer*, the Court took the view that the taxpayer sold a mere right to interest for a lump sum — that lump sum being received in exchange for, and as the present value of, the future interest it would have received. The taxpayer simply converted future income into present income.

A subsequent leading case on the issue of whether there is a profit-making scheme is *Westfield v FCT* [1991] FCA 97.

Westfield v FCT [1991] FCA 97

Facts: This case involved the purchase of land by the taxpayer to develop and run a shopping centre. The core business of the taxpayer was the construction and management of shopping centre developments. At the time of the purchase, the taxpayer intended to construct a shopping centre on the land and manage it thereafter. However, the taxpayer subsequently determined this was not a viable project and sold the land. The purchaser then engaged the taxpayer to develop the shopping centre on the site.

The question for the Court was whether the profits from the sale of the land were assessable income or a capital receipt for realisation of a capital asset.

Held: The sale of land was not in the ordinary course of the taxpayer's business. The question was, therefore, whether the profits were assessable as part of a profit-making scheme. The Court held they were not. This is because although the taxpayer had a general profit-making intention when it purchased the land, a general profit motive is not enough to constitute a profit-making scheme. To be a profit-making scheme, the scheme generating the profits must be the same as the scheme in contemplation at the time the transaction was entered into. This was not the situation in this case.

An interesting contrast with the *Westfield* case is the case of *Moana Sand Pty Ltd v FCT* discussed next. This was also a case in which the taxpayer did not generate profits in the precise manner it had contemplated at the time it acquired a property, but nonetheless the Court was satisfied that the proceeds from the sale were assessable as income from a profit-making scheme.

Facts: Moana Sand purchased a property with a view to mining and selling the sand on the property and subsequently subdividing and selling the land for profit. However, once the sand was all gone, the taxpayer was unable to get Council approval to subdivide the land. Ultimately, the land was resumed by the Coastal Protection Board. The Commissioner sought to assess the profits from the resumption of the land by the Coastal Protection Board either as ordinary income or as income from a profit-making scheme.

Held: Although the proceeds from the sale of the land were not derived from a subdivision as envisaged when the land was purchased, the proceeds were still within the scope of the initial intent when purchasing the land which was ultimately to sell the land for a profit once the supply of sand on the land had been exhausted. Accordingly, the proceeds were within the scope of the original profit making scheme.

3.7 Property income

LEARNING OBJECTIVE 3.7 Describe the assessability of property income.

Some property assets are used to generate returns that are clearly assessable income — for example, rental from investment properties or dividend receipts from share investments. The issue becomes a little blurred where there are questions surrounding the proceeds of the sale of the underlying capital assets. In most cases, these will not be considered ordinary income, with the proceeds being assessed under the provisions of the CGT. However, there can be situations where the underlying capital asset, such as land or shares, is central to the business of the taxpayer — for example, property developers or share market stock traders. In such cases, profits from the sales of the property assets can be considered ordinary income. This is where the preceding discussion of isolated transactions leads us neatly into a discussion of property income. This is because many cases involve proceeds from isolated transactions generated from the sales of property and similar considerations such as whether the sale is a mere realisation of a capital asset or is part of a profit-making scheme.

An early case illustrating this point is *Californian Copper Syndicate v Harris (Surveyor of Taxes)* [1904] 41 SLR 691.[36] This case involved a company established for purchasing copper-bearing land. However, the company did not have enough money to mine the land and ultimately decided to sell the land to another company in return for shares in that company. In doing so, the taxpayer made a large profit. The question for the Court was whether this profit was assessable as income or simply constituted a capital receipt from realisation of a capital asset. The Court decided the profit was assessable income. Key to this decision was the Court's view that the company from the outset was established for the purpose of buying and selling land as it never had enough capital to actually mine the land itself. Hence, the sale of the land was not a mere realisation of a capital asset; it was a trading transaction in operating a business of carrying out a profit-making scheme.

The following extract from the judgement of Lord Justice-Clerk in *Californian Copper* gives a good starting insight into the difficulties of determining whether the sale of a capital asset is a mere realisation or a profit-making scheme:

> It is quite a well-settled principle in dealing with questions of assessment of income-tax, that where the owner of an ordinary investment chooses to realise it and obtains a greater price for it than he originally acquired it at, the enhanced price is not profit ... assessable to income-tax. But it is equally well established that enhanced values obtained from realisation or conversion of securities may be so assessable where what is done is not merely a realisation or change of investment, but an act done in what is truly the carrying on or carrying out of a business ...

> What is the line which separates the two classes of cases may be difficult to define, and each case must be considered according to its facts, the question to be determined being, is the sum of gain that has been made a mere enhancement of value by realising a security, or is it, again, made by an operation of business in carrying out a scheme for profit-making.[37]

---

35 The link to this case is at: http://www.austlii.edu.au/cgi-bin/sinodisp/au/cases/cth/FCA/1988/401.html?query=.
36 The link to this case is at: https://www.bailii.org/scot/cases/ScotCS/1904/41SLR0691.html.
37 *Californian Copper Syndicate v Harris (Surveyor of Taxes)* [1904] 41 SLR 691, 694.

A more recent case illustrating when proceeds from a sale of property will be considered assessable is *FCT v Whitfords Beach* [1982] HCA 8. The case illustrates a situation where an isolated property transaction can be viewed as a business of itself and the proceeds assessable as income on that basis.

FCT v Whitfords Beach [1982] HCA 8

Facts: The taxpayer was a company originally formed in 1954 and owned by a group of fishermen to purchase a very large parcel of beachside land next to fishing shacks to give them easy access to the beach. Thirteen years later the shares in the company were purchased by property developers who changed the constitution of the company to reflect a new intention to develop and sell the land. The company, now owned by the property developers, subsequently subdivided the land and sold the lots for significant profits.

The ATO sought to assess the company on these profits either as income in the ordinary course of business or as part of a profit-making scheme. The taxpayer argued that the profits were simply from the realisation of the company's land assets in the most advantageous way — hence they were a capital receipt and not assessable as income.

Held: The majority of the High Court considered the proceeds were assessable as income in the ordinary course of business. Although the three judges differed in their reasoning in reaching this conclusion, Mason and Wilson JJ held that the massive scale of the property development activities meant the transaction could not be considered a mere realisation of an asset, but was more appropriately characterised as a stand-alone property development business.

Mason J observed:

> I do not agree with the proposition which appears to be founded on remarks in some of the judgments that sale of land which has been subdivided is necessarily no more than the realization of an asset merely because it is an enterprising way of realizing the asset to the best advantage. That may be so in the case where an area of land is merely divided into several allotments. But it is not so in a case such as the present where the planned subdivision takes place on a massive scale, involving the laying out and construction of roads, the provision of parklands, services and other improvements. All this amounts to development and improvement of the land to such a marked degree that it is impossible to say that it is mere realization of an asset.[38]

Subsequent cases have elaborated on additional factors which are relevant considerations in determining whether the proceeds from a property development transaction will be considered a capital receipt from a mere realisation of an asset or will constitute assessable income. These include factors such as the degree of personal involvement in the project by the taxpayer, and the extent to which the development of the land went beyond the minimum required to gain the relevant statutory approvals for the development. The cases of *Statham & Bickerton v FCT* [1988] FCA 463 and *Casimaty v FCT* (1997) 37 ATR 358 illustrate these points.

Statham & Bickerton v FCT [1988] FCA 463[39]

Facts: The taxpayers were trustees of a deceased estate. The dispute concerned the subdivision of the property of the deceased initially acquired for farming purposes. The subdivision work was carried out by the local Council. This included all sewerage, road works, earthworks and electrical works. The sale of the 105 subdivided lots was managed and carried out by a local real estate agent. The taxpayers had no involvement in any of these activities associated with the subdivision and sale of the subdivided lots.

Held: The Federal Court held that the proceeds from the sales of the subdivided lots were capital proceeds from the mere realisation of the land rather than assessable as ordinary income, despite the relatively large size of the subdivision. Key to the Court's ruling was the complete lack of involvement in the subdivision by the taxpayers. This helped inform the characterisation of the subdivision as simple and having few hallmarks of a business enterprise. Other relevant factors included the fact that the taxpayers had unsuccessfully tried to dispose of the land as a single parcel prior to resorting to subdivision, the very limited clearing and earthworks involved, and the lack of any business organisation, manager, office, secretary, etc.

---

38 *FCT v Whitfords Beach* [1982] HCA 8, [37].
39 The link to this case is at: http://www8.austlii.edu.au/cgi-bin/viewdoc/au/cases/cth/FCA/1988/463.html.

Facts: For decades, the taxpayer was a farmer on land gifted to him by his father in 1955. However, due to deteriorating health and financial problems, the taxpayer was compelled to sell the farm. The taxpayer proceeded with a series of subdivisions between 1975 and 1995 to sell off parts of the farm, doing only the bare minimum amount of development to the land in order to comply with the requirements of the development approval. The taxpayer did not involve himself in the sale and marketing of the subdivided blocks.

Held: The taxpayer's activities amounted to no more than a mere realisation. Hence, the proceeds were not assessable as ordinary income. Key to the Federal Court's conclusion was the minimal level of development of the land coupled with the taxpayer's minimal involvement in the subdivision project.

Another common context in which the issue of whether there is a mere realisation of a capital asset or the operation of a business in a property context is where sales of shares or other property investment transactions and activities are concerned.

Where, for example, trading in shares is concerned, in the event that the facts indicate that a taxpayer is in the business of share-trading, the shares will be considered trading stock of the business and the trading stock rules will apply. In essence, this will mean that the cost of acquiring the shares will be deductible and profits made from the sale of shares will be assessable as ordinary income. We cover trading stock rules in detail in a later chapter. Where the sales of shares are not considered to be in the context of business, then the proceeds from their sale will be dealt with under the capital gains tax rules which we also cover in a later chapter. For present purposes, however, *AAT Case 4083* [2011] AATA 545 illustrates some of the challenges in determining whether a taxpayer in engaged in a business of share trading or is merely a passive investor.

AAT Case 4083 [2011] AATA 545[40]

Facts: The taxpayer was a successful business man who spent approximately two hours each day engaged in investing in the share-market in his own name. He claimed that these activities amounted to a business of share trading. The Commissioner alleged the taxpayer was merely a passive investor, pointing to relatively infrequent share trading, and an overall lack of system and organisation to the share-trading activities.

Held: The taxpayer was operating a share-trading business. The Tribunal accepted that the taxpayer was not engaged in a passive academic or recreational pursuit in his investment activities. The taxpayer had subscribed to stock market bulletins to help him identify companies he thought were undervalued by the market. He would research those companies using publicly available information from a range of sources. He would read books from well-known businessmen like Warren Buffett and George Soros to help inform his investment strategy. Although the number of transactions was small during the period in question he claimed, this was due to the Global Financial Crisis rather than evidence that he had any long-term passive investment strategy. In addition, his investments were substantial — well in excess of $1 million.

On the question of whether the taxpayer's activities were operated in a business-like manner, the Tribunal made the following interesting observations:

> The question of whether or not the taxpayer operated in a 'business-like manner' is a curious one, if only because the concept is becoming increasingly fluid. One must be careful of stereotypes in cases like this — especially given the advances in information technology that have changed concepts like 'place of business' and 'office'. I have already noted the taxpayer was a thoroughly modern business-man who relied on his lap-top and internet connection (and increasingly his mobile phone, complete with apps) to do business from where he was located at any given time. Research and transactions were conducted over the phone or online. Even his record-keeping occurred online. He had entered into arrangements with a broker and Commsec, including a margin-lending facility. That implied a degree of sophistication and a business purpose.[41]

---

40 The link to this case is at: http://www6.austlii.edu.au/cgi-bin/viewdoc/au/cases/cth/aat/2011/545.html.
41 *AAT Case 4083* [2011] AATA 545, [21].

An interesting current and emerging challenge is where various forms of transacting in cryptocurrencies is concerned. The ATO recently issued guidance for tax practitioners and taxpayers on the issue, affirming that key factors to determine whether trading in cryptocurrencies will be considered a business or mere realisation of property assets include factors such as the nature and purpose of the taxpayer's cryptocurrency activities, the repetition, volume and regularity of their activities, and whether they have a business plan and their activities are organised in a business-like way.[42] However, it is worth exploring a little more deeply the potential uncertainties and challenges in determining the appropriate tax treatment of cryptocurrency transactions for both taxpayers and their advisers.

TECHNOLOGY IN ACTION

Blockchain beyond Bitcoin

Blockchain is more than just Bitcoin. Although blockchain technology has gained substantial attention since 2008 due to Satoshi Nakamoto's Bitcoin whitepaper,[43] the on-chain 'metaverse' is continuing to expand as more and more use cases emerge and more and more blockchains emerge. The Bitcoin blockchain itself is limited in its functionality; it enables the cryptocurrency Bitcoin to operate without the need for a central authority. However, other blockchains have increasing functionality. The Ethereum blockchain, for example, was introduced in 2015 and due to the more complex smart contracts that can be executed, there has been exponential growth in experimentation of decentralised applications (DApps), non-fungible tokens (NFTs), decentralised finance (DeFi) and decentralised autonomous organisations (DAOs).[44]

Not only can a taxpayer invest in Bitcoin, but they can participate in a multitude of communities. Cryptoassets may represent social tokens and credentialling, including membership to virtual clubs, gaming tokens (such as a shield for battle or race car), artwork, or even governance tokens for participation in the DAO (i.e. enable voting for changes to protocols). The taxpayer may even be working for a DAO or receive their wages in cryptoassets instead of Australian dollars.

Moreover, with the evolution of DeFi, there are now decentralised alternatives for traditional financial products (such as derivatives, forward and futures contracts, options and swaps).[45] For example, on-chain, taxpayers can participate in 'yield farming' (where the taxpayer uses cryptoassets to earn returns) via 'Uniswap' or other decentralised exchanges; or invest in DeFi derivatives such as 'Synthetix'.[46] The tax implications are more complex and may incorporate not only assessable income (somewhat similar to earning interest), but the acquisition of CGT assets (i.e. when income is derived in the form of new cryptoassets) and also the potential technical disposal of the cryptoassets invested in DeFi platforms.[47]

With this in mind, a tax practitioner needs to closely examine their clients' activities to be able to apply the tax law correctly. What exactly is the client doing on blockchain? Are they an investor, speculator, experimenter, gamer or entrepreneur? What cryptoassets are they interacting with? What platforms are they on? What protocols are they delving into? Each asset, each protocol, is likely to have differing characteristics, differing terms and conditions and therefore have the potential for differing tax consequences. Are they carrying on a business (if so, what kind of business — trading, mining, gaming, art, music)? Or does their activity merely amount to a hobby, with real tax consequences that they may not understand?

REFLECTION

If, at this point, you are thoroughly confused, that's okay! A lot of tax practitioners have been too. This is reflective of an emerging technology moving quickly for which there is a lot of regulatory uncertainty. What skills do you think are important for a tax practitioner to have when attending to clients who undertake blockchain-related activities? Consider the TASA Code of Professional Conduct.

---

42 The link to this case is at: https://www.ato.gov.au/Tax-professionals/TP/Cryptocurrency---investment-or-personal-use-asset.

43 Satoshi Nakamoto, *Bitcoin: a Peer-to-Peer Electronic Cash System* (White Paper, 31 October 2008) https://bitcoin.org/bitcoin.pdf.

44 For a detailed explanation of these, see Vitalik Buterin, 'DAOs, DACs, Das and More: An Incomplete Terminology Guide' *Ethereum Foundation Blog* (Web Page, 6 May 2014) https://blog.ethereum.org/2014/05/06/daos-dacs-das-and-more-an-incomplete-terminology-guide.

45 These financial products are beyond the scope of this text.

46 Litepaper, *Synthetix* (Web Page, March 2020) https://docs.synthetix.io/litepaper.

47 This is depending on the interpretation of the smart contract terms. For example, in Uniswap, the taxpayer invests their cryptoassets and receives either LP tokens or LP-NFTs representing their investment. This provides a right to earn a return on that investment; however, there is some debate over whether the act of investing in Uniswap represents a disposal of the original cryptoassets held. See, eg, the discussion in Joni Pirovich, 'Shifting to more equitable and DAO-based global economies: the case for micro auto-taxing standards and a framework for auto-taxing revenue sharing' (2021) 50(4) *Australian Tax Review* (forthcoming).

3.8 Compensation and reimbursements

LEARNING OBJECTIVE 3.8 Explain the tax treatment of isolated transactions and compensation payments.

When dealing with the income tax treatment of compensation receipts it is very important to work out the reason for which the compensation is being paid. In particular, you need to work out whether the compensation is for loss of income or for loss of assets. As a general principle, if the compensation is for loss of income, the compensation will be considered assessable as ordinary income. Conversely, if the compensation is for loss of a capital asset, the proceeds will be considered a capital receipt rather than ordinary income. In such cases, the question of whether the proceeds are assessable is determined by applying the provisions of the CGT. This stems from a principle known as the **replacement principle**: compensation will generally take the same character as what it replaces.[48]

In *FCT v Dixon* [1952] HCA 65, discussed at length previously (section 3.5.1) in the context of personal services income, Fullagar J concluded the payments of a top-up salary by an employer to encourage employees to enlist in the army were ordinary income on the grounds that they were a 'substitute' for wages and, as such, acquired the same assessable character as the wages they replaced. His Honour observed that if a payment is intended as an equivalent or a substitute for salary or wages '… it must be income, even though it is paid voluntarily and there is not even a moral obligation to continue making the payments. It acquires the character of that for which it is substituted and that to which it is added'.[49]

The tax treatment of compensation for loss of other assets will depend on the nature of the asset. For example, compensation for pain and suffering or for loss of physical ability is usually considered a capital receipt. The cases discussed in sections 3.8.1 and 3.8.2 give examples of the treatment of other types of compensation, including compensation for loss of office and compensation for discrimination for physical disability respectively.

In the business context, complex issues can arise in determining whether the compensation is for harm affecting the business structure (in which case the payment is considered a capital payment) or simply for damage to trading activities or trading stock of the business (in which case the payment is properly characterised as assessable income). The distinction can be a subtle one and the cases discussed in section 3.8.3 illustrate how courts have addressed the issue.

3.8.1 Compensation for loss of office

In some situations, compensation is paid for early termination of an income-earning appointment — for instance, as a company director. In these situations, courts will be more likely to deem that the compensation is income where the payment is periodic and paid in the same amounts and on the same terms as if the contract had not been terminated. Two cases — *Scott v FC of T* (1935) 35 SR (NSW) 215 and *FCT v Phillips* [1936] HCA 11 — provide good examples of how these principles are applied in practice.

In *Scott v FC of T* (1935) 35 SR (NSW) 215, the taxpayer was paid compensation for early cancellation of his appointment as chair of the Metropolitan Meat Industry Board after the board was abolished by legislation. The sum paid was equivalent to the amount payable for services had the contract continued for its full term. The taxpayer argued the payment was a capital payment for loss of opportunity to earn income. The Court agreed, characterising the payment as a price for being prevented from continuing in employment. The amount paid was calculated to be an amount equal to that which would have been payable had the taxpayer brought a claim for wrongful dismissal.

In contrast to the *Scott* case, in *FCT v Phillips* [1936] HCA 11, payments made as compensation for termination of the taxpayer's contract as a managing director of a theatre company were deemed by the High Court to be assessable income. In this case, the payments were paid periodically in the same amounts and the same times as the income that would have been payable to the taxpayer had the contract not been terminated. In these circumstances, the High Court applied the replacement principle — the payments were a direct replacement for the salary that would have been payable under the terminated contract — and the payments 'must … be regarded as of the same nature as the payments which they replace'.

---

48 *FCT v Dixon* [1952] HCA 65.
49 Ibid [7].

3.8.2 Compensation for discrimination or for physical disability

Compensation for discrimination or for physical disability will normally not be considered assessable as ordinary income. However, in some cases, questions can arise about whether the payment is really compensation for income lost rather than for the injury suffered by the taxpayer. A good example of the former is *FCT v DP Smith* (1981) 147 CLR 578. This case concerned compensation received by a medical doctor for injury received in a car accident. The compensation was paid as a monthly amount under an insurance policy until he was well enough to return to work. The High Court held the payments were assessable income, deeming the payments as compensation for loss of income. The Court called upon the familiar 'fruit and tree' analogy in reaching this conclusion:

> If the ability to earn is the tree, and income the fruit thereof, a policy of insurance against impairment of the fruit-bearing capacity of the tree may well take the form of providing the fruit until such time as the tree recovers its proper role.[50]

Certain annuities and lump sums paid for personal injury under 'structured settlements' may be exempt from income tax (Division 54 of the ITAA97). There are also exemptions from CGT that apply to some compensation payments under section 118-37 of the ITAAA97.

3.8.3 Compensation for business losses

From the application of the replacement principle, we can conclude the following.
1. Compensation received by a taxpayer for breach of trading contracts or loss of trading stock is assessable as ordinary income.
2. Compensation for breaches of contract that harm the business structure are usually capital receipts rather than ordinary income.
3. Compensation for breaches of ordinary trading contracts will be considered assessable as ordinary income because it is a replacement for trading income.

Heavy Minerals P/L v FCT [1966] HCA 60[51]

Facts: A company that mined the mineral rutile entered into a long-term contract to supply rutile to overseas purchasers. Due to a slowdown in demand for rutile, the overseas purchasers subsequently negotiated a cancellation of their contracts and the company received compensation payments. The company temporarily ceased operations but continued to pursue other options for selling its product overseas — albeit, without success

Held: The compensation payments were income, as the company was not put out of business by the cancellation of its overseas contracts. The company was free to continue to sell its rutile to new customers. Windeyer J put this conclusion in the following terms:

> The taxpayer's business was mining rutile and dealing in rutile. Its capital assets were the mining lease and the plant. After the contracts were cancelled it still had these. It was free to mine its rutile and to sell it if it could find buyers: and it tried to do so. The taxpayer was not put out of business by the cancellation of its overseas contracts. It did not go out of business when they were cancelled. What happened is that because the price of rutile had drastically fallen it could not carry on its business at a profit.

Allied Mills Industries Pty Ltd v FCT [1989] FCA 110[52]

Facts: A payment was received as compensation for the termination on an agency agreement relating to the distribution of 'Vita Weet' biscuits. The agency agreement was one of several contracts that the

---

50 *FCT v DP Smith* (1981) 147 CLR 578, 583.

51 The link to this case is at: https://www.ato.gov.au/law/view/document?DocID=JUD/115CLR512/00002&PiT=9999123123 5958.

52 The link to this case is at: http://www.austlii.edu.au/cgi-bin/sinodisp/au/cases/cth/FCA/1989/110.html?query=.

company held. The business of the taxpayer was not confined to distribution activities but also included separate divisions engaged in the provision of raw materials to other food product manufacturers.

Held: The compensation payment was income as the agency constituted one section of the company's many business activities. The payment was essentially the loss of anticipated profits from the agency agreement which was entered into in the course of carrying on business.

The Federal Court explained its reasoning as follows.

> The activities and structures of the appellant as a whole must be considered in determining whether the rights of the appellant which were terminated by the 1977 agreement constituted a structural asset. Normally in order for a contract to be regarded as a capital asset it must be a contract which is of substantial importance to the structure of the business itself. This is a factual matter and inevitably a matter of degree. Here the appellant was not parting with a substantial part of its business or ceasing to carry on business …

In contrast, compensation for harm caused to the fundamental structure of the business would be considered a capital receipt. This usually applies in situations where the compensation is for an event that effectively results in the termination of the business — for example, where the compensation is for a manufacturer paying compensation to a distributor of their product in return for terminating the distribution contract. The following case provides an example of this.

Californian Oil Products Ltd v FCT [1934] HCA 35

Facts: A company entered into a 5-year contract with an overseas supplier which gave it sole rights to distribute its oil products in Australia. The agency was Californian Oil's sole business. The overseas supplier terminated the agreement and paid the company an amount as compensation for the termination of the contract. Its whole business ceased, and the company went into liquidation.

Held: The compensation payment was capital in nature. It was compensation for abandoning the only business that the company conducted. It was not income earned while carrying on business.

Courts have also drawn a distinction between compensation for loss of profits (which would be considered assessable income) and compensation for loss or destruction of profit-making capital assets (which are considered capital payments, even if the amount of compensation is calculated by reference to the forgone profits which could have been gleaned from the asset had it not been surrendered or destroyed).

Glenboig Union Fireclay Co Ltd v IR Commissioners (1922) 12 TC 427

Facts: The taxpayer was paid compensation for agreeing to give up its rights to mine clay for brick-making from fields next to a railway line which were causing the railway line to be undermined. The amount of compensation was calculated as an amount equivalent to the profit the taxpayer would have expected to make had it been permitted to continue its clay mining operations from the fields next to the railway line until all the clay had been mined.

Held: The payment was a capital payment even though it was calculated by reference to taxable profits the taxpayer would otherwise have earned. The Court considered the payment was for destruction of an asset of the taxpayer's business and the mere fact that the amount of the payment was calculated by reference to profit did not give the payment the character of income. The payment was not for loss of profits — it was for destruction of the profit-making asset.

Where compensation is for loss of trading stock, the receipt will be considered assessable as ordinary income. Please note that loss of trading stock is also assessable as statutory income under section 70-115 of the ITAA97.

Facts: A farmer was paid compensation for destruction of his herd of dairy cattle by a public authority due to a disease outbreak.

The taxpayer contended the payment was not assessable income as it was a capital receipt.

Held: The High Court disagreed, characterising the payment as a payment for loss of trading stock. The Court applied the replacement principle — namely, that 'moneys recovered from any source representing items of a revenue account must be regarded as received by way of revenue ...'.[53] Note that section 70-10 of the ITAA97 expressly includes livestock in the definition of trading stock for tax purposes.

3.8.4 Reimbursement of previously deducted expenses

The application of the replacement principle does not extend to making reimbursements of amounts that have previously been claimed as tax deductions by the taxpayer's automatically assessable income. Whether or not the reimbursement is assessable as income will depend on whether the reimbursement itself, considered at the time it is received by the taxpayer, is properly considered income. The leading Australian case is *FCT v Rowe* [1997] HCA 16.

FCT v Rowe [1997] HCA 16

Facts: The taxpayer received an ex gratia payment from the Queensland Government as reimbursement of legal costs he had incurred in bringing a successful unfair dismissal claim against his employer, the Livingstone Shire Council. He had received a tax deduction for these costs. The issue for the Court was whether the reimbursement of these previously deducted expenses in the form of the payment from the Queensland Government was assessable income.

Held: A receipt does not bear the character of assessable income simply by reason of its relationship with a deductible loss or outgoing. The character of a receipt is assessed by reference to its character in the hands of the taxpayer, not the character of the expenditure which produces the payment to the taxpayer. The High Court majority agreed with the following characterisation of the payment to the taxpayer.

> The payment was in no sense a reward for his services during his employment by the Council, which had long since been determined. It was a recognition of the wrong done to him, and also of the fact that he had been forced to shoulder the task of sharing in an Inquiry undertaken by the government for public purposes. The payment was not a remuneration, but a reparation. Of course, it was far from being a complete reparation, since he had had to bear the costs, which were reimbursed without interest in the currency of some years later.[54]

For a further example, see *Allsop v FCT* [1965] HCA 48, a case involving a payment under a deed of settlement for erroneously collected trucking fees. These were considered a capital receipt to settle a claim rather than income. The Commissioner of Taxation's argument that the refund of a previously deductible amount was assessable as income in the hands of the taxpayer was rejected by the High Court.

Division 20 of the ITAA97 now includes certain reimbursed deductible expenses as statutory income where they would not otherwise be considered assessable as ordinary income. Reimbursements of employee expenses by an employer are dealt with under the fringe benefits tax (FBT). This is discussed further in a later chapter. Where the FBT provisions apply, the FBT treatment takes priority over any different income tax treatment.

---

53 *FCT v Wade* [1951] HCA 66, [13].
54 *FCT v Rowe* [1997] HCA 16, [29].

3.8.5 Undissected lump sum compensation

In some cases, compensation will take the form of an 'undissected' lump sum which, although it is compensation for both capital and income amount, does not specify in what proportions. In these situations, courts have held that the entire amount will be characterised as wholly capital sum and non-assessable as ordinary income.

This principle was affirmed by the High Court in *McLaurin v FCT* [1961] HCA 9. In this case, the taxpayer received a lump sum payment for destruction of its farm property in a fire. The payment was in settlement of all claims against the railway company that had caused the fire. This included claims for revenue items such as loss of livestock and loss of capital assets such as buildings and equipment. The Court held that the whole amount was a capital sum as it was an undissected lump sum and in these circumstances was not possible to apportion the compensation.

Although not assessable as ordinary income, remember that such sums may be treated as statutory income under the CGT provisions.

SUMMARY

3.1 Explain the importance of the concept of assessable income to the income taxation system.

Assessable income is one of the key components of taxable income (the other being deductions). Each receipt must be tested to determine if it is assessable income — either ordinary income or statutory income. Whether a receipt is ordinary or statutory income has consequences for the tax treatment of the income.

3.2 Apply the tests for determining whether an amount is ordinary income.

Ordinary income is not precisely defined by the legislation. Over time various tax cases have developed a series of general indicators of ordinary income that should be considered depending on the factual issues of the particular case. The general indicators include that the income must be derived by the taxpayer, there must be a sufficient nexus between the income and earning activity, the benefit must be cash or convertible to cash, and the mutuality principle must be satisfied.

3.3 Apply the tests for determining whether an amount is statutory income.

Amounts that are not ordinary income but are included in your assessable income by provisions about assessable income, are called statutory income. These provisions are found throughout the ITAA Acts. Statutory income can relate to various employment-related items such as allowances, return to work payments, and accrued leave entitlements; royalties; profit-making schemes; insurance payments, and capital gains.

3.4 Differentiate between income and capital.

Ordinary income excludes capital receipts. The distinction is important because the tax treatment differs. However, the distinction can be problematic in regard to payments in return for giving up valuable right/restrictive covenants; payments in compensation for injury or wrong to the person, reputation or loss of income-earning capacity; and compensation for loss of business contracts, franchise rights or agency agreement.

3.5 Describe the assessability of personal services and employment income.

Personal service income is income generally considered personal to the individual who performed the service. The key test for determining whether a payment is income from personal services is whether the payment can be considered a 'product' or 'incident' of the employment. Under the ITAA97 ruling, it is generally taxable in the hands of the person who carried out the service and cannot be redirected to be taxable in the hands of somebody else. This does not apply if the income is derived as part of a personal service business, which can be determined by application of various tests.

3.6 Describe the assessability of business income.

The assessability of business income depends on (1) whether the taxpayer is carrying on a business; (2) whether the sum received by the taxpayer is within the scope of the taxpayer's business; and (3) whether the sum received is for activities outside the scope of the taxpayer's business, and whether the sum received resulted from a 'profit-making scheme'. Income arising from illegal business activities can still be assessable. Isolated transactions — those not part of the business's usual activities, may also be assessable income if they were prompted by a profit-making motive.

3.7 Describe the assessability of property income.

Some property assets are used to generate ordinary income. Usually, the sale of the underlying capital assets will not be ordinary income but will be assessed under CGT provisions. If the underlying capital asset is central to the business of the taxpayer, profits from the sale can be considered ordinary income.

3.8 Explain the tax treatment of isolated transactions and compensation payments.

Compensation paid for loss if income is generally considered assessable as ordinary income. Compensation is paid for loss of a capital asset is generally considered a capital receipt. This is known as the 'replacement principle'.

KEY TERMS

alienation Alienation in a legal context is a term used to describe the transfer of your legal rights over property to somebody else.

assessable income Gross income including salary and wages, dividends, interest and rent before any deductions are allowed. Assessable income also includes net capital gains, eligible termination payments and other amounts that are not ordinarily classed as income.

capital receipt Proceeds from the sale of a capital asset; not part of ordinary income.

isolated transaction A transaction that is not part of the usual daily activities of the business but can give rise to assessable income which is ordinary income where there was a profit-making motive for entering the transaction.

mere gift A windfall gain not arising from any income-earning activity and thus not ordinary income.

mutuality The principle that payment, if it is to be ordinary income, must derive from a source other than the taxpayer; a payment to oneself is not ordinary income.

normal proceeds Proceeds that arise from the regular, ordinary and expected incident of the taxpayer's business activities.

ordinary income Income according to ordinary concepts — reflecting common usage and common, everyday meaning.

personal service income Income generally considered personal to the individual who performed the service; generally personal service income is taxable in the hands of the person who carried out the service — it cannot be redirected to be taxable in the hands of somebody else.

personal services business (PSB) An individual or personal services entity (PSE) is a PSB where the individual or PSE has a PSB determination from the Commissioner of Taxation in force, or the individual or PSE satisfies the results test, or less than 80 per cent of the PSI is derived from a single source and the individual or PSE satisfies one of the other three PSB tests.

replacement principle Compensation generally takes the same character as what it replaces.

restrictive covenant A contractual commitment to either do or not do something in return for a payment.

statutory income Amounts that are not ordinary income but are included in assessable income by provisions about assessable income in the ITAA Acts.

sufficient nexus Whether the item is sufficiently connected to an earning activity or a product of employment — a core test for determining whether an item is ordinary income.

QUESTIONS

3.1 Why is it important to determine assessable income and to distinguish between ordinary income and statutory income?

3.2 What are key factors that courts have used to assist in determining whether an amount has a sufficient nexus with an earning activity or is a product of employment?

3.3 Describe the traditional distinction between income and capital. Is this distinction justified?

3.4 A longstanding client of your accounting firm decides to leave you $10 000 in their will 'for being such a great adviser and friend over the years'. Is the amount assessable income? What additional information would you need to help you answer this question?

3.5 Which of the following amounts are assessable income under section 6-5?

    (a) Weekly wages

    (b) Profits on the sale of shares by an individual investor and by an individual share trader

    (c) Profit on the sale of vacant land

    (d) Funds borrowed as part of financing of real property

    (e) Winnings from regular betting on horse racing.

3.6 Which of the following are assessable as ordinary income?

    (a) Rambo is an army whistleblower and he receives a lump sum of $10 000 for the exclusive rights to his story from a television station.

    (b) Southern Biscuits receives a lump sum of $50 000 for termination of the exclusive rights to distribute 'Oateez' biscuits in Australia. Southern biscuits also distributes other biscuits; however, Oateez was their most profitable product so after a year of drastically reduced sales in the wake of the termination of the Oateez contract, the owners of Southern Biscuits decide to close down the business altogether.

(c) Eddie is director of a company. His directorship is terminated a year early, and he receives a lump sum amount equal to what he would have received if the contract had not been terminated early.

(d) Sakiya is a star basketball player. She is so good, one of the leading Victorian basketball teams pays her $100 000 in return for her agreeing *not* to play in the Victorian A-grade basketball competition.

3.7 Explain the replacement principle and its relevance to determining whether an item is assessable income.

3.8 Annika runs a chicken farm, and sells eggs to local restaurants, friends and family. One of her restaurant customers does not pay cash for the eggs but instead pays for the eggs by providing prepared restaurant meals to Annika equal to the value of the eggs. Last year this amounted to $5000 worth of meals. Another of her customers is the principal of the school her children attends and Annika agrees for the amount owing for the eggs to simply be deducted from the amount owing to the school for her children's school fees. Last year, this resulted in a $1000 reduction in the school fees. Annika claims neither amount is assessable income as she never actually received any money for the sales of the eggs. Advise Annika.

3.9 What is a 'profit-making scheme' for tax purposes? How is it relevant to determining whether an amount is assessable income?

3.10 Slim has always loved gambling. He bets on everything he can, but he particularly likes betting on the outcome of football matches. His bets are regular and large — last year his winnings totalled over $1 million. He has developed his own computer program to predict which team will win a match, based on a range of factors including home ground advantage, weather conditions, particular combinations of players and historical results. He also owns a football team and is heavily involved in coaching and player management activities. The Tax Office alleges his winnings are assessable income from a gambling business. Are they right?

PROBLEMS

3.11 Explain, giving reasons, whether any of the following amounts are assessable and, if so, the amount to be included in assessable income. Indicate what, if any, additional information would assist in deciding.

(a) John works as a grocery delivery driver. At Christmas time, John received a case of wine from his employer. The wine has a retail value of $250. However, his employer was able to obtain it through his suppliers for $100.

(b) Ali works at a restaurant as a waiter on a part-time basis while he completes his university accounting degree. In addition to his salary, Ali receives about $50 per week in tips from customers.

(c) Vismi is a full-time student. She can afford to go to university because she receives a scholarship of $3000 a year from a company in her hometown. The terms of the scholarship require Vismi to work for the company for a minimum of 3 years after graduation.

(d) Walter is a drug dealer. This year has been a particularly good year and his drug sales bring in $100 000.

(e) Sonaldo Rent-a-Car receives $20 000 from the sales of cars from their car hire business at the end of their useful life as rental vehicles.

(f) Tarla received $5000 last year after posting a series of videos of her cat on YouTube that went viral.

3.12 Giuseppe, an Australian resident, received the following amounts for the year ended 30 June 2022:

(a) $35 000 salary and wages from sources in Australia

(b) $1500 from being a part-time Uber driver and an additional $500 in tips from his Uber passengers

(c) a bonus of $2500 from his employer paid into his bank account on 2 July 2022

(d) a payment of $20 000 to compensate him for legal fees he incurred in successfully suing his previous employer. He has already claimed a tax deduction for the legal fees.

(e) $10 000 in prizes after a series of appearances on a reality TV show

(f) $50 000 in compensation from his insurer for the loss of livestock and destruction of shedding and fencing on a small farming property that he owns.

Calculate Giuseppe's assessable income for the year ended 30 June 2022.

3.13 Francesco and Maria are getting old. They live on a 20-acre lifestyle property they purchased in 1975. While they are both still fit and healthy, they realise that the property is starting to get too much for them to look after. Their eldest son, Giovanni, a lawyer with an extensive investment property portfolio, makes some enquiries and discovers that the Council recently changed the zoning of the land to permit subdivision of the land into blocks no smaller than one acre. He suggests that they subdivide the land into 20 one-acre lots and sell those lots to fund their move into town. The Council has advised that in order to give development consent they would require the blocks to be fully fenced, and for a sealed road, guttering, extensive drainage works and street-lighting to be installed in the development. Francesco and Maria tell their son they are happy to proceed provided they can leave all the arrangements and the work to him, and that the development of the land is no more than necessary to satisfy Council requirements. Advise Francesco and Maria on whether the proceeds from the sale of the blocks will be defined as assessable as ordinary income.

3.14 Ariana runs a successful chain of cafés. She prides herself on being a generous and sympathetic employer. However, when a global pandemic hits she is left with no choice but to terminate the employment of her staff and close her cafés. She feels terrible and decides she will pay all her staff during the closure in the hope she will be able to re-employ them when the pandemic is over. Are the following payments assessable in the hands of the terminated employees?

(a) Periodical amounts equal to what they would have been paid had they continued to be employed during the period of the pandemic.

(b) Equal lump sum payments of $5000 to each former staff member 3 years after the pandemic is over and the staff are now working somewhere else.

(c) Payments made in coffee beans and food vouchers rather than cash.

3.15 Vinh is an accountant. He lives on a small rural acreage and over the years has enjoyed growing tomatoes. Over time, word has spread about Vinh's tomatoes being the tastiest in the region. Gradually, he has grown more and more tomatoes and now sells the tomatoes and tomato juice at local and regional markets. Recently, restaurants have begun to place regular orders. His knowledge of tomato growing has been passed down from his father and he credits his success on his particularly fertile plot of land. He doesn't employ anybody and doesn't record his sales or expenses other than keeping all his receipts in a shoe box in his house. Even though he estimates he is now making a profit, he says growing the tomatoes keeps him fit and sane. He envisages he will probably grow tomatoes full time when he retires from his accounting job. Are the proceeds from Vinh's tomato sales assessable income?

3.16 Rohan is obsessed with cryptocurrencies. Although he is a full-time teacher, he spends all his spare time learning all he can about various cryptocurrencies. Although he has no formal business plan or investment strategy, he subscribes to a number of online registries where he accesses detailed information for tracking and predicting the performance of various cryptocurrencies. He also keeps meticulous electronic records of his investments. Over the course of the last year, he has conducted over 1000 trades. However, his trades are small and his total investments currently stand at $50 000. His profits from his activities in the last financial year total $20 000. He claims this amount is not assessable income as his cryptotrading is simply a hobby. Advise Rohan.

3.17 Bronnie Pty Ltd carries on a business manufacturing power tools. It also derives income from the rental of a large number of properties it owns. Last financial year, Bronnie Pty Ltd assigned to an unrelated party its right to receive rental income from the properties in return for a lump sum. Is the lump sum assessable income?

3.18 As a tax adviser, what advice would you give your clients to ensure you comply with your ethical and legal responsibilities where they indicate they are involved in earning money from sharing economy activities but insist on not declaring the proceeds from their activities on the basis that they consider those activities as simply a hobby?

ACKNOWLEDGEMENTS

Extracts: © Federal Register of Legislation. Licensed under CC BY 4.0.
Extracts: © High Court of Australia
Extract: © Incorporated Council of Law Reporting for England and Wales
Extracts: © Federal Court of Australia. Licensed under CC BY 3.0.
Extract: © The Board of Taxation. Licensed under CC BY 3.0.
Extract: © Scottish Court of Session Decisions. Public Domain.
Extract: © Australian Taxation Office

CHAPTER 4

Capital gains tax

LEARNING OBJECTIVES

After studying this chapter, you should be able to:

4.1 explain how taxpayers pay tax on their capital gains in Australia

4.2 define CGT assets

4.3 describe the major types of CGT events

4.4 determine the cost base or reduced cost base of CGT assets

4.5 describe and apply CGT exemptions

4.6 calculate the net capital gain or loss from all CGT events for an income year

4.7 understand SBE concessions in relation to CGT

4.8 understand the CGT treatment of cryptocurrencies.

Overview

This chapter provides a detailed explanation and discussion of the Australian capital gains tax (CGT) regime which was introduced on 20 September 1985. CGT was introduced to tax taxpayers on any gains they made that were capital in nature. For a CGT liability to arise there must be a CGT event — for example, the disposal of a CGT asset. This chapter starts with a discussion on the key concepts involved in the Australian CGT regime. Although the word 'tax' is included in the name, unlike other tax regimes, such as FBT or GST, CGT is not a separate tax; instead, any taxable capital gains are included in the taxpayers' assessable income and the taxpayers are taxed in the income tax system.

The operation of CGT is subject to certain exemptions where the capital gains are exempt from CGT, and these exemptions are discussed in this chapter. However, the main focus is on the calculation of net capital gains or losses for a taxpayer in a tax year, which is a procedure that involves two stages. The CGT concessions for small business entities (SBEs) will also be discussed.

4.1 Australian capital gains tax (CGT) regime and its operation

LEARNING OBJECTIVE 4.1 Explain how taxpayers pay tax on their capital gains in Australia.

The Australian **capital gains tax (CGT)** regime was introduced on 20 September 1985 by the then Labor Government with the aim to tax taxpayers on the gains that are generated from the transactions or events that involve capital assets. Figure 4.1 presents an overview of the CGT regime and also reflects the overall structure of this chapter. Each component of the regime will be discussed in the following sections.

FIGURE 4.1 Overview of the Australian CGT regime

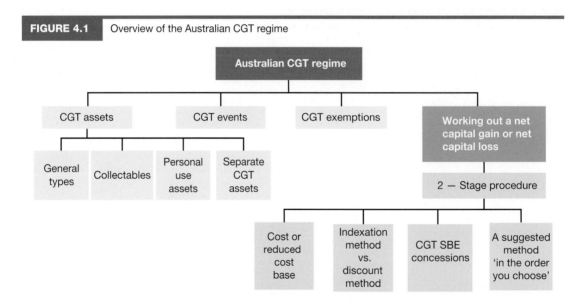

Before the introduction of the CGT regime, the concepts of capital gains and capital losses were not defined in the ITAA36. This law only covered a limited number of types of gains that were not income in nature in a few unrelated former sections, including sections 15-15, 26AAA, 26C, 36AA and 124P. They also did not strictly govern the taxation on those gains and tax could be easily avoided. For example, the former section 26AAA of the ITAA36 stated that the assessable income of the taxpayer should include the profit arising from property purchased and sold within 12 months. This provision was avoided by taxpayers who sold properties they had held for a period longer than 12 months. Similarly, section 15-15 states that your assessable income includes profits arising from the carrying on or carrying out of a profit-making undertaking or plan; therefore, if you sold a property you acquired for profit-making purposes, it would be part of assessable income. Taxpayers could avoid this by simply stating the property was acquired for other purposes, such as for investment purposes. The other major types of gains that were capital in nature and were generated from transactions or events other than the disposal of property or shares/securities were not captured by the former ITAA36. For example, compensation payments for the cancellation of structural business contracts were found to be capital in nature and not assessable income in various cases.[1]

Under the current CGT regime, which is systematically covered in Divisions 100 to 104 of the ITAA97, capital gains are taxed according to various facts and circumstances, explained throughout this chapter.

Interestingly, although the word 'tax' is included in its name, unlike FBT or GST, CGT is not a separate tax from income tax. Any taxable net capital gains are included in a taxpayer's assessable income, as a form of statutory income, and accordingly the taxpayers are taxed in accordance with income tax law. If a net capital loss is incurred in an income[2] year, it could generally be carried forward to be offset against any capital gains in the future year(s), which will reduce the taxpayers' income tax liability. The working out of the net capital gains and losses, which is a two-stage procedure,[3] is briefly summarised in table 4.1.

TABLE 4.1 **The two-stage procedure of working out net capital gain or loss for an income year**

	Steps	Explanation of key terms or steps in the procedure	ITAA97 provisions
Stage I	Working out the capital gain or loss for each CGT transaction/event for the income year.	• A capital gain is obtained when the amounts received from the transaction/event (capital proceeds) exceeds the total cost associated with the asset and the transaction (cost base). • A capital loss is incurred when the total cost associated with the asset and the transaction (reduced cost base) exceeds the capital proceeds. • An example of a CGT transaction or event is the sale of shares or a residential property.	s 100-45 s 100-35 s 100-40
Stage II	Step 1 Subtract the capital losses from the capital gains worked out from stage I.	• If the capital losses exceed the capital gains, the difference is the net capital loss for the income year. • If there are any capital gains remaining, proceed to step 2 at this stage II.	s 100-50 s 102-5 s 102-10
	Step 2 Further reduce any capital gains remaining from step 1 by any capital losses carried forward from previous years.	• If the capital losses carried forward from previous years exceed the remaining capital gains from step 1, the capital gains for the income year are reduced to nil and the remaining capital losses from previous years will be further carried forward to future income years. • If any capital gains remain for the income year, proceed to step 3.	
	Step 3 Apply the applicable discount percentage to any discount capital gains for any capital gains remaining after the first two steps.	• The discount applies only to individual taxpayers, complying superannuation funds and trusts for the capital gains generated from the disposal of the CGT assets that are held for more than 12 months (discount capital gains). • The discount percentage is 50% for eligible individual taxpayers and trusts, and 33.3% for complying superannuation funds.	

(continued)

---

1 See, eg, *Californian Oil Products Ltd (In Liq) v Federal Commissioner of Taxation* [1934] HCA 35; *Van den Berghs Ltd v Clark (Inspector of Taxes)* [1935] AC 431.
2 ITAA97 section 102-5.
3 Sections 100-45, 100-50, 102-5 and 102-10.

TABLE 4.1   (continued)

Steps	Explanation of key terms or steps in the procedure	ITAA97 provisions
Step 4 Apply the small business concessions to further reduce the capital gains if the taxpayer is a small business entity (SBE).	• For the concessions to apply, the taxpayer must be a CGT SBE and the CGT event involves an active asset. • The SBE concessions in relation to CGT are discussed further in detail in section 4.7 on 'Special CGT rules on SBEs'.	
Step 5 Add up any remaining non-discount capital gains and any remaining discount capital gains to work out the net capital gain for the income year.	Non-discount capital gains include: • the capital gains generated by taxpayers other than individuals, trusts or complying superannuation funds, or • the capital gains generated by individuals, trusts or complying superannuation funds from the transactions that involve the CGT assets that are held for less than 12 months.	

This procedure of calculating the net capital gain will be discussed in detail in a later section in this chapter.

A taxpayer is considered to have made a **capital gain** or **capital loss** only when a **CGT event** happens.[4] A summary of the CGT events is provided in section 104-5 of the ITAA97, which contains more than 50 different types of CGT events. This chapter provides detailed explanation and discussion of the common and major types of CGT events, such as the disposal of CGT assets (CGT event A1), the loss or destruction of CGT assets (CGT event C1) and other types of CGT events (CGT event D1).

The operation of the CGT regime is subject to many exemptions. CGT only applies to the CGT assets that were acquired on or after 20 September 1985, which are called **post-CGT assets**. Capital gains and losses relating to **pre-CGT assets**, which are the assets acquired before the introduction of CGT on 20 September 1985, are generally disregarded.[5]

Other major types of CGT exemptions, including the main residence exemption,[6] motor vehicle exemption,[7] personal assets and collectables exemptions,[8] depreciating assets exemptions[9] etc. will also be discussed later in this chapter.

4.1.1 Record-keeping

Taxpayers must maintain records of capital gains and losses made. The records need to be kept in English, be readily accessible, and retained for 5 years after it is certain that no CGT event can happen for which those records could be expected to be relevant in determining the capital gain or loss (section 121-25).

4.2 CGT assets

LEARNING OBJECTIVE 4.2   Define CGT assets.

In general, section 108-5 ITAA97 defines a **CGT asset** as 'any kind of property' or 'a legal or equitable right that is not property'. A note to this section provides some common examples of the CGT assets. These include land and buildings; an equity or debt interest, such as goodwill, shares or debts, in a business that could be a company, a partnership or a trust; as well as foreign currencies. Division 108 of the ITAA97 also contains some special types of CGT assets and the related rules on them, including collectables (Subdivision 108-B), personal use assets (Subdivision 108-C) and separate CGT assets relating to capital improvement (section 108-70), which are discussed in detail next.

---

4 ITAA97 sections 100-20(1) and 102-20.
5 See, eg, section 104-10(5).
6 ITAA97 section 118-110.
7 ITAA97 section 118-5.
8 ITAA97 section 118-10.
9 ITAA97 section 118-24.

4.2.1 Collectables

A collectable is defined in section 108-10(2) of the ITAA97 as:

(a) artwork, jewellery, an antique or a coin or medallion; or

(b) a rare folio, manuscript or book; or

(c) a postage stamp or first day cover;

that is used or kept mainly for your (or your associate's) personal use or enjoyment.

A collectable is only subject to capital gains and losses if it is acquired for $500 or more. Section 108-10(1) of the ITAA97 includes a special rule that applies to the CGT assets of collectables, according to which any capital losses that are incurred from collectables can only be offset against any capital gains that are generated from collectables (the **collectables-to-collectables rule**). This is demonstrated in example 4.1.

EXAMPLE 4.1

Collectables-to-collectables rule

During the 2021–22 income year, Joe sold some shares that he acquired 2 years earlier and made a gain of $3000. He also incurred a loss of $500 from the sale of a painting and generated a gain of $300 from the sale of an antique chair. Consequently, Joe made a net capital gain of $3000 from the sale of shares and a net capital loss of $200 from collectables, which is calculated as the gain of $300 (antique chair) minus the loss of $500 (the painting).

What is Joe's assessable income in relation to these transactions for the 2021–22 income year?

The net capital gain of $3000 will be included in Joe's assessable income for this income year. Joe cannot reduce this net capital gain by the $200 capital loss from collectables in this income year. Instead, he will need to carry forward this capital loss of $200 from collectables into the future income year(s) to offset any future capital gains from collectables (sections 108-10(1) and (4)).

4.2.2 Personal use assets

A **personal use asset** is mainly used for a taxpayer's personal use or enjoyment but cannot be a collectable or a piece of land or a building.[10] The common examples of personal use assets include furniture, boats, electronic goods and other household appliances. Importantly, any capital losses that are incurred from personal use assets are disregarded, which means that they cannot be applied to reduce other capital gains in working out the net capital gain or loss for the income year.[11] A personal use asset is only subject to capital gains if it was acquired for more than $10 000. This principle is demonstrated in example 4.2.

EXAMPLE 4.2

Capital losses from the sale of personal use assets

Maria purchased a speed boat several years ago for $15 000 which she sold within the 2021–22 income year for $8000, thus making a capital loss of $7000. During the same year, she earned a capital gain of $10 000 from the sale of her investment property.

What is the appropriate tax treatment of the transactions?

Maria has made a capital gain of $10 000 from the sale of her investment property. She *cannot* reduce this capital gain by the $7000 capital loss from the sale of her personal items. Further, Maria *cannot* carry forward this loss into future income years because the law disregards this type of capital loss.

How would your answer change if the speed boat cost $9500?

In this situation, as the speed boat value is less than $10 000, capital gains does not apply to the sale of the speed boat.

There are two reasons for this law. First, these assets, such as a TV or a washing machine, are for 'personal' use, rather than for the purpose of generating income. Therefore, they fall within the second negative limb in section 8-1(2) of the ITAA97 (discussed in a later chapter) that prevents any related

---

10 ITAA97 sections 108-20(2) and (3).
11 ITAA97 section 108-20.

expenses or losses from being deductible. Second, it is common for individual taxpayers to incur a loss from the sale of these personal or domestic items, such as in a garage sale for example. If this capital loss from personal use assets is taken into consideration in the calculation of the net capital gain or loss, it would provide a way for individual taxpayers to reduce their tax liability and the costs relating to tax compliance and administration would be significantly increased.

4.2.3 Separate CGT assets — building or structure on land, capital improvement

Some assets are recognised by law as **separate CGT assets**. A building or structure on land that a taxpayer acquired on or after 20 September 1985 is regarded as a separate CGT asset from the land if any balancing adjustment provisions[12] apply to the building or structure.[13] For example, if John constructed a building on land that he has owned since July 1987, and the building is subject to a balancing adjustment when disposed of or destroyed, this building will be treated as a separate CGT asset from the land. In other cases, a building or structure that is constructed on a pre-CGT land (acquired before 20 September 1985) will also be treated as a separate CGT asset if the construction started or the contract to the construction was entered into on or after 20 September 1985. For instance, Linda purchased a piece of land on 5 May 1983 and started constructing a building on 10 June 1988 — this building will also be taken as a separate CGT asset from the land.

Similarly, any capital improvements to the existing or so-called original CGT assets could also be treated as separate CGT assets if the conditions in sections 108-70(1) and (2) are satisfied. A capital improvement is generally a structural change that is added to an existing CGT asset or the reconstruction or replacement of the entire existing CGT asset. A capital improvement will enhance the value, or improve the efficiency, of the existing asset. Examples include a house extension or the installation of an additional part to existing equipment.

Specifically, section 108-70 applies in the following situations.
- When it is a capital improvement to post-CGT land, or if the contract to the improvement is entered into on or after 20 September 1985, or the capital improvement starts on or after that day when there is no contact, and if certain balancing adjustment provisions apply to such improvement.
- When it is a capital improvement to a pre-CGT asset, such improvement can still be taken as a separate CGT asset if the cost base of the improvement at the time when a CGT event occurs — for example, the whole asset was sold, is more than the improvement threshold for the income year when the CGT event occurs and is more than 5 per cent of the proceeds that the taxpayer receives from the CGT event. The improvement threshold is a dollar value threshold that is indexed annually (section 108-85 of the ITAA97) taking into consideration inflation and is published by the ATO Commissioner in the Taxation Determination (TD) before the beginning of each financial year. The improvement threshold is $155 849 for the 2020–21 income year and is $156 784 for the 2021–22 income year.
- In addition, if the capital improvement is treated as a separate CGT asset, the capital proceeds received from the CGT event should be apportioned between the original asset and the capital improvement.[14] Example 4.3 illustrates different scenarios that involve capital improvements.

EXAMPLE 4.3

Capital improvements

In September 1983, Vicki purchased a Melbourne investment property with 3 rooms for $95 000, which consisted of $60 000 for the land and $35 000 for the house. In order to enhance the value of the property and increase the rental income, she extended the house in 1991 by adding another 3 rooms with the same

---

12 A balancing adjustment is associated with depreciating assets that are dealt with under the capital allowance regime (Division 40 ITAA97). A balancing adjustment occurs when a depreciating CGT asset is disposed of, where the net value of the asset (after deducting the total amount of depreciations that have been claimed as tax deductions, the adjustable value) and the capital proceeds received from the disposal (termination value) will be compared. Under such adjustment, if the termination value is greater than the adjustable value, the difference is included in the taxpayer's assessable income (section 40-285(1)). Otherwise, the taxpayer can claim a deduction for the difference if the termination value is less than the adjustable value (section 40-285(2)).

13 Section 108-55(1).

14 ITAA97 section 116-40.

size and quality to the existing ones in 1991. This extension cost $75 000. Vicki sold the property in August 2021 for $760 000. During this transaction, a licenced property valuer indicated that the land was valued at $400 000 and the house was valued at $360 000, with the 3 newer rooms and the 3 original ones in highly similar conditions. The improvement threshold is $156 784 for the 2021–22 income year.

Scenario 1

If the cost base of the extension (capital improvement) at the time of sale in August 2021 (when the CGT event occurs) is $140 000, the extension is not treated as a separate CGT asset as the value is below the improvement threshold (section 108-70(2) of the ITAA97). Therefore, section 116-40 of the ITAA97 does not apply and Vicki does not need to apportion the capital proceeds between the original house and the extension. Even though Vicki has made a capital gain of $665 000 (being calculated as the proceeds of $760 000 minus the original value $95 000), she does not include this capital gain in her assessable income for the 2021–22 income year, because the whole house is a pre-CGT asset (section 104-10(5)).

Scenario 2

If the cost base of the extension, at the time of sale, is $160 000, the extension will be taken to be a separate CGT asset because it meets the two threshold tests contained in section 108-70(2) of the ITAA97. That is, the value is above the improvement threshold, $156 784, and it is greater than 5 per cent of the capital proceeds pertaining to this CGT event.

According to section 116-40 of the ITAA97, Vicki needs to apportion the capital proceeds that she received from the sale between the original house and the extension. As per the facts stated in the case, the added 3 rooms are the same size and quality as the original rooms, and they were in highly similar conditions according to the licensed property valuer. Therefore, it would be reasonable to apportion the proceeds pertaining to the 6-room house on a 50/50 basis, being $180 000 (half of the value of the house, $360 000 each to the original house and the extension).

Based on the discussion, the calculation of Vicki's taxable capital gain relating to this transaction will be as follows.

CGT assets	Original value/cost incurred $	Capital proceeds $	Capital gain or loss $
Original asset (land and original 3 rooms)	95 000	580 000*	0**
Capital improvement (the added 3 rooms)	75 000	180 000	105 000***
Total			**105 000**

* ($400 000 + $180 000).
** This original house is a pre-CGT asset. Therefore, any capital gains or losses are disregarded (section 104-10(5)).
*** This extension is treated as a separate CGT asset. Thus, apportionment applies (sections 116-40 and 104-10(4)).

4.3 CGT events

LEARNING OBJECTIVE 4.3 Describe the major types of CGT events.

A list of more than 50 different types of CGT events is provided in section 104-5 of the ITAA97. This part of the chapter deals with the most common types of CGT events, including the disposal of a CGT assets (CGT event A1) and the loss or destruction of a CGT asset (CGT event C1), as well as other types of more common CGT events, such as creating contractual or other rights (CGT event D1).[15]

It is important to understand whether a CGT event has occurred because it determines if the taxpayer has made a capital gain or loss and it will in turn affects the taxpayer's income tax liability. Sections 100-20(1) and 102-20 both state that a capital gain or loss arises only if a CGT event occurs.

Example 4.4 demonstrates how a CGT event must have occurred in order for a capital gain or loss to arise.

---

15 Note that event numbers are used to indicate different CGT events. For example, the letter (A, B, C etc.) indicates a category of CGT events; the number after the letter indicates a specific CGT event within the category.

Identifying CGT events

Michael purchased 3000 AGL shares in July 2015 at $16 per share. The share price reached $27 in May 2022 resulting from AGL's share buyback program. Suppose Michael sold the 3000 shares at $27 in May 2022.

Has a CGT event occurred?

A CGT event (an A1 event in this case) has occurred, where a capital gain arose and was able to be calculated as $33 000, which must be included in Michael's assessable income in this income year. If Michael had held the shares in May 2022 as he believed the price would keep increasing, no CGT event would have occurred at this point and no capital gain or loss would have arisen. Hence, Michael's income tax liability for this income year would not be affected.

4.3.1 CGT events — categories

Section 104-5 contains a summary of CGT events. The table sets out different categories of CGT events. It then provides the basic information such as (1) what is the event; (2) the section which contains detailed information regarding the event and the time the event arises; and (3) how a capital gain or loss is calculated. The events are grouped into categories:

A Disposal of an asset

B Use of an asset before passing title

C Loss or ending of an asset

D Creation of CGT assets

E Trust-related events

F Leases

G Company-related events

H Special payments received

I Ceasing residency

J Reversal of Rollovers

K Other CGT events

L Consolidated group events

Where more than one event can apply to a particular situation, it is necessary to choose the one which is most relevant.

4.3.2 CGT event A1 — disposal of a CGT asset

This type of CGT event is dealt with in Subdivision 104-A of the ITAA97. According to section 104-10(2), disposal of a CGT asset occurs when the ownership over the asset is changed and the taxpayer stops being the legal and beneficial owner. The timing of the event is determined as when the taxpayer enters into the contract for the disposal, or when the change of ownership occurs if there is no contract.[16] This is illustrated in example 4.5.

Timing of disposal of a CGT asset

Sara entered into a contract to sell a building in October 2020. The contract was officially settled in August 2021 and Sara made a capital gain of $300 000.

When was the capital gain made?

According to section 104-10(3), this capital gain was made in the 2020–21 income year when the contract was entered, rather than the 2021–22 income year when the settlement of the contract occurred.

---

16 ITAA97 section 104-10(3).

What happens if the contract fell through prior to settlement?

Note 1 of section 104-10(3) states that there is no CGT event A1 if the contract falls through before settlement. As Sara has already lodged her 2021 income tax return, to report the CGT event she will need to amend that return to disregard the CGT event.

4.3.3 CGT event C1 — loss or destruction of a CGT asset

When a CGT asset is lost or destroyed, a C1 type of CGT event happens.[17] This type of event is deemed to have happened when the taxpayer receives a compensation for the loss or destruction of the CGT asset, or when the loss is discovered or the destruction happened.[18] This is illustrated in example 4.6.

EXAMPLE 4.6

Timing of loss or destruction of a CGT asset

Troy purchased a J-200 Gibson Guitar which was used by Elvis Presley in the 1960s for $300 000 in May 2016. Unfortunately, this guitar was destroyed by a bushfire accident in January 2022. If Troy insured this guitar as a collectable and was compensated for this loss by his insurer for $380 000 in July 2022, then a CGT event C1 occurs in July 2022 and Troy makes a capital gain of $80 000 in the 2022–23 income year. However, if insurance was not arranged for this collectable, the CGT event occurs in January 2022 when the loss happened and Troy incurs a capital loss of $300 000 in the 2021–22 income year.

4.3.4 Other CGT events

A CGT event could also happen in other cases, such as when a contractual or other legal or equitable right is created by the taxpayer in another entity, and this event (CGT event D1) happens when the contract or the right is created.[19] When entering into this kind of contract or agreement, a taxpayer normally gives up a certain right, such as the right for a business operation, in exchange for a capital gain payment. At the same time, a contractual or legal right (a CGT asset) has been created in another party to take legal action against the taxpayer in case if the contract or agreement is breached by the taxpayer.

This is demonstrated in example 4.7.

EXAMPLE 4.7

CGT events — contractual rights

In June 2022, David sold his milk bar business called '7am Everyday' to Jack for $160 000. This amount included $20 000 for David not to operate another milk bar or similar business within a distance of 10 kilometres from '7am Everyday'. David consulted his lawyer regarding this separate arrangement from the sale of the milk bar and incurred a cost of $1200. In this case, two types of CGT events took place: the sale of the milk bar, which is a CGT event A1; and the separate agreement of non-operation within 10 kilometres, which is a CGT event D1. In this CGT event D1, David gave up his right to run a similar business within the agreed area in exchange for a payment of $20 000. This also created a contractual right in favour of Jack because Jack now has the right to sue David if David opens another similar business within the agreed area. Lastly, David made a capital gain of $140 000 from the sale of '7am Everyday' and another capital gain for $18 800 from entering into the special agreement with Jack. This is calculated as the capital proceeds from creating the right ($20 000) minus the incidental costs and the legal costs of $1200 incurred to consult the lawyer relating to this special agreement (see section 104-35(3)).

---

17 ITAA97 Subdivision 104-C.
18 ITAA97 section 104-20.
19 ITAA97 sections 104-35(1) and (2).

A lease premium is a one-off amount paid by a lessee to a lessor at the commencement of the lease (CGT event F1).[20] The lessor will make a capital gain if the capital proceeds received from granting the lease exceed any costs involved. It is not to be confused with lease rental payments which are paid fortnightly or monthly and treated as normal income in the hands of the lessor and deductible under section 8-1 to the lessee.

If a liquidator or administrator declares shares or financial instruments of a company worthless, this will crystallise a capital loss for the shareholders (CGT event G3).[21]

CGT event H1[22] happens if a deposit paid to the taxpayer is forfeited because the prospective sale or transaction does not proceed. The most common example is where the deposit is forfeited under contract for the sale of the land. The time of the event is when the deposit is forfeited. The vendor will have a capital gain which is the difference between the amount of the deposit received and any expenses incurred in connection with the prospective sale. This specific event is required as there is no change in ownership of the asset. The purchaser may realise a capital loss on the forfeiture of a deposit under either CGT event C1 or H1.

CGT event H2[23] is described as the 'residual catch-all event'. The event exists to capture any capital proceeds received in relation to a CGT event which was not covered by any other event or did not result in an adjustment of the cost base or reduced cost base of the CGT asset. An example of this would be the receipt of a lump sum as an inducement to the owner of land to commence construction earlier than planned. The time of the CGT event is when the act, transaction or event occurs.

Another important CGT event we should consider is when an individual or company stops being an Australian resident for tax purposes and what the consequences are for CGT purposes (CGT event I1[24]). The taxpayer must look at each CGT asset, with the exception of taxable Australian property, that the taxpayer owned just before residency ended to determine whether a capital gain or loss arises. Taxable property is essentially a direct or indirect interest in real property located in Australia or an asset that is used in carrying on a business through a permanent establishment in Australia.

---

20 ITAA97 section 104-110.
21 ITAA97 section 104-145.
22 ITAA97 section 104-150.
23 ITAA97 section 104-155.
24 ITAA97 section 104-160.

Broadly, an indirect interest in Australian real property arises when an individual holds an interest in an entity, where the entity's main assets are interests in Australian real property, and together with associates holds more than 10 per cent of the interposed entity. Australian real property always maintains a connection with Australia and therefore, Australia will always have taxation rights over property located in Australia.

Unfortunately, this event can have cash flow implications for taxpayers when they cease to be residents as they are required to pay tax on capital gains for which there has been no actual sale and therefore no actual proceeds received. Section 104-165 gives individual taxpayers an option to disregard these gains until the asset is actually sold or the taxpayer becomes a resident again. The disadvantage of using this deferral is that any capital gain which accrues on that asset will be taxable and will lose the 50 per cent general discount for the period of non-residency.

EXAMPLE 4.10

CGT events — non-residency

Kate has been a resident of Australia for tax purposes at all times up to 15 March 2022 and on that date she took up a contract to work in France for 4 years and was considered to be a foreign resident (non-resident) of Australia from 15 March 2022.

Kate owned a main residence in Brisbane that cost her $300 000 when she purchased it on 17 March 2001 and it had a market value of $520 000 on 15 March 2022.

She also owns a house in Paris that she purchased for $350 000 on 23 August 2021 and it had a market value of $395 000 on 15 March 2022.

As a result of her becoming a foreign resident (non-resident), what CGT event will apply and what capital gain will she derive?

CGT event I1 will occur on the date she leaves Australia.

The house in Australia is taxable Australian real property and will not be affected.

The house in Paris will be subject to CGT based on its market value.

Capital proceeds	$395 000
Cost base	350 000
Net capital gain	$ 45 000

4.4 Cost base and reduced cost base of a CGT asset

LEARNING OBJECTIVE 4.4 Determine the cost base or reduced cost base of CGT assets.

In order to accurately work out the amount of a capital gain or loss from each transaction or event, another important factor that must be determined is the cost base or the reduced cost base of a CGT asset, which is mainly dealt with in Subdivision 110-A of the ITAA97. A **cost base** is relevant when calculating the capital gain from a CGT event; a **reduced cost base** is used in working out the capital loss from a CGT event.

4.4.1 Elements of the cost base

In general, section 110-25(1) states that the cost base of a CGT asset consists of five elements, which are illustrated in figure 4.2.

4.4.1.1 First element (section 110-25(2))

The first element of the cost base refers to the money that the taxpayer paid, or is required to pay, in acquiring the CGT asset; or the market value of any property or properties that the taxpayer gave out, or is required to give out, in order to acquire the CGT asset.

This is illustrated in example 4.11.

Cost base of a CGT asset =

1. Money paid or property given for the CGT asset	s 110-25(2)

+

2. Incidental costs of acquiring the CGT asset or that relate to the CGT event	s 110-25(3)

+

3. Cost of owning CGT asset	s 110-25(4)

+

4. Capital costs to increase or preserve the value of your asset or to install or move it	s 110-25(5)

+

5. Capital costs of preserving or defending your title or rights to your CGT asset	s 110-25(6)

Source: Adapted from Australian Taxation Office, 'Cost base of assets' (Web Page, 4 August 2021) https://www.ato.gov.au/individuals/capital-gains-tax/calculating-your-cgt/cost-base-of-assets.

EXAMPLE 4.11

Cost base — first element

Matt purchased 3000 CBA shares in 2017 and paid $255 000 ($85 per share). In another transaction, Matt transferred a building with a market value of $1.5 million to Julie in exchange for a piece of land.

What is the first element of the cost base of Matt's CBA shares and of Matt's land?

The first element of the cost base of Matt's CBA shares will be $255 000. The first element of the cost base of the land to Matt will be $1.5 million.

If the taxpayer does not incur any expenditure for the acquisition (e.g. the taxpayer inherits a property or receives an asset as a gift, or the transaction is not done at arm's length), a 'market value substitution rule' is used to determine the first element of the CGT asset. According to this rule, the first element of the cost base of a CGT asset is its market value at the time the acquisition takes place.[25]

This is demonstrated in example 4.12.

---

25 ITAA97 section 112-20.

Market value substitution rule

Sally inherited her grandmother's two-storey house in Box Hill, Melbourne. The house had a market value of $2.2 million.

If a CGT event happens later, what is the first element of the cost base of this CGT asset to Sally?

The first element of the cost base will be the market value of $2.2 million — the value at the time when Sally acquired the property.

4.4.1.2 Second element (section 110-25(3))

The second element of the cost base is the 'incidental costs' associated with the acquisition of a CGT asset. In general, incidental costs are the costs associated with or incidental to the acquisition or disposal of CGT assets.[26] Sections 110-35(2) to (10) provide further explanations and examples for this second element of the cost base of a CGT asset. They include:

- the remuneration for any legal, property valuation, accounting, brokerage and real estate agency services provided by the relevant professionals, including the advice provided by a registered tax adviser
- costs of the transfer of the CGT assets
- stamp duties
- advertising or marketing costs
- conveyancing costs
- borrowing expenses associated with a mortgage, such as the application or discharge fee.

4.4.1.3 Third element (section 110-25(4))

The third element of the cost base is any costs incurred for owning a CGT asset that was acquired after 20 August 1991.[27] Specifically, this type of cost includes:

- interest expense incurred for the money borrowed to acquire a CGT asset
- maintenance and repair expenditures incurred during the ownership period
- insurance costs
- council rates or land tax
- interest expense incurred to refinance the money borrowed for the acquisition of the CGT asset
- interest on the money borrowed to finance the capital expenditure that the taxpayer incurred in order to enhance the value of the CGT asset.

Note that the third element does not apply to certain types of CGT assets, including personal use assets or collectables.[28]

If you have claimed a deduction previously you cannot deduct the amount in the cost base for the calculations of the CGT.

4.4.1.4 Fourth element (section 110-25(5))

The fourth element of the cost base includes:

- any capital expenditure that a taxpayer incurred with the purpose, or the expected effect, of increasing or preserving the value of a CGT asset
- expenditure in regard to installing or moving the asset.

Example 4.13 illustrates the fourth element.

---

26 ITAA97 section 110-35(1).

27 This is the day when the *Taxation Laws Amendment (No. 3) Act 1991* was introduced, and section 68 of this Act amended the previous provision in relation to the third element of a CGT asset's cost base, section 160ZH of the ITAA36. This 1991 amendment inserted these types of costs that comprise the third element of a CGT asset's cost base into the law.

28 ITAA97 sections 108-117 and 108-30.

Capital expenditure on investment property

In May 2017, Eric purchased an investment property for $400 000. In July 2021, he spent $50 000 renovating the kitchen, bathroom and backyard. The value of this renovation was verified by a licensed property valuer.

If later a CGT event relating to this investment property occurs, what will be the cost base for calculating a capital gain or loss?

The cost base will be $450 000. The renovation costs will be included in the cost base, as these costs are capital in nature and would not be allowed as an immediate deduction against the assessable income of the investment property.

4.4.1.5 Fifth element (section 110-25(6))

The fifth element of the cost base is any capital expenditure that a taxpayer incurs in order to establish or defend his or her title to, or right over, a CGT asset. This is illustrated in example 4.14.

Capital expenditure — legal costs

As a result of a court decision in November 2021, Jean was compensated for $12 000 by her neighbour after her neighbour built a fence that encroached on Jean's property. Jean incurred a cost of $9000 for all the services provided by her lawyer in the lawsuit.

If Jean sells this property or any other type of CGT event happens later, how will the legal costs affect the cost base?

The legal cost of $9000 will be included in the cost base of the property. The $12 000 compensation paid by the neighbour would result in a capital gain under CHT event H2 (act or transaction in relation to a CGT asset).

4.4.1.6 A taxation laws amendment on the element in the cost base

If a taxpayer can claim a tax deduction for an expenditure, then the taxpayer cannot include that expenditure in the cost base for the purposes of calculating a capital gain for assets acquired after 7:30 pm (Australian Eastern Standard Time) on 13 May 1997.[29] This situation is illustrated in example 4.15.

Cost base — adjusted for capital works deductions

Adam acquired a rental property on 1 June 2002. The property was sold in August 2021 for $1 010 000 and the total cost base of the property at the time of sale was $230 000. During the ownership period, Adam claimed a total deduction of $20 000 for capital works.

How will the cost base be adjusted in working out a capital gain?

The cost base will be adjusted for the capital works deduction to $210 000 in working out a capital gain.

As described in figure 4.3, the sum of the five elements described constitutes the reduced cost base of a CGT asset.

---

29 This is the time when the Taxation Laws Amendment Bill (No. 6) 1997 was passed, which includes the amendments in Schedule 7, and such amendments were announced in the 1997–98 Federal Budget. The purpose of this amendment is to prevent double tax benefit for taxpayers. If those deductible expenditures were included in the cost base, the taxpayers would have generated lower capital gains, as the cost base would be higher, and at the same time they also receive the tax benefit of lower tax resulted from more deductions.

FIGURE 4.3   Elements of the reduced cost base

Reduced cost base of a CGT asset =

1. Money paid or property given for the asset   s 110-25(2)

\+

2. Incidental costs of acquiring the CGT asset or that relate to the CGT event   s 110-25(3)

\+

3. Balancing adjustment amount, that is, any amount that is assessable because of a balancing adjustment for the asset or that would be assessable if certain balancing adjustment relief were not available   s 110-55

\+

4. Capital costs to increase or preserve the value of your asset or to install or move it   s 110-25(5)

\+

5. Capital costs to preserving or defending your title or rights to your asset   s 110-25(6)

Source: Adapted from Australian Taxation Office, 'Cost base of assets' (Web Page, 4 August 2021) https://www.ato.gov.au/individuals/capital-gains-tax/calculating-your-cgt/cost-base-of-assets.

4.4.2 Reduced cost base (Subdivision 110-B)

As mentioned earlier, a reduced cost base is used in working out the capital loss from a CGT event. The reduced cost base of a CGT asset also has five elements.[30] These are similar to the cost base, but there is one difference which is related to the third element.[31] Specifically, in working out a capital loss, the third element of the reduced cost base includes any amount that the taxpayer has included in his or her assessable income as a result of a balancing adjustment for this CGT asset. Again, a balancing adjustment occurs when a depreciating CGT asset is sold, under which the termination value and the adjustable value of the CGT asset will be compared. This is represented by figure 4.4. Section 110-55(2) notes that the five elements are the same as the cost base, except for element 3, which is included in section 110-55(3).

Also, certain amounts are not included in the reduced cost base, such as any costs that the taxpayer has incurred and for which they have or could have claimed a tax deduction.[32]

This is illustrated in example 4.16.

---

30 ITAA97 section 110-55(1).
31 ITAA97 section 110-55(3).
32 ITAA97 sections 110-55(4) and (5).

FIGURE 4.4   Working out the net capital gain or loss for an income year

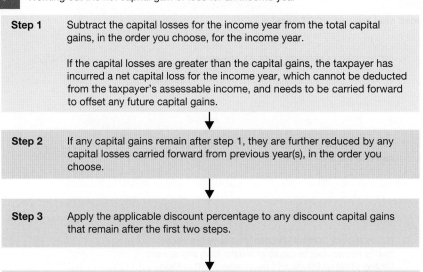

Step 1	Subtract the capital losses for the income year from the total capital gains, in the order you choose, for the income year. If the capital losses are greater than the capital gains, the taxpayer has incurred a net capital loss for the income year, which cannot be deducted from the taxpayer's assessable income, and needs to be carried forward to offset any future capital gains.
Step 2	If any capital gains remain after step 1, they are further reduced by any capital losses carried forward from previous year(s), in the order you choose.
Step 3	Apply the applicable discount percentage to any discount capital gains that remain after the first two steps.
Step 4	Apply the small business concessions to further reduce the taxpayer's capital gains if the taxpayer is carrying on small business.
Step 5	Add up the remaining non-discount capital gains and the remaining discount capital gains, if any, to arrive at the net capital gain for the income year.

EXAMPLE 4.16

Reduced cost base — determining capital loss

Julia purchased an income-producing asset for her business in January 2015 for $90 000. During the years that she held this asset, Julia claimed deductions for capital works for this asset of $12 000. She sold this asset for $60 000 in January 2022. In this case, the reduced cost base is calculated by subtracting the deductions of $12 000 that she claimed for capital works from the original cost base of $90 000, which is adjusted to $78 000.

What is Julia's capital loss for the 2021–22 income year?

Julia's capital loss for the 2021–22 income year will be $18 000, being the capital proceeds of $60 000 minus the reduced cost base of $78 000.

4.4.3 Modifications to cost base and capital proceeds

4.4.3.1 Capital proceed modifications

Section 116-10 states the following.

(1) There are 6 modifications to the general rules that may be relevant. The table in section 116-25 lists which ones may be relevant to each CGT event.

Explanation of modifications

(2) The first is a market value substitution rule. [We discussed this in section 4.4.1.1.]

(3) The second is an apportionment rule. It is relevant if a payment you receive in connection with a transaction relates in part only to a CGT event. Example: you sell 3 CGT assets for a total of $900,000. The $900,000 needs to be apportioned between the 3 assets.

(4) The third is a non-receipt rule. It is relevant if you do not receive, or are not likely to receive, some or all of the capital proceeds from a CGT event. [This rule will only apply if the non-receipt did not arise as a result of anything done or not done by the taxpayer and all reasonable steps were taken to enforce

the payment. The sale proceeds from the sale of a business are often paid in instalments. This is known as 'vendor finance'. This modification applies if one or more of the instalments is not received by the vendor. The date the contract is signed is the date of the CGT event. The vendor has paid tax on the capital gain even though not all the capital proceeds have been received.

When it becomes obvious that some of the purchase price will never be received, the vendor can request an amendment to reduce the capital proceeds on the sale and therefore reduce the capital gain.]

(5) The fourth is a repaid rule. It is relevant if you are required to repay some or all of the capital proceeds from a CGT event.

In some sales of a business, part of the proceeds will need to be repaid if the business does not achieve specified criteria or if some aspect of the information provided relating to the sale is incorrect. The vendor may need to refund some of the capital proceeds to the purchaser.

If this occurs, the capital proceeds will be reduced and the vendor will request an amendment to reduce the capital gain which arose when the CGT event arose, which might have been some years previously.

(6) The fifth is relevant only if another entity assumes a liability in connection with a CGT event.

[The capital proceeds will include any liabilities taken over from the vendor — for example, if the purchaser takes over a loan of the vendor, and the loan relates to the operation of the business, the purchaser may take over leases which the vendor had entered.]

(7) The sixth relates to misappropriation by an employee or agent. It is relevant if your employee or agent misappropriates all or part of the capital proceeds from a CGT event.

4.4.3.2 Cost base — general modification rules

Section 112-5 contains the modifications to the general rules that may be relevant for cost and reduced cost bases for CGT purpose.

Explanation of modifications

Market value substitution (section 112.20), apportionment rules (section 112-30) and assumption of liability rules (section 112-35) are the reverse of the capital proceeds provisions discussed earlier.

Section 112-25 governs what happens when assets are either split or merged. As the taxpayer remains the owner of the asset, no CGT event occurs so there is no gain or loss arising. When assets are merged, all the cost base elements are added together. This would occur when a taxpayer buys a number of properties and then merges them to form one large property. When assets are split, it will be necessary to apportion the cost base among each new asset on a reasonable basis.

ETHICS IN PRACTICE

Ethics in capital gains tax

Your client has recently sold their investment property and has asked you to work out the CGT that will be applicable. During the ownership of the property, the client has been claiming the capital works deduction against the assessable income generated by this property. You explain to the client that you will need to adjust the cost base of the property to reflect the amount that has already been claimed. The client is not happy about this, as they argue they will be paying more tax on the sale of the property than they wanted to, and give instructions for you not to undertake this reduction on the cost base.

What considerations would you take into account in resolving this ethical dilemma?

Are you meeting your requirements under the TPB Code of Conduct as a registered tax agent?

Would your behaviour be ethical and in line with your professional obligations if you followed the client's wishes?

What could you do to advise your client of their taxation responsibilities?

Would losing the client and their fee be an option if they stood by their decision to not reduce the cost base?

4.5 CGT exemptions and some special rules

LEARNING OBJECTIVE 4.5 Describe and apply CGT exemptions.

The CGT regime is subject to some major exemptions, which means that a capital gain or loss is disregarded under certain circumstances.

4.5.1 Pre-CGT exemption (section 104-10(5)(a))

The first major exemption applies to the assets acquired before the introduction of the CGT regime (20 September 1985), which are known as 'pre-CGT assets', and any capital gains or capital losses made or incurred on those assets are disregarded.

4.5.2 Main residence exemption (Subdivision 118-B)

The main residence exemption states that, in general, a capital gain or loss that a taxpayer makes in relation to his or her dwelling that was the taxpayer's main residence throughout the ownership period is disregarded.[33] A dwelling is defined in section 118-115 to include a unit of accommodation that is a building or is contained in a building and which consists wholly or mainly of residential accommodation. It also includes such things as caravans, houseboats and mobile homes. The land under such units of accommodation is also included.

Land adjacent to the house will be exempt, providing it is not more than 2 hectares and is used principally for private or domestic purposes (section 118-120).

This is illustrated in example 4.17.

EXAMPLE 4.17

Main residence exemption

Hudson purchased a house in Adelaide in 1990 for $115 000 and has lived in it with his family since then. In 2022, he sold the house for $890 000. During this period, this house was not rented out or used for generating any assessable income.

What is the CGT treatment of the sale?

This capital gain of $775 000 is disregarded, as it is treated by law as Hudson's main residence.

However, this exemption may not apply in full if the dwelling is the taxpayer's main residence during only part of the taxpayer's ownership period, or if the dwelling is partly used for producing assessable income.[34] According to section 118-145(2), if the taxpayer uses part of his or her dwelling for an income-producing purpose, the taxpayer can still treat it as his or her main residence if the dwelling is used for that purpose for only up to 6 years. Also, according to the second part of this section (section 118-145(2)), a taxpayer is entitled to another period of up to 6 years each time the dwelling becomes and ceases to be the main residence.

This is demonstrated in example 4.18.

EXAMPLE 4.18

Main residence exemption

In January 2003, Mark acquired a house in Sydney and lived in it immediately. He rented it out in May 2006 because he was transferred overseas for a business project until April 2010 (4 years of absence). Mark then moved back into this house upon his return to Sydney in 2010. In 2015, he was again posted overseas for another project for 4 years and he rented the house out again during this period. When he returned in 2021, Mark sold the house. During this whole period from 2003 to 2021, Mark did not have any other main residence.

What is the CGT treatment of the sale of the house?

In this case, Mark is entitled to the full main residence exemption and the capital gain that he earned from this transaction is fully disregarded because each of his absences was shorter than 6 years.

Section 118-145(2) often works in conjunction with other sections, such as section 118-185, where partial exemption applies. Under section 118-185(1), an individual taxpayer will only receive a partial

---

33 ITAA97 section 118-110(1).
34 ITAA97 sections 118-145(2), 118-185 and 118-190.

exemption when a CGT event occurs to his or her dwelling that was the taxpayer's main residence for only part of the total ownership period. This is illustrated in the example 4.19.

EXAMPLE 4.19

Partial main residence exemption

In August 2009, Tanya bought a 5-bedroom house to live in. She rented it out in August 2012 as she got a job in another city. The house was sold in August 2021 and Tanya made a capital gain of $12 000. In this case, Tanya's total ownership period includes 12 years from August 2009 to August 2021. During this period, she rented the house out for 9 years from August 2012 to August 2021.

What is the CGT treatment of the sale?

According to section 118-145, Tanya can choose to treat this house as her main residence for the first 6 years in the total rental period of 9 years, for which she receives the partial main residence exemption. Therefore, Tanya is considered to have made a capital gain for the 3 years when the house is not her main residence and the calculation is as follows.[35]

$$\text{Capital gain} = \$12\,000 \times \frac{365 \times 3}{365 \times 12}$$
$$= \$3000$$

4.5.2.1 Use of dwelling to produce assessable income

If the main residence is used partially for earning assessable income then, to that extent, a capital gain or loss will arise. This will mainly affect taxpayers who run a business from home and set aside an area of the home for this purpose.

The apportionment of the gain or loss is made on the area of the home used for income-earning purposes.

Note that this apportionment requirement to being able to deduct interest in respect of the income-earning activities. This will preclude people who set aside one room of a home as a home study.

EXAMPLE 4.20

Use of dwelling to produce assessable income

Yee Fen ran her own business in public relations. She used 20 per cent of her house to operate the business. When she eventually sold the house, she made a capital gain of $30 000. Only 20 per cent of the gain ($6000) will be assessable.

4.5.2.2 Section 118-192: Cost base of residence used to earn assessable income

A property used as a principal residence (and therefore exempt from CGT) may subsequently be used to earn assessable income — for example, rented out. This happens when the taxpayer has lived in the property and then buys a second property in which to live and rents out the first property. Section 118-192 deems the cost base of the property to be the market value at the date it ceases to be the principal residence.

EXAMPLE 4.21

Principal residence used to earn assessable income

Andrew bought his home for $340 000. Some years later, when its market value was $530 000, he rented it out. He sold the house for $600 000 18 months later.

The capital gain is only $70 000, as the cost base is deemed to be $530 000.

---

35 The calculation of a capital gain or capital loss in relation to partial main residence exemption is stated in section 118-185(2).

4.5.2.3 Foreign residents' access to the main residence exemption

Changes in the CGT regime were introduced at 7:30 pm (AEST) on 9 May 2017 in relation to foreign tax residents' access to the main residence exemption.[36]

For dwellings that were acquired and held as the main residence before the introduction of the new changes (7:30 pm (AEST) on 9 May 2017):

- those taxpayers who became foreign tax residents could still claim the main residence exemption when they disposed of the properties on or before 30 June 2020 if other requirements for this exemption were met
- those foreign tax residents' access to the main residence exemption is denied if they dispose of the properties after 30 June 2020, *unless* they were foreign tax residents for a continuous period of 6 years or less and during the period one of the following life events happened:
    - those foreign tax residents, their spouse or child under 18, had a terminal medical condition
    - their spouse or child under 18 died
    - the CGT event was resulted from divorce or separation and the distribution of assets was involved.

For dwellings that were acquired and held as the main residence at or after 7:30 pm (AEST) on 9 May 2017:

- those foreign tax residents' access to the main residence exemption is denied *unless* they were foreign tax residents for a continuous period of 6 years or less and during the period one of the life events listed occurred.

It is reasonable to conclude that those previous Australian tax residents who became foreign tax residents for longer than 6 years and sold their main residences in Australia had no intention to come back. Therefore, they will not receive the same tax benefits in terms of this main residence exemption if they did not contribute to Australian society by paying Australian tax within this substantial period and have no intention to do so in the future.

4.5.3 Depreciating asset exemption (section 118-24)

A capital gain or loss that is generated from a CGT event in relation to a depreciating asset is generally disregarded if the asset was held by an individual taxpayer, or a partnership or a trust where the taxpayer is a partner or a beneficiary, and used solely for such a purpose. The taxpayers can claim deductions for the decline in value of such assets in the years they are used and any gain from a CGT event, such as a disposal, relating to a depreciating asset will be calculated in the form of 'assessable balancing charge' under the balancing adjustment rule in section 40-285. CGT would apply to the depreciating assets that are for private use.

4.5.4 Motor vehicle exemption (section 118-5)

A capital gain or loss that a taxpayer makes from a motor vehicle, such as a car or a motorcycle, is also disregarded. This is because a capital loss is generally incurred when a taxpayer sells a used car or motorcycle. If not disregarded, this would be another major means for taxpayers to lower their income tax liabilities as it is quite common that a second-hand motor vehicle is sold at a price that is much lower than its purchase price.

4.6 Calculation of net capital gains or net capital losses

LEARNING OBJECTIVE 4.6 Calculate the net capital gain or loss from all CGT events for an income year.

The procedure of calculating a net capital gain or a net capital loss for an income year is stated in sections 100-45 and 100-50 of the ITAA97.

---

36 These new rules that deny foreign residents' access to the main residence exemption were first announced in the 2017–18 Federal Budget on 9 May 2017 and further amended in the Treasury Laws Amendment (Reducing Pressure on Housing Affordability Measures) Bill 2019.

4.6.1 Stage 1 — capital gain or loss for most CGT events (section 100-45)

A taxpayer will need to separately calculate the capital gains or capital losses that he or she generates or incurs for each CGT event during the year, while taking account of certain applicable CGT exemptions. To do so, the cost base or the reduced cost base of a CGT asset is subtracted from the capital proceeds received from the CGT event. A capital gain is generated when the capital proceeds exceed the cost base; while a capital loss is incurred if the reduced cost base is greater than the capital proceeds. In certain cases, there will be neither a capital gain nor a capital loss if the capital proceeds is less than the cost base but greater than the reduced cost base. In general, this step has been illustrated by the many examples discussed.

During this first step, a taxpayer can use either the 'indexation method' (Division 114) or the 'discount method' (Division 115) depending on the timing of the CGT event and whether the taxpayer is an individual, complying superannuation fund, a trust or a company. Specifically, the indexation method can be used by all types of taxpayers, including companies, if the following two conditions are met:
1. the CGT assets were acquired at or before 11:45 am (by legal time in the Australian Capital Territory) 21 September 1999[37] (section 114-1), and
2. the CGT assets have been held for more than 12 months (section 114-10(1)).[38]

In contrast, the discount method can only be used if the taxpayer is an individual, or a complying superannuation fund, or a trust (section 115-10) if the following conditions are met:
1. the capital gains must be made after 11:45 am (by legal time in the Australian Capital Territory) on 21 September 1999 (section 115-15), and
2. the cost base that is used in working out the capital gain does not include indexation (section 115-20), and
3. the CGT assets have been held more than 12 months before the CGT event happens (section 115-25).

Eligible taxpayers, including individuals, complying superannuation funds and trusts can choose between these two methods and select the one that will generate a lower capital gain if the relevant conditions are met. For the assets that were acquired after that date, only the discount method can be used. Companies are not eligible to use the discount method and can only use the indexation method if the two conditions that are contained in sections 114-1 and 114-10(1) are met. These two methods are discussed in the next examples.

4.6.1.1 Indexation method (Division 114)

Under the **indexation method**, the cost base of a CGT asset acquired at or before 11:45 am on 21 September 1999 (by legal time in the Australian Capital Territory) includes indexation of the elements of the cost base, except for the third element, which is the non-capital costs of ownership.[39] The purpose of including the indexation is to adjust the cost base for inflation, which indicates the decreased purchasing power of money that causes prices to increase, but the actual product value does not change. For example, a taxpayer purchased an asset for $100 5 years ago and sold it for $120 now. If the current market price for the asset of the same quality is $105, where the increase of $5 is just because of inflation, rather than the real increase in the value of the asset, then according to Division 114, the cost base of this asset is adjusted as $105 and the taxpayer has made a capital gain of $15. Otherwise, without such indexation for inflation, the taxpayer would have been taxed for a higher capital gain of $20. Such indexation could be viewed as a tax benefit and an allowance for inflation.

The indexation applies subject to the following additional rules contained in the notes to section 114-1.
- Indexation does not apply to inflation after 30 September 1999, which means that if a CGT event happens on or after 11:45 am (by legal time in the Australian Capital Territory) on 21 September 1999, the taxpayer can only index the relevant elements in the cost base up to 30 September 1999.
- Indexation is not relevant to expenditures incurred after 11:45 am (by legal time in the Australian Capital Territory) on 21 September 1999 in the acquisition of a CGT asset.

In addition, indexation is not included in the elements of the reduced cost base in working out a capital loss.[40]

---

37 On 21 September 1999, the New Business Tax System (Capital Gains Tax) Bill 1999 was announced in the Treasurer's Press Release No. 58, which introduced the discount method in order to simplify the calculation procedure and to provide taxpayers with more tax benefits in terms of the lower capital gains.

38 This could be interpreted as a discouragement for any market opportunistic behaviour.

39 ITAA97 sections 110-36(1) and 114-1.

40 TAA97 section 110-55.

To use this method, the cost base is indexed by multiplying it by its indexation factor (section 960-270(1)), which is calculated by referring to the quarterly Consumer Price Index (CPI) published between 1985 and 30 September 1999.[41] Applying section 960-275, the indexation factor is calculated by using the following formula.

$$\text{Indexation factor} = \frac{\text{CPI for the quarter ending on 30 September 1999}}{\text{CPI for the quarter in which the expenditure was incurred}}$$

Then, the cost base is indexed as:

$$\text{Indexed cost base} = \text{Cost base} \times \text{Indexation factor}$$

Example 4.22 illustrates the calculation of a capital gain using the indexation method.

EXAMPLE 4.22

Indexation method

Scott Johnson purchased a rental property on 20 June 1994 for $98 000 and sold the property for $830 000 on 25 September 2021.

What is the capital gain using the indexation method?

The calculation is as follows.

$$\text{Indexation factor} = \frac{68.7 \,(\text{CPI for the quarter ending on 30 September 1999})^{\dagger}}{61.9 \,(\text{CPI for the quarter ending on 30 June 1994})}$$
$$= 1.11$$

† As mentioned earlier, indexation does not take into account the inflation after 30 September 1999 when a CGT event happens after 11:45 am (by legal time in the ACT) on 21 September 1999.

Thus, the indexed cost base of Scott's investment property will be:

$$\text{Indexed cost base} = \$98\,000 \times 1.11 = \$108\,780$$

Lastly, capital gain = $830 000 – $108 780 = $721 220.

$721 220 is the capital gain that Scott generated from this CGT event, which he will need to include in the further calculation of his net capital gain or loss for the income year. Clearly, if the indexation is not included, he would have to pay higher tax on this transaction for a capital gain of $732 000 (being calculated as the capital proceeds of $830 000 minus the original unindexed cost base $98 000).

In addition, the CPIs published in the valid period for the indexation method are provided in table 4.2.

TABLE 4.2   CPIs published using the indexation method — September 1985 to September 1999

CPIs within the indexation valid period — September 1985 to September 1999				
Year/quarter ending	31 March	30 June	30 September	31 December
1999	67.8	68.1	68.7	
1998	67.0	67.4	67.5	67.8
1997	67.1	66.9	66.6	66.8
1996	66.2	66.7	66.9	67.0
1995	63.8	64.7	65.5	66.0
1994	61.5	61.9	62.3	62.8
1993	60.6	60.8	61.1	61.2
1992	59.9	59.7	59.8	60.1
1991	58.9	59.0	59.3	59.9

---

41 This is the period that starts with the introduction of the CGT regime and ends on the day when the indexation method was frozen.

1990	56.2	57.1	57.5	59.0
1989	51.7	53.0	54.2	55.2
1988	48.4	49.3	50.2	51.2
1987	45.3	46.0	46.8	47.6
1986	41.4	42.1	43.2	44.4
1985			39.7	40.5

4.6.1.2 Discount method (Division 115)

The **discount method** means to discount a capital gain by a discount percentage if certain requirements are met (Subdivisions 115-A and 115-B). In order to discount a capital gain, there are four major requirements that must be met.

1. The first requirement states the types of taxpayers who can discount their capital gains. Specifically, the capital gain must be made by an individual taxpayer, or a complying superannuation fund, or a trust, or a life insurance company that is involved in a CGT event with a complying superannuation fund.[42]
2. The capital gain must be made or, in other words the CGT event must have happened, after 11:45 am (by legal time in the Australian Capital Territory) on 21 September 1999 when the discount method was introduced.[43]
3. An indexation must not be included in the cost base of the CGT asset when calculating a discount capital gain.[44] A possible interpretation for this requirement is that the capital gain will be lowered if the cost base is increased by including an indexation. When a discount is further applied, the taxpayer would receive double tax benefits.
4. The CGT assets must be held for at least 12 months before the related CGT event.[45] Further, the discount method cannot be used for certain CGT events, such as CGT event D1.[46] If these four requirements are met, the capital gain is called a 'discount capital gain'.

Once all the major requirements are met, different types of taxpayers can apply different discount percentages in order to discount their assessable capital gains.[47] The discount percentage is 50 per cent for individual taxpayers and trusts; 33.33 per cent for complying superannuation funds or the life insurance companies that made capital gains in the CGT events with complying superannuation funds.

The discount method is much simpler than the indexation method, which can be demonstrated by using the same details as in example 4.23.

EXAMPLE 4.23

Discount method

Scott Johnson is an individual taxpayer who acquired an investment property before 21 September 1999 and sold this property on 25 September 2021. Thus, before this CGT event, Scott held this asset for much longer than the required 12-month ownership period. Therefore, Scott would be allowed to use the discount method and his discount percentage is 50 per cent.

$$\text{Capital gain} = \$830\,000 \ - \ \$98\,000 \ \text{(the cost base that does not include the indexation)}$$
$$= \$732\,000$$

---

42 ITAA97 section 115-10.
43 ITAA97 section 115-15.
44 ITAA97 section 115-20(1).
45 ITAA97 section 115-25.
46 ITAA97 section 115-25(3).
47 ITAA97 section 115-100.

When a 50 per cent discount is applied:

$$\text{Discount capital gain} = \$732\,000 \times 50\% = \$366\,000$$

Therefore, the assessable capital gain that Scott generated in this transaction is $366 000, which is much lower than the one under the indexation method. Scott should then choose the discount method, which helps him lower his income tax liability for the income year ending 30 June 2022.

4.6.2 Stage 2 — calculate the net capital gain or loss from all CGT events (section 100-50)

After calculating the capital gains and losses from most CGT events, a taxpayer will then need to follow a 5-step procedure in order to work out a net capital gain or a net capital loss for a certain income year. These five steps are stated in section 100-50 and presented in figure 4.4.

Note that steps 1 and 2 in figure 4.4 mention 'in the order you choose'. As the law differentiates between the discount capital gains and non-discount capital gains, there is a suggested method which will help to lower the amount of net capital gain for an income year.

The 5-step method is as follows.

1. Analyse each CGT transaction and separate the discount capital gains and non-discount capital gains.
2. Subtract the current capital losses first from any non-discount capital gains, then subtract the remaining capital losses, if any, from the discount capital gains.
3. Subtract the capital losses from previous year(s), if any, first from the non-discount capital gains, when applicable, and then subtract the remaining capital losses from previous year(s), if any, from the discount capital gains.
4. Apply the discount percentage to any remaining discount capital gains.
5. Any remaining net capital gain will be included in the taxpayer's assessable income.

The idea for this suggestion is to eliminate the non-discount capital gains as much as possible because the discount percentage cannot be applied to those gains, which will help to generate a lower net capital gain. This suggested procedure is an application of the wording of 'in the order you choose' given in the law provisions in relation to the first two steps in stage 2 and illustrated in example 4.24.

EXAMPLE 4.24

Calculating the net capital gain

One of your long-standing clients, Ms Amanda Ross who is an Australian resident for tax purposes, contacted you to seek your advice on her income tax liability for the income year 2021–22 and she included a list of CGT transactions she entered into during this income year.

1. On 10 July 2021, Amanda sold 2000 shares at the price of $85 per share. She acquired those shares in September 2020 for a total price of $96 000.
2. On 3 January 2022, she sold her rental property for $850 000 that she bought in 2010 with a total cost base of $380 000.
3. On 23 May 2022, she received $230 000 from the disposal of other shares that she had purchased in 2018 for $340 000.
4. She had a net capital loss of $160 000 from prior years that she could carry forward to offset other capital gains.

Amanda is an individual taxpayer and qualifies for the use of the discount method according to section 115-10. From the first transaction, Amanda earned a capital gain of $74 000.[48] However, this is a non-discount capital gain (NDCG) as she held those shares for less than 12 months (section 115-25). She made a discount capital gain (DCG) for $470 000 in the second transaction, and a capital loss of $110 000 in the third one.

How should the net capital gain be calculated?

---

48 $85 × 2000 − $146 000

The following table summarises the calculation of the net capital gain using the suggested method.

	NDCG $	DCG $
Capital gains	74 000	470 000
Less: Capital loss in current year	(74 000)	(36 000)[49]
	0	434 000
Offset the remaining capital gain by prior capital loss		(160 000)
Notional capital gain		274 000
Apply the discount % for individuals (50%)		(137 000)
The net capital gain to be included in assessable income		**137 000**

The following table illustrates the method that does not follow the above suggested method providing a clear comparison between the two methods.

	NDCG $	DCG $
Capital gains	74 000	470 000
Less: Capital loss in current year		(110 000)
		360 000
Offset the remaining capital gain by prior capital loss		(160 000)
Notional capital gain	74 000	200 000
Apply the discount % for individuals (50%)		(100 000)
The net capital gain to be included in assessable income		**174 000**[50]

4.7 Special CGT rules on SBEs

LEARNING OBJECTIVE 4.7 Understand SBE concessions in relation to CGT.

If an entity is recognised by law as a small business entity (SBE) for CGT purposes — a **CGT small business entity (CGT SBE)** the entity is allowed to disregard or defer some or all of a capital gain generated from the disposal of an active asset used in the business.

An entity is recognised as a CGT SBE if:
- it carries on a business in the current income year (section 328-110), and
- its annual turnover is less than $2 million (section 152-10(1AA)), or
- the net value of the assets owned and used in the business does not exceed $6 million (section 152-15).

A CGT asset (either tangible or intangible) is an **active asset** if it is a tangible asset owned by the taxpayer and it is used or held ready for use in the course of carrying on a business (section 152-40(1)(a)) or if it is an intangible asset owned by the taxpayer and it is inherently connected with the business that the taxpayer carries on (section 152-40(1)(b)), and either of the following two conditions is met (section 152-35):

1. when the asset has been owned for up to 15 years, it is an active asset for at least half of the test period, or

---

49 Subtract the current capital loss from the NDCG first, and then subtract any balance from the DCG. Therefore, $36 000 is calculated as the total current capital loss, $110 000, minus $74 000.

50 $174 000 is calculated by adding up the DCG of $100 000 and the NDCG of $74 000.

2. when the asset has been owned for more than 15 years, it is an active asset for at least 7 and half years during the test period.

The test period (section 152-35(2)) begins with the acquisition of the assets, and ends at the earlier of:

(i) the CGT event, and

(ii) the cessation of the business if the business ceased in the 12 months before the CGT event.

This is demonstrated in example 4.25.

EXAMPLE 4.25

Active assets

Belinda opened a printing business in July 2000 and closed the business in January 2022. She sold a printing machine that she acquired in October 2003 and used in the business until January 2022.

Is the printing machine an active asset?

Belinda owned the business for 21 and a half years, and she owned and used the printing machine for more than 18 years. This printing machine is an active CGT asset because it meets the required conditions.

There are four exemption or deferral rules that allow a CGT SBE to disregard or defer some of all of a capital gain generated from a CGT event that involves an active asset, which are discussed as follows.

4.7.1 Small business concessions

This section will look at the four deferral rules that allow a CGT SBE to defer some or all of a capital gain generated from a CGT event that involves an active asset (see table 4.3).

TABLE 4.3   Small business concessions available to SBEs

Rule	Conditions	Concession
15-year exemption Subdivision 152B	The business must have continuously owned the active asset for at least 15 years just before the CGT event. The taxpayer is aged 55 or over and the CGT event occurs in connection with retiring or permanent incapacitation.	100% exempt.
50% small business asset reduction Subdivision 152C	n/a	50% reduction of the capital gain on an active asset. (This reduction is in addition to the 50% CGT discount if applicable, and thus the total reduction is 75%.) The small business retirement exemption and small business rollover relief may also apply.
Retirement exemption Subdivision 152D	The capital proceeds from the CGT must be used in connection with your retirement. Lifetime limit of $500 000. If the taxpayer is under 55, the exempt amount must be paid into a complying superannuation fund or a retirement savings account. If the taxpayer is over 55, the exempt amount can be taken automatically.	Capital gains from the sale of active assets are exempt up to a lifetime limit of $500 000.

Rollover exemption Subdivision 152E	Within two years of the CGT event, the taxpayer must use the rolled over amount to acquire a replacement active asset and/or make capital improvements to an existing active asset. (Failure to meet this condition results in reversal of the rollover.)	The taxpayer may elect to defer the making of a capital gain from a CGT event.

Source: Adapted from Federal Register of Legislation, '*Income Tax Assessment Act 1997*: Information from Division 152' (Web Page, 20 March 2020) www.legislation.gov.au/Details/C2020C00113.

4.7.2 Small business 15-year exemption (Subdivision 152-B)

A CGT SBE is able to disregard any capital gain generated from a CGT event that involves an active asset if the following conditions are met (section 152-105):
- the CGT SBE is carried on by an individual, or if it is a company or a trust that has a significant individual who has more than 20 per cent ownership or voting power in the company or the trust (sections 152-70 and 152-110), and
- the active asset was continuously owned for the 15-year period before the CGT event, and
- the individual who carries on the business or the significant individual in the company or the trust is 55 years old or over and is retiring or permanently incapacitated at the time of the CGT event.

This exemption rule has priority over the other three exemption or deferral rules, which means that if a CGT SBE can entirely disregard a capital gain, there is no need to apply any further deduction or discount (sections 152-215, 152-330 and 152-430).

4.7.3 Small business 50 per cent reduction (Subdivision 152-C)

A CGT SBE can apply a further 50 per cent reduction to any remaining capital gains arising from a CGT event that involves an active asset after applying the applicable discount percentage from step 3 in stage 2 (sections 100-50 and 102-5).

In addition, if a CGT SBE can use the 50 per cent deduction, the entity may still be eligible for another two exemptions (the retirement and the roll-over exemptions) and can choose the order in applying the three exemptions in order to reduce the capital gains to the largest extent (section 152-210).

4.7.4 Small business retirement exemption (Subdivision 152-D)

An individual who carries on a CGT SBE, or a company or a trust that has a significant individual, can choose to disregard the capital gains arising from a CGT event that involves an active asset for up to $500 000 (sections 152-305 and 152-320). If the individual is under 55 years old, the disregarded amount must be paid into a complying superannuation fund or a retirement saving account (RSA) (section 152-305(1)(b)).

4.7.5 Small business roll-over (Subdivision 152-E)

This rollover rule allows a CGT SBE to defer all or part of a capital gain arising from a CGT event that involves an active asset for 2 years, or longer if:
- an asset is acquired to replace the active asset involved in the CGT event — that is, being disposed of, or
- the SBE incurs capital improvement expenditure on an existing asset that replaces the active asset involved in the CGT event (section 152-410).

4.7.5.1 CGT event J5

Occurs where the taxpayer chose to apply the CGT small business roll-over to disregard a capital gain that arose in relation to a CGT asset in an income year and by the end of the replacement asset period either:
- the taxpayer has not acquired a replacement asset or had not incurred fourth element expenditure in relation to a CGT asset, or
- the replacement asset does not satisfy the replacement asset conditions.

The timing of this event is at the end of the replacement asset period.

The capital gain from this event is equal to the amount of the capital gain that was disregarded previously under the small business roll-over concession.

The capital gain under this event cannot be discounted by the general discount provisions or the 50 per cent active asset reduction. Only the retirement concessions can reduce the gain.

4.7.5.2 CGT event J6

Occurs where the taxpayer chose to apply the CGT small business roll-over to disregard a capital gain that arose in relation to a CGT asset in an income year and, by the end of the replacement asset period, the value of the replacement asset or fourth element expenses is less than the original amount of capital gains disregarded.

The timing of this event is at the end of the replacement asset period.

The capital gain under this event cannot be discounted by the general discount provisions or the 50 per cent active asset reduction. Only the retirement concessions can reduce the gain.

EXAMPLE 4.26

CGT event J6

Cody applied the CGT small business roll-over to disregard a capital gain of $900 000 arising from CGT event A1 which occurred on 16 January in Year 1.

On 15 June in Year 1, Cody acquired the land on which he conducted his security business for $400 000. Cody incurred incidental costs on the acquisition of $20 000. On 7 September in Year 2, Cody built a second building on the land to provide further space to conduct his business. The cost of this improvement was $300 000. The cost of the capital improvement was fourth element expenditure.

On 15 January in Year 3, being the end of the replacement asset period:

- Cody had acquired the land as a replacement asset and incurred fourth element expenditure
- the property was an active asset of Cody's
- the total of the first element of the cost base ($400 000), the incidental costs ($20 000) and the fourth element expenditure ($300 000) was $720 000, being less than the capital gain of $900 000 previously disregarded.

Accordingly, CGT event J6 will happen to Cody on 15 January in Year 3. The capital gain will be equal to $180 000 ($900 000 – $720 000).

4.7.6 Small business CGT concessions — additional considerations

There are important concepts we need to understand in relation to the SBE CGT concessions.

4.7.6.1 Maximum net asset value test

This test requires that the total net value of the CGT assets held by a taxpayer and their connected entities at the time of making the gain is less than $6 million.

The test looks at 3 groups of assets:

1. the taxpayer's net assets
2. the net assets of a small business CGT affiliate to the taxpayer
3. the net assets of other entities connected to the taxpayer.

A small business CGT affiliate of a taxpayer is any individual or company that, in relation to their own business affairs, acts or could reasonably be expected to act in accordance with the taxpayer's directions or wishes.

An entity is 'connected to' another entity if:

1. either entity controls the other, or
2. both entities are controlled by the same third entity.

The net assets of the other entities and the business affiliate that need to be included are those assets that are used in a business only.

4.7.6.2 Meaning of net value of CGT assets

The net value of the CGT assets of an entity is the sum of the market values of those assets, less any liabilities of the entity that are related to those assets. Assets to be included in determining the net value of CGT assets are not restricted to business assets and include all CGT assets of the entity.

Where the taxpayer is an individual the following assets are excluded from the net value of CGT:

- assets of a private or personal nature
- assets solely for the personal use and enjoyment of the individual of a small business CGT affiliate (e.g. family home)
- rights to capital amounts payable out of a superannuation fund or approved deposit fund
- rights to an asset of a superannuation fund or approved deposit fund
- life insurance policies.

Note: Although gains from depreciating assets are treated as income rather than capital gains, depreciating assets are still CGT assets and are therefore included in the calculation of net asset value.

Amendments have been made to the net asset value test and they are as follows.

1. Negative net assets: Section 152-10(1) has been amended to clarify that the calculation of net value of the assets can allow for an entity to have a negative net asset value.
2. Liabilities: Section 152-10 will now allow in the definition of liabilities to include provisions for annual leave, long service leave, unearned income and tax liabilities.
3. Private dwellings: These are excluded from the net asset value test even if it is used to produce an amount of assessable income, provided no deduction is (or would be) available in relation to interest incurred on money borrowed to acquire the dwelling. Section 152-20 was amended so that an individual only includes in their net assets the current market value of a dwelling to the extent that it is reasonable, having regard to the amount that the dwelling has been used to produce assessable income which gives rise to the deductions for interest payments.
4. Partnerships: The maximum net asset value test when applied in relation to partnership assets only counts the assets of each relevant partner and not the partnership as a whole.

4.7.6.3 Active assets

Shares and interest in trusts can also be active assets if the taxpayer owns the trust and the total of:

- the market values of the company's/trust's active assets, and
- any capital proceeds that the company/trust received during the 2 years before the time from the CGT event happening to its active assets, and which the company/trust holds in the form of cash or debt pending the acquisition of a new active assets is 80 per cent or more of the market value of all the assets of the company/trust.

Cash and financial instruments are not active assets but they count towards the satisfaction of the 80 per cent test provided they are inherently connected with the business.

The 80 per cent test is met if the 80 per cent requirement is tested at some stage and it is reasonable to assume that the test will continue to be passed at a later time. If there has been significant changes and the 80 per cent test is reapplied and is not met, the share/trust interest will still be an active asset if the failure is only temporary.

The following are a list of assets that are considered to not be active assets:

- interest in a connected entity
- shares in companies and trusts (i.e. public companies and listed trusts)
- financial instruments (e.g. loans, debentures, bonds, promissory notes, future contracts, forwards contracts, currency swap contracts, rights and options)
- an asset whose main use in the course of carrying on a business is to derive passive income — (e.g. interest, annuity, rent, royalties).

4.7.6.4 Significant individual test

If the asset being disposed of is a share in a company or an interest in a trust, the entity must satisfy the significant individual test and the entity claiming the concession must be a CGT concession stakeholder in the company or trust.

This test can be applied directly or indirectly through one or more interposed entities. The benefit of this indirect tracing is that an entity disposing of an asset can now make 15-year exemption payments and retirement exemption payments directly to the ultimate significant individuals in relation to the disposing entity.

An individual is a significant individual in a company or a trust if the individual has a small business participation percentage of at least 20 per cent. This can be made up of direct and indirect percentages.

An entity's direct small business participation percentage in a company is the lower of the percentage of:
- voting power that the entity is entitled to exercise
- any dividend payment that the entity is entitled to receive
- any capital distribution that the entity is entitled to receive.

EXAMPLE 4.27

Small business participation

Peter has shares that entitle him to 30 per cent of any dividends and capital distribution of Coffee Co. The shares do not carry any voting rights. Peter's direct small business participation in Coffee Co is 0 per cent.

For a fixed trust, an entity's small business participation percentage is the lower of the percentage of:
- any distribution of income that the trustee may make to which the entity would be beneficially entitled
- any distribution of capital that the trustee may make to which the entity would be beneficially entitled.

For a discretionary trust, an entity's small business participation interest is the lower of the percentage of distributions of income or capital that the entity is beneficially entitled to during the income year. If the trust did not make a distribution of income or capital during the year, it will not have a significant individual in relation to that income year.

An entity's indirect small business participation percentage in a company or trust is calculated by multiplying together the entity's direct participation interest in an interposed entity and the interposed entity's total participation percentage (both direct and indirect) in the company or trust.

EXAMPLE 4.28

Participation percentage

An individual owns 80 per cent of a private company. A discretionary trust distributes 90 per cent of its income to the company. The discretionary trust owns 60 per cent of a unit trust.

The individual's participation percentage is as follows: 80% × 90% × 60% = 43.2%.

Therefore, the individual's total participation percentage is more than 20 per cent, so they can access the concessions.

4.7.6.5 Concession stakeholders

An individual is a CGT concession stakeholder of a company or trust if the individual is:
- a significant individual of that company or trust, or
- the spouse of a significant individual, but the spouse must have a participation percentage in the company or trust that is greater than nil. The participation percentage can be held either directly or indirectly and is worked out on the same basis as for the significant individual test.

4.7.6.6 Additional conditions for company shares and trust interests

Previously, only individuals could access the small business CGT concessions due to the definition of a concession stakeholder but, under the amendments, interposed entities can now access the concessions. This is due to the alternative test which requires that CGT concession stakeholders in the company or trust being disposed of together have a small business participation percentage in the disposing company or trust of at least 90 per cent.

The three conditions that apply to allow the CGT Concessions on these types of interests are:
1. the entity must be a CGT small business entity with an aggregated turnover of less than $2 million, or satisfy the $6 million net asset value test,
2. the CGT asset must be an active asset, and
3. where the asset is a share in a company or an interest in a trust, there must be a CGT concession stakeholder (small business participation percentage of at least 20 per cent) in the object company or trust; or CGT concession stakeholders in the object company or trust together have a small business participation percentage in the entity claiming the concession of at least 90 per cent.

4.8 CGT treatment of cryptocurrencies

LEARNING OBJECTIVE 4.8 Understand the CGT treatment of cryptocurrencies.

The term **cryptocurrency** is what is used to describe a digital asset in which encryption techniques are used to regulate the generation of additional units and verify transactions on a blockchain.

Cryptocurrencies are classified as property in most countries, and property is an 'asset' for tax purposes; therefore, cryptocurrencies are subject to CGT provisions. A digital wallet often is used by taxpayers to maintain their cryptocurrencies, which may be made up of many different types of currency. For CGT purposes, each cryptocurrency is a separate CGT asset.

In Australia, CGT provisions will apply, meaning a taxpayer can either make a capital loss or a capital gain on a CGT event that is connected to the cryptocurrency. If the cryptocurrencies are classified as a personal use asset then the gain/loss is disregarded.

If the cryptocurrency is held for more than 12 months, then the taxpayer can apply the CGT general discount provisions.

4.8.1 Cryptocurrency events

In Australia, these types of disposals can generate a CGT event:
- exchanging cryptocurrencies
- selling cryptocurrencies
- gifting cryptocurrencies
- using cryptocurrencies to purchase goods and services
- converting cryptocurrencies to flat currency (this is a currency established by government regulation or law, e.g. Australian dollars).

EXAMPLE 4.29

Exchanging cryptocurrency

On 5 July 2021, Katrina acquired 100 Coin A for $15 000. On 15 November 2021, through a reputable digital currency exchange, Katrina exchanged 20 of Coin A for 100 of Coin B. Using the exchange rates on the reputable digital currency exchange at the time of the transaction, the market value of 100 Coin B was $6000. For the purposes of working out Katrina's capital gain for her disposal of Coin A, her capital proceeds are $6000.

Katrina's CGT calculations will be:

Capital proceeds	$6 000
Cost base	
$15 000/100 × 20	3 000
CGT gain	$3 000

As the asset was not held for more than 12 months, no discounting applies.

4.8.2 Personal use assets

Some capital gains or losses that arise from the disposal of a cryptocurrency that is a personal use asset may be disregarded. Cryptocurrency is a personal use asset if it is kept or used mainly to purchase items for personal use or consumption.

Where cryptocurrency is acquired and used within a short period of time to acquire items for personal use or consumption, the cryptocurrency is more likely to be a personal use asset.

However, where the cryptocurrency is acquired and held for some time before any such transactions are made, or only a small proportion of the cryptocurrency acquired is used to make such transactions, it is less likely that the cryptocurrency is a personal use asset. In those situations, the cryptocurrency is more likely to be held for some other purpose and may be subject to either the CGT provisions or income tax.

The relevant time for working out if an asset is a personal use asset is at the time of its disposal.

Only capital gains made from personal use assets acquired for less than $10 000 are disregarded for CGT purposes. However, all capital losses made on personal use assets are disregarded.

EXAMPLE 4.30

Personal use asset

Michael wants to attend a concert. The concert provider offers discounted ticket prices for payments made in cryptocurrency. Michael pays $270 to acquire cryptocurrency and uses the cryptocurrency to pay for the tickets on the same day.

Under the circumstances in which Michael acquired and used the cryptocurrency, the cryptocurrency is a personal use asset.

EXAMPLE 4.31

Non-personal use asset

Peter has been regularly keeping cryptocurrency for over 6 months with the intention of selling at a favourable exchange rate. He has decided to buy some goods and services directly with some of his cryptocurrency. Because Peter used the cryptocurrency as an investment, the cryptocurrency is not a personal use asset.

4.8.3 Loss or theft of cryptocurrency

You may be able to claim a capital loss if you lose your cryptocurrency private key or your cryptocurrency is stolen.

In this context, the issue is likely to be whether the cryptocurrency is lost, whether you have lost evidence of your ownership, or whether you have lost access to the cryptocurrency.

Generally, where an item can be replaced, it is not lost. A lost private key can't be replaced. Therefore, to claim a capital loss you must be able to provide the following kinds of evidence:

- when you acquired and lost the private key
- the wallet address that the private key relates to
- the cost you incurred to acquire the lost or stolen cryptocurrency
- the amount of cryptocurrency in the wallet at the time of loss of the private key
- that the wallet was controlled by you (e.g. transactions linked to your identity)
- that you are in possession of the hardware that stores the wallet
- transactions to the wallet from a digital currency exchange for which you hold a verified account or is linked to your identity.[51]

---

51 This resource has been used extensively in this section: Australian Taxation Office, 'Tax treatment of cryptocurrencies' (Web Page, 30 March 2020) https://www.ato.gov.au/general/gen/tax-treatment-of-crypto-currencies-in-australia—specifically-bitcoin.

Cryptoactivities, CGT complexities and tax reform

According to the Final Report of the Australia as a Technology and Financial Centre Committee (hereafter the 'Bragg Report'),[52] there are as many as 25 per cent of Australians who have held (whether currently or previously) cryptoassets. Cryptoassets are not limited to Bitcoin or other more traditional forms of cryptocurrencies. In recent years, there has been an explosion of activity in what is described as the 'metaverse'. For example, non-fungible tokens (NFTs) can represent anything from artwork, gaming or other unique property, or bundles of rights. Unlike Bitcoin, each NFT is unique and, through scarcity and verifiability, they yield intrinsic value, like that of a piece of artwork.[53]

Where taxpayers hold cryptoassets for investment purposes, cryptoassets are considered CGT assets and their disposals as CGT events.[54] Tax practitioners need to appreciate what crypto-related activities their clients may have undertaken to appropriately determine whether the specific categories of CGT asset apply (personal use asset or collectable) and therefore any relevant special rules or exemptions. Many taxpayers have been perhaps disappointed to learn that the $10 000 threshold for personal use assets will not apply unless, for example, they have acquired Bitcoin to simply buy a pizza! In contrast, could an NFT that represents a digital piece of artwork meet the definition of a collectable?[55]

Determining a taxpayer's CGT consequences can become challenging due to a number of factors, including the frequency in which a taxpayer can transact, the varying characterisation of activities possible, as well as the types of arrangements entered into that can lead to a multitude of CGT events. For example, to acquire a CGT asset such as an NFT, the taxpayer generally needs another cryptoasset to do so (e.g. ETH on the Ethereum blockchain). The acquisition of the NFT triggers a disposal of the ETH, as ETH is not money or currency. Taxpayers may be operating layers and layers away from dollars and never 'cash in'. Due to this use of cryptoassets as a means of payment, this invokes the principles of barter transactions, requiring market values to be used[56] (which can be challenging to determine for many cryptoassets). Third-party tax crypto-calculators can assist both taxpayers and tax practitioners.[57]

The Committee agreed that the number of taxable events (i.e. CGT events A1) created by blockchain protocols is problematic and not all should result in taxable events.[58] In response to the growing challenges faced within the crypto-economy and its metaverse, the Bragg Report recommended that the CGT regime be amended to ensure that digital asset transactions only create a CGT event when they 'genuinely result in a clearly definable capital gain or loss'.[59] This could be achieved via a new kind of CGT asset or new kind of CGT event.[60] The Report also highlighted the need for Treasury and the ATO to be proactive and keep pace with the developments in this space.[61]

....

REFLECTION

What progress has been made, if any, on reforming the CGT regime with respect to digital asset transactions? If none, what do you think a possible CGT event or CGT asset category could look like for cryptoassets to balance simplicity for taxpayers whilst ensuring government objectives are met?

---

52 Select Committee on Australia as a Technology and Financial Centre, 'The Senate Select Committee on Australia as a Technology and Financial Centre' (Final Report, October 2021) ix https://www.aph.gov.au/Parliamentary_Business/Committees/Senate/Financial_Technology_and_Regulatory_Technology/AusTechFinCentre/Final_report ('Bragg Report').

53 See, eg, Hashmasks (Web Page) https://www.thehashmasks.com.

54 See, eg, Australian Taxation Office, 'Income tax: is bitcoin a "CGT asset" for the purposes of subsection 108-5(1) of the *Income Tax Assessment Act 1997*?' (TD 2014/26, 28 November 2019) https://www.ato.gov.au/law/view/document?DocID=TXD/TD201426/NAT/ATO/00001.

55 See ITAA97 section 108-110.

56 Australian Taxation Office, 'Income tax: barter and countertrade transactions' (IT 2668) [15]. See more general guidance at Australian Taxation Office, 'Tax treatment of cryptocurrencies', (Web Page, 30 March 2020) https://www.ato.gov.au/general/gen/tax-treatment-of-crypto-currencies-in-australia—specifically-bitcoin.

57 See, eg, *Crypto Tax Calculator* (Web Page) https://cryptotaxcalculator.io/au; and *Crypto Tax Calculator for Australia* (Web Page) https://koinly.io/au. See the chapter on tax avoidance and evasion for further discussion on tech solutions for crypto-related activities.

58 Bragg Report, 139–140.

59 Bragg Report, 140.

60 Bragg Report, 140. See also Elizabeth Morton, 'The Bragg Report's Agenda for Reforming Capital Gains Tax for the Crypto Economy', *Austaxpolicy* (Blog, 26 November 2021) https://www.austaxpolicy.com/the-bragg-reports-agenda-for-reforming-capital-gains-tax-for-the-crypto-economy.

61 Bragg Report, 140.

SUMMARY

4.1 Explain how taxpayers pay tax on their capital gains in Australia.

Unlike FBT or GST, CGT is not a separate tax from income tax. Any taxable net capital gains are included in a taxpayer's assessable income, as a form of statutory income, and the taxpayers are taxed pursuant to income tax law, accordingly.

Taxpayers must maintain records of capital gains and losses made. The records need to be kept in English, be readily accessible and retained for 5 years after it is certain that no CGT event can happen for which those records could be expected to be relevant in determining the capital gain or loss (section 121-25).

4.2 Define CGT assets.

In general, section 108-5 of the ITAA97 defines a CGT asset as 'any kind of property' or 'a legal or equitable right that is not property'. A note to this section provides some common examples of the CGT assets, which include land and buildings; an equity or debt interest, such as goodwill, shares or debts, in a business that could be a company, a partnership or a trust; as well as foreign currencies. Division 108 of the ITAA97 also contains some special types of CGT assets and the related rules on them, including collectables (Subdivision 108-B), personal use assets (Subdivision 108-C) and separate CGT assets relating to capital improvement (section 108-70).

4.3 Describe the major types of CGT events.

Sections 100-20(1) and 102-20 both state that a capital gain or loss arises only if a CGT event happens. A list of more than 50 different types of CGT events is provided in section 104-5 of the ITAA97, and this chapter discusses the most common types of CGT events, including the disposal of a CGT asset (CGT event A1) and the loss or destruction of a CGT asset (CGT event C1), as well as other types of CGT events, such as creating contractual or other rights (CGT event D1).

4.4 Determine the cost base or reduced cost base of CGT assets.

Section 110-25 (1) states that the cost base of a CGT asset consists of five elements:

- The first element of the cost base refers to the money that the taxpayer paid, or is required to pay, in acquiring the CGT asset; or the market value of any property or properties that the taxpayer gave out, or is required to give out, in order to acquire the CGT asset.
- The second element of the cost base is the 'incidental costs' associated with the acquisition of a CGT asset. In general, incidental costs are the costs associated with or incidental to the acquisition or disposal of CGT assets.
- The third element of the cost base is any costs incurred for owning a CGT asset that was acquired after 20 September 1991.
- The fourth element of the cost base includes:
  - any capital expenditure that a taxpayer incurred with the purpose, or the expected effect, of increasing or preserving the value of a CGT asset, and
  - expenditure in regard to installing or moving the asset.
- The fifth element of the cost base is any capital expenditure that a taxpayer incurs in order to establish or defend his or her title to, or right over, a CGT asset.

4.5 Describe and apply CGT exemptions.

The CGT regime is subject to some major exemptions, which means that a capital gain or loss is disregarded under certain circumstances. These major exemptions include pre-CGT exemption (section 104-10(5)(a)), main residence exemption (Subdivision 118-B), depreciating asset exemption (section 118-24) and motor vehicle exemption (section 118-5).

4.6 Calculate the net capital gain or loss from all CGT events for an income year.

The cost base or the reduced cost base of a CGT asset is subtracted from the capital proceeds received from the CGT event. A capital gain is generated when the capital proceeds exceed the cost base; while a capital loss is incurred if the reduced cost base is greater than the capital proceeds.

A taxpayer can use either the indexation method (Division 114) or the discount method (Division 115) depending on the timing of the CGT event and whether the taxpayer is an individual, a complying superannuation fund, a trust or a company in working out the capital gain or capital loss.

4.7 Understand SBE concessions in relation to CGT.

If an entity is recognised by law as a small business entity (SBE) for CGT purpose, the entity is allowed to disregard or defer some or all of a capital gain generated from the disposal of an active asset used in the business. These concessions include a 15-year exemption (Subdivision 152-B), 50 per cent reduction (Subdivision 152-C), retirement exemption (Subdivision 2 152-D) and small business roll-over (Subdivision 2 152-E). If an entity is recognised by law as a small business entity (SBE) for CGT purpose, the entity is allowed to disregard or defer some or all of a capital gain generated from the disposal of an active asset used in the business. These concessions include a 15-year exemption (Subdivision 152-B), 50 per cent reduction (Subdivision 152-C), retirement exemption (Subdivision 2 152-D) and small business roll-over (Subdivision 2 152-E).

4.8 Understand the CGT treatment of cryptocurrencies.

In Australia CGT provisions ensure that a taxpayer can either make a capital loss or a capital gain on a CGT event that is connected to cryptocurrency. If the cryptocurrency is classified as a personal use asset, then the gain/loss is disregarded. If the asset (cryptocurrency) is held for more than 12 months, the taxpayer can apply the CGT general discount provisions.

In Australia these types of disposals can generate a CGT event: exchanging, selling or gifting cryptocurrencies, using cryptocurrencies to purchase goods and services, and converting crypto-currencies to fiat currency.

Taxpayers must maintain records of capital gains and losses made.

KEY TERMS

active asset A tangible asset owned by the taxpayer used or held ready for use in the course of carrying on a business or an intangible asset owned by the taxpayer and inherently connected with the business that the taxpayer carries on *and* either, when the asset has been owned for up to 15 years, it is an active asset for at least half of the test period; or when the asset has been owned for more than 15 years, it is an active asset for at least 7 and a half years during the test period.

capital gain The extent to which the proceeds of the sale of a capital asset exceed the cost of acquiring it.

capital gains tax (CGT) A part of income tax, paid on a capital gain (the extent to which the proceeds of the sale of a capital asset exceed the cost of acquiring it).

capital loss The extent to which the proceeds of the sale of a capital asset fall short of the cost of acquiring it.

CGT asset Any kind of property or a legal or equitable right that is not property.

CGT event An event, described in section 104-5 of the ITAA97, that triggers a capital gain or loss.

CGT small business entity (CGT SBE) A business entity that meets certain requirements and can therefore disregard or defer some or all of a capital gain generated from the disposal of an active asset used in the business.

collectables-to-collectables rule Any capital losses that are incurred from collectables can only be offset against any capital gains that are generated from collectables.

cost base Relevant when a capital gain is made, the cost of the asset when you bought it, plus certain other costs associated with acquiring, holding and disposing of the asset.

discount method For a CGT asset, the discounting of a capital gain by a discount percentage if certain requirements are met.

indexation method For a CGT asset acquired at or before 11:45 am 21 September 1999, the indexation of the elements of the cost base, except for the third element. This is intended to adjust the cost base for inflation.

personal use asset An asset mainly used for a taxpayer's personal use or enjoyment, but not a collectable or a piece of land or a building.

post-CGT assets Capital assets acquired after the introduction of CGT (20 September 1985).

pre-CGT assets Capital assets acquired before the introduction of CGT (20 September 1985).

reduced cost base Relevant when a capital loss is made, the cost of the asset when you bought it, plus certain other costs associated with acquiring, holding and disposing of the asset.

separate CGT assets The recognition by law that buildings or structures (or capital improvements to them) are separate assets to the land for the purposes of balancing adjustment provisions applied to the building or structure.

QUESTIONS

4.1 Explain why the CGT regime was introduced in Australia, and how taxpayers are taxed on the capital gains.

4.2 Define a CGT asset and name one example for each of the general type and specific types of CGT assets.

4.3 What is a CGT event? Give some examples of the common CGT events and explain if a capital gain can be generated when there is no CGT event.

4.4 What are the major CGT exemptions?

4.5 Explain the special rules contained in section 118-145(2) in relation to the main residence exemptions.

4.6 Explain the concepts of cost base and reduced cost base, list the elements that comprise a cost base or reduced cost base, and describe the situations under which a cost base and reduced cost base is used.

4.7 Describe how to use the indexation method and the discount method, identify which type(s) of taxpayers are eligible to use the discount method, and explain how companies determine the cost base of their CGT assets involved in the CGT events.

4.8 Briefly describe the two-stage procedure of working out a net capital gain or net capital loss and describe the suggested method 'in the order you choose'.

4.9 Explain how a taxpayer could be recognised as a CGT SBE.

4.10 Describe under what circumstances does each of the four small business exemptions apply to a CGT SBE.

PROBLEMS

4.11 In November 2021, Michelle Jayden sold the following items to a local Money Converters shop:
- a painting by a famous artist sold for $5000, which she purchased in 2005 for $1200
- a Panasonic smart TV sold for $600, which she purchased in December 2017 for $2800.

Advise Michelle of the tax consequences in relation to the transactions. Provide explanation with reference to the relevant law provisions and calculations.

4.12 Ashley Jones inherited a beach house from her mother and immediately rented it out in 2006, and the market value of the house at that time was $125 000. She sold the house for $230 000 in September 2021. During the ownership period, she incurred the following expenses:
- legal costs associated with the inheritance process in 2006 and the disposal of the property in 2021 (total $3800)
- repair and maintenance costs, as well as the renovation expenditures (total $29 800) but she claimed deductions for those expenditures in the years that they were incurred
- legal costs of $25 000 in 2007 from her involvement in a lawsuit with one of her cousins who was trying to take over the ownership of the property
- premiums for an insurance policy over the property every year (total $18 200).

Determine the cost base of Ashley's beach house that was involved in the CGT transaction. Support each step in your calculation by the relevant CGT provisions.

4.13 Brad Johnson purchased a two-bedroom house as an investment property in June 1981 for $73 000. In order to increase the value of the property and the rental income, Brad built an extension of two additional bedrooms with the same size to the original ones in September 1998 and incurred a total expenditure of $58 000. At the same time, he paid $20 000 to repair and redecorate the original two bedrooms, and he claimed deductions for this capital works expenditure during the 1998–99 income year.

In July 2021, Brad sold this property for $785 000. At the time of sale, a licensed property valuer issued a report indicating that the land had a value of $460 000 and the balance is the value of the house, and the 4 bedrooms were in the same quality and condition. Furthermore the market price for such an extension of two bedrooms was $160 000.

What are the tax consequences of the transactions? Provide an explanation with reference to the relevant law provisions and calculations.

4.14 Sharna, a resident in Melbourne, purchased a three-bedroom house to live in with her family in May 2009 for $420 000. The price included the property and any incidental costs. She rented it out in May 2011 as she started a new business based in Sydney. The house was sold in May 2022 and Sharna received an amount of $860 000 after deducting all the fees associated with the transaction. Assume she did not incur any other fees during the ownership period.

Determine if Sharna has made any capital gain from this CGT event. Show calculations and support with the relevant law provisions.

4.15 As a tax accountant, you are trying to prepare the income tax return for one of your clients, Jennifer Gallen, for the 2021–22 income year and she included a list of CGT transactions that she entered into during this income year.

- On 1 October 2021, she sold 1800 shares at the price of $76 per share. She acquired those shares in September 2017 for a total price of $88 000.
- On 30 December 2021, she sold her rental property for $920 000 after deducting all the fees and costs associated with the transaction. She bought the property in 2010 with a total cost base of $430 000.
- On 3 April 2022, she received $450 000 from the disposal of other shares that she purchased in June 2021 for $320 000.
- In May 2022, a painting by a famous artist, which was owned by Jennifer, was stolen. Unfortunately, she did not insure this painting. She bought the painting in 2015 for $1300 and the current market value of this painting was $2600.
- Also, she had a net capital loss of $230 000 from prior years that she could carry forward to offset other capital gains.

Calculate the net capital gain or loss for Jennifer and apply the relevant law provisions to minimise her tax liability when relevant.

4.16 Stephanie, an Australian resident up until 29 June 2022, became a foreign resident on 30 June 2022 (Year 9) and has provided you with the following information.

- Her Perth residential investment property was purchased for $200 000 in Year 1 (post-September 1999). It had a market value of $550 000 as at 30 June 2022.
- Her antique car was acquired for $80 000 in Year 6. As at 30 June 2022, it had a market value of $85 000.
- Her London (United Kingdom) residential investment property was purchased for $175 000 on 12 April in Year 8. It had a market value of $190 000 as at 30 June 2022.
- She made a capital gain of $10 000 from selling some shares in a listed company in January 2022. The shares were acquired in November 2021.

Assume that Stephanie has not made any elections. Calculate the minimum net capital gain or capital loss for Stephanie for the year ended 30 June 2022.

Show all workings. Provide the relevant section references for any exclusions.

4.17 Tom owns a boat that he and his family use for water-skiing. The boat cost Tom $40 000 when he purchased it on 12 September 2021. Tom insured the boat for damage and loss.

On 23 December 2021, because of a severe storm, Tom's boat was smashed against the rocks off the coast and was damaged beyond repair. There was no injury or loss of life.

Tom received $42 000 from his insurance company because of the accident. Which CGT event occurs because of the accident?

4.18 Oscar sells his business to Baxter on 1 July (Year 10). He had a cost base of $123 000 and the contract for sale showed a sale price of $1 300 000. Baxter paid $750 000 on settlement and agreed to pay the remaining $550 000 in equal instalments on the anniversary of the sale.

Oscar receives the first 3 payments on time, but Baxter advises him that the business has not succeed and he cannot pay anything further.

What are the implications of this information? What can Oscar do? How does this affect Baxter's cost base or reduced cost base if he is able to sell the business?

4.19 Morgan's Pty Ltd (100% owned by Annette) owns the following assets:

- a residential investment property which it rents out
- a guest house which operates as a bed and breakfast and
- a hardware store.

Required

(a) Are the small business concessions available for the sale of these properties, and if not, what has to be done to satisfy the tests?

(b) Are the small business concessions available for the sale of the shares in the company and, if not, what has to be done to satisfy the tests?

(c) What would be the position if Morgan's was 100% owned by a holding company that was wholly owned by Annette?

4.20 Henry disposed of an active asset for $20 000 and derived a capital gain of $4000. Henry acquires two replacement assets for $12 000 and $8000 and elects for small business roll-over relief. Both assets are different types of active assets to the asset that was disposed of.

Two years later, Henry sells the $8000 roll-over asset for $10 000, which results in a capital gain on that asset of $2000. Henry does not apply for roll-over relief.

What are the CGT implications to Henry?

ACKNOWLEDGEMENTS

Figures 4.2, 4.3: © Australian Taxation Office

Extracts: © Federal Register of Legislation. Licensed under CC BY 4.0.

CHAPTER 5

Fringe benefits tax

LEARNING OBJECTIVES

After studying this chapter, you should be able to:

5.1 describe the operation of the fringe benefit tax regime in Australia

5.2 apply the three steps for calculating fringe benefits tax liability

5.3 apply the 'otherwise deductible rule' and understand the effect of employee contributions on the calculation of the FBT liability

5.4 describe the common types of fringe benefits and calculate the related fringe benefits tax liabilities

5.5 describe and apply common fringe benefits tax exemptions

5.6 describe the concepts of reportable fringe benefits and salary packaging

5.7 describe the range of FBT administration matters.

Overview

This chapter provides a detailed explanation and discussion of the Australian fringe benefits tax (FBT) regime. Figure 5.1 presents an overview of the components of the FBT regime.

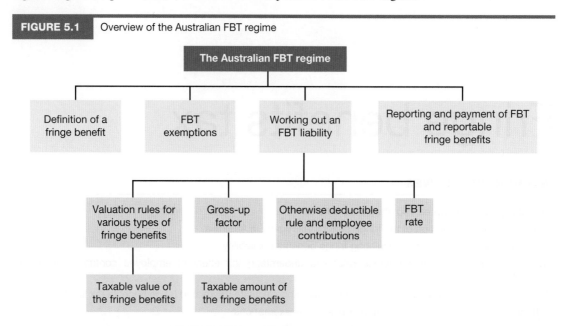

FIGURE 5.1 Overview of the Australian FBT regime

Generally speaking, a business should not pay an employee's private expenses from its business bank account. However, in some instances, this does happen and the **employer** provides an **employee** with a private benefit. This is referred to as a **fringe benefit**.

Fringe **benefits tax** operates separately to income tax. This chapter will firstly provide an overview of the fringe benefits tax regime and how an employer's fringe benefits tax liability is calculated.

Second, this chapter outlines the various categories of fringe benefits and how the **taxable value** of each category is calculated. The chapter then goes onto discuss some of the most common benefits which are exempt from FBT followed by a discussion of the reportable fringe benefit amount. The chapter concludes with a brief overview of the concept of salary packaging and FBT administration.

5.1 The Australian FBT regime

LEARNING OBJECTIVE 5.1 Describe the operation of the FBT regime in Australia.

Employers can reward their employees a number of ways. By far, the most common form of remuneration is the payment of salaries and wages. Other forms of remuneration include the payment of cash allowances, such as a clothing or travel allowance, or bonuses. These amounts are assessable income in the hands of the employee by virtue of either section 6-5(1) or section 15-2 of the ITAA97.

An employer may also provide their employees with non-cash benefits. This may involve, for example, paying the employee's private medical bills, home electricity bills or children's school fees.

Prior to 1 July 1986, the employee was required to include in their assessable income the value of all non-cash (or fringe) benefits received in respect of employment. However, on 1 July 1986, the *Fringe Benefits Tax Assessment Act 1986* (Cth) was introduced. From this date onwards, where an employer provides non-cash (or fringe) benefits to employees that are private in nature, FBT may apply.

Australia is one of only three countries in the world to apply an FBT regime. The other two countries are New Zealand and India.

Essentially, fringe benefits tax is a tax payable by employers on the value of fringe (or private) benefits provided to their employees or their associates in respect of employment.

FBT is a tax payable by the employer regardless of whether the employer is an individual, partnership, company, trust, incorporated association or government department. The tax is levied at a flat rate of 47 per cent on the grossed-up taxable value of the fringe benefits provided.

Where an employer pays FBT, they are able to claim an income tax deduction under section 8-1 of the ITAA97 for both the cost of the fringe benefit provided to the employee as well as the FBT paid.

Furthermore, where the benefit provided to the employee includes GST, the employer is able to claim back the GST input tax credits in respect of the fringe benefit.

Unlike income tax, where the income year is 1 July to 30 June, the **FBT year** runs from 1 April to 31 March. Where an employer provides fringe benefits to their employees, the employer is required to lodge an annual FBT return with the ATO by 21 May, or 25 June if lodged by a registered tax agent. However, if it is lodged electronically by a registered tax agent, payment is due by 28 May.

As the tax is payable by the employer, from the perspective of the employee, any fringe benefits they receive are treated as **non-assessable non-exempt (NANE) income** (section 23L of the ITAA36) and are not included in their assessable income.

5.1.1 What is a fringe benefit?

According to section 136(1) of the *Fringe Benefit Tax Assessment Act 1986* (Cth) (FBTAA86), a **fringe benefit** is defined as a non-salary/wages benefit provided by the employer or an **associate** of the employer to the employee or an associate of the employee, in respect of their employment, during and for the FBT year.

Common examples of fringe benefits include:
- provision of a company-owned car to the employee who takes the car home and uses it for private purposes
- payment of an employee's home telephone or electricity bills
- payment of an employee's private health insurance premiums or medical bills
- payment of an employee's children's school fees or childcare fees
- provision of a low or interest-free loan to the employee, and
- provision of entertainment, including taking the employee out to a restaurant for lunch, or buying a ticket for the employee to attend a concert, musical, opera or sporting event.

5.1.2 Benefits not considered fringe benefits

Section 136(1) outlines those benefits that do not give rise to any FBT liability. These include:
- **exempt benefits** expressly provided for in the FBTAA86
- salary or wages (this includes cash bonuses and allowances, other than a living-away-from-home allowance)
- most superannuation fund contributions
- payments from certain superannuation funds
- benefits arising under employee share schemes under Division 83A of the ITAA97
- employment termination payments
- capital payments for enforceable contracts in restraint of trade
- capital payments for personal injury
- payments deemed to be dividends for income tax purposes and loans that comply with the deemed dividend provisions in the ITAA36
- a benefit that is specifically made exempt under the FBTAA86.

Many of the benefits listed are specifically exempt from FBT largely because they are taxed under other provisions of the ITAA36 and ITAA97.

TECHNOLOGY IN ACTION

Is the provision of cryptocurrency to an employee a fringe benefit?

There may be situations where an employer provides cryptocurrency to an employee as a form of remuneration. The question is whether cryptocurrency is considered cash or is it a fringe benefit and therefore, subject to fringe benefits tax?

In December 2014, the ATO released Taxation Determination TD 2014/28, *FBT: Is Bitcoin a Fringe Benefit?* This provided guidance as to whether the provision of Bitcoin by an employer to an employee in respect of their employment is a fringe benefit. The ATO concluded that Bitcoin (and cryptocurrency in general) is not considered cash, and as such, does not fall within the definition of salary and wages.

Instead, the ATO's stated position was that the provision of Bitcoin to an employee meets the definition of a property fringe benefit, and as such, is subject to FBT.

▶

However, since the release of the 2014 taxation determination, the ATO has subsequently revised its interpretation. The ATO now considers that the appropriate treatment of cryptocurrency depends on whether a valid **salary sacrifice arrangement** is in place.

Put simply, where a valid salary sacrifice arrangement has been put in place between the employer and the employee, the FBT regime will apply and the cryptoassets will be treated as a property fringe benefit. The taxable value of the cryptoassets provided is based on the market value of those cryptoassets on the date they are provided to the employee.

On the other hand, where there is no valid salary sacrifice arrangement in place, the cryptoassets constitute ordinary income to the employee, and, hence, form part of salary and wages. PAYG obligations will be imposed on the employer based on the Australian dollar value paid.

The issue of salary sacrificing/salary packaging is specifically covered later in this chapter.

REFLECTION

Contemplate whether it is worthwhile for an employer to provide $20 000 worth cryptocurrency to an employee who is on a base salary of $80 000.

5.1.3 Provided by the employer or an associate of the employer

A fringe benefit arises when the employee's employer (or their associate) provides the benefit. An employer includes a current, former and future employer.

FBT applies regardless of whether the employer is a sole trader, partnership, trustee, corporation, unincorporated association, government or government authority (sections 165 and 166 of the FBTAA86).

A fringe benefit also arises if the benefit is provided by an associate of the employer. An associate of an employer typically includes a subsidiary of the employer or a related company (section 318 of the ITAA36).

5.1.4 Benefit provided to the employee or their associate

To be a fringe benefit, a benefit must be provided to an employee or to an associate of the employee. For FBT purposes, an employee is defined as a person who receives, or is entitled to receive, salary and wages in return for work or services provided, or for work under a contract that is wholly or principally for the person's labour. An employee includes a current, former and future employee.

The term 'employee' includes company directors. However, an employee does not include genuine contractors, or other non-employees, such as clients, customers, shareholders and suppliers. Hence, benefits provided to contractors and/or clients will not be subject to FBT.

FBT also applies to an 'associate' of the employee. Section 318 of the ITAA36 defines an associate as including relatives of the employee, such as the taxpayer's spouse, children, parents, brothers, sisters, grandparents, uncles, aunties and cousins etc.

5.1.5 Benefit provided in respect of employment

According to section 148 of the ITAA36, in order for a benefit to be a fringe benefit, it must be provided to the employee or their associate 'in respect of employment'. This means that in order to qualify as a fringe benefit, the benefit must be provided on the basis of the employment of the employee — meaning that there must be a 'nexus'

Therefore, a benefit cannot qualify as a fringe benefit if it is not sufficiently linked with the employment of the employee. Hence, benefits provided to clients, customers, consultants or suppliers would not qualify as fringe benefits.

The issue of consumer loyalty programs (including frequent flyer points) was discussed in *Payne v FCT* 96 ATC 4407. The Court held that benefits (such as free flights received under frequent flyer or consumer loyalty programs) are not subject to FBT as the benefits provided did not arise from an employer/employee relationship, but a supplier/customer relationship. In other words, the benefits (being free flights) did not arise 'in respect of employment'.

5.1.6 Impact on employers

As previously mentioned, FBT is a tax payable by the employer. However, the employer is able to claim an income tax deduction for not only the fringe benefit provided to the employee but also for the amount of fringe benefits tax paid to the ATO under section 8-1 of the ITAA97.

The interrelationship between fringe benefits tax, income tax and the GST is summarised in table 5.1.

TABLE 5.1   Relationship between FBT, income tax and GST

Expense incurred	Business expense	Private expense
Has a fringe benefit been provided to an employee?	✗	✔
FBT is payable by the employer at 47%	✗	✔
Income tax deduction (for the FBT tax paid and the private expense)	✔	✔
GST input tax credit is claimed (if GST has been charged)	✔	✔

5.1.7 Impact on employees

According to section 23L(1A) of the ITAA36, where a taxpayer receives a fringe benefit, this constitutes non-assessable, non-exempt (NANE) income to the employee for income tax purposes. Hence, fringe benefits are not included in the assessable income of the employee.

However, as discussed in section 5.7.1 of this chapter, the **reportable fringe benefits amount** must be included on each employee's Income Statement (formerly called PAYG payment summary) in respect of fringe benefits provided to the employee (or their associate) for the relevant FBT year.

5.2 Calculating FBT in general

LEARNING OBJECTIVE 5.2 Apply the three steps for calculating fringe benefits tax liability.

According to section 66 of the FBTAA86, an employer is required to pay fringe benefits tax at 47 per cent on the fringe benefits taxable amount (i.e. the 'grossed-up amount') of fringe benefits provided to employees and their associates during the relevant FBT year.

The FBT rate is effectively equivalent to the top marginal tax rate for individuals (currently 45 per cent plus the 2 per cent Medicare Levy). The FBT tax rate will change whenever the top marginal tax rate and/or the Medicare Levy changes.

There are three distinct steps in calculating an employer's FBT liability. These three steps are summarised in figure 5.2.

These three steps are explained as follows.

- *Step 1: Calculate the fringe benefits taxable value.*

  The first step is to calculate the fringe benefits taxable value of each fringe benefit provided to employees and their associates. The fringe benefits taxable value is the GST-inclusive amount of the fringe benefit provided (where applicable). In the case where GST-free or input-taxed benefits are provided, then the GST-exclusive amount is used as this was the amount paid.

  The fringe benefits taxable value is established from a series of specific valuation rules. There are 12 categories of fringe benefits and each has its own specific rules for calculating the taxable value. These 12 categories are further discussed in section 5.5 of this chapter.

- *Step 2: Calculate the fringe benefits taxable amount (grossed-up amount).*

  Once the fringe benefits taxable value has been determined, the second step is to gross-up these benefits using one of two gross-up rates to derive the 'fringe benefits taxable amount'. This is also referred to as the 'grossed-up amount'.

  The two gross-up rates that an employer must use in respect of each fringe benefit provided to an employee or their associate are summarised as follows.

  (a) *Type 1 fringe benefits* are those benefits where the employer is entitled to claim an input tax credit in respect of the GST paid on the fringe benefit provided to the employee. Type 1 benefits are grossed up by a factor of 2.0802 (GST).

Typical Type 1 fringe benefits include:

- payment of an employee's home electricity or home telephone bills
- payment of an employee's gym membership fees
- payment of an Australian holiday for the employee
- payment of a meal or payment to buy movie tickets, concert or musical tickets or sporting event tickets for an employee.

(b) *Type 2 fringe benefits* are those benefits where the employer is not entitled to claim an input tax credit in respect of the fringe benefit provided to the employee. Type 2 benefits are grossed up by a factor of 1.8868 (no GST). Type 2 fringe benefits encompass the provision of both GST-free benefits under Division 38 of the *A New Tax System (Goods and Services Tax) Act 1999* (Cth) (GST Act) and input-taxed benefits arising under Division 40 of the GST Act.

The most common types of GST-free benefits include:

- payment of an employee's private health insurance premiums or medical bills
- payment of an employee's children's school fees or childcare fees, and
- payment of an overseas private holiday for the employee.

The most common types of input-taxed benefits include:

- payment of an employee's residential rent
- payment of an employee's home mortgage loan repayments, and
- provision of loans to employees.

According to section 5B of the FBTAA86, an employer's aggregate fringe benefits taxable amount is the sum of the total of the Type 1 and Type 2 aggregate fringe benefits amounts.

- *Step 3: Calculate fringe benefits tax payable.*

The third involves calculating the amount of FBT payable, which is 47 per cent of the grossed-up amount (from Step 2).

These three steps are mirrored at Items 14 to 16 of the FBT return (see figure 5.3). Item 14A requires disclosure of the taxable value of Type 1 fringe benefits. Item 14B requires disclosure of the taxable value of type 2 fringe benefits. This is the equivalent to Step 1 in our three-step process.

Once these amounts are entered, the FBT return preprints the two gross-up rates (being 2.0802 and 1.8868), such that the grossed-up amounts are calculated and shown at Labels A and B on the far right hand-side of Item 14.

These amounts are subsequently added together (Item 15) to derive the 'fringe benefits taxable amount' (or grossed-up amount). This is the equivalent to Step 2 in our three-step process.

Finally, Item 16 calculates the amount of fringe benefits tax owing. As the form shows, this amount is simply 47 percent of the fringe benefits taxable amount (or grossed-up amount). This is the equivalent to Step 3 in our three-step process.

FIGURE 5.2   Three steps in calculating the amount of FBT payable

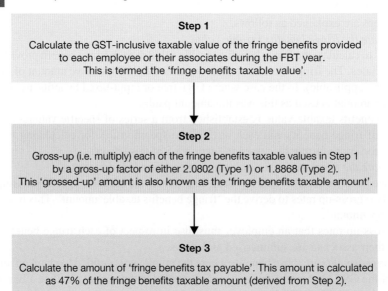

Step 1

Calculate the GST-inclusive taxable value of the fringe benefits provided to each employee or their associates during the FBT year.
This is termed the 'fringe benefits taxable value'.

Step 2

Gross-up (i.e. multiply) each of the fringe benefits taxable values in Step 1 by a gross-up factor of either 2.0802 (Type 1) or 1.8868 (Type 2).
This 'grossed-up' amount is also known as the 'fringe benefits taxable amount'.

Step 3

Calculate the amount of 'fringe benefits tax payable'. This amount is calculated as 47% of the fringe benefits taxable amount (derived from Step 2).

Return calculation details

❯ Visit ato.gov.au/FBT2022 for more information.

14 Calculated fringe benefits taxable amounts (whole dollars only)

A Type 1 aggregate amount $ ☐☐☐,☐☐☐,☐☐☐·00 ×2.0802 = $ ☐☐☐,☐☐☐,☐☐☐·00 A

B Type 2 aggregate amount $ ☐☐☐,☐☐☐,☐☐☐·00 ×1.8868 = $ ☐☐☐,☐☐☐,☐☐☐·00 B

C Aggregate non-exempt amount (hospitals, ambulances, public benevolent institutions and health promotion charities only) **or** $ ☐☐☐,☐☐☐,☐☐☐·00 C

15 Fringe benefits taxable amount *(A + B)* **or** C $ ☐☐☐,☐☐☐,☐☐☐·00

16 Amount of tax payable (47% of item 15 amount) $ ☐☐☐,☐☐☐,☐☐☐·☐☐

Source: Australian Taxation Office, 'Fringe benefits tax (FBT) return' (Web Page, 2022) https://www.ato.gov.au/uploadedFiles/Content/SPR/downloads/FBT_return_form_2022_n1067.pdf.

Example 5.1 illustrates the application of these three steps.

EXAMPLE 5.1

Steps in calculating FBT

Orion Holdings Pty Ltd provides the following two fringe benefits to one its employees, William during the course of the 2022 FBT year:

(i) Payment for a LED television set costing $1100 (inclusive of $100 GST).
(ii) Payment of medical bills for William's wife, Rebecca, totalling $3000 (no GST).

You are required to do the following.

(a) Calculate the fringe benefits taxable value of each of the two fringe benefits.
(b) Calculate the fringe benefits taxable amount of each benefit (i.e. the 'grossed-up' amount).
(c) Calculate the amount of FBT payable by Orion Holdings Pty Ltd.
(d) How much is tax-deductible to Orion Holdings Pty Ltd?
(e) How much GST input tax credits can be claimed back by Orion Holdings Pty Ltd?

The calculations for the various amounts are as follows.

(a) The fringe benefits taxable value of the LED television set is $1100 (inclusive of $100 GST), whilst the fringe benefits taxable value of the medical fees is $3000 (no GST).
(b) The fringe benefits taxable amount (i.e. the 'grossed-up' amount) is calculated as follows:
Type 1: LED television set: $1100 × 2.0802 = $2288.22
Type 2: Medical bills: $3000 × 1.8868 = $5660.40
The total fringe benefits taxable amount is the sum of these two benefits. Hence:

	$
Type 1 aggregate fringe benefit	2 288.22
Type 2 aggregate fringe benefit	5 660.40
Fringe benefits taxable amount (i.e. 'grossed-up' amount)	7 948.62

(c) The amount of FBT payable by Orion Holdings Pty Ltd is $3735.85 (i.e. $7948.62 × 47%).
(d) Orion Holdings Pty Ltd is entitled to claim each expense as an allowable deduction (i.e. GST-exclusive amount of $1000 and $3000) as well as the FBT paid of $3735.85 under section 8-1 of the ITAA97. Hence, the total tax-deductible amount comes to $7735.85.
(e) Orion Holdings Pty Ltd is entitled to claim back GST of $100 paid in relation to the purchase and provision of the LED television set to William.

5.3 The 'otherwise deductible rule' and employee contributions

LEARNING OBJECTIVE 5.3 Apply the 'otherwise deductible rule' and understand the effect of employee contributions on the calculation of the FBT liability.

5.3.1 The 'otherwise deductible rule'

It will be remembered that FBT only applies to those fringe (or non-cash) benefits provided by an employer to an employee in respect of employment that are private in nature. For instance, FBT will apply if the employer provides the employee with benefits which are not related to the derivation of assessable income, and for which no income tax deduction would be allowed to the employee. For example, FBT applies where the employer pays for a private holiday for the employee. However, FBT would not apply in the case where the employer were to pay for the employee to attend a work-related conference that was directly relevant to their job. This concept is referred to as the **otherwise deductible rule (ODR)**. Essentially, this rule is based on the premise that where an employer provides their employee with a benefit that would be 'otherwise deductible' to the employee, then the fringe benefits taxable value is reduced.

The ODR provides that if the employee (but not their associate) would have been able to claim a once-only tax deduction for the item in question in their personal tax return if they had incurred the expenditure themselves, the item is not subject to FBT. A once-only deduction means a deduction for the whole expense (or portion of the expense) is allowed as an income tax deduction during the year of income. It excludes deductions for depreciable items as this does not result in a once-only deduction (see section 52(1)(b) and TD 93/46).

The resultant effect of the ODR is that only the private component of any fringe benefit provided to the employee is subject to FBT.

In order for the employer to benefit from the ODR the employee must provide the employer with a declaration which declares that the employee has used the benefit for deductible work-related or deductible income-producing purposes. A sample expense payment declaration is shown in figure 5.4.

The ODR can only be used to reduce the taxable value of the following categories of fringe benefits:
- loan fringe benefits
- expense payment fringe benefits
- board fringe benefits
- property fringe benefits
- residual fringe benefits.

The application of the ODR is shown in example 5.2.

FIGURE 5.4   Sample expense payment declaration

> **Expense payment benefit declaration**
>
> I, _____ declare that
>   (name of the employee)
>
> _____
> (show nature of expense e.g. telephone rental and/or calls)
> were provided to me by or on behalf of my employer during the period from
> _____ 20 _____ to _____ 20 _____ and the expenses were
> incurred by me for the following purpose(s)
>
> _____
>
> _____
>
> (Please give sufficient information to demonstrate the extent to which the expenses were incurred by you for the purpose of earning your assessable income.)
>
> I also declare that the percentage of those expenses incurred in earning my assessable income was _____%.
>
> Signature _____
>
> Date _____

The otherwise deductible rule

On 19 January 2022, Isabella's employer pays her home telephone bill totalling $540. Isabella goes through her telephone bill and determines that 25 per cent of these calls (amounting to $135) were work-related calls to the office and to clients. Isabella provides the appropriate declaration to her employer to this effect.

The taxable value of the fringe benefit is calculated as follows.

	$
Payment of telephone bill	540
Less: Otherwise deductible amount (25% work-related component)	(135)
Taxable value of the fringe benefit (i.e. 75% private component)	405

As the telephone bill is a taxable supply and the employer can claim back the GST input tax credit, the relevant gross-up factor is 2.0802 (Type 1).

FBT is payable on the grossed-up taxable amount of $842.48 (i.e. $405 × 2.0802). Assuming there are no other fringe benefits, the FBT payable is $395.97 (i.e. $842.48 × 47%).

5.3.2 Employee contributions

Another way that the fringe benefits taxable value can be reduced is for the employee that has received the fringe benefit to reimburse the employer for the amount of the benefit. This is what the FBT legislation refers to as an **employee contribution**.

For the employee contribution to reduce the taxable value of the fringe benefit, it must be an after-tax contribution. Hence, a pre-tax salary sacrifice employee contribution does not constitute a valid employee contribution and, therefore, cannot reduce the taxable value of the fringe benefit.

An employee contribution represents a reimbursement by the employee back to their employer in respect of payment of the private expenses made by the employer on behalf of the employee.

The amount of the employee contribution is considered assessable income to the employer. This amount is specifically required to be reported in the employer's income tax return (see extract of the 2021 trust income tax return as follows). Furthermore, an employee is unable to claim a deduction for their contribution in their personal income tax return where the contribution is used to reduce the FBT taxable value (see section 51AF of the ITAA36).

Source: Australian Taxation Office, 'Trust tax return' (Web Page, 2021) https://www.ato.gov.au/uploadedFiles/Content/IND/Down loads/Trust-tax-return-2021.pdf.

Employee contributions

On 7 September 2021, Christian's employer, pays his golf club membership totalling $3400. Christian made an after-tax contribution of $600 to his employer in respect of the payment.

The taxable value of the fringe benefit is calculated as follows.

	$
Payment of golf club membership (100% private)	3 400
Less: Employee contribution	(600)
Taxable value of the fringe benefit	2 800

As the golf club membership fees are a taxable supply and the employer can claim back the GST input tax credit, the relevant gross-up factor is 2.0802 (Type 1).

FBT is payable on the grossed-up taxable amount of $5824.56 (i.e. $2800 × 2.0802). Assuming there are no other fringe benefits, the FBT payable is $2737.54 (i.e. $5824.56 × 47%).

5.4 Categories of fringe benefits

LEARNING OBJECTIVE 5.4 Describe the common types of fringe benefits and calculate the related FBT liabilities.

There are several categories of fringe benefits, each having its own specific rules for calculating the taxable value. The various categories of benefits are shown in figure 5.5.

FIGURE 5.5 Categories of fringe benefits

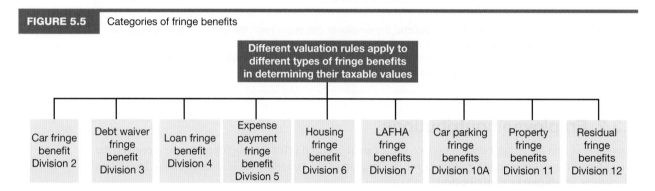

These fringe benefit categories are mirrored in Item 23 of the FBT return (see figure 5.6).

FIGURE 5.6 Extract of Item 23 of the 2022 FBT return

23 Details of fringe benefits provided

Type of benefits provided (1 April 2021 to 31 March 2022)		Number	WHOLE DOLLARS ONLY			
			Gross taxable value (a)	Employee contribution (b)	Value of reductions (c)	Taxable value of benefits (a) − (b) − (c)
Cars using the statutory formula	A					
Cars using the operating cost method	B					
Loans granted	C					
Debt waiver	D					
Expense payments	E					
Housing – units of accommodation provided	F					
Employees receiving living-away-from-home allowance (show total paid including exempt components)	G					
Board	J					
Property	K					
Income tax exempt body – entertainment	L					
Other benefits (residual)	M					
Car parking	N					
Meal entertainment	P					

Source: Australian Taxation Office, 'Fringe benefits tax (FBT) return' (Web Page, 2022) https://www.ato.gov.au/uploadedFiles/Content/SPR/downloads/FBT_return_form_2022_n1067.pdf.

These specific rules are contained in the mentioned FBTAA86 provisions and are discussed and illustrated with examples in this section.

5.4.1 Car fringe benefits (Division 2)

Cars are the largest and most popular type of fringe benefits provided by employers to employees in Australia. Car fringe benefits are covered in Division 2 (sections 7 to 13) of the FBTAA86.

A **car fringe benefit** arises when three conditions are met:

(a) a car

(b) has been held (acquired) by the employer, and

(c) is used, or has been made available for the employee to use for private purposes.

5.4.1.1 What is a 'car'?

For FBT purposes, a 'car' is not defined in the FBTAA86. Instead, the definition of a 'car' is taken from the definition contained in section 995-1 of the ITAA97.

A **car** is defined as a motor car, station wagon, panel van, utility truck or any other road vehicle (including a four-wheel-drive vehicle) that is designed to carry a load of less than one tonne and fewer than nine passengers.

Motorcycles are specifically excluded from the definition (see Miscellaneous Taxation Ruling MT 2022). However, the provision of a motorcycle to an employee will be regarded as a **residual fringe benefit**.

Furthermore, vehicles designed to carry a load of 1 tonne or more, or greater than 9 passengers, do not come under the car fringe benefit provisions, but may be subject to FBT as a residual fringe benefit (see Miscellaneous Taxation Ruling MT 2034).

5.4.1.2 Car must be held by the employer

To give rise to a car fringe benefit, the car must be 'held' by the employer, or by an associate of the employer. A car is 'held' by the employer if it is owned outright or leased by the employer.

5.4.1.3 Is the car used by the employee for private purposes?

A car fringe benefit subsequently arises where the car is either used for private purposes by the employee or their associate or made available for private use.

If the car is actually used by the employee for private purposes, it is subject to FBT. However, according to section 7(2), a car is also subject to fringe benefits tax if it is 'available for private use'. This means that even if the car is not actually used for private purposes by the employee, it is taken to be available for private use if the car was garaged or kept at or near a place of residence of the employee or their associate at any time on a given day. In this situation, the car was available for private use by the employee who could have used the car for private purposes should they have wished to do so.

In applying these rules, a car is considered to be available for private use if the car is garaged at the employee's residence and they have custody and control of the vehicle (i.e. if they have the keys in their possession).

Once a car fringe benefit arises, there are two methods for calculating the taxable value of a car benefit:

(a) statutory formula method (section 9), and

(b) operating cost method (section 10).

The valuation rules regarding the car fringe benefits are contained in various FBT law provisions, including sections 9, 10, 11 and 12 of the FBTAA86.

An employer has the choice of changing each method each year. Furthermore, an employer may choose the statutory formula for one car and the **operating cost method** for another car. The choice of method must be made by the employer when the FBT return is lodged (section 10(1)). Where no choice is made, the **statutory formula method** is deemed to apply.

In order to minimise the amount of FBT payable, it is generally prudent to calculate the taxable value of the car fringe benefit under both methods and choose the one which results in the lowest taxable value.

5.4.1.4 Statutory formula method

Section 9(1) states that the taxable value of a car fringe benefit under the statutory formula method is worked out by using the following formula:

$$\left(0.2 \times \begin{array}{c} \text{Base value of} \\ \text{the car} \end{array} \times \frac{\begin{array}{c} \text{No. of days during the FBT year on which the car} \\ \text{fringe benefits were provided} \end{array}}{\text{No. of days in the FBT year}} \right) - \begin{array}{c} \text{Amount (if any) of payment} \\ \text{made by the benefit} \\ \text{recipient} \end{array}$$

Section 9(2) provides the interpretations of the components that are contained in the statutory formula. The **base value** of the car is the sum of the following amounts:

- the GST-inclusive cost of the car
- non-business accessories, such as headlight protectors, leather protection, window tinting, customised wheels, seat covers and sunroofs, and
- dealer delivery charges.

However, the following costs are not included, and do not form part of the base value of the car:

- stamp duty,
- registration (regarded as an operating cost), and
- insurance (regarded as an operating cost).

In determining the base value of the car, the depreciation car cost limit of $60 733 for the 2022 FBT year is fully ignored. It does not apply in the case of calculating a car fringe benefit. In other words, the full GST-inclusive cost of the car forms the base value.

Furthermore, where the car has been owned or leased for four full FBT years, the cost of the car for FBT purposes will be reduced to two-thirds of its cost. The one-third reduction applies from the start of the FBT year following the fourth anniversary of the date the car was first owned or leased (see TD 94/28).

Once the base value of the car has been determined, it is multiplied by a single flat rate of 20 per cent (0.2), regardless of the number of kilometres travelled during the relevant FBT year.

The formula also takes into account the number of days that the car fringe benefit was provided. This means the number of days that the car was made available for the private use of the employee during the FBT year. If the car was garaged at the employer's premises or being repaired at a workshop during the FBT year, this reduces the number of days that the car was provided to the employee.

Finally, the taxable value of the car fringe benefit is reduced by the amount of the recipient's payment (i.e. employee contribution). This must be a post-tax contribution, not a salary sacrifice pre-tax contribution.

After calculating the taxable value of the car fringe benefit, this amount will be grossed-up by either 1.8868 (Type 2) or 2.0802 (Type 1). If the car was bought from a GST-registered entity and GST was charged, then assuming that the entity acquiring the car is also registered for the GST and can claim a GST input tax credit back on acquisition, then the relevant gross-up rate is 2.0802 (i.e. Type 1).

On the other hand, if the motor vehicle was acquired as a result of a private sale (i.e. from a non-GST registered entity), then as no GST was charged on the transaction, the entity acquiring the motor vehicle is not able to claim back GST input tax credits. In this case, the relevant gross-up rate is 1.8868 (i.e. Type 2).

Once the fringe benefits taxable amount has been calculated, the amount of FBT payable is simply 47 per cent of the grossed-up amount.

EXAMPLE 5.4

Statutory formula method

Assume that a new car is purchased by a GST-registered employer on 19 September 2021 for $50 000 from a GST-registered car dealer. For the 194 days from 19 September 2021 to 31 March 2022, the car is made available for the private use of an employee.

The employee makes an after-tax cash contribution of $2600 to the employer towards the cost of the car. The fringe benefits taxable value of the car using the statutory formula method is calculated as follows.

$$\text{FBTV} = \left(0.2 \times \$50\,000 \times \frac{194\ \text{days}}{365\ \text{days}} \right) - \$2600 = \$2715$$

As the car was purchased from a GST-registered car dealer, the employer is able to claim an input tax credit for the GST paid to acquire the car. Hence, the gross-up factor is 2.0802 (Type 1).

The grossed-up amount is $5647.74 (i.e. $2715 × 2.0802). The FBT payable comes to $2654.44 (i.e. $5467.74 × 47%).

5.4.1.5 Operating cost method

According to section 10, the taxable value of a car fringe benefit under the operating cost method is the sum of all the operating costs of the year relating to the car multiplied by the private use percentage. The formula for the operating cost method is:

$$\text{FBTV} = C \times (100\% - \text{BP}) - R$$

In this formula:

C: the total operating costs of the car during the period when the car is provided as a fringe benefit

BP: the percentage of the business use of the car

R: the amount that has been paid by the benefit recipient and not been reimbursed by the employer, which has the same definition as the amount of the recipient's payment as in the statutory formula (i.e. the employee contribution).

There are distinct two steps in determining the taxable value of a car fringe benefit under the operating cost method.

- *Step 1: Determine the operating costs of the car.*

  The first step is to total the operating costs of the car during the FBT year. According to section 10(3), the operating costs of a car include:
  - registration
  - insurance
  - petrol and oil, and
  - repairs and maintenance.

  For FBT purposes, the above operating costs are to be included at their GST-inclusive amounts (where relevant).

  In addition to these operating costs, if the car is owned by the employer, two additional costs need to be calculated and included, namely:
  - depreciation on the GST-inclusive opening written down value of the car (at 25 per cent diminishing value), and
  - imputed (or notional) interest on the GST-inclusive opening written down value of the car (where owned — at 4.52 per cent for the 2022 FBT year).

  However, if the car is leased instead of owned outright, then the amount of the lease payments are included as part of the operating costs of the car, instead of depreciation and imputed interest.

  For the purposes of calculating depreciation and imputed interest on the car, once again, for FBT purposes, the depreciation car cost limit of $60 733 for the 2022 FBT year is ignored. Both of these figures are determined on the full GST-inclusive cost of the car.

- *Step 2: Determine the extent of private use of the car.*

  The second step under the operating cost method is to determine the extent of private use of the car.

  A logbook is required to be maintained for at least 12 consecutive weeks and is valid for 5 years provided there is no change in the pattern of usage. If no logbook is maintained, all travel is considered to be private.

  At the end of the 12-week period, the taxpayer calculates the business use percentage by dividing the total number of business kilometres travelled by the total number of kilometres travelled and multiplying this amount by 100. The private percentage is simply the difference between 100 per cent and the business use percentage. For example, if the business use percentage is 60 per cent, then the private use percentage is 40 per cent.

  To calculate the taxable value of the car fringe benefit using the operating cost method, the total operating costs of the car are multiplied by the private use percentage of the car.

  Finally, the taxable value of a car fringe benefit can also be reduced by the amount of the recipient's payment (i.e. the employee contribution).

  After calculating the taxable value of the car fringe benefit, this amount will be grossed-up by either 1.8868 (Type 2) or 2.0802 (Type 1). As in the case of the statutory formula method, if the car was bought from a GST-registered entity and GST was charged, then assuming that the entity acquiring the car is also registered for the GST and can claim a GST input tax credit back on acquisition, then the relevant gross-up rate is 2.0802 (i.e. Type 1).

  On the other hand, if the motor vehicle was acquired as a result of a private sale (i.e. from a non-GST registered entity), then as no GST was charged on the transaction, the entity acquiring the motor vehicle is not able to claim back GST input tax credits. In this case, the relevant gross-up rate is 1.8868 (i.e. Type 2).

EXAMPLE 5.5

Operating cost method

Assume the same facts as example 5.4. It will be remembered that the car was purchased outright by a GST-registered employer for $50 000 on 19 September 2021 from a GST-registered car dealer.

The operating costs of the vehicle consisted of:

	$
Registration	712
Insurance	994
Petrol and oil	2 780
Repairs and maintenance	242

Assume that the car is made available for the private use by an employee, who takes the company car home every night for the 194-day period from 19 September 2021 to 31 March 2022.

Furthermore, assume that the employee has maintained a 12-week logbook during the 2022 FBT year, which revealed that the car travelled a total of 6600 kilometres, of which 4488 kilometres were work-related.

Lastly, assume that the employee makes an after-tax cash contribution of $2600 to the employer towards the cost of the car.

The fringe benefits taxable value of the car using the operating cost method is calculated as follows.

	$
Registration	712
Insurance	994
Petrol and oil	2 780
Repairs and maintenance	242
Depreciation ($50 000 × 25% DV × 194/365 days)	6 644
Imputed interest ($50 000 × 4.52% × 194/365 days)	1 201
Total operating costs	**12 573**

According to the logbook maintained by the employee during the 2022 FBT year, the business use percentage of the car can be calculated as follows:

$$\frac{4488 \text{ business kilometres}}{6600 \text{ total kilometres}} = 68\%$$

Therefore, the private use percentage is 32 per cent. The taxable value of the car fringe benefit under the operating cost method is calculated as follows:

$$\text{FBTV} = (\$12\,573 \times 32\%) - \$2600 = \$1423$$

As the car was purchased from a GST-registered car dealer, the employer is able to claim an input tax credit for the GST paid to acquire the car. Hence, the gross-up factor is 2.0802 (Type 1).

The grossed-up amount is $2960.12 (i.e. $1423 × 2.0802). The FBT payable comes to $1391.26 (i.e. $2960.12 × 47%).

As the **fringe benefits tax payable** of $1391.26 under the operating cost method is lower than the amount owing under the statutory formula method of $2654.44, the employer should elect to use the operating cost method.

5.4.2 Loan fringe benefits (Division 4)

Loan fringe benefits are covered in Division 4 (sections 16 to 19) of the FBTAA86. According to section 16(1), a **loan fringe benefit** arises where an employer lends money to an employee (or their associate) at an interest rate that is less than the statutory (or benchmark) interest rate for the relevant FBT year published by the ATO.

This is summarised in yellow the following formula.

$$\text{Taxable value of a loan fringe benefit} = \text{The loan principal} \times \left(\begin{array}{c} \text{Statutory} \\ \text{interest rate} \end{array} - \begin{array}{c} \text{Interest rate} \\ \text{offered by} \\ \text{employer} \end{array} \right)$$

A loan fringe benefit exists in any year in which the recipient is under an obligation to repay the whole or any part of the loan. For the year ended 31 March 2022, the **statutory interest rate** for the FBT purposes is 4.52 per cent.

Section 18 provides that the taxable value of a loan fringe benefit is calculated as the difference between the statutory interest rate for the relevant FBT year and the actual interest rate charged to the employee. For example, if the actual interest rate under the loan provided to the employee was 2.00 per cent, then the taxable interest rate of the loan fringe benefit is 2.52 per cent (i.e. 4.52 per cent – 2.00 per cent).

As loans are an input-taxed supply, the gross-up factor to be used on all loan fringe benefits is 1.8868 (Type 2).

EXAMPLE 5.6

Loan fringe benefit

On 27 November 2021, Ashleigh is provided with a loan from her employer totalling $400 000 at an interest rate of 1.00 per cent. Ashleigh uses these funds to assist in purchasing the family home for herself and her family.

Assume that Ashleigh did not make any loan repayments for the 125 days from the date of the loan to 31 March 2022.

The taxable value of the loan fringe benefit is calculated as follows.

	$
Statutory interest ($400 000 × 4.52% × 125/365 days)	6192
Actual interest ($400 000 × 1.00% × 125/365 days)	(1370)
Taxable value of the loan fringe benefit (i.e. $400 000 × 3.52% × 125/365 days)	4822

As interest on a loan is input-taxed and not subject to GST, the relevant gross-up factor is 1.8868 (Type 2). FBT is payable on the grossed-up taxable amount of $9098.15 (i.e. $4822 × 1.8868). FBT payable is $4276.13 (i.e. $9098.15 × 47 per cent).

5.4.3 Reduction in the fringe benefits taxable value

The fringe benefits taxable value is calculated based on the extent of the loan used by the employee for non-income producing (or private) purposes. In other words, if the loan is used for income-producing purposes, then the application of the ODR will apply to reduce the taxable value of the loan fringe benefit such that only the private component of the loan is subject to FBT (section 19(2)).

In order for the employer to benefit from the ODR, the employee must provide the employer with a loan fringe benefits declaration which states that the employee has used the benefit for employment purposes. A declaration is required for each fringe benefit and must be submitted to the employer prior to lodgment of the FBT return.

EXAMPLE 5.7

Reduction in value of loan fringe benefit

On 19 June 2021, Isaac is provided with a loan from his employer totalling $250 000 at an interest rate of 1.50 per cent. Isaac uses $200 000 of these funds to buy shares in ASX-listed companies that pay dividends and used the remaining $50 000 to take himself and his family on a round-the-world cruise.

▶

Assume that Isaac did not make any loan repayments for the 286 days from the date of the loan to 31 March 2022.

As Isaac used $200 000 of the $250 000 loan for income-producing purposes, the application of the ODR means that this component of the loan is not subject to FBT. Only the component of the loan that was used for private purposes (being $50 000) will be subject to FBT.

The taxable value of the loan fringe benefit is calculated as follows.

	$
Statutory interest ($50 000 × 4.52% × 286/365 days)	1 771
Actual interest ($50 000 × 1.50% × 286/365 days)	(588)
Taxable value of the loan fringe benefit (i.e. $50 000 × 3.02% × 286/365 days)	1 183

As interest on a loan is input-taxed and not subject to GST, the relevant gross-up factor is 1.8868 (Type 2). FBT is payable on the grossed-up taxable amount of $2232.08 (i.e. $1183 × 1.8868). FBT payable is $1049.08 (i.e. $2232.08 × 47 per cent).

5.4.4 Expense payment fringe benefits (Division 5)

Expense payment fringe benefits are covered in Division 5 (sections 20 to 24) of the FBTAA86. An **expense payment fringe benefit** arises where:

(a) the employer directly pays the expense to a third party on behalf of the employee, or

(b) the employer reimburses the employee for the expense incurred and paid for by the employee.

Examples of expense payment fringe benefits include payment of:

- home telephone and electricity expenses
- school fees or childcare fees on behalf of the children of employees
- private health insurance premiums, and
- personal holidays.

The taxable value of an expense payment fringe benefit is the GST-inclusive amount of the expenditure paid by the employer.

A cash allowance paid to an employee, such as a travel allowance or a clothing allowance, is not an expense payment fringe benefit. Being a cash allowance, the amount of the allowance will be included in the assessable income of the employee by virtue of section 15-2 of the ITAA97.

The fringe benefit benefits taxable value of an expense payment fringe benefit can be reduced in two ways:

(a) by applying the application of the 'otherwise deductible rule', and/or

(b) if an employee makes an after-tax employee contribution.

An expense payment fringe benefit is grossed up at 1.8868 (Type 1) if the benefit provided to the employee or their associate did not include GST (e.g. payment of an employee's private health insurance premium, or education or childcare fees) or 2.0802 (Type 1) if the benefit provided to the employee or their associate included GST (e.g. payment of home telephone and electricity bills and payment of gym membership fees).

However, once again, in order for the employer to benefit from the ODR, the employee must provide the employer with an expense payment fringe benefit declaration which states that the employee has used the benefit for employment purposes.

EXAMPLE 5.8

Expense payment fringe benefit

On 22 February 2022, Grace's employer pays her home telephone bill of $120. Grace provides the appropriate declaration to her employer confirming that 20 per cent of this amount is work-related (i.e. $24).

The taxable value of the expense payment fringe benefit is calculated as follows.

	$
Payment of the telephone bill	120
Less: Otherwise deductible amount ($120 × 20% work-related)	(24)
Taxable value of the expense payment fringe benefit	96

As the telephone bill is a taxable supply and the employer can claim back the GST input tax credit, the relevant gross-up factor is 2.0802 (Type 1).

FBT is payable on the grossed-up taxable amount of $199.70 (i.e. $96 × 2.0802). Assuming there are no other fringe benefits, the FBT payable is $93.86 (i.e. $199.70 × 47 per cent).

5.4.5 Housing fringe benefits (Division 6)

Housing fringe benefits are covered in Division 6 (sections 25 to 28) of the FBTAA86. A housing fringe benefit arises where an employee or their associate is provided with a right to use a unit of accommodation as the person's usual place of residence. The unit of accommodation is normally owned or leased by the employer.

A unit of accommodation is defined in section 136(1) to include a house, flat or home unit, a caravan, mobile home, an apartment or a room in a hotel, motel, hostel or guesthouse.

The fringe benefits taxable value of a housing fringe benefit depends on whether the housing benefit is provided within or outside of Australia and, in the case of where the housing benefit is provided within Australia, whether it is in a remote or non-remote area.

If the unit of accommodation provided is a hotel, motel, hostel, guesthouse, caravan or mobile home, the taxable value of the housing fringe benefit is the market value of the accommodation, less any consideration paid by the employee. In the case where the unit of accommodation is similar to, or identical to, that provided by paying guests in the ordinary course of business, the taxable value is equal to 75 per cent of the market value of rental of the accommodation, reduced by any consideration paid by the employee.

The market value rental is based on the occupancy rate charged to long-term guests rather than the daily rate charged to casual guests.

If the unit of accommodation provided is a house, the taxable value of the housing fringe benefit is determined by reference to the market value of the unit of accommodation provided.

However, instead of calculating the market value every year, the taxable value for the second and subsequent FBT years can be calculated based on the first year's market rental value and indexing it by a relevant factor.

The indexation factors are published by the ATO annually and vary for different states and territories. The factors for the current and previous FBT year are contained in table 5.2.

TABLE 5.2	Housing indexation factors							
FBT year ending	NSW	VIC	QLD	SA	WA	TAS	NT	ACT
31 March 2022	0.975	1.000	0.998	1.011	0.991	1.043	0.947	1.018
31 March 2021	1.000	1.017	1.002	1.010	0.969	1.056	0.948	1.029

Source: Australian Taxation Office, 'Fringe benefits tax — rates and thresholds' (Web Page, 2022) https://www.ato.gov.au/rates/fbt.

Example 5.9 demonstrates how housing FBT is applied.

If the unit of accommodation is located outside Australia or in an external territory, such as the Australian Antarctic Territory or Christmas Island, the taxable value will be the amount (if any) by which the market value exceeds the rent paid by the employee (section 26(1)(a)).

If this benefit is provided in a remote area, which is not an eligible urban area, this housing benefit will be an exempt benefit from FBT (section 58ZC). This could be viewed as a government incentive to encourage the economic growth in the remote areas.

In the case of commercial accommodation, such as a hotel, motel, hostel, guesthouse, caravan or mobile home, the **Type 1 gross-up rate** of 2.0802 applies as commercial accommodation is generally subject to GST.

Conversely, where the housing benefit comprises residential accommodation such as a house, apartment or flat, then the **Type 2 gross-up rate** of 1.8868 will apply as residential accommodation is input-taxed.

EXAMPLE 5.9

Housing fringe benefit

On 1 April 2020, a company provided its employee Amelia with the use of a two-bedroom apartment in Adelaide. During the FBT year ending on 31 March 2021, the market rental rate for this apartment was appraised to be $450 per week ($23 400, annually). Amelia paid $150 per week ($7800 annual rent payment). The weekly market rental in the FBT year ending on 31 March 2022 increased to $520 ($27 040 annual total rental); however, the company did not increase Amelia's weekly rental contribution of $150 per week.

What is the employer's FBT liability on the accommodation?

For the 2021–22 FBT year, the statutory annual value of this accommodation for Amelia (before her $7800 contribution) could be either:

(a) $27 040, which is the current market value for the 2021–22 FBT year, or

(b) $23 657, which is the market value for the previous 2021–2022 FBT year ($23 400) indexed by the indexation factor of 1.011 for South Australia.

In this case, option (b) should be selected for the calculation of the related FBT for the company as it results in a lower taxable value.

The fringe benefits taxable value of the housing fringe benefit is calculated as follows.

$$\text{Taxable value} = \$23\,657 - \$7800 = \$15\,857$$

As the unit of accommodation is a flat, and constitutes residential accommodation, the relevant gross-up factor is 1.8868 (Type 2). FBT is payable on the grossed-up taxable amount of $29 918.99 (i.e. $15 857 × 1.8868). FBT payable is $14 061.93 (i.e. $29 918.99 × 47%).

5.4.6 Living away from home allowance (LAFHA) fringe benefits (Division 7)

Living-away-from-home allowances (LAFHA) are covered in Division 7 (sections 30 and 31) of the FBTAA86. A **LAFHA fringe benefit** arises where an employer pays a cash allowance to the employee to compensate them for the additional living expenses (including accommodation and food) that the employee incurs while living away from home to perform their employment duties (section 30(1)). This allowance is in the nature of compensation because the employee is unable to claim deductions for these additional living expenses as they are private in nature.

Generally, an employee will be considered to be living away from home where the employee temporarily moves away from their home (i.e. their usual place of residence) in order to take up a residence in a new (but temporary) work location so that they can carry out their work duties. There is an intention that the employee will return to their former location at the end of their temporary appointment.

A LAFHA is not a travel allowance. A travel allowance is usually paid to an employee who is travelling on a short-term basis carrying out their employment-related duties. No change in job location actually occurs.

On 11 August 2021, the Commissioner of Taxation released TR 2021/4 *Income tax and fringe benefits tax: employees: accommodation and food and drink expenses, travel allowances and living-away-from-home allowances*.

The ruling provides guidance as to when an employee can deduct accommodation and food and drink expenses under section 8-1 of the ITAA97 when they are travelling for work as well as the FBT implications where an employee is reimbursed for accommodation and food and drink expenses, or where the employer provides or pays for these expenses. The ruling also provides clarity on the criteria for determining whether an allowance is a travel allowance or a LAFHA.

A LAFHA is not subject to income tax in the employee's hands. However, the employer may be liable to pay FBT on the following components of the allowance:

(a) the accommodation component

(b) the food component, and

(c) the incidentals component.

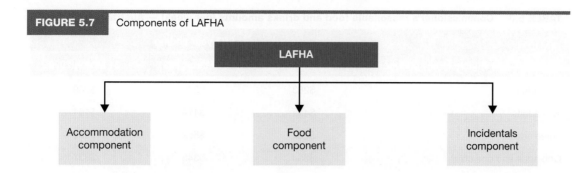

FIGURE 5.7   Components of LAFHA

The taxable value of a LAFHA is generally the full amount of the allowance paid to the employee. However, the taxable value of the accommodation and food components of a LAFHA is able to be reduced if the employee satisfies three conditions (sections 31(1) and 31(2)).

1. The employee must maintain a home in Australia, which means the employee or spouse has an ownership interest in the unit of accommodation that he or she usually resides, and that this accommodation continues to be available to the employee while he or she lives away from it to perform the duties or employment (section 31C). This means that they cannot rent out, sell or surrender the lease on their normal place of residence even whilst living away from home.
2. The concessional FBT treatment will only continue to apply where an employee is living away from home for a maximum period of 12 months at any particular work location (section 31D(1)). Any period in excess of 12 months will not be subject to the concessional treatment for FBT purposes. However, this 12 month-limit is reset if the employee's work location changes.
3. The employee must provide their employer with a living-away-from-home declaration providing details including the address that the employee is residing at whilst living away from home for work and a statement that the employee has satisfied the requirements of maintaining a home in Australia where they usually reside when not working away which is available for their immediate use and enjoyment (section 31F).

5.4.6.1 The accommodation component

The exempt accommodation component is equal to the amount actually incurred and substantiated by the employee by receipts etc. Where the accommodation allowance is greater than the actual accommodation expense, the excess is subject to FBT.

5.4.6.2 The food component

The food component represents the amount that employees would ordinarily spend on food regardless of where they reside. In determining how much of the food component of LAFHA is subject to FBT, it is necessary to determine the following two amounts:
• the statutory food amount, and
• the reasonable food component.

We now discuss each of these two components in turn.

1. *The statutory food amount*
   The 'statutory food amount' is the amount that the employee would normally expend on food and drink if the employee remained at their usual residence instead of living away from home. The statutory food amount is set it $42 per week. This equates to 21 meals per week at $2 per meal (based on a 7-day week). For a child under the age of 12, the statutory food amount is $21.
2. *The reasonable food amount*
   The 'reasonable food component' is so much of the allowance that the Commissioner considers reasonable for a person to spend on food and drink whilst travelling per week. The allowance is based on a 7-day week.
   Each year, the ATO publishes figures setting out the 'reasonable food component' of LAFHA. The amounts for the FBT year ended 31 March 2020 to 31 March 2022 are set out in table 5.3.

TABLE 5.3   Commissioner's reasonable food and drinks amounts (per week) — Australia

Employee and eligible family member	FBT year ending		
	31 March 2022	31 March 2021	31 March 2020
One adult	$283	$276	$269
Two adults	$425	$414	$404
Three adults	$567	$552	$539
One adult and one child	$354	$345	$337
Two adults and one child	$496	$483	$472
Two adults and two children	$567	$552	$540
Two adults and three children	$638	$621	$608
Three adults and one child	$638	$621	$607
Three adults and two children	$709	$690	$675
Four adults	$709	$690	$674
Each additional adult	$142	$138	$135
Each additional child	$71	$69	$68

Source: Australian Taxation Office, 'Fringe benefit tax – rates and thresholds' (Web Page, 2022) https://www.ato.gov.au/rates/fbt.

Where the amount of the food allowance paid to an employee is equal to or less than the reasonable food allowance (as per table 5.3), no substantiation is required.

However, where the amount of the food allowance paid to an employee is more than the reasonable food allowance (as per table 5.3), the employee is required to substantiate all of their food costs, not just the excess over and above the reasonable food component.

5.4.6.3 The incidentals component

In some cases, an employer may also provide an incidentals allowance to the employee to cover incidentals (e.g. telephone calls, lost socks etc.). The entire amount of any incidentals component of LAFHA is subject to FBT.

The fringe benefits taxable value of a LAFHA is grossed-up at the Type 2 rate of 1.8868 as the employer is paying a cash allowance.

Example 5.10 demonstrates the calculation of LAFHA.

EXAMPLE 5.10

Living-away-from-home allowance

On 1 June 2021, Marc, who lives in Perth, is transferred by his employer, Maximus Pty Ltd, to Melbourne. Marc's transfer is for a period of 8 months, after which he intends to return to his home in Perth.

Marc is paid a total LAFHA of $1600 per week for the 32-week period from 1 June 2021 to 11 January 2022. The LAFHA allowance is broken down as follows (per week).

	$
Accommodation component	1 190
Food component (to cover all of his food costs)	400
Incidentals component	10
Total	**1 600**

Marc has kept receipts substantiating the accommodation whilst in Melbourne for the 32-week period. However, unfortunately, Marc did not keep receipts substantiating his food costs whilst away.

The fringe benefits tax implications of each component is determined as follows.

(a) Accommodation component: $1190 per week

The exempt accommodation component is equal to the amount actually incurred and substantiated by the employee. Hence, as Marc has kept receipts to substantiate his accommodation whilst in Melbourne, the entire accommodation component of $1190 per week is exempt from FBT.

(b) Food component: $400 per week

In terms of the food allowance, we are told that Marc was provided with a $400 per week food allowance to cover all of his food costs whilst away.

As this was more than the reasonable food allowance of $283 per week (based on the rate for one adult) for the year ended 31 March 2022, in order for the food allowance to be exempt from FBT, Marc needed to have kept receipts. If he had, then the entire $400 per week food allowance would have been exempt from FBT (apart from the first $42 statutory food amount).

However, we are told that Marc has failed to keep any receipts in respect of his food costs. As such, only part of the $400 food allowance per week will be exempt from FBT.

The first $42 is always taxable. The amount in excess of $283 per week is also subject to FBT. Hence, a further $117 per week will be taxable (i.e. $400 – $283).

Consequently, the taxable value of the LAFHA in respect of the food component will be $159 per week (i.e. $42 + $117).

(c) Incidentals component: $10 per week

There is no FBT exemption for the incidentals component of a LAFHA. Hence, the entire amount of $10 per week is subject to FBT.

The total taxable value of the LAFHA equates to $169 per week, which is comprised of the food component of $159 per week plus the incidentals component of $10 per week.

As Marc was away from home for 32 weeks during the 2022 FBT year, the taxable value of the LAFHA is $5408 (i.e. $169 per week × 32 weeks).

As Maximus Pty Ltd cannot claim back the input tax credits, the relevant gross-up rate is 1.8868. Hence, the taxable value of $5408 will be grossed-up at a rate of 1.8868 (Type 2).

FBT is payable on the grossed-up taxable amount of $10 203.81 (i.e. $5408 × 1.8868). The FBT tax payable is $4795.79 (i.e. $10 203.81 × 47%).

5.4.7 Car parking fringe benefits (Division 10A)

Car parking fringe benefits are covered in Division 10A (sections 39A to 39GH) of the FBTAA86.

A **car parking fringe benefit** arises in relation to each day (including weekends) where the employer provides a car parking space for an employee and all of the following conditions outlined in section 39A are met:

- the car is parked on the business premises, which is either the primary place of the employee's employment or in the vicinity of the primary place of employment, owned or leased by the employer or associate
- a commercial parking station is located within a one kilometre radius of the business premises where the employee's car is parked
- the lowest parking fee charged by any commercial parking station to the public for 'all-day parking' on the first business day of the FBT year (i.e. 1 April) is more than the 'car parking threshold' for that year. For the 2022 FBT year, the car parking threshold is $9.25. In other words, if there are two commercial parking stations located within one kilometre of the business premises, and one charges $9 per day and the other charges $16 per day (as at 1 April 2021), then a car parking fringe benefit arises as there is at least one commercial parking station that charges a fee for all day parking more than the car parking threshold of $9.25 for the 2022 FBT year. The definition of a commercial car parking facility includes shopping centres, hospitals, hotels, airports and sports stadiums (see TR 2021/2 *Car Parking Benefits*). However, on 29 March 2021, the Government announced that it will consult stakeholders with a view of amending the definition of a commercial car parking station to exclude these facilities
- the parking is provided in relation to the employee's employment
- the car is owned by, leased or controlled by the employee or provided by the employer
- the car is parked at, or in the vicinity of, the employee's primary place of employment
- the car is parked for more than four hours between 7:00 am and 7:00 pm on that day. The four hours do not have to be a continuous period, and
- the car is used by the employee to travel between home and work (or vice versa) at least once that day.

If any of these conditions are not satisfied, no car parking fringe benefit arises.

The car parking fringe benefit thresholds that are published by ATO for the past 3 FBT years are contained in table 5.4.

TABLE 5.4 **Car parking thresholds**

FBT year ending	Thresholds
31 March 2022	$9.25
31 March 2021	.$9.15
31 March 2020	$8.95

Source: Australian Taxation Office, 'Fringe benefits tax — rates and thresholds' (Web Page, 2022) https://www.ato.gov.au/rates/fbt.

5.4.7.1 Calculating the taxable value of a car parking fringe benefit

Once a car parking fringe benefit has arisen, there are 5 methods that can be used to calculate the taxable value of a car parking fringe benefit. These methods are:

- commercial parking station method
- market value basis
- average cost method
- statutory formula method
- 12-week register method.
  Each of these methods is discussed as follows.

5.4.7.2 Commercial parking station method (section 39C)

Under this method, the taxable value of a car parking fringe benefit is the lowest fee charged for all-day parking on that day by any commercial parking station within a 1-kilometre radius of the premises on which the car is parked. The taxable value is reduced by any amount paid by the employee.

The commercial parking station method is demonstrated in example 5.11.

EXAMPLE 5.11

Commercial parking station method

Lin is a full-time employee of Ariadne Pty Ltd. She drives her car to work each day and is allowed to park her car in the basement of the company's building. She is required to pay her employer $3 per day.

There are two commercial parking stations within a one kilometre radius of the employer's premises. One charges $14 per day, whilst the other charges $16 per day. During the 2022 FBT year, Lin worked 208 days.

What is the value of this car parking fringe benefit using the commercial parking station method?

In this case, a car parking fringe benefit arises as all the conditions described are satisfied. There is at least one commercial parking station within a one kilometre radius of the employer's business premises that charges more than the car parking threshold for the 2022 FBT year of $9.25 per day.

However, the company can choose to value the car parking fringe benefit using the lowest commercial parking station charge (being $14 per day). Hence, the taxable value of each car parking fringe benefit will be $14.

The taxable value of the car parking fringe benefit is calculated as follows.

$$TV = (\$14 - \$3 \text{ per day}) \times 208 \text{ days worked}$$
$$TV = \$2288$$

As the provision of car parking is a taxable supply and the employer can claim back the GST input tax credit, the relevant gross-up factor is 2.0802 (Type 1).

FBT is payable on the grossed-up taxable amount of $4759.50 (i.e. $2288 × 2.0802). Assuming there are no other fringe benefits, the FBT payable is $2236.97 (i.e. $4759.50 × 47 per cent).

5.4.7.3 Market value basis (section 39D)

Under this method, the taxable value of the benefit is the amount that the employee could reasonably be expected to pay the employer for the car parking. This market value is determined by a suitably qualified independent valuer who must provide a valuation report to the employer before the valuation date. Once again, the taxable value is reduced by any employee contribution. The market value basis method is demonstrated in example 5.12.

EXAMPLE 5.12

Market value method

Refer to the facts of example 5.11. This time, assume that Ariadne Ltd engaged an independent valuer to value the car parking fringe benefit provided to their employee, Lin. According to the valuer's report, the market value of this car parking spot was determined to be $12 per day for all-day parking during the FBT year ending on 31 March 2022.

What is the value of this car parking fringe benefit using the market value method?

If the company elects to use the market value basis, the calculation is as follows.

$$TV = (\$12 - \$3 \text{ per day}) \times 208 \text{ days worked}$$
$$TV = \$1872$$

As the provision of car parking is a taxable supply and the employer can claim back the GST input tax credit, the relevant gross-up factor is 2.0802 (Type 1).

FBT is payable on the grossed-up taxable amount of $3894.13 (i.e. $1872 × 2.0802). Assuming there are no other fringe benefits, the FBT payable is $1830.24 (i.e. $3894.13 × 47%).

5.4.7.4 Average cost method (section 39DA)

Under the average cost method, the taxable value of a car parking fringe benefit is calculated by reference to an average of the lowest fees charged by a commercial operation within a 1-kilometre radius of the employer on the first and last day of the FBT year on which a benefit was provided. If the employer elects to use this method, the fees chosen by the employer in calculating the taxable value of the fringe benefit must be representative.

Once again, the taxable value is reduced by the amount of the employee's contribution, if any, towards the benefit.

The average cost method is demonstrated in example 5.13.

EXAMPLE 5.13

Average cost method

Refer to the facts of example 5.11. This time, assume that the lowest fee charged by the commercial car park that is located within 1 kilometre of Ariadne Ltd's premises was $13 on 1 April 2021 and $17 on 31 March 2022.

What is the value of this car parking fringe benefit using the average cost method?

If the company elects to use the average cost method, the calculation is as follows.

$$TV = ((\$13 + \$17)/2 - \$3 \text{ per day}) \times 208 \text{ days worked}$$
$$TV = \$2496$$

As the provision of car parking is a taxable supply and the employer can claim back the GST input tax credit, the relevant gross-up factor is 2.0802 (Type 1).

FBT is payable on the grossed-up taxable amount of $5192.18 (i.e. $2496 × 2.0802). Assuming there are no other fringe benefits, the FBT payable is $2440.32 (i.e. $5192.18 × 47%).

5.4.7.5 Statutory formula method (section 39F)

Under the statutory formula method, the taxable value of the car parking fringe benefits is calculated by referring to the number of car parking spaces available to employees; thus, it is also called 'the spaces method'.

Under this method, it is assumed that there are 228 car parking fringe benefits arising from each car parking space during the course of the FBT year. This is reduced proportionately if the number of employees is less than the number of car parks.

The calculation of the taxable value under the statutory formula differs under two situations:

1. when the number of parking spaces available to employees is *less* than the number of employees
2. when the number of parking spaces available to employees is *greater* than the number of employees.

Under the first situation, the taxable value of the benefit is worked out following a three-stage procedure that involves a statutory formula (section 39FA(4)) as follows.

- *Stage 1:* work out an amount using the statutory formula for each parking space on which at least one car parking benefit is provided to an employee.

$$\text{Daily rate amount} \times \text{Number of days in availability periods in relation to the space} \times 228 \times 366$$

Note that 366 days is always used as the denominator every year (even where the FBT year is not a leap year) as per section 39GB of the FBTAA86.

In this formula, 'daily rate amount' for each parking space is the taxable value of the car parking fringe benefit worked out using one of the three methods (the commercial parking station method; the market value method; or the average cost method (section 39FC), and the employee's contribution is not included in the daily rate amount. The availability period is the period during the FBT year in which each parking space is provided to an employee as the fringe benefit (section 39FD).

- *Stage 2:* work out the total statutory benefit amount by summing the amounts calculated from step 1 for all parking spaces that are provided to employees as the car parking fringe benefits.
- *Stage 3:* deduct any contributions paid by the employees from the total statutory benefit amount calculated from step 2.

The statutory formula method is demonstrated in example 5.14.

EXAMPLE 5.14

Statutory formula method

Zeus Ltd employs 60 employees. The company has 45 car parking spaces on the company's business premises, which were provided to employees for the 216 workdays during the 2022 FBT year.

Using the market value method, the daily rate of each car parking space has been determined to be $13. Zeus Ltd requires each employee to contribute $2 per day for each car parking space used.

What is the value of this car parking fringe benefit using the statutory formula method?

It will be observed that the number of car parking spaces (being 45) is less than the number of employees (being 60). In this instance, if the company elects to use the statutory formula method, the fringe benefits taxable value is calculated as follows.

$$TV = \$A \times B / 366 \times 228$$

where:

A = $13 (being the daily rate)
B = 216 days

Therefore, the fringe benefits taxable value is:

$$TV = \$13 \times 216\,\text{days} / 366\,\text{days} \times 228 = \$1749$$

As 45 car parking benefits have been provided, the total taxable value is:

$$TV = \$1749 \times 45\,\text{spaces} = \$78\,705$$

Finally, the employee contribution is then applied to reduce the fringe benefits taxable value as follows.

$$TV = \$78\,705 - (2\,\text{per day} \times 216\,\text{days} \times 45\,\text{car parking spaces})$$
$$TV = \$78\,705 - \$19\,440$$
$$TV = \$59\,265$$

As the provision of car parking is a taxable supply and the employer can claim back the GST input tax credit, the relevant gross-up factor is 2.0802 (Type 1).

FBT is payable on the grossed-up taxable amount of $123 283.05 (i.e. $59 265 × 2.0802). Assuming there are no other fringe benefits, the FBT payable is $57 943.03 (i.e. $123 283.05 × 47%).

Under the second situation when the number of parking spaces available to employees is greater than the number of employees, it is reasonable to assume that not all parking spaces are provided as the car parking fringe benefit to the employees. Therefore, the total statutory benefit amount that is calculated in stage 2 of section 39FA(4) will be reduced (section 39FB). The reduction is worked out in the following way (section 39FB(2)).

$$\text{Total statutory benefit amount} \times \frac{\text{Average number of employees}}{\text{Average number of eligible parking spaces}}$$

In this formula, the average number of employees is worked out as (section 39FB(3)):

$$\frac{\text{Number of employees covered by the election at the beginning of the parking period} + \text{Number of employees covered by the election at the end of the parking period}}{2}$$

The average number of eligible parking spaces is worked out as (section 39FB(4)):

$$\frac{\text{Number of eligible spaces at the beginning of the parking period} + \text{Number of eligible spaces at the end of the parking period}}{2}$$

The parking period is the availability period as defined in stage 1 of section 39FA(4). To be able to elect to use this method under this situation, the number of employees and the number of spaces must be representative as a measure of anti-tax avoidance (section 39FB(6)).

5.4.7.6 12-week register method (section 39G)

Under this method, the number of car parking fringe benefits is calculated for a continuous 12-week period (section 39GE(1)). This 12-week period is then used to calculate the number of car parking benefits provided for the full FBT year. The 12-week period selected and contained in the register must be representative (section 39GE(2)).

The details that must be included in the register include the date on which each car was parked, whether the car was parked for more than 4 hours, whether the car was used for travel between the employee's place of residence and the primary place of employment, and the place where the car was parked (section 39GG(1)). The employer must also specify whether this method covers all the employees, or a class of employees, or particular employees (section 39GA(2)).

Under the 12-week register method, the total taxable value of the car parking fringe benefits is worked out using the following formula (section 39GB).

$$\left[\begin{array}{c}\text{Total value of car}\\\text{parking benefits} \times \dfrac{52}{12}\\\text{(register)}\end{array}\right] \times \frac{\text{Number of days in car parking availability periods}}{366}$$

Note that 366 days is always used as the denominator every year (even where the FBT year is not a leap year) as per section 39GB of the FBTAA86.

In this formula, the *total value of car parking benefits (register)* is calculated by using one of the three methods outlined — the commercial parking station method, the market value method or the average cost method (section 39GC). The 12-week register method is demonstrated in example 5.15.

EXAMPLE 5.15

12-week register method

Instant Copy Pty Ltd provided car parking fringe benefits to its employees for the 244 workdays during the 2022 FBT year.

The company elected to use the 12-week register method, which showed a total value of car parking benefits of $26 400, which was worked out using the average cost method after deducting the employee contributions.

What is the value of this car parking fringe benefit using the 12-week register method?

Step 1: The taxable value of the car parking fringe benefit is calculated as follows:

$$\left[\begin{array}{c}\text{Total value of car}\\\text{parking benefits} \times \dfrac{52}{12}\\\text{(register)}\end{array}\right] \times \frac{\text{Number of days in car parking availability periods}}{366}$$

$$\text{TV} = [\$26\,400 \times 52/12] \times 244/366$$
$$\text{TV} = \$76\,267$$

As the provision of car parking is a taxable supply and the employer can claim back the GST input tax credit, the relevant gross-up factor is 2.0802 (Type 1).

FBT is payable on the grossed-up taxable amount of $158 650.61 (i.e. $76 267 × 2.0802). Assuming there are no other fringe benefits, the FBT payable is $74 565.79 (i.e. $158 650.61 × 47%).

5.4.7.7 Exempt car parking fringe benefits

Certain car parking fringe benefits are exempt if they are provided by the following employers:
- scientific institutions (non-profit)
- religious institutions
- charitable institutions
- public educational institutions, and
- government bodies in relation to employees engaged exclusively in or in connection with public educational institutions.

Furthermore, under section 58GA of the FBTAA86, car parking fringe benefits provided by small business employers are exempt if the following conditions are satisfied:
- the car parking is not provided in a commercial car park
- the employer is not a government body or a listed public company (or a subsidiary thereof), and
- the employer's total assessable income for the year ending most recently, before the start of the relevant FBT year, was less than $50 million.

5.4.8 Property fringe benefits (Division 11)

Property fringe benefits are covered in Division 11 (sections 40 to 44) of the FBTAA86. A **property fringe benefit** arises where an employer or their associate provides free or sells discounted property to an employee or their associate (section 40). Property is widely defined in section 136(1) as both tangible and intangible property and includes:
- goods (e.g. computer and furniture)
- real property (e.g. land and buildings), and
- rights to property (e.g. shares, bonds and other securities).

If the benefits are provided to the employee on a working day and on the employer's business premises, this benefit will be exempt because the property is provided to the employee for business purposes (section 41(1)). This exemption does not apply to food or drink provided to the employee under a salary packaging arrangement (section 41(2)).

The taxable value of a property fringe benefit is dependent upon whether the property benefit is an in-house or external property fringe benefit.

5.4.8.1 In-house property fringe benefits

An **in-house property fringe benefit** arises when the benefits provided are similar to those goods normally provided and sold by the employer to customers in the ordinary course of their business. The calculation of the taxable value of different types of in-house property fringe benefits is summarised in table 5.5.

TABLE 5.5   Taxable values of various in-house property fringe benefits

In-house property fringe benefits	Taxable value of the property fringe benefits is	FBTAA86 section
The property was acquired/purchased by the employer who is a retailer	The cost price of the goods less any employee contribution	s 42(1)(b)
The property is manufactured, produced, processed or treated by the employer who sells these items to other manufacturers, wholesalers or retailers who sell to the public in the ordinary course of business	The lowest selling price at of the property less any employee contribution	s 42(1)(a)(i)
The property is manufactured, produced, processed or treated by the employer who sells these items to directly to the public	75% of the lowest price at which that property was sold to a member of the public less any employee contribution	s 42(1)(a)(ii)

Furthermore, in the case of in-house property fringe benefits, section 62 of the FBTAA86 provides that the first $1000 of aggregate taxable value of in-house property fringe benefits provided by an employer or their associate to each employee or their associate per FBT year is exempt. However, the $1000 in-house exemption does not apply where the goods are provided to an employee through a salary packaging arrangement.

The gross-up rate applicable in determining the FBT payable on an in-house property fringe benefit depends on whether the property was acquired by the employer or manufactured by the employer.

Where the property was purchased by the employer and the employer is registered for GST, the Type 1 gross-up rate of 2.0802 applies. Conversely, where the property was manufactured by the employer, the Type 2 gross-up rate of 1.8868 applies because the employer does not hold a tax invoice for purchasing the goods.

EXAMPLE 5.16

In-house property fringe benefit

Ethan works for Oz Furniture Pty Ltd, a furniture retailer. During the 2022 FBT year, the company gave Ethan a dining room table and four dining room chairs. This was not part of a salary packaging arrangement.

The cost price of these items was $1600. The retail price of the dining room tables and chairs is $2800.

As Oz Furniture Pty Ltd is a retailer and sells items of furniture to the public, the provision of a dining room table and chairs to Ethan constitutes an in-house property fringe benefit. According to section 42(1)(b), the taxable value of the fringe benefit is calculated as the cost of the property to the employer, less any amount paid by the employee.

We are told that Oz Furniture Pty Ltd acquired the dining room table and chairs for $1600. This is the cost price of the items. Ethan did not pay any amount to acquire the furniture. Hence, the taxable value of the in-house fringe benefit is $1600.

As per section 62, the first $1000 of in-house property fringe benefits per employee is exempt. Hence, the taxable value is reduced from $1600 to $600.

As Oz Furniture Pty Ltd acquired the dining room table and chairs, this constitutes a taxable supply and the employer can claim back the GST input tax credit, the relevant gross-up factor is 2.0802 (Type 1).

FBT is payable on the grossed-up taxable amount of $1248.12 (i.e. $600 × 2.0802). Assuming there are no other fringe benefits, the FBT payable is $586.62 (i.e. $1248.12 × 47%).

5.4.8.2 External property fringe benefits

An **external property fringe benefit** is one which is not considered to be an in-house benefit. The taxable value of an external property fringe benefit arises when the property is sold by the employer, or their associate, to the employee or their associate below cost price or where the item of property is given away to the employee.

The calculation of the taxable value of external property fringe benefits is summarised in table 5.6.

TABLE 5.6   **Taxable values of external property fringe benefits**

External property fringe benefits	Taxable value of the property fringe benefits is	FBTAA86 section
The property was acquired/ purchased by the employer	The cost price of the goods less any employee contribution	s 43(1)(a)

The $1000 reduction in the taxable value per employee does not apply in the case of external property fringe benefits.

Once again, the taxable value of an external property fringe benefit is reduced where the employee or their associate makes a contribution towards the benefit (section 42(1)).

EXAMPLE 5.17

External property fringe benefit

Assume the same facts as in example 5.16. However, this time, assume that Oz Furniture Pty Ltd bought and gave Ethan a jet ski. This was not part of a salary packaging arrangement. The company does not sell jet skis to the public in the ordinary course of its business.

The company was able to buy the jet ski for $2500 from one it its suppliers. The retail price of the jet ski at jet ski retailers at is $3400.

▶

The jet ski is an external property fringe benefit as this item is not sold in the ordinary course of Oz Furniture Pty Ltd's business. According to section 43, the taxable value of an external property fringe benefit is the cost of the property to the employer, less any amount paid by the employee.

Hence, the taxable value of the jet ski is $2500, which is the cost of the jet ski to Oz Furniture Pty Ltd. There is no $1000 reduction, as this only applies to in-house property fringe benefits.

As Oz Furniture Pty Ltd acquired the jet ski, this constitutes a taxable supply and the employer can claim back the GST input tax credit, the relevant gross-up factor is 2.0802 (Type 1).

FBT is payable on the grossed-up taxable amount of $5200.50 (i.e. $2500 × 2.0802). Assuming there are no other fringe benefits, the FBT payable is $2444.24 (i.e. $5200.50 × 47%).

5.4.9 Residual fringe benefits (Division 12)

Residual fringe benefits are covered in Division 12 (sections 45 to 52) of the FBTAA86. According to section 45, a residual fringe benefit is a benefit provided by an employer to an employee which does not fall within any of the other twelve categories of benefit within the FBTAA86 and includes any right, privilege, service or facility provided in respect of employment.

Essentially, a residual fringe benefit is a 'catch-all' provision. Common examples of residual fringe benefits include:

- the provision of services (e.g. provision of investment advice or legal advice or dry cleaning of employee's clothing)
- the use of an employer's property (e.g. use of an employer's equipment at home), and
- the provision of a vehicle owned or held by the employer that does not qualify as a car (e.g. a motorcycle or truck) to an employee who uses the vehicle for work purposes.

The taxable value of a residual fringe benefit is dependent upon whether the benefit is an external or in-house residual fringe benefit.

(a) *In-house residual fringe benefits*

In-house residual fringe benefits are those where the services provided by the employer to the employee are of a kind that the employer sells or provides to the customers in the ordinary course of business.

The taxable value of an in-house residual fringe benefit is calculated as 75 per cent of the lowest selling price charged to the public for the same type of services under an arm's length transaction, less any amount, if any, paid by the employee or their associate.

Furthermore, in the case of in-house residual fringe benefits, section 62 provides that the first $1000 of the aggregate taxable value of 'in-house' residual fringe benefits provided by an employer to each employee per FBT year is exempt from FBT.

The gross-up rate applicable in determining the FBT payable on an in-house residual fringe benefit depends on whether the item in question was acquired by the employer or provided as a service as part of their business.

Where an employer provides an in-house residual fringe benefit (e.g. discounted professional advice by a law firm to an employee), the benefit will always be treated as a Type 2 benefit, and, therefore, grossed-up at a rate of 1.8868.

(b) *External residual fringe benefits*

External residual fringe benefits are those where the services provided by the employer to the employee are not ordinarily provided to the general public in the ordinary course of the employer's business.

The taxable value of an external residual fringe benefit is the amount of expenditure incurred by the employer less any employee contribution. The $1000 reduction in the taxable value per employee does not apply in the case of external residual fringe benefits.

5.5 Exempt fringe benefits

LEARNING OBJECTIVE 5.5 Describe and apply common fringe benefits tax exemptions.

Exempt fringe benefits are covered in Division 13 of the FBTAA86 (sections 53 to 58ZE). Section 58, in particular, outlines a number of exemptions which apply where a benefit is provided to the employee or their associate. Some of the more common exemptions are shown in table 5.7.

TABLE 5.7 Common FBT exemptions under section 58

Section	Exemption
58A	Car, expense payment, property or residual benefits provided in respect of employment interviews or selection tests.
58B-58F	Exempt relocation expenses which include: • removal and storage of household effects • incidental costs on the sale and/or purchase of a home • costs of connecting or reconnecting gas, electricity and telephone at a new home • the transport costs associated with relocating • temporary accommodation and meals.
58G	Some motor vehicle parking benefits provided by or in connection with scientific, religious, charitable and public educational institutions.
58H	The provision of newspapers and periodicals used for business purposes.
58J	Benefits provided because an employee has suffered a compensable work-related trauma.
58K	The provision of in-house health care facilities for employees.
58L	The benefit relates to travel to obtain medical treatment where the employment is in a foreign country.
58LA	The benefit relates to travel on the compassionate grounds of the death or illness of a close family member.
58M	The benefit consists of work-related medical examinations, medical screening, preventative health-care, counselling or migrant language training.
58N	The provision of emergency assistance for health care expenses.
58P	The provision of infrequent and irregular minor benefits with a taxable value of less than $300 (GST-inclusive).
58Q	The provision of long service leave awards granted in recognition of at least15 years service up to $1000 (GST-inclusive). For each year, the amount increases by $100 per year.
58R	The provision of safety awards whose value does not exceed $200 per annum.
58S	Some benefits provided to trainees engaged under the Australian Traineeship system.
58T	Live-in domestic workers employed by religious institutions.
58U	Live-in help for elderly and disadvantaged persons.
58V	Food and drink for non-live in domestic employees.
58W	Deposits under the *Small Superannuation Accounts Act* (Cth) (1995).
58X	Eligible work-related items provided to employees, that are used primarily for use in the employee's employment purchased. The FBT exemption is limited to one item of each type per employee per FBT year unless it is a replacement item. The list of FBT-exempt work-related items include: • a portable electronic device (including mobile phones, electronic diaries or personal digital assistants, laptop computers, portable printers designed for use with laptop computers and other electronic portable devices • an item of computer software • an item of protective clothing • a briefcase, and • a tool of trade (including a calculator).
58Y	Exempt fees and subscriptions paid by an employer for an employee's: • subscription to a trade or professional journal • membership for a corporate credit card, or • membership fees for an airport lounge subscription (e.g. Qantas Club membership).
58Z	The provision of a single taxi or ride-source sharing ride trip (including an Uber, Ola or Didi) for an employee starting or ending at the employee's place of work or for sick employees for travel home or to any other place to which it is necessary or appropriate for the employee to go as a result of illness or injury (e.g. to a doctor or a relative).

In the Federal Budget handed down on Tuesday 29 March 2022, the Federal Government announced that the costs of taking a COVID-19 test to attend a place of work would be tax deductible for individuals and exempt from fringe benefits tax from 1 July 2021.

5.6 Reportable fringe benefits and salary packaging

LEARNING OBJECTIVE 5.6 Describe the concept of reportable fringe benefit and salary packaging.

5.6.1 Reportable fringe benefits

Employers are required to include the reportable fringe benefits amount on each employee's Income Statement (formerly known as a PAYG payment summary) where the total GST-inclusive taxable value is more than $2000 per employee (section 135P).

No amount needs be reported on the employee's Income Statement where the total taxable value of fringe benefits provided to the employee during the relevant FBT year is $2000 or less.

The amount to be reported on the employee's 2022 Income Statement is in respect of the FBT year (i.e. 1 April 2021 to 31 March 2022).

The relevant extract from the employee's income statement showing the reportable fringe benefits amount is shown in figure 5.8.

| FIGURE 5.8 | Extract from the employee's income statement showing the reportable fringe benefits amount |

Australian Government
Australian Taxation Office

Name
TFN

Other amounts

Reportable employer super contributions
Community Development Employment projects payments
Reportable fringe benefits — total

Source: Adapted from Australian Taxation Office, 'myGov' (Web Page) https://www.ato.gov.au/general/online-services/in-detail/mygov/ato-and-the-mygov-inbox.

Where the fringe benefits taxable value exceeds $2000, the amount that must be included on the employee's Income Statement (and therefore, included in their individual tax return) is the fringe benefits taxable value grossed up at the rate of 1.8868 irrespective of whether a Type 1 or Type 2 fringe benefit has been provided to the employee or their associate.

The reportable fringe benefits amount is calculated as the fringe benefits taxable value multiplied by the 1.8868 gross-up rate irrespective of whether a Type 1 or Type 2 fringe benefit has been provided to the employee or their associate.

While these benefits are required to be shown on each employee's Income Statement, they are not subject to income tax in the employee's hands. Instead, the reportable fringe benefits amount is added to the employee's taxable income in order to determine the taxpayer's liability to surcharges and availability of offsets such as:

- the Medicare levy surcharge
- determining entitlement to the private health insurance tax offset
- determining whether the taxpayer is liable for Division 293 tax for superannuation contributions
- determining the taxpayer's eligibility for the government co-contribution for personal superannuation co-contributions made
- determining the taxpayer's eligibility for the low-income super tax offset for concessional (before tax) superannuation contributions paid into the employee's superannuation fund
- determining whether the taxpayer can offset their business loss against other income (non-commercial losses)
- working out whether the taxpayer is entitled to reduce their employee share scheme discount
- working out the amount the taxpayer must repay against their Higher Education Loan Program (HELP), Student Financial Supplement Scheme (SFSS), Student Start-up Loan (SSL), ABSTUDY Student Start-up Loan (ABSTUDY SSL) or Trade Support Loan (TSL) debt

- determining the taxpayer's entitlement to a range of tax offsets such as the dependant invalid and carer tax offset, zone or overseas forces tax offset, the seniors and pensioners tax offset and the tax offset for superannuation co-contributions made on behalf of a spouse
- determining the taxpayer's eligibility for family assistance payments (Family Tax Benefit Part A and Part B), Child Care Subsidy, Parental Leave Pay, and Dad and Partner Pay), and
- working out the taxpayer's child support obligations.

Exempt fringe benefits are not reported on an employee's Income Statement. As exempt fringe benefits have no taxable value, they do not form part of the reportable fringe benefits arrangements.

EXAMPLE 5.18

Reportable fringe benefits amount

Abracadabra Pty Ltd provides one its employees, Steve, with three individual fringe benefits during the 2022 FBT year.

	$
Payment of private health insurance premium	2 720
Provision of an Apple iPad used exclusively for work-purposes	890
Payment of Netflix subscription	510
Total	**4 120**

The provision of the Apple iPad used exclusively for work purposes is an exempt fringe benefit under section 58X(2). Being an exempt fringe benefit, this is not taken into account in calculating Steve's reportable fringe benefit amount.

The total taxable value of the remaining two fringe benefits comes to $3230 (being $2770 + $510). As this amount exceeds $2000, a reportable fringe benefits amount needs to be shown on Steve's 2022 Income Statement.

The reportable fringe benefits amount to be included on Steve's 2022 Income Statement is $6094 (i.e. $3230 × 1.8868). This amount is required to be included in Steve's individual tax return even though he does not pay tax on this amount.

5.6.2 Salary packaging (or salary sacrificing)

Despite the introduction of the FBT legislation in 1986, employees often will still prefer to take a fringe benefit rather than taking a cash salary. This is called 'salary packaging' or 'salary sacrificing'.

The terms 'salary packaging' or 'salary sacrificing' mean where an employer and employee enter into an arrangement whereby the employee agrees to forgo (or sacrifice) part of their gross salary or wage in the form of non-cash or fringe benefits. Importantly, to be an 'effective' salary sacrificing arrangement, this arrangement must be entered into before the employee has performed their employment services (see TR 2001/10).

The purpose of a salary packaging arrangement is to enable the employee to have certain benefits paid from their pre-tax salary, rather than from post-tax dollars. This can then improve the after-tax cash in hand position for the employee.

However, the employer is now liable to pay fringe benefits tax on the provision of these benefits. Whilst the employer is liable for (and pays the FBT owing), in most cases, the employer will pass this cost onto the employee as a reduction from the employee's pre-tax salary.

Thus, the employer should be in the same net after-tax position as they would have been if a cash salary been paid.

To achieve the maximum benefit from salary sacrificing, employees should consider packaging benefits in the following order:

(a) superannuation. This is because superannuation is not subject to FBT and is generally fully tax-deductible
(b) benefits which are exempt from FBT, such as laptop computers

(c) benefits with no taxable value, such as where the taxable value of a benefit is reduced to $nil by virtue of employee contributions or application of the 'otherwise deductible rule'

(d) concessionally taxed fringe benefits, such as cars whose taxable value may be calculated under the statutory formula method, thereby giving a lower fringe benefits taxable value, and

(e) benefits which are fully taxable (i.e. payment of an employee's private health insurance, childcare fees etc.).

There can be considerable benefits to both the employer and employee in salary packaging.

From the employer's perspective, the salary package does not cost any more than just providing the salary and the compulsory superannuation. By allowing staff to salary package, the employer can attract new and continue to retain staff by offering a range of salary packaging items.

From the employee's perspective, the major benefit of salary packaging is that the employee can receive more after-tax disposable income. Due to a lower cash salary, the employee may be pushed into a lower tax bracket, meaning they pay less tax on their cash salary. Furthermore, the employee also benefits from having the benefit paid for from pre-tax dollars, instead of post-tax dollars, thereby saving tax.

5.7 FBT administration

LEARNING OBJECTIVE 5.7 Describe the range of FBT administration matters.

The FBT year starts on 1 April and ends on 31 March of the following year. The FBT is based on a system of self-assessment, and the employer must prepare and lodge an annual FBT return either by 21 May or by 25 June if the FBT return is lodged electronically by a registered tax agent.

When the FBT return is lodged manually, payment of any FBT owing is due no later than 21 May. However, if it is lodged electronically by a registered tax agent, payment is due by 28 May.

An FBT return is not required to be lodged if an employer's fringe benefits taxable amount for the FBT year is $Nil. However, if the employer is registered for FBT purposes, but is not required to lodge an FBT return, the employer should complete a 'Notice of Non-Lodgement Fringe Benefits Tax Return' and lodge it with the ATO.

Where the FBT liability is less than $3000, the tax is paid when the FBT return is lodged (section 111 FBTAA86). Conversely, where the FBT liability is $3000 or more, then the FBT liability is payable in quarterly instalments on the Business Activity Statement.

An employer must keep records to identify and explain all transactions and acts relevant to ascertaining its FBT liability (section 132 of the FBTAA86). This includes receipts, invoices etc. The records must be in English or readily accessible and convertible into English.

Such records must be kept for five years from the date of assessment, or any dispute on the assessment has been finalised.

Failure to do so constitutes an offence under section 132 and may result in the imposition of a penalty of $6660 (being 30 penalty units). One penalty unit is currently the equivalent of $222 (*Crimes Act 1914* (Cth) section 4AA).

ETHICS IN PRACTICE

Private holiday and FBT implications

You are employed as a manager of a chartered accounting firm in Sydney. One of your clients, Simon, is the sole director and sole shareholder of a real estate agency company based in Sydney.

Simon advises you that, in May 2022, the company paid $5000 for him to attend a 'business' trip in Singapore. This comprised return airfares, accommodation, meals, entertainment and various taxi fares.

When you question Simon about the purpose of this trip, he advises that there was no official reason, other than to observe the Singaporean property market and meet up with a few Singaporean real estate agents that he has known from his high school days.

Simon has not kept a travel diary but has provided you with all of his receipts. You instantly observe that Simon has spent a considerable amount on food and drinks at high-end restaurants with his real estate friends. There are also several receipts from golf courses and sightseeing trips.

You express concerns to Simon as to the purpose of the trip, as it appears that the primary purpose of the trip was private/social in nature, with little business conducted. You advise him that, as the purpose of the trip was primarily private in nature, the trip will be considered a fringe benefit and, therefore, subject to fringe benefits tax.

Simon finally confesses to you that the trip was purely social in nature, but states 'The company pays its fair share of tax. After all, how would the ATO know it was primarily social?'

Simon instructs you to claim the entire amount of the trip as a business deduction for the company and avoid the fringe benefits tax issues altogether.

What should you do? What ethical considerations need to be considered?

It is apparent that the trip to Singapore was not a business trip, and instead, was social/private in nature. Hence, no deduction should be claimed for the cost of the airfares, accommodation, meals, entertainment and taxis totalling $5000. Instead, the cost of the trip is subject to fringe benefits tax.

Section 120 of APES 110 *Code of Ethics for Professional Accountants* requires the tax agent to act with objectivity, whilst section 130 also requires the tax advisor to act with professional competence and due care. This means that the tax advisor cannot simply 'turn a blind eye' to the client's request to treat the trip as a business trip as 'the ATO would not know'.

Furthermore, section 4 of APES 220 *Taxation Services* requires members to ensure that they prepare and/or lodge tax returns in accordance with the relevant taxation law. Hence, claiming a deduction for $5000 travel and asserting that it was a business trip, when in reality it was a personal trip, would not only be ethically wrong but would be legally incorrect, as the second negative limb of section 8-1(2) of the ITAA97 states that losses and outgoings of a private or domestic nature are not deductible.

Finally, section 7 of APES 220 requires that members shall not, under any circumstances, become associated with any tax return or submission on behalf of a client if it contains incorrect or misleading information.

For all of these reasons, you should not claim the $5000 as a tax deduction, but instead, advise Simon that unless he reimburses the company for the full cost of the trip, it will be subject to fringe benefits tax. If Simon refuses to do so, then you should refuse to continue to act as his tax agent and resign from the engagement immediately.

SUMMARY

5.1 Describe the operation of the fringe benefit tax regime in Australia.

Fringe benefits tax (FBT) was introduced on 1 July 1986. The relevant legislation is the *Fringe Benefits Tax Assessment Act 1986.*

Essentially, fringe benefits tax is a tax payable by employers on the value of fringe (or non-cash) private benefits provided to their employees or their associates in respect of employment.

The tax is paid by the employer regardless of whether they are individuals, partnerships, companies, trusts, incorporated associations or government departments. The tax is levied at a flat rate of 47 per cent on the 'grossed-up' taxable value of the fringe benefits provided during the FBT year, which runs from 1 April to 31 March (not 1 July to 30 June).

It is important to note that fringe benefits tax is a separate tax from income tax, meaning that FBT is payable by the employer regardless of whether the employer makes a profit or a loss for income tax purposes.

5.2 Apply the three steps for calculating fringe benefits tax liability.

There are three distinct steps in calculating the amount of FBT payable.

The first step involves calculating the GST-inclusive taxable value of the fringe benefits provided to each employee or their associates during the FBT year. This is termed the 'fringe benefits taxable value'. The fringe benefits taxable value is established from a series of specific valuation rules. There are twelve categories of fringe benefits and each has its own specific rules for calculating the taxable value.

The second step involves grossing-up (or multiplying) each of the fringe benefits taxable values by a gross-up factor of either 2.0802 (Type 1) or 1.8868 (Type 2). Type 1 fringe benefits are those benefits where the employer is entitled to an input tax credit in respect of the GST paid on the benefit.

Conversely, Type 2 fringe benefits are those benefits where the employer is not entitled to an input tax credit in respect of any GST paid on the benefit. This 'grossed-up' amount is also known as the 'fringe benefits taxable amount'.

The third, and final step involves multiplying the grossed-up amount by the FBT rate of 47 per cent. The resultant amount is the fringe benefits tax payable.

5.3 Apply the 'otherwise deductible rule' and understand the effect of employee contributions on the calculation of the FBT liability.

Fringe benefits tax applies to fringe (or non-cash) benefits provided by an employer to an employee in respect of employment and more specifically, is principally designed to tax only the 'private' component of each benefit which is provided.

Where an employer provides an employee with a benefit that would be otherwise deductible to the employee, then the fringe benefits taxable value is reduced. This is referred to as the 'otherwise deductible rule'.

The otherwise deductible rule provides that 'if the employee (but not their associate) would have been able to claim a once-only tax deduction for the item in question if they had incurred the expenditure themselves, the item is not subject to fringe benefits tax'. In other words, the otherwise deductible rule does not apply to benefits provided by an employer to an associate the employee.

Where an employee makes an after-tax cash contribution towards a benefit which is subject to FBT, the taxable value of the fringe benefit is reduced accordingly.

In effect, an employee contribution represents a reimbursement by the employee back to their employer in respect of payment of the private expenses made on behalf of the employee.

Furthermore, an employee is unable to claim a deduction for their contribution in their personal income tax return where the contribution is used to reduce the FBT taxable value (see section 51AF of the ITAA36).

5.4 Describe the common types of fringe benefits and calculate the related fringe benefits tax liabilities

There are twelve categories of fringe benefits, each having its own specific rules for calculating the taxable value. The twelve categories of benefits are shown in the following table.

	Fringe benefit category	FBTAA Division
1.	Car fringe benefits	2
2.	Debt waiver fringe benefits	3
3.	Loan fringe benefits	4
4.	Expense payment fringe benefits	5
5.	Housing fringe benefits	6
6.	Living-away-from-home fringe benefits	7
7.	Board fringe benefits	9
8.	Meal entertainment fringe benefits	9A
9.	Tax-exempt body entertainment fringe benefits	10
10.	Car parking fringe benefits	10A
11.	Property fringe benefits	11
12.	Residual fringe benefits	12

5.5 Describe and apply common fringe benefits tax exemptions.

Some fringe benefits are expressly excluded as fringe benefits and do not give rise to any FBT liability. Section 136(1) of the FBTAA86 outlines the major exclusions, being:
- the payment of salary and wages
- cash allowances (except a living-away-from-home allowance)
- cash superannuation contributions on behalf of employees
- payments from superannuation funds
- benefits arising under employee share schemes under Division 83A of the ITAA97
- employment termination payments, and
- a benefit that is specifically made exempt under the FBTAA86. These include portable electronic devices provided to employees for employment purposes, such as mobile phones and laptop computers, minor fringe benefits, airline lounge memberships and taxi and Uber travel to and from the workplace and home.

5.6 Describe the concepts of reportable fringe benefits and salary packaging.

Employers are required to include the reportable fringe benefits amount on each employee's Income Statement where the total GST-inclusive taxable value is more than $2000 per employee (section 135P).

The reportable fringe benefits amount is calculated as the fringe benefits taxable value multiplied by the 1.8868 gross-up rate irrespective of whether a Type 1 or Type 2 fringe benefit has been provided to the employee or their associate.

Whilst the reportable fringe benefits amount is required to be shown on each employee's Income Statement (and therefore, included in their individual tax return), this amount is not subject to income tax in the employee's hands. Instead, the reportable fringe benefits amount is added to the employee's taxable income in order to determine the taxpayer's liability to a range of surcharges.

The terms 'salary packaging' or 'salary sacrificing' mean where an employer and employee enter into an arrangement whereby the employee agrees to forgo (or sacrifice) part of their gross salary or wage in the form of non-cash or fringe benefits. To be an 'effective' salary sacrificing arrangement, this arrangement must be entered into before the employee has performed their employment services.

The purpose of a salary packaging arrangement is to enable the employee to have certain benefits paid from their pre-tax salary, rather than from post-tax dollars. This can then improve the after-tax cash in hand position for the employee. Due to a lower cash salary, the employee may be pushed into a lower tax bracket, meaning they pay less tax on their cash salary.

5.7 Describe the range of FBT administration matters.

The FBT year starts on 1 April and ends on 31 March of the following year. The FBT is based on a system of self-assessment, and the employer must furnish an annual FBT return either by 21 May or by 25 June if the FBT return is lodged electronically by a registered tax agent.

When the FBT return is lodged manually payment of any FBT owing is due no later than 21 May. However, if it is lodged electronically by a registered tax agent, payment is due by 28 May.

Where the FBT liability is less than $3000, the tax is paid when the FBT return is lodged. Conversely, where the FBT liability is $3000 or more, then the FBT liability is payable in quarterly instalments on the Business Activity Statement or Instalment Activity Statement.

KEY TERMS

associate An associate includes people and entities closely associated with the employee, such as relatives, or closely connected companies or trusts.

base value The base value of a car owned is the sum of the original purchase price paid plus the costs of any fitted accessories that are not required for business use of the car, for example, car stereo or air conditioner and dealer delivery charges, excluding registration and stamp duty charges.

car A car is defined as a motor-powered road vehicle, including a motor car, station wagon, panel van, utility truck or any other road vehicle (including a four-wheel drive vehicle), that is designed to carry a load of less than one tonne and fewer than nine passengers.

car fringe benefit Arises when a car that is held by the benefit provider (an employer or associate) is provided for the employee or associate's private use in respect of the employment of the employee.

car parking fringe benefit Car parking provided by the employer when a series of conditions are satisfied.

employee An employee is generally someone who receives, or is entitled to receive, salary and wages in return for work or services provided, or for work under a contract that is wholly or principally for the person's labour. An employee includes company directors, office holders, common law employees and recipients of compensation payments. Includes a current, future and former employee.

employer An employer is defined as a current employer, a future employer or a former employer.

employee contribution This is also known as a recipient's payment. Generally, the payment is an after-tax cash contribution made by the employee to their employer.

expense payment fringe benefit Arises where the employer directly pays the expense to a third party on behalf of the employee or reimburses the employee for the expense incurred and paid for by the employee.

external property fringe benefit Arises where goods are provided to employees that are not normally provided and sold by the employer in the ordinary course of their business

exempt benefits Exempt benefits are those benefits which are specifically made exempt under the FBTAA86. The list of exempt fringe benefits are contained in Division 13 of the FBTAA86.

FBT year The FBT year runs from 1 April to 31 March.

fringe benefit A fringe benefit is defined as any benefit provided at any time during the FBT year by the employer or an associate of the employer to an employee or their associate in respect of the employee's employment.

fringe benefits tax The tax imposed by the FBTAA86 on employers at the rate of 47 per cent of the aggregated fringe benefits taxable amount (or 'grossed-up' amount.)

fringe benefits taxable amount Also known as the 'grossed-up' amount. This amount multiplies taxable amount the fringe benefits taxable value by a gross-up rate of either 2.0802 (Type 1) or 1.8868 (Type 2).

fringe benefits tax payable The amount of FBT owing to the ATO. This amount is calculated at 47 per cent of the fringe benefits taxable amount (or 'grossed-up' amount).

in-house property fringe benefit Arises where goods are provided to an employee where those goods are normally provided and sold by the employer in the ordinary course of their business (i.e. trading stock).

LAFHA fringe benefit Arises where an employer pays a cash allowance to employee to compensate them for the additional non-deductible living expenses, such as accommodation and food suffered because the employee (and/or their family) is required to live away from their normal residence in order to perform their employment duties.

loan fringe benefit Arises where an employer lends money to an employee (or their associate) and the interest rate on the loan is less than the statutory (or benchmark) FBT interest rate for the relevant FBT year. For the year ended 31 March 2022, the statutory interest rate for the FBT purposes is 4.52 per cent.

operating cost method The operating cost method is also known as the log book method. The taxable value of a car fringe benefit under the operating cost method is the sum of all the operating costs of the year relating to the car multiplied by the private percentage.

otherwise deductible rule (ODR) Refers to the situation whereby the taxable value of a fringe benefit may be reduced where the benefit is used for employment-related purposes. This occurs where the employee (but not their associate) would have been able to claim a 'once-only' income tax deduction for the item in question if they had incurred the expenditure themselves.

property fringe benefit Arises where an employer (or their associate) provides free or sells discounted property (i.e. an asset) to an employee or their associate (section 40). Property is defined as both tangible and intangible property and includes goods (e.g. computer and furniture), real property (e.g. land and buildings) and rights to property (e.g. shares, bonds and other securities).

reportable fringe benefits amount The reportable fringe benefits amount is the grossed-up amount of taxable value of fringe benefits provided to the employee and their associates during the relevant FBT year (at 1.8868). The reportable amount must be included on each employee's Income Statement where the total GST-inclusive taxable value of fringe benefits provided to each employee (and the associate) exceeds $2000 per employee.

residual fringe benefit Any fringe benefit that does not fit into one of the other 12 categories of fringe benefits is called a residual benefit.

salary sacrifice arrangement A salary sacrifice arrangement is an arrangement between an employer and an employee, whereby the employee agrees to forgo part of their future entitlement to salary or wages in return for the employer or associate providing them with benefits of a similar value.

statutory formula method The effect of the statutory formula is to value a car fringe benefit by applying a statutory fraction to the base value of the car.

statutory interest rate The statutory interest rate is also known as the benchmark interest rate. This interest rate is published by the Commissioner of Taxation each year and must be used to calculate the taxable value of a fringe benefit provided by way of a loan or a car fringe benefit where an employer chooses to value the benefit using the operating cost method. For the 2022 FBT year, the statutory percentage is 4.52 per cent.

taxable value This is the GST-inclusive value of fringe benefits that are provided to each employee or their associate during the FBT year. There are different rules for calculating the taxable value of the different types of fringe benefits.

Type 1 gross-up rate Type 1 fringe benefits are those benefits where the employer is entitled to an input tax credit in respect of the GST paid on the benefit provided to the employee. Type 1 benefits are grossed up (i.e. multiplied) by a rate of 2.0802.

Type 2 gross-up rate Type 2 fringe benefits are those benefits where the employer is not entitled to an input tax credit in respect of any GST paid on the benefit provided to the employee. Type 2 benefits are grossed up (i.e. multiplied) by a rate of 1.8868.

QUESTIONS

5.1 Discuss how the fringe benefits tax regime operates in Australia.

5.2 Provide some examples of fringe benefits.

5.3 List those benefits that are exempt from FBT.

5.4 What are the three steps in calculating the amount of FBT payable.

5.5 What are the two FBT gross-up rates? Explain how and why each gross-up rate is used. Provide three examples of fringe benefits that are grossed-up by each gross-up rate.

5.6 What are some of the common FBT exemptions under section 58 of the FBTAA86?

5.7 When is an employer required to include an amount in the 'reportable fringe benefits amount' on the employee's annual income statement? Does an employee pay income tax on this amount?

5.8 When is the FBT year-end? When is an employer required to lodge their annual FBT tax return and pay any outstanding FBT owing to the ATO?

5.9 How long are employers required to retain their FBT records for? What penalties apply for those employers that do not keep or maintain appropriate records?

PROBLEMS

5.10 Vulcan Enterprises Pty Ltd provides the following two fringe benefits to one its employees, Melinda, during the course of the 2022 FBT year:

1. Payment of annual gym membership fees totalling $2200 (inclusive of $200 GST).
2. Payment of childcare fees for Melinda's 5-year-old daughter, Charlotte three days per week totalling $8000 (no GST).

Required

(a) Calculate the fringe benefits taxable value of each of the fringe benefits.
(b) Calculate the fringe benefits taxable amount of each benefit (i.e. the 'grossed-up' amount).
(c) Calculate the amount of FBT payable by Vulcan Enterprises Pty Ltd.
(d) How much is tax-deductible to Vulcan Enterprises Pty Ltd?
(e) How much GST input tax credits can be claimed back by Vulcan Enterprises Pty Ltd?

5.11 What is the taxable value for FBT purposes of each of the following payments made by an employer on behalf of an employee?

Transaction	Payment by employer	Tax deduction had employee paid
Work-related conference	$ 700	$ 700
Private health insurance premiums	$2 600	$ Nil
HECS-HELP fees	$4 860	$ Nil
Qantas airport lounge membership	$ 600	$ 600
Body corporate fees for a rental property in the taxpayer's name	$3 180	$3 180

5.12 On 18 August 2021, Icehouse Pty Ltd, a GST-registered company, purchased a new Toyota Camry costing $44 000 (GST-inclusive) from a GST-registered car dealership and immediately provided it for the exclusive use to one of its employees, Jessica.

The $44 000 cost included stamp duty of $1200 (GST-inclusive) and dealer delivery charges of $900 (GST-inclusive).

The car was also garaged each night at Jessica's home during this period.

Jessica kept a logbook for the entire 226-day period from 18 August 2021 to 31 March 2022. The logbook revealed that the vehicle travelled a total of 12 000 km of which 6960 km were business-related.

Jessica made after-tax cash contributions of $380 (GST-inclusive) towards the running costs of the vehicle during this 226-day period.

Motor vehicle costs incurred (and paid for) by Icehouse Pty Ltd for the period 18 August 2021 to 31 March 2022 are as follows.

	$
Registration (GST-free)	680
Insurance (GST-inclusive)	812
Petrol and oil (GST-inclusive)	2 780
Repairs and maintenance (GST-inclusive)	110

Required

(a) Calculate the taxable value of the car fringe benefit using both the statutory formula method and the operating cost method.
(b) Which method should be used assuming that Icehouse Pty Ltd wishes to minimise its FBT liability?
(c) Calculate the amount of fringe benefits tax payable by Icehouse Pty Ltd in respect of the FBT year ended 31 March 2022.

5.13 Elizabeth is an employee of Misty Rain Pty Ltd. On 19 October 2021, Elizabeth is provided with a $800 000 10-year loan by her employer at an annual interest rate of 2.00 per cent p.a.

Katrina uses the $700 000 to acquire a rental property in her own name and the remaining $100 000 to pay off personal credit cards.

Elizabeth did not make any repayments during the 164 days from 19 October 2021 to 31 March 2022.

Required

(a) Calculate the taxable value of the loan fringe benefit.

(b) Calculate the amount of fringe benefits tax payable by Misty Rain Pty Ltd in respect of the FBT year ended 31 March 2022.

5.14 Consider each of the following scenario.

During the 2022 FBT year, *The Mirror*, a newspaper publisher, provided the following benefits to one if its employees, Joshua, a newspaper reporter.

	$
Payment of income protection insurance premiums	2 420
Payment of home electricity bills (20 percent work-related)	1 960
Purchase of a laptop computer exclusively for work purposes	1 850

Required

(a) Calculate the taxable value of each of the fringe benefits.

(b) Calculate the amount of fringe benefits tax payable by The Mirror in respect of the FBT year ended 31 March 2022.

5.15 Consider each of the following scenario.

On 19 February 2022, Gigantor Ltd, a civil engineering company, paid for its CEO, Adrian Gardiner, to attend a 1-week international engineering conference in Berlin. The cost was as follows.

	$
Return airfares from Brisbane to Berlin	3 280
Conference registration fee	1 560
Accommodation and meals (in Berlin)	2 490
One-day Berlin sightseeing trip	340

All amounts shown are expressed in Australian dollars.

Required

(a) Calculate the taxable value of each of the fringe benefits.

(b) Calculate the amount of fringe benefits tax payable by Gigantor Ltd in respect of the FBT year ended 31 March 2022.

5.16 On 1 July 2021, Joanne, who lives in a 3-bedroom house in Brisbane, is transferred by her employer, Ace Jewellery Pty Ltd, to Sydney. Joanne's transfer is for a period of 6 months, after which she intends to return to her home in Brisbane.

Joanne is paid a total LAFHA of $1400 per week for the 26-week period from 1 July 2021 to 30 December 2021.

The LAFHA allowance is broken down as follows (per week).

	$
Accommodation component	1 000
Food component (to cover all of her food costs)	380
Incidentals component	20
Total	**1 400**

Joanne has kept receipts substantiating the accommodation whilst in Sydney for the 26-week period. Unfortunately, Joanne did not keep receipts substantiating her food costs whilst away.

Required

(a) Calculate the taxable value of the LAFHA for the year ended 31 March 2022.

(b) Calculate the FBT payable by Ace Jewellery Pty Ltd in relation to the LAFHA paid to Joanne.

5.17 Styx Pty Ltd employs 30 employees. The company has 20 car parking spaces on the company's business premises, which were provided to employees for the 260 work days during the 2022 FBT year.

Using the market value method, the daily rate of each car parking space has been determined to be $10. Styx Pty Ltd requires each employee to contribute $5 per day for each car parking space used.

Styx Pty Ltd elects to use the statutory formula method in the 2022 FBT year.

Required

(a) Calculate the taxable value of the car parking fringe benefits using the statutory formula method.

(b) Calculate the FBT payable by Ace Jewellery Pty Ltd in relation to the car parking fringe benefits.

5.18 Consider each of the following two independent scenarios.

(a) Fridge World Ltd is a retailer of whitewoods including refrigerators, freezers washing machines, dishwashers and dryers. During the 2022 FBT year, the company allowed each staff member to take $1700 worth of whitewoods for their own personal use. This price represents the actual cost of the items to the retailer. This is the only fringe benefit provided to each staff member during the 2022 FBT year. This was not part of any salary sacrificing arrangement. A total of 20 staff members took clothing from the store for their own personal use.

(b) BBQ's Direct Pty Ltd manufactures BBQs. The company sells BBQs directly to the public through a factory outlet in Newcastle. On 13 February 2022, the company sold one of its deluxe BBQs to an employee, Trevor, for $1200. This particular BBQ normally retails to the public for $5000. The lowest selling price of this particular BBQ sold to the general public during the 2022 FBT year was in the post-Christmas sale, where it was advertised and sold for $4000. This was the only fringe benefit provided to each staff member during the 2022 FBT year. This was not part of a salary sacrificing arrangement.

Required

(a) Calculate the taxable value of each of the property fringe benefits.

(b) Calculate the amount of fringe benefits tax payable by each employer in respect of the FBT year ended 31 March 2022 for each of the fringe benefits.

5.19 Neil Anderson is employed as the CEO of ABC Ltd. He joined the firm on 1 April 2021. He receives a base salary of $120 000 plus the following benefits.

(a) A new Mitsubishi Lancer that was purchased by ABC Ltd on 1 April 2021 from a GST-registered car dealership and immediately provided to Neil. The base value of the car is $52 000 (GST-inclusive). Neil advises you that he did not maintain a logbook during the 2022 FBT year.

(b) As part of his salary package, on 1 April 2021, Neil receives a low interest housing loan of $200 000 at a rate of 1.00 per cent. Neil used this money to buy a house which he uses as his main residence.

(c) The firm paid Neil an entertainment allowance of $5000 to help cover the cost entertainment associated with wining and dining some of their largest clients.

(d) Neil also has his golf membership fees of $3600 (GST-inclusive) paid for by ABC Ltd. This was paid on 10 June 2021.

(e) On 31 December 2021, due to the company recording a record profit, Neil receive a cash bonus of $10 000. The bonus was paid to Neil on 14 January 2022.

Required

(a) Calculate the taxable value of each of the benefits.

(b) Calculate the amount of fringe benefits tax payable by ABC Ltd in respect of the FBT year ended 31 March 2022.

5.20 Summer is employed as a human resource manager with a large law firm, McKenzie Brackman. She receives a base salary of $100 000 plus the following benefits.

		$
(i)	Payment for an Australian holiday	3 400
(ii)	Payment of Qantas Club airport lounge subscription	560
(iii)	Payment of a clothing allowance in compensation for purchasing a company uniform bearing the firm's logo	400
(iv)	Payment of her son Ethan's school fees	6 800

Based on this information, calculate the reportable fringe benefits amount to be recorded on Summer's 2022 Income Statement.

ACKNOWLEDGEMENTS

Figures 5.3, 5.6: © Australian Taxation Office
Figure 5.8: © myGov Australia
Tables 5.2–5.4: © Australian Taxation Office

5.20 Suzanne is employed as a maintenance manager with a large law firm, McKenzie Beckman. She receives a base salary of $100,000 plus the following benefits:

(i)	Personal use of an Australian holiday	$3,000
(ii)	Payment of her children's private school tuition	$8,000
(iii)	Payment of a clothing allowance in remuneration for purchasing a compulsory uniform bearing the firm's logo	$5,000
(iv)	Payment of her golf club subscription fees	$4,000

Based on this information, calculate the reportable fringe benefits amount to be recorded on Suzanne's 2021 Income Statement.

ACKNOWLEDGEMENTS

Figures 5.3, 5.5: © Australian Taxation Office
Figure 5.8: © Andrew Sundholm
Table 5.2, 5.3: © Australian Taxation Office

CHAPTER 6

General deductions

LEARNING OBJECTIVES

After studying this chapter, you should be able to:

6.1 differentiate the general deduction provision from specific deductions and explain the loss or outgoing and apportionment concepts

6.2 apply the two positive limbs of the general deduction provision

6.3 apply the four negative limbs of the general deduction provision

6.4 explain the substantiation requirements in order to claim a deduction.

Overview

The previous chapters have focused mostly on the income component of taxable income. We now move to consider the expenditure component of the equation: general and specific deductions.

Under section 8-1 of the ITAA97, a taxpayer can deduct from their assessable income any loss or outgoing to the extent that it is incurred in gaining or producing assessable income (such as wages and salaries), or necessarily incurred in carrying on a business, for the purpose of gaining or producing the taxpayer's assessable income (such as renting office space).

We will discuss the two 'positive limbs', at least one of which must be met for a loss or outgoing to be deductible under this provision, and the four 'negative limbs' that deny or limit deductibility. This chapter will lead you through key judicial decisions to gain a working understanding of the general deduction provision and conclude with a review of the necessary substantiation requirements.

6.1 Locating the general deduction provision

LEARNING OBJECTIVE 6.1 Differentiate the general deduction provision from specific deductions and explain the loss or outgoing and apportionment concepts.

The basic formula for taxable income is assessable income less allowable deductions.[1] Division 8 of the ITAA97 deals with the tax treatment of the deductions side of the equation. Taxation rests upon a different legislative framework to accounting and thus the accounting concept of expenses cannot necessarily be applied to tax issues. Consequently, a solid understanding of 'deductions' from a taxation viewpoint must be established.

Section 995-1 of the ITAA97 defines **deduction** as simply 'an amount that you can deduct' and refers to Division 8 for further explanation, as follows.

8-1 General deductions

(1) You can *deduct* from your assessable income any loss or outgoing to the extent that:
   (a) it is incurred in gaining or producing your assessable income, or
   (b) it is necessarily incurred in carrying on a business for the purpose of gaining or producing your assessable income.

   Note: Division 35 prevents losses from non-commercial business activities that may contribute to a tax loss being offset against other assessable income.

(2) However, you cannot deduct a loss or outgoing under this section to the extent that:
   (a) it is a loss or outgoing of capital, or of a capital nature, or
   (b) it is a loss or outgoing of a private or domestic nature, or
   (c) it is incurred in relation to gaining or producing your exempt income or your non-assessable non-exempt income, or
   (d) a provision of this Act prevents you from deducting it.

   For a summary list of provisions about deductions, see section 12-5.

(3) A loss or outgoing that you can deduct under this section is called a *general deduction*.

...

8-5 Specific deductions

(1) You can also *deduct* from your assessable income an amount that a provision of this Act (outside this Division) allows you to deduct.
(2) Some provisions of this Act prevent you from deducting an amount that you could otherwise deduct, or limit the amount you can deduct.
(3) An amount that you can deduct under a provision of this Act (outside this Division) is called a *specific deduction*.

...

8-10 No double deductions

If two or more provisions of this Act allow you deductions in respect of the same amount (whether for the same income year or different income years), you can deduct only under the provision that is most appropriate.

---

1 ITAA97 section 4-15.

Note that section 12-5 of the ITAA97 outlines a list of provisions about deductions and, where the taxpayer is registered for GST (see the chapter on GST). Division 27 outlines the effect of GST in working out deductions.

In interpreting the words of Division 8, we need to appreciate and consider how the courts have interpreted their meaning. As such, this chapter relies both on the legislation and case law.

As can be seen from Division 8, deductions are broken up into **general deductions** (section 8-1) and specific deductions (section 8-5). We can thus view the taxable income formula as shown in figure 6.1.

FIGURE 6.1   Extending the taxable income formula

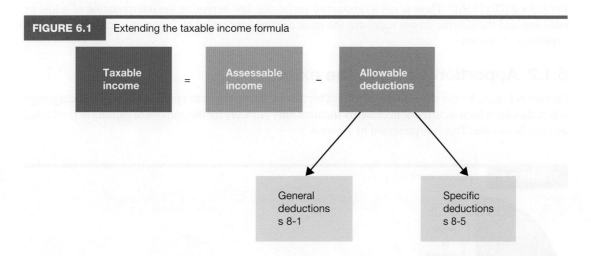

This chapter focuses on general deductions — any loss or outgoing that is deductible under section 8-1 is known as a general deduction.[2] (The chapter on specific deductions and applications of deductibility outlines specific deductions and reviews common categories of losses and outgoings.) When assessing losses or outgoings, if an amount fails to meet the general deduction provision requirements, then the specific deduction provisions should be considered. There is overlap between the two, so a deduction may satisfy both general and specific criteria. Despite this, a deduction cannot be claimed twice against assessable income — double deductions are disallowed by section 8-10. In such a circumstance, the most appropriate provision would be relied upon, and often this will be the specific provision.

The general deduction provision, section 8-1, includes **positive limbs** and **negative limbs**. Positive limbs represent what the legislation brings into deductibility and negative limbs specify what cannot be deducted under section 8-1. This is represented in figure 6.2.

FIGURE 6.2   Limbs of deductibility

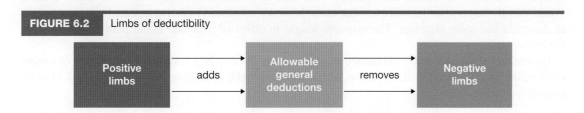

The interpretation of the positive and negative limbs in the general deduction provision relies heavily on case law. Hence, it is necessary to be able to identify both commonalities and differences between a taxpayer's particular facts and circumstances and those presented in the case law. Note that a substantial portion of the case law that is explored and discussed in this chapter refers to the former section 51(1) of the ITAA36, which was superseded by section 8-1 of the ITAA97. Despite this, the case law is equally applicable to section 8-1 (although it refers to section 51(1)).

Before examining the positive and negative limbs in detail in sections 6.2 and 6.3 respectively, some key terms are explored first. These are found within section 8-1: what a 'loss' or 'outgoing' represents, and what is meant by the phrase 'to the extent'.

---

2 ITAA97 section 8-1(3).

6.1.1 A 'loss' or 'outgoing'

Unlike accounting standards and practice, the tax legislation does not refer to 'expenses'. Instead, Division 8 describes a 'loss' or 'outgoing'. These are undefined in the legislation, but there is no need for substantial concern in relation to the meaning of what constitutes a loss or an outgoing. Importantly, losses and outgoings are not limited to monies outlaid or paid ('outgoing'). They may also involve less direct circumstances where no monies may have been paid, or even an involuntary action such as theft, that has resulted nonetheless in a depletion of resources ('loss') as confirmed by *Charles Moore & Co (WA) Pty Ltd v FCT* (1956).[3] There is not a substantial set of case law exploring the interpretation of a loss or outgoing and these terms do not represent the main area of concern when it comes to characterising an expense as deductible.

6.1.2 Apportionment: 'to the extent'

Section 8-1 includes the term 'to the extent'. This allows the taxpayer to apportion losses and outgoings where they have been incurred or necessarily incurred only *partially* for the purpose of gaining or producing assessable income. This is represented by figure 6.3.

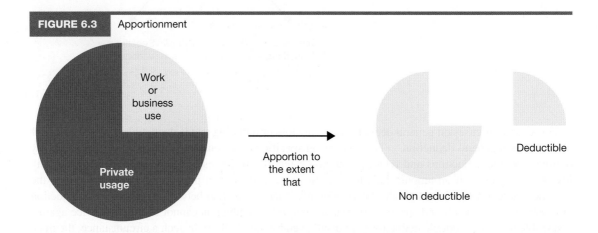

FIGURE 6.3 Apportionment

Work or business use

Private usage

Apportion to the extent that

Non deductible

Deductible

There is no exact approach or formula that must be followed in apportioning a loss or outgoing. The apportionment must, however, be determined on a *reasonable basis* rather than arbitrarily. This is a principle long established by *Ronpibon Tin NL v FCT* (1949).[4] Here, the taxpayer was a no-liability mining company registered in Victoria that operated a tin mine in Thailand (formerly known as Siam). During World War II, the taxpayer lost access to the mine; however, continued to derive income from investments in Australia and incur expenses. The taxpayer sought to claim all expenses rather than a proportion of the costs.

Depending on what kind of items require apportionment, this may be a reasonably simple task or a more challenging one. Latham CJ, Rich, Dixon, McTiernan and Webb JJ in *Ronpibon Tin NL v FCT* (1949)[5] considered this specifically:

> ... the problem is to apportion outgoings which have a double aspect, outgoings that are in part attributable to the gaining of assessable income and in part to some other end or activity. It is perhaps desirable to remark that there are at least two kinds of items of expenditure that require apportionment. *One kind consists in undivided items of expenditure in respect of things or services of which distinct and severable parts are devoted to gaining or producing assessable income and distinct and severable parts to some other cause.* In such cases it may be possible to divide the expenditure in accordance with the applications which have been made of the things or services. [emphasis added][6]

---

3 95 CLR 344.
4 *Ronpibon Tin NL v FCT* (1949) 78 CLR 47.
5 78 CLR 47.
6 Ibid 59.

The kind of expenditure described in this extract of the judgement is one that, despite being undivided (e.g. a taxpayer receives a bill of $300), is made up of distinct and severable parts, enabling the taxpayer to determine with relative ease what proportion (e.g. of the $300) directly relates to income-earning activities and what proportion relates to private or domestic purposes. This is demonstrated in example 6.1.

Apportionment: work-related and personal phone calls

Lee is required to have a mobile phone for work purposes. He incurred expenditure of $1250 on phone calls during the current tax year. On inspection of his bills, he notes that 30 per cent relate to personal phone calls and the balance are work-related calls.

What can Lee claim?

Lee can claim the expenditure to the extent that it is incurred in gaining or producing assessable income. He cannot claim the personal phone calls; however, this does not prevent him from claiming a proportion of the expense. He can claim 70 per cent of the expenses, which equates to $875.

Through applying the principles of apportionment, the taxpayer claims only what is directly attributable to the income-earning activities. Apportionment, however, can be more challenging when there is no clear distinction between the costs relating to income-earning activities and those that are private in nature. Latham CJ, Rich, Dixon, McTiernan and Webb JJ in *Ronpibon Tin NL v FCT* (1949)[7] went on to describe the second kind of expenditure requiring apportionment:

> The other kind of apportionable items consists in those involving a *single outlay or charge which serves both objects indifferently* … It is an indiscriminate sum apportionable, but hardly capable of arithmetical or ratable division because it is common to both objects.[8]

In this instance, there is a greater challenge in determining the *fair and reasonable*[9] apportionment between income-producing activities (deductible) and private purposes (not deductible). A 'reasonable' approach is required, as shown in example 6.2.

Apportionment: work-related and personal travel

Lee (from example 6.1) went on a 2-week study tour for both income-earning and private purposes. The package cost $2100.

What can Lee claim?

Rather than claiming the full $2100, Lee needs to consider the extent to which he can claim the expenditure. Making this more challenging, unlike in example 6.1, Lee cannot directly attribute the outgoings to each activity (income-earning or private activities). Instead, Lee needs to consider a reasonable basis to apportion the costs involved.

If, for example, Lee undertook the tour equally for income-earning purposes and private purposes, it would be reasonable for Lee to claim half of $2100, being $1050.

On the other hand, if one particular purpose was merely incidental then it is unlikely to require apportionment.

- If the private purposes were merely incidental, then Lee may be able to claim the full amount of $2100.
- If the income-earning purposes were merely incidental, then Lee is unlikely to be able to claim any of the $2100.

Note that the Commissioner of Taxation does not necessarily consider whether the taxpayer ought to have spent a certain amount in order to earn income.[10] It is for the taxpayer to decide whether to spend commercially reasonable or unreasonable amounts. Taxpayers, for example, can choose to purchase first

---

7 Ibid.
8 Ibid 59.
9 Ibid.
10 *Ronpibon Tin NL v FCT* (1949) 78 CLR 47.

class plane tickets instead of economy, or even make bad business choices! What is important, expanded upon in the following section and subsections, is that a nexus (connection) with income-earning activities be established. However, the Commissioner will step in if the expenditure is grossly excessive,[11] or where there are mixed purposes,[12] including where expenditure is structured to obtain tax benefits.

Furthermore, there are instances where caps are established for certain categories of expenditure. One important example is the luxury car limit, which limits the depreciable amount of a motor vehicle as well as GST credits claimable.

6.2 Positive limbs

LEARNING OBJECTIVE 6.2 Apply the two positive limbs of the general deduction provision.

The general deduction provision begins with taxpayers being able to claim a loss or outgoing to the extent that it meets the requirements of the first and/or second limb:

(a) it is incurred in gaining or producing your assessable income [*first positive limb, all taxpayers*]
(b) it is necessarily incurred in carrying on a business for the purpose of gaining or producing your assessable income [*second positive limb, business taxpayers only*].[13]

The first positive limb captures all taxpayers, whereas the second positive limb applies only to those taxpayers carrying on a business (see figure 6.4). As such, not all taxpayers need to consider the second limb; however, those taxpayers carrying on a business will clearly fall within both positive limbs. Substantial case law exists to interpret the meaning of the words contained within each limb, largely pursuant to the former section 51(1) of the ITAA36. As such, the parameters of the deduction provision have become well established, although complexity still remains.

| FIGURE 6.4 | The positive limbs |

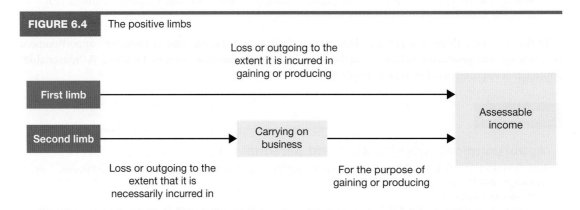

We will now examine the requisite nexus required between the incurring of expenditure and income-earning activities (or carrying on a business).

6.2.1 Nexus: 'incurred' and 'necessarily incurred'

When examining the positive limbs of section 8-1, it is necessary to assess the nexus between the loss or outgoing and assessable income (or carrying on a business in terms of the second positive limb). This relationship focuses on interpreting the terms 'incurred' (first positive limb) and 'necessarily incurred' (second positive limb) (see figure 6.4).

These terms are not defined within the legislation. For the first positive limb, there needs to be a direct nexus between income-earning activities and the loss or outgoing, whereas a less direct nexus is required by the second limb. If the taxpayer applies the second limb, they need only to establish that the expense was incurred in the course of carrying on the business. If the expenditure forms part of the ordinary operations of business, then it is likely to satisfy the requisite nexus, whether or not the expenditure is required by legal necessity. Thus, a broader interpretation is offered by the second limb. Note, however, that this assumes

---

11 *Robert G Nall Ltd v FCT* (1937) 57 CLR 695.
12 *Ure v FCT* (1981) 81 ATC 4100.
13 ITAA97 section 8-1(1).

that the taxpayer is *carrying on a business* (as opposed to non-business income-earning activities, or even the carrying on of a *hobby*).

In assessing whether a sufficient nexus exists, the courts have applied several tests in considering the first positive limb.[14] Some of these include the 'incidental and relevant' test, the 'essential character' test, the 'purpose test' and the 'occasion of the expenditure' test. Note that, in making their assessment, the courts have not been so concerned with establishing a nexus between the loss or outgoing and a *particular* amount of assessable income, nor with the *timing* of assessable income. The nexus needs only to be of a general nature and can conceivably relate to the production of income in prior or future years. The following subsections describe a selection of tests applied by the courts.

6.2.1.1 Incidental and relevant test

Courts have considered whether the expense is 'incidental and relevant' to the income-producing or business activities of the taxpayer. Expenditure may not on its own produce income, but nonetheless be appropriately incurred for a deduction to be allowed. For example, in *W Nevill & Co Ltd v FCT* (1937) 56 CLR 290, the taxpayer sought a tax deduction in relation to the termination of a managing director. The Court concluded that an outlay may be incurred to reduce future expenses and increase the efficiency of business operations, thereby being incidental and relevant to the production of future income.[15] The following judicial decisions and examples exemplify the incidental and relevant test.[16]

Herald and Weekly Times Ltd v FCT (1932) 48 CLR 113

Facts: The publisher of a newspaper claimed a deduction for damages paid arising from defamatory matter it had published. The Commissioner denied the deduction on the basis that the expenditure was not wholly and exclusively incurred in producing assessable income.

Held: The deduction was allowed pursuant to the former section 51(1) of the ITAA36.

Comment: The Court concluded that there was a sufficient nexus between the expenditure and the production of assessable income. As per Gavan Duffy CJ and Dixon J:

> None of the libels or supposed libels was published with any other object in view than the sale of the newspaper. The liability to damages was incurred, or the claim was encountered, because of the very act of publishing the newspaper. The thing which produced the assessable income was the thing which exposed the taxpayer to the liability or claim discharged by the expenditure. It is true that when the sums were paid the taxpayer was actuated in paying them, not by any desire to produce income, but, in the case of damages or compensation, by the necessity of satisfying a claim or liability to which it had become subject, and, in the case of law costs, by the desirability or urgency of defeating or diminishing such a claim. But this expenditure flows as a necessary or a natural consequence from the inclusion of the alleged defamatory matter in the newspaper and its publication. Expenditure in which the taxpayer is repeatedly or recurrently involved in an enterprise or exertion undertaken in order to gain assessable income cannot be excluded … simply because the obligation to make it is an unintended consequence which the taxpayer desired to avoid. No point is made of the fact that the publication took place in a former year, and properly so. The continuity of the enterprise requires that the expenditure should be attributed to the year in which it was actually defrayed.[17]

EXAMPLE 6.3

Incidental and relevant

A government employee, Omar, travelled overseas to study structural engineering of bridges in order to enhance his skill and knowledge in his role as a Project Engineer.

Is Omar's travel likely to be deductible under section 8-1?

Omar's travel is incidental and relevant to his employment. It is incurred for educational purposes to increase his professional skill and knowledge, which will likely enable him to better carry out his role working for the government. Thus, Omar's travel is likely to be deductible under section 8-1.[18]

---

14 See, eg, *St George Bank Ltd v FCT* (2009) ATC 9620, 9631 (Perram J).
15 *W Nevill & Co Ltd v FCT* (1937) 56 CLR 290.
16 See also *Ronpibon Tin NL v FCT* (1949) 78 CLR 47.
17 Ibid 118.
18 See also *FCT v Finn* (1961) 106 CLR 60.

Facts: The taxpayer was a company that carried on the business of a departmental store in Perth. Two employees of the company (cashier and escort) would take the previous days takings to the bank about 200 metres away on a daily basis. On one occasion, the employees were held up at gun point and robbed of the daily takings amounting to approximately £3031. The money was not insured; therefore, the taxpayer did not receive compensation and the money was not subsequently recovered. The takings were made up of cash sales, customer accounts (mail orders, letters of credit, lay-by payments and deposits, payments on delivery and staff ledger accounts and customers' current trading accounts)and sundry receipts. The taxpayer claimed the stolen receipts as an allowable deduction against its assessable income. The Commissioner disallowed the deduction.

Held: The £3031 was found to be deductible under former section 51(1) of the ITAA36.

Comment: The loss incurred was incidental and relevant to the taxpayer's income-earning activities. Incidental and relevant relate to their nature or character — their connection with operations undertaken to gain or produce assessable income. As per Dixon CJ, Williams, Webb, Fullager and Kitto JJ:

> In the case of a large departmental store such as the taxpayer carries on, the ordinary course of business requires that, day by day and as soon as may be, the takings shall be deposited in the bank. It is as necessary to the conduct of the business as it is to place goods on the shelves or to deliver them to the customers. They are all operations in the course of gaining or producing the assessable income by means of carrying on the business.[19]

The very nature of having to carry money to a bank gave rise to the risk of robbery in *Charles Moore*: an unavoidable, involuntary loss. The Court highlighted that it is pertinent to consider the kinds of misfortune or mischance that can arise from a particular trade or business activity. Dixon CJ, Williams, Webb, Fullager and Kitto JJ continued:

> … [T]he phrase 'incidental and relevant' when used in relation to the allowability of losses as deductions do not refer to the frequency, expectedness or likelihood of their occurrence or the antecedent risk of their being incurred, but to their nature or character. What matters is their connection with the operations which more directly gain or produce the assessable income.[20]

Consider therefore, if the employee was doing something other than simply walking from the place of business to the bank, such as making an unrelated personal diversion, could the requisite characterisation of incidental and relevant be broken? It is likely to be difficult for the nexus to be severed simply by stopping to have a coffee along the way; however, if the money was taken and lost through gambling, it would have been more difficult to claim the loss was incidental and relevant.

6.2.1.2 Essential character test

As well as the incidental and relevant test, courts have considered the essential character of the expenditure itself, whether it is essentially income-producing or of a private nature. This was already considered in *Charles Moore* in terms of describing the incidental and relevant nature of the expense being related to the character of the expense, rather than 'the frequency, expectedness or likelihood of their occurrence or the antecedent risk of their being incurred'.[21]

For example, travel to and from work is a function of where you choose to live rather than being essentially related to earning income. In particular, the decisions in *Lunney and Hayley v FCT* (1958)[22] reject the proposition that travel between home and work is incurred in gaining or producing income on the basis that travel was a prerequisite to do so. We can therefore characterise such travel as *private or domestic* and not deductible.

Similarly, in *Lodge v FCT* (1972),[23] the taxpayer was denied costs for sending her children to a nursery school allowing her the ability to carry out her duties. The essential character of the nursery fees was determined to be of a personal or living expense and therefore were held not to be deductible. The

---

19 Ibid 349.
20 Ibid 351.
21 *Charles Moore & Co (WA) Pty Ltd v FCT* (1956) 95 CLR 344, 351.
22 100 CLR 478.
23 128 CLR 171.

expenditure did not have the requisite character of an expense, despite it being incurred in order for the taxpayer to earn income.

Similarly, the private or domestic characterisation has been found to extend to food for a sportsperson, even where the expenditure is specifically at the direction of their coach: *FCT v Cooper* (1991).[24]

FCT v Cooper (1991) 29 FCR 177

Facts: The taxpayer, a professional rugby player, claimed deductions for additional food and drink consumed on the instruction of his coach to maintain an optimum playing weight and retain strength. Weight loss impacted his ability to play rugby at the necessary level and therefore maintaining weight and strength related directly to his income-earning activities. The coach's instructions stated for the taxpayer to consume the following.

1. 1.3 kilos of steak, only medium cooked.
2. Potatoes at each meal, 1 kilo per week.
3. Bread at each meal, at least three loaves per week.
4. Beer is an excellent method of increasing weight, therefore at least 1 dozen cans per week.
5. At least one glass of Sustagen per day.[25]

The Commissioner denied the deduction for the additional food and drink.

Held: The deduction pursuant to the former section 51(1) of the ITAA36 was denied.

Comment: The Court concluded that despite outlays for additional food and drink being for the purposes of playing professional football (and thereby earning assessable income), the taxpayer was paid to train and play football rather than for the consumption of food and drink. As per Hill J:

> Food and drink are ordinarily private matters, and the essential character of expenditure on food and drink will ordinarily be private rather than having the character of a working or business expense. However, the occasion of the outgoing may operate to give to expenditure on food and drink the essential character of a working expense in cases such as those illustrated of work-related entertainment or expenditure incurred while away from home. No such circumstance, however, intervenes here. In particular, the mere fact that Mr Masters [the coach] suggested or even directed Mr Cooper [the taxpayer] to eat particular food, does not convert the essential character of the food as private into a working expense.[26]

As will be further outlined when considering the negative limbs of section 8-1,[27] private expenditure is often considered to be incurred *too soon*, instead putting the taxpayer in a position to earn income rather than being incurred in gaining or producing income. See example 6.4 to consider when a loss or outgoing may not be considered to be incurred *too soon*.

EXAMPLE 6.4

Essential character

Kelly has a YouTube account reviewing, discussing and playing video games, and has gained more than 20 000 followers. She regularly purchases games, has early access to beta versions, and records her experiences playing the games, posting videos online. Kelly earns some sponsorship and advertising income from this activity.

Do Kelly's game purchases meet the essential character test?

In considering the essential character of the game purchases, Kelly is more likely to be able to distinguish her circumstances from the previous cases,[28] as there is a direct nexus with earning income and the outgoings. The essential character of the outgoings reflects an integral — or essential — part of the activities Kelly carries out to earn her assessable income.

---

24 91 ATC 4396.
25 *FCT v Cooper* (1991) 29 FCR 177.
26 Ibid 201.
27 ITAA97.
28 See, eg, *Lunney and Hayley v FCT* (1958); *FCT v Cooper* (1991).

6.2.1.3 Purpose test

The courts have assessed the purpose of the expenditure to establish the nexus between the loss or outgoing and the producing of income. This is particularly noteworthy in terms of tax schemes, where the subjective purpose (what the taxpayer seeks to achieve) of the taxpayer is considered to characterise the loss or outgoings.[29] This will more likely be the case where there has been a lack of assessable income generated or a disproportionate level of losses or outgoings.[30] This relates specifically to issues such as tax minimisation schemes, such as the losses or outgoings considered in *Ure v FCT* (1981).[31]

Ure v FCT (1981) 81 ATC 4100

Facts: The taxpayer acquired four loans, with interest rates ranging from 7.5 per cent to 12.5 per cent. The funds were on-lent to his wife and family company at an interest rate of 1 per cent to discharge the mortgage on the family home. The taxpayer declared the 1 per cent interest income in his tax return and claimed the interest expense in its entirety.

Held: The Court allowed a deduction pursuant to the then section 51(1) of the ITAA36; however, only to the extent of the interest income.

Comment: The Court concluded that the purpose of the arrangement was private and domestic in nature. Following *Ronpibon Tin NL v FCT* (1949),[32] the Court apportioned the expenditure, allowing a deduction only to the extent of the interest income. Note that if the taxpayer had instead used the funds to acquire some income-generating assets, the full interest expense may have been deductible. However, it is important to note the tax minimisation motivations in the taxpayer's arrangement and such a disparity in the interest rates are indicative of a purpose other than income generation.

6.2.1.4 Occasion of the expenditure test

The 'occasion of the expenditure' test considers the nexus between expenditure and income-earning activities in terms of the question: 'Is the occasion of the outgoing found in whatever is productive of actual or expected income?'[33] This test is exemplified through considering the quasi-legal expenses incurred by the taxpayer in *FCT v Day* (2008).[34]

FCT v Day (2008) 236 CLR 163

Facts: The taxpayer, a customs officer, incurred and claimed legal expenses to defend against allegations of misconduct under the *Public Services Act 1922* (Cth). The Commissioner denied the deduction on the basis they were not incurred in the course of gaining or producing assessable income.

Held: The majority of the High Court allowed the deduction.

Comment: Gummow, Hayne, Heydon and Kiefel JJ stated that the legal expenses 'must be considered in the context of the special position which such an officer holds, the extent of the duty owed by the officer and the legislative provision for the enforcement and regulation of such duty'.[35] The occasion of the expense arose from his position as a customs officer and therefore was deductible under section 8-1. Importantly, the Court distinguished between legal expenses incurred in relation to charges against a specific law, which places direct obligations on an employee, and legal expenses incurred in relation to criminal or civil charges, which instead may consequently impact employment or income-earning activities. This case exemplifying the former being deductible, while it may be challenging for the latter to be found deductible. Clearly there are shades of grey in establishing the deductibility of quasi-private or personal expenditure.

---

29 *Ure v FCT* (1981) 81 ATC 4100.
30 *Fletcher v FCT* (1991) 173 CLR 1.
31 81 ATC 4100.
32 78 CLR 47.
33 236 CLR 163.
34 Ibid.
35 Ibid 180.

Example 6.5 applies the occasion of the expenditure test to an alternative set of circumstances.

Occasion of the expenditure

Mina earns income from two unrelated sources located in two different places. She is seeking to claim a deduction for the travel between locations.

Can Mina claim the travel expenditure?

Mina is unlikely to be able to claim a deduction in accordance with the general deduction provision because the travel expenditure is to put her in a position to earn income rather than in a position of earning income. For similar circumstances, the High Court in *FCT v Payne* [2001][36] noted that:

> … neither the taxpayer's employment as a pilot nor the conduct of his business farming deer occasioned the outgoings for travel expenses. These outgoings were occasioned by the need to be in a position where the taxpayer could set about the tasks by which assessable income would be derived.[37]

The travel is comparable to travel between home and work, being private or domestic in nature. However, Mina may be able to claim a deduction arising from the specific deduction provisions. Refer to the chapter on specific deductions and applications of deductibility for further details.

6.2.2 'Necessarily' incurred

Notably, when considering the second positive limb, the word **necessarily** is not given its strict dictionary meaning. Instead, the courts have interpreted it to mean 'no more than clearly appropriate or adapted for'.[38] The courts allow a generous interpretation of 'necessarily incurred' and look to the taxpayer's business as to what would be considered reasonable and reflecting commercial judgement.[39] Many business expenses will clearly meet both positive limbs, such as voluntary outgoings, involuntary or compulsory losses or outgoings, unexpected or abnormal events and so forth. The phrase 'necessarily incurred' is examined in *FCT v Snowden and Willson Pty Ltd* (1958).[40]

FCT v Snowden and Willson Pty Ltd (1958) 99 CLR 431

Facts: The taxpayer, a speculative house builder, incurred legal and advertising expenses to counter negative press reports as well as legal costs arising from legal representation before a Royal Commission following allegations of misconduct.

Held: Outgoings were deductible pursuant to the former section 51(1) of the ITAA36.

Comment: This expenditure was necessarily incurred and therefore deductible under the second limb, and possibly the first limb. Dixon CJ stated that 'necessarily' does not mean legal or logical necessity:

> Logical necessity is not a thing to be predicated of business expenditure. What is meant by the qualification is that the expenditure must be dictated by the business ends to which it is directed, those ends forming part of or being truly incidental to the business.[41]

The Court continued in describing the press attacks as having the ability to seriously affect the business. As such, the taxpayer 'could do nothing else but defend itself, if it was to sustain its business and continue carrying it on in anything like the same volume or according to the same plan'.[42] The outgoings were incurred in carrying on that business and necessarily so because there was a business imperative that demanded so.[43]

---

36 202 CLR 93.

37 202 CLR 93, 14.

38 *Ronpibon Tin NL v FCT* (1949) 78 CLR 47.

39 *FCT v Snowden and Willson Pty Ltd* (1958) 99 CLR 431.

40 Ibid.

41 Ibid 437.

42 Ibid.

43 Ibid 444.

> It would naturally seem essential to the company's directors that a vigorous effort should be made to repel those attacks, and no defence could have any prospect of being effective which did not involve the expenditure of substantial sums of money.[44]

Such outgoings are now well accepted as being deductible in the carrying on of a business. Similarly, legal expenses have been deductible even when they relate to criminal charges.[45] This can be observed in *Magna Alloys & Research Pty Ltd v FCT* (1980).[46]

Magna Alloys & Research Pty Ltd v FCT (1980) 11 ATR 276

Facts: The taxpayer, a company, incurred legal expenses in defending against criminal charges imposed on the company itself, a number of its directors and its agents for alleged secret commissions pursuant to the *Crimes Act 1958* (Vic). Ultimately the charges against the company were abandoned, while the directors and agents were convicted. The taxpayer sought to deduct the legal expenditure, including the amounts relating to the directors and agents. The Commissioner disallowed the deduction. Initially the Supreme Court held the expenditure to be of a private nature, however the taxpayer appealed to the Federal Court.

Held: The legal fees were deductible pursuant to the former section 51(1) of the ITAA36.

Comment: The legal fees were necessarily incurred in carrying on a business. Despite having personal motivations by the directors, the outgoings were reasonably capable of being seen as desirable and appropriate in the pursuit of the taxpayer's business, with the taxpayer's reputation under attack. Despite the criminal nature of the charges, the outgoings were not of a private nature as they arose from commercial activities. According to Deane and Fisher JJ:

> Business outgoings may be properly and necessarily incurred in pursuit of indirect and remote, as well as direct and immediate, advantages. The fact that the business advantage sought is indirect or remote will not of itself preclude the pursuit of that advantage from characterising the outgoing as an outgoing necessarily incurred in carrying on the relevant business.[47]

Example 6.6 applies the necessarily incurred requirement to a further set of circumstances.

EXAMPLE 6.6

Necessarily incurred

Una runs an accounting firm in Darwin. Recently, she incurred legal fees in suing an employee who had breached their employment contract restricting their ability to work within a radius of Una's firm and to not use company confidential information, including client lists. The employee stole numerous clients from the firm, resulting in substantial losses in anticipated revenues.

Could Una deduct the legal fees?

Following *Snowden's*[48] case, Una could argue that all she could do was defend her business in order to sustain and continue on as she had done before the former employee's actions. In doing so, the legal fees are necessarily incurred as there was a business imperative for the outgoings to be incurred.[49]

6.2.3 Timing between income derivation and incurring of expenditure

The income tax legislation does not require taxpayers to match income and expenses in the way traditionally done so in accounting practice. Rather, the determination of deductibility looks to the *nexus* as described previously. Although temporality may be relevant, it is one of a number of factors that need

---

44 Ibid.
45 11 ATR 276.
46 Ibid.
47 Ibid 296.
48 *FCT v Snowden and Willson Pty Ltd* (1958) 99 CLR 431, 437.
49 Ibid.

to be considered when determining the existence of a necessary connection between the incurring of an outgoing and the actual or projected income receipt. This was noted by Gleeson CJ, Gaudron and Gummow JJ in *Steele v DFCT* (1999) 161 ALR 201 at 212:

> The temporal relationship between the incurring of an outgoing and the actual or projected receipt of income may be one of a number of facts relevant to a judgment as to whether the necessary connection might, in a given case, exist, but contemporaneity is not legally essential, and whether it is factually important may depend upon the circumstances of the particular case.

Steele considered interest expenses in relation to land acquired for a motel that never eventuated but derived income via agistment.

Steele v DFCT (1999) 161 ALR 201

Facts: The taxpayer purchased a block of land in 1980 with an intention to develop a motel. Despite this intention, a number of problems arose, such as zoning rejections and disputes with relevant parties, and by the late 1980s the land was sold. During the period of ownership, the taxpayer earned a small amount of income through horse agistment and incurred various holding costs, including interest throughout the ownership period. As a result, the taxpayer claimed interest deductions, which were denied by the Commissioner. The issues raised were twofold: (1) whether there was a sufficient nexus (first positive limb), and (2) whether the interest was capital or of a capital nature (first negative limb).

Held: The interest was deductible pursuant to the former section 51(1) of the ITAA36.

Comment: The Court confirmed that the interest was deductible on revenue account and a sufficient nexus existed, irrespective of whether the outgoings were used to acquire a capital asset and, moreover, even where it was not expected that assessable income would be earned until the future (and even though the motel development did not eventuate). Gleeson CJ, Gaudron and Gummow JJ confirmed at 209:

> In the usual case, of which the present is an example, where interest is a recurrent payment to secure the use for a limited term of loan funds, then it is proper to regard the interest as a revenue item, and its character is not altered by reason of the fact that the borrowed funds are used to purchase a capital asset.

This does not preclude, however, interest expenses to be found to be on capital account. This may occur even when the expense is recurrent.[50]

Importantly, expenditure may not be deductible if incurred too soon; however, it may be deductible despite income-earning activities ceasing in prior years. This will occur if the expenditure can be directly related to the prior activities.

6.2.3.1 Expenditure incurred *before* commencement

It is difficult to establish a sufficient nexus between expenditure and income production (or business activities) when the activities or business are yet to commence. Costs incurred before a business has commenced may include feasibility studies and will generally be non-deductible under section 8-1.[51] This position is comparable to the previously discussed issues regarding private or domestic expenditure, such as travel to and from work. These costs are considered *too soon*, placing the taxpayer in a position to earn assessable income rather than being incurred in earning assessable income.[52] Key authority for this proposition can be found in *Softwood Pulp and Paper Ltd v FCT* (1976).[53]

Softwood Pulp and Paper Ltd FCT (1976) 7 ATR 101

Facts: The taxpayer was incorporated for the purposes of establishing a mill complex in South Australia to produce paper, craft board and associated products. Expenditure was incurred on a feasibility study

---

50 See, eg, Perram J in *St George Bank Ltd v FCT* (2009) ATC 9620, 9631.
51 *Softwood Pulp and Paper Ltd v FCT* (1976) 76 ATC 4339.
52 *Lunney and Hayley v FCT* (1958) 100 CLR 478.
53 76 ATC 4339.

and, based on its findings, the project did not go ahead. The taxpayer sought to claim the outgoings and the Commissioner denied the deduction on the basis it was too preliminary in nature and not incurred in gaining or producing assessable income or in the course of carrying on a business.

Held: The deduction pursuant to the former section 51(1) of the ITAA36 was denied.

Comment: The Court agreed with the Commissioner in that the expenditure was of a preliminary nature, being incurred before the commencement of the business or the earning of assessable income. This decision can be compared to *FCT v Osborne* (1990),[54] in which a farmer leased and fertilised land in order to grow chestnuts, but the venture was abandoned before the trees were planted. The taxpayer claimed outgoings for rent, depreciation and labour with the Court determining that these outgoings were deductible as the steps taken to fertilise the land in order to plant the chestnut trees was regarded as carrying on a business.

Even if the business has commenced, feasibility studies relating to the establishment of a new component of the business will similarly be non-deductible under the general deduction provision.[55] However, these costs may be deductible through other provisions, such as the blackhole provisions found within Division 40.

6.2.3.2 Expenditure incurred *after* cessation

Irrespective of whether a business has ceased, expenditure incurred may still be deductible provided the requisite nexus with the former activity can be established.[56] Early case law suggested that a complete cessation of business activity would mean that the nexus with expenditure could no longer be established and therefore the deduction would be disallowed.[57] This could be compared with a temporary closure, where assets continued to be maintained in good order and condition.[58] However, later decisions found that a complete cessation of business activity does not necessarily result in the nexus being severed.[59] Importantly, the current authority confirms that obligations can *spring* from business that had formerly been carried on.[60]

A number of cases provide useful examples of where losses or outgoings incurred after the cessation of business activity have been found to be deductible. First, consider *Placer Pacific Management Pty Ltd v FCT* (1995),[61] which related to a warranty attached to goods sold by a business which was no longer in operation.

Placer Pacific Management Pty Ltd v FCT (1995) 31 ATR 253

Facts: The taxpayer was in the business of manufacturing conveyor belts. In 1981, the business was sold with the condition that the taxpayer would remain liable for any uncompleted contracts. Of particular relevance was the supply and installation of a conveyor belt in 1979. The customer of the conveyor belt commenced legal proceedings in 1981 (subsequent to the sale of the business), on the basis that the conveyor belt was defective. The proceedings were settled 8 years later. The taxpayer then proceeded to claim a deduction for the settlement and associated legal fees in the 1989 year, which the Commissioner disallowed based on the conveyor belt business having already been sold.

Held: The deduction was allowed pursuant to the former section 51(1) of the ITAA36.

Comment: The Court allowed the deduction under the second limb of section 51(1).[62] In reaching their decision, Davies, Hill and Sackville JJ interpreted the earlier judgement in *AGC (Advances) Ltd v FCT* (1975)[63] as establishing the proposition that the discontinuance of the business did not prevent the expenditure being deductible:

54 21 ATR 888.
55 See, eg, *Griffin Coal Mining Co Ltd v FCT* (1990) 21 ATR 819.
56 *AGC (Advances) Ltd v FCT* (1975) 132 CLR 175; *Placer Pacific Management Pty Ltd v FCT* (1995) 31 ATR 253; *FCT v Jones* (2002) ATC 4135; *FCT v Brown* (1999) 99 ATC 4600.
57 *Amalgamated Zinc (De Bavay's) Ltd v FCT* (1935) 54 CLR 295.
58 *Queensland Meat Export Co Ltd v FCT* (1939) 5 ATD 176.
59 Barwick CJ in *AGC (Advances) Ltd v FCT* (1975) 132 CLR 175, 187 indicated that the early case law was incorrect.
60 *AGC (Advances) Ltd v FCT* (1975) 132 CLR 175.
61 31 ATR 253.
62 ITAA36.
63 132 CLR 175.

> ... Provided the occasion of a business outgoing is to be found in the business operations directed towards the gaining or production of assessable income generally, the fact that that outgoing was incurred in a year later than the year in which the income was incurred and the fact that in the meantime business in the ordinary sense may have ceased will not determine the issue of deductibility ... [T]he occasion of the loss or outgoing ultimately incurred in the year of income was the business arrangement entered into between Placer [the taxpayer] and NWCC [the customer] for the supply of the conveyor belt which was alleged to be defective. The fact that the division had subsequently been sold and its active manufacturing business terminated does not deny deductibility to the outgoing.[64]

The Court in *Placer Pacific Management Pty Ltd v FCT* (1995)[65] highlighted the inequity and unjust result that would arise in the future if such long-tailed liabilities were denied, as such liabilities are often generated in the considerable future. We can see this when we look to the cases of *FCT v Brown* (1999)[66] and *FCT v Jones* (2002).[67]

FCT v Brown (1999) 43 ATR 1

Facts: The taxpayer carried on a delicatessen in partnership with his wife. In 1988, they had acquired a loan to fund its purchase. On selling the business in 1990, the proceeds received were insufficient to discharge the balance of the loan and therefore the taxpayer was required to continue to make repayments until 1995 when the loan was fully repaid. Of concern is the interest payments made subsequent to the sale of the delicatessen. The Commissioner denied the deductions for the interest on the basis that, by selling the business, the occasion of the outgoings no longer could be found in the business operations.
Held: The interest was deductible pursuant to the former section 51(1) of the ITAA36.
Comment: In line with *AGC (Advances)* and *Placer Pacific*, the occasion of the expenditure was found in the acquisition of the loan in order to carry on the delicatessen business. The sale of the business did not sever the requisite nexus.

This decision in *FCT v Brown* (1999) was followed by *FCT v Jones* (2002),[68] where a business was similarly carried on in partnership by a husband and wife and that partnership obtained loans to acquire equipment. The husband subsequently passed away in 1992, resulting in the wife (the taxpayer) taking up employment as a nurse and unsuccessfully repaying all debts. Furthermore, in 1996, the loan was refinanced to obtain a lower interest rate. The Commissioner denied the interest deduction from 1992 when the partnership ceased, but the Court disagreed. The interest was allowed, irrespective of the partnership ceasing and the loan being refinanced. The refinanced loan simply took on the character of the original loan.[69]

Note that the precedent established does not mean that there will never be a severing of the nexus on cessation of business activity and the incurring of interest expenses. Each set of facts and circumstances should be considered on their own merits to determine whether the occasion of the outgoings rest with the former business activity.

EXAMPLE 6.7

Expenditure incurred after the business has ceased

Christian was an electrical engineer operating just outside of Melbourne. His business ceased operating 3 years ago due to his ill health. Unfortunately, one of Christian's utility providers argued that Christian never paid an account and demanded payment from Christian. After a long negotiation, Christian paid $25 000 in the current tax year to settle the account.
    Can Christian claim the expenditure under section 8-1?

▷

---

64 *Placer Pacific Management Pty Ltd v FCT* (1995) 31 ATR 253, 259.
65 31 ATR 253.
66 99 ATC 4600.
67 2002 ATC 4135.
68 2002 ATC 4135.
69 2002 ATC 4135, [18].

> Despite the business ceasing to operate a number of years ago, Christian is likely to be able to establish the nexus between the utilities expense and the former business activity following authority in *FCT v Brown* (1999)[70] and *FCT v Jones* (2002).[71]

We have now concluded the review of the positive limbs of section 8-1. If the taxpayer's expenditure fails both positive limbs, then they do not need to consider the negative limbs. However, the analysis should not conclude in its entirety at this stage. There may be specific deductions that are available to the taxpayer, considered in more detail in the chapter on specific deductions and applications of deductibility. In contrast, if the taxpayer's expenditure meets the requirements of the positive limbs, the expenditure should then be considered in terms of the negative limbs. If these negative limbs prove problematic, again there may be a specific deduction available to the taxpayer. It is important to remember that where a loss or outgoing is deductible under both the general deduction provision and a specific provision, the expenditure should be claimed under the most appropriate provision.

6.3 Negative limbs

LEARNING OBJECTIVE 6.3 Apply the four negative limbs of the general deduction provision.

The negative limbs of section 8-1 specifically exclude from deductibility losses or outgoings that:
- are of a capital nature
- are private or domestic in nature
- have a nexus with exempt or non-assessable non-exempt income (as opposed to assessable income)
- are explicitly denied by a provision within the legislation (e.g. under the ITAA36 or ITAA97).

As such, after determining whether a particular loss or outgoing meets the requirements of one of the positive limbs, consideration must be given to whether there is a negative limb that will disallow the deduction. Specifically, section 8-1(2) states that you cannot deduct a loss or outgoing to the extent that:

(a) it is a loss or outgoing of capital, or of a capital nature; or
(b) it is a loss or outgoing of a private or domestic nature; or
(c) it is incurred in relation to gaining or producing your exempt income or your non-assessable non-exempt income; or
(d) a provision of this Act prevents you from deducting it.

The role of the negative limbs is summarised in figure 6.5.

In practice, multiple negative limbs may apply to any particular expenditure. As soon as one applies, the deduction cannot be claimed to the extent that the negative limb applies. Ensure you consider specific or limiting provisions that may impact deductibility, as well as the substantiation requirements outlined later in this chapter.

FIGURE 6.5   Negative limbs

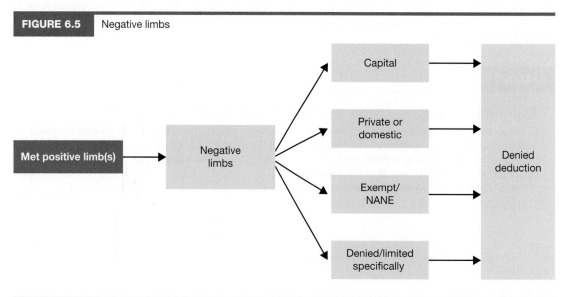

---

70 99 ATC 4600.
71 2002 ATC 4135.

6.3.1 First negative limb: capital or of a capital nature

Section 8-1(2)(a) requires you to ask the question *is the loss or outgoing of a capital or revenue nature?* Those of a capital nature are not deductible, as shown in figure 6.6.

FIGURE 6.6 The revenue–capital distinction

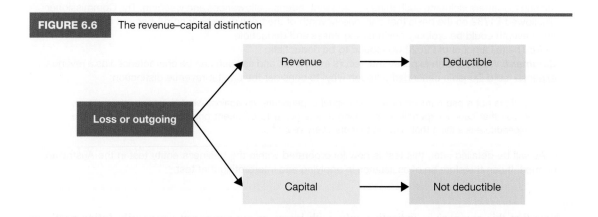

The distinction between a loss or outgoing being of a capital or revenue nature is an area of substantial struggle. Over time, the courts have grappled with developing tests such as the 'once and for all' test, the 'enduring benefits' test and the 'business entity' test to assist the interpretation and characterisation of losses and outgoings. The first two tests were developed in the United Kingdom, while the latter test reflects the key Australian authority on the matter. Although these tests have assisted in the capital–revenue classification of expenditure, this area has continued to be a challenging area of tax law. Table 6.1 lists prominent Australian cases that have considered the distinction, and whether the relevant loss or outgoings were of a capital nature or a revenue nature.

TABLE 6.1 Australian cases considering the revenue–capital distinction

Capital	Revenue
Strick (Inspector of Taxes) v Regent Oil Co Ltd (1966) AC 295	*BP Australia v FCT* (1965) 112 CLR 386
John Fairfax & Sons Pty Ltd v FCT (1959) 101 CLR 30	*Hallstrom Pty Ltd v FCT* (1946) 72 CLR 634
Broken Hill Theatres Pty Ltd v FCT (1952) 85 CLR 423	*National Australia Bank Ltd v FCT* (1997) 37 ATR 378
Sun Newspapers Ltd & Associated Ltd v FCT (1938) 61 CLR 337	*FCT v Snowden and Willson Pty Ltd* (1958) 99 CLR 431
Mount Isa Mines Ltd v FCT (1992) 176 CLR 142	*FCT v Citylink Melbourne Limited* (2006) 228 CLR 1
FCT v Star City Pty Ltd (2009) 72 ATR 431	

The following subsections briefly outline each test.

6.3.1.1 'Once and for all' test

The 'once and for all' test establishes that capital expenditure is a loss or outgoing that is spent once and for all, as opposed to something that is recurring on a regular basis reflecting a more continuous demand, which is more appropriately characterised as a revenue expense.[72] The leading authority for this test is *Vallambrosa Rubber Company Ltd v Farmer (Surveyor of Taxes)* [1910].[73]

---

72 *Vallambrosa Rubber Company Ltd v Farmer (Surveyor of Taxes)* [1910] SC 519. See also *Ounsworth v Vickers Ltd* (1915) 6 TC 671.
73 SC 519.

Facts: The taxpayer owned a rubber plantation to cultivate and produce rubber and other tropical products for the purposes of sale. Among the expenses incurred, the taxpayer claimed £2022 deductions relating to matters including such things as superintendence, allowances and weeding. The Commissioner disallowed £1732 on the basis that only one-seventh of the trees were bearing rubber and therefore only one-seventh could be ordinary business expenses and deductible.

Held: The full amount of £2022 was found to be deductible.

Comment: Weeding is an expense that recurs every year, and as such can be characterised as a revenue expense. Lord Dunedin described a 'rough way' to consider the capital-revenue distinction:

> ... [I]t is not a bad criterion of what is capital expenditure, as against what is income expenditure, to say that capital expenditure is a thing that is going to be spent once and for all, and income expenditure is a thing that is going to recur every year.[74]

As will be detailed later, this test is now incorporated within the business entity test in the Australian context. It can therefore be of assistance in applying and interpreting that test.

Note that this approach is indicative only, with losses or outgoings not necessarily fitting neatly or consistently within this test. It is critical to understand the particular facts and circumstances of each relevant taxpayer.

Example 6.8 applies the 'once and for all' test.

EXAMPLE 6.8

Once and for all test

A television station incurred expenditure in acquiring a licence to televise a documentary, allowing it to broadcast the program over 3 years. The station obtains program licences from numerous networks and production companies, with each licence varying in length from 1 to 7 years. Each licence requires a separate agreement and payment within 30 days of signing.

Would this pass the once and for all test?

There is some argument that the expenditure on the licence is once and for all, given the lasting benefit obtained; however, the expenditure incurred will likely be of a revenue nature. The outgoing does not represent a once and for all expense due to the necessity of the business to frequently and continually acquire these program licences. Therefore, the expenditure may be characterised as recurrent, reflective of the cost of carrying out the business operation.[75]

6.3.1.2 'Enduring benefits' test

The 'enduring benefits' test looks to whether the expenditure brings into existence an asset of an 'enduring' nature — a lasting nature. If so, then the loss or outgoing is capital in nature. The origin of the enduring benefits test is *British Insulated & Helsby Cables Ltd v Atherton* (1926),[76] where Viscount Cave characterised a capital outgoing in the following manner:

> When an expenditure is made, not only once and for all, but with a view to bringing into existence an asset or an advantage for the enduring benefit of a trade, I think that there is a very good reason (in the absence of special circumstances leading to the opposite conclusion) for treating such an expenditure as properly attributable not to revenue but to capital.[77]

Numerous cases have applied the enduring benefits test in the United Kingdom.[78] However, in Australia, the courts have often diverged from such strict characterisation through the application of the business entity test formulated by Dixon J in *Sun Newspapers Ltd & Associated Ltd v FCT* (1938).[79]

---

74 Ibid 536.
75 Australian Taxation Office, *Income Tax: television program licences* (IT 2646, 11 July 1991).
76 10 TC 155.
77 Ibid 192–193.
78 *Southern v Borax Consolidated Ltd* [1940] 4 AII ER 412; *C of T v Nchanga Consolidated Copper Mines Ltd* [1964] 1 AII ER 208.
79 61 CLR 337.

6.3.1.3 'Business entity' test

The 'business entity' test distinguishes losses and outgoings between those that can be characterised as relating to the taxpayer's profit-yielding subject (structure) or those that relate to the process of operating it, as shown in figure 6.7. Where the losses and outgoings relate to the structure, they will be characterised as capital and therefore not deductible under the general deduction provision. If the loss or outgoing relate to the process, then it will be deductible as a revenue expense.

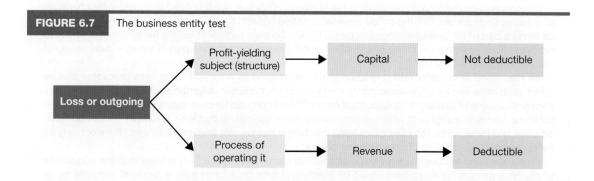

FIGURE 6.7 The business entity test

The origin of this test can be found in *Sun Newspapers Ltd & Associated Ltd v FCT* (1938),[80] in which the taxpayer paid a competitor, by instalment, a sum of money for an agreement to not publish a newspaper for 3 years, as well as making available certain plant for use. The High Court concluded that the outgoing was of a capital nature.

Dixon J, in *Sun Newspapers Ltd & Associated Ltd v FCT* (1938),[81] formulated the business entity test through deliberating on both the once and for all test and the enduring benefits test established in the United Kingdom, and then looking at the purpose of the expenditure:

> The distinction between expenditure and outgoings on revenue account and on capital account corresponds with the distinction between the *business entity, structure, or organisation set up or established* for the earning of profit and the *process by which such an organisation operates* to obtain regular returns by means of regular outlay, the difference between the outlay and returns representing profit or loss …

> As general *conceptions* it may not be difficult to distinguish between the *profit-yielding subject* and the *process of operating it*. In the same way expenditure and outlay upon establishing, replacing and enlarging the profit-yielding subject may in a general way appear to be of a nature entirely different from the continual flow of working expenses which are or ought to be supplied continually out of the returns or revenue.[82]

Dixon J further provided three matters to consider in guiding the distinction between the profit-yielding subject and the process of operating it:

> … (a) the character of the advantage sought, and in this its lasting qualities may play a part, (b) the manner in which it is to be used, relied upon or enjoyed, and in this and under the former head recurrence may play its part, and (c) the means adopted to obtain it, that is, by providing a periodical reward or outlay to cover its use or enjoyment for periods commensurate *with* the payment or by making a final provision or payment so as to secure future use or enjoyment.[83]

This test has become the leading test to distinguish between revenue and capital expenditure in Australia. Example 6.9 applies the test to the acquisition of equipment at an olive farm.

---

80 Ibid.
81 Ibid. Reiterated in Dixon J's dissenting judgement in *Hallstrom Pty Ltd v FCT* (1946) 72 CLR 634.
82 61 CLR 337, 359–360 (emphasis added).
83 Ibid 363.

An olive farm and the business entity test

The taxpayer is an olive farm producing olive oil, operating west of Melbourne, Victoria. During the current income year, it acquires an olive processor — a machine that presses the olives in the first stage of olive oil production.

Does the acquisition of the machine satisfy the business entity test?

When assessing the outgoing in terms of the business entity test, we first need to consider *the character of the advantage sought*.[84] If the outlay provides a lasting benefit, then it is more likely to be characterised as being a part of the profit-yielding structure. These outgoings represent lasting benefits — the ability to process olives into olive oil. These pieces of machinery or equipment form part of the structural set up of the profit-making enterprise.

We then need to *consider how it is to be used, relied upon or enjoyed*.[85] The olive processor can be relied upon once and for all. In assisting your interpretation, consider *Vallambrosa Rubber Company Ltd v Farmer (Surveyor of Taxes)* [1910] described earlier.[86] This can also be contrasted with the electricity used for those pieces of equipment, which requires recurrent outgoings. In that way, electricity cannot be relied on once and for all, while the olive processing machinery can be. We therefore can describe electricity as forming part of the process of operating the business.

Finally, we need to consider *the means adopted to obtain the benefit*.[87] It is likely that the acquisition of the olive processing equipment would be purchased through a lump sum, a series of instalments, or a loan. Lump-sum type payments are more readily capital in nature, compared to recurrent outgoings. Arrangements to pay in instalments make it more difficult to establish the third limb of the business entity test. For example, this can be contrasted with a lease arrangement where, instead of purchasing the equipment outright, it was leased from a third party.

It can be concluded that the olive processing equipment can be characterised as relating to the profit-yielding structure and therefore of a capital nature, in contrast with electricity and other recurrent outgoings. Consequently, the equipment is not deductible under section 8-1 of the ITAA97.

Figure 6.8 represents this relationship visually.

FIGURE 6.8   The distinction between the profit-yielding subject and the process of operating it

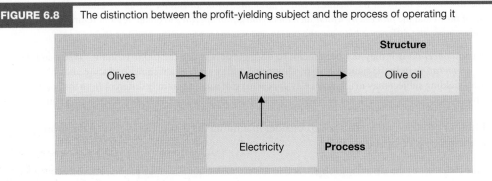

If a taxpayer has established that their outgoing is of a capital nature, they should consider the capital allowance provisions, which are detailed in a later chapter. In particular, there are certain allowances for low cost assets for non-business taxpayers as well as concessions for small business entities that may offer an immediate deduction for capital outlays. Otherwise, expenditure should be considered in terms of the remaining negative limbs.

6.3.2 Second negative limb: private or domestic nature

Section 8-1(2)(b) requires an answer to the question: *is the loss or outgoing of a private or domestic nature?* As outlined in section 6.2.1 of this chapter, to pass the positive limbs of section 8-1 of the ITAA97, a nexus between the expenditure and either income production (first positive limb) or business activity (second positive limb) is required. In carrying out that analysis, the essential character of the

---

84 Ibid.
85 Ibid.
86 SC 519.
87 *Sun Newspapers Ltd & Associated Ltd v FCT* (1938) 61 CLR 337, 363.

loss or outgoing can be found to be private or domestic in nature and the deduction denied. Therefore, the need of this negative limb is debatable. Arguably, this limb acts to prevent rare instances where this expenditure may satisfy the positive limbs of section 8-1.[88] This is irrespective of whether expenditure is practically required to enable the taxpayer to derive income or carry on a business (e.g. travel to/from work, consumption of food, or payment of childcare fees[89]). Often such expenditure is incurred *too soon*. Table 6.2 lists some of the leading cases characterising expenditure as private or domestic in nature.

TABLE 6.2   **Examples of private or domestic expenditure**

Expenditure	Case	Outcome
Travel between home and work	*Lunney and Hayley v FCT* (1958) 100 CLR 478	Not-deductible
Child-minding costs in order to undertake income-earning activities	*Lodge v FCT* (1972) 128 CLR 171; *Martin v FCT* (1984) 15 ATR 808	Not-deductible
Additional food consumed by rugby player on the instruction of coach	*FCT v Cooper* (1991) 21 ATR 1616	Not-deductible
Relocation costs due to relocation of employment	*Fullerton v FCT* (1991) 22 ATR 757	Not-deductible

This does not mean that all expenses that would otherwise be described as private or domestic will always be denied. As seen in the chapter on specific deductions and applications of deductibility, when we consider common expenses such as clothing, home office and travel, certain expenditure can be found to be deductible. The following example provides one of these contrasting sets of circumstances.

EXAMPLE 6.10

Food and drink

Hannah is an Instagram influencer. Her activities include critiquing bars and cafes, uploading photos of various food and drinks she has tasted, along with a written review and other online materials. She has been able to leave her full-time job, earning enough money from these activities (through advertising and sponsorships).

Are Hannah's purchases of food and drink deductible?

In analysing her situation, it is likely to be argued that the food and drink are not prevented from being deducted by section 8-1(2)(b). Her income-earning activities are directly related to the purchase and consumption of food; the food and drink are not putting Hannah in a position to earn income. The character of the food and drink are therefore distinguished from *FCT v Cooper* (1991).[90]

6.3.3 Third negative limb: nexus with exempt income or non-assessable non-exempt income

In accordance with section 8-1(2)(c), a loss or outgoing incurred in gaining or producing exempt or non-assessable non-exempt income will not be an allowable deduction.[91] This is logical given neither form of receipt amounts to a form of 'assessable income'.[92] As such, the third negative limb of section 8-1 does not add much to the analysis of allowable deductions. Note, however, a loss or outgoing will be non-deductible only to the *extent* it relates to exempt or non-assessable non-exempt income; as such, the provision does not prevent apportionment.[93]

---

88 *Magna Alloys & Research Pty Ltd v FCT* (1980) 11 ATR 276.
89 See section 6.2.1.2 of this chapter, as well as section 7.8 'Applications of deductibility to common expenditures' in the chapter on specific deductions.
90 91 ATC 4396.
91 ITAA97 section 8-1(2)(c).
92 See, eg, ITAA97 sections 6-1(3), 6-15.
93 See, eg, *Ronpibon Tin NL v FCT* (1949) 78 CLR 47.

6.3.4 Fourth negative limb: specifically denying provisions

Section 8-1(2)(d) denies losses or outgoings to the extent that a provision within either the ITAA36 or ITAA97 prevents the deduction. This outcome occurs irrespective of whether the expenditure is incorporated within accounting profit or whether the taxpayer financially incurs an economic burden.

A large proportion of the limiting or denying provisions are found within Division 26 of the ITAA97. The exploration of a selection of non-deductible or limited deductions follows. Note, however, that for business taxpayers with employees an exception can apply if the expense is subject to fringe benefits tax (FBT). In that case, the expense may then be an allowable deduction for income tax purposes and the employer (business taxpayer) will also be liable to pay FBT on the benefits provided pursuant to the *Fringe Benefits Tax Assessment Act 1986* (Cth) (FBTAA86). Think of this as an 'all in' or 'all out' position. Take time to consider the social perspective on these restrictions to the general deduction provision.

6.3.4.1 Penalties (section 26-5)

Section 26-5 specifically denies the deduction for penalties arising from Australian or foreign laws as well as court-ordered payments arising from convictions of an entity for an offence against an Australian or foreign law. This does not apply against, for example, a local library fee for late returns, but does apply to parking tickets and fines for speeding. This provision has been constructed to prevent taxpayers benefiting from breaking the law. There is existing case law that suggests that irrespective of section 26-5, such infringements are in any case not deductible under the general deduction provision due to the personal nature of the punishment distinguished from the taxpayer's trading activities. Gavan Duffy CJ and Dixon J state in *Herald & Weekly Times Ltd v FCT* (1932):[94]

> The penalty is imposed as a punishment of the offender considered as a responsible person owing obedience to the law. Its nature severs it from the expenses of trading. It is inflicted on the offender as a personal deterrent, and it is not incurred by him in his character of trader.[95]

In *Madad Pty Ltd v FCT* (1984),[96] for example, the Court relied on this proposition to deny penalties under the *Trade Practices Act 1974* (Cth) arising from various motoring offences. Such penalties can be contrasted to the outgoings found to be deductible in *Herald & Weekly Times Ltd v FCT* (1932).[97]

Example 6.11 demonstrates the application of the fourth negative limb to penalties.

EXAMPLE 6.11

Penalties

Speedy Deliveries Ltd is a delivery business serving the greater Brisbane area. The business delivers packages to customers with a 3-day delivery guarantee. During the current tax year, their drivers incurred $15 000 in toll road fees and $3300 in speeding fines in delivering packages.

What expenses can Speedy Deliveries Ltd claim?

The company will be able to claim the $15 000 in toll road fees in accordance with section 8-1 of the ITAA97. The expense is necessarily incurred in carrying on the business (second limb). However, despite the speeding fines also having the requisite nexus with the income-earning activities, section 26-5 of the ITAA97 will deny the $3300 in speeding fines from being deducted. The fines amount to a penalty arising from Australian law. They would, therefore, appear in Speedy Deliveries' accounting profit or loss statement, but would be excluded from the calculation of taxable income.

6.3.4.2 Leave payments (section 26-10)

Provisions for long service leave, annual leave, sick and other leave cannot be claimed unless the amount has been paid. The principle that leave payments are not yet incurred was established in cases including *FCT v James Flood Pty Ltd* (1953).[98] In that case, provisions were established reflecting employee entitlements to holiday pay; however, deductions for those provisions were denied as the taxpayer was yet to be completely subjected to the expense. Similarly, in *Nilsen Development Laboratories Pty Ltd*

---

94 48 CLR 113, 120.
95 Ibid.
96 15 ATR 1118.
97 48 CLR 113.
98 88 CLR 492.

---

v FCT (1981),[99] long service leave and holiday leave provisions were found to be non-deductible as no liability presently existed. The employees had *not* taken the leave, nor had any requisite event occurred (e.g. death or termination of employment) that would bind the employer to make the payments.[100] The operation of this principle is demonstrated in example 6.12.

Leave payments

Nano Robotics Ltd is an IT firm employing 12 technology specialists. The company's financial statements show that the company has a provision for long service leave of $25 000 for the current year; however, it has only paid $8000 in long service leave to its employees.

What is the allowable deduction for Nano Robotics?

Only $8000 is an allowable deduction in the current tax year. Section 26-10 specifically denies the provision to the extent that is not paid.

6.3.4.3 Rebatable benefits (section 26-19)

Section 26-19 denies a loss or outgoing to the extent it is incurred in gaining or producing a **rebatable benefit.** This includes use of property, such as deprecation arising from a laptop used in gaining or producing the rebatable benefit.[101] A rebatable benefit includes government allowances such as Youth Allowance (Student), Youth Allowance (Jobseeker), ABSTUDY Living Allowance, Austudy Living Allowance, and Newstart Allowance.[102] This provision in essence removes the ability of recipients of government allowances to be able to use related expenditure as deductions against non-government assessable income. This provision was introduced following the decision in *FCT v Anstis* [2010].[103]

6.3.4.4 Assistance to students (section 26-20)

Section 26-20 specifically denies student contributions and payments to higher education under the *Higher Education Support Act 2003* (Cth). An exception applies when the taxpayer provides the payments as a fringe benefit. However, in doing so, the employer would be liable for fringe benefits tax. Consider example 6.13.

Assistance to students

Syed is studying a Bachelor of Commerce (Accounting) while working as an accountant at a local accounting firm. During the year, Syed pays $5000 in HECS-HELP repayments.

Can Syed deduct the expense?

Although there is a nexus with his income-earning activities, section 26-20 specifically denies the $5000 from being deducted against his employment income. This provision operates to reflect government funding for higher education places in Australia and therefore prevents further benefits arising.

If Syed's employer paid the HECS-HELP fees, the $5000 may be treated as a fringe benefit and therefore may be deductible for his employer.

6.3.4.5 Political contributions and gifts (section 26-22)

Political contributions and gifts to a political party or individual candidates in an election are specifically denied for taxpayers. There is an exception, however, for individual taxpayers in Division 30: An individual who is not making the contribution in the course of carrying on a business (see section 30-242) is allowed to deduct up to $1500 in contributions and gifts.[104] The operation of this exception is illustrated by example 6.14.

---

99 144 CLR 616.
100 Ibid 621.
101 ITAA97 section 26-19(2).
102 Refer to ITAA36 section 160AAA(1) for definition.
103 241 CLR 443.
104 Section 30-243.

Political contributions and gifts

During the year, Josephine contributed $2000 towards a candidate running in the NSW elections.
Is her contribution deductible?

Josephine is not specifically impacted by section 26-22, given she is an individual taxpayer. However, Josephine must instead consider Division 30. Assuming her contribution meets the requirements of Division 30, she can claim $1500 against her assessable income; however, Josephine cannot claim the balance pursuant to section 30-243. If the donation was made by a business taxpayer, section 26-22 would deny the full $2000.

Refer to the chapter on specific deductions and applications of deductibility for more in-depth coverage of Division 30.

6.3.4.6 Relative's travel expenses (section 26-30)

It is a common occurrence for taxpayers to be accompanied by a partner or spouse for work- or business-related travel. Section 26-30 specifically denies a loss or outgoing to the extent it is attributable to the relative's travel. An exception applies here if the expenditure was provided as a fringe benefit. Furthermore, section 26-30 does not apply to the extent the family member performed substantial duties as the taxpayer's employee and it is reasonable to conclude that they would have accompanied you irrespective of the personal relationship.

6.3.4.7 Travel related to use of residential premises as residential accommodation (section 26-31)

Section 26-31 prevents taxpayers claiming a loss or outgoing insofar as it relates to travel to residential premises being used for income-producing purposes and not carrying on a business. It is largely aimed at the individual taxpayer where concerns arise regarding landlords claiming private travel, rather than for companies or self-managed superfunds.

6.3.4.8 Reducing deductions for amounts paid to related entities (section 26-35)

According to section 26-35, taxpayers can only deduct reasonable amounts paid to related entities. What is considered reasonable refers to what the Commissioner considers reasonable. A **related entity** refers to the taxpayer's relative or a partnership in which the taxpayer's relative is a partner.[105] Section 26-35(3) provides further examples of related entities for partnerships.

This is particularly relevant given the extent of small family businesses in Australia. If the taxpayer employs a spouse or child, the question required to be asked is would the taxpayer have paid an unrelated employee the same amount? If the taxpayer compensated their partner for work performed to the same extent that they would be willing to pay someone 'at arm's length' to do the same, then there is not a problem.[106] The problem arises only with excessive payments, especially tax-effective payments to use the spouse's tax-free threshold, for example.[107]

If section 26-35 applies to payments to a related entity, then to the extent it applies, the related entity does not include the receipt in their assessable income. It is neither assessable income, exempt income nor exempt income.[108] In essence, the related entity would treat the amount as a gift.

Example 6.15 applies section 26-35 to a set of circumstances.

Payments to related entities

Karen runs an online store and employs her daughter Lulu on a casual basis. During the school holidays, Lulu worked 15 hours processing and posting purchases. Karen paid her wages of $3000.

---

105 ITAA97 section 26-35(2).
106 R Caldwell, *Taxation for Australian businesses* (Wrightbooks, 2014)
107 Ibid.
108 ITAA97 section 26-35(4).

6.3.4.9 Recreational club expenses (section 26-45)

Section 26-45 denies taxpayers deductions for expenditure incurred in obtaining or maintaining membership of a recreational club or the rights to enjoy recreational club facilities. It does not matter whether the expenditure is incurred for the taxpayer themselves, or someone else (e.g. a client or employee). The legislation defines a **recreational club** as:

> A recreational club is a company that was established or is carried on mainly to provide facilities, for the use or benefit of its members, for drinking, dining, recreation or entertainment.[109]

An example of a membership that would be denied under section 26-45 includes a golf club.

Note that the definition looks at what the entity was established mainly for. For example, section 26-45 does not capture employer's entitlement to claim a deduction under section 8-1 for airport lounge membership fees, where the membership arises out of the employment relationship.[110] It does not matter that the membership may be used substantially for private use, or that there is some drinking, dining, recreation or entertainment while it is being used.

There can be some overlap regarding this provision with the limitations imposed by Division 32 (entertainment).[111] The airport lounge clubs do not meet the definition of an entertainment[112] nor recreational club[113] because:

> Airport lounge clubs provide business facilities (such as meeting rooms, individual workstations and Wi-Fi access) and services relating to the travel of their members (such as a streamlined checking in process). Although the clubs also provide some food, drink and recreation, the provision of a lounge membership is not properly characterised as a provision of 'entertainment'. Similarly, airport lounge clubs could not properly be said to be clubs that are carried on 'mainly to provide facilities ... for drinking, dining, recreation or entertainment'.[114]

Exceptions do apply, however, if denied expenditure is incurred in providing a fringe benefit that is not exempt;[115] however, airport lounge memberships are specifically excluded from fringe benefits tax under section 58Y of the FBTAA86.[116]

6.3.4.10 Expenditure relating to illegal activities (section 26-54)

Under section 26-54, losses or outgoings are denied where they relate to offences against Australian law. Note that section 26-54 is not intended to apply to a taxpayer who is carrying on a lawful business activity but who is convicted of illegal activities during those business undertakings.[117] The law is intended to apply to activities that are wholly illegal, such as drug dealing and people smuggling.[118] Furthermore, if the conviction occurs after the submission of the taxpayer's tax return, the Commissioner can amend their assessment any time within 4 years after the conviction in order to give effect to section 26-54(2).[119] Note that there are complementary provisions relating to illegal activities within the CGT provisions.

---

109 ITAA97 section 26-45(2).
110 Australian Taxation Office, *Income tax: Is an employer entitled to a deduction under section 8-1 of the Income Tax Assessment Act 1997 for the annual fee incurred on an airport lounge membership for use by its employees?* (TD 2016/15, 27 July 2016).
111 ITAA97.
112 See section 32-5.
113 See section 26-45(2).
114 Australian Taxation Office, *Income tax: Is an employer entitled to a deduction under section 8-1 of the Income Tax Assessment Act 1997 for the annual fee incurred on an airport lounge membership for use by its employees?* (TD 2016/15, 27 July 2016), [7] (citations omitted).
115 Section 26-45(3).
116 Australian Taxation Office, *Income tax: Is an employer entitled to a deduction under section 8-1 of the Income Tax Assessment Act 1997 for the annual fee incurred on an airport lounge membership for use by its employees?* (TD 2016/15, 27 July 2016).
117 Tax Laws Amendment (Loss Recoupment Rules and Other Measures) Bill 2005 Explanatory Memorandum, 147.
118 Ibid 146.
119 Section 26-54(2).

This denying provision was introduced after the controversial decision in *FCT v La Rosa* (2003).[120] The outcome of the case resulted in the then Commonwealth Treasurer, Peter Costello, announcing that the law would be amended to deny losses and outgoings relating to illegal activities:

> The income tax law will be amended to deny deductions for losses and outgoings to the extent that they are incurred in the furtherance of, or directly in relation to, activities in respect of which the taxpayer has been convicted of an indictable offence.[121]

FCT v La Rosa (2003) 53 ATR 1

Facts: Frank La Rosa was a charged and convicted heroin and amphetamines dealer. The taxpayer had been burying the proceeds of his criminal activity in his backyard and in May 1995 dug up $220 000 intending to carry out a drug deal. However, during the deal with an unknown person, the money was stolen. The money was lost during activities directly connected with carrying on an illicit drug dealing business for the purpose of acquiring trading stock (drugs). Through being prosecuted for the criminal offences, the Commissioner of Taxation became aware of the taxpayer's financial affairs. This resulted in the taxpayer being issued default assessments for 7 years of income, arising from the taxpayer not having submitted his tax returns. The taxpayer objected to these assessments on the basis that his taxable income had been overstated. The taxpayer argued that the stolen $220 000 was deductible under section 51(1)of the ITAA36 (equivalent to section 8-1 of the ITAA97) for the 1995 income year. The Commissioner argued that the amount should not be deductible as it was an attempt to affect an illegal transaction, that the loss was of a capital nature, and that the policy of the law was not served by allowing a loss that was of a criminal nature to be deducted.

Held: The $220 000 was found to be deductible under the former section 51(1) of the ITAA36.

Comment: It did not matter that the activities were illegal. Putting aside legality, there was sufficient nexus with income-earning activities and the drug deal. Recall *Charles Moore & Co (WA) Pty Ltd v Federal Commissioner of Taxation* (1956) 95 CLR 344. Given the loss related to the acquisition of trading stock, the loss was of a revenue nature. In concluding, the Court described that with regard to the policy of the law, one must refer to criminal law in order to seek punishment for illegal activities and wrongdoing rather than tax law.[122] Note that the $220 000 was also included in the taxpayer's assessable income.

6.3.4.11 Limits on deductions (section 26-55)

Section 26-55 of the ITAA97 sets limits on deductions a taxpayer can claim with respect to pensions, gratuities or retiring allowances (section 25-50); gifts or contributions (Division 30); conservation covenants (Division 31); and for personal superannuation contributions (section 290-150). In essence, these expenses are only deductible to the extent that they do not add or create a tax loss. For example, if a taxpayer had derived assessable income of $20 000 and deductions of $20 000 pursuant to section 8-1 of the ITAA97 and $1000 deductions pursuant to Division 30, section 26-55 would operate to reduce the Division 30 deductions to nil. If, on the other hand, the section 8-1 deductions were $19 500, then section 26-55 would reduce the Division 30 deduction to $500.

6.3.4.12 Expenses associated with holding vacant land (section 26-102)

Section 26-102 of the ITAA97 limits deductions for losses or outgoings incurred in relation to holding vacant land. This restriction extends to interest or any other ongoing costs in relation to borrowing funds to acquire the land. This limit relates to land that has no substantial or permanent structure in use or available for use. The restriction does not apply to the loss or outgoing to the extent that the land is in use, or available for use, in carrying on a business.

6.3.4.13 Non-compliant payments for work and services (section 26-105)

Section 26-105 of the ITAA97 denies deductions for non-compliant payments for work and services. Non-compliant payments refer to those payments that are subject to withholding provisions pursuant to the *Taxation Administration Act 1953* (Cth) Schedule 1. These include, for example, payments to employees that do not comply with the pay as you go (PAYG) withholding and reporting requirements, as well as

---

120 2003 ATC 4510.
121 Peter Costello, 'Media releases: Income tax deductions to be denied for illegal activities' www.petercostello.com.au/press/2005/2827-income-tax-deductions-to-be-denied-for-illegal-activities [5].
122 *FCT v La Rosa* (2003) 2003 ATC 4510.

contractors that hold Australian business numbers (ABNs). This limiting deduction is in addition to existing penalties that may apply under the PAYG withholding system.[123]

6.3.4.14 Input tax credits (Division 27)

There needs to be a particular consideration given to the relationship between GST and deductions. Division 27 provides specific rules on this matter. Importantly, section 27-5 denies a deduction to the extent it relates to an input tax credit to which the taxpayer is entitled. The outcome of applying this provision is that a double benefit (tax deduction and input tax credit) is prevented from arising from the same amount. Note that this does not apply where the tax entity is not registered for GST. Where the tax entity is not registered, they are entitled to a deduction for the GST component of a deductible amount.

6.3.4.15 Entertainment (Division 32)

Special rules can be found within Division 32[124] relating to entertainment expenditure. **Entertainment** is defined as:

(a) entertainment by way of food, drink or recreation; or
(b) accommodation or travel to do with providing entertainment by way of food, drink or recreation.[125]

In particular, section 32-5 specifically denies entertainment expenditure and section 32-15 extends the restriction to property used in providing entertainment (e.g. denying repairs and decline in value for said property). Furthermore, it does not matter if business discussions or transactions occur during the provision of entertainment, such as at a business lunch or social function.[126]

However, it is important to consider the essential character of the provision.[127] For example, a business lunch with a client would not be deductible for a solicitor. However, if the solicitor was having a meal during business travel, then the meal could be deductible. Or, if instead of a solicitor, the taxpayer was a food writer, then the expenditure on the meal would not be considered the provision of entertainment.

Moreover, there are numerous exceptions and exemptions that apply to entertainment. One of the key exceptions is if the entertainment is provided by way of a fringe benefit.[128] Further exceptions can be found in Subdivision 32-B, with key terms found in Subdivision 32-C, anti-avoidance provisions in Subdivision 32-E, as well as special rules applicable to companies and partnerships in Subdivision 32-F.

6.3.4.16 Reimbursements (section 51AH)

Employees are often in a position where they incur work-related expenses and these may then be reimbursed by the employer. Generally speaking, fringe benefits that can arise in these circumstances should be considered. However, in characterising the loss or outgoing, section 51AH of the ITAA36 makes it certain that the employee cannot claim the expense as a deduction if it has been reimbursed, or to the extent it has been reimbursed.

Before moving onto the substantiation requirements, take a moment to reflect on taking reasonable care to ascertain a taxpayer's state of affairs as a tax practitioner (Code Item 9, under the TASA Code of Professional Conduct). Recall from an earlier chapter that registered tax practitioners are required to comply with the Code. In this example, we explore what this may look like in considering the principles of deductibility examined so far in this chapter.

ETHICS IN PRACTICE

Ethics in deductions

Taking reasonable care
Miku is a registered tax agent, who has been engaged by Amy to lodge her income tax return. Amy works for a retail chain as a store manager. Miku obtains Amy's income statement from the prefill report, which shows Amy earned $45 000 during the income year. Amy explains that she has motor vehicle expenses of ▶

---

123 See Australian Taxation Office, 'Removing tax deductibility of non-compliant payments' (Web Page, 30 October 2019) https://www.ato.gov.au/general/gen/removing-tax-deductibility-of-non-compliant-payments/?page=1#Types_of_payments_affected.
124 ITAA97.
125 Section 32-10(1).
126 Section 32-10(2).
127 See, eg, *FCT v Amway Australia Ltd* [2004] 141 FCR 40.
128 Section 32-20.

$8000 to claim. Miku has been engaging with Amy over a number of years and this is the first time Amy's claims have exceeded $1000.

Under Code Item 9 of the TASA Code of Conduct, Miku is required to take reasonable care to ascertain Amy's state of affairs.[129] Miku should exercise her professional judgement as a starting point to consider Amy's claims. This requires knowledge, skills and experience.[130]

Do you think Miku would consider Amy's claims of $8000 credible? Should Miku accept Amy's claim without further action?

If Miku determined that the claim is credible and without basis for doubt,[131] Miku may discharge her responsibility without further enquiries. However, it is likely that Miku would not consider the motor vehicle expenses as credible without asking further questions of Amy and/or obtaining records to ascertain Amy's tax affairs. Not only does the level of expenditure appear inconsistent with prior claims, but an unusually high claim, particularly given her occupation and income level. It is unlikely that Miku could discharge her responsibility under Code Item 9, without further enquiries. If Miku does not do so, she will be in breach of the Code and may have sanctions imposed.

After asking Amy for further information, Miku determines that Amy's expenses are not deductible. In particular, Miku has ascertained that the motor vehicle expense of $8000 reflects the purchase of a second-hand car. As such, this is a capital acquisition so would not be deductible under the first negative limb: section 8-1(2)(a) of the ITAA97. Moreover, Miku confirms that the car is used to travel to and from work only, and thus the essential character of the outgoing is private and lacks the requisite nexus with her income earning activities.

Miku therefore explains to Amy that she is not entitled to claim the $8000, nor outgoings related to the vehicle.

6.4 Substantiation

LEARNING OBJECTIVE 6.4 Explain the substantiation requirements in order to claim a deduction.

The next step in determining a general deduction is substantiation, as shown in figure 6.9. When claiming deductions, it is imperative to consider substantiation of the taxpayer's claims. Division 900 of the ITAA97 details rules regarding written evidence of various expenses for *individuals* and *partnerships* only; while, more generally, taxpayers carrying on a business are required to make and retain tax-related records in accordance with section 262A of the ITAA36. There are also specific provisions relating to, for example, retaining GST-related[132] records and FBT-related records.[133] The following subsections consider Division 900 and section 262A.

FIGURE 6.9   Substantiation

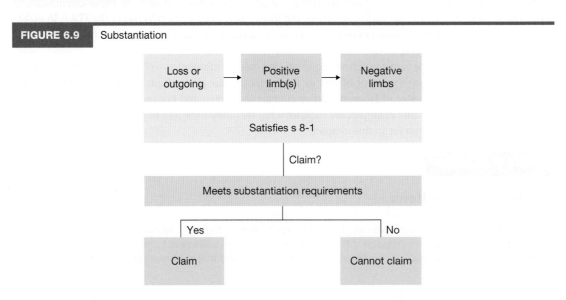

---

129 See TASA2009 section 30-10(9).
130 Tax Practitioners Board, 'TPB(I) 17/2013 Code of Professional Conduct – Reasonable care to ascertain a client's state of affairs' (Web Page, 20 November 2019) https://www.tpb.gov.au/reasonable-care-ascertain-clients-state-affairs-tpb-information-sheet-tpbi-172013.
131 Ibid.
132 See, eg, section 382-5 of Schedule 1 of the *Taxation Administration Act 1953* (Cth).
133 See, eg, section 132 of the *Fringe Benefits Assessment Act 1986* (Cth).

6.4.1 Division 900 of the ITAA97

Division 900 of the ITAA97 details rules regarding written evidence of various expenses for *individuals* and *partnerships*, particularly in relation to substantiating work expenses (Subdivision 900-B), substantiating car expenses (Subdivision 900-C) and substantiating business travel expenses (Subdivision 900-D). Critically, if the taxpayer cannot adequately substantiate the deduction, then the loss or outgoing cannot be claimed against assessable income, irrespective of whether it may or may not meet the criteria of section 8-1. This is depicted in figure 6.9.

The Australian Tax Office often describes the requirement as being the 'three golden rules':
1. the taxpayer 'must have spent the money themselves and weren't reimbursed'
2. the loss or outgoing 'must be directly related to earning their income'
3. the taxpayer 'must have a record to prove it'.[134]

The following subsections explore the substantiation requirements for work expenses, travel expenses and business expenses, therefore briefly outlining the requirements for retaining and producing related records. First, however, 'written evidence' is briefly outlined.

6.4.1.1 What is written evidence?

Usually when the substantiation provisions refer to written evidence, it is referring to the receipt of an invoice, which generally sets out the:
- name of the supplier (whether an individual's name or a business name)
- amount of the expense (presented in the currency in which the expense was incurred)
- nature of the goods or services
- day the expenditure was incurred
- document date (invoice or receipt date).[135]

In some instances, you may find the payment date or nature of the goods or services missing. In these circumstances, you may use bank statements or other reasonable evidence to show when the expense was paid, or you may write the nature of the goods or services onto the document.[136] In some circumstances, the nature and amount of a work expense may be shown on a taxpayer's payment summary provided by their employer. In such a circumstance, the taxpayer can use the payment summary as written evidence.[137] These may include donations to charities, or union fees, for example.

6.4.1.2 Substantiating work expenses (Subdivision 900-B)

Work expenses relate to those losses or outgoings incurred in producing salary or wages, withholding payments, and travel and meal expenditure incurred when the travel or meals are covered by a travel or meal allowance.[138] Following the introduction of the Treasury Laws Amendment (Cost of Living Support and Other Measures) Bill 2022, section 900-30(7) includes the newly enacted specific deduction for COVID-19 tests (see section 25-125 of the ITAA97, and refer to the next chapter for further information). Subdivision 900-B does not apply to motor vehicle expenses, unless incurred in respect to travel outside of Australia or relate to a taxi fare or similar loss or outgoing.[139] In practice, the treatment and substantiation of most losses or outgoings relating to motor vehicles are found within Division 28 and Subdivision 900-C.

Section 900-15 requires the taxpayer to obtain written evidence in order to deduct a loss or outgoing that qualifies as a deduction in accordance with other provisions within the Act. Specifically, if the taxpayer cannot substantiate the loss or outgoing, it will not be an allowable deduction despite otherwise meeting the requirements for deductibility.

If the taxpayer is travelling away from their ordinary residence for more than six nights in a row, **travel records** are required pursuant to Subdivision 900-F.[140] Subdivision 900-F explains how to keep travel records, which are records of activities undertaken during the taxpayer's travel.[141] The record must include the following information entered in English:
- the nature of the activities undertaken
- the day and approximate time of when the activities began

---

134 For an example, visit: Australian Taxation Office, 'Work-related expenses' (Web Page) www.ato.gov.au/Tax-professionals/ Your-practice/Tax-and-BAS-agents/Risk-assessment/Work-related-expenses.
135 Section 900-115.
136 Section 900-115.
137 Section 900-135.
138 Section 900-30.
139 Section 900-30(6).
140 Section 900-20.
141 Section 900-140.

- how long the activities lasted
- where the taxpayer engaged in the activities.[142]

Note that you do not need to record any other kind of activity beyond income-producing activities, but you may do so.[143] For example, if you undertake both income-producing activities (such as attend a conference) and also attend a friend's home for dinner (private activity) you may choose to include details of only the conference attendance in the record. Note that you may also need to keep a logbook in accordance with Division 28 (car expenses) in addition to a travel diary (see the example in table 6.3). Division 28 will be discussed in the chapter on specific deductions and applications of deductability.

TABLE 6.3   Example travel diary

Date	Start time	End time	Activity	Location
6 June 2020	6:00 pm	9:00 pm	Travel from Ballarat to Inverloch	In transit
			Overnight at Inverloch hotel	Inverloch
7 June 2020	9:30 am	5:30 pm	Attend accounting conference	Inverloch
	6:30 pm	7:30 pm	Attend welcome reception	Inverloch
			Overnight at linverloch hotel	Inverloch
8 June 2020	9:30 am	5:30 pm	Attend accounting conference	Inverloch
	7:00 pm	11:00 pm	Attend conference dinner	Inverloch
			Overnight at Inverloch hotel	Inverloch
9 June 2020	9:30 am	5:30 pm	Attend accounting conference	Inverloch
			Overnight at Inverloch hotel	Inverloch
10 June 2020	10:00 am	12:00 pm	Site visits to accounting firm #1	Melbourne
	2:00 pm	5:00 pm	Site visit to accounting firm #2	Melbourne
			Overnight at Melbourne hotel	Melbourne
11 June 2020	10:00 am	4:00 pm	Workshop on digital technology	Melbourne
			Overnight at Melbourne hotel	Melbourne
12 June 2020	9:00 am	11:00 am	Committee meeting	Melbourne
	11:30 am	1:00 pm	Travel from Melbourne to Ballarat	In transit

6.4.1.2.1 Exceptions

There are several exceptions to the general requirement to substantiate all losses and outgoings. Importantly, these do not create an automatic right to minimum deductions; they only allow taxpayers to reduce their compliance burden, which include the following.

- If the total of all your work expenses does not exceed $300, you do not need written evidence or travel records. However, the taxpayer *must* still be able to explain the claim if the ATO enquires. Note that for this threshold, work expenses *include* laundry expenses but *exclude* travel and meal allowance expenses (including car expenses). Once expenditure exceeds $300, you are required to substantiate *all* work expenses.[144]
- You can claim up to $150 in laundry expenses without written evidence.[145] Laundry expenditure includes washing, drying or ironing clothing such as uniforms. It explicitly excludes dry cleaning.[146] Importantly, this exception is included within the $300 limit. As such, a taxpayer cannot claim $450 of unsubstantiated costs. Note that you can calculate on a reasonable basis the laundry expenditure based

---

142 Section 900-150.
143 Section 900-155(2).
144 Section 900-35.
145 Section 900-40.
146 Section 900-40(4).

on \$1 per load of if the load is only made up of work-related clothing (this rate includes washing, drying and ironing), or \$0.50 per load if the load includes both work-related and other clothing. Clothing expenditure will be discussed further in the chapter on specific deductions and applications of deductibility.

- If an individual loss or outgoing costs \$10 or less, you can rely on your own record as written evidence (such as a diary entry), instead of a supplier document. You must document the same information as would be provided by a supplier,[147] as this does not reflect the same level of relief as the \$300 exception. You can claim up to \$200 deductions applying this exception.[148] Critically, if the \$200 threshold is exceeded, all purchases must be accompanied by the standard substantiation requirements. This exception is not dependent on whether the \$300 exception is satisfied.[149]

    It is therefore plausible to claim a number of deductions without formal supplier receipts. However, the taxpayer will need to be able to rely on appropriately applicable rules or rates (e.g. laundry rate per wash)[150] or by preparing the equivalent documentation (e.g. the small claims noted).

- Exceptions apply for both domestic and international travel allowance expenses. Written evidence or travel records may not be required where the Commissioner considers the total of the losses or outgoings claimed is reasonable.[151] Relevant losses or outgoings include accommodation, food or drink and incidentals and the travel must be covered by a travel allowance. However, for international travel, the exception does not apply to accommodation and the taxpayer is still required to keep travel records where the taxpayer is away from their ordinary residence for six or more nights in a row.[152] The Commissioner releases annual amounts for reasonable travel and overtime meal allowances.[153]

- A similar exception applies to expenses incurred in buying food or drink where the taxpayer receives an overtime meal allowance and the purchases are in connection with overtime worked.[154]

- Where the Commissioner considers it unreasonable to obtain written evidence, regardless of whether the expense is more than \$10, the taxpayer may be able to create their own written evidence in accordance with section 900-125.[155]

6.4.1.3 Substantiating car expenses (Subdivision 900-C)

As already noted, the treatment and substantiation of most motor vehicles losses or outgoings are found within Division 28 and Subdivision 900-C. Depending on the method relied upon, substantiation may be in the form of written evidence or odometer readings.

- When the taxpayer uses the 'log book' method, written evidence is required to substantiate expenses.[156] An exception applies to fuel or oil, in that the taxpayer may choose to rely on odometer records to establish and estimate average fuel and oil costs.

- When the taxpayer uses the 'cents per kilometre' method, taxpayers are required to reasonably estimate the business kilometres and are not required to comply with any substantiation rules.

6.4.1.4 Substantiating business travel expenses (Subdivision 900-D)

Similar to work expenses, a taxpayer is required to substantiate business travel expenses with written evidence and travel records are required for travel involving being away from the taxpayer's ordinary residence for six or more nights in a row.[157] The key difference between Subdivision 900-B and Subdivision 900-D, is that the travel expense relates to the production of assessable income other than salary or wages.[158]

---

147 Section 900-125.
148 Section 900-35.
149 Section 900-125 Note 2.
150 See also PS LA 2005/7 *Substantiating an individual's work-related expenses*. Note that there is also a home office hourly rate.
151 Section 900-50(1); section 900-55(1).
152 Sections 900-55(1),(3).
153 For an example, review TD 2019/11 *Income tax: what are the reasonable travel and overtime meal allowance expense amounts for the 2019–20 income year?*
154 Section 900-60. Also review TD 2019/11 *Income tax: what are the reasonable travel and overtime meal allowance expense amounts for the 2019–20 income year?*
155 Section 900-130.
156 Section 900-70.
157 Section 900-85.
158 Section 900-95.

6.4.1.5 Retaining and producing records

Written records are required to be retained for 5 years, known as the 'retention period'.[159] The 5 years start on the due day for lodging the income tax return, or the date of lodgement if later.[160] The Commissioner may tell you to produce your records, however you do not have to produce records if the retention period is over.[161] Archiving of business records is a normal part of your annual cycle and should be done on a regular basis. The 5-year rule in tax is a common requirement and should be adhered to for all records whether or not they have a direct bearing on your tax position.[162] Note that the retention period can be extended — for example, when there is a dispute with the Commissioner relating to the expense.[163] Once the dispute is resolved the extension ends.[164]

The Commissioner also has the discretion to allow claims, where the taxpayer has failed to substantiate, and the Commissioner is satisfied that the expense was incurred and that the taxpayer is entitled to the deduction.[165] There may also be circumstances where documents are lost or destroyed. In those instances, section 900-205 may offer assistance to the taxpayer, whether by accepting complete copies of the original document(s), or in the case of travel records, not requiring any replacement.

6.4.2 Section 262A ITAA36

General record-keeping requirements are found in section 262A of the ITAA36, which requires a person (including a company) who carries on a business to keep records and explain all transactions and other acts engaged in by the person that are relevant for income tax purposes. These records must be in English, or otherwise capable of being converted into English.[166] The period of retention is generally 5 years; however, some exceptions do apply (not detailed here).[167] Further guidance can be found in the following tax rulings.

- TR 96/7[168] details those records that are considered acceptable for the purpose of satisfying section 262A. It discusses records arising from cash registers, receipt books and credit cards for example, as well as when there are no source records.
- TR 2018/2[169] details acceptability around electronic records, including issues such as encryption and cloud storage.

TECHNOLOGY IN ACTION

Record-keeping for cryptoassets

The Australian Taxation Office (ATO) provides some guidance on recording-keeping for cryptoassets.[170] In particular, the ATO outline the core records that a taxpayer needs to retain in table 6.4.

Taxpayers can approach recording-keeping in a number of ways, including using a basic spreadsheet to compile records, or use professional programs or applications. The ATO, for example, offers a free application called *myDeductions* that can be downloaded onto smart devices.[171] This app can be used to record expense details (as well as photos of receipts), with the expense details then able to be uploaded to prefill *myTax* when proceeding to submit the taxpayer's tax return. Alternatively, the details can be emailed to the taxpayer's tax agent. For individual taxpayers, the app can be used for a multitude of expenses, including car, travel, uniform, self-education, gifts or donations, costs related to managing tax affairs, interest, dividend and other deductions. Sole traders with simple tax affairs can also use the app.[172]

---

159 Section 900-25(1); section 900-90; section 900-165.
160 Section 900-25(2).
161 Section 900-175.
162 R Caldwell, 'Taxation for Australian businesses' (Wrightbooks, 2014).
163 Section 900-25(3); section 900-170.
164 Section 900-170.
165 Section 900-195.
166 ITAA36 section 262A(3).
167 ITAA36 section 262A.
168 *Income tax: record keeping — section 262A — general principles.*
169 *Income tax: record keeping and access — electronic records.*
170 Ether is the cryptocurrency on the Ethereum blockchain. This is comparable to Bitcoin being the cryptocurrency on the Bitcoin blockchain.
171 Australian Taxation Office, 'Cryptocurrency and tax' (Web Page, 8 December 2021) https://www.ato.gov.au/General/Other-languages/In-detail/Information-in-other-languages/Cryptocurrency-and-tax.
172 Australian Taxation Office, 'myDeductions' (Web Page, 4 August 2021) https://www.ato.gov.au/General/Online-services/ATO-app/myDeductions/?=redirected_myDeductions.

TABLE 6.4   Core records for cryptoassets

Buying/acquiring	Owning/holding	Disposing

Either:
• records of receipts of transactions
• documents that display:
  – the cryptocurrency
  – the purchase price in Australian dollars
  – the date and time of the transaction
  – what the transaction was for.
 	
And records showing:
• commission or brokerage fees on the purchase
• agent, accountant and legal costs
• exchange records.
	Records showing:
	• software costs related to managing tax affairs
	• digital wallet records and keys
	• documents showing the date and quantity of cryptocurrency received via staking or airdrop.
		Either:
		• records of receipts of sale or transfer
		• documents that display:
		  – the cryptocurrency
		  – the sale or transfer price in Australian dollars
		  – the date and time of the transaction
		  – what the transaction was for.
		
		And records showing:
		• commission or brokerage fees on the sale or transfer
		• exchange records
		• Calculation of capital gain or loss.

Source: Australian Taxation Office, Cryptocurrency and tax (Web Page, 8 December 2021) https://www.ato.gov.au/misc/downloads/pdf/qc67444.pdf

REFLECTION

What challenges do you think will arise in record-keeping for cryptoassets, reflecting the perspectives of both the taxpayer and the tax practitioner? What records will be most challenging to ascertain?

173 Australian Taxation Office, 'Add your expenses' (Web Page, 26 May 2021) https://www.ato.gov.au/General/Online-services/In-detail/myDeductions/Using-myDeductions/?anchor=Addyourexpenses#Addyourexpenses.

SUMMARY

6.1 Differentiate the general deduction provision from specific deductions and explain the loss or outgoing and apportionment concepts.

The general deduction provision is found in section 8-1 of the ITAA97. This provision is made of 'positive limbs' and 'negative limbs', which bring a loss or outgoing into deductibility or remove it, respectively. What constitutes a loss or outgoing is more than merely what is outlaid or paid by a taxpayer, it is also the depletion of resources. Where there is dual purpose in a particular loss or outgoing, rather than having an inability to claim the amount, the taxpayer can apportion the amount and claim the loss or outgoing to the extent that it relates to income-earning activities.

6.2 Apply the two positive limbs of the general deduction provision.

The two positive limbs of section 8-1 offer comparable approaches to establish the nexus with a taxpayer's loss or outgoings. The first establishes the conditions for all taxpayers, and the second positive limb applies only to business taxpayers. Extensive and complex case law attempts to refine the key tests to establish whether the requisite nexus exists, whether in terms of being 'incurred' (first positive limb) or 'necessarily incurred' (second positive limb). For the first limb, there is a need to establish that nexus directly with income-earning activities, but for the second positive limb, this needs only to be established with the carrying on of a business. As such, the second limb offers a broader interpretation for taxpayers to establish the requisite nexus.

The courts have applied several tests in interpreting what it means to be 'incurred'; including the 'incidental and relevant test', 'the essential character test', 'the purpose test' and 'the occasion of the expenditure test'. The courts have shown that there need not be a temporal nexus such as found in accounting practice; deductions have been allowed despite income-earning activities having ceased.

6.3 Apply the four negative limbs of the general deduction provision.

The four negative limbs reduce opportunities for deductions where the loss or outgoing is of a capital nature; private or domestic nature; has nexus with exempt or non-assessable non-exempt income; or is explicitly denied through specific provisions of the legislation outside of section 8-1.

The courts have struggled over characterising a loss or outgoing as capital, and therefore not deductible; or a revenue expense, and therefore deductible (pursuant to the remaining negative limbs). Though numerous tests exist, such as the 'once and for all test' and the 'enduring benefits test', Australia settled on 'the business entity test'. This test characterises losses and outgoings by distinguishing between the 'profit-yielding subject' (structure) of a taxpayer and 'the process of operating it', with the latter leading to a revenue expense deductible pursuant to section 8-1 (as long as no other limb prevents it).

The second negative limb denies deductibility of expenses to the extent that they are of a private or domestic nature. Here, common expenditure to be characterised this way includes travel between home and work, child minding costs and food or drink. To be private or domestic will often mean that the loss or outgoing may not have been able to satisfy the positive limbs to begin with — a similar logical conclusion could be made with the third negative limb; losses or outgoings related to exempt income or non-assessable non-exempt income.

The final negative limb denies deductibility where a specific provision in either the ITAA36 or ITAA97 prevents the deduction. Many of these are found within Division 26 of the ITAA97. It is critical to appreciate that expenditure here may well be otherwise deductible under section 8-1 if not for these provisions.

6.4 Explain the substantiation requirements in order to claim a deduction.

Irrespective of whether a loss or outgoing meets the requirements of section 8-1, if the taxpayer cannot adequately substantiate the amount, the deduction will not be allowed. It is therefore important to be aware of legislative requirements in terms of individuals and partnerships (Division 900) and taxpayers more generally (section 262A of the ITAA36), to appropriately substantiate claims, including the preparation and retention of written records.

KEY TERMS

deduction An amount that you can deduct.

entertainment Section 32-10(1) of the ITAA97 defines entertainment as (a) providing food, drink or recreation as entertainment, or (b) providing accommodation or travel for entertainment that involves food, drink or recreation.

general deduction Any loss or outgoing that is deductible under section 8-1 of the ITAA97 is known as a general deduction.

necessarily The word 'necessarily' is not given its strict dictionary meaning. Instead, the courts have interpreted it to mean something probably 'no more than clearly appropriate or adapted for'.

negative limb Specifies what cannot be deducted under section 8-1 of the ITAA97.

nexus Can be defined as an important connection between the parts of a system or a group of things.

positive limb Represents what the legislation brings into deductibility under section 8-1 of the ITAA97.

rebatable benefit Includes government allowances such as Youth Allowance (Student), Youth Allowance (Jobseeker), ABSTUDY Living Allowance, Austudy Living Allowance and Newstart Allowance.

recreational club Section 26-45(2) of the ITAA97 defines a recreational club as 'a company that was established or is carried on mainly to provide facilities, for the use or benefit of its members, for drinking, dining, recreation or entertainment'.

related entity According to section 26-35 of the ITAA97, a related entity is a relative or partnership in which your relative is a partner. The provision further defines related parties in the context of partnerships.

travel record According to section 900-140 of the ITAA97, a travel record is a record of activities undertaken during travel.

QUESTIONS

6.1 Briefly outline the difference between the positive limbs and negative limbs of section 8-1 of the ITAA97.

6.2 Determine whether the following statements are true or false.
   (a) Outgoings must be incurred in the same year as the related assessable income.
   (b) If the loss or outgoing meets the requirements of a general and specific deduction, the taxpayer can claim under both sections.
   (c) *Charles Moore & Co (WA) Pty Ltd v FCT* (1956) confirmed that losses, such as stolen earnings, can be deductible under the general deduction provision.
   (d) Food and drink will always be classified as private or domestic in nature.
   (e) The business entity test is the key test in Australia to distinguish between capital and revenue expenses.
   (f) If a loss or outgoing meets the requirements of section 8-1 of the ITAA97, it can be claimed irrespective of records kept.

6.3 Can a business taxpayer rely on both positive limbs of section 8-1 of the ITAA97, or are they restricted to falling within the second limb only?

6.4 What does the business entity test outlined by Dixon J in *Sun Newspapers Ltd & Associated Ltd v FCT* (1938) seek to determine?

6.5 The fourth negative limb denies losses or outgoings to the extent that a provision in the Acts prevent the deduction. Identify and provide an explanation of three denying provisions according to Division 26. You may use examples to assist in your explanation.

6.6 If a business, which ceased operation numerous years ago, was left with outstanding debts related to those operations, will the related interest expense for the debt likely be deductible under section 8-1 of the ITAA97?

6.7 Political contributions and gifts are specifically denied under section 26-22 of the ITAA97, except in what instance with reference to Division 30?

6.8 What is the effect of the application of section 27-5 of the ITAA97?

6.9 Outline the five pieces of information required for a piece of written evidence, such as a receipt, to be compliant with Division 900 of the ITAA97.

6.10 Perry, a fellow student is a little confused over the substantiation rules. He has provided the following details. Determine if they are true or false.

(a) Expenses that cost less than $10 do not need supplier invoices. Instead, equivalent records can be created by the taxpayer.

(b) Taxpayers can claim $300 against their assessable income automatically.

(c) Taxpayers can claim laundry expenses of up to $150 without receipts; however, this excludes dry cleaning.

(d) The $300 limit excludes car expenses and expenses relating to allowances for meals and travel.

(e) Division 900 of the ITAA97 applies to all taxpayers.

(f) When substantiating car expenses using the logbook method, written evidence is required for all expenditure.

PROBLEMS

6.11 Brianna owns a residential investment property in Inverloch, which she has been renting out to tenants for the last 3 years. Brianna lives in Sydney and travels once a year to inspect the rental property. In the current tax year, she incurred $1400 in travel expenses, including flights, hire car, accommodation, food and incidentals. The travel related solely to attending the property to undertake the annual inspection.

(a) Explain whether or not the outgoings will be deductible to Brianna.

(b) Will your response in (a) differ if, instead of Brianna herself undertaking the travel, she arranged for a property manager to undertake the inspection?

(c) Will your response to (a) differ if the taxpayer was a corporate taxpayer?

6.12 Chris runs an advertising business in Heidelberg. His employees are occasionally required to travel around Australia as part of their job. Rather than paying for them to travel economy, he pays for them to travel business class. This usually adds around $500–$1000 to each trip. Jacob, his friend points out that the Commissioner is likely to question the deduction and only allow what is reasonable: an estimate of economy pricing. Advise Chris.

6.13 Stephan is a building designer operating out of Daylesford, near Melbourne, Victoria. He produces drawings and designs for new builds, minor renovations and extensions. He completed several projects in the last 12 months. However, one disgruntled client argued that the design was faulty and led to major delays in the construction of his dwelling. Stephan was taken to court and ultimately settled, paying $12 000 in damages to the client. He then spent a further $15 000 on advertising to overcome a small amount of negative press arising from the events. Advise Stephan of the deductibility of the settlement and advertising.

6.14 Sia is required to attend a 3-day conference in Sydney. The travel is directly related to her income-earning activities. She travels with her husband Bobby. Sia incurs the following travel expenditure.

- Flights: $150 per person return.
- Airport transfers: $40 per person return.
- Accommodation: $320 per room per night.
- Conference ticket: 1 ticket for $650.
- Guest ticket to welcome event: 1 ticket for $90.

Determine, based upon section 26-30 of the ITAA97, the deduction allowed for Sia in accordance with section 8-1 of the ITAA97. Present a detailed explanation of your calculation.

6.15 In example 6.4, it was explained that Kelly has a YouTube account reviewing, discussing and playing video games. She has successfully gained over 20 000 followers. Kelly regularly purchases games, has early access to beta versions, and records her experiences playing the games, posting them online. Kelly earns some sponsorship and advertising income from this activity.

It was argued that the expenditure on games was not of a private nature. Explain the relevance in terms of this characterisation and complete the analysis of whether the game purchases will be deductible under section 8-1 of the ITAA97.

6.16 Kevin Andrews is a regular client of Bradley, a registered tax agent. Kevin is a dental nurse in regional New South Wales and provided Bradley with an income statement showing $65 000 in gross income for the tax year. Kevin explains to Bradley that he wants to claim $3000 in travel costs. With respect to the TASA Code of Professional Conduct, discuss Bradley's responsibilities under Code Item 9 and what he may do to discharge this responsibility.

ACKNOWLEDGEMENTS

Table 6.4: © Australian Taxation Office
Extracts: © Federal Register of Legislation. Licensed under CC BY 4.0.
Extracts: © High Court of Australia
Extracts: © Federal Court of Australia. Licensed under CC BY 3.0.
Extract: © UK Court of Appeal. Licensed under OGL v3.0.
Extract: © Australian Taxation Office

Specific deductions and applications of deductibility

LEARNING OBJECTIVES

After studying this chapter, you should be able to:

7.1 explain the relationship between general and specific deductions

7.2 apply common specific deductions set out in Division 25

7.3 apply deductions related to car expenses as set out in Division 28

7.4 apply deductions related to donations as set out in Division 30

7.5 apply deductions related to non-compulsory uniforms as set out in Division 34

7.6 describe the deductibility of tax losses as set out in Division 36

7.7 describe the deductibility of non-commercial losses as set out in Division 35

7.8 describe the general and specific deductibility of the more common losses and outgoings.

Overview

As described in the chapter on general deductions, the ITAA97 breaks deductions into general (section 8-1) and specific deductions (section 8-5). Having described general deductions in that chapter, in this chapter we examine the specific deduction provisions.

Specific deduction provisions offer further opportunities to claim losses or outgoings, whether they perhaps already meet the requirements of the general deduction provision (you cannot, however, claim a deduction twice) or when a loss or outgoing fails one of the limbs (e.g. where a loss or outgoing is found to be of a capital nature).

At the conclusion of the chapter, we consider the more common losses and outgoings experienced by taxpayers and outline the deductibility in terms of the general deduction provision and specific provisions where applicable. In that way, we bring together numerous aspects of the legislation and case law relevant to deductions.

7.1 Relationship between general and specific deductions

LEARNING OBJECTIVE 7.1 Explain the relationship between general and specific deductions.

The ITAA97 provides for general deductions in section 8-1 and specific deductions in section 8-5. Specific deductions reflect particular kinds of expenditure that the legislation *specifically* permits.

A loss or outgoing may be eligible to be a specific deduction whether or not it qualifies as a general deduction (see figure 7.1). A loss or outgoing that meets the positive limbs described in the previous chapter may be a general deduction as well as a specific deduction. However, this does not mean that a taxpayer can claim the loss or outgoing twice (ITAA97 section 8-10); instead, the most appropriate provision will apply — in most cases, this is the specific deduction provision. Additionally, where a loss or outgoing meets the positive limbs, but is removed by the negative limbs, it will not be an allowable deduction under the general deduction provision but may still be deductible according to a specific deduction provision. Hence, any loss or outgoing should be assessed against not only the general deduction provision, but also the specific deduction rules.

FIGURE 7.1   Extending the general deduction provision

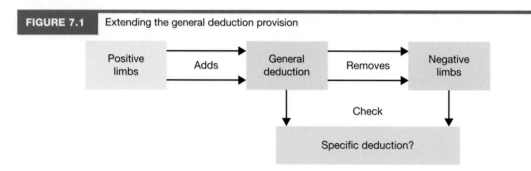

Numerous sections of the ITAA97 outline specific deductions. Section 12-5 lists deductions and many specific deductions are cited in Divisions 25 to 30. Section 8-5 provides for these provisions to be deducted against taxpayer's assessable income and applies the label **specific deduction** to these losses or outgoings:

Specific deductions

(1) You can also deduct from your assessable income an amount that a provision of this Act (outside this Division) allows you to deduct.

(2) Some provisions of this Act prevent you from deducting an amount that you could otherwise deduct, or limit the amount you can deduct.

(3) An amount that you can deduct under a provision of this Act (outside this Division) is called a specific deduction.

Note: If you receive an amount as insurance, indemnity or other recoupment of a deductible expense, the amount may be included in your assessable income: see Subdivision 20-A.

In the following sections, we outline a selection of the more common specific deduction and limiting provisions:

- Division 25: Some amounts that you can deduct
- Division 28: Car expenses
- Division 30: Gifts or contributions
- Division 34: Non-compulsory uniforms
- Division 36: Tax losses of earlier income years
- Division 35: Deferral of losses from non-commercial business activities.

7.2 Division 25 — Specific deduction provisions

LEARNING OBJECTIVE 7.2 Apply common specific deductions set out in Division 25.

Division 25 sets out amounts that may be deducted. The following subsections describe some of the more commonly used deductions allowed under Division 25.[1] In reviewing these specific deductions, it should be recognised that the general rules in Division 8 (discussed in the chapter on general deductions) 'may also apply'.

7.2.1 Tax-related expenses (section 25-5)

According to section 25-5, a taxpayer can deduct expenditure relating to the managing of their tax affairs, including, for example, obligations imposed by a Commonwealth law (insofar it relates to the taxpayer's tax affairs). This section is available to a wide variety of entity types, including individuals, bodies corporate, partnerships and companies. Without this provision, payment to a tax agent for the preparation and lodgement of an individual's tax return would be considered private in nature.

Section 995-1 describes **tax affairs** as affairs relating specifically to income tax. This restricts section 25-5 to income tax matters only, not matters relating to other forms of taxation, such as GST and FBT (for these, taxpayers will need to refer to the general deduction provision instead). Furthermore, the services in relation to tax affairs are only deductible if provided by a recognised tax adviser.[2] A **recognised tax adviser** is a registered tax agent, BAS agent or tax (financial) adviser, or legal practitioner.[3]

Despite these restrictions, section 25-5 has broad applicability in terms of capturing a wide range of compliance activities. Some examples are described in table 7.1.[4]

Example 7.1 considers the deductibility of the cost of managing tax affairs pursuant to section 25-5 specifically.

EXAMPLE 7.1

Deductibility of cost of managing tax affairs

A taxpayer incurs costs seeking advice from a recognised tax adviser. They seek advice on obtaining a private ruling regarding whether an item of property can be depreciated, the preparation of an objection to a fringe benefits tax assessment, the winding up of an entity and the preparation and submission of their tax return.

To what extent can the taxpayer claim the costs of the tax adviser's services?

The taxpayer can claim the costs to the extent they are in relation to the managing of their tax affairs. This would include the advice on a private ruling (see the example in subsection 25-5(4)) and the preparation and submission of their tax return. The taxpayer will not be able to rely on section 25-5 for the objection for the fringe benefits assessment or the winding up of an entity. These do not fall within the scope of tax affairs covered by section 25-5, which is limited to income tax only.

---

1 ITAA97 section 25-1.
2 ITAA97 section 25-5(2)(e).
3 ITAA97 section 995-1.
4 See also Matthew Eakin, Phillip Browne and Kaylene Hubbard, 'Section 25-5: More than meets the eye?' (2012) 46(9) *Taxation in Australia* 401–403, which considers the broad scope of section 25-5.

TABLE 7.1   **Example deductibility of expenditure according to section 25-5**

Deductible under section 25-5	Not-deductible under section 25-5
• Preparation and lodgement of income tax returns, income activity statements by a recognised tax adviser. • Advice relating to the taxpayer's income tax affairs, irrespective of whether capital/revenue nature. • Decline in value of capital expenditure pursuant to Division 40, to the extent used for managing tax affairs.[5] • Associated expenditure incurred, including travelling to the recognised tax adviser, accommodation, meals, taxi fares etc.[6] • Responding to an audit, assessment or determination in relation to income tax matters. • Payment of the general interest charge (GIC), shortfall interest charges (SIC). • Obtaining certain valuations.	• The income tax obligation itself, amounts withheld or payable under the PAYG system. • Capital expenditure (e.g. cost of a computer for the purposes of managing your tax affairs). • Expenditure for borrowing money for the purposes of paying income tax and other related obligations, such as PAYG withholding (e.g. interest). • Responding to an audit, assessment or determination in relation to GST or FBT. • Tax shortfall, administrative penalties. • Expenditure incurred in managing tax affairs paid to someone other than a recognised tax adviser. • Advice regarding the commission of an offence against an Australian or foreign law. • Expenditure that is specifically denied or limited by a provision other than section 8-1.

7.2.2 Repairs (section 25-10)

Section 25-10 allows the taxpayer to claim a deduction for repairs to premises, part of premises, or a depreciable asset (plant, machinery, tools, articles) insofar as it is held or used for producing assessable income. Whether repairs are deductible according to section 25-10 depends on considering whether the expenditure meets the definition of a 'repair', whether it is of a capital nature, and the extent to which it is incurred in producing assessable income.

A decision chart for whether expenditure is deductible as repairs is presented in figure 7.2.

FIGURE 7.2   Mapping repairs

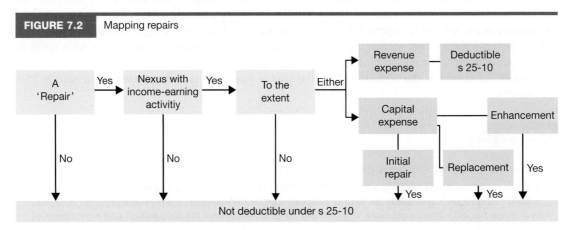

Note that figure 7.2 is for section 25-10 only. Capital allowances/capital works (covered in Divisions 40 and 43) should also be assessed, particularly where the outgoing is found to be of a capital nature. See the chapter on capital allowances for more detail.

7.2.2.1 What constitutes a 'repair'

The expenditure needs to reflect an actual 'repair'. Given that the Act does not define what 'repair' means, it takes on its ordinary meaning. As such, what constitutes a repair generally reflects some activity of restoration or renewal of decayed, worn out or broken parts, or re-fixing what is loose or detached, as opposed to 'maintenance'. There needs to be a link with some form of wear and tear, or damage and

---

5 Its use is deemed to be property used for the purpose of producing assessable income according to ITAA97 sections 25-5(5), (6).

6 See Australian Taxation Office, *Income tax: Is the cost of travelling to have a tax return prepared by a 'recognised tax adviser' deductible under section 25-5 of the Income Tax Assessment Act 1997* (ITAA 1997)? (TD 2017/8, 29 March 2017).

making good of such defects to its former condition, therefore restoring the efficiency or function, and without changing its character.[7] Jenkinson J in *BP Oil Refinery (Bulwer Island) Ltd v FCT*[8] said:

> Work will not be considered repair unless it includes some restoration of something lost or damaged, whether function or substance or some other quality or characteristic.

This can be contrasted with *maintenance*, which generally prevents the defects, damage or deterioration from occurring. Maintenance expenses are not allowable under section 25-10 but may be deductible under the general deduction provision.

The same conditions apply to works undertaken in accordance with requirements of a regulatory body.[9]

Expenditure to remove substances such as asbestos is not a 'repair' under section 25-10, unless the Commissioner is of the view that there is a genuine need for repair (defect, damage, deterioration).[10] However, a deduction may be allowable under section 40-755.

The meaning of repair is demonstrated in example 7.2, which relates to environmental protection activities.

EXAMPLE 7.2

Repairs

Graeme Constructions Ltd runs a business of constructing caravans. The business was required to remove asbestos insulation from its factory walls due to the health risks associated with asbestos. The insulation was otherwise in good condition and was not in need of repair. The business replaced the insulation with equivalent non-dangerous insulation material.

Is the work deductible under section 25-10?

This expenditure is not deductible according to section 25-10. It is not rectifying a physical or mechanical defect as the insulation is functionally efficient as insulation; instead, the works relate to health risks. However, a deduction may be available under section 40-755[11] (environmental protection activities).[12]

Repairs are commonly claimed for rental properties. Figure 7.3 is an ATO flow chart mapping deductibility relating to repairs in this context. We can map out the legislative basis to this chart beginning with outlays for repairs that are deductible according to section 25-10, compared with maintenance (more likely to be deductible under section 8-1 rather than section 25-10), and capital outlays such as initial repairs, capital works and depreciable assets. Note that where an outlay is of a capital nature, taxpayers need to refer to other sections of the tax legislation, such as the capital allowance provision (Division 40) and capital works provision (Division 43). These are discussed in the chapter on capital allowances.

7.2.2.2 Requisite nexus with income-earning activities

Repairs must be in connection with an income-producing asset and are claimable only to the extent the relevant asset or premises is used for that income-producing purpose. Note, however that it is possible to claim repairs when they are carried out after the cessation of income-earning activities as long as the expenditure is incurred within the same income year, as noted in Taxation Ruling IT 180:

> A deduction may be allowed for the cost of repairs to property providing:
>
> (a) the necessity for the repairs can be related to a period of time during which the premises have been used to produce assessable income of the taxpayer, and
>
> (b) the premises have been used in the production of such assessable income of the year of income in which the expenditure is incurred.[13]

---

7 See, eg, *W Thomas & Co Pty Ltd v FCT* (1965) 115 CLR 58, 72.

8 *BP Oil Refinery (Bulwer Island) Ltd v FCT* 92 ATC 4031, 4039 (Jenkinson J).

9 Australian Taxation Office, *Income tax: deductions for repairs* (TR 97/23, 3 December 1997) [24]-[25] ('TR 97/23').

10 Ibid [26].

11 ITAA97.

12 Based on the example in TR 97/23, [27].

13 Australian Taxation Office, *Repairs to property carried out after cessation of income production* (IT 180, 10 December 1964), [4].

Are you replacing something that is worn out, damaged or broken as a result of renting out the property?	This is likely to be a **REPAIR**	E.g. replacing part of the fence damaged in a storm or getting in a plumber to fix a leaking tap	This should be claimed at **Repair and Maintenance** on the rental schedule
Are you preventing or fixing deterioration of an item that occurred while renting out the property?	This is likely to be **MAINTENANCE**	E.g. getting faded interior walls repainted or having a deck re-oiled	This should be claimed at **Repair and Maintenance** on the rental schedule
Are you repairing damage that existed when the property was bought (whether it was known about at the time of purchase or not)?	This is likely to be an **INITIAL REPAIR**	E.g. fixing floorboards that had damage when the property was bought	This should be claimed at **Capital Works** or **Capital Allowances** on the rental schedule
Are you replacing an entire structure that is only partly damaged? Or are you renovating or adding a new structure to the property?	This is likely to be a **CAPITAL WORKS**	E.g. replacing all the fencing, not just the damaged portion, or adding a carport	This should be claimed at **Capital Works** on the rental schedule
Are you installing a brand new appliance or floor/window covering?	This is likely to be a **DEPRECIATING ASSET**	E.g. buying a brand new dishwasher or installing new carpet	This should be claimed at **Capital Allowance** on the rental schedule

Source: Australian Taxation Office, NAT 75208-08.2019 DE-5271.

Section 25-10 is silent in terms of the taxpayer owning the property in question. This means that if the taxpayer is a lessee of property and incurs genuine repair costs, they continue to be entitled to a deduction under section 25-10 for those repairs.

7.2.2.3 Capital repairs

Consistent with the general deduction provision, a taxpayer is denied a deduction according to section 25-10(3) to the extent the repairs are of a capital nature. In other words, you cannot claim capital 'repairs' under section 25-10. When characterising outgoings as repairs, the taxpayer needs to ensure that what they are doing does not amount to improvements, replacements or initial repairs. In those instances, the outgoings are appropriately characterised as capital and therefore are not deductible under section 25-10(3). Furthermore, if the taxpayer adds something to the asset in question (e.g. an extension to a property), then it too will not be of a capital nature and not a repair.

Where an outlay is found to be capital in nature, the taxpayer will need to look elsewhere for deductibility. For example, the capital allowance provisions in accordance with Division 40 or the capital works provisions in Division 43.

7.2.2.3.1 Initial repairs

An initial repair reflects acquisition activities. When the property is acquired with some pre-existing damage, deterioration or defect (i.e. is in need of repair), repair expenditure is classed as an 'initial repair'. The need to repair in this instance does not arise from the operations of the taxpayer, rather the need to repair forms part of the acquisition cost and having the asset ready and able to be used by the taxpayer. This was examined in *W Thomas & Co Pty Ltd v FCT.*

Facts: The taxpayer, a flour miller and grain merchant, incurred substantial expenditure on repairs to a dilapidated building that the taxpayer had recently acquired. The renovations were required before the taxpayer could use the building and sought a deduction for the expenditure.

Held: The Court found the expenditure was not deductible under the former section 53 of the ITAA36 (currently section 25-10 of the ITAA97).

Comment: The Court concluded that the outgoings were of a capital nature. Kitto J said:

> It is an expense of a revenue nature when it is to repair defects arising from the operations of the person who incurs it. But if when a thing is bought for use as a capital asset in the buyer's business it is not in good order and suitable for use in the way intended, the cost of putting it in order suitable for use is part of the cost of its acquisition ...[14]

This decision reaffirmed the decision set out in *Law Shipping Co Ltd v IRC* (1923)[15] that repairs on newly acquired premises will be capital outlays. The repairs are not attributable to the wear and tear by the taxpayer's operation, but instead reflect the cost of acquiring the asset.

Importantly, *W Thomas & Co Pty Ltd v FCT* (1965)[16] confirms that the taxpayer does not need to be aware of pre-existing defects in the asset.

7.2.2.3.2 Improvements

Improvements will be capital outgoings rather than repairs. Where the outlays result in the item as a whole becoming functionally better than what it was, it is considered an improvement rather than a repair under section 25-10. Importantly, the use of modern materials or the degree of technological enhancement may lead to a characterisation of improvement rather than a mere repair, where they lead to improvements in the operating efficiency of the assets that are not immaterial. Where the taxpayer simply restores the asset to its original state, it will not amount to an improvement.[17] This was examined in *FCT v Western Suburbs Cinemas Ltd*.

Facts: The taxpayer, a theatre, replaced the ceiling that was in a state of disrepair with different and better material due to the unavailability of original materials.

Held: The Court concluded that the outgoings amounted to a capital improvement and were not deductible as a revenue expense under the former section 53 of the ITAA36 (currently section 25-10 of the ITAA97).

> It did much more than meet a need for restoration; it provided a ceiling having considerable advantages over the old one, including the advantage that it reduced the likelihood of repair bills in the future ...[18]

Comment: Kitto J concluded that the replacement of the ceiling did not amount to a repair. In the contemporary setting, the taxpayer would be able to make use of the capital works deductions in accordance with Division 43 or form part of the cost base of the CGT asset.[19]

The scope of improvement — that it does not include replacement or improvement beyond renewal or replacement of subsidiary parts and minor and incidental improvements[20] — is demonstrated in example 7.3.

---

14 *W Thomas & Co Pty Ltd v FCT* (1965) 115 CLR 58, 72 (Kitto J).
15 12 TC 621.
16 115 CLR 58.
17 *Rhodesia Railways Ltd v CIT Bechuanaland* [1933] AC 368.
18 86 CLR 102, 105.
19 See ITAA97 Division 110.
20 *Lurcott v Wakely & Wheeler* [1911] 1 KB 905, 924.

EXAMPLE 7.3

Improvements

Worn out motor vehicle engines can be rebuilt to restore original functioning. Consider a car owner who has an engine rebuilt and as part of the process the mechanic replaces the damaged cast-iron pistons with alloy pistons. Alloy pistons are commonly used in modern engines. They are slightly more efficient because they are lighter, more resistant to wear and produce less friction.

Is the work related to the pistons a repair or an improvement?

Whether the work is a repair or an improvement depends on whether the functionality of the engine has been restored/only enhanced in a minor and incidental way or whether the pistons make the engine functionally better.

The alloy pistons do not change the engine's essential efficiency of function or character of the engine.[21] Expenditure in replacing the pistons is therefore deductible under section 25-10.

7.2.2.3.3 Replacements

The replacement of the whole, or substantially the whole, will be an improvement. Specifically, if a taxpayer replaces merely a part of the whole asset (due to its state of deterioration or damage), it will generally be deductible under section 25-10.[22] However, if the taxpayer replaces or reconstructs the entirety, or substantially the entirety, it will generally be capital in nature. As noted in *Lurcott v Wakely & Wheeler*:

> ... the question of repair is in every case one of degree, and the test is whether the act to be done is one which in substance is the renewal or replacement of defective parts, or the renewal or replacement of substantially the whole.[23]

This issue was also examined in *Lindsay v FCT*.

Lindsay v FCT (1960) 106 CLR 197

Facts: The taxpayer, a boat slip proprietor and ship repairer, incurred expenditure to reconstruct a slipway that had substantially deteriorated. The taxpayer sought to claim a deduction for the expenditure on the basis that the slipway was a part of the larger facility being the business premises and therefore a repair of a part not the entirety.

Held: The Court concluded that the expenditure was a renewal of the entirety not a part and thus was not deductible under the former section 53 of the ITAA36 (currently section 25-10 of the ITAA97).

Comment: The slipway represented an asset in itself rather than forming a part of the facilities and as such the expenditure did not amount to a repair.[24]

The expenditure was therefore of a capital nature. This decision can be compared with *Rhodesia Railways Ltd v CIT Bechuanaland* [1933],[25] in which 74 miles of railway were renewed with new sleepers and rails. The deduction was allowed as it represented only a part of the entirety (588-mile-long railway). However, it is important to note that in that case timber sleepers were replaced with concrete sleepers, so it would likely be capital if held in Australia due to enhancing the functionality of the asset. Relevantly, with such a characterisation, taxpayers can look towards Divisions 40 or 43 of the ITAA97 to seek deductions over the life of the asset (whether a depreciating asset or as capital works).

7.2.3 Borrowing expenses (section 25-25)

Section 25-25 of the ITAA97 allows a deduction for expenditure incurred in borrowing money, excluding the interest component, to the extent that the money is borrowed for income-producing purposes. This is not generally an immediate deduction of the full cost of borrowing; instead the expenditure is spread over the period of the loan as outlined next. The period of the loan refers to the shorter of the original loan contract or 5 years. Note, however, that if the borrowing expenses are of $100 or less, they can be immediately deducted (see subsection 25-25(6)).

---

21 Example in TR 97/23, [91].
22 ITAA97.
23 1 KB 905, 924.
24 385.
25 AC 368.

Section 25-25 allows for losses or outgoings that would otherwise be non-deductible in accordance with the general deduction provision due to their capital nature. Example expenditure covered by this section includes bank establishment fees. As section 25-25 does not apply to interest expense, taxpayers should consider interest deductibility in accordance with section 8-1.[26]

To determine the deduction allowed under section 25-25, the following steps should be applied. The 'maximum amount' allowed as a deduction for an income year can be determined as follows (ensure the maximum amount is apportioned for part purposes):

Step 1. Work out the *remaining expenditure* as follows:

- For the income year in which the period of the loan begins, it is the amount of the expenditure.
- For a later income year, it is the amount of the expenditure reduced by the maximum amount that you can deduct for the expenditure for each earlier income year.

Step 2. Work out the *remaining loan period* as follows:

- For the income year in which the period of the loan begins, it is the period of the loan (as determined at the end of the income year).
- For a later income year, it is the period from the start of the income year until the end of the period of the loan (as determined at the end of the income year).

Step 3. Divide the remaining expenditure by the number of days in the remaining loan period.

Step 4. Multiply the result from Step 3 by the number of days in the remaining loan period that are in the income year.[27]

Figure 7.4 presents a visualisation of this method and the process is demonstrated in example 7.4.

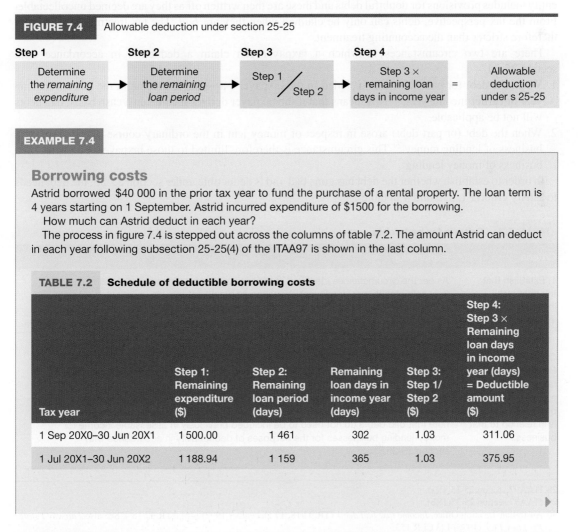

FIGURE 7.4 Allowable deduction under section 25-25

EXAMPLE 7.4

Borrowing costs

Astrid borrowed $40 000 in the prior tax year to fund the purchase of a rental property. The loan term is 4 years starting on 1 September. Astrid incurred expenditure of $1500 for the borrowing.

How much can Astrid deduct in each year?

The process in figure 7.4 is stepped out across the columns of table 7.2. The amount Astrid can deduct in each year following subsection 25-25(4) of the ITAA97 is shown in the last column.

TABLE 7.2 Schedule of deductible borrowing costs

Tax year	Step 1: Remaining expenditure ($)	Step 2: Remaining loan period (days)	Remaining loan days in income year (days)	Step 3: Step 1/ Step 2 ($)	Step 4: Step 3 × Remaining loan days in income year (days) = Deductible amount ($)
1 Sep 20X0–30 Jun 20X1	1 500.00	1 461	302	1.03	311.06
1 Jul 20X1–30 Jun 20X2	1 188.94	1 159	365	1.03	375.95

26 See, eg, *FCT v Munro* (1926) 38 CLR 153.
27 ITAA97 section 25-25(4).

Tax year	Step 1: Remaining expenditure ($)	Step 2: Remaining loan period (days)	Remaining loan days in income year (days)	Step 3: Step 1/ Step 2 ($)	Step 4: Step 3 × Remaining loan days in income year (days) = Deductible amount ($)
1 Jul 20X2–30 Jun 20X3	812.99	794	365	1.02	372.30
1 Jul 20X3–30 Jun 20X4	440.69	429	365	1.03	375.95
1 Jul 20X4–31 Aug 20X4	64.74	64	64	1.01	64.74
					1 500.00

Note: Dollar amounts in this table have been rounded at each step.

7.2.4 Bad debts (section 25-35)

Section 25-35 allows for taxpayers to claim a deduction for a debt or part of a debt that is written off in the income year. Importantly, the tax treatment is distinct from accounting practice. In accounting practice, the entity includes provisions for doubtful debts and these are then written off as they are deemed uncollectable. From the tax perspective, debts can only be claimed when they are *bad*. The tax treatment for debts is therefore stricter than the accounting treatment.

There are two circumstances in which a taxpayer can claim a deduction in accordance with section 25-35.

1. When the debt (or part debt) was included in the taxpayer's assessable income in the current income year or earlier income year.[28] This means that if the taxpayer derives income on a cash basis, bad debts will not be applicable.
2. When the debt (or part debt) arose in respect of money lent in the ordinary course of the taxpayer's business of lending money.[29] This circumstance is therefore limited to those taxpayers that carry on a business of money lending.

In order to establish whether the debt has gone bad and is deductible under section 25-35, the debt needs to satisfy criteria 1, 2, 3 *and* 4 in table 7.3.

TABLE 7.3	Criteria for bad debts

Criteria	Explanation
1. Establish that the debt was included previously in assessable income.	As per the circumstances identified, if the taxpayer derives income on a cash basis (e.g. sole practitioner, employee), the taxpayer would not include uncollected receipts in their assessable income and therefore not be entitled to claim a deduction under section 25-35. This can be contrasted with a taxpayer deriving income on an accrual's basis (e.g. larger professional practice or retailer).
OR Establish that the taxpayer carries on a money-lending business and the debt is in relation to that business.	The taxpayer is required to have been in the business of money lending at the time the loan was made, however not at the time the debt was written off. As to whether a taxpayer is carrying on a business of money lending is a question of fact, however is not limited to those ready and willing to lend moneys to the public at large, but also merely certain classes of borrowers.[30] Once established, it is important to note that bad debts do not need to be included previously in assessable income for money-lending businesses for the purposes of deductibility in accordance with section 25-35.[31]

28 ITAA97 section 25-35(1)(a).
29 ITAA97 section 25-35(1)(b).
30 Australian Taxation Office, *Income tax: bad debts* (TR 92/18, 17 December 1992) [46] ('TR 92/18'). See also *Fairway Estates Pty Ltd v FCT* (1970) 123 CLR 153.
31 *FCT v National Commercial Banking Corporation of Australia Ltd* (1983) 83 ATC 4715.

2. Establish the existence of the debt.	A debt refers to a sum of money due from one person to another.[32] At the time the taxpayer writes off the debt, the taxpayer is required to have some form of legal or equitable right in the debt. For example, no debt would exist if the taxpayer forgives or releases the debtor from the debt before it is written off.[33]

3. Establish that the debt is 'bad'.

The taxpayer needs to conclude that the debt is irrecoverable and not merely doubtful or simply considered bad because of an elapsed period of time.[34] The Commissioner states that: 'What is necessary is that the creditor make a bona fide assessment, based on sound commercial considerations, of the extent to which the debt is bad'.[35]

The Commissioner provides the following guidance in establishing that a debt is bad.

31. A debt may be considered to have become bad in any of the following circumstances:
   (a) the debtor has died leaving no, or insufficient, assets out of which the debt may be satisfied,
   (b) the debtor cannot be traced and the creditor has been unable to ascertain the existence of, or whereabouts of, any assets against which action could be taken,
   (c) where the debt has become statute barred and the debtor is relying on this defence (or it is reasonable to assume that the debtor will do so) for non-payment,
   (d) if the debtor is a company, it is in liquidation or receivership and there are insufficient funds to pay the whole debt, or the part claimed as a bad debt,
   (e) where, on an objective view of all the facts or on the probabilities existing at the time the debt, or a part of the debt, is alleged to have become bad, there is little or no likelihood of the debt, or the part of the debt, being recovered.

32. While individual cases may vary, as a practical guide a debt will be accepted as bad under category (e) above where, depending on the particular facts of the case, a taxpayer has taken the appropriate steps in an attempt to recover the debt and not simply written it off as bad. Generally speaking, such steps would include some or all of the following, although the steps undertaken will vary depending upon the size of the debt and the resources available to the creditor to pursue the debt:
   (i) reminder notices issued and telephone/mail contact is attempted
   (ii) reasonable period of time has elapsed since the original due date for payment of the debt. This will of necessity vary depending upon the amount of the debt outstanding and the taxpayers' credit arrangements (e.g. 90, 120 or 150 days overdue)
   (iii) formal demand notice is served
   (iv) issue of, and service of, a summons
   (v) judgement entered against the delinquent debtor
   (vi) execution proceedings to enforce judgement
   (vii) the calculation and charging of interest is ceased and the account is closed (a tracing file may be kept open; also, in the case of a partial debt write-off, the account may remain open),
   (viii) valuation of any security held against the debt,
   (ix) sale of any seized or repossessed assets.[36]

4. Establish that the debt has been written off.	The taxpayer is required to write off the debt in the year of income before the debt can be claimed as a bad debt in accordance with section 25-35. This can be achieved through accounting entries in the books of accounts, or alternatively board meeting minutes or written recommendations by the financial controller. Importantly, this criterion is *not* satisfied if the debt is written off after the year end, at the time when the books of account are being prepared.[37] Nor will it be satisfied if the debt has already been settled, compromised, extinguished or assigned.[38]

The provision does impose several further restrictions on bad debts, including for company taxpayers that have failed the ownership tests in accordance with Subdivisions 165-C and 166-C.[39] For further guidance refer to TR 92/18 *Income tax: bad debts*.

---

32 TR 92/18, [25].
33 See, eg, *Point v FCT* (1970) 119 CLR 453.
34 TR 92/18, [30].
35 Ibid [29].
36 Ibid [31]–[32].
37 Ibid [37]; *Point v FCT* (1970) 119 CLR 453, 458.
38 TR 92/18, [38]; *Point v FCT* (1970) 119 CLR 453; *Franklin's Selfserve Pty Ltd v FCT* (1970) 125 CLR 52.
39 See ITAA97 section 25-35(5).

7.2.5 Loss by theft etc. (section 25-45)

A problematic occurrence is loss of money arising through theft, stealing, embezzlement, larceny, defalcation or misappropriation. Section 25-45 allows the taxpayer to claim such a loss arising from the taxpayer's employee or agent as an allowable deduction. In order to claim such a loss, the taxpayer needs to have discovered the loss in the income year and have included the money in their assessable income in either the current income year or a prior income year.[40] Note that if the loss is recouped, the amount may be included in assessable income.[41]

Importantly, this provision only applies to money, which includes for example currency, promissory notes and bills of exchange.[42] Taxpayers should consider for example section 25-47 and Division 40 for depreciable assets and the trading stock provisions for trading stock (Division 70).

7.2.6 Payments to associations (section 25-55)

Section 25-55 provides for a deduction for payments in respect of memberships for trade, business and professional associations (e.g. memberships to the Chartered Accountants of Australia and New Zealand, CPA Australia, Institute of Public Accountants and the Tax Institute). Note that if the payment to an association is otherwise deductible under section 8-1 of the ITAA97, the taxpayer can claim the full amount. Section 25-55 will generally apply when the membership would fail to meet the requirements of section 8-1. For example, if the taxpayer was retired or on maternity/paternity leave, the necessary nexus to income-earning activities would not be established. The taxpayer may still want to keep their membership up to maintain their industry connections, and they may be earning other assessable income (e.g. interest, dividend income). In those cases, section 25-55 can be relied upon. However, unlike section 8-1, the deduction is a limited deduction. The taxpayer can only claim $42 per association. This is demonstrated in example 7.5. For additional guidance, see TR 2000/7.[43]

EXAMPLE 7.5

Payments to associations

Jeremy is a graduate engineer working in a Canberra firm. He has recently joined Engineers Australia, the professional body for the industry. He incurred $560 for his membership to the engineering professional body. He had been previously working as an accountant and so also has memberships with other related professional bodies and he is not ready to give these up. As such, he renewed his membership with two accounting and taxation associations. The costs of these renewals were $600 and $700 respectively.

How much can Jeremy claim under sections 8-1 and 25-55?

Jeremy can claim $560 in full in accordance with section 8-1 for the engineering membership. The engineering association has a direct nexus with his income-earning activities. However, he does not have the required nexus with the accounting and taxation associations. As such, he must rely on section 25-55 in order to obtain a deduction. Accordingly, he can claim a total of $84 for the accounting and taxation memberships ($42 for each association). He cannot claim the remaining $1216 for these particular memberships. As such, Jeremy can claim deductions totalling $644.

7.2.7 Travel between workplaces (section 25-100)

Section 25-100 of the ITAA97 provides a deduction for individual taxpayers who travel between two workplaces to engage in unrelated income-earning activities or to carry on a business for the purposes of gaining or producing assessable income. Ordinarily, this travel would not be considered to have been incurred in gaining or producing assessable income in respect of section 8-1, as it would be putting the taxpayer in a position *to* earn that income.[44]

---

40 ITAA97 section 25-45(a) and (c).
41 ITAA97 section 25-45. Also see Subdivision 20-A.
42 For the full definition, refer to section 195-1 of *A New Tax System (Goods and Services Tax) Act 1999* (Cth).
43 *Income tax: subscriptions, joining fees, levies and contributions paid to associations by individuals.*
44 *FCT v Payne* (2001) 202 CLR 93.

Figure 7.5 presents various scenarios and maps them against the requirements of section 25-100, with an illustration presented in example 7.6. A review of travel expenses is outlined in a later section.

FIGURE 7.5 Mapping deductible travel between workplaces under section 25-100

Panel A: Deductible direct travel   Panel B: Non-deductible indirect/private travel   Panel C: Non-deductible travel workplace/residence

EXAMPLE 7.6

Travel between workplaces

Carmen works two part-time jobs. She has shift work as a security guard and works as a call centre operator. Often Carmen is required to go from one to the other within the same day so catches the bus directly between jobs.

Can Carmen claim the travel between jobs under section 25-100?

Carmen can claim the cost of travel between the two part-time jobs under section 25-100; however, she cannot claim the travel from home and back. This reflects an application of Panel A in figure 7.5. Importantly, without section 25-100, the travel would not be deductible under section 8-1 as the occasion of the travel is to put Carmen in the position to earn income rather than in earning income.[45] Moreover, if Carmen diverts between the two places of work (e.g. to stop home to collect a uniform) rather than travelling directly to the second place of employment, the travel will not be deductible (visualised in Panel B of figure 7.5).

FCT v Payne (2001) 202 CLR 93

Facts: The taxpayer, a farmer and pilot, operated a deer farm at his home in NSW. He would travel between his home (the deer farm) and Sydney airport, in which he would fly out of as a pilot for Qantas. The issue in question was whether the travel between home/farm and the airport was deductible.

Held: The Court determined that the travel was not deductible.

Comment: The Court concluded that the travel was not incurred in the course of deriving income as either a farmer or as a pilot. The travel occurred between two income-producing activities and therefore was incurred in travelling *to* work, rather than *for* work. Section 25-100 of the ITAA97 was introduced after *Payne*'s case; however, *Payne* would not have been able to find relief in this provision. The fact that the deer farm was also his home, disqualified him from the particular claim.[46] This is representative of Panel C in figure 7.5.

7.2.8 COVID-19 tests (section 25-125)

The Federal Budget 2022 reaffirmed its aim to ensure the tax deductibility of COVID-19 tests, where the acquisition is incurred in order to attend a place of work, effective from 1 July 2021.[47] This measure was initially announced in February 2022[48] to resolve the potential private/domestic characterisation of the outgoings (recall the discussion in an earlier chapter on this important characterisation). Following

---

45 Ibid.
46 Refer to ITAA97 section 25-100(3).
47 Commonwealth of Australia, *Budget Paper No. 2 2022–23* (Web Page, 29 March 2022) 18 https://budget.gov.au/2022-23/content/bp2/download/bp2_2022-23.pdf. Similarly, making these acquisitions exempt from FBT: Ibid.
48 Michael Sukkar, 'Tax deductibility of COVID-19 test expenses' (Web Page, 8 February 2022) https://ministers.treasury.gov.au/ministers/michael-sukkar-2019/media-releases/tax-deductibility-covid-19-test-expenses.

Budget night, Treasury Laws Amendment (Cost of Living Support and Other Measures) Bill 2022 passed both Houses on the 30 March 2022. Having subsequently received royal assent, section 25-125 has been introduced to ITAA97 as follows.

(1) You can deduct a loss or outgoing to the extent it is incurred in gaining or producing your assessable income if:
   (a) you are an individual; and
   (b) the loss or outgoing is incurred in respect of testing you for the novel coronavirus SARS-CoV-2 that causes COVID-19 using a test covered by subsection (3); and
   (c) the purpose of testing you is to determine whether you may attend or remain at a place where you:
      (i) engage in activities to gain or produce your assessable income; or
      (ii) engage in activities in the course of carrying on a business for the purpose of gaining or producing your assessable income.
(2) However, you cannot deduct a loss or outgoing under this section to the extent that it is a loss or outgoing of capital, or of a capital nature.
(3) This subsection covers a test that:
   (a) is a polymerase chain reaction test; or
   (b) is a therapeutic good (within the meaning of the Therapeutic Goods Act 1989) that:
      (i) is included in the Australian Register of Therapeutic Goods maintained under section 9A of that Act; and
      (ii) has an intended purpose, accepted in relation to that inclusion, that relates to the detection of the novel coronavirus SARS-CoV-2 that causes COVID-19.

Section 25-125 therefore removes doubt on the deductibility where purchased in relation to a taxpayers work. There must be a sufficient connection between the testing for COVID-19 and the assessable income of the taxpayer — focusing on the taxpayer attending or remaining at their place of work.[49] As the Explanatory Memorandum explains, 'The amendments cover circumstances where a taxpayer's positive COVID-19 status means that they cannot attend their place of work at all, or will instead work from home if they are able to'.[50] It is not intended to include outgoings in respect to the prospect of future employment[51] or ancillary costs acquiring the tests;[52] however, may include for example credit card fees, postage and handling.[53] Where a pack of tests are used for both private and work purposes, the cost is required to be apportioned.[54]

Importantly, if the work-related expense is not able to be substantiated then the taxpayer cannot claim the cost of COVID-19 tests. Given that this newly enacted deduction applies from 1 July 2021, it is likely that not all taxpayers have retained their receipts from purchasing COVID-19 tests. As such, despite its introduction, this may not necessarily result in the taxpayer being able to claim it. Recall though, as outlined in the previous chapter, there are some exceptions to the general substantiation rules. For example, where a taxpayer's total work expenses total $300 or less, then written evidence is not required. As outlined in the previous chapter, in section 6.4.1.2, COVID-19 tests pursuant to section 25-125 are made explicitly within the scope of work expense exceptions.[55] This is not a giveaway though, the taxpayer is still required to be able to explain the claim if the ATO asked.

7.3 Division 28 — Car expenses

LEARNING OBJECTIVE 7.3 Apply deductions related to car expenses as set out in Division 28.

Division 28 of the ITAA97 provides specific rules regarding the claiming of car expenditure. This division only applies to individuals and partnerships that include at least one natural person (individual).[56] Note that the taxpayer does not need to legally own the car: this division can be applied to a car that is leased or

---

49 Explanatory memorandum, Treasury Laws Amendment (Cost of Living Support and Other Measures) Bill 2022, 22.
50 Ibid 22-3.
51 Ibid 23.
52 Ibid.
53 Ibid.
54 Ibid.
55 Ibid 24.
56 ITAA97 section 28-10. This means the partnership cannot have only corporate partners; one of the partners must be a natural person.

hired under a hire purchase agreement.[57] **Car expenses** include a loss or outgoing to do with operating a car as well as the decline in value of a car; however, it excludes car expenses incurred in respect of overseas travel as well as taxi fares or similar.[58]

Taxpayers can claim car expenses under one of two methods:

1. the 'cents per kilometre' method[59]
2. the 'log book' method.[60]

The cents per kilometre method allows the taxpayer to avoid more extensive paperwork but may result in a lower deduction. There is flexibility in which method is chosen: taxpayers can switch between methods each year, or even change their choice, and taxpayers can apply different methods to different cars within the same income year.[61] Figure 7.6 is a decision chart to guide the choice between the two methods.

FIGURE 7.6 Choosing between methods

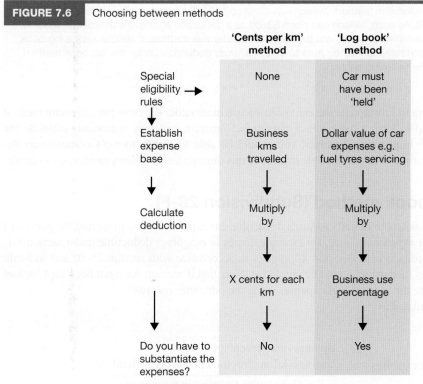

Source: Income Tax Assessment Act 1997 (Cth) section 28-15.

7.3.1 The cents per kilometre method (Subdivision 28-C)

You can claim the business kilometres you have travelled in the income year up to 5000 km using the cents per kilometre method. Business kilometres refer to those kilometres travelled to produce assessable income or to travel between workplaces.

The formula is set out in subsection 28-25(1):

$$\begin{array}{l} \text{Number of business kilometres} \\ \text{travelled by the car in the} \\ \text{income year} \end{array} \times \text{Rate of cents per kilometre}$$

The rate of cents per kilometre is updated from time to time.[62] For the 2020–2021 and 2021–2022 income years, the rate is 72 cents per kilometre. This rate considers operating expenses for a car, such

---

57 ITAA97 section 28-1.
58 ITAA97 section 28-13.
59 ITAA97 Subdivision 28-C.
60 ITAA97 Subdivision 28-F.
61 ITAA97 section 28-20.
62 ITAA97 section 28-25(4). See, eg, *Income Tax Assessment Act 1997 — Cents per Kilometre Deduction Rate for Car Expenses 2020.* As per Income Tax Assessment — Cents per Kilometre Deduction Rate for Car Expenses Determination 2022, the proposed rate from 1 July 2022 is 75 cents per kilometre.

as fuel, maintenance, registration, insurance and depreciation. By claiming using this method you do not claim any individual car expenses. This method is demonstrated in example 7.7.

Cents per kilometre method

Nelson is a sole trader running a liquor licensing consulting business. He travels around regional and metropolitan Victoria to meet with various clients who run cafes, bars and restaurants. During the year, Nelson travelled 8500 business kilometres.

The current rate of cents per kilometre is 72 cents.

How much can Nelson claim using the cents per kilometre method?

Under the cents per kilometre method, Nelson can claim up to 5000 kilometres. This can be calculated as $5000 \times 0.72 = \$3600$. As such, Nelson can claim $3600 as a deduction against his assessable income.

The remaining 3500 kilometres would not be deductible under this method. If Nelson kept a log book and record of his expenditure, he may be able to obtain a larger deduction under the log book method. This is considered in the following section.

There is no requirement to substantiate the car expenses you incur under the cents per kilometre method and you are not required to keep a log book of your travel. Instead, you may reasonably estimate the number of kilometres.[63] Importantly however, you should be able to justify to the Commissioner the claimed kilometres if required. You may be able to achieve this through keeping diary entries, for example.

7.3.2 The log book method (Subdivision 28-F)

The log book method looks more directly towards deductible car expenses[64] you incur and the pattern of car usage. Deductible car expenses include, for example, losses or outgoings deductible under section 8-1, decline in value in accordance with Division 40, repairs in accordance with section 25-10 and so forth. Clearly, capital outgoings themselves would be precluded. Note that if receipts have not been kept for fuel and oil, you may estimate the average fuel expenses using the odometer records.[65]

The deduction is calculated as:[66]

$$\text{Car expenses} \quad \times \quad \frac{\text{Business use percentage:}}{\text{Business kilometres travelled in period held}}{\text{Total kilometres travelled in that period}}$$

Importantly, the business use percentage is established through the log book records kept in accordance with Subdivision 28-G, and odometer readings in accordance with Subdivision 28-H of ITAA97. In particular, the log book needs to be kept for a continuous period of 12 weeks for the first income year for which you use the log book method.[67] The log book is then valid for the following 4 years, unless the Commissioner directs you to keep a new log book or you acquire an additional car that you also wish to apply the log book method for.[68] Additionally, estimating business kilometres needs to also consider other records kept, variations in patterns of use and any change in cars used.[69] The log book itself is required to record the journeys made in the car and the information included must be compliant with section 28-115. More generally, all car expenses must comply with the substantiation rules found within Subdivision 900-C of the ITAA97.

The log book method is demonstrated in example 7.8.

---

63 ITAA97 section 28-28.

64 ITAA97 section 28-90(2).

65 Refer to Australian Taxation Office, *Income tax: substantiation: car expenses: how do you calculate the cost of fuel and oil when using the 'one-third of actual expenses' method or the 'log book' method, if you have not kept written evidence of the expense?* (TD 97/19, 30 July 1992).

66 ITAA97 section 28-90.

67 ITAA97 sections 28-110, 28-115.

68 ITAA97 section 28-115.

69 ITAA97 section 28-90(5).

Log book method

Continuing example 7.7, we determined that Nelson has kept a log book of his car usage. It reveals that his business use percentage is 55 per cent. He has also kept his receipts for travel.

	$
Petrol	2 600
Registration	550
Insurance	620
Servicing	360
Interest	300
Decline in value	4 375
Total car expenses	8 805

How much can Nelson claim?

Applying the log book method, Nelson can claim $8805 × 55% = $4843. Note that this is a greater deduction than using the cents per kilometre method and more accurately reflects expenditure incurred by Nelson. However, the substantiation and record-keeping requirements are more onerous under this method.

7.4 Division 30 — Donations

LEARNING OBJECTIVE 7.4 Apply deductions related to donations as set out in Division 30.

Unlike many of the expenses discussed so far, Division 30 of the ITAA97 allows taxpayers tax deductions for certain gifts and contributions, despite having no requisite nexus with income-earning activities. In allowing taxpayers such deductions, the government encourages and rewards philanthropy within the community. The Division 30 provisions are somewhat complicated, with sets of rules set out for claiming gifts for different categories of recipients and the different ways in which taxpayers can gift money or property.

7.4.1 Donations to deductible gift recipients (DGRs)

Subdivision 30-A outlines a taxpayer's ability to claim deductions to a number of different recipients.[70] The focus of this chapter is donations to recipients captured by Subdivision 30-B specifically or endorsed in accordance with Subdivision 30-BA as deductible gift recipients (DGRs). Subdivision 30-B provides tables of recipients for deductible gifts, categorised as:

- health (section 30-20)
- education (sections 30-25 to 30-37)
- research (section 30-40)
- welfare and rights (sections 20-45 to 30-46)
- defence (section 30-50)
- environment (sections 30-55 to 30-60)
- industry, trade and design (section 30-65)
- the family (sections 30-70 to 30-75)
- international affairs (sections 30-80 to 30-86)
- sports and recreation (section 30-90)
- philanthropic trusts (section 30-95)
- cultural organisations (section 30-100)
- fire and emergency services (section 30-102)
- other recipients (section 30-105).

---

70 See the table in section 30-15 of the ITAA97. Recipient categories include a fund, authority or institution covered by an item in any of the tables in Subdivision 30-B (particular ancillary funds; the Australiana Fund; Australian public libraries, museum or art galleries; the Commonwealth (for the purposes of Artbank); state and territory National Trusts or Australian Council of National Trusts; and certain deductible gift recipients).

The tables provide for both specific organisations listed by name (e.g. 'The Royal Australian and New Zealand College of Obstetricians and Gynaecologists'[71]) as well as general categories (e.g. 'a public hospital'[72]).[73]

More specifically, DGRs are organisations that are specifically registered for and to receive donations.[74] Often charities will be endorsed as DGRs; however, not all charities are in fact DGRs and therefore gifts to those recipients would not be deductible under Division 30. However, from 14 December 2021, all non-government DGRs will need to register as charities.[75] Similarly, donations to popular crowd-funding platforms and campaigns, unless run by DGRs, are not deductible in accordance with this provision. Moreover, in order for a taxpayer to claim donations to DGRs, whether of money or property, they must satisfy several conditions listed in table 7.4.

TABLE 7.4   Key characteristics or conditions of deductible donations

Characteristic or condition	Explanation
The recipient must be a DGR	Specifically listed in Subdivision 30-B or otherwise endorsed as a DGR in accordance with Subdivision 30-BA.
The gift must be a *true* gift	For a gift to be considered a 'true gift', it must be made voluntarily by the donor and without the donor receiving any material benefit.[76]
	Voluntarily
	The transfer of the gift must be 'the act and will of the giver, and there must be nothing to interfere with or control the exercise of that will'.[77] Note that a moral obligation does not preclude the gift being voluntary; however, a gift will not be considered voluntary if, for example, it is made for consideration or a prior obligation is imposed on the giver, or it is given in order to discharge or reduce obligations.[78]
	Without material benefit
	Material benefit refers to something that has a monetary value. For example, in *FCT v McPhail* (1968),[79] the taxpayer made contributions to their child's school building fund and in return was able to access reduced school fees. The Court found that the reduced fees amounted to a material benefit and therefore the contribution was not deductible.
	In applying this principle more generally, if you receive a simple token item, such as a pin, daffodil, sticker or wristband (such as found at charity stalls in shopping centres and supermarkets), these goods will not be considered to amount to a material benefit. The fact that they will provide promotional benefits to the DGR is not an issue either (e.g. red noses for Red Nose Day). As such, receiving token items for donations would not preclude the gift being deductible under Division 30.
	However, if the donor receives something of utility or value, such as a keyring, concert tickets, chocolates, mugs, pens or raffle tickets for example, these will amount to a material benefit and therefore affect deductibility under Division 30.

---

71 ITAA97 section 30-20(2) item 1.2.1.

72 ITAA97 section 30-20(1) item 1.1.1.

73 In the 2021–22 Federal Budget, the Government announced that they would establish a new general DGR category for funding pastoral care and analogous wellbeing services delivered to students in primary and secondary schools: more detail can be found at this link: https://budget.gov.au/2021-22/content/myefo/download/myefo-2021-22.pdf.

74 Whether or not an entity is endorsed as DGR can be checked via the Australian Business Register: www.abn.business.gov.au/Tools/DgrListing.

75 Australian Taxation Office, 'Non-government DGRs required to register as a charity' (Web Page, 9 December 2021) https://www.ato.gov.au/Non-profit/Newsroom/Running-your-organisation/Non-government-DGRs-required-to-register-as-a-charity.

76 117 CLR 11.

77 Australian Taxation Office, *Income tax: tax deductible gifts — what is a gift* (TR 2005/13, 2005) ('TR 2005/13') [23].

78 TR 2005/13, [23]–[26].

79 *FCT v McPhail* (1968) 117 CLR 11.

	An exception applies in this regard if there is a considerable disproportion between value of the donation and the material benefit. For example, donating $4000 and receiving a keyring. In such a circumstance, the keyring would be considered immaterial (unless the keyring is made of valuable materials or have some other particular feature that would lead to a substantial value in itself).[80]
	Similarly, material benefits can be in the form of marketing and advertising benefits (for example, sponsorships by commercial entities). In those instances, the outgoings by the donor may be deductible under the general deduction provision rather than Division 30.
	Special rules apply to when you make contributions for fundraising events.[81]
Money or property	*Money* The value of the donation must be a minimum amount of $2. The value being the amount donated. *Property* Property, including trading stock and shares, can be donated. There are separate rules relating to different categories of property. For example, whether the property was purchased during the 12 months before the gift is made; whether the property is valued at over $5000; whether the property is shares and valued at over $5000; or whether the property is trading stock. Generally, the value of the donation will be either the market value of the property at the time the property was donated, or the amount paid for the property. In some instances, the value is determined by the Commissioner's valuation.
Receipt of gift	You need written evidence of your donation. There is one exception however: bucket donations. Up to $10 can be claimed without receipt if one or more donations of at least $2 was made to approved organisations for natural disasters (bushfires, severe storms, floods).

For further guidance, refer to TR 2005/13 *Income tax: tax deductible gifts — what is a gift*.

It should be noted that certain DGRs have additional conditions imposed on gifts, on top of the criteria listed in table 7.4, and as such should be considered before claiming donations to those organisations. Lastly, taxpayers should note that deductions under Division 30 cannot add to or create a tax loss.[82]

TECHNOLOGY IN ACTION

Crypto-donations

As already seen, the mere fact that cryptoassets are not money or currency create challenges for taxpayers to apply principles of tax law. In a recent article, Morton and Curran consider the implications of non-business taxpayers donating cryptoassets to deductible gift recipients (DGRs).[83] They note that, although it may appear comparable donating with cryptoassets with Australian currency, Division 30 of the ITAA97 outlines separate conditions with respect to property.[84]

Importantly, depending on the category of property, different rules apply. One category, for example, are shares in a listed public company. For property more generally, such as cryptoassets, categorisation (and therefore tax treatment) is based on factors including the way they were obtained (purchased or acquired in some other way); whether they were obtained within 12 months, or at least 12 months prior; and whether their value is either (1) $5000 or less, or (2) more than $5000.[85] Depending on the combination of factors (and assuming the recipient is a DGR and the gift is a 'true gift'), a taxpayer may be able to claim a tax deduction based on either:

• a valuation obtained from the Commissioner, or
• the lesser of the market value on the day of donation and the amount paid for the cryptoassets.[86]

---

80 TR 2005/13, [169].
81 See ITAA97 section 30-15 item 7.
82 ITAA97 section 26-55(1)(ba).
83 Elizabeth Morton and Michael Curran, 'Crypto-donations and tax deductibility' (2021) 25(2) *The Tax Specialist*, 54 ('Morton and Curran').
84 Ibid. See also section 108-5(1)(a) of the ITAA97 and paragraph 7 of the Australian Taxation Office, *Income tax: is bitcoin a 'CGT asset' for the purposes of subsection 108-5(1) of the Income Tax Assessment Act 1997?* (TD 2014/26).
85 See Morton and Curran, 57, for a summary of factors outlined in Subdivision 30-B of the ITAA97.
86 ITAA97 section 30-15(2) item 1; ITAA97 section 30-212.

However, in some instances, there will be no valid approach to claim a tax deduction — for example, where the property (in this context, cryptoassets) is:
- not purchased but acquired in some other way, and
- regardless of the length of time held, is also valued at less than $5000.[87]

Importantly, given cryptoassets will often be a CGT assets,[88] the taxpayer must also consider the CGT implications for donating cryptoassets. As Morton and Curran note, where cryptoassets are donated, although there may be a tax deduction available, there may also be a taxable gain to report (i.e. donating cryptoassets will likely result in CGT event A1).[89] As such, tax compliance for crypto-donations can quickly become more complex, particularly when compared with the donation of Australian dollars.

REFLECTION

Depending on the characterisation of the cryptoassets gifted, do you imagine that the resulting impact on taxable income could vary substantially? Consider how.

7.5 Division 34 — Non-compulsory uniforms

LEARNING OBJECTIVE 7.5 Apply deductions related to non-compulsory uniforms as set out in Division 34.

Special rules in Division 34 apply to non-compulsory uniforms worn by employees and individuals who receive certain withholding payments in accordance with Schedule 1 of the *Taxation Administration Act 1953* (Cth).[90]

A **uniform** is defined as:

> One or more items of clothing (including accessories) which, when considered as a set, distinctively identify you as a person associated (directly or indirectly) with (a) your employer; or (b) a group consisting of your employer and one or more of your employer's associates.[91]

Uniforms are considered non-compulsory *unless*:

> ... your employer consistently enforces a policy that requires you and the other employees (except temporary or relief employees) who do the same type of work as you:
>
> (a) to wear the uniform when working for your employer, and
> (b) not to substitute an item of clothing not included in the uniform for an item of clothing included in the uniform when working for your employer,
>
> except in special circumstances.[92]

With this in mind, Division 34 limits or restricts expenditure related to non-compulsory uniforms to those that are firstly allowable in accordance with section 8-1 and that the design of the non-compulsory uniform is on the *Register of Approved Occupational Clothing*.[93]

Importantly, occupation-specific clothing (e.g. nurse uniform, chef's checked pants) and **protective clothing** (e.g. hard hats, apron) are excluded from the restrictions in Division 34.[94] These are discussed in more detail in a later section.

---

87 Morton and Curran, 57. See also Australian Taxation Office, 'Gift types, requirements and valuation rules' (Web Page, 25 July 2017) https://www.ato.gov.au/non-profit/gifts-and-fundraising/claiming-tax-deductions/gift-types,-requirements-and-valuation-rules.
88 As discussed in the *Technology in practice* box in the chapter on capital gains tax.
89 See ITAA97 Subdivision 104-A; Morton and Curran, 58.
90 See ITAA97 section 34-5.
91 ITAA97 section 34-15(1).
92 ITAA97 section 34-15(2).
93 ITAA97 section 34-10(1).
94 ITAA97 section 34-10(3).

7.6 Division 36 — Treatment of tax losses

LEARNING OBJECTIVE 7.6 Describe the deductibility of tax losses as set out in Division 36.

A **tax loss** refers to when a taxpayer has more deductions than income for an income year (the loss year).[95] Division 36 allows taxpayers to carry forward their tax losses and deduct them against assessable income in future income years. Tax losses cannot generally be carried back to prior years; however, they can be carried forward indefinitely. Note special rules apply to corporate tax entities that can restrict the ability to carry forward losses. In 2020, the Government introduced a temporary 'carry back' mechanism. This was a response to the COVID-19 pandemic to spur on economic recovery and was subsequently extended in the Government's 2021–22 Federal Budget to be available until the 2022–23 year.[96] The mechanism is discussed further in the chapter on taxation of companies. This section focuses on the application of losses to non-corporate tax entities.

7.6.1 How to calculate a tax loss

Section 36-10 of the ITAA97 outlines the calculation of a tax loss as follows:

(1) Add up the amounts you can deduct for an income year (except tax losses for earlier income years).
(2) Subtract your total assessable income.
(3) If you derived *exempt* income, also subtract your net exempt income (worked out under section 36-20).
(4) Any amount remaining is your tax loss for the income year, which is called a loss year.

Recall that exempt income does not form part of assessable income. Income is 'exempt' if a provision in the ITAA36, ITAA97 or other Commonwealth law makes it so (section 6.20 of the ITAA97). Subdivision 11-A of the ITAA97 provides a list of classes of exempt income. To clarify, **net exempt income** for resident taxpayers refers to the amount by which your total exempt income from all sources exceeds the total of the losses and outgoings (excluding capital losses and outgoings) incurred in deriving that exempt income as well as any taxes payable outside Australia on that exempt income.[97] As such, despite exempt income not forming part of assessable income, it indirectly impacts a taxpayer's income tax calculation by way of soaking up available losses. It is also important to recognise that section 26-55 of the ITAA97 outlines certain deductions that cannot create or add to a tax loss (e.g. gifts).

The calculation of a tax loss is demonstrated in example 7.9.

EXAMPLE 7.9

Calculating a tax loss

Harold earned assessable income of $55 000 and incurred allowable deductions of $80 000. He also derived net exempt income of $5000.

What is Harold's tax loss?

Harold's tax loss can be calculated as follows.

	$
Allowable deductions	80 000
Assessable income	(55 000)
Net exempt income	(5 000)
Tax loss	20 000

As such, Harold has a tax loss of $20 000, which he can carry forward to future years.

---

95 ITAA97 section 36-01.
96 The Government, in its 2021–22 Federal Budget, announced it would extend the temporary mechanism to 2022–23.
97 ITAA97 section 36-20(1).

Extending this example with respect to section 26-55, if in his deductions was a donation of $1000 in accordance with Division 30, it would not be able to be included in the tax loss. Therefore, the tax loss would be revised to $19 000.

	$
Allowable deductions	79 000
Assessable income	(55 000)
Net exempt income	(5 000)
Tax loss	19 000

7.6.2 Deducting a tax loss for non-corporate taxpayers

Non-corporate taxpayers, such as individual taxpayers, can carry forward their tax losses and apply them against future assessable income. If the taxpayer has no net exempt income in that future income year, the prior year tax loss carried forward is applied against the excess of assessable income over total deductions: subsection 36-15(2) of the ITAA97. If the taxpayer has net exempt income in that future year, the particular process depends on whether income exceeds deductions or vice versa. See subsections 36-15(3) and (4) the ITAA97, as outlined as follows.

(3) If you have net exempt income for the later income year and your total assessable income (if any) for the later income year exceeds your total deductions (except tax losses), you deduct the tax loss:
   (a) first, from your net exempt income; and
   (b) secondly, from the part of your total assessable income that exceeds those deductions.
(4) However, if you have net exempt income for the later income year and those deductions exceed your total assessable income, then:
   (a) deduct the tax loss from any net exempt income that remains.
   (b) secondly, from the part of your total assessable income that exceeds those deductions.

This is illustrated in figure 7.7.

Example 7.10 demonstrates where the taxpayer has net exempt income for the later income year and their total assessable income for the later income year exceeds their total deductions.[98]

EXAMPLE 7.10

Applying carried forward losses from prior years

Continuing with Harold's example (example 7.9), in year 2 Harold earned assessable income of $125 000 and incurred allowable deductions of $95 000. He also derived net exempt income of $15 000.

What is Harold's taxable income for year 2?

We can apply the carried forward loss as follows (assuming he did not in fact have deductible donations as per the prior example extension).

	$
Assessable income	125 000
Allowable deductions	(95 000)
Net exempt income	15 000
Carried forward losses	(20 000)
Remaining carried forward losses	(5 000)
Taxable income	25 000

As such, Harold has taxable income of $25 000 for year 2.

---

98 ITAA97 section 36-15(3).

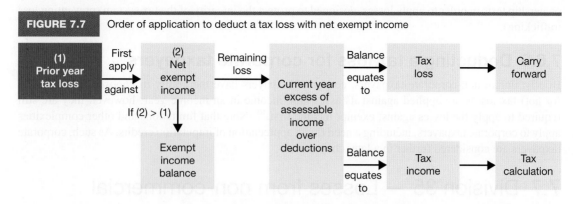

Panel A: Current year income exceeds deductions

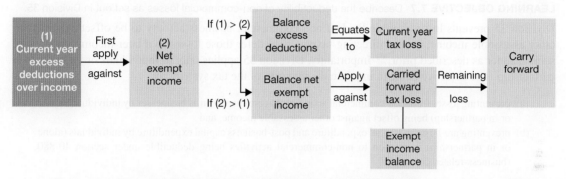

Panel B: Current year deductions exceed income

However, in contrast, if there is insufficient assessable income to exceed total deductions, the current year excess deductions are applied to the current year net exempt income before the carried forward losses are applied to the remaining exempt income.[99] This situation is shown in example 7.11.

EXAMPLE 7.11

Carrying forward prior year and current year losses

Referring back once more to Harold's examples (examples 7.9 and 7.10), assume instead of making a profit in year 2 Harold earned assessable income of $85 000, along with incurring deductions of $95 000 and net exempt income of $15 000.

How would the loss be carried forward?

We would apply the carried forward loss as follows.

	$
Net exempt income	15 000
Allowable deductions	(95 000)
Assessable income	85 000
Excess of deductions over income	(10 000)
	5 000
Carried forward losses	(20 000)
Tax loss	15 000

As such, Harold has a tax loss of $15 000 that can be carried forward to future years. Note that individual taxpayers cannot choose when to apply their tax losses. This is contrary to corporate taxpayers.

Note that if a taxpayer has two or more tax losses, then they must be deducted in the order in which they were incurred: first in first out.[100] It is therefore pertinent for adequate record-keeping and documentation. This becomes particularly important when corporate tax entities are considered as they are required to meet

---

99 ITAA97 section 36-15(4).
100 ITAA97 section 36-15(5).

ownership tests in order to apply losses, designed to protect the integrity of the tax system (preventing loss trafficking).

7.6.3 Deducting a tax loss for corporate taxpayers

Briefly, unlike non-corporate taxpayers, corporate taxpayers have the ability to *choose* to what extent (or not) tax losses are applied against its assessable income in an income year; however, they are still required to apply the losses against exempt income first.[101] Note that limitations and other complexities apply to corporate taxpayers, including a need for an appreciation of imputation credits. As such, corporate taxpayers are considered further in a later chapter.

7.7 Division 35 — Losses from non-commercial activities

LEARNING OBJECTIVE 7.7   Describe the deductibility of non-commercial losses as set out in Division 35.

Division 35 prevents losses from individual non-commercial business activity to be offset against their other assessable income, instead directing taxpayers to defer those losses to a later income year, in the same manner as described prior.[102] Importantly, Division 35 applies only to individuals or individuals in partnership. The objective being to improve the integrity of the tax system, by:

(a) preventing losses from non-commercial activities that are carried on as businesses by individuals (alone or in partnership) being offset against other assessable income, and

(b) preventing pre-business capital expenditure and post-business capital expenditure by individuals (alone or in partnership) in relation to non-commercial activities being deductible under section 40-880 (business-related costs).[103]

In essence, this provision will most often apply to start-ups or activities that may be borderline hobby in nature.

7.7.1 Deferring 'non-commercial business activity'

Division 35 is not intended to apply to passive investment activities or other non-business activities (such as negative gearing). Instead, it captures 'non-commercial business activity', which refers to where expenditure attributable to a business activity exceeds the business income. Where there is an excess of expenditure, that excess is treated as if it were not incurred in that income year and deferred to the next income year in which the activity is carried on.[104] Furthermore, amounts deductible under section 40-880 of the ITAA97 related to the business activity are also captured by this provision (including pre-business and post-business activities).[105] Note that exempt income is applied against losses before applying Division 35.[106] This is demonstrated in example 7.12.

EXAMPLE 7.12

Deferring losses from non-commercial activities

Matilda has a salaried job working for the Australian Taxation Office (ATO), and she also carries on a business activity consisting of selling 3D printed wall hangings.

Year 1: Matilda starts the 3D printing activities on 1 July 2020, and for the 2020–21 income year, the business activity produces assessable income of $8000 and deductions of $10 000. Although Matilda has assessable income derived from her salaried work at the ATO (less any allowable deductions), Matilda has a non-commercial business activity amounting to $2000 (excess of the $10 000 expenditure less $8000

---

101 ITAA97 section 35-17.
102 ITAA97 section 35-1.
103 ITAA97 section 35-5.
104 ITAA97 section 35-10(2).
105 ITAA97 sections 35-10(2A), (2B).
106 ITAA97 section 35-15. Further modifications apply if the taxpayer is bankrupt: see section 35-20 of the ITAA97.

business income). The activity does not pass any of the exceptions (outlined in the following section), so the $2000 excess is required to be quarantined as a non-commercial business activity loss. Therefore, this loss is carried over to the next income year in which the activity is carried on in line with Division 35. This means that Matilda cannot apply the non-commercial loss to her salary income (not shown here).

A deduction may be allowed for the cost of repairs to property providing:

(a) the necessity for the repairs can be related to a period of time during which the premises have been used to produce assessable income of the taxpayer, and
(b) the premises have been used in the production of such assessable income of the year of income in which the expenditure is incurred.

	$
Allowable deductions	10 000
Assessable income	(8 000)
Non-commercial loss carried forward	2 000

Year 2: For the 2021–2022 income year, the 3D printing business activity produces assessable income of $9000 and deductions of $10 000 (excluding the $2000 excess from 2020–21). Again, whilst Matilda derives assessable income from her salaried work, the 3D printing business activity is determined to be a non-commercial of $1000 ($10 000 expenditure less $9000 business income). No exception applies and so Division 35 requires her to defer the non-commercial losses rather than applying the losses against her salary income. $3000 is carried over to the next income year (comprising the $1000 excess for the current year, plus the previous year's $2000 excess) when the activity is carried on.[107] Again, Matilda cannot apply the non-commercial losses to her salary income (not shown here).

	$
Allowable deductions	10 000
Assessable income	(9 000)
Current year non-commercial loss	1 000
Prior year non-commercial loss	2 000
Non-commercial losses carried forward	3 000

Year 3: During the 2022–2023 income year, on top of her salary income, Matilda's 3D printing business activity generates assessable income of $13 000 and deductions of $11 000 (excluding the prior year losses carried forward from years 1 and 2). Now, Matilda can apply the prior year losses to the extent of current year business income produced, with the balance being carried forward to future income. This results in the 3D printing business activity contributing zero income to Matilda's taxable income position (i.e. Matilda's taxable income will be made up of assessable income derived from her ATO salary less any allowable deductions (not shown here)).

	$	$
Assessable income		13 000
Allowable deductions		(11 000)
Current year business income		2 000
Prior year non-commercial losses	3 000	
Applied prior year non-commercial losses	2 000	2 000
Taxable income		0
Non-commerical loss carried forward	1 000	

Note that, following subsection 36-15(5) of the ITAA97, tax losses are applied in the order in which they were incurred: first in first out basis. This means that the remaining losses to be carried forward would equate to the year 2 losses (rather than the year 1 losses).

7.7.2 Exceptions to deferment

There are a number of exceptions that apply to Division 35 in order for deferment of losses to be avoided. If a taxpayer satisfies one of the exceptions, then they are not required to defer non-commercial losses to

---

107 Adapted from example in section 35-10(2) of the ITAA97.

future years and instead can apply losses against other assessable income. The available exceptions include that the:

- taxpayer meets the income and commercial activity threshold: the taxpayers adjusted taxable income is below the required threshold (income test) and their activity meets one of four activity tests (assessable income test, profits test, real property test, other assets test (see table 7.5)[108]
- Commissioner exercises discretion[109]
- business activity amounts to a primary production business or professional arts business and assessable income from other unrelated sources (e.g. wages, excluding net capital gains) are less than $40 000 (see table 7.6).[110]

TABLE 7.5   Applying the income and commercial activity tests

Test	Reference (ITAA97)	Explanation
Income test	Subsection 35-10(2E)	The taxpayer passes this test if their adjusted taxable income is less than $250 000. Adjusted taxable income includes for the year: • taxable income • reportable fringe benefits • reportable superannuation contributions • total net investment losses. Disregard the excess deductions that are subject to Division 35 in applying this test.
And pass one of the following		
Assessable income test	Section 35-30	The taxpayer passes this test if their assessable income from the business activity is at least $20 000 for the year.
Profits test	Section 35-35	The taxpayer passes this test if for at least three of the past five income years (including the current income year), assessable income exceeded deductions for the business activity (i.e. a profit was made in three of five income years).
Real property test	Section 35-40	The taxpayer passes this test if the real property used on a continuous basis in carrying on the business activity is at least $500 000 in value. In determining the total assets included, this test excludes a dwelling and adjacent land used mainly for private purposes as well as fixtures owned by the taxpayer as a tenant.[111]
Other assets test	Section 35-45	The taxpayer passes this test if certain assets used on a continuous basis in carrying on the business activity is at least $100 000 in value. Assets included in this assessment include depreciable assets, trading stock, leased assets, trademarks, patents, copyrights and similar rights.[112] Assets that are excluded from this test include real property, cars, motorcycles and similar vehicles.[113]

---

108 ITAA97 section 35-10(1)(a).
109 ITAA97 sections 35-10(1)(b), 35-55.
110 ITAA97 sections 35-10(1)(c), 35-10(4), 35-10(5).
111 ITAA97 section 3540(4).
112 ITAA97 section 3545(2).
113 ITAA97 section 3545(4).

TABLE 7.6   **Defining primary production business and professional arts business**

Business activity	Defined in ITAA97	Definition
Primary production business	Section 995-1	Includes a business the taxpayer carries on, for example: (a) cultivating or propagating plants, fungi or their products or parts (b) maintaining animals for the purpose of selling them or their bodily produce (including natural increase) (c) manufacturing dairy produce.
Professional arts business	Subsection 35-10(5)	Defined as a business the taxpayer carries on as: (a) the author of a literary, dramatic, musical or artistic work (b) a performing artist (c) a production associate.

Example 7.13 demonstates exceptions to deferment.

EXAMPLE 7.13

Exceptions to deferment

Referring to Matilda's situation in example 7.12, we can extend her circumstances to consider the exceptions as follows for the 2020–21 income year. To do this, let us imagine that her adjusted taxable income is $120 000, that she undertakes her business activity from her family home, and that other assets amount to $25 000.

Assess whether an exception applies to Matilda's deferment of losses.

Applicable test	Matilda's circumstances	Test outcome
Assessable income test	Adjusted taxable income: $120 000, which is below the income test threshold of $250 000.	Passed
And one of:		
Assessable income test	As per the main facts: $8000, which is below the minimum assessable income level for this test.	Failed
Profits test	New business commenced current year: loss year, therefore Matilda cannot show sufficient profit-making activity.	Failed
Real property test	As per the additional facts: Family home (excluded), therefore Matilda cannot meet the requisite minimum threshold of $500 000 in real property used on a continuous basis.	Failed
Other assets test	As per the additional facts: $25 000, which is below the minimum level of other assets required of $100 000.	Failed

Based on the analysis, despite Matilda meeting the assessable income test, she does not meet one of the commercial activity tests. As such, as per in the example 7.13, Matilda is required to carry forward the losses.

7.8 Applications of deductibility to common expenditures

LEARNING OBJECTIVE 7.8 Describe the general and specific deductibility of the more common losses and outgoings.

As a final consideration of deductions, before bringing this chapter to a close, we bring together aspects of general deductibility and specific deductibility to consider common business and non-business expenses incurred by taxpayers. There is clearly going to be a wide range of expenses taxpayers will likely incur in gaining assessable income. Many of these will be industry and environment specific. Often expenses incurred in the business setting can include salary and wages, rent, interest, utilities (water, electricity), payroll tax, fringe benefits tax, bookkeeping and accounting, insurance, telephone and internet and so forth. For an individual taxpayer, such as a wage earner, they can include phone and internet charges, tools and equipment, professional association and journal subscriptions, etc. Often these expenses will be prima facie deductible, although denying and limiting provisions may apply, or specific provisions may prescribe the extent or enable certain expenditure to be claimed. Tax Ruling TR 2020/1 *Income tax: employees: deductions for work expenses under section 8-1 of the Income Tax Assessment Act 1997* is a useful guide for general principles of deductibility for employees. Some common categories of deductions are expanded on next.

7.8.1 Clothing expenses

A common cost incurred by taxpayers is the purchase and maintenance of clothing, footwear and uniforms — whether conventional, protective or occupation-specific. Taxpayers need to establish a sufficient nexus with such expenditure and the income-producing activities to be considered deductible according to section 8-1. Otherwise, expenditure on clothing is considered private in nature. Consequently, there have been numerous court cases to examine the deductibility of such clothing and some general principles have been therefore established. Beyond section 8-1, taxpayers are required to consider the applicability of Division 34 (non-compulsory uniforms), section 51AH (if expenditure has been reimbursed), as well as Division 900 substantiation requirements and exceptions (such as specific laundry rates as discussed in the chapter on general deductions).

Table 7.7 summarises the deductibility of different categories of clothing.

TABLE 7.7   Categories of clothing

Category	Example	Deductibility
Conventional clothing	Suits, jeans, black t-shirts and label clothing.	Not deductible. *Exceptions:* *FCT v Edwards* (1994) 94 ATC 4255 *Mansfield v FCT* (1995) 96 ATC 4001
Occupation-specific clothing	Chef's hat, chequered pants, white jacket, barrister's robes and cleric's ceremonial gowns.	Generally deductible due to distinctive characteristics, but consider whether capital in nature.
Compulsory uniform	Employment policy expressly prescribes distinctive uniform to be worn by class of employees. Can include shoes, socks and stockings.	Generally deductible due to distinctive and compulsory characteristics, but consider whether capital in nature.
Protective clothing	Overalls, aprons, goggles, hard hats and safety boots.	Generally deductible when worn to protect the wearer, but consider whether capital in nature.
Non-compulsory uniform	Optional employment policy regarding distinctive uniform *or* compulsory uniform not strictly enforced. Can include accessories, such as belts, ties, scarves and hats but excludes underwear, short socks, stockings and shoes.[114]	Not-deductible unless meets requirements per Division 34.

It is also important to consider whether the outgoing on clothing is of a capital nature. More generally, clothing is not seen to be of a capital nature as the benefits enjoyed tend to last only a couple of years. However, this is not the case for all clothing acquisitions. For example, the purchase of ceremonial robes for a judge would be considered a capital outlay and therefore would not be deductible under section 8-1. However, taxpayers can then consider Division 40 to consider claiming the decline in value of such a capital acquisition.

---

114 Australian Taxation Office, *Income tax and fringe benefits tax: work related expenses: deductibility of expenses on clothing, uniform and footwear* (TR 97/12, 18 June 1997), [92] ('TR 97/12').

Moreover, in certain circumstances, clothing may have a dual purpose: partly used for work purposes and partly for private purposes. As such, the taxpayer should apportion the expenditure and claim only to the extent that the outgoing satisfies the requisite nexus.

7.8.1.1 Conventional clothing

Generally speaking, taxpayers cannot claim costs of purchasing, repairing, laundering everyday plain conventional clothing. Conventional clothing is inherently private in nature as there is an insufficient nexus between the expenditure and the income-earning activities.[115] Conventional clothing can be compared to other costs of living, such as food and drink, or shelter.[116] It does not matter that an employer may require a particular type (or brand) of conventional clothing to be worn.[117] For example, clothing such as black t-shirts for a barista or business attire (suits) for a solicitor, are not deductible.

This is illustrated in example 7.14.

EXAMPLE 7.14

Conventional clothing

Alec works part time for a high-end retail clothing and sportswear business. His employer requires him to wear either the branded clothing sold at the store or plain white or black t-shirts. Alec spent $750 on brand clothing through the year and $150 on plain t-shirts.

Can Alec claim the costs of this clothing?

Alec cannot claim the costs of either the brand clothing or the plain t-shirts. Nor can Alec claim laundering or other related expenditure. This is despite being instructed by his employer. As Hill J stated in *FCT v Cooper* (1991):

> … the fact that the employee is required, as a term of his employment, to incur a particular expenditure does not convert expenditure that is not incurred in the course of the income-producing operations into a deductible outgoing.[118]

The clothing amounts to everyday clothing and are therefore private in nature.

It is well established that conventional clothing is generally not deductible. However, as with generally all applications of the tax law, there is no universal proposition. In *rare* circumstances, conventional clothing may be deductible: *FCT v Edwards* (1994).[119] Importantly though, special facts existed in this case, and any taxpayer should be cautioned on relying too heavily on this case without due consideration of the circumstances and a high level of similarity with the precedent.

FCT v Edwards (1994) 49 FCR 318

Facts: The taxpayer in question was the personal secretary to Lady Campbell, the wife of the then Governor of Queensland, and was expected to accompany and attend on Lady Campbell at official occasions and dress appropriately. The taxpayer ultimately attended over 150 events throughout the year. As such, the taxpayer required an extensive wardrobe of high-quality clothes to dress in a manner compatible with the Governor's wife, sometimes requiring multiple changes of clothing per day. The taxpayer, for example, required hats, gloves and full evening dresses.

Held: The Court allowed the deduction. Consequently, the Court allowed the claims, finding that the expenditure was not of a private nature.

Comment: The quantity and quality of the acquired clothing was in excess of the taxpayer's normal everyday requirements. The essential character of the expenditure was to be the gaining or producing of assessable income. Although the taxpayer's first set of clothing of the day meets her personal requirements, the additional changes of clothing served solely the work-related purposes.

Example 7.15 contrasts where a deduction may and may not be allowed.

---

115 *Mansfield v FCT* 96 ATC 4001.
116 See, eg, TR 97/12, [12].
117 *Mansfield v FCT* 96 ATC 4001; *FCT v Cooper* 91 ATC 4396.
118 *FCT v Cooper* 91 ATC 4396, [48].
119 *FCT v Edwards* (1994) 49 FCR 318.

Deductibility of clothing

Let's compare two contrasting taxpayers, Janice and Eva, and consider how their differing circumstances are likely to lead to differing outcomes for their clothing claims.

- Janice is an undercover police officer working in Sydney, New South Wales. As part of her work, Janice is required to play a 'role' to try to infiltrate a drug ring. This role requires Janice to wear certain pieces of clothing that are necessary and peculiar to her undercover role. She does not wear the clothing to and from work, or for private purposes. The clothing is only worn for her role in the undercover activities.
- Eva is a marriage celebrant who claims expenditure on dress suits, accessories and footwear. She contends that the wardrobe of hats and garments, including shoes and stockings, ranging from the highly formal to the informal, is far more extensive than she would ordinarily acquire.

Can Janice and Eva claim their clothing costs?

Janice's expenditure on undercover clothing is additional to her normal needs and has a direct connection with her income-producing activities as an undercover police officer. The clothing expenditure will therefore be deductible according to section 8-1.[120] For Eva, however, even if her additional clothing is worn solely for performing her duties as a marriage celebrant, her income-earning activities do not turn upon her wearing the additional clothes. The clothing, accessories and footwear are not specific and suited only to her celebrant activities. Despite having an extensive wardrobe, Eva's duties do not involve multiple daily changes of clothing. On the facts, the expenditure remains purely private in nature and is therefore not deductible according to section 8-1.[121]

Following on from example 7.15, where the purchases reflect the particular working conditions imposed on the taxpayer, clothing may be deductible.

Facts: The taxpayer was a flight attendant who incurred expenditure on shoes (a part of the uniform and half a size bigger to cope with cabin pressure), hosiery (a part of the compulsory uniform), moisturiser/conditioner (to cope with dehydration effects of the pressurised environment and lack of humidity), and hairdressing (to be well groomed).

Held: Except for the hairdressing, deductions allowed under the former subsection 51(1) of the ITAA36.

Comment: The Court determined that the clothing reflected the particular working conditions imposed on the taxpayer. With respect to the acquisition of the shoes, the fact that they were not able to be worn outside of work due to their sizing, assisted the Court in concluding that the occasion of the outgoing was found in the flight attendant duties. The hosiery was a part of the compulsory uniform that was important to the image of the airline, therefore the essential character was work-related. The necessity of the moisturisers was brought about by the harsh conditions of employment and therefore would not have been used otherwise. As such, the outgoings were incidental and relevant to the taxpayer's occupation of a flight attendant. The hairdressing expenses, however, was a personal choice not occasioned by her employment and therefore was characterised as a private expense.

7.8.1.2 Occupation-specific clothing, uniforms and protective clothing

Taxpayers can generally claim expenses for compulsory uniforms, occupation-specific clothing and protective clothing, as the nexus with income earnings activities are more readily established. Deductible outgoings include the acquisition of the clothing, footwear and uniforms, as well as the costs of cleaning and maintenance (e.g. laundry, dry-cleaning, repairing).

Occupation-specific clothing includes clothing that distinctively identifies the taxpayer as belonging to a particular profession, trade, vocation, occupation or calling.[122] These can include such items as a traditional chef's clothing: hat, chequered pants and white jacket. Similarly, a barrister's or judge's gowns, or a cleric's ceremonial robes: these are distinct to their occupations respectively. If, however, a piece of clothing could be worn across several occupations, then it will not be deductible unless, for example, it is protective in nature. In the case of a pharmacist wearing a white coat and white trousers to give

---

120 ITAA97. Janice's circumstances are adapted from an example in TR 97/12, [62].
121 ITAA97. Eva's circumstances are adapted from an example in TR 97/12, [63].
122 ITAA97 section 34-20(1).

the appearance of a health worker, this clothing is not sufficiently distinctive to confirm their specific occupation as a pharmacist. It would therefore not be classified as occupation-specific clothing; but, may be instead considered protective clothing.[123]

Similarly, **compulsory uniforms** satisfy the requirements of section 8-1 due to their distinctive and compulsory characteristics.[124] Distinctiveness is more than style and colour, but of a nature that clearly identifies the taxpayer as an employee of, or the products or services provided by, a particular employer.[125] As such, the distinctiveness provides the requisite nexus. With respect to the compulsory nature, according to the Commissioner:

32. A compulsory uniform must be prescribed by the employer in an expressed policy which makes it a requirement for a particular class of employees to wear that uniform while at work, and which identifies the relevant employer. The employer's compulsory uniform policy guidelines should stipulate the characteristics of the colour, style and type of the clothing and accessories that qualify them as being a distinctive part of the compulsory uniform. Also, the wearing of the uniform generally should be strictly and consistently enforced.

33. In our view, it is only in these strict regimes for compulsory and distinctive uniforms that expenditure on these items is likely to be regarded as work related rather than private in nature.[126]

For example, in *Mansfield v FCT* (1995),[127] the taxpayer's employer strictly enforced a uniform policy that included distinctive stockings and shoes. As such, expenditure on those items were also deductible. For those regimes that are not strictly enforced, or the regime is optional, taxpayers must consider the operation of Division 34.

While **protective clothing** includes clothing of a kind that the taxpayer mainly uses to protect oneself, or someone else, from risk of death, disease, injury, damage to clothing or damage to an artificial limb or other artificial substitute, or to a medical surgical or other similar aid or appliance.[128] Examples of protective clothing include overalls, aprons, goggles, hard hats and safety boots, when worn to protect the wearer.[129] The deductibility of protective clothing is confirmed in *Morris v FCT* (2002),[130] where a number of taxpayers were engaged in outdoor occupations and claimed expenditure for sun protection (sun screen, hats, sunglasses). The Court concluded that the expenditure was deductible: protection was necessary for the taxpayers to perform their duties, increased their productivity and protected them from exposure, which could result in sunburn and skin cancer. The Court was satisfied that there was a close nexus between the expenditure and the income-earning activities.

TR 2020/1 lists and summarises the guidance provided by the ATO on the deductibility of work-related clothing, laundry and dry-cleaning expenses, as well as protective items, cosmetics and personal grooming expenses.

- Taxation Ruling TR 97/12 *Income tax and fringe benefits tax: work related expenses: deductibility of expenses on clothing, uniform and footwear*
- Taxation Determination TD 1999/62 *Income tax: what are the criteria to be considered in deciding whether clothing items constitute a compulsory corporate uniform/wardrobe for the purposes of paragraph 30 of Taxation Ruling TR 97/12?*
- Taxation Ruling TR 98/5 *Income tax: calculating and claiming a deduction for laundry expenses*
- Taxation Ruling TR 2003/16 *Income tax: deductibility of protective items*
- Taxation Ruling TR 96/16 *Income tax: work-related expenses: deductibility of expenses on compulsory uniform shoes, socks and stockings*
- Taxation Ruling TR 94/22 *Income tax: implications of the Edwards case for the deductibility of expenditure on conventional clothing by employees*
- Taxation Determination TD 93/111 *Income tax: is expenditure on dinner suits and other similar clothing worn by members of an orchestra deductible?*[131]

---

123 See the example in TR 97/12, [68].
124 See, eg, TR 97/12, [31].
125 See TR 97/12, [79].
126 TR 97/12, [32]-[33].
127 96 ATC 4001.
128 ITAA97 section 34-20(2).
129 Ibid.
130 50 ATR 104.
131 Australian Taxation Office, *Income tax: employees: deductions for work expenses under section 8-1 of the Income Tax Assessment Act 1997* (TR 2020/1, 1 April 2020) Appendix 1, [69] https://www.ato.gov.au/law/view/document?DocID=TXR/TR20201/NAT/ATO/00001&PiT=99991231235958 ('TR 2020/1').

- Taxation Ruling TR 2003/16 *Income tax: deductibility of protective items*
- Taxation Ruling IT 2477 *Income tax: deductibility of tinted eye glasses used by a visual display unit (VDU) operator*[132]
- Taxation Ruling TR 96/18 *Income tax: cosmetics and other personal grooming expenses*[133]

7.8.2 Travel expenses

Travel has already been raised as an issue that can create blurring between travel that is of a private and domestic nature and travel that meets the necessary nexus with income-earning or business activity. Here we sum up some of the key categories of travel, their deductibility with respect to section 8-1 of the ITAA97 and the common exemptions to being characterised as private or domestic. Furthermore, we summarise some of the key provisions with the Acts that allow further travel expenditure to be claimed by a taxpayer.

Generally, travel between home and work are considered private in nature and are not deductible. As outlined in the previous chapter, the Court in *Lunney and Hayley v FCT* (1958) 100 CLR 478 rejected the proposition that travel between home and work is incurred in gaining or producing income. Such expenditure puts the taxpayer in a position to earn income. This is so even if there is a substantial distance between home and work, or if the work is done outside of normal business hours. However, the point at which a taxpayer travelling to work transitions to travelling in the course of their employment can be challenging to ascertain. For example, in *John Holland Group Pty Ltd v FCT* [2015] FCAFC 82, the Full Federal Court determined that the taxpayer would have been able to deduct the cost of flights between Perth and Geraldton when considering the 'otherwise deductible rule'. The taxpayer worked remotely under a fly-in fly-out arrangement and was required to travel to the airport, from which the employer paid for flights to the various remote locations (and thus a residual fringe benefit under section 52 of the FBTAA). Although the taxpayer was travelling to work to get to the airport, once checked in, the taxpayer was travelling in the 'course of their employment'.

Circumstances in which travel expenditure may be able to be claimed includes where travel is required to different workplaces or if there is a need to carry bulky equipment or tools. Furthermore, if travel overnight is required for income-producing purposes, claims can be made for accommodation, flights, airport transfers, car hire, taxi fares, meals and incidental costs. Note that the travel needs to be somewhere other than to the usual place of work and consideration should be had of any private activities that could create a dual purpose to the travel.

The deductibility of various types of travel is summarised in table 7.8 and illustrated in example 7.16.

TABLE 7.8   Categories of travel

Category	Example	Deductibility
Travel to work	Travel between home and work.	Not-deductible under section 8-1 of the ITAA97 as private in nature, too soon. Puts the taxpayer in a position to earn income rather than being incurred for work: *Lunney and Hayley v FCT* (1958) 100 CLR 478.
Note exceptions:		
	Travelling from/to home to visit clients, for rostered business travel.	Generally deductible under section 8-1 of the ITAA97. In these circumstances, travel is considered to be undertaken 'in the course of' work: *FCT v Ballesty* 77 ATC 4181. The taxpayer was a professional rugby player that was required to travel between sports grounds for training and matches. Whilst the occasion of Ballesty's travel was to comply with the terms of his contract, this can be contrasted with *FCT v Maddalena* (1971) 2 ATR 541. The taxpayer was denied a deduction for the cost of travel to a new football club to obtain a contract. The travel was too soon.

132 Ibid [76].
133 Ibid [75].

Travel between home and work when on stand-by or on call.	Generally deductible under section 8-1 of the ITAA97. As above, in these circumstances, travel is considered for work: *FCT v Collings* 76 ATC 4254. The computer consultant was 'on call' after hours for trouble shooting problems. When the taxpayer was not able to resolve issues remotely, they would return to the office. This travel was found to be incurred in the course of her work.
Transporting heavy, bulky, cumbersome items or equipment.	If equipment is bulky and transport is essential, then it is generally deductible under section 8-1 of the ITAA97. Importantly, the equipment needs to be sufficiently bulky and have no alternative means of storage: *FCT v Vogt* (1975) 75 ATC 4073; *Crestani v FCT* 98 ATC 2219; *Case 43/94* (1994) 94 ATC 387. In *Vogt*, the taxpayer was a professional musician and was required to transport instruments and associated equipment between home and gigs.
Itinerant workers, travelling sales-person.	Generally, travel from home is deductible as long as the taxpayer can establish the necessary connection with income-earning activities: *FCT v Wiener* (1978) 78 ATC 4006. However, merely having numerous places of work will generally be insufficient: see factors outlined in TR 95/34.[134]

Other categories and restrictions already considered:

Relative's travel	Partner accompanies taxpayer on business trip.	Specifically denied under section 26-30 of ITAA97 (exceptions apply).
Travel related to residential rental properties	Travel to/from rental premises to undertake inspection.	Specifically denied under section 26-31[135] of ITAA97 (exceptions apply).
Travel between workplaces	Direct travel.	Deductible according to section 25-100 of ITAA97. See section 7.2.7 of this chapter.
	Indirect travel. Dual workplace/residence.	Not-deductible. Not-deductible.
Car expenses	Special rules apply.	Deduction determined in accordance with Division 28. See section 7.3 of this chapter.

EXAMPLE 7.16

Deductibility of travel

Henry is a teacher and as part of his role he is required to teach at five different schools across the city. As such, he uses his home as the basis for preparing lessons as well as to keep his teaching materials. His sister, Anika, is also a teacher, but she is required to teach only at a single school. Her travel therefore only includes travel to and from home and work and she has an office at the school for lesson preparation and storing of materials.

Describe the deductibility of Henry's and Anika's travel.

Henry's employment would be described *as itinerant*. The travel, including from home at the beginning of the day and to home at the end of the day, would be aptly characterised as travelling for work and therefore deductible under section 8-1 of the ITAA97: *FCT v Wiener* (1978) 78 ATC 4006. Note that the travel between two places of work that relate to the same income-earning activity will likely be deductible under section 8-1 of the ITAA97, while deductible under section 25-100 of the ITAA97 if they are distinct places of work. This can be compared with Anika's travel, which can be characterised as private or domestic in nature: Anika is travelling *to* work, rather than *for* work and therefore not deductible.

---

134 See factors outlined in Australian Taxation Office, *Income tax: employees carrying out itinerant work — deductions, allowances and reimbursements for transport expenses* (TR 95/34, 8 July 1996) [7].
135 ITAA97.

TR 2020/1 lists and summarises the guidance provided by the ATO on the deductibility of work-related travel and car expenses.

- Taxation Ruling TR 2021/1 *Income tax: when are deductions allowed for employees' transport expenses?*
- Taxation Ruling TR 2021/4 *Income tax and fringe benefits tax: employees: accommodation and food and drink expenses travel allowances, and living-away-from-home allowances*
- Taxation Ruling TR 95/34 *Income tax: employees carrying out itinerant work — deductions, allowances and reimbursements for transport expenses*
- Taxation Ruling IT 2543 *Income tax: transport allowances: deductibility of expenses incurred in travelling between home and work*
- Miscellaneous Taxation Ruling MT 2027 *Fringe benefits tax: private use of cars: home to work travel*
- Taxation Ruling IT 2199 *Income tax: allowable deductions: travelling expenses between place(s) of employment and/or place(s) of business*
- Taxation Ruling IT 2481 *Income tax: travelling expenses of an employee moving to a new locality of employment*
- Taxation Determination TD 96/42 *Income tax: is the cost of travel between a taxpayer's residence, being a property on which the taxpayer carries on a business of primary production and a place of employment or business, deductible?*
- Taxation Determination TD 94/71 *Income tax: where a person provides 'consultancy services' as an employee of an interposed entity (such as a non-arm's length company, trust or partnership which has its base of practice at the employee's place of residence), are travel expenses incurred by the person in travelling between his or her place of residence and a place where the person performs the services deductible?*
- Taxation Ruling IT 2566 *Income tax: deductibility of travelling expenses of employee, spouse and family incurred by employer in relocating the employee*
- Taxation Ruling IT 2614 *Income tax and fringe benefits tax: employee expenses incurred on relocation of employment*
- Law Administration Practice Statement PS LA 1999/2 *Calculating joint car expense deductions*
- ATO Interpretative Decision ATO ID 2002/1005 *Travel expenses incurred in respect of work-related items*
- ATO Interpretative Decision ATO ID 2004/614 *Deduction: installing a portable global positioning system in a motor vehicle*
- ATO Interpretative Decision ATO ID 2001/329 *Overseas travel expenses — airfares*
- ATO Interpretative Decision ATO ID 2004/847 *Deductions: work related travel — privately accrued consumer loyalty points*
- ATO Interpretative Decision ATO ID 2001/615 *Deductibility of travel insurance*[136]

Before moving onto self-education expenses, take a moment to reflect on tax practitioners acting 'lawfully' in the best interest of their clients — a requirement under Item 4 of the TASA Code of Professional Conduct. Recall from an earlier chapter that registered tax practitioners are required to comply with the Code. In this ethics example, we extend the ethical practice considered in the previous chapter by considering when clients may request a tax practitioner to claim a deduction the client is not entitled to.

ETHICS IN PRACTICE

Ethics in specific deductions and applications of deductibility

Pursuant to Item 4 of the TASA Code of Professional Conduct, Miku is required to act lawfully in the best interests of the client.[137] Recall in the previous chapter that Miku, a registered tax agent, was engaged by Amy to lodge her income tax return. Amy works for a retail chain as a store manager. Miku obtains Amy's income statement from the prefill report, which shows Amy earned $45 000 during the income year. Amy explained that she had motor vehicle expenses of $8000 to claim. After asking Amy for further information, Miku determines that Amy's expenses were not deductible. Miku ascertained that the motor vehicle expense reflected the purchase of a second-hand car. As such, it is a capital acquisition and not

136 TR 2020/1 Appendix 1, [68].
137 TASA 2009 section 30-10(4).
138 Taxation Practitioners Board, 'TPB(I) 01/2010 Code of Professional Conduct' (Explanatory Paper TPB 01/2010, 18 October 2021) 14 https://www.tpb.gov.au/sites/default/files/tpb_ep_01_2010_code_of_professional_conduct.pdf?v=1634551124. See also *Burnett and Tax Practitioners Board* [2014] AATA 687.

deductible under the first negative limb: section 8-1(2)(a) of the ITAA97. Miku also confirmed that the car is used to travel to and from work only, and thus the essential character of the outgoing is private and lacks the requisite nexus with her income-earning activities.

Miku explained to Amy that she is not entitled to claim the $8000, nor outgoings related to the vehicle. However, Amy asks Miku to claim the deduction anyway.

Focusing on the responsibility to act lawfully pursuant to Item 4 of the Code, what should Miku do?

Item 4 requires Miku to act in Amy's best interests only to the extent that Miku's actions are consistent with the law: Miku cannot disregard the law.[138] As outlined in the Explanatory Memorandum to the Tax Agent Services Bill 2008 at 3.33:

> As tax agents and BAS agents are agents of their clients, they must act in the best interests of their clients. However, tax agents and BAS agents also operate as an intermediary between taxpayers and the tax administration and therefore owe duties not only to their clients but also to the community. As such, their obligations to their clients must be subject to the law.

Miku should not follow Amy's instructions to claim the deduction and Miku should advise Amy accordingly.

7.8.3 Self-education expenses

There are a range of expenses that can be incurred when a taxpayer undertakes self-education that are potentially deductible under section 8-1 of the ITAA97 or other provisions of the Acts. These include, for example:

- course/tuition fees, including those paid to attend conferences or seminars
- books, journals and stationery, printing and other consumables
- travel and related costs (including flights, accommodation, meals, incidentals) to attend conferences, seminars or educational institutions (excludes travel when not required to sleep away from home)
- interest on money borrowed for self-education expenses
- decline in value of depreciating assets used for self-education purposes
- other expenses that are not as directly discernible, including home office running costs, internet usage and phone calls.

It should be noted that there is an automatic cross-over with respect to what has already been covered in this and earlier chapters (e.g. travel/car expenses, the capital-revenue distinction and the need to claim outgoings to the extent they are incurred for self-education and not private usage). What needs to be established is that the self-education activities have a sufficient nexus with the taxpayer's income-earning activities. Generally speaking, this can be in terms of maintaining or improving the taxpayer's skill or knowledge[139] or activities that lead to (or are likely to lead to) increases in the taxpayer's income from current income-earning activities.[140] Self-education activities that are aimed at obtaining new employment, or opening up new income-earning activities, will not be allowable deductions.[141]

FCT v Finn (1961) 106 CLR 60

Facts: The taxpayer, a government architect, travelled overseas to study architecture. As he travelled, he compiled documentation, such as notes, sketches, photographs, and reports. The taxpayer used his leave entitlements to undertake the travel and his employer covered some of the expenditure on the basis that the taxpayer would extend the trip to enable further locations to be visited. All of the activities undertaken during the trip were devoted to architecture. The taxpayer claimed the costs on the basis that the travelling would improve his ability to perform the duties required of him. The Commissioner disallowed the claim.
Held: The expenses were found to be deductible in accordance with the former section 51 of the ITAA36.

---

139 *FC of T v Finn* (1961) 106 CLR 60; *FCT v Studdert* (1991) 22 ATR 762.
140 *FCT v Hatchett* 71 ATC 4184; *FCT v Studdert* (1991) 22 ATR 762.
141 *FCT v Maddalena* (1971) 2 ATR 541.

> **Comment:** The outgoings were incidental and relevant to the taxpayer's employment as an architect. The trip allowed the taxpayer, to improve his chances of promotion, was supported by his employer, and was well documented to clearly indicate the devotion of activities to architecture. Kitto J explained that:
>
> > ... a taxpayer who gains income by the exercise of his skill in some profession or calling and who incurs expenses in maintaining or increasing his learning, knowledge, experience and ability in that profession or calling necessarily incurs those expenses in carrying on his profession or calling.[142]
>
> Importantly, Dixon J further explained that acquiring skill and knowledge are not considered to be a capital asset:
>
> > Unfortunately, skill and knowledge of most arts and sciences are not permanent possessions: they fade and become useless unless the art or the science is constantly pursued or, to change the metaphor, nourished and revived. They do not endure like bricks and mortar.[143]

A number of denying or limiting provisions nonetheless apply to self-education expenditure.

- Expenditure related to rebatable benefits (e.g. Youth Allowance) are denied (section 26-19 of the ITAA97). The introduction of section 26-19 followed the High Court's decision in *FCT v Anstis* [2010] HCA 40. Here, the Court found that the requisite nexus between self-education expenses (textbooks, student administration fees, travel costs and other supplies) and derivation of assessable income had been satisfied despite the taxpayer not being employed. The taxpayer was a full-time student studying a teaching degree and was in receipt of Youth Allowance. The requirements of Youth Allowance included being enrolled at a minimum three-quarters of a normal full-time load at an educational institution and making satisfactory progress. The taxpayer was successful in arguing that the expenses were incurred *in* retaining rights to Youth Allowance (i.e. deriving assessable income), as opposed to being incurred too soon (such as in the case of *Lunney* and *Hayley* (i.e. being of a private or domestic nature)). In response to the High Court's decision, section 26-19 was introduced effective from 1 July 2011 to prevent such deductions.
- Tuition fees: contributions paid to a higher education provider under the *Higher Education Support Act 2003* are specifically denied under section 26-20(1)(ca) of the ITAA97.
- The first $250 of certain self-education expenses that fall within the definition of section 82A of the ITAA36 are denied. However, in the 2021–22 budget it was announced that the threshold will be removed pending enabling legislation.[144]

It is also relevant to note that Treasury undertook consultation on the education and training expense deductions for individuals after it was announced in the 2020–21 Federal Budget that a new deduction may be introduced for education and training where the expense is not related to the current employment of the taxpayer. Consultation was open until January 2021.[145]

Furthermore, in the Federal Budget 2022, the Government announced that small business (those with a turnover less than $50 million) will receive a skills and training boost. Eligible businesses will be able to deduct an additional 20 per cent of expenditure on external training courses provided to their employees, whether in Australia or online, as long as they are delivered by entities registered in Australia and incurred between 7:30 pm AEDT 29 March 2022 and 30 June 2024.[146]

Table 7.9 summarises the deductibility of various types of self-education expenses.

---

142 *FC of T v Finn* (1961) 106 CLR 60, 70.

143 *FC of T v Finn* (1961) 106 CLR 60, 69 (Dixon J).

144 Note that non-deductible expenses, such as capital outlays, can go towards this $250 threshold: TR 98/9 *Self-education expenses*. The removal of this threshold will come into effect from the first income year after Royal Assent is received.

145 Commonwealth of Australia, 'Education and training expense deductions for individuals' (Web Page, 2020) https://treasury.gov.au/consultation/c2020-131250.

146 Commonwealth of Australia, *Budget Paper No. 2 2022–23* (29 March 2022) 26 https://budget.gov.au/2022-23/content/bp2/download/bp2_2022-23.pdf. It was also announced that those eligible businesses will be able to deduct an additional 20 per cent of the cost incurred on business expenses and depreciable assets between 7:30 pm AEDT 29 March 2022 and 30 June 2023, which support digital adoption, including portable payment devices, cybersecurity systems or cloud-based subscription services capped to $100 000 annually: Ibid 27.

TABLE 7.9   Categories of self-education

Category	Explanation
Self-education for current occupation: maintains or improves chances of advancing, which improves efficiency.	Generally deductible under section 8-1 of the ITAA97 where the expenditure increases the taxpayer's knowledge or proficiency in their current occupation. This may or may not lead to increased wages or income. For example: • Overseas architecture study tour found to be deductible: *FCT v Finn* (1961) 106 CLR 60. • Outgoings related to a schoolteacher's Teacher's Higher Certificate found to be deductible: *FCT v Hatchett* (1971) 71 ATC 4184. Here, Menzies J takes the view that equipping the mind to enable increased earning capacity is not regarded as capital in nature: '[I]t has no reference to a man's body, mind, or capacity... human capacity is entirely different from "capital" ...' [at 4186]. This view is consistent with Dixon CJ in *Finn*, noting 'You cannot treat an improvement of knowledge in a professional man as the equivalent of the extension of plant in a factory' [at 69]. As detailed above, Dixon CJ highlighted that skills and knowledge fade; they do not endure as bricks and mortar do. • Outgoings related to a dentist (general practice) obtaining post-graduate degree (Master of Science in Periodontics) found to be deductible: *FCT v Highfield* (1982) 82 ATC 4463. The Court concluded that the additional knowledge/skill acquired could enable the taxpayer to expand their abilities as a practitioner and charge higher fees, which would be acceptable to their client given the increase in skills [Lee J at 4471]. • Flight engineer's costs incurred to receive flying lessons found deductible: *FCT v Studdert* (1991) 22 ATR 762. The Court determined that the lessons could improve the proficiency of the taxpayer's current occupation. It need not result in an increase in income, despite the factor playing a part in the decision of *Highfield* above.
Self-education for another occupation: to obtain employment, new employment, or new opportunities for income-earning activities.	If a taxpayer is not presently in a particular occupation that they are incurring self-education expenditure for, they will not generally be entitled to a tax deduction for those outgoings. In these instances, the taxpayer will not be able to establish a nexus between the loss or outgoing and the income-earning activities: the expenditure is incurred too soon.[147] For example: • A public service clerk incurred expenditure to complete a law degree and later obtained a position as a legal officer. The self-education expenses were determined to be incurred too soon: *Case Z1* [1991] ATC 101. The decision followed the reasoning by Menzies J in *FCT v Maddalena* (1971) 71 ATC 4161 in that the expenses were incurred in obtaining work as an employee rather than in doing the work [at 4163]. • A mining engineer/manager was retrenched and subsequently undertook a Master of Business Administration in the US. The taxpayer was re-employed on his return by a different company and at a higher salary. He was denied a deduction for the self-education costs incurred as the self-education expenses were concluded to be incurred in obtaining *new* employment: *FCT v Roberts* (1992) ATC 4787.

TR 2020/1 lists and summarises the guidance provided by the ATO on the deductibiliy of work-related self-education expenses.

- Taxation Determination TR 98/9 *Income tax: deductibility of self-education expenses incurred by an employee or a person in business*
- Taxation Determination TD 93/175 *Income tax: is expenditure incurred by an employee in applying for a promotion deductible under subsection 51(1) of the Income Tax Assessment Act 1936?*
- ATO Interpretative Decision ATO ID 2005/26 *Deductions: self-education — course fees paid from FEE-HELP loan funds*
- ATO Interpretative Decision ATO ID 2005/27 *Deductions: self-education — payments made to reduce FEE-HELP debt*

---

147 ITAA97. See also TR 2020/1.

- ATO Interpretative Decision ATO ID 2003/84 *Self-education expenses — personal development course*
- ATO Interpretative Decision ATO ID 2003/614 *Deductions: self-education — personal development course*
- ATO Interpretative Decision ATO ID 2012/65 *Deductions: student services and amenities fee*
- ATO Interpretative Decision ATO ID 2002/517 *Self-education expenses: driver education course*
- ATO Interpretative Decision ATO ID 2005/69 *Self education expenses: cancellation of enrolment of study*
- ATO Interpretative Decision ATO ID 2002/902 *Deductibility of damages paid for breach of employment contract — repayment of self-education expense*[148]

7.8.4 Home office expenses

An increasingly frequent area of concern is when the home office, or areas of the home more generally, are used as a place for income-earning activities. Such use raises the pertinent question of whether home office expenditure is deductible under section 8-1.[149] There are an increasing number of taxpayers whose employment contracts do not provide a place of work and are expected to telecommute, work remotely or hot desk.[150] The ATO has in recent years raised the red flag on the increasing prevalence and opportunity for taxpayers to work from home and the need to be vigilant in how and what they claim as a tax deduction.[151]

Generally, the home is not within the bounds of section 8-1 of the ITAA97, given its inherently domestic nature. Moreover, it is critical to appreciate the inherent impact business use may have on the main residence exemption. The law is somewhat well established, and we can articulate some general propositions in the extent of deductibility in accordance with section 8-1 of the ITAA97. It is firstly pertinent to consider what expenditure we are referring to. These can generally be categorised into two distinct and discrete categories (see table 7.10).

TABLE 7.10   Categories of home office expenditure

Category	Explanation	Examples (to the extent that...)
Occupancy expenses	The ATO defines this as: 'Expenses relating to ownership or use of a home which are not affected by the taxpayer's income-earning activities'.[152] Aickin J in *Handley v FCT* (1981) adds that 'these expenses can otherwise be described as those relating to the building and/or land as a whole. They related to the building and/or land as a whole and are not affected in any way at all by reason of the fact that the taxpayer performs professional work on the premises. They would remain the same whether or not he worked at home'.[153]	Interest on mortgages if the property is owned by the taxpayer, rent if the taxpayer is the tenant of the home. Additionally: water rates, council rates, land taxes and home building insurance.

---

148 TR 2020/1 Appendix 1, [70].

149 Mining engineer/manager, *FCT v M I Roberts* (1992) 24 ATR 479; Public service clerk, Case Z1 92 ATC 101; AAT Case 7541 (1991) 22 ATR 3549.

150 Dale Boccabella and Kathrin Bain, 'The age of the home worker — part 1: Deductibility of home occupancy expenses' (2018) 33(4) *Australian Tax Forum*, 827, 829.

151 Australian Taxation Office, 'Shortcut method' (Web Page, 2018) https://www.ato.gov.au/Individuals/Income-and-deductions/ Deductions-you-can-claim/Working-from-home-expenses/Shortcut-method. A thorough analysis of this area of tax deductibility has been compiled by Dale Boccabella and Kathrin Bain from UNSW Business School. See 'The age of the home worker — part 1: Deductibility of home occupancy expenses' (2018) 33(4) *Australian Tax Forum* 827; and 'The age of the home worker – part 2: Calculation of home occupancy expense deductions, deduction apportionment and partial loss of CGT main residence exemption' (2019) 34(1) *Australian Tax Forum* 65.

152 Australian Taxation Office, *Income tax: deductions for home office expenses* (TR 93/30, 30 September 1993) [6] ('TR 93/30').

153 *Handley v FCT* (1981) 148 CLR 182, 202.

| Running expenses | The ATO defines this as:
'Expenses relating to the use of facilities within the home'.[154]

These expenses can otherwise be described as those occasioned by the income-earning activities.

'These are items of expenditure, the occasion of which is indeed the work that Mr Ovens [the taxpayer] undertook in his home office. It is by reason of his working in the home office that he would switch on the gas heater in that area. It is by reason of his working in the home office that he would turn on the lights, and consume electricity through the use of the various items of electronic equipment that he had deployed in that room … '.[156] | Electricity, heating, cooling, lighting, cleaning, decline in value, leasing, repairs for depreciable assets (e.g. furniture, fittings and equipment), home contents insurance, consumables and stationery. Note that non-business taxpayers can claim immediately the cost of depreciable assets under $300.[155] |

For many expenses, it will be a straightforward task to categorise into each category, although in certain circumstances it can be challenging. A consideration of the facts and circumstances are warranted in all situations. Importantly, this distinction between occupancy and running expenses (both predominantly concepts under the positive limbs of the general deduction provision) is not referent to the capital-revenue distinction. A running or occupancy expense that is capital (e.g. the purchase price of a depreciable asset) will not be deductible under section 8-1 but may attract a deduction under the capital allowance rules.[157]

In practice, for a taxpayer to claim occupancy expenditure, they need to establish:

- a high degree of almost exclusive usage of the home office for income-earning purposes, and
- that the home office is not being used as an office of mere convenience (lack of necessity determined in terms of availability of another work location).[158]

In *Swinford v FCT* (1984), the Court determined that a proportion of their rent (an occupancy expense) was deductible. Hunt J made it clear that simply being associated with their home, did not preclude it from being characterised as used for business use (as opposed to a matter of convenience). This can be compared with *Handley* and *Forsyth*, where the home office usage was found to be a matter of convenience. These cases are outlined as follows.

Swinford v FCT (1984) 84 ATC 4803

Facts: The taxpayer was a self-employed script writer who worked exclusively from home. The taxpayer set up a separate room to undertake her writing. The premises were also used for meetings with television station staff. Situated within the room was also a wardrobe to store long pieces of clothing used by the taxpayer. The taxpayer claimed a proportion of rent as a tax deduction.
Held: Rent was held to be deductible.
Comment: The Court concluded that there was no alternative place to work. The Court distinguished the taxpayer's circumstances from *Handley*[159] and *Forsyth*[160] on the basis that the taxpayer did not have a separate place of business. Hunt J stated that:

> Whilst in most cases a home office will not constitute business premises unless, like the doctor's surgery, it is physically distinct from the area used as a home, I would not be prepared to say that a home office cannot, as a matter of law, amount to business premises … The work done … was not done at her home rather than elsewhere as a matter of convenience … This was the only place where she did carry out her writing activities. This was the base, and the only base, of the taxpayer's operations …[161]

---

154 TR 93/30, [6].
156 *Ovens v FCT* (2009) 75 ATR 479, 487.
155 *FCT v M I Roberts* (1992) 24 ATR 479; *Case Z1* 92 ATC 101; AAT Case 7541 (1991) 22 ATR 3549.
157 Dale Boccabella and Kathrin Bain, 'The age of the home worker — part 1: Deductibility of home occupancy expenses' (2018) 33(4) *Australian Tax Forum* 827, 832.
158 See, eg, *Handley v FCT* (1981) 148 CLR 182; *FCT v Forsyth* (1981) 148 CLR 203; *Swinford v FCT* 84 ATC 4803.
159 *Handley v FCT* (1981) 148 CLR 182.
160 *FCT v Forsyth* (1981) 148 CLR 203.
161 *Swinford v FCT* 84 ATC 4803, 4806.

Facts: The taxpayer, a barrister, used his home study for work purposes for approximately 20 hours per week for 45 weeks of the year. The room was also used on occasion for private purposes. The study was used in addition to his chambers in the city. The taxpayer claimed interest, utilities and rates proportionally against his assessable income.

Held: Deductions were denied.

Comment: The Court concluded that the study remained inherently part of the family home and that the expenditure was private in nature. *FCT v Forsyth* (1981)[162] similarly concluded that the 'essential character' of such expenditure was private.[163] The rooms were not used exclusively for income-earning activities, and the taxpayer needs to consider the extent to which the space is separated (or integrated) with the remaining house. To be able to claim occupancy expenses, the space needs to lose its private or domestic character through being a physically discrete space and be used nearly exclusively for income-earning activities. Note that minor private or domestic usage, such as a wardrobe in the corner of a room may not deny the characterisation.[164] However, this case did not distinguish between occupancy and running expenses. Running expenditure, such as utilities, are now generally accepted as deductible without changing the characterisation of the home office. Such expenditure is seen as additional costs relating to the use of the room for income-earning purposes.[165]

TR 93/30[166] provides the following factors to consider in assessing whether home office usage would shift that usage from private or domestic to commercial or business:

- an alternative place for conducting income-earning activities
- a clearly identifiable area as a place of business
- the area is not readily suitable or adaptable for use for private or domestic purposes in association with the home generally
- the area is used exclusively or almost exclusively for carrying on a business, and
- the area is used regularly for visits of clients or customers.[167]

It is generally difficult for many employees, particularly knowledge workers, to establish entitlement to claim occupancy expenses. This is irrespective of minimal working conditions being provided.[168]

If the taxpayer has been required to work from home during the COVID-19 pandemic, this may reflect a shift in the way in which the home office is used, as well as in the mix of work-related expenses. For example, taxpayers are perhaps going to have travelled less; however, incurred more eligible expenses relating to the home office. Although, just because the taxpayer is not going into the office, this does not mean their home office will necessarily be characterised as a genuine home office.[169] The space is required to be used exclusively for work purposes. Unless there is a dedicated space, the more than mere convenience of working from home will not be sufficient.

For running expenditure, there is greater scope for deductibility. The taxpayer is able to claim deductions (e.g. for depreciation) if the room is exclusively used for income-earning activities and to the extent the outgoings relate to that particular space.[170] If other family members also use the space, then this needs to be considered in calculating the deductible proportion.

It is important to note the implications of income-earning activities on the capital gains tax exemption on a taxpayer's main residence. The previously mentioned cases occurred prior to the introduction of capital gains tax, and, since its introduction, taxpayers are ordinarily less inclined to claim occupancy expenses as that forms part of a re-characterisation of the home space to a place of income-earning activities and therefore the main residence exemption is directly impacted.

---

162 148 CLR 203.
163 Recall *Lunney v FCT* (1958) 100 CLR 478.
164 *Swinford v FCT* 84 ATC 4803.
165 *FCT v Faichney* (1972) 129 CLR 38.
166 *Income tax: deductions for home office expenses.*
167 TR 93/30.
168 Dale Boccabella and Kathrin Bain, 'The age of the home worker — part 1: Deductibility of home occupancy expenses' (2018) 33(4) *Australian Tax Forum* 827–871.
169 For further consideration of the implications of COVID-19 on home occupancy expenses, see Elizabeth Morton, Michael Curran and Sarah Hinchliffe, 'COVID-19 responses and the contemplative worker's home occupancy expense claim' (2021) 50(2), *Australian Tax Review* 81. See also Dale Boccabella and Kathrin Bain, 'The age of the home worker — part 1: Deductibility of home occupancy expenses' (2018) 33(4) *Australian Tax Forum* 827.
170 *FCT v Faichney* (1972) 129 CLR 38.

Briefly, the consequences of characterising the home office as a place of business is the partial removal of the main residence exemption: section 118-110 of the ITAA97. Although the exemption is discussed in depth in an earlier chapter, it is relevant to briefly outline it here. In its most simple form, the taxpayer's main residence will be exempt from capital gains tax to the extent it is not used for the production of assessable income. As such, the proportion of the dwelling that is taken up as a genuine home office enables occupancy expenses to be claimed. It is therefore pertinent for a taxpayer to fully appreciate whether or not their use of their home office amounts to a shift away from domestic or private to a commercial or business characterisation as it will not only lead to differences in deductibility of home office expenses but have a possible impact on the taxable status of the dwelling.

As usual, deductibility is further dependent on substantiation requirements. Taxpayers are required to keep records and written evidence to claim the correct proportion of expenditure (and not claim to the extent that the expenditure is private/domestic).[171] These may include invoices as well as entries on bank or credit card statements in the taxpayer's name.[172]

Note that for depreciable assets, decline in value is in accordance with Division 40 of the ITAA97.

An alternative to claiming the actual costs of a taxpayer's home office (actual cost method), the Commissioner allows a rate of $0.52 per hour for home office expenses (fixed rate method). This rate includes average energy costs (heating, lighting, cooling), cleaning, and the value of common furniture (but not the decline in value for computers and other similar equipment). It does not include phone and internet expenditure, consumables and stationery.[173] In essence the taxpayer needs to establish the additional costs of running expenses: if the taxpayer has a dedicated office space this will equate to a higher claim than if the taxpayer simply works from the kitchen table.[174]

Additionally, taxpayers can claim a deduction of up to $50 for phone and internet expenses based on $0.25 for each work call made from a landline, $0.75 for each call made from a mobile and $0.10 for each text message sent from the mobile. Although there are fewer requirements for documentation using this method, the taxpayer should still be able to justify the claim. Alternatively, the actual expenses can be claimed via the itemised bill.

This is demonstrated in example 7.17.

EXAMPLE 7.17

Home office expenses

Bjorn's work-related activities mean that he is eligible to claim running expenses. He works from his home office three days a week for two hours per day, for 46 weeks of the year.

How much can Bjorn claim?

Using the Commissioner's fixed rate, he can claim (3 × 2 × 46) × 0.52 = $143.52. This includes running expenses such as the electricity and decline in value for his furnishings. Alternatively, Bjorn instead could calculate his claim based on the actual expenditure. He could also claim under the shortcut method.

Note that for the income year 1 March 2020 to 30 June 2020, as well as the 2020–21 and 2021–22 income years, the Government allows for a temporary 'shortcut method' in response to the COVID-19 pandemic to be used. This allows taxpayers to claim a higher rate of $0.80 cents per hour (compared with the fixed rate method), where the taxpayer was required to work from home. When the taxpayer uses this rate, they cannot claim any other expenses (including the purchase of equipment) and is instead of the $0.52 hourly rate or the actual cost method. The shortcut method includes expenses such as phone, internet, decline in value for furniture and equipment, as well as electricity and gas expenses. When using this method, the taxpayer should include 'COVID-19 hourly rate' in the description under 'Other work-related expenses'.[175] Note that this may not result in the highest possible claim — a trade-off occurring between substantiating actual costs and simplicity in determination of tax deduction.

---

171 See Practice Statement Law Administration PS LA 2001/6 *Verification approaches for home office running expenses and electronic device expenses.*
172 Ibid section 3.
173 Ibid.
174 https://www.ato.gov.au/Individuals/Income-and-deductions/Deductions-you-can-claim/Working-from-home-expenses/Shortcut-method.
175 https://www.ato.gov.au/Individuals/Income-and-deductions/Deductions-you-can-claim/Working-from-home-expenses/Shortcut-method

7.8.5 Other relevant expenditure

There are a number of other common outgoings. Interest is one of the most common financing costs incurred by taxpayers with the deductibility dependent generally on its 'use': *FCT v Munro* (1926) 38 CLR 153. Deductibility of interest is permitted even when deductions exceed assessable income, as is the case for negative gearing. Table 7.11 summarises the deductibility of interest, rent/lease payments and legal fees.

TABLE 7.11 **Other common losses or outgoings**

Category	Deductible	Not-deductible
Interest	• Generally deductible according to section 8-1 of the ITAA97 to the extent the borrowed funds are used for income-producing purposes (nexus): *FCT v Munro* (1926) 38 CLR 153 • The nexus may not require the interest outgoings to generate income in the year incurred: *Steele v DFCT* (1999) 197 CLR 459 • Interest incurred after a business has ceased may still be deductible: *FCT v Brown* (1999) 43 ATR 1; *FCT v Jones* (2002) 49 ATR 188.[176] • May also be deductible as an element forming the cost base of a depreciable asset or CGT asset.	• To the extent the borrowed funds are not used for income-producing purposes, irrespective if those borrowings enable the taxpayer indirectly to maintain income-producing assets.[177] • May be found to be capital in nature in certain circumstances. • Interest of a capital nature may be deductible in accordance with the blackhole provisions.[178]
Lease/rent payments	• Generally deductible in accordance with section 8-1 of the ITAA97 to the extent the asset under lease (e.g. land, building, depreciable assets etc.) is used for income-producing purposes over the term of the lease (nexus). • Lease preparation expenditure: section 25-20 of the ITAA97. • Capital expenditure to terminate lease etc.: section 25-110 of the ITAA97.	• To the extent the leased asset is not used for income-producing purposes. • May be found to be capital in nature in certain circumstances.[179] • Rental premiums to secure a lease/license are likely to be capital in nature.[180] • Lease/rent of a capital nature may be deductible in accordance with the blackhole provisions.[181]

---

176 See also the previous chapter.
177 *Ure v FCT* (1981) 11 ATR 484; *FCT v Munro* (1926) 38 CLR 153.
178 ITAA97 section 40-880.
179 *FCT v South Australian Battery Makers Pty Ltd* (1978) 14 CLR 645.
180 *FCT v Star City Pty Ltd* (2009) 72 ATR 431.
181 ITAA97 section 40-880.

| Legal fees | • Generally deductible in accordance with section 8-1 of the ITAA97 to the extent the fees are incurred for income-producing purposes (nexus). For example, debt recovery expenditure, defending/settling charges, disputes, libel action, etc.[182]
• Legal fees incurred in relation to managing tax affairs: section 25-5 of the ITAA97.
• Lease preparation expenditure: section 25-20 of the ITAA97.
• Borrowing expenses: section 25-25 of the ITAA97.
• May also be deductible as an element forming the cost base of a depreciable asset or CGT asset. | • May be found to be capital in nature where the fees relate to the preservation and protection of the taxpayer's business.[183]
• Note that capital expenditure may be instead deductible under the blackhole provisions.[184] |

182 See, eg, *Herald & Weekly Times Ltd v FCT* (1932) 48 CLR 113; *Magna Alloys & Research Pty Ltd v FCT* (1980) 11 ATR 276; *Hallstrom Pty Ltd v FCT* (1946) 72 CLR 634.
183 *Broken Hill Theatres Pty Ltd v FCT* (1952) 85 CLR 423.
184 ITAA97 section 40-880.

SUMMARY

7.1 Explain the relationship between general and specific deductions.

The ITAA97 provides for general deductions in section 8-1 and specific deductions in section 8-5. A loss or outgoing qualifies for a general deduction if it meets the positive limbs and is not disallowed by the negative limbs. A specific deduction is one allowed by a specific provision in the ITAA97. A loss or outgoing may be one or the other or both, but the same loss or outgoing cannot be claimed as a deduction more than once.

7.2 Apply common specific deductions set out in Division 25.

Division 25 of the ITAA97 is titled 'Some amounts that you can deduct' and describes various available specific deductions and the conditions under which they are deductible. These include, for example, deductions for costs relating to management of tax affairs, repairs to premises or a depreciable asset when used to generate income, expenses related to certain types of borrowing, the cost of bad debts, loss by theft, payments to associations and certain travel between workplaces.

7.3 Apply deductions related to car expenses as set out in Division 28.

Division 28 of the ITAA97 is titled 'Car expenses' and describes specific deductions for car-related expenses and the conditions under which they are deductible. Taxpayers can claim car expenses using the cents per kilometre method or the log book method. The cents per kilometre method involves multiplying a reasonable estimate of the business kilometres travelled by the rate of cents per kilometre allowed under the ITAA97. The log book method involves keeping records of losses and outgoings (over a representative part of the year) and then apportioning them on the basis of business versus private kilometres travelled.

7.4 Apply deductions related to donations as set out in Division 30.

Division 30 of the ITAA97 is titled 'Gifts or contributions' and describes specific deductions for donations. The deduction is intended to encourage and reward philanthropy and does not require a nexus to income-producing activities. There are, however, somewhat complex rules relating to which recipients qualify a donation for deductibility.

7.5 Apply deductions related to non-compulsory uniforms as set out in Division 34.

Division 34 of the ITAA97 is titled 'Non-compulsory uniforms' and describes specific deductions for employees and individuals for non-compulsory uniforms under strict conditions. Occupation-specific clothing and protective clothing are dealt with under the general deduction provision of the legislation.

7.6 Describe the deductibility of tax losses as set out in Division 36.

Division 36 of the ITAA97 is titled 'Tax losses of earlier income years' and describes specific deductions for carried forward tax losses and which deductions can and cannot be included in calculation of a tax loss. The rules differ for individual taxpayers and corporate taxpayers.

7.7 Describe the deductibility of non-commercial losses as set out in Division 35.

Division 35 of the ITAA97 is titled 'Losses from non-commercial business activities' and requires losses from individual non-commercial business activity to be offset only against income from those activities in a later income year. Generally, with a few exceptions, losses for non-commercial activities cannot be offset against other assessable income.

7.8 Describe the general and specific deductibility of the more common losses and outgoings.

Taxpayers incur a wide range of expenses in gaining assessable income. Often these expenses will be prima facie deductible, but denying and limiting provisions may apply, and specific provisions may prescribe the extent or enable certain expenditure to be claimed. Some of the most common deductions that need to be carefully assessed are clothing expenses, travel expenses, self-education expenses and home office expenses.

KEY TERMS

car expenses Losses or outgoings to do with operating a car as well as the decline in value of a car. However, it excludes car expenses incurred in respect of overseas travel as well as taxi fares or similar.

compulsory uniform Distinctive clothing and accessories that must be worn as expressed in a formal policy established by an employer.

net exempt income The amount by which a resident taxpayer's total exempt income from all sources exceeds the total of the losses and outgoings (excluding capital losses and outgoings) incurred in deriving that exempt income as well as any taxes payable outside Australia on that exempt income.

occupation-specific clothing Clothing that distinctively identifies the taxpayer as belonging to a particular profession, trade, vocation, occupation or calling.

protective clothing Clothing of a kind that the taxpayer mainly uses to protect oneself, or someone else, from risk of death, disease, injury, damage to clothing or damage to an artificial limb or other artificial substitute, or to a medical surgical or other similar aid or appliance.

recognised tax adviser A registered tax agent, BAS agent or tax (financial) adviser, or legal practitioner.

specific deduction A deduction allowed by a specific provision in the ITAA97.

tax affairs Affairs relating to tax, specifically income tax.

tax loss A situation where the taxpayer has a negative taxable income. A tax loss is defined as the situation where allowable deductions exceed assessable and net exempt income. A tax loss can be carried forward indefinitely by the taxpayer and in the case of a company can be used to offset future taxable income provided one of two tests are met.

uniform One or more items of clothing (including accessories) which, when considered as a set, distinctively identify you as a person associated (directly or indirectly) with (a) your employer, or (b) a group consisting of your employer and one or more of your employer's associates.

QUESTIONS

7.1 Review the following expenses and determine whether they will be deductible or not deductible pursuant to section 25-5 of the ITAA97.
   (a) Tax return prepared by Jacob using *myTax*. Jacob is a fellow business student working part time at the local café.
   (b) Train fare incurred in travelling to registered tax agent to obtain advice on the tax implications of selling cryptocurrencies.
   (c) Interest on loan obtained to pay the prior year's income tax obligation.
   (d) Payment of general interest charge.

7.2 Specify whether the following will more likely or less likely be a 'repair' under section 25-10 of the ITAA97.
   (a) Replacing a picket fence with a brick fence.
   (b) Replacing broken pickets along a fence.
   (c) Replacing an awning that is in good condition.
   (d) Mending a damaged awning.
   (e) Replacing a worn-out motor in a truck.
   (f) Vehicle servicing, oil top ups.
   (g) Regular re-painting of internal/external areas.
   (h) Painting internal/external walls to make good deterioration on newly acquired property.

7.3 Specify whether the following will more likely be a 'part' or the 'entirety', when contemplating deductibility of repairs pursuant to section 25-10 of the ITAA97.
   (a) A chimney in a factory is replaced.
   (b) Repairs are made to guttering of a building.
   (c) Replacement of a floor of a house.
   (d) Replacement of the roof of a factory.
   (e) Replacement of sleepers and rails on a railway line.

7.4 In respect to claiming a deduction pursuant to section 25-35 of the ITAA97, explain how a taxpayer can establish that a debt is bad.

7.5 Olive recently obtained a second job at a winery to supplement her income as an arborist for a local council. Each day from Thursdays and Sundays, Olive catches a bus straight from her council position to the winery. However, on occasion, Olive meets her friends for dinner in the city before travelling to the winery. Explain the extent that Olive can claim the travel expenditure.

7.6 Markus has been working for 30 years in education and decided to take 18 months off work to travel with his family. While he is on leave, he continues to pay for his memberships to two professional bodies, paying $340 and $560 respectively. Advise Markus whether he can claim the expenditure against his taxable income (which is made up of investment income only).

7.7 Kelly has used her car throughout the income year for work purposes; however, she has failed to keep records of her expenses. Her work diary confirms that she has attended numerous client meetings off site. In triangulating her diary entries with addresses, Kelly has determined that she has travelled 8700 km in the income year. Explain to what extent Kelly can claim her travel expenses.

7.8 Mathew donated the following amounts to a number of charities and institutions. Briefly confirm whether they are deductible or not deductible under Division 30 of the ITAA97.

(a) Mathew donated $800 to Oxfam.

(b) His friend Jakub completed Dry July raising money for the Cancer Council, Mathew donated $300.

(c) His aunt started a 'GoFundMe' page to help raise money for their cousin who lost his house in recent bushfires. Mathew donated $50.

(d) Mathew dropped $12 dollars of change into a bushfire donation tin. He does not have records for this.

(e) Mathew donated $20 to an online charity, receiving a jumper in return.

(f) Mathew donated $500 to a local club with the agreement that his architecture business will be included in brochures and signage at an upcoming event.

7.9 Ingrid is currently studying an Arts degree and to fund her living expenses recently obtained a part time job at a clothing store. Ingrid was required by her employer to wear the brand clothing whilst on shift. Ingrid has spent $350 on the store brand clothing, including hoodies, leggings and various t-shirts. A further $80 was also spent on the brand sunglasses; however, her employment does not require her to be outside. Advise Ingrid as to the deductibility of the items acquired.

7.10 Lulu is currently employed as a personal assistant in a rural law firm. Specify whether the following will more likely or less likely be a deductible self-education expense for Lulu.

(a) Lulu is currently finishing her marketing degree part-time. She eventually wishes to start her own marketing business.

(b) Lulu is required by her employer to complete several short courses designed to equip her with the requisite knowledge of the document management system used by the firm and basic training in law to be able to negotiate queries and tasks. Lulu attends three workshops throughout the income year and her employer reimburses her for the outgoings associated.

(c) Lulu becomes somewhat overwhelmed with her study and work responsibilities so decides to complete a time management course. Lulu paid for the course herself and attended the course after work hours.

PROBLEMS

7.11 Amy borrowed $120 000 in 2020 to fund the purchase of a business. The loan term is 3 years starting on 31 October 2020. Amy incurred expenditure of $3000 for the borrowing. Outline the yearly deduction available to Amy in accordance with section 25-25 of ITAA97.

7.12 Mackenzie is a casual employee. Mackenzie is rostered to work various shifts at various locations within commuting distance of her home, taking her anywhere between ten minutes and one hour depending on the location. Occasionally she is required to commute between locations and in doing so uses her own car; however, travel is not a fundamental part of her employment. There is no requirement for Mackenzie to work from home. She is paid an annual salary and is not provided a travel allowance or reimbursed for her travel expenses.

Mackenzie is required to have available at the commencement and duration of the rostered shift protective eyewear, gloves, face mask, high visibility vest, helmet, coveralls, and safety boots. She is also required to wear a supplied uniform. These items are transported by Mackenzie in a small overnight bag, which when packed weighs approximately 12 kg. At each location there are lockers available for storage.

(a) Is the travel between home and work deductible?

(b) Is the travel between workplaces deductible?

7.13 'Mammoth Videos' is a store run by Garry as a sole trader. Due to natural disasters in the prior year (year 1), Garry's store has experienced a significant downturn. In reviewing his records, he notes that he received $10 000 in exempt income arising from a government grant on top of $220 000 in ordinary income and $300 000 in allowable deductions in Year 1.

(a) Determine Garry's taxable income (loss) for the prior year (year 1).

(b) In the current year, Garry's business earned $460 000 in ordinary income and incurred $310 000 in allowable deductions. Again, Garry received exempt income of $10 000 in addition to his ordinary income. Determine Garry's taxable income (loss) for the current year (year 2).

(c) If Garry had an additional $100 000 in tax losses from an earlier income year (year 0), how would the calculation in (b) differ and what, if any, loss year (year 0, year 1) would be represented in carried forward losses?

Disregard the commercial loss rules.

7.14 Continuing on from the prior example, Garry earns an additional $80 000 per year as a consultant for the Commonwealth Government. Consider whether Garry could have applied the losses from 'Mammoth Videos' incurred in year 1 against his wages in that year based on the following additional information.

- Garry had been making profits in his business prior to year 0.
- Garry has reportable fringe benefits of $3000.
- Real property used to carry on his business is valued at $360 000.
- Assets used to carry on his business are valued at $180 000, made up of depreciable assets of $95 000 and vehicles valued at $85 000.

7.15 Axil is a full-time staff member of 'The Reptile Room' pet store company in the administration department. Axil originally was based on the premises of the 'The Reptile Room' in Northcote, Melbourne. However, in 2022, the department moved to South Australia. The remaining sites in Victoria are all retail shopfronts. 'The Reptile Room' agreed for Axil to establish a home office in mid-2022.

Axil lives in Footscray, Melbourne. His residence consists of three bedrooms, one bathroom, one lounge room and one kitchen. Additionally, there is a loft space in the roof that Axil cordoned off as the home office space. The area represents approximately one-quarter of the house area. He acquired standard office furniture to furnish the space, including a desk, chair, lamp, filing cabinet, printer and other general office supplies. He does not install any signage to suggest from the street front that the office is present. He continues to use the laptop and phone that his employer provides.

No clients or colleagues visit the home or home office and there is no available space for car parking if clients were to visit the premises. Axil works from home 4 days per week to achieve a 32-hour work week. He uses the office space for his employment only and no personal effects are stored in the room except for a piano that remains in one corner.

(a) Is Axil eligible to claim a deduction for a proportion of occupancy expenses in relation to the home office space?

(b) Is Axil eligible to claim a deduction for a proportion of running expenses in relation to the home office space?

(c) What impact does the home office space have on the main residence exemption?

7.16 Anthony is a client of Lan's, a registered tax agent. Anthony is a real estate agent in central Queensland and has requested that Lan claim $4000 in home office expenditure in his tax return this year. Lan has already ascertained that the $4000 is not credible (Code Item 9). Lan explained to Anthony that, based on his circumstances, he is entitled to claim $400 in running expenses only. Despite this, Anthony instructs Lan to claim the full $4000. In accordance with Item 4 of the TASA Code of Professional Conduct, what should Lan do?

ACKNOWLEDGEMENTS

Figure 7.3: © Australian Taxation Office
Figure 7.6: © Federal Register of Legislation. Licensed under CC BY 4.0.
Extracts: © Federal Register of Legislation. Licensed under CC BY 4.0.
Extracts: © CCH Australia Limited
Extracts: © Australian Taxation Office
Extract: © Public Domain

CHAPTER 8

Capital allowances

LEARNING OBJECTIVES

After studying this chapter, you should be able to:

8.1 outline depreciation concepts in accordance with Division 40 of the ITAA97

8.2 calculate decline in value using the prime cost method and the diminishing value method

8.3 describe the different taxation depreciation rules for individual taxpayers, small business entities, medium-size business entities and large business taxpayers

8.4 apply the special depreciation rules in relation to computer software

8.5 determine the assessability/deductibility when a depreciating asset is disposed

8.6 determine the CGT implications when selling a CGT asset

8.7 apply the Division 43 capital allowance rules in respect of buildings, structural improvements, extensions, alterations and capital improvements made to buildings

8.8 apply section 40-880 to certain types of business-related capital expenditure incurred by businesses.

Overview

This chapter outlines the taxation rules relating to capital allowances. 'Capital allowances' is a broad term that refers to the taxation treatment of depreciable assets under Division 40 and Division 43 of the ITAA97. This term also encompasses the special rules afforded to businesses that incur certain types of business-related capital expenditure in accordance with section 40-880 of the ITAA97.

The chapter provides an overview of Division 40, including the general rules allowing a taxpayer a deduction for the decline in the value of a 'depreciating asset' that is owned and used by a taxpayer in the course of gaining or producing assessable income. Two methods for calculating decline in value are explained — the prime cost method and the diminishing value (DV) method.

The depreciation rules contained in Division 40 differ depending on the type of taxpayer. This chapter outlines the depreciation rules applicable to individual taxpayers, small business entities, medium-size business entities and large business taxpayers.

The tax treatment of computer software is also looked at briefly as, while it is an intangible asset, it is considered a depreciating asset for tax purposes.

The chapter discusses the taxation implications where a depreciating asset is sold that generates a gain and/or loss for accounting purposes. It also briefly discusses how CGT can apply when a depreciating asset is sold at higher than its original cost.

Buildings are not considered depreciable assets for taxation purposes under Division 40. However, a special claim for buildings and capital improvements to buildings can be made under Division 43 of the ITAA97. Division 43 provides a deduction (called 'capital works allowance') in respect of buildings, structural improvements, extensions, alterations and capital improvements made to buildings.

This chapter concludes by discussing the application of section 40-880 which provides a deduction for capital expenditure that would not be otherwise deductible under section 8-1. Under section 40-880, a taxpayer that is carrying on a business is entitled to a deduction over a 5-year period in relation to costs incurred in setting up the business, capital raising and costs incurred in closing down the business. This equates to a deduction of 20 per cent each year over 5 years. Small business entities are permitted to claim an immediate 100 per cent deduction on certain capital expenditures incurred when setting up their business.

8.1 Depreciation — basic concepts

LEARNING OBJECTIVE 8.1 Outline depreciation concepts in accordance with Division 40 of the ITAA97.

Capital allowances is a generic term that refers to the taxation treatment of depreciable assets under Division 40 and Division 43 of the ITAA97. The term also encompasses section 40-880 which provides a special deduction for certain capital-related business expenditure that would not otherwise be deductible under other provisions of the ITAA36 and ITAA97.

As discussed in an earlier chapter, under section 8-1(2) of the ITAA97, a taxpayer is denied an immediate deduction for any outgoing of a capital nature. This is referred to as the second negative limb. However, Division 40 of the ITAA97 allows a taxpayer a deduction for the decline in the value of a depreciating asset that is owned and used by a taxpayer while gaining or producing assessable income.

The key operative provision for depreciation is section 40-25(1) of the ITAA97 which states:

> You can claim an amount equal to the decline in value for an income year (as worked out under this Division) of a depreciating asset that you held for any time during the year.

Note that the term **decline in value** means *depreciation*. In order to claim a tax deduction for depreciation, the taxpayer must use the asset for income-producing purposes (section 40-25(2)). If the asset is used partly for income-producing purposes and partly for private purposes, the depreciation claim is apportioned for the income-producing use. For the rest of this chapter, the term 'depreciation' will be used instead of the term 'decline in value'.

FIGURE 8.1   Extract of depreciation claim in the 2021 company tax return

Source: Australian Taxation Office, *Company tax return 2021* (Web Page, 2021) https://www.ato.gov.au/uploadedFiles/Content/IND/Downloads/Company-tax-return-2021.pdf.

8.1.1 Who is the holder of a depreciating asset?

A deduction for depreciation is available to the 'holder' of a depreciating asset. In most cases, the legal owner is the holder of the asset. However, there are some exceptions to this general rule.

Section 40-40 contains a table detailing the entity that is treated as the holder of a depreciating asset. This is reproduced as table 8.1.

TABLE 8.1	Identifying the holder of a depreciating asset	
Item	**This kind of depreciating asset ...**	**... is held by this entity**
1	A car in respect of which a lease has been granted that was a luxury car when the lessor first leased it.	The lessee.
2	A depreciating asset that is fixed to land subject to a quasi-ownership right where the owner has a right to remove the asset.	The owner of the right (while the right exists).
3	An improvement to land subject to a quasi-ownership right, made, or itself improved, by the owner of the right.	The owner of the right (while the right exists).
4	A depreciating asset that is subject to a lease where the asset is fixed to land.	The lessor.
5	A hire purchase agreement.	The economic owner (i.e. the entity using the asset), not the legal owner.
6	Any other depreciating asset subject to an agreement, where the economic owner rather than the legal owner possesses the asset and holds a right, which if exercisable, will allow them to become the legal owner.	The economic owner (i.e. the entity using the asset), not the legal owner.
7	A depreciating asset that is a partnership asset.	The partnership itself and not the individual partner.
8	Mining, quarrying or prospecting information that an entity has and is relevant to mining, exploration or prospecting activities.	The entity.
9	Other mining, quarrying or prospecting information that an entity has and is not generally available.	The entity.
10	Any depreciating asset.	The owner, or the legal owner, if there is both a legal and equitable owner.

Source: ITAA97 section 40-40.

8.1.2 What is a depreciating asset?

According to section 40-30(1), a **depreciating asset** is defined as an asset that has a limited effective life and can reasonably be expected to decline in value over the time it is used. This definition captures the meaning of plant (such as machinery).

For accounting purposes, virtually all tangible non-current assets are considered depreciable assets. However, land, trading stock and many intangible assets are specifically excluded from the definition of a depreciating asset. Section 40-30(2) of the ITAA97 provides that the following intangible assets are considered depreciating assets, provided they are not trading stock:

- mining, quarrying or prospecting rights
- mining, quarrying or prospecting information
- items of intellectual property (such as a trademarks)
- IRUs (indefeasible rights to use international telecommunications submarine cable systems), and
- telecommunications site access rights.

The following assets are specifically excluded from Division 40 of the ITAA97:

- capital works, including income-producing buildings and capital improvements made to income-producing buildings (section 40-45(2) of the ITAA97). However, the building may qualify for the special capital works write-off provided for under Division 43 of the ITAA97. This Division is discussed in a later section in this chapter

- depreciating assets associated with investments in Australian films where deductions are claimable under the former film concessions in Divisions 10B or 10BA of the ITAA97, and
- cars, where the taxpayer has elected to use the 'cents per kilometre' method to claim a deduction for the car expenses in that income year (section 40-55 of the ITAA97).

8.1.3 Determining the cost of a depreciating asset

The decline in value of a depreciating asset is calculated on the basis of the 'cost' of the asset. According to section 40-175, the cost of a depreciating asset comprises:
1. the first element (section 40-180) which consists of the initial purchase price, and
2. the second element (section 40-190) which comprises those incidental costs incurred to bring the asset to its present condition and location.

Hence, the cost of a depreciating asset not only includes its purchase price, but also the initial costs incurred when acquiring the asset and getting it to its intended location, installed and ready for use. These costs include customs duty, delivery costs, in-transit insurance and installation costs (see Taxation Ruling IT 2197).

This is a similar concept for accounting purposes under AASB 116 *Property, Plant and Equipment*, where incidental costs are added to the cost of the asset in the balance sheet.

The concept of the cost of a depreciable asset is shown in figure 8.2.

FIGURE 8.2	Cost of a depreciable asset under Division 40

Cost of a depreciable
asset (s 40-175)

1st element: Purchase price (s 40-180) + 2nd element: Incidental costs (s 40-190)

If an entity is registered for the goods and services tax (GST), then the cost of the asset excludes the GST input tax credit, as this would have been claimed back in the Business Activity Statement (BAS).

8.1.4 When does depreciation start?

According to section 40-60(1), a depreciating asset starts to decline in value from its start time. The **start time of a depreciating asset** is the earlier of the dates on which the taxpayer:
- first uses the asset (for any purpose whatsoever), or
- has the asset installed ready for use, for any purpose (taxable or non-taxable).

If a depreciating asset is not used for a taxable purpose from its start time, then there is no tax deduction for its decline in value. A deduction for depreciation can only be claimed from when the asset was first used for a taxable purpose (section 40-25(2)). The cost of the depreciable asset is the amount determined based on the 'cost' of the asset as per section 40-60.

A taxable purpose essentially means that the asset is used for the purpose of gaining or producing assessable income.

Example 8.1 demonstrates the importance of the start time in terms of depreciation and the time from when a deduction can be claimed.

EXAMPLE 8.1

Claiming a deduction for depreciation

On 9 August 2021, Alan buys a car at a cost of $42 000. He immediately uses it for private purposes. On 19 May 2022, Alan commences his own business as a financial planner. He begins using the car exclusively for income-producing purposes from this date onwards.

When can Alan claim a deduction for depreciation of the car?

The 'start time' of the car is 9 August 2021 (i.e. the date on which Alan first starts using the car). The fact that the car is used for private purposes is not relevant. Depreciation will still be calculated from this time; however, Alan is not able to claim any tax deduction for depreciation in respect of the car from 9 August 2021 to 19 May 2022, as the vehicle was not used for income-producing purposes.

From 19 May 2022 onwards, Alan began using the vehicle for income-producing purposes. Hence, from this date onwards, Alan is entitled to claim a tax deduction for depreciation in respect of the car.

8.1.5 Determining the effective life of a depreciating asset

The effective life of a depreciating asset is determined differently under accounting and taxation rules.

8.1.5.1 Accounting

According to paragraph 50 of AASB 116 *Property, Plant and Equipment*, a depreciable asset must be systematically depreciated over its estimated useful life (expressed in years). The definition of 'useful life' in paragraph 6 means the estimated period over which the future economic benefits are expected to be consumed by the entity.

AASB 116 does not provide any specific guidance to assist the entity to determine the useful lives of its assets. In practice, the entity assesses the lives of its assets based on several factors, including historical records of how long it has held similar assets, the warranty period and company policy on how long it intends holding the asset before disposing (or replacing) it.

8.1.5.2 Taxation

For taxation purposes, the decline in value of a depreciating asset is calculated under Division 40 of the ITAA97 based on the asset's effective life (expressed in years).

According to section 40-95(1) of the ITAA97, a taxpayer has one of two choices in determining a depreciating asset's **effective life**:

1. self-assess and determine the effective life based on how long the asset could be used if it were kept in a reasonably good working order (section 40-105), or
2. rely on the Commissioner's determination of effective life (section 40-100).

This choice must be made at the time the asset is first used by the taxpayer for any purpose or is installed ready for use (section 40-60(2) of the ITAA97).

Note that the effective life for certain intangible assets (e.g. patents, copyrights and in-house software) is prescribed in the legislation and the taxpayer cannot self-assess. These intangible assets and their statutory lives are listed in sections 40-95(7) of the ITAA97 and are discussed further in this chapter.

To assist taxpayers in determining the useful (or effective) lives of depreciable assets, in January 2001, the Commissioner published his own determination of the effective lives of depreciating assets. This listing is included in a Taxation Ruling which is updated and re-issued every year.[1]

The latest version, TR 2021/3, was issued by the Commissioner on 30 June 2021 and applies in respect of income years beginning on or after 1 July 2021. This 280-page ruling contains the effective lives of a range of depreciating assets. The ruling consists of two tables: Table A and Table B.

Table A is an industry table which contains assets under industry headings generally derived from the Australian and New Zealand Standard Industry Classification (ANZSIC) subject categories. This table is only to be used by members of the specified industries. Taxpayers not in those industries must use Table B.

Table A covers business taxpayers specifically involved in the following industries:

- agriculture, forestry and fishing
- mining
- manufacturing
- electricity, gas, water and waste services
- construction
- wholesale trade
- retail trade

---

1 The version at the time of writing was TR 2021/3, issued by the Commissioner on 30 June 2021 and applicable in respect of income years beginning on or after 1 July 2021. This 280-page ruling can be accessed at the ATO's website.

- accommodation and food services
- transport, postal and warehousing
- information media and telecommunications
- financial and insurance services
- rental, hiring and real estate services
- professional, scientific and technical services
- administrative and support services
- education and training
- health care and social assistance
- arts and recreation services, and
- other services.

If an asset used by an industry member is not listed under its industry heading, either specifically or under the general functional group/class, then the entity should use the effective life of the asset listed in Table B.

If an item appears in both Table A and Table B, industry members must use Table A and non-industry members must use Table B. The assets listed in Table B are common assets (e.g. rental property assets, cars, computers, etc.) used by a broader range of taxpayers (including salary and wage earners, landlords, small businesses, etc.). For example, according to Table B, the Commissioner considers the effective life of a desktop computer to be 4 years, a laptop computer to be 2 years, a photocopying machine to be 5 years and a motor vehicle to be 8 years.

Finally, if an asset does not appear in either table, then the Commissioner has not made a determination of the asset's effective life. Accordingly, the taxpayer must determine the effective life of the asset themselves.

Figure 8.3 is an extract from Table A and figure 8.4 is an extract from Table B.

| FIGURE 8.3 | TR 2021/3 Table A extract — effective lives, agriculture, forestry and fishing |

AGRICULTURE, FORESTRY AND FISHING (01110 to 05290)			
Asset	Life (years)	Reviewed	Date of application
All terrain vehicles (ATVs) used in primary production activities	5	*	1 Jul 2007
Environmental control structures (including glasshouses, hothouses, germination rooms, plastic clad tunnels and igloos)	20	*	1 Jul 2006
Fences (excluding stockyard, pen and portable fences): Being fencing constructed at a time for a particular function (e.g. a line of fencing forming a side of a boundary or paddock) not being in the nature of a repair:			
General (incorporating anchor assemblies, intermediate posts, rails, wires, wire mesh and droppers)	30	*	1 Jul 2008
Electric	20	*	1 Jul 2008
Fence energisers for electric fences:			
Mains power	10	*	1 Jul 2008
Portable	5	*	1 Jul 2008
Fertigation systems:			
Pumps	3	*	1 Jul 2008
Tanks	10	*	1 Jul 2008
Grading and packing line assets used on farm:			
Banana assets:			
Air rams	3	*	1 Jul 2008
Bunch lines	10	*	1 Jul 2008
Choppers/mulchers	8	*	1 Jul 2008

Asset	Life (years)	Reviewed	Date of application
Rails (including points)	15	*	1 Jul 2008
Scrap conveyors	5	*	1 Jul 2008
Tops	8	*	1 Jul 2008
Water troughs	10	*	1 Jul 2008

Source: Australian Taxation Office, *Income tax: effective life of depreciating assets* (TR 2021/3, 1 July 2021) https://www.ato.gov.au/law/view/view.htm?docid=TXR/TR20213/NAT/ATO/00023&PiT=99991231235958.

FIGURE 8.4 TR 2021/3 Table B extract — effective lives (asset categories)

Asset	Life (years)	Reviewed	Date of application
Accommodation units in caravan/tourist parks being articles, not fixtures, and used for a specified purpose:[46]			
Relocatable homes and tourist park cabins constructed with chassis	20	*	1 Jul 2015
Other accommodation units (e.g. manufactured homes)	30	*	1 Jul 2015
Additive manufacturing printers (including 3D printers)	3	*	1 Jul 2016
Advertising signs:			
Billboard assets:			
Billboard lighting:			
HID/Metal halide lighting systems	5	*	1 Jul 2015
LED lighting systems (including solar powered LED lighting systems)	10	*	1 Jul 2015
Solar power generating assets — see Table B Solar photovoltaic electricity generation system assets			
Billboard steel structures (incorporating electrical systems, footings, scaffolding and walking platforms and steel frame sign panels)	20	*	1 Jul 2015
Computer hardware — see Table B Computers			
Digital LED screens	6	*	1 Jul 2015
Electronic message centre (EMC) units	3	*	1 Jul 2015
Mobile billboard assets:			
Digital LED screens	4	*	1 Jul 2015
Mobile billboard trucks and trailers — see Table B Motor vehicles and trailers			
Floor mounted internal advertising panels (used in airports and shopping centres etc.)	7	*	1 Jul 2015
Kiosks and other external standalone advertising panel structures	15	*	1 Jul 2015
LED advertising screens (used in office tower foyers etc.)	5	*	1 Jul 2015

Source: Australian Taxation Office, *Income tax: effective life of depreciating assets* (TR 2021/3, 21 July 2021) https://www.ato.gov.au/law/view/view.htm?docid=TXR/TR20213/NAT/ATO/00023&PiT=99991231235958.

If the taxpayer chooses to self-assess the effective life of a depreciating asset, they must be able to prove to the Commissioner how they have come up with their estimate and why it differs from the Commissioner's estimate of effective life contained in TR 2021/3. This is based on a number of factors, including historical records, company policy on when assets are replaced, as well as how long the entity intends to hold the asset.

Figure 8.5 is an extract from Item 9 of the 2021 company tax return, where taxpayers indicate whether they have self-assessed the effective lives themselves.

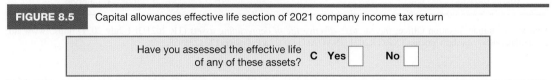

FIGURE 8.5 Capital allowances effective life section of 2021 company income tax return

Source: Australian Taxation Office, *Company tax return 2021* (Web Page, 2021) https://www.ato.gov.au/uploadedFiles/Content/IND/Downloads/Company-tax-return-2021.pdf.

8.1.5.3 Intangible assets that have a statutory life

Certain intangible assets have been determined to have specific statutory lives for income tax purposes. These statutory effective lives override any other assessments of effective lives determined by the Commissioner of Taxation in various taxation rulings and/or by the taxpayer themselves through their own self-assessment processes.

These intangible assets are listed in section 40-95(7) of the ITAA97 and are shown in table 8.2.

TABLE 8.2 Intangible assets that have a statutory life

Intangible asset	Statutory effective life
1. Standard patent	20 years
2. Innovation patent	8 years
3. Petty patent	6 years
4. Registered design	15 years
5. Copyright (except copyright in a film)	The shorter of: (a) 25 years from when you acquire the copyright, or (b) the period until the copyright ends.
6. A licence (except one relating to a copyright or in-house software)	The term of the licence
7. A licence relating to a copyright (except copyright in a film)	The shorter of: (a) 25 years from when you become the licensee, or (b) the period until the licence ends.
8. In-house software	5 years
9. Spectrum licence	The term of the licence
14. Telecommunications site access right	The term of the right

Note: A trademark (as distinct from a patent, registered design or copyright) is not considered a depreciating asset (see section 40-30 ITAA97).

Source: ITAA97 section 40-95(7).

Each of these assets other than items 6 and 7 must be depreciated using the prime cost depreciation method. The taxpayer may choose between the prime cost depreciation method and the diminishing value depreciation method for items 6 and 7.

Generally, assets that have statutory effective lives cannot be self-assessed, despite the fact that some assets may have a different economic life than the statutory rate listed in section 40-95(7). However, in May 2021, the Federal Government announced that it would draft legislation to allow taxpayers to self-assess the tax effective lives of certain depreciating intangible assets, such as patents, copyrights and in-house software. This forms part of the Government's $1.2 billion Digital Economy Strategy.

On 3 December 2021, the Government released the Treasury Laws Amendment (Measures for Consultation) Bill 2021: Intangible Asset Depreciation. The Bill and accompanying exposure draft proposes to allow taxpayers to self-assess the effective life of intangible depreciating assets listed in the table in subsection 40-95(7) rather than using the statutory effective life specified in the table 8.2.

The intangible assets to which this choice will apply are:

- a standard patent
- an innovation patent
- a registered design
- a copyright (except copyright in film)
- a licence relating to a copyright (except copyright in a film)
- in-house software
- a spectrum licence, and
- a telecommunications site access right.

If this legislation is passed, the choice can be made in relation to intangible assets the taxpayer starts to hold on or after 1 July 2023.

8.2 Calculating the decline in the value of depreciating assets

LEARNING OBJECTIVE 8.2 Calculate decline in value using the prime cost method and the diminishing value method.

The calculation of the decline in value of depreciating assets is different between the accounting standards and the tax law.

According to paragraph 62 of AASB 116, there are three acceptable methods of calculating depreciation for accounting purposes. These are:

1. straight-line,
2. diminishing balance, or
3. units-of-production method.

All methods are acceptable under AASB 116 as they progressively allocate the cost of the asset on a systematic basis to the Income Statement over the useful life of the asset.

On the other hand, for taxation purposes, the decline in value of a depreciating asset is calculated under Division 40 of the ITAA97 based on the asset's effective life (expressed in years).

For taxation purposes, section 40-65(1) permits only one of two methods in calculating the decline in the value of a depreciating asset:

1. the prime cost method (section 40-75), or
2. the diminishing value method (section 40-70).

A taxpayer may choose either the prime cost or diminishing value method for each depreciating asset. However, the choice of method for a particular asset applies for that income year and all later years in which the taxpayer claims a deduction for the decline in value of that asset (section 40-130). In other words, the taxpayer cannot change depreciation methods for a particular asset once a particular method is initially chosen.

8.2.1 The prime cost method

The **prime cost method** for taxation purposes is similar to the straight-line method for accounting purposes. The prime cost depreciation rate is calculated by dividing 100 per cent of the asset's cost by the effective life of the item. This is represented in figure 8.6.

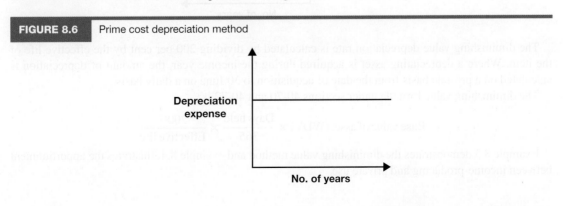

FIGURE 8.6   Prime cost depreciation method

Where a depreciating asset is acquired during the income year, the amount of depreciation is calculated on a pro-rata basis from the date of acquisition to 30 June on a daily basis. The prime cost formula under section 40-75 is:

$$\text{Asset's cost} \times \frac{\text{Days held}}{365} \times \frac{100\%}{\text{Effective life}}$$

It should be noted that the denominator of 365 days is specified in the legislation, meaning that it must be used each year, regardless of whether the year is a leap year or not.

Example 8.2 demonstrates the prime cost method.

EXAMPLE 8.2

Prime cost method

On 31 March 2022, a taxpayer buys a desktop computer costing $4000. The desktop computer is exclusively used for income-producing purposes. According to TR 2021/3 (Table B, Category C), the effective life of a desktop computer is 4 years.

What is the depreciation in the 2022 and 2023 tax years under the prime cost depreciation method? There are 92 days from 31 March 2022 to 30 June 2022.

The decline in value of the desktop computer for the years ended 30 June 2022 and 30 June 2023 under the prime cost depreciation method is shown next.

2022:

$$\text{Depreciation} = \$4000 \times \frac{92\,\text{days}}{365\,\text{days}} \times \frac{100\%}{4\,\text{year}} = \$252\,(\text{rounded})$$

2023:

$$\text{Depreciation} = \$4000 \times \frac{365\,\text{days}}{365\,\text{days}} \times \frac{100\%}{4\,\text{year}} = \$1000$$

8.2.2 The diminishing value method

The **diminishing value method** for taxation purposes equates to the diminishing balance method for accounting purposes. The diminishing value method involves applying a percentage rate initially to the original cost of the item, but subsequently to the base value (i.e. written down value) at the commencement of each year thereafter. This is represented in figure 8.7.

FIGURE 8.7   Diminishing value depreciation method

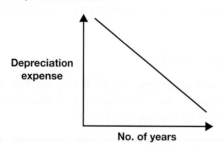

The diminishing value depreciation rate is calculated by dividing 200 per cent by the effective life of the item. Where a depreciating asset is acquired during the income year, the amount of depreciation is calculated on a pro-rata basis from the date of acquisition to 30 June on a daily basis.

The diminishing value formula under sections 40-70 and 40-72 is:

$$\text{Base value of asset (WDV)} \times \frac{\text{Days held}}{365} \times \frac{200\%}{\text{Effective life}}$$

Example 8.3 demonstrates the diminishing value method and example 8.4 illustrates the apportionment between income-producing and private use.

EXAMPLE 8.3

Diminishing value method

Assume the same facts as example 8.2. On 31 March 2022, a taxpayer buys a desktop computer costing $4000. The desktop computer is exclusively used for income-producing purposes. According to TR 2021/3 (Table B, Category C), the effective life of a desktop computer is 4 years.

What is the depreciation in the 2022 and 2023 tax years under the diminishing value depreciation method?

The decline in value of the desktop computer for the years ended 30 June 2022 and 30 June 2023 under the diminishing value depreciation method is shown next.

2022:

$$\text{Depreciation} = \$4000 \times \frac{92\,\text{days}}{365\,\text{days}} \times \frac{200\%}{4\,\text{years}} = \$504\,(\text{rounded})$$

2023:

$$\text{Base value (or WDV)} = (\$4000 - \$504) = \$3496$$

$$\text{Depreciation} = \$3496 \times \frac{365\,\text{days}}{365\,\text{days}} \times \frac{200\%}{4\,\text{years}} = \$1748$$

The base value at 30 June 2023 is calculated at $1748 (being $3496 − $1748). Depreciation in 2023–24 will be based on this figure.

Table 8.3 shows a comparison of the two tax depreciation methods using example 8.3. It will be observed that, over the 4-year period, the total depreciation claimed comes to $4000, being the cost of the depreciating asset.

TABLE 8.3   Comparison of tax depreciation methods

Income year	Prime cost depreciation ($)	Diminishing value depreciation ($)
2022	252	504
2023	1 000	1 748
2024	1 000	874
2025	1 000	437
2026	748	437
Total	**4 000**	**4 000**

EXAMPLE 8.4

Apportionment between business and private use

As in examples 8.2 and 8.3, on 31 March 2022, a taxpayer buys a desktop computer costing $4000. However, assume now that the taxpayer used the desktop computer for 80 per cent of the time for income-producing purposes and 20 per cent of the time for private purposes.

According to TR 2021/3 (Table B, Category C), the effective life of a desktop computer is 4 years.

What is the depreciation in the 2022 and 2023 tax years under the diminishing value depreciation method?

As the desktop computer was not used exclusively for income-producing purposes, the depreciation needs to be apportioned. As the desktop computer was used 80 per cent of the time for business purposes, consequently only 80 per cent of the depreciation can be claimed as a tax deduction.

Hence, the depreciation claim for each year is shown next (using the depreciation figures calculated in example 8.3).

2022:

$$\$504 \times 80\% = \$403$$

2023:

$$\$1748 \times 80\% = \$1398$$

Where the asset is not used exclusively for income-producing purposes, there are two calculations required. The first step is to calculate the depreciation for the asset 'as if' it were used 100 per cent for income-producing purposes.

Once the depreciation figure has been ascertained, then this figure is subsequently multiplied by the business percentage to arrive at the amount that is tax deductible.

8.3 Special rules for different types of taxpayers

LEARNING OBJECTIVE 8.3 Describe the different taxation depreciation rules for individual taxpayers, small business entities, medium-size entities and large business taxpayers.

Special rules relating to deductions for the decline in value of depreciating assets apply to various categories of taxpayers. These taxpayers are split into:

1. individual taxpayers
2. small business entities (SBEs)
3. medium-size entities, and
4. large business taxpayers.

8.3.1 Depreciation rules for individual taxpayers

The depreciation rules for individual taxpayers are summarised as follows.

(a) According to section 40-80(2), an immediate 100% deduction applies in respect of depreciating assets costing $300 or less used by non-business taxpayers in deriving assessable income.[2]

(b) For depreciating assets costing more than $300 but less than $1000, two options are available to the individual taxpayer:

(i) The assets may be allocated to a **low-value pool** and depreciated at:
- 18.75% depreciating value (DV) in the first year, and
- 37.5% DV in the second and subsequent years.

Once a low-value pool has been created, then all depreciable capital assets costing between $300 and $1000 must be allocated to that low-value depreciation pool and the business must continue to use the low-value pool method until all value in that pool has been diminished. In other words, once an item is allocated into this low-value pool, it must remain there.

(ii) If the taxpayer elects not to use a low-value pool, then the normal depreciation rules contained in (c) apply.

(c) Depreciating assets costing $1000 or more are depreciated over their effective lives as outlined by the Commissioner in TR 2021/3 using either the prime cost or diminishing value depreciation methods.

There are three advantages of pooling.

1. There is no need to self-assess the individual effective life of each depreciating asset or refer to the effective life of each individual asset as per the Commissioner of Taxation's TR 2021/3. If a taxpayer has multiple depreciable assets, this could prove to be very time-consuming as each asset has a different effective life for tax purposes.

2. There is no need to calculate the number of ownership days as there is no need to apportion the depreciation for the number of days in the initial ownership year (i.e. from the date of purchase to 30 June in that first year).

3. Only two depreciation rates need to be used. One rate for depreciating assets purchased during the income year (being 18.75%), and a second rate for assets held since the end of the prior income year (being 37.5%).

---

2 ITAA97 section 40-80(2).

The main disadvantage of pooling is that the asset loses its individual identity in the pool. What is depreciated is the total of the asset pool and not the individual assets themselves. Many owners/directors want to know the original cost and written down values of individual assets that their entity owns. This information is often required for internal business management purposes.

Example 8.5 examines the issues to consider in choosing an approach to depreciation.

EXAMPLE 8.5

Calculating depreciation for an individual taxpayer

Summer, an individual taxpayer, works as a journalist for a newspaper. During the 2022 income year, she purchased the following assets for exclusive use for her job.

Item	Date	Asset	No. days	TR 2021/53 effective life	Amount ($)
(a)	7 September 2021	Portable laser printer	297	5 years	240
(b)	19 February 2022	Multi-function machine	132	5 years	880
(c)	2 May 2022	Desktop computer	60	4 years	1 200

Calculate Summer's decline in value (depreciation) claim in respect of the mentioned assets for the year ended 30 June 2022. Assume that Summer wishes to *maximise* any depreciation deduction claimed in 2022.

(a) The portable laser printer cost $240. As this amount is less than $300, Summer can claim the entire amount as a tax deduction under section 40-80(2) of the ITAA97.

(b) The multi-function machine cost $880. As this amount is between $300 and $1000, Summer has the choice of depreciating the asset using the effective life of 5 years (as per Table B of TR 2021/3) and apportion for the number of days to 30 June 2022, *or* allocate the asset to a low-value pool and depreciate it at the rate of 18.75% DV in the first year (with no apportionment for the number of days).

Both calculations are shown as follows.

Pooling:

$$\$880 \times 18.75\% \text{ DV} = \$165$$

Depreciation as per TR 2021/3

$$\$880 \times \frac{132 \text{ days}}{365 \text{ days}} \times \frac{200\%}{5 \text{ years}} = \$127 \text{ (rounded)}$$

As pooling gives the greater deduction, Summer should *pool* the multi-function machine. However, if Summer elects to pool this asset, all subsequent assets purchased costing between $300 and $1000 must be pooled.

(c) In terms of the desktop computer, as this amount is more than $1000, it must be depreciated in accordance with the Commissioner's effective life of 4 years as per Table B of TR 2021/3. The decline in value of the desktop computer is calculated as follows.

$$\$1200 \times \frac{60 \text{ days}}{365 \text{ days}} \times \frac{200\%}{4 \text{ years}} = \$99 \text{ (rounded)}$$

Summer's total depreciation claim for 2022 comes to $504 (i.e. $240 + $165 + $99).

Figure 8.8 summarises the depreciation rules for individual taxpayers under Division 40.

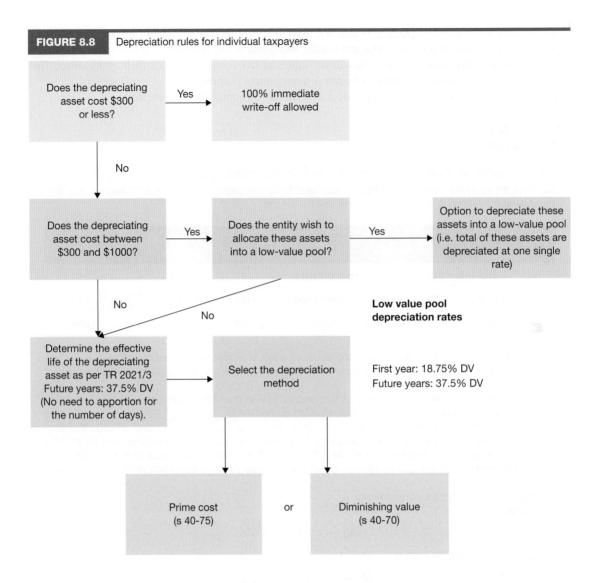

FIGURE 8.8 Depreciation rules for individual taxpayers

8.3.2 Depreciation rules for small business entity (SBE) taxpayers

Special depreciation rules are available to small business entity (SBE) taxpayers who elect to take advantage of simplified depreciation concessions.

According to section 328-110 of the ITAA97, a business is classified as a **small business entity** if:

- it carries on business in that year, and
- its aggregated turnover for the year is less than the specified 'annual SBE turnover'.

For the year ended 30 June 2022, the specified 'annual SBE turnover' is $10 million.

There are two components of these SBE simplified depreciation concessions:

1. an instant write-off for certain 'low cost' assets, and
2. the ability to group all other depreciable assets into a 'small business pool' for simpler depreciation calculation.

If a small business chooses to use the simplified small business depreciation rules, then it must apply these rules to all its depreciating assets.

If a small business chooses not to use these special depreciation rules, then it must use the depreciation rules for large business entities as outlined in a later section of this chapter. This means that newly acquired assets are not added into the general small business pool and are instead depreciated under Division 40. Second, the small business pool still exists and it will continue to be depreciated at 30 per cent until the pool has been fully extinguished and reduced to a $nil balance.

The simplified depreciation rules for SBEs are shown in figure 8.9.

FIGURE 8.9 Depreciation rules for small business entities (SBEs)

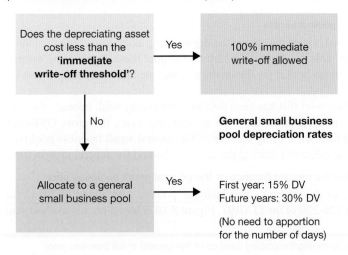

The **immediate write-off threshold** (also known as the 'instant write-off threshold') depends on when the depreciating asset was acquired. The relevant thresholds are summarised in table 8.4.

TABLE 8.4 Immediate write-off thresholds for SBE depreciation

Date of acquisition of depreciating asset	Immediate write-off threshold	Annual SBE turnover
Before 12 May 2015	$1 000	< $2 million
12 May 2015 to 28 January 2019	$20 000	< $10 million
29 January 2019 to 2 April 2019	$25 000	< $10 million
3 April 2019 to 11 March 2020	$30 000	< $10 million
12 March 2020 to 6 October 2020	$150 000	< $10 million
6 October 2020 to 30 June 2023	Unlimited	< $10 million
After 1 July 2023	$1 000	< $10 million

As outlined in the next section, medium-size entities are also eligible for the immediate write-off concession.

8.3.2.1 General small business pool rules

Where the cost of the depreciating asset (including computer software not allocated to a software development pool) costs more than the 'immediate write-off threshold' outlined in table 8.4, then the SBE is required to pool (i.e. lump) these depreciating assets and depreciate them in a **general small business pool**.

According to section 328-190(2), any new depreciating assets acquired during an income year are allowed half-a-year's depreciation for that income year (i.e. 15 per cent) and are allocated to the appropriate pool at the end of that year (section 328-185(4)) so that they can then be depreciated at the full rate in the subsequent year.

The annual depreciation deduction for the pool is calculated under section 328-190(1) by multiplying the pool's opening balance by the depreciation rate of 30 per cent.

Once the balance of the pool has decreased below the immediate write-off threshold, the balance can be fully written-off in the subsequent income tax year.

Due to the temporary full expensing rules enacted by the Federal Government effective from 6 October 2020 to 30 June 2023, the SBE closing general small business pool at 30 June 2021 and 30 June 2022 would have been written-off and claimed in full. Due to the impact of the temporary full expensing rules, an SBE taxpayer will not have an opening general small pool balance at 1 July 2021 and will not allocate depreciating assets to the pool during the 2022 and 2023 income years. If, and when, the temporary full expensing rules expire on 30 June 2023, the general small business pools will recommence in the 2023/24 income years.

8.3.2.1.1 Disposal of pooled assets

As previously discussed, where the cost of the depreciating asset costs more than the 'immediate write-off threshold' outlined in table 8.3, the SBE is required to pool these depreciating assets and depreciate them in a general small business pool at the diminishing value rate of 30 per cent per year (15 per cent DV in the first year).

When a depreciating asset that has been pooled is ultimately sold, instead of calculating the individual gain or loss arising from the disposal of the depreciating asset, the gross GST-exclusive sale proceeds are simply deducted from the closing balance of the general small business pool (section 328-200 of the ITAA97). This has the effect of reducing the amount claimed for depreciation in future years.

8.3.2.1.2 Determining the closing balance of the general small business pool

The closing balance of the general small business pool is determined by using the method statement contained in section 328-200 of the ITAA97. Figure 8.10 is based on this method statement.

FIGURE 8.10	Determining the closing balance of the general small business pool

Opening general small pool balance for the year
+
Additions to the pool (i.e. new assets acquired during the income year). This does not include assets that were immediately written off under the write-off threshold
+
Any cost addition amounts including improvements made to assets in the pool during the year
=
Subtotal
−
Depreciation on opening pool balance (@ 30% diminishing value)
−
Depreciation on any additions during the income year at half-rate (@ 15% diminishing value)
−
Disposals of assets during the income year (gross sale proceeds)
=
Closing general pool balance for the year

Source: Adapted from ITAA97 section 328-200.

Should the closing balance of the general small business pool become a negative amount (i.e. when the sale proceeds from disposal of depreciating assets exceeds the remaining balance of the pool), then the closing balance of the pool is regarded as assessable income of the taxpayer (section 328-215(4)).[3]

8.3.2.1.3 What happens if the balance of the general small business pool falls below the instant asset write-off threshold?

Should the closing balance of the general small business pool fall below the instant asset write-off threshold (before calculating depreciation for the income year), the entire balance may be claimed as a deduction (section 328-210). However, as mentioned previously, due to the temporary full expensing rules enacted by the Federal Government effective from 6 October 2020 to 30 June 2023, the SBE closing general small business pool at 30 June 2021 and 30 June 2022 would have been written-off and deducted in full.

8.3.2.2 Disclosure of SBE simplified depreciation in the income tax return

If an SBE has elected to adopt the simplified depreciation regime, this will be reflected in the business's tax return. All tax returns have a section entitled 'Small business entity simplified depreciation'.

If this section has been completed by the entity's accountant or tax agent, then this indicates that the entity has adopted the simplified depreciation regime afforded to SBEs. An extract of the company tax return is shown in figure 8.11.

Label A at Item 10 shown in figure 8.11 entitled 'Deduction for certain assets' is the sum of those assets that were acquired during the year, which have been claimed in full. Label B entitled 'Deduction for general small business pool' is the sum of depreciation claimed for those assets that were subject to the 15 per cent or 30 per cent DV rates during the income year.

---

3 ITAA97 section 328-215(4).

| 10 Small business entity simplified depreciation | Deduction for certain assets | **A** $ ☐☐,☐☐☐,☐☐☐,☐☐☐ ⋅☒ |
| | Deduction for general small business pool | **B** $ ☐☐,☐☐☐,☐☐☐,☐☐☐ ⋅☒ |

Source: Australian Taxation Office, *Company tax return 2021* (Web Page, 2021) https://www.ato.gov.au/uploadedFiles/Content/IND/Downloads/Company-tax-return-2021.pdf.

8.3.3 Depreciation rules for medium-size entity taxpayers

On 2 April 2020, as part of the Coronavirus Stimulus Package, the Federal Government announced that the 'immediate write-off threshold' would be expanded to include all businesses with an annual turnover of between $10 million and $500 million. These entities are referred to as medium-size entities. In the Federal Budget handed down on 6 October 2020, the Government amended the definition of a medium-size entity to one with an annual turnover of less than $5 billion.

At the same time, the Federal Government announced that medium-size entities with an annual turnover of less than $5 billion can claim the full cost of an eligible new depreciating asset purchased on or after 7:30 pm on 6 October 2020 and 30 June 2023. These rules allow a deduction for the full cost of eligible new depreciating assets of any value, acquired from 7:30 pm AEDT on 6 October 2020 and first used or installed ready for use by 30 June 2023.

This is what the Federal Budget refers to as 'temporary full expensing' (and is not limited to an eligible asset with a cost of less than $150 000). This means that an entity with an annual turnover of less than $5 billion can claim the entire cost of any depreciable asset as a tax deduction. The Federal Government estimated that approximately 3.5 million businesses would be eligible for the scheme in a move set to encourage spending among businesses.

For businesses with an aggregated turnover of less than $50 million, temporary full expensing also applies to the business portion of eligible second-hand depreciating assets.

Eligible depreciating assets do not include:
- assets allocated to a low-value pool or a software development pool
- certain primary production assets, including water facilities, fencing, horticultural plants or fodder storage assets
- buildings and other capital works for which are deductible under Division 43
- assets that either will never be located in Australia or will not be used principally in Australia for the principal purpose of carrying on a business.

If the business has an aggregated turnover of $50 million or more, it is excluded from immediately deducting the cost of an eligible asset that is a second-hand asset.

As well as claiming an immediate deduction for the business portion of the cost of an eligible asset, a medium-sized entity taxpayer can also claim an immediate deduction for the business portion of the cost of any improvements to an eligible asset if it is incurred before 30 June 2023. The claim also covers improvements to existing assets.

Furthermore, following amendments passed by Federal Parliament on 10 December 2020, businesses have the option to opt out of this measure on an asset-by-asset basis. Businesses which opt out or are ineligible to claim the temporary full expensing concession for certain assets may still be eligible for other concessions including the original 'instant-asset write-off' concession and the backing business investment accelerated depreciation measure.

The depreciation rules for medium-size entities are shown in figure 8.12.

It is important to note that businesses with an annual turnover of $5 billion or more are not eligible to use the instant asset write-off as they are considered 'large business taxpayers'. The depreciation rules for large business taxpayers are explained in the next section of this chapter.

As announced in the Federal Budget handed down on Tuesday 29 March 2022, the Federal Government will introduce a technology investment boost to support digital adoption by small and medium-size businesses.

The Government has proposed that businesses with annual turnover of less than $50 million will be able to deduct an additional 20 per cent of the cost incurred on business expenses and depreciating assets that support its digital adoption, such as portable payment devices, cybersecurity systems or subscriptions to cloud-based services.

FIGURE 8.12 Depreciation rules for medium-size business entities

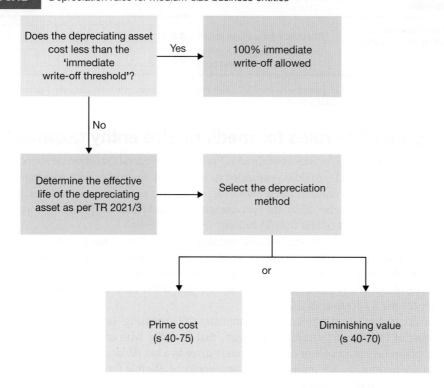

An annual cap will apply in each qualifying income year so that expenditure up to $100 000 will be eligible for the boost. The boost will apply to eligible expenditure incurred from 29 March 2022 until 30 June 2023. The boost for eligible expenditure incurred by 30 June 2022 will be claimed in tax returns for the following income year. The boost for eligible expenditure incurred between 1 July 2022 and 30 June 2023 will be included in the income year in which the expenditure is incurred.

8.3.4 Depreciation rules for large business entities

A **large business taxpayer** is defined as a business that is not a small business entity (SBE), nor a medium-size entity. For the year ended 30 June 2022, a large business taxpayer is one that has an annual turnover of more than $5 billion. Large business taxpayers are subject to the following depreciation rules.

Furthermore, the depreciation rules for large business taxpayers outlined also apply to those SBEs that elect not to take advantage of the simplified depreciation rules described in the previous section.

The depreciation rules for large business taxpayers that acquire depreciating assets (including computer software that is not allocated to a software development pool) are summarised as follows.

(a) An immediate 100 per cent deduction applies in respect of depreciating assets costing $100 or less (e.g. hole punches, staplers, calculators, labelling machines, document holders).

(b) For depreciating assets costing more than $100 but less than $1000, two options are available.
   (i) The assets may be allocated to a low-value pool and depreciated at the following rates:
      – 18.75% DV in the first year, and
      – 37.5% DV in the second and subsequent years.
      Once a low-value pool has been created, then all depreciable capital assets costing between $100 and $1000 must be allocated to that low-value depreciation pool and the business must continue to use the low-value pool method until all value in that pool has been diminished. In other words, once an item is allocated into this low-value pool, it must remain there.
   (ii) If the taxpayer elects not to use a low-value pool, then the normal depreciation rules in (c) apply.

(c) Depreciating assets costing $1000 or more, or those assets not placed into a low-value pool, are depreciated over their effective lives as outlined by the Commissioner in Taxation Ruling TR 2021/3 using either the prime cost or diminishing value depreciation methods.

Figure 8.13 summarises the depreciation rules for large business taxpayers and those SBEs that choose not to adopt the simplified depreciation method.

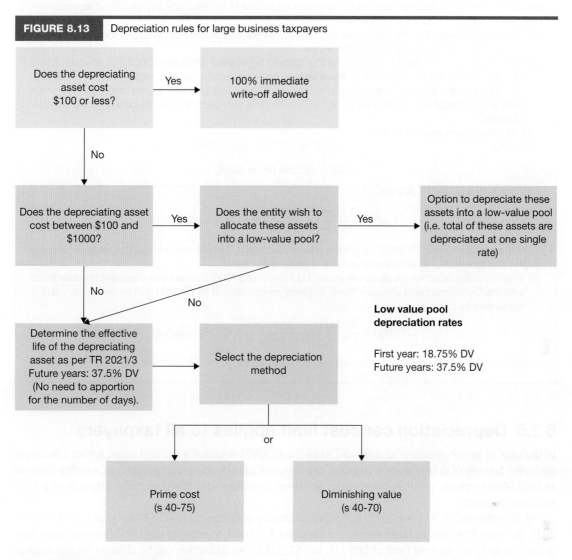

FIGURE 8.13 Depreciation rules for large business taxpayers

Example 8.6 demonstrates these rules.

EXAMPLE 8.6

Calculating depreciation for a large business taxpayer

Tait Manufacturing Ltd operates a chocolate manufacturing plant in Geelong.

The company's annual turnover is $6.2 billion, making it a large business taxpayer, as its annual turnover for the year ended 30 June 2022 is more than $5 billion.

During the 2022 income year, the company purchased the following assets for exclusive use in the business.

Item	Date	Asset	No. days	TR 2021/3 effective life	Amount ($)
(a)	14 July 2021	Paper shredder	352	15 years	87
(b)	19 September 2021	Electronic whiteboard	285	5 years	560
(c)	3 April 2022	Industrial robot	89	10 years	750 000

Calculate Tait Manufacturing Ltd's decline in value claim in respect of the mentioned assets for the year ended 30 June 2022. Assume that Tait Manufacturing Ltd wishes to *maximise* any depreciation deduction claimed in 2022.

(a) The shredder cost $87. As this is less than $100, Tait Manufacturing Ltd can claim the entire amount as a tax deduction in the current income year.

(b) The electronic whiteboard cost $560. As this amount is between $100 and $1000, Tait Manufacturing Ltd has the choice of depreciating the asset using the effective life of 5 years (as per Table B of TR 2021/3) and apportion for the number of days to 30 June 2022, or allocate the asset to a low-value pool and depreciating it at the rate of 18.75 DV in the first year (with no apportionment for the number of days).

Both calculations are shown next.

Pooling:

$$\$560 \times 18.75\% \text{ DV} = \$105$$

Depreciation as per TR 2021/3:

$$\$560 \times \frac{285 \text{ days}}{365 \text{ days}} \times \frac{200\%}{5 \text{ years}} = \$175 \text{ (rounded)}$$

As depreciation under TR 2021/3 gives the greater deduction, Tait Manufacturing Ltd should individually depreciate the electronic whiteboard instead of pooling the asset.

(c) In terms of the industrial robot, as this amount is more than $1000, it must be depreciated in accordance with the Commissioner's effective life of 10 years as per Table B of TR 2021/3. The decline in value is calculated as follows.

$$\$750\,000 \times \frac{89 \text{ days}}{365 \text{ days}} \times \frac{200\%}{10 \text{ years}} = \$36\,575 \text{ (rounded)}$$

Tait Manufacturing Ltd's total depreciation claim for 2022 comes to $36 837 (i.e. $87 + $17 + $36 575).

8.3.5 Depreciation car cost limit applies to all taxpayers

In the case of motor vehicles, section 40-230 of the ITAA97 imposes a car cost limit, which effectively limits the amount of depreciation a taxpayer can claim as a tax deduction (regardless of whether they are an individual taxpayer, small business entity taxpayer, a medium-size business entity taxpayer or a large business taxpayer).

For the year ended 30 June 2022, the depreciation car cost limit is $60 733 (for year ended 30 June 2021, this was $59 136). In other words, if a car costs $125 000, a taxpayer can only claim an immediate deduction up to the car cost limit of $60 733, *not* $125 000. No deduction can be claimed for any amount in excess of $60 733.

A car is defined in section 995-1 of the ITAA97 as a motor vehicle (including a motor car, station wagon, panel van, utility truck or any other road vehicle, including a four-wheel drive that is designed to carry a load of less than one tonne and fewer than nine passengers (excluding motor cycles)).

Therefore, for other vehicles, the car limit has no application. Hence, utes and trucks with a carrying capacity of more than one tonne may be eligible for full depreciation in the year that they are acquired and used in the business.

ETHICS IN PRACTICE

Ethics in capital allowances

Jason is a resident individual taxpayer. He works as an engineer for a large engineering firm in Sydney. You are his tax agent. In early June 2022, Jason purchased a desktop computer costing $3600 to use while working from home.

Jason asks you how much he can claim as a tax deduction in respect of the desktop computer as he has heard from friends and colleagues about the Federal Government's instant asset write-off rules.

However, you explain to Jason that these rules only apply when the taxpayer is carrying on business and does not apply to individual taxpayers who are employees. Instead, Jason will be eligible to claim depreciation in respect of the desktop computer over a period of 4 years, as per the Commissioner's guidelines contained in TR 2021/3.

Jason is not impressed with this, as the amount of depreciation claimed will be rather minimal as he will need to apportion his depreciation claim for the number of days to 30 June 2022 and then write the asset off over 4 years.

Jason prefers a larger depreciation claim and when you advise that it is also possible to self-assess the effective life, Jason immediately says 'That's great. Let's use one year, as this will give me the 100% tax deduction that I am after'. You subsequently discover that Jason has no intention whatsoever of replacing the desktop computer in one year's time but, instead, intends to hold it for approximately 4 years.

What advice would you provide to Jason?

You should make it clear to Jason that taxpayers are entitled to self-assess and determine the effective life of depreciable assets themselves as per section 40-105. However, the effective life must be based on objective evidence and represent the period that the taxpayer intends to use the asset and then dispose (or replace) the asset.

Jason has stated that he wants you to use an effective life of 1 year, instead of 4 years, being the period that he actually intends holding and using the asset for. Jason's primary motivation in using a shorter effective life of 1 year is purely to obtain a larger depreciation deduction for the 2022 income year.

Section 120 of APES 110 *Code of Ethics for Professional Accountants* requires the tax agent to act with objectivity, whilst section 130 also requires the tax advisor to act with professional competence and due care. This means that the tax advisor cannot simply 'turn a blind eye' to the client's request.

Furthermore, section 6 of APES 220 *Taxation Services* warns that any use of estimates must be reasonable and objectively determined. Where estimates are not reasonable, the member must advise the client or employer of the risks and consequences of using estimates.

In addition, section 7 of APES 220 requires that members shall not, under any circumstances, become associated with any tax return or submission on behalf of a client if it contains incorrect or misleading information.

For all of these reasons, the tax agent needs to ensure that the effective life of the desktop computer accurately reflects the period of time that Jason will hold the asset, being 4 years. It is not acceptable to use an effective life of 1 year so as to maximise Jason's depreciation claim for the 2022 income year.

8.4 Computer software

LEARNING OBJECTIVE 8.4 Apply the special depreciation rules in relation to computer software.

For accounting purposes, computer software is considered an intangible asset and comes within the provisions of AASB 138 *Intangible Assets*.

Items of computer hardware are clearly depreciating assets and are subject to the ordinary capital allowance rules. Such items include computers, screens and backup drives. For taxation purposes, computer software is also considered to be a depreciating asset and special depreciation rules relate to depreciable computer software. The rules depend on the classification of computer software. For taxation purposes, there are four main classifications of computer software:

1. in-house software (includes purchased software)
2. internally developed software
3. software acquired under a recurring licence, and
4. software acquired for the purposes of resale (i.e. trading stock).

These rules are summarised in the following sections.

8.4.1 In-house software (includes purchased software)

Section 995-1 of the ITAA97 defines **in-house software** as computer software that is acquired or developed by the taxpayer for its own internal use.

For example, word processing software purchased off-the-shelf (or downloaded from the internet) is an example of in-house software.

If expenditure on the computer software is deductible under another provision of the ITAA97 (e.g. under section 8-1 in the case of software acquired under a monthly licence) then the software is not considered in-house software (see section 8.4.3).

According to item 8 of section 40-95(7), in-house software that is purchased off-the-shelf, or expenditure incurred in developing computer software that is not allocated to a software development pool, is required to be depreciated over 5 years using the prime cost depreciation method. This translates to a depreciation rate of a flat 20 per cent per year. The diminishing value method is not allowed to be used (per section 40-70(2)).

Example 8.7 applies the depreciation rules to in-house software.

In-house software

On 14 May 2022, Jessica (an individual taxpayer) purchased Adobe Acrobat Pro DC for $1280 for exclusive use in her job as a graphic designer.

Calculate the decline in value of the computer software for the year ended 30 June 2022. There are 48 days from 14 May 2022 to 30 June 2022.

The acquired (or off-the-shelf) software qualifies as in-house computer software and is required to be depreciated over 5 years under the prime cost depreciation method.

The decline in value is calculated as follows.

$$\$1280 \times \frac{48\,\text{days}}{365\,\text{days}} \times \frac{100\%}{5\,\text{years}} = \$34\,(\text{rounded})$$

8.4.1.1 Relationship between section 40-95(7) and special depreciation rules for taxpayers

As previously mentioned, computer software is a depreciating asset under Division 40 but is subject to special rules.

In the case where an entity (whether it be an individual, SBE or large business entity) elects to allocate depreciating assets into a pool, then all depreciating assets (including computer software) must be allocated into that pool.

In other words, if a low-value or SBE pool is created, then the pooling rules override the special computer software rules contained in Division 40, and the computer software must be allocated to that respective pool. Furthermore, if a SBE or medium-size entity acquires computer software, then the instant asset rule/temporary full expensing rules override section 40-95(7), meaning that the computer software can be claimed as an immediate tax deduction in the year that it is acquired.

8.4.2 Internally developed software

Software developed internally by the entity also meets the definition of 'in-house software'. For internally developed software, the taxpayer has two choices.

1. Capitalise all expenditure on the software during the development phase, and when the software becomes fully operational, depreciate the software at the flat 20 per cent prime cost depreciation rate allowed for in-house software (as previously mentioned).
2. Pool the expenditure into a **software development pool**. If the taxpayer elects to pool the internally developed software, section 40-455 provides that the pooled software must be depreciated over 5 years using the following rates:
   – 0% for the first year
   – 30% in the second year
   – 30% in the third year
   – 30% in the fourth year, and
   – 10% in the fifth year.

Once again, the prime cost method must be used. The diminishing value method is *not* allowed to be used (section 40-70(2)).

8.4.3 Software acquired under a recurring licence

The Commissioner of Taxation accepts that annual license fees are deductible under section 8-1 rather than having the expenditure capitalised and then depreciated as part of the cost of in-house software.

This would apply, for instance, in the case where a business makes monthly payments for the right to use a computerised accounting package such as MYOB or Xero under a monthly subscription service (e.g. $100 per month).

This issue was addressed in the ATO's Interpretative Decision ID 2010/14. It was concluded that accounting and tax software acquired under a recurring annual licence will be fully tax-deductible under section 8-1 because the fees are not capital or capital in nature.

8.4.4 Software acquired for the purposes of resale

If the computer software has been acquired for the purposes of resale, then the purchase of the software will be tax-deductible under section 8-1 and the stock balances may also be subject to the trading stock provisions contained in Division 70 of the ITAA97.

TECHNOLOGY IN ACTION

Cryptocurrency

With the increasing interest in blockchain technology, many Australians are actively involved in crypto-trading, or even cryptomining.

Where a taxpayer's activities focus on cryptomining, although they have not purchased cryptoassets, their mining activities are not without cost. What about the equipment used for mining? For large-scale mining activities, a taxpayer may have made significant investments in equipment, such as computer hardware and computer software.

REFLECTION

If you had a client undertaking a cryptomining business, what are the Division 40 implications? (The special depreciation rules outlined in section 8.3 of this chapter will apply depending on the type of taxpayer (i.e. small business entity taxpayer, medium-size entity or large business taxpayer).)

8.5 Disposals of depreciating assets

LEARNING OBJECTIVE 8.5 Determine the assessability/deductibility when a depreciating asset is disposed.

In some instances, a taxpayer may dispose of a depreciating asset. In accounting terminology, this may give rise to a gain or loss on sale. For taxation purposes, this is referred to as a **balancing adjustment** event (section 40-295).

According to section 40-285(1) of the ITAA97, if the **termination value** (i.e. sale proceeds) of a depreciating asset is more than its **adjustable value** (i.e. written down value), the difference (i.e. a gain on sale) is assessable in the year of sale. This is referred to as an **assessable balancing adjustment**.

Conversely, according to section 40-285(2) of the ITAA97, if the termination value (i.e. sale proceeds) of a depreciating asset is less than its adjustable value (i.e. written down value), the difference (i.e. a loss on sale) can be claimed as a deduction in the year of sale. This is referred to as a **deductible balancing adjustment**.

A comparison of the accounting and taxation terminology is shown in table 8.5. Example 8.8 illustrates the tax treatment of the disposal of depreciating assets.

TABLE 8.5 Accounting and taxation terms

Accounting term	Taxation term
Sale proceeds	Termination value
Written down value	Adjustable value
Gain on sale	Assessable balancing adjustment
Loss on sale	Deductible balancing adjustment

EXAMPLE 8.8

Disposals of depreciating assets

Orion Financial Planners Pty Ltd owns a colour photocopier. On 17 April 2022, the company sold its colour photocopier for $1000. The written down value of the photocopier on this date is $1400.

Orion Financial Planners Pty Ltd will record a loss on sale (i.e. a deductible balancing adjustment) of $400 ($1400 – $1000). This amount is an allowable deduction in accordance with section 40-285(2) of the ITAA97.

On the other hand, if Orion Financial Planners Pty Ltd sold the colour photocopier for $1600, then it will record a gain on sale (i.e. an assessable balancing adjustment) of $200 ($1600 – $1400) in accordance with section 40-285(1) of the ITAA97.

8.6 CGT and depreciable assets

LEARNING OBJECTIVE 8.6 Determine the CGT implications when selling a CGT asset.

A capital gain or capital loss arising from the sale of a depreciating asset used solely for income-producing purposes is disregarded (section 118-24). However, a capital gain may arise under CGT event K7 where a depreciating asset is disposed of that was partly used for income-producing purposes and partly for private (non-taxable) purposes. In this situation, the capital gain under CGT event K7 is calculated based on the difference between the assets sale proceeds and its original cost (section 118-240). This concept is illustrated in example 8.9.

EXAMPLE 8.9

CGT and depreciable assets used partially for income-producing purposes

Laura is a resident individual taxpayer. She works as a journalist for a television station. On 1 July 2021, she acquires a desktop computer costing $4000. According to records maintained by Laura, she uses the computer 80 per cent of the time for business purposes and 20 per cent for private purposes.

Assume that Laura depreciates the desktop computer over 4 years using the prime cost depreciation method. Hence, the amount of depreciation claimed for the 2022 income year came to $800 (being $4000 × 365 days/365 days × 100%/4 years = $1000 × 80% taxable purpose).

The amount of private depreciation (being the non-taxable purpose) for the 2022 income year came to $200 (being $4000 × 365 days/365 days × 100%/4 years × 20% non-taxable purpose).

The written down value of the desktop computer at 30 June 2022 was therefore $3000 (being $4000 – $1000). Assume that, on this date, a colleague offers Laura $4400 for the desktop computer, which she accepts.

As Laura has sold the depreciating asset ($4400) for more than what she bought it for ($4000), and has used the depreciating asset partly for a taxable purpose (80%) and partly for a non-taxable (or private) purpose, CGT event K7 applies.

8.6.1 Calculation of CGT event K7

The capital gain under CGT event K7 is calculated as follows:

$$\frac{[\text{Sale proceeds} - \text{Original cost}] \times \text{Non-taxable (private) depreciation}}{\text{Total depreciation}}$$

Hence:

$$[\$4400 - \$4000] \times \frac{\$200}{\$1000}$$
$$\$400 \times 20\%$$
$$= \$80$$

8.6.2 Calculation of assessable balancing adjustment (i.e. gain on sale)

A gain on sale (or assessable balancing adjustment) will also arise in respect of the taxable component of the desktop computer under section 40-285(1). The assessable balancing adjustment is calculated as follows:

$$\frac{[\text{Sale proceeds} - \text{Written down value}] \times \text{Taxable (business) depreciation}}{\text{Total depreciation}}$$

Hence, the assessable balancing adjustment (or gain on sale) is calculated as follows:

$$[\$4400 - \$3000] \times \frac{\$800}{\$1000}$$
$$[\$1400] \times \frac{\$800}{\$1000}$$
$$\$1400 \times 80\%$$
$$= \$1120$$

8.7 Division 43: Deduction for capital works expenditure

LEARNING OBJECTIVE 8.7 Apply the Division 43 capital allowance rules in respect of buildings, structural improvements, extensions, alterations and capital improvements made to buildings.

As previously mentioned, for taxation purposes, a taxpayer is not entitled to claim depreciation in respect of income-producing buildings under Division 40 of the ITAA97.

However, Division 43 allows a taxpayer to claim a deduction for capital works expenditure incurred on the original construction cost of income-producing buildings and other capital works.

Division 43 of ITAA97 applies to both residential and non-residential income-producing buildings. Income-producing residential buildings include units, apartments, flats, hotels, motels and guesthouses while income-producing non-residential buildings include shops, offices, casinos, convention centres and shopping centres (section 43-20(3)).

While the term 'capital works' is not defined, Division 43 applies to:
- buildings
- structural (capital) improvements
- environmental protection earthworks, and
- extensions, alterations, or capital improvements to any of the listed items (e.g. refurbishment of a kitchen or bathroom to a rental property owned by a taxpayer).

It is important to note that the deduction is not based on what the taxpayer acquired the building for, but on the original construction cost.

The rate of deduction depends on the year in which the construction commenced, in addition to the use of the building and/or capital works.

The applicable rates of deduction for construction expenditure are shown in table 8.6.

TABLE 8.6   Division 43 capital works allowance rates

Type of construction	Start of construction	Deduction rate	Years
Industrial buildings	After 26 February 1992	4.0%	25
Short-term traveller accommodation (e.g. backpackers and youth hostels)	22 August 1979 to 21 August 1984	2.5%	40
	22 August 1984 to 15 September 1987	4.0%	25
	16 September 1987 to 26 February 1992	2.5%	40
	After 26 February 1992	4.0%	25
Other residential accommodation (e.g. residential units, apartments, flats and houses)	18 July 1985 to 15 September 1987	4.0%	25
	After 15 September 1987	2.5%	
Other non-residential buildings (e.g. commercial premises)	20 July 1982 to 21 August 1984	2.5%	40
	22 August 1984 to 15 September 1987	4.0%	25
	After 15 September 1987	2.5%	40
Structural improvements	After 26 February 1992	2.5%	40
Environmental protection earthworks	After 18 August 1992	2.5%	40

Unlike Division 40, where the taxpayer can elect to use either the prime cost or diminishing value method, under Division 43 only the prime cost depreciation method can be used.

As with depreciation, a deduction is only allowable to the extent that the building and/or capital works is used for income-producing purposes. Like depreciation, the calculation under Division 43 (at either 2.5 per cent or 4 per cent) needs to be performed on a daily basis starting from (and, therefore including) the first date that the property was used to derive assessable income.

The claim for Division 43 capital works deduction is made at Label I at Item 9 of the company tax return.

FIGURE 8.14 Capital works deductions section of 2021 company tax return

Capital works deductions   I $ ☐☐,☐☐☐,☐☐☐,☐☐☐ .00

Source: Australian Taxation Office, *Company tax return 2021* (Web Page, 2021) https://www.ato.gov.au/uploadedFiles/Content/IND/Downloads/Company-tax-return-2021.pdf.

8.7.1 What is construction expenditure?

As previously mentioned, the Division 43 write-off is not based on the original purchase price of the asset to the taxpayer, but on its **construction expenditure**.

Construction expenditure includes:

- the original construction costs of the building or capital improvement
- preliminary expenses such as architect's fees, engineering fees and costs associated with obtaining approval for the building
- the cost of structural features that are an integral part of the building (e.g. retaining walls, fences, atriums and lift wells).

However, according to section 43-70(2), construction expenditure does not include costs incurred in:

- acquiring the land
- clearing the land
- demolishing existing structures
- pre-construction site clearance (e.g. clearing, levelling, filling or draining), and
- landscaping.

The question is how one determines the original construction cost.

TR 97/25 states that where the taxpayer is unable to precisely determine the actual cost of construction, the ATO will accept estimates from:

- a clerk of works (i.e. a project manager for major building projects)
- a supervising architect who approves payments at each stage in major projects or smaller contracts
- a builder who is experienced in estimating costs of similar building projects, or
- quantity surveyors.

Real estate valuers, estate agents, accountants and solicitors will *not* be accepted unless they have other relevant qualifications.

Finally, it is important to note that depreciable plant and equipment is excluded. These may be claimed at separate (generally higher) depreciation rates under Division 40.

Example 8.10 demonstrates the calculation of a claim under Division 43.

EXAMPLE 8.10

Calculating the Division 43 claim

On 5 September 2021, Miranda acquires a 3-bedroom apartment in Caloundra for $820 000. She immediately rents this property out to tenants at $760 per week.

Based on a quantity surveyor's report, she is advised that the apartment was built by Taylor Builders in June 2014. The original construction cost of her 3-bedroom apartment was $360 000.

What deduction can Miranda claim under Division 43?

Miranda is entitled to an annual deduction of $9000 per year under Division 43. This is based on the original construction cost of $360 000 divided by 40 years (or 2.5% per annum). However, for the year ended 30 June 2022, Miranda's Division 43 claim must be prorated for the number of days from 5 September 2021 (being the date that it was first rented out to tenants) to 30 June 2022 (being 299 days).

Her claim for 2022 therefore comes to $7373 (based on $360 000 × 2.5% × 299/365 days).

> If the 3-bedroom apartment came furnished (e.g. carpets, blinds, curtains, dishwasher, washing machine, lounge, chairs and tables), these items constitute depreciable items. Miranda would have been entitled to a depreciation claim for these items under the depreciation rules contained in Division 40 if she had purchased this property before 9 May 2017. However, as Miranda had acquired this property after 9 May 2017, no deduction would be available for any depreciable items that were part of the acquisition of the property as, from this date, the legislation was amended to provide that depreciation in respect of depreciable plant (i.e. second-hand property) acquired from a previous owner is not able to be claimed as a tax deduction by the new owner.

8.7.2 Distinction between Division 40 and Division 43

In reality, the distinction between Division 40 (depreciation) and Division 43 (capital works allowance) is a difficult one to differentiate in practice.

For example, in a rental property, items such as outdoor furniture, washing machines, stoves, furniture, rugs, carpets and microwave ovens are considered depreciable assets and subject to depreciation over their effective lives as per Division 40.

On the other hand, items such as the building structure, electrical wiring, the outdoor deck, built-in kitchen cupboards and shelving, windows, floor tiles, doors, the toilet and bath are considered to form part of the building, and as such qualify for the capital works allowance as per Division 43.

The guidelines in table 8.7 can help determine whether a capital asset qualifies for deduction under Division 40 or Division 43.

TABLE 8.7   Division 43 capital works allowance rates

Question	Division 40	Division 43
Can the item of property in question be easily removed and taken with the taxpayer without damaging the item?	Yes	No
Is the item of property permanently affixed to the building and form part of the building?	No	Yes
Is the item of property specifically listed in TR 2021/3?	Yes	No

Table 8.8 summarises various assets and whether they fall under the provisions of Division 40 or Division 43.

TABLE 8.8   Division 40 versus Division 43

Item	Division 40	Division 43
Air-conditioning plant (not attached to building)	✓	
Architect's fees (preliminary expenses)		✓
Alarms	✓	
Car park (sealed)		✓
Carpet	✓	
Ceiling fan	✓	
Cupboards (built-in)		✓
Cupboards (free-standing)	✓	
Door handles and deadlocks		✓
Ducted heating		✓
Electrical wiring		✓

(continued)

TABLE 8.8 *(continued)*

Item	Division 40	Division 43
Exit/emergency lights		✓
Fence		✓
Fire extinguishers	✓	
Floor tiles		✓
Floor coverings (i.e. linoleum and vinyl)	✓	
Furniture and fittings	✓	
Garbage disposal unit	✓	
Gas insulation		✓
Gates		✓
Gutters and downpipes		✓
Insulation		✓
Lifts	✓	
Liftwell		✓
Light fittings mounted to building		✓
Light fittings not mounted to building	✓	
Pipes, pipelines, wash basins and taps		✓
Plumbing		✓
Power points		✓
Refrigerator	✓	
Retaining wall		✓
Security door and security system		✓
Smoke detectors	✓	
Spa and in-ground swimming pool		✓
Telephone installation		✓
Toilet and bidet		✓
Wall safe		✓

8.8 Section 40-880 blackhole expenditure

LEARNING OBJECTIVE 8.8 Apply section 40-880 to certain types of business-related capital expenditure incurred by businesses.

As outlined in the chapter on general deductions, many business expenses are non-deductible under section 8-1 largely for two reasons.

1. The costs are considered non-deductible as they have been incurred 'too soon' (i.e. before the business has started generating income) and not incurred while gaining or producing assessable income.
2. The costs are capital in nature, and thus not deductible under the first negative limb of section 8-1.

However, from 1 July 2001, certain types of business-related capital expenditure — termed **blackhole expenditure** — are specifically made deductible by virtue of section 40-880 of the ITAA97.

Section 40-880 is intended to provide a deduction for capital expenditure that is not otherwise deductible under section 8-1 or any other provision of the Act. In this respect, it is referred to as the 'section of last resort'. On 1 July 2005, the section was amended to broaden the list of business-related costs that can be claimed as a deduction.

Examples of business-related costs deductible under section 40-880 include:

- costs to establish your business structure (e.g. costs of incorporation, establishing a trust, registering a business name)
- costs to convert your business structure to a different structure
- costs of investigation into the viability of a business, such as feasibility studies and market research
- expenses that are a necessary precedent to the business being carried on, such as costs of market testing or preparing a tender
- costs to raise equity for your business (including costs of preparing a prospectus, legal fees, printing fees, underwriting costs)
- costs to defend your business against takeover (including legal and accounting fees, stockbrokers' fees, printing and mailing expenses)
- costs to your business of unsuccessfully attempting a takeover
- costs of liquidating a company that carried on a business and of which you are a shareholder, and
- costs to stop carrying on your business.

None of these costs are deductible under section 8-1.

However, under section 40-880, a taxpayer who is carrying on a business (or is proposing to carry on a business) is entitled to a deduction over a 5-year period in relation to costs incurred in setting up the business, capital raising and costs incurred in closing down the business.

The deduction cannot be claimed outright but can be claimed over 5 years (equivalent to an annual tax deduction of 20 per cent per annum). The expenditure is not apportioned or pro-rated for the number of days if it is incurred part way through a year.

For example, if a taxpayer spends $5000 to set up a company that is used as the business structure through which their business operates, they will be entitled to claim a tax deduction of $1000 in the first year and $1000 in each of the subsequent four income years. The claim for section 40-880 is made at Label Z of the company tax return (see figure 8.15).

FIGURE 8.15 | Section 40-880 deduction of 2021 company tax return

Immediate deduction for capital expenditure Z $ ☐☐,☐☐☐,☐☐☐,☐☐☐ .00

Source: Australian Taxation Office, *Company tax return 2021* (Web Page, 2021) https://www.ato.gov.au/uploadedFiles/Content/IND/Downloads/Company-tax-return-2021.pdf.

8.8.1 Small business entities — 100 per cent write-off

From 1 July 2015, small business entities (SBEs) can claim an immediate 100 per cent write-off for certain professional expenses associated with establishing a new business.

Recall that, according to section 328-110 of the ITAA97, a business is classified as a 'small business entity' if:

- it carries on business in that year, and
- its aggregated turnover for the year is less than $10 million.

From 1 July 2020, this concession has been expanded to businesses with a turnover of less than $50 million.

According to section 40-880(2A), for SBEs, immediate deductibility will be available for only two categories of expenditure.

1. Expenditure incurred in obtaining advice or services relating to the structure or proposed operation of the business. This would include:
   - professional advice relating to the proposed business structure (e.g. accounting and legal advice)
   - advice regarding legal arrangements or business systems
   - the viability of the proposed business (including due diligence where an existing business is being purchased)
   - the development of a business plan, and
   - costs associated with raising capital (whether debt or equity) for the operation of the proposed business.

2. Payments to an Australian Government agency. This would include:
   – costs associated with establishing the entity (e.g. ASIC incorporation fees), and
   – costs associated with transferring assets to the new entity (e.g. stamp duty).
   Example 8.11 demonstrates the section 40-880 100 per cent write-off for SBEs.

SBE 100 per cent write-off for SBE taxpayers

On 2 February 2022, Lucas starts his own business as a motor mechanic. He anticipates that his turnover will be in the vicinity of approximately $300 000 to $400 000 per annum.

Lucas incurred the following expenses:

1. $2600 in legal costs provided by a firm of solicitors on 21 January 2022 on setting up his business
2. $1200 costs incurred to incorporate the company on 2 February 2022, and
3. $3400 paid to his accountant for drafting a business plan on 10 February 2022.

What amounts (if any) are deductible under section 40-880 of the ITAA97?

All the mentioned costs would not be deductible under section 8-1 of the ITAA97. However, all three items qualify for deductibility under section 40-880(1)(a).

Normally, an entity can claim a deduction for these items over 5 years under section 40-880(1)(a). However, as Lucas's business qualifies as a small business entity (SBE), he is entitled to claim an immediate 100 per cent deduction for these costs under section 40-880(2A).

Hence, Lucas's total claim under section 40-880 comes to $7200 (i.e. $2600 + $1200 + $3400).

SUMMARY

8.1 Outline depreciation concepts in accordance with Division 40 of the ITAA97.

Under section 8-1(2) of the ITAA97, a taxpayer is denied an immediate deduction for any outgoing of a capital nature. However, Division 40 of the ITAA97 allows a taxpayer a deduction for the decline in value of a depreciating asset that is owned and used by a taxpayer while gaining or producing assessable income.

8.2 Calculate decline in value using the prime cost method and the diminishing value method.

The decline in value for tax purposes is calculated under Division 40 of ITAA97 based on the asset's effective life in years.

The prime cost depreciation rate is calculated by dividing 100 per cent of the asset's cost by the effective life of the item. Depreciation is pro-rated if it is held for income-producing for only part of the year. Hence:

$$\text{Asset's cost} \times \frac{\text{Days held}}{365} \times \frac{100\%}{\text{Effective life}}$$

The diminishing value depreciation method applies a percentage rate initially to the original cost of the item, and subsequently to the base value (i.e. written down value) at the commencement of each year thereafter.

The diminishing value depreciation rate is calculated as dividing 200 per cent of the base value by the effective life of the item. Again, depreciation is pro-rated if it is held for income-producing for only part of the year. Hence:

$$\text{Base value of asset (WDV)} \times \frac{\text{Days held}}{365} \times \frac{200\%}{\text{Effective life}}$$

8.3 Describe the different taxation depreciation rules for individual taxpayers, small business entities and large business taxpayers.

For individuals:

- An immediate 100% deduction applies in respect of depreciating assets costing $300 or less used by non-business taxpayers in deriving assessable income.
- For depreciating assets costing more than $300 but less than $1000, the assets may be allocated to a low-value pool and depreciated at 18.75% DV in the first year and 37.5% DV in the second and subsequent years, or the depreciation rules for assets costing $1000 or more may be applied.
- Depreciating assets costing $1000 or more are depreciated over their effective lives using either the prime cost or diminishing value depreciation methods.
- For small business entities, optional simplified depreciation concessions are available:
- An immediate 100% write-off applies in respect of depreciating assets costing less than the immediate write-off threshold.
- For depreciating assets costing more than the immediate write-off threshold, the assets may be allocated to a low-value pool and depreciated at 15% DV in the first year and 30% DV in the subsequent years.
  For large business taxpayers:
- An immediate 100% deduction applies in respect of depreciating assets costing $100 or less.
- For depreciating assets costing more than $100 but less than $1000, the assets may be allocated to a low-value pool and depreciated at 18.75% DV in the first year and 37.5% DV in the second and subsequent years, or the depreciation rules for assets costing $1000 or more may be applied.
- Depreciating assets costing $1000 or more are depreciated over their effective lives using either the prime cost or diminishing value depreciation methods.
  Motor vehicle depreciation is capped at a car cost of $60 733 for all taxpayers.

8.4 Apply the special depreciation rules in relation to computer software.

In-house software, including purchased software, is depreciated over 5 years using the prime cost depreciation method.

Expenditure on the development phase of internally developed software may be capitalised and then depreciated at 20 per cent prime cost over 5 years from when the software becomes operational. Alternatively, internally developed software may be placed in a software development pool and depreciated over 5 years at 0 per cent for the first year, 30 per cent for years two to four, and 10 per cent for year five.

Software acquired under a recurring licence or acquired for the purpose of resale is not subject to the depreciation rules.

Software acquired for the purposes of resale is subject to the trading stock provisions contained in Division 70 of the ITAA97.

8.5 Determine the assessability/deductibility when a depreciating asset is disposed.

The sale of a depreciating asset generates a balancing adjustment event and has taxation implications. A gain on sale (known as an 'assessable balancing adjustment') is assessable in the year of sale and a loss on sale (also known as a 'deductible balancing adjustment') is deductible in the year of sale.

8.6 Determine the CGT implications when selling a CGT asset.

A capital gain or capital loss arising from the sale of a depreciating asset used solely for income-producing purposes is disregarded. However, a capital gain may arise under CGT event K7 where a depreciating asset is disposed of that was partly used for income-producing purposes and partly for private (non-taxable) purposes.

In this situation, the capital gain under CGT event K7 is calculated based on the difference between the assets sale proceeds and its original cost.

8.7 Apply the Division 43 capital allowance rules in respect of buildings, structural improvements, extensions, alterations and capital improvements made to buildings.

Buildings are not considered depreciable assets for taxation purposes under Division 40. However, Division 43 permits a taxpayer to claim a deduction (capital works allowance) in respect of buildings, structural improvements, extensions, alterations and capital improvements made to buildings.

However, unlike depreciation under Division 40, which is based on the purchase price of the asset, Division 43 permits a deduction based on the original construction cost. The rate of deduction (either 2.5 or 4 per cent) depends on the year in which the construction commenced in addition to the use of the building and/or capital works.

8.8 Apply section 40-880 to certain types of business-related capital expenditure incurred by businesses.

Section 40-880 is referred to as the 'section of last resort' as it provides a tax deduction for certain items of capital expenditure that would otherwise not be deductible under section 8-1.

Under section 40-880, a taxpayer that is carrying on a business (or is proposing to carry on a business) is entitled to a deduction over 5 years in relation to costs incurred in setting up the business, capital raising and costs incurred in closing down the business. The deduction is claimed over 5 years (equivalent to an annual tax deduction of 20 per cent per annum).

However, small business entities with an annual turnover of less than $50 million are permitted to claim an immediate 100 per cent deduction on certain capital expenditure incurred when setting up their business.

KEY TERMS

adjustable value A taxation term that refers to the value of a depreciable asset net of depreciation as at the date of disposal. Referred to as the 'book value', 'carrying amount' or 'written down value' for accounting purposes. Also known as 'base value' for taxation purposes.

assessable balancing adjustment Calculated when a depreciating asset is sold and the termination value (i.e. gross proceeds) is more than the adjustable value (i.e. written down value) as at the date of disposal. An assessable balancing adjustment is included in the assessable income of the taxpayer in the year of sale. Referred to as a 'gain on sale' for accounting purposes.

balancing adjustment Refers to the difference between the termination value (i.e. gross proceeds) of a deprecating asset and its adjustable value. A balancing adjustment may be an 'assessable balancing adjustment' or a 'deductible balancing adjustment'.

blackhole expenditure A term that refers to section 40-880 of the ITAA97. Under this section, from 1 July 2001, certain types of business-related capital expenditure (termed 'blackhole expenditure') are specifically made deductible by virtue of section 40-880 of the ITAA97. These costs are deductible over five years or immediately deductible in the case of small business entities (SBEs).

capital allowances A generic term that refers to the taxation treatment of depreciable assets under Division 40, Division 43 and section 40-880 of the ITAA97.

construction expenditure For the purpose of Division 43, includes the original construction costs of the building or capital improvement; preliminary expenses such as architect's fees, engineering fees, and costs associated with obtaining approval for the building; and the cost of structural features that are an integral part of the building (e.g. retaining walls, fences, atriums and lift wells).

decline in value Referred to as 'depreciation' for accounting purposes. This term is used in Division 40 of the ITAA97. A taxpayer can claim a tax deduction equal to the decline in value of a depreciating asset held for any time during the income year. For taxation purposes, taxpayers are permitted to use either the prime cost or diminishing value depreciation methods.

deductible balancing adjustment Calculated when a depreciating asset is sold and the termination value (i.e. gross proceeds) is less than the adjustable value (i.e. written down value) as at the date of disposal. A deductible balancing adjustment can be claimed as an allowable deduction by the taxpayer in the year of sale. Referred to as a 'loss on sale' for accounting purposes.

depreciating asset An asset with a limited effective life and that declines in value over the time the asset is used.

diminishing value method One of two depreciation methods permitted to be used under Division 40. The diminishing value method is an example of an accelerated depreciation method. It assumes that the asset will yield more service potential in the earlier years than in the later years. Hence, it allocates greater amounts of depreciation in the earlier years of the asset's life than in the later years. It does this by applying a percentage rate initially to the original cost of the item, but subsequently to the base value (i.e. written down value) at the commencement of each year thereafter. The diminishing value depreciation rate is calculated by dividing a percentage (being 200 per cent) by the useful life of the asset.

effective life The effective life of a depreciating asset is the estimated period of time expressed in years) during which the asset is expected to be used by the entity. This is used in determining the depreciation rate of the depreciable asset. This is a similar concept to the useful life for accounting purposes.

general small business pool A depreciation pool created specifically for small business entities (SBEs) that allows them to pool depreciating assets costing more than a certain threshold (termed the 'immediate write-off threshold') and depreciate them at the diminishing value rate of 30 per cent per year (15 per cent diminishing value in their first year). However, due to the temporary full expensing rules enacted by the Federal Government effective from 6 October 2020 to 30 June 2023, the SBE closing general small business pool at 30 June 2021 and 30 June 2022 would have been written-off and deducted in full. If, and when, the temporary full expensing rules expire on 30 June 2023, the general small business pools will recommence in the 2023–24 income years.

immediate write-off threshold Also known as the 'instant write-off threshold'. This threshold applies to small business entities (SBEs) and medium-size entities. If an SBE or MSE purchases a depreciating asset (including computer software) below this threshold, they are entitled to an immediate 100 per cent deduction, instead of depreciating the asset over its effective life. For depreciating assets acquired between 12 March 2020 and 6 October 2020, the immediate write-off threshold is $150 000. From 6 October 2020 to 30 June 2023, there is no threshold, meaning that an SBE or MSE can write-off the cost of any eligible depreciating asset. This is referred to as 'temporary full expensing'.

in-house software Computer software that is acquired or developed by the business for their own internal use. Software purchased off-the-shelf (or downloaded from the internet) is an example of 'in-house software'.

large business taxpayer Defined as a business that is not a small business entity (SBE). For the year ended 30 June 2022, a large business entity is defined as any entity with an annual turnover of more than $5 billion.

low-value pool An optional taxation depreciation system for individual and non-SBE taxpayers who wish to pool depreciating assets whose opening adjustable value (i.e. opening written down value) for the current year has declined in value under the diminishing value method to less than $1000. These assets are depreciated at a rate of 37.5 per cent diminishing value. Once an asset has been allocated to a low-value pool, it must remain in the pool.

medium-size business entities An entity that carries on business during the income year and between 12 March 2020 to 31 December 2020 had an annual turnover of between $10 million and $500 million. In the Federal Budget handed down on 6 October 2020, the definition of a medium-sized entity increased from an annual turnover of $500 million to $5 billion. For depreciating assets acquired between 12 March 2020 and 6 October 2020, the immediate write-off threshold is $150 000. From 6 October 2020 to 30 June 2023, there is no threshold, meaning that MSE can write-off the cost of any eligible depreciating asset. This is referred to as 'temporary full expensing'.

prime cost method One of two depreciation methods permitted to be used under Division 40. The prime cost depreciation rate is calculated by dividing 100 per cent by the effective life of the item. This is similar to the straight-line depreciation method used for accounting purposes.

small business entity Also known as an SBE. This term is defined in Division 328 of the ITAA97. A small business entity is defined as one that carries on business during the income year and has an aggregated turnover of less than the 'annual SBE turnover' threshold. For the year ended 30 June 2022, the relevant SBE threshold is $10 million. This means that an SBE is defined as any entity with an annual turnover of $10 million or less. A small business entity has the option to adopt a simplified depreciation regime instead of using the depreciation rules applicable for large business entities.

software development pool An optional pool that applies to 'in-house software'. If the taxpayer elects to pool the internally developed software, the pooled software must be depreciated over five years; being 0 per cent for the first year; 30 per cent in years two to four; and 10 per cent in the fifth year. Only the prime cost depreciation method can be used.

start time of a depreciating asset The earlier of the dates on which the taxpayer first uses the asset (for any purpose whatsoever) or has the asset installed ready for use, for any purpose.

termination value Means the gross sale proceeds received from the sale of a depreciable asset. Referred to as 'sale proceeds' for accounting purposes.

QUESTIONS

8.1 What is depreciation for taxation purposes and who is entitled to claim depreciation?

8.2 What are the two depreciation methods for tax purposes? Can a taxpayer change methods each year? If the taxpayer wishes to minimise their taxable income in the first year, what method should they adopt?

8.3 How are intangible assets depreciated for tax purposes?

8.4 What are the depreciation rules for individual taxpayers?

8.5 What are the depreciation rules for small business entity taxpayers?

8.6 What are the depreciation rules for large business taxpayers?

8.7 What are the two main types of computer software for depreciation purposes? What are the depreciation rules for computer software?

8.8 How can the disposal of a depreciating asset give rise to a captial gain?

8.9 Is a building a depreciating asset for tax purposes? If not, what deductions can a taxpayer claim in respect of income-producing buildings?

8.10 What is the difference between Division 40 and Division 43 of ITAA97? What criteria can a taxpayer use to differentiate between the two divisions?

8.11 What is the objective of section 40-880 of ITAA97? What types of deductions does this section apply to? How are deductions calculated under section 40-880 for business taxpayers?

PROBLEMS

8.12 Emily, an individual taxpayer, works as a lawyer for a law firm. During the 2022 income year, she purchased the following assets for exclusive use for her job.

Item	Date of acquisition	No. days	TR 2021/3 effective life	Cost ($)
Anti-virus software	9 November 2021	234	5 years	120
Apple iPad	24 February 2022	127	2 years	780
Motor vehicle*	14 June 2022	17	8 years	68 000

* According to a log book maintained by Emily, the motor vehicle was used 60% of the time for income-producing purposes.

Required

Calculate Emily's decline in value (depreciation) claim in respect of the mentioned assets for the year ended 30 June 2022. Please round all calculations to the nearest whole dollar. Assume that Emily wishes to maximise any depreciation deduction claimed in 2022.

8.13 Coconut Burst Pty Ltd manufacturers coconut water drinks to sell directly to Australian retailers, including convenience stores, supermarkets, health stores and gymnasiums. The company's annual turnover is $6.5 million making it a small business entity taxpayer, as its annual turnover for the year ended 30 June 2022 is less than $10 million. During the 2022 income year, the company purchased the following assets for exclusive use in the business.

Item	Date of acquisition	Cost ($)
Desktop computer	11 October 2021	2 600
Manufacturing equipment	2 February 2022	220 000
Motor vehicle	2 May 2022	88 000

Required

Calculate Coconut Burst Pty Ltd's decline in value (depreciation) claim in respect of the mentioned assets for the year ended 30 June 2022. Please round all calculations to the nearest whole dollar. Assume that the company elects to adopt the simplified depreciation rules available to SBE taxpayers.

8.14 Consider each of the following independent transactions in the case of Ace Jewellers Pty Ltd, a company that runs and operates several jewellery stores throughout south-east Queensland. For the year ended 30 June 2022, the company's annual turnover is $4.2 million making it a small business taxpayer for depreciation purposes, as its annual turnover for the year ended 30 June 2022 is less than $10 million. During the 2022 income year, the company purchased the following assets for exclusive use in the business.

Item	Date of acquisition	Cost ($)
Motor vehicle	16 July 2021	104 000
Jewellery equipment	9 December 2021	180 000
Computer equipment	14 March 2022	21 000
Fit-out of retail premises	8 April 2022	150 000
Computer software	9 May 2022	8 200

Required

Calculate Ace Jewellers Pty Ltd's decline in value (i.e. depreciation) claim in respect of the mentioned assets for the year ended 30 June 2022. Please round all calculations to the nearest whole dollar. Assume that the company elects to adopt the simplified depreciation rules available to SBE taxpayers.

8.15 Oz Wines Pty Ltd manufactures Australian wines and sells them to wine wholesales both within Australia and overseas. The company's annual turnover is $32 million making it a medium-size entity taxpayer, as its annual turnover for the year ended 30 June 2022 is more than $10 million but less than $5 billion. During the 2022 income year, the company purchased the following assets for exclusive use in the business.

Item	Date of acquisition	Amount ($)
Colour photocopier	15 September 2021	10 800
Wine manufacturing equipment	19 February 2022	460 000
Motor vehicle	4 June 2022	110 000

Required

Calculate Oz Wines Pty Ltd's decline in value (depreciation) claim in respect of the mentioned assets for the year ended 30 June 2022. Please round all calculations to the nearest whole dollar.

8.16 Giant Manufacturing Ltd is a large business taxpayer. It operates a food processing manufacturing plant in Fremantle. The company's annual turnover is $5.8 billion making it a large business taxpayer, as its annual turnover for the year ended 30 June 2022 is more than $5 billion. During the 2022 income year, the company purchased the following assets for exclusive use in the business.

Asset	Date of acquisition	No. days	TR 2021/3 effective life	Amount ($)
Calculator	2 August 2021	333	10 years	92
Apple iPad	13 January 2022	169	2 years	940
Industrial robot	11 May 2022	51	10 years	1 240 000

Required

Calculate Giant Manufacturing Ltd's decline in value (depreciation) claim in respect of the mentioned assets for the year ended 30 June 2022. Please round all calculations to the nearest whole dollar. Assume that Giant Manufacturing Ltd wishes to maximise any depreciation deduction claimed in 2022.

8.17 Consider each of the following independent transactions in the case of Phone World Ltd, a retailer of mobile phones and accessories. The company's annual turnover is $7.2 billion making it a large business taxpayer, as its annual turnover for the year ended 30 June 2022 is more than $10 million. During the 2022 income year, the company purchased the following assets for exclusive use in the business.

Item	Date of acquisition	Accounting useful life	Cost ($)
Colour photocopier	3 August 2021	4 years	7 800
Motor vehicle	19 October 2021	5 years	104 000
Copyright	10 January 2022	20 years*	100 000
Trademark	16 March 2022	20 years	80 000
Accounting software acquired	15 May 2022	4 years	960
Commercial office building	10 June 2022	25 years	6 million**

*The period that the copyright ends.

**The figure of $6 million shown in the table is the original construction cost as determined by a qualified quantity surveyor. The office building was constructed in March 2010. Phone World Ltd purchased the building on 10 June 2022 for $10 million.

Wherever possible, the company would like to self-assess the effective lives of these depreciable assets for taxation purposes rather than use the Commissioner's determination of effective life contained in TR 2021/3. The company would like to use the same useful life values for taxation purposes for the depreciable assets as they are using for accounting purposes as shown in the table.

Required

Calculate Phone World Ltd's decline in value (i.e. depreciation) claim in respect of the mentioned assets for the year ended 30 June 2022. Please round all calculations to the nearest whole dollar.

8.18 On 17 September 2021, Genisis Holdings Pty Ltd acquires a property (consisting of a large block of land and a commercial office building) for an amount of $7.4 million.

The company engaged a quantity surveyor to determine the breakdown of the costs relating to the property. The quantity surveyor's report reveals the following cost information.

The company leased the commercial office building to tenants on 1 October 2021. It was rented out to tenants from 1 October 2021 to 30 June 2022 inclusive.

	$
Cost of land	1 800 000
Demolition of old building on site (May 2012)	80 000
Pre-construction site clearance (May 2012)	210 000
Construction of new building (July 2015)	3 400 000
Landscaping (August 2016)	68 000

Required

Calculate Genisis Holdings Pty Ltd's deduction for capital works expenditure for the year ended 30 June 2022. Please quote appropriate sections of the ITAA97 in your answer. Please round all calculations to the nearest whole dollar.

8.19 Joshua has been working for a large dental practice for the past 12 years. In March 2022, Joshua resigns and decides to go into business for himself. He incurs the following amounts:

(a) preparation of a business plan costing $6000 incurred on 28 March 2022

(b) company incorporation costs of $960 paid to incorporate a company 'Queen Street Dental Pty Ltd' on 14 April 2022

(c) legal fees of $1400 paid to a lawyer on 16 April 2022 for advice given in relation to the legal issues involved in setting up his business

(d) purchase of a desktop computer on 22 April 2022 costing $2800

(e) printing of business cards, stationery and letterhead costing $820 on 4 May 2022.

Joshua anticipates that the turnover of his company will be in the vicinity of $1.2 million to $1.3 million per annum.

Required

What amounts (if any) are deductible under section 40-880 of the ITAA97? If the amount is not deductible under section 40-880, please indicate what section (if any) the item may be deductible under and the amount. Please round all calculations to the nearest whole dollar.

8.20 Scorpion Boat Builders Ltd is an Australian boat manufacturer. The company's annual turnover is $6.6 billion making it a large business taxpayer, as its annual turnover for the year ended 30 June 2022 is more than $5 billion. On 19 February 2021, the company acquired new manufacturing equipment totalling $780 000. On the same date, the company incurred the additional following costs.

	$
Insurance and transport of manufacturing equipment	24 000
Installation and testing of manufacturing equipment	8 200
Removal of old manufacturing equipment	16 800
Maintenance of the equipment (to be completed in June 2021)	3 400

The manufacturing equipment was installed, ready for use on the day of purchase (i.e. 19 February 2021). At the same time, the company also entered into an annual maintenance agreement on 19 February 2021 with the company that installed and tested the manufacturing equipment.

The effective life of the manufacturing equipment for taxation purposes is estimated to be 10 years.

Unfortunately, due to a sudden downturn in the boat building industry in 2022, Scorpion Boat Builders Ltd decided to restructure and has consequently sold the manufacturing equipment on 17 May 2022 for $568 000.

Required

(a) Calculate the total initial depreciable cost of the new manufacturing equipment.

(b) Calculate the decline in value (i.e. depreciation) of the new manufacturing equipment for the years ended 30 June 2021 and 30 June 2022. Assume that Scorpion Boat Builders Ltd elects to use the diminishing value depreciation method in respect of the manufacturing equipment. Please round all calculations to the nearest whole dollar.

(c) Calculate the amount that is assessable/deductible to Scorpion Boat Builders Ltd in relation to the sale of the manufacturing equipment on 17 May 2022.

ACKNOWLEDGEMENTS

Figures 8.1, 8.3, 8.4, 8.5, 8.11, 8.14, 8.15: © Australian Taxation Office
Figure 8.10: © Federal Register of Legislation. Licensed under CC BY 4.0.
Tables 8.1, 8.2: © Federal Register of Legislation. Licensed under CC BY 4.0.
Extract: © Federal Register of Legislation. Licensed under CC BY 4.0.

CHAPTER 9

Tax accounting and trading stock

LEARNING OBJECTIVES

After studying this chapter, you should be able to:

9.1 explain the difference between the accounting treatment and income tax treatment of revenues and expenses

9.2 determine when income is derived for taxation purposes, including the various rules that apply to each type of income

9.3 determine when losses and outgoings are incurred for taxation purposes, including the various rules that apply to each type of loss and outgoing

9.4 describe the trading stock provisions of the ITAA97

9.5 explain when trading stock becomes on hand for both accounting and taxation purposes

9.6 apply the rules for determining the assessability/deductibility of trading stock under both the periodic and perpetual inventory systems

9.7 use the valuation rules permitted in valuing closing stock on hand at year-end and the special valuation rules that apply to obsolete stock

9.8 describe various special rules applying to trading stock, including the special trading stock provisions for small business entities.

Overview

The first part of this chapter explains the concept of tax accounting — how accounting for taxable income for tax purposes differs from accounting for net profit in accordance with the accounting standards. One of the key differences is the timing of when income is derived and when losses or outgoings are incurred.

Case law has established that the correct basis of accounting for tax purposes (i.e. cash or accruals) is dependent upon the type of income derived, not the type of taxpayer. In terms of deductions, for taxation purposes a loss of outgoing is deductible when 'incurred'. There are special rules relating to employee entitlements, such as annual leave and long service leave, the taxation treatment of provisions, such as warranties, and taxation relating to prepayments.

The second part of the chapter provides an overview of the taxation rules relating to trading stock contained in Division 70 of the ITAA97. For taxation purposes, trading stock includes anything produced, manufactured or acquired by a business with the intention of resale in the ordinary course of business.

The chapter outlines the taxation rules relating to trading stock in determining the amount assessable or deductible under both the periodic and perpetual inventory systems. The valuation of trading stock is also discussed.

Finally, the chapter concludes with special trading stock rules relating to small business entities.

9.1 Differences between accounting income and taxable income

LEARNING OBJECTIVE 9.1 Explain the difference between the accounting treatment and income tax treatment of revenues and expenses.

For accounting purposes, a company's net profit is calculated as the difference between income and expenses, calculated in accordance with the AASB Accounting Standards. In other words:

$$\text{Net Profit} = [\text{Income} - \text{Expenses}]$$

For taxation purposes, a company's taxable income is determined by the principles set out in both the ITAA36 and ITAA97. According to section 4-15 of the ITAA97:

$$\text{Taxable income} = [\text{Assessable income} - \text{Allowable deductions}]$$

While the two figures may produce similar results, they are not necessarily the same. There are several reasons why the net profit for accounting purposes does not necessarily equal taxable income.

9.1.1 Revenues/assessable income

While most items of revenue are assessable for tax purposes, this is not always the case. There are some items of accounting revenue that are not assessable for income tax purposes (e.g. exempt income).

Conversely, there may be some items that are assessable for taxation purposes but are not included as revenue for accounting purposes. For example, while a franked dividend is recorded as revenue in the income statement, the franking credit should not be included in the financial statements (either as revenue or as a receivable).

9.1.2 Expenses/allowable deductions

In terms of deductions, several expenses recorded in the income statement are not tax-deductible (e.g. provisions for bad debts, annual leave, meal entertainment provided to clients).

Conversely, there may be some items that are deductible for income tax but are not shown as an expense in the income statement; rather they are recorded in the balance sheet (e.g. prepayments).

In practice, a statement is prepared to reconcile the net profit for accounting purposes to the taxable income. The statement is typically referred to as a **tax reconciliation**. An example of a tax reconciliation is contained in the chapter on taxation of companies.

9.1.3 Cash vs accruals basis of accounting

For accounting purposes, transactions of a business are typically prepared under the accrual accounting concepts.

Under the **accrual basis of accounting**, revenues are recorded in the period in which the business sells the goods or performs the services. This may or may not be the same as the accounting period in which the cash is received. In other words, under the accrual accounting concepts, revenue is recognised in the period in which the revenue has been derived, not when the cash has been received.

Similarly, expenses are recognised in the period when the expenses have been incurred or consumed. This may or may not be the same accounting period in which the cash is paid. The effect of this is that under the accrual accounting concepts, revenues and expenses are effectively matched in the same accounting period. This is referred to as the 'matching principle'.

Under the **cash basis of accounting**, revenues are recorded in the period in which the cash is received, not the period in which the goods have been sold or services have been provided. Similarly, expenses are recorded in the period in which the cash is paid, not the period in which the expenses have been incurred.

9.1.4 Timing of income and expenses

When income has been 'derived' for income tax purposes under section 6-5 of the ITAA97 and when a loss or outgoing has been 'incurred' for income tax purposes under section 8-1 of the ITAA97 is a matter to be determined under taxation concepts, which may not necessarily accord with accounting principles. Where differences exist, this is broadly defined as **tax accounting**.

9.2 When is income derived?

LEARNING OBJECTIVE 9.2 Determine when income is derived for taxation purposes, including the various rules that apply to each type of income.

The concept that ordinary income must be 'derived' was introduced in the chapters on residency and assessable income. This section extends that discussion.

Section 6-5(2) of the ITAA97 states:

> If you are an Australian resident, your assessable income includes the ordinary income you derived directly or indirectly from all sources whether in or out of Australia during the income year.

The concept of derivation is about timing — *when* has the income been derived? Derivation determines which income year an amount will be assessed in. There is no formal definition of *derivation* in either the ITAA36 or ITAA97. Hence, we need to turn our attention to common law principles. The guiding principle on this matter was in the case of *FCT v Clarke* (1927) 40 CLR 246.

FCT v Clarke (1927) 40 CLR 246

Facts: The taxpayer, Clarke, was assessed for Commonwealth income tax in respect of profits arising from dealings in shares in companies. Profits were received by or on behalf of various members of Clarke's family.

The Commissioner of Taxation disallowed the objection.

Clarke appealed to the Supreme Court of Victoria arguing that those profits were derived by or on behalf of various members of his family when the right to receive the profits originated, not when the cash was received by those family companies.

Held: The issue was when the taxpayer derived the business profits. According to Isaacs J at 261, the word derived means 'obtained', 'got' or 'acquired'. The Commissioner of Taxation argued that the word 'derived' meant 'received'. However, Isaacs J stated that the word 'derived' did not mean 'received'. In fact, it is quite possible for a taxpayer to have derived income even though it has not been received.

9.2.1 Which accounting method to use?

Two alternative methods have been judicially accepted by which a taxpayer may recognise income.
1. The cash basis accounting method (also called the receipts method) recognises income when a taxpayer actually receives cash.
2. The accrual basis accounting method (also called the earnings method) recognises income when a taxpayer accrues the legal right to receive income. This is normally when the goods are delivered to the customer or the services have been performed for the client.

The decision as to whether a choice exists as to which method a taxpayer should use in recognising income was initially outlined by the Full High Court in *C of T (SA) v Executor Trustee and Agency Co of South Australia Ltd* ('*Carden's* case') (1938) 63 CLR 108.

C of T (SA) v Executor Trustee and Agency Co of South Australia Ltd ('*Carden's* case') (1938) 63 CLR 108

Facts: Dr Carden operated a medical practice as a sole practitioner and, until the year ended 30 June 1929, returned, and was assessed on income calculated on an earnings (accruals) basis. Thereafter he returned his income on a receipts (cash) basis.

All subsequent income tax assessments up to and including the year ended 30 June 1935, were made on the receipts (cash) basis. Dr Carden died in November 1935 and at the date of his death, he was owed substantial professional fees.

The Commissioner assessed the income under the accruals basis. The taxpayer asserted that the cash basis was the appropriate method.

Held: Dixon J (at 158) disagreed with the Commissioner and held that Dr Carden's income was properly assessed on a receipts (cash) basis and a little later held that there was no foundation for the Commissioner's attempted substitution of the earnings basis in respect of the 1935 assessment.

Dixon J went onto state at 151-2 that:

> One view suggested is that a choice between the two methods is permitted by law and that choice lies with the Commissioner. The question whether one method of accounting or another should be employed in assessing taxable income derived from a given pursuit is one the decision of which falls within the province of courts of law.

In other words, *Carden's* case established that it is for the courts to determine the appropriate basis of accounting, not the Commissioner or the taxpayer. The principle established by the courts is that the correct basis of accounting (i.e. cash or accruals) is dependent upon the type of income derived, not the type of taxpayer.

Many of the principles on which the determination may be made have been summarised by the Commissioner in Taxation Ruling TR 98/1.

The following sections summarise the derivation rules based on the type of income derived.

9.2.2 Income from personal exertion

Income from personal exertion (i.e. salary and wages and other consulting income) is deemed to be derived when received, whether the amount is payment for past or current services.

This means that income from personal exertion is to be recognised on a cash basis (see *Brent v FCT* 71 ATC 4195).

9.2.3 Business (trading) income

Trading income (i.e. income from carrying on a business) must be brought to account on the *accruals basis*. Taxpayers carrying on a business are required to recognise assessable income in the period in which the income has been earned, not when the cash is received (see *Henderson v FCT* (1970) 119 CLR 612).

9.2.4 Revenue received in advance (unearned income)

Some entities receive monies from clients or customers in advance of performing the services. In this case, while the cash has been received from the customer, no service has been performed.

From an accounting perspective, no revenue is recognised at this point as the entity has not provided any services to the customer. Instead, a liability account entitled 'revenue received in advance' is created to reflect the future obligation of the entity to provide the services. This account is also sometimes referred to as 'unearned income'.

The taxation implications of revenue received in advance were decided by the High Court of Australia in *Arthur Murray (NSW) Pty Ltd v FC of T* (1965).

Facts: The taxpayer company provided dancing lessons for payment. A discount was offered to encourage prepayment and customers often paid for dancing lessons in advance. Although the contracts expressly provided that no refunds were available in respect of the prepaid dance lessons, the general practice of the taxpayer was to give refunds where not all dance lessons were taken.

Upon initial receipt of the monies from the dance students, the taxpayer's bookkeeper debited the 'cash at bank' account and credited the 'unearned income' current liability account as per generally accepted accounting principles. Revenue was then progressively recognised at the completion of each dance lesson.

However, the Commissioner treated the taxpayer as having derived its income on a receipts (cash) basis. Accordingly, the Commissioner included the advance payments as assessable income in the year in which the fees were received notwithstanding that the taxpayer had not provided dance lessons in respect of some of those fees.

Held: The Full High Court disagreed with the Commissioner and held that the payments received up-front were *not* income even though the monies had been received by the taxpayer. Instead, the receipts were assessable in the income year in which the dance lessons were provided. Hence, the *accruals basis* of accounting was appropriate. According to Barwick CJ:

> ... it would be out of accord with the realities of the situation to hold, that the amount received has the quality of income derived by the company. This conclusion accords with established accountancy and commercial principles. We have not been able to see any reason which should lead the court to differ from accountants and commercial men on this point.

The accruals basis treatment described in *Arthur Murray (NSW) Pty Ltd v FC of T* is only granted where:
- the taxpayer's accounts are prepared on an accruals basis and where the amounts received in advance are credited to the liability account 'revenue received in advance'
- there is a possibility of refunds being provided to customers.

Hence, if the up-front receipts are non-refundable, the entire amount will be regarded as assessable income in the year of receipt (see Taxation Ruling TR 95/7).

9.2.5 Income from professional practices

The correct basis of accounting for income tax purposes for professional practice income (i.e. income derived by solicitors, accountants, doctors, dentists, optometrists, architects, engineers etc.) is not as precise as with income from personal exertion and trading income.

The correct basis of accounting (i.e. cash or accruals) depends on several factors, the most important of which is the size of the professional practice.

9.2.5.1 Smaller professional practices

In the case of smaller professional practices, the cash basis of accounting is considered appropriate as the earning of income is seen to be more akin to personal exertion income rather than carrying on a business. This was also examined in *Carden's* case, discussed earlier.

Facts: The taxpayer, Dr Carden, had been conducting a business as a sole medical practitioner. From 1929 to 1935, he returned his income using the cash basis of accounting.

The Commissioner disagreed with Dr Carden's approach and assessed his income using the accruals method, thereby including fees for work that had been performed and invoiced before the end of the income year, but for which payment had not yet been received.

Held: The Court held that the cash basis was the appropriate basis for accounting because the income was substantially personal services income.

A similar decision was handed down in *FCT v Firstenberg* 76 ATC 4141. The taxpayer was a solicitor who conducted his business as a sole practitioner. His only employee at the time was a secretary.

He returned income from the practice on a cash basis. The Commissioner assessed the taxpayer on the accruals basis arguing that it was the appropriate basis. Once again, the Court disagreed with the Commissioner and held that the cash basis was the appropriate basis. The Court held that the taxpayer derived income as a result of his professional skill and experience — his personal exertion.

9.2.5.2 Larger professional practices

For larger professional practices, where the derivation of professional income constitutes the carrying on of business, the accruals method is considered the appropriate basis. The professional income derived is seen as being akin to trading income, particularly where the scale of operations is substantial. This was examined in *Henderson v FCT* (1970).

Henderson v FCT (1970) 119 CLR 612

Facts: The taxpayer was a partner in a large accounting firm in Western Australia. The partnership consisted of 19 partners, 65 associates and 295 employees, of whom approximately 150 were qualified accountants. Fees earned annually exceeded $1 million.

For the year ended 30 June 1964, the partnership prepared its accounts and lodged its partnership tax return on the cash basis. For the years ended 30 June 1965 and 30 June 1966, the partnership changed its method of accounting to the accruals basis of accounting.

The Commissioner refused to accept the change of method and continued to assess the taxpayer according to the cash basis. The taxpayer objected to the Commissioner's arguments, arguing that the accruals basis of accounting was the appropriate method.

Held: The Court agreed with the taxpayer and held that the accruals basis was the appropriate method of income recognition for the years ended 30 June 1965 and 1966. The Court held that the size, structure and method of operation of the accountancy partnership were relevant factors in determining that the accruals basis was more appropriate as it was akin to carrying on a business.

The Court in *Henderson v FCT* distinguished the case with hundreds of employees from a sole practitioner like that in *FCT v Firstenberg* (see section 9.2.5). *Henderson* and *Firstenberg* represent the extremes, and most professional practices lie somewhere in between. In borderline cases, the ATO would normally expect that the accruals method would be the most appropriate to adopt.

In TR 98/1, the Commissioner outlines the factors that the ATO will follow in determining whether a professional practice should account for its income on a cash or accruals basis. These factors include:
- the size of the professional practice
- the number of employees
- the extent of involvement by the owners of the business in doing the work or overseeing the work
- the number of clients of the practice
- the degree to which the taxpayer vigorously pursues unpaid invoices, and
- whether the business involves trading stock.

In *Barratt v FCT* (1992) 92 ATC 4275, a partnership of 5 medical practitioners carried on a pathology practice that used various service companies to help treat over 92 000 patients and which generated fees of more than $8 million. The practice provided pathology services requiring sophisticated equipment and employed 26 qualified medical technicians and laboratory assistants and 67 general assistants who operated under the supervision of the partners. The Full Federal Court held the circumstances suggested that the accruals basis was the appropriate method.

9.2.6 Income from property

Income from property may arise in various forms, including interest, dividends or rent — each of which is described in the following sections.

9.2.6.1 Interest

Interest is generally derived for tax purposes when it is credited into the bank account (i.e. the cash basis). An exception applies where the taxpayer is carrying on a business of money lending (e.g. banks and financial institutions), in which case the accruals basis is considered appropriate.

9.2.6.2 Dividends

In the case of dividends, section 44(1) of the ITAA36 provides that dividends are derived when they are paid to the taxpayer (i.e. the cash basis). According to section 6(1) of the ITAA36 'paid' means credited or paid by cheque.

9.2.6.3 Rent

Rent is generally derived for tax purposes when it is received (i.e. the cash basis). An exception applies where the taxpayer is carrying on business as a landlord, in which case the accruals basis is considered appropriate.

The mentioned derivation rules are summarised in table 9.1.

TABLE 9.1	Summary of rules relating to derivation of income
Type of income	**Derivation rule**
Income from personal exertion	Cash
Trading (business) income	Accruals
Revenue received in advance	Accruals (provided refunds are given)
Income from professional practices	Small (cash); large (accruals)
Income from property	Cash

Remember that the rules apply to the type of income derived by the taxpayer, *not* the type of taxpayer. In other words, the fact that a taxpayer derives trading income does not mean that all of their income is to be treated on an accruals basis. So, for example, a shoe store that sells goods (i.e. shoes) would account for its trading income on an accruals basis. However, if it earned residual interest income or dividend income, these would be regarded as income in the period when the cash was received (i.e. the cash basis).

9.2.7 The doctrine of constructive receipt

It is not necessary that money actually be paid over to the taxpayer. Instead, income may be dealt with at the taxpayer's direction on their behalf.

This principle is recognised in section 6-5(4) of the ITAA97 which states:

> You are taken to have received the amount as soon as it is applied or dealt with in any way on your behalf as you direct.

This is referred to as the **doctrine of constructive receipt**. This applies in the situation where the taxpayer invests their money into a term deposit (e.g. $10 000). At the expiry of the term deposit date, instead of receiving the interest as cash (e.g. $100), the taxpayer contacts the bank and asks for the principal of $10 000 plus the interest derived of $100 to be rolled over into another term deposit.

Even though the taxpayer did not receive the $100 interest in cash, they have instructed the bank to roll over the interest as part of a new term deposit. The interest is assessable to the taxpayer when they instructed the bank to roll over the interest, even though they have not received the cash.

As the taxpayer has 'dealt with' the interest, they are taken to have derived the interest income. This is an example of the doctrine of constructive receipt.

9.3 When are losses and outgoings incurred?

LEARNING OBJECTIVE 9.3 Determine when losses and outgoings are incurred for taxation purposes, including the various rules that apply to each type of loss and outgoing.

According to section 8-1(1) of the ITAA97:

> You can deduct from your assessable income any loss or outgoing to the extent that:
>
> (a) it is incurred in gaining or producing your assessable income, or
> (b) it is necessarily incurred in carrying on a business for the purpose of gaining or producing assessable income.

Section 8-1 requires that the loss or outgoing be 'incurred' before it will qualify for deduction. Whether or not a loss or outgoing has been incurred is a question of fact.

The word 'incurred' is not defined in either the ITAA36 or ITAA97 and we therefore need to look at case law to determine the meaning of this word. Various principles arising in the case law that help interpret the meaning of 'incurred' are described in the following section. The important point to note is that when a loss or outgoing has been 'incurred' for the purposes of section 8-1, it is not based on the type of taxpayer. In other words, the timing of when a deduction is incurred applies regardless of whether the taxpayer is an individual, a small business entity or a large business taxpayer.

9.3.1 Not synonymous with the word 'paid'

Over the years, the courts have held that 'incurred' is not synonymous with 'paid'. As stated by Latham J in *W Nevill & Co Ltd v FCT* (1937) 56 CLR 290 at 302:

> The word used in the legislation is 'incurred' and not 'paid'. The language lends colour to the suggestion that, if a liability to pay an outgoing comes into existence, section 8-1 is satisfied, even though the liability has not actually been discharged at the relevant time.

Hence, if a taxpayer receives a telephone bill dated 28 June 2022 and pays that bill on 16 July 2022, the taxpayer has incurred the telephone expense on 28 June 2022 (i.e. the date of the telephone bill) and, as such, can claim a deduction for the telephone bill in their 2022 income tax return (assuming that the telephone bill relates exclusively to work-related telephone calls).

Therefore, provided the liability has been incurred prior to the end of the income year and the amount is quantifiable, it will be regarded as 'incurred' even though it is not paid until the following income year. This is the case where an invoice has been received before year end and also in cases where an invoice may not have been provided but the expense has been incurred prior to year-end as long as the taxpayer is able to reliably measure the amount owing.

9.3.2 Taxpayer must be 'totally committed' to making the payment

The courts have held that as long as the taxpayer is 'totally committed' to making the payment and has no choice but to make the payment, the loss or outgoing is incurred, even though it may remain unpaid (or even unbilled) at the end of the income year. In other words, the taxpayer must have a legal obligation to pay the amount owing as per the invoice.

9.3.3 Discretionary payments

Discretionary payments are payments that are not necessitated by a pre-existing liability and include such items as:
- gifts/donations
- insurance premiums
- licence renewals, and
- motor vehicle registration fees.

There may be an expectation that the discretionary item may be renewed but there is no legal liability between the parties for the payment to be made unless the consumer wishes to renew the service that is being provided (e.g. membership or subscription fees).

As there is no pre-existing liability to renew the contract and as there is no 'total commitment' to making the payment (until the payment is made), the Commissioner considers that these expenses are only deductible when paid.[1]

The Commissioner of Taxation has issued TR 97/7 setting out their views on the word 'incurred' for the purposes of section 8-1 of the ITAA97.

These views are based upon the various propositions which have been developed by the courts over the years and which have been discussed.

---

1 See paragraph 21 of TR 97/7.

Generally:

- a taxpayer need not actually have paid any money to have incurred (a loss or) outgoing provided the taxpayer is definitely committed in the year of income
- a taxpayer may have a presently existing liability, even though the liability may be defeasible (i.e. when a payment is subject to a legal dispute)
- in the case of discretionary payments (i.e. payments not necessitated by a liability), the expense is incurred when the expense is paid
- a taxpayer may have a presently existing liability, even though the amount of the liability cannot be precisely ascertained, provided it is capable of reliable estimation (based on probabilities).[2]

The Commissioner of Taxation accepts that the discussed principles apply regardless of whether the taxpayer uses the cash or accruals basis of accounting for recognising their income.

Thus, a taxpayer who uses the cash basis of accounting need not necessarily have paid or borne a loss or outgoing before claiming a deduction for it.

9.3.4 Employee entitlements

Employee entitlements include annual leave, long service leave and sick leave. In the case of annual leave, most employment agreements and/or awards entitle employees to 4 weeks of annual leave per year.

From an accounting perspective, at 30 June each year, AASB 119 *Employee Benefits* requires the entity to recognise an expense and a corresponding provision (being a liability) for leave entitlements, such as annual leave or long service leave.

An interesting question arises from a taxation perspective as to whether employee entitlements such as provision for annual leave, long service leave and sick leave accrued at year-end by an employer are 'incurred' for the purposes of section 8-1.

This matter was addressed in *FCT v James Flood Pty Ltd* (1953).[3] The Court held that provisions for annual leave and long service leave accrued at the end of the income year were not incurred for the purposes of section 8-1 as the employees were not immediately eligible to take their leave at that time.

Hence, the employer was therefore not committed to making the expenditure at that time. The liability arose when the employees actually took their leave and were paid.

Section 26-10 has subsequently been inserted into the ITAA97 to specifically provide that no deduction for employee entitlements is allowed until such time as the employee entitlements had been paid.

9.3.5 Other provisions

The same taxation principle applies to other provisions, such as warranties expense. From an accounting perspective, an entity that provides warranties to its customers for goods manufactured or sold is required to estimate the amount of warranties that it expects to pay out to customers who may return faulty items or damaged goods.

This requires the entity to recognise the warranties expense and corresponding provision for warranties based on the estimated amount of warranties to be paid out in a subsequent accounting period.

However, from a taxation perspective, section 8-1 of the ITAA97 confirms that warranties are only 'incurred' (and therefore, deductible) when paid out.

9.3.6 Prepaid expenses

There are some instances where a taxpayer may choose to prepay certain expenditure.

From an accounting perspective, under accrual accounting principles, an expense is recognised in the period during which it is used or consumed, not in the period in which the cash is paid. The remaining amount of the cost that is yet to be consumed is reported in the balance sheet as an asset called 'prepaid expense', since it represents a future economic benefit to be used in future reporting periods.

From a taxation perspective, the general premise is that a taxpayer is not entitled to claim a deduction for prepaid expenditure (as the actual service needs to be incurred, and not just paid). As such, sections 82KZL to 82KZO of the ITAA36 require that any deduction for prepaid expenditure is required to be spread (apportioned) over the relevant (eligible) service period. However, there are several exceptions to this general rule which allow all taxpayers to claim a deduction for prepaid expenditure.

---

2 Paragraph 6 of TR 97/7.
3 88 CLR 492.

A taxpayer (including a large business taxpayer) is entitled to claim a deduction for prepaid expenditure if any one of the following conditions apply. These are referred to 'excluded expenditure' in section 82KZL(1):

(a) the expenditure is less than $1000;
(b) the expenditure is deductible under a provision other than section 8-1 (e.g. prepaid tax agent fees under section 25-5);
(c) the expenditure is required to be made by law. This includes payments such as workers compensation premiums, business name renewals and payments for land tax; or
(d) the expenditure is paid under a contract of service. This includes the prepayment of salary and wages.

If none of these 4 exceptions apply, then the amount of the prepaid expenditure must be apportioned over the period that the prepayment relates up to a maximum of 10 years (called the 'eligible service period').

Furthermore, in addition to these four requirements, individual taxpayers and small business entities (SBEs) are also entitled to an immediate tax deduction where certain conditions are met.

9.3.6.1 Individual taxpayers not carrying on a business

Individual taxpayers that are not carrying on a business include those taxpayers deriving salary and wage income or those taxpayers that derive rental income or interest income from passive investments, such as a rental property or shares.

According to section 82KZM of the ITAA36, an individual taxpayer is also entitled to claim an immediate tax deduction for prepaid expenditure provided the period covered by the expenditure is 12 months or less (regardless of the amount). If the taxpayer is not entitled to an immediate deduction, then the amount of the prepaid expenditure must be apportioned over the period that the prepayment relates up to a maximum of 10 years (called the 'eligible service period').

9.3.6.2 Small business entities

Special rules apply to small business taxpayers. These rules are outlined as follows.

For the year ended 30 June 2022, a business is classified as a small business entity (SBE) if:
- it carries on business in that year, and
- its aggregated turnover for the year is less than $10 million.[4]

An entity's annual turnover for an income year is the total ordinary income that the entity derives in the income year in the ordinary course of carrying on a business.

According to section 82KZM of the ITAA36, in addition to the four requirements contained earlier in (a) to (d), a small business entity (SBE) taxpayer is also entitled to claim an upfront tax deduction for the amount of prepayment (regardless of the amount) provided that the period covered by the prepayment:
- does not exceed 12 months, and
- ends in the next income year.

If the SBE is not entitled to an immediate deduction because the length of the prepayment made was more than 12 months, then the amount of the prepaid expenditure must be apportioned over the period that the prepayment relates up to a maximum of 10 years (called the 'eligible service period').

The application of SBE rules is demonstrated in example 9.1.

EXAMPLE 9.1

Small business taxpayer and prepaid rent

On 30 June 2022, Christie Allen prepays 2 months rent of $2500 per month for her cafe (total of $5000). Under accrual accounting principles, the entire $5000 will be debited to the prepaid rent account in the balance sheet.

What can Christie's business claim as a tax deduction if it is a:
(a) small business entity; and
(b) a large business?

Small business entity

If Christie's cafe is a small business entity, she would be entitled to claim an immediate tax deduction for the entire $5000 prepaid rent on 30 June 2022, despite the fact that the rent relates to July and August 2022 (i.e. in the next financial year, being 2023). The prepaid rent was only for 2 months (being less

---

4 According to section 328-110 of the ITAA97.

than 12 months) and ends in the 2023 income year. Hence, it is fully deductible to Christie in the 2022 income year.

Large business entity

On the other hand, if Christie were a large business taxpayer, she would not be entitled to any tax deduction for her rent prepayment in the 2022 income year as none of the requirements contained in (a) to (d) outlinedin section 82KZL(1) would apply. Instead, the whole amount of the rent prepayment of $5000 would be deductible to Christie in the 2023 income year.

9.4 Definition of trading stock

LEARNING OBJECTIVE 9.4 Describe the trading stock provisions of the ITAA97.

The trading stock divisions are found in Division 70 of the ITAA97. **Trading stock** is defined in section 70-10 of the ITAA97 as including:

(a) anything produced, manufactured or acquired that is held for purposes of manufacture, sale or exchange in the ordinary course of a business, and
(b) livestock.

Trading stock refers to goods that are purchased by a business with the intention of resale. Accountants refer to trading stock as **inventory**.[5]

Inventory can be a substantial asset for a business. For most retailers, inventory can represent one of their largest (if not, their largest) assets.

Table 9.2 provides examples of trading stock.

TABLE 9.2	Examples of trading stock
Type of item	**Trading stock**
Clothes	Clothes bought and held for sale by a clothes retailer.
Alcohol	Alcohol, consisting of wine, beer, champagne, spirits held for sale by a bottle shop, as well as alcohol held by a licensed restaurant for sale to customers when dining in.
Fish	Tropical and freshwater fish held by an aquarium store for sale to customers.
Land	Capable of being trading stock in the hands of the land dealer (see *St Hubert's Island Pty Ltd* 78 ATC 4104). To be trading stock, the land must be held for resale and a business activity which involves dealing in land must have commenced. Where a large area of land is acquired for subdivision and resale, an individual block will only be a separate article of trading stock when it is converted to a subdivisible state which can be marketed (see TD 92/124).
Shares	Can be trading stock if frequently traded (see *Investment and Merchant Finance Corporation Limited v FCT* 71 ATC 4140).
Retirement village	Can be trading stock where the property developer develops a retirement village for the purpose of sale to a village operator.
Computer software	Computer software that is produced or developed for sale by a software manufacturer or developer, is considered trading stock. Computer software developed for licence is not trading stock.
Crops/plants	Standing or growing crops, timber or fruit are not considered to be trading stock (see TR 95/6). Crops, timber and fruit become trading stock only when they are severed (i.e. cut) from the land in which they are growing. Similarly, wool only becomes trading stock once the fleece is shorn from the sheep.

(continued)

---

5 See AASB 102 *Inventories*.

TABLE 9.2	*(continued)*
Type of item	**Trading stock**
Livestock	Livestock includes all animals owned by a taxpayer carrying on a business of primary production, but excludes animals used as beasts of burden or working beasts in a business other than primary production (e.g. racehorses). Domestic pets are not livestock. Racehorses are livestock if used for breeding, but not if used for racing (see TR 93/26). Freshwater crayfish kept and bred on farms or for sale and live pearl oysters used in a business of pearl culture are livestock (see Taxation Ruling IT 2667).
Work in progress	Work in progress of a manufacturer is considered trading stock, but work in progress under a long-term construction project is not trading stock of the builder (see Taxation Ruling IT 2450). Work in progress of a professional partnership does not constitute trading stock.

9.5 Meaning of 'stock on hand'

LEARNING OBJECTIVE 9.5 Explain when trading stock becomes on hand for both accounting and taxation purposes.

This section discusses the concept of 'stock on hand' from both an accounting and income tax perspective.

9.5.1 Accounting purposes

For accounting purposes, whether inventory is 'on hand' at the end of the financial year depends on who has legal power to dispose of the inventory (i.e. the buyer or the seller). This depends on the terms of shipping rather than who physically has possession of the goods at year end.

The freight concept of **free on board (FOB)** is important in determining who is the legal owner of goods being shipped.

Where the terms of the shipment are **FOB shipping point**, the legal title to the goods passes to the buyer at the point of shipping. This is represented in figure 9.1.

FIGURE 9.1	FOB shipping point

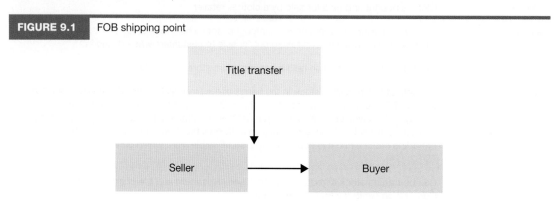

Conversely, if the terms of the shipment are **FOB destination**, the legal title to the goods remains with the seller until the goods are received by the buyer at the point of destination (figure 9.2).

FIGURE 9.2	FOB destination

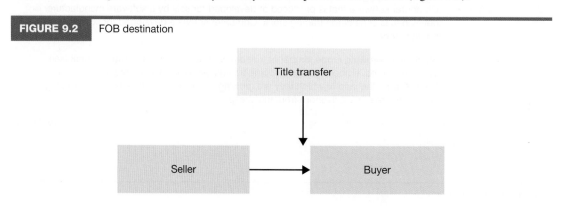

9.5.2 Taxation purposes

From a taxation perspective, the Commissioner considers trading stock to be 'on hand' when the taxpayer has dispositive power (i.e. the power to deal with it as if it were his or her own).[6] In other words, stock on hand is *not* a question of physical possession. The crux lies with whether the taxpayer has the legal power to dispose of the goods.

For this reason, the Commissioner accepts that the same principles that exist in accounting apply to taxation. The terms of shipment (i.e. FOB shipping point or FOB destination) are crucial. This principle was confirmed by the court in *All States Frozen Foods Pty Ltd v FCT* (1990) 90 ATC 4175.

All States Frozen Foods Pty Ltd v FCT (1990) 90 ATC 4175

Facts: The taxpayer carried on business as a wholesaler dealer in a variety of frozen foods in Australia. The taxpayer purchased frozen foods from an overseas supplier. On 30 June 1985, the shipping containers of frozen foods which the taxpayer had ordered and paid for were in transit to Australia. The bill of lading specified that the goods were shipped FOB shipping point, meaning that the risk in the goods had passed to the taxpayer on 30 June 1985. The stock did not arrive until after 30 June 1985.

The taxpayer claimed a deduction for the purchase of the stock, which the Commissioner allowed. However, the taxpayer argued that the stock en route to Australia by sea at 30 June 1985 was not 'on hand' as it did not have physical possession of the good and therefore, not available for sale in the ordinary course if its business. The Commissioner disagreed and asserted that the stock was 'on hand' for tax purposes under the former section 28 of the *ITAA36*.

The issue before the Court was whether the trading stock was 'on hand' at 30 June 1985.

Held: The Court held that stock in transit was 'on hand' at the end of the income year, notwithstanding that the stock had not been physically delivered to the taxpayer. Accordingly, the stock in transit was required to be included as part of the taxpayer's closing stock at 30 June 1985.

The Court held that 'stock on hand' for the purposes of section 28 meant where the taxpayer has the power to dispose of the stock on its own account. Under the bill of lading, the taxpayer was in a position to dispose of the stock and, as such, the stock was 'on hand' at 30 June 1985. It did not matter that, in the ordinary course of business, the taxpayer did not have physical possession. The key criteria was that the taxpayer has 'dispositive power' over the stock.

9.6 Determining what is assessable or deductible

LEARNING OBJECTIVE 9.6 Apply the rules for determining the assessability/deductibility of trading stock under both the periodic and perpetual inventory systems.

A retailer keeps track of inventory using an inventory system to determine how much is available for sale and how much has been sold. There are two generally accepted inventory systems:
1. periodic
2. perpetual.

Each inventory system has differing taxation implications, which are discussed in the following sections.

9.6.1 Periodic inventory method

This section describes the periodic inventory method for accounting purposes and for taxation purposes.

9.6.1.1 Accounting purposes

Under the **periodic inventory system**, detailed records of inventory movements are not maintained. There is no continuous record of how much inventory is on hand at any particular point in time. The only way that the amount of inventory on hand can be ascertained is by performing a physical stocktake (i.e. counting the inventory on hand).

When inventory is acquired throughout the year, the 'purchases' account is debited. When an item of inventory is sold, 'revenue' is credited.

---

6 See *FCT v Suttons Motors* (1985) 16 ATR 567.

In order to determine the amount of cost of goods sold during the reporting period, a schedule of cost of goods sold needs to be prepared detailing the opening balance of the inventory account, adding all purchases acquired during the period and then deducting the closing inventory to calculate this value.

This concept is illustrated in example 9.2.

EXAMPLE 9.2

Periodic inventory system (accounting treatment)

Southside Electronics Pty Ltd is an electronics retailer. It buys and sells a range of electronic equipment, such as television sets, Blu-ray players and sound systems.

For the year ended 30 June 2022, the business derived gross sales of $2 400 000. Its purchases totalled $1 480 000.

Opening stock at 1 July 2021 was $320 000 and closing stock at 30 June 2022 (based on a stocktake) was $380 000.

What is the cost of goods sold and gross profit for the year ended 30 June 2022?

	$	$
Gross sales		2 400 000
Less: Cost of goods sold		
Opening stock	320 000	
Add: Purchases	1 480 000	
Cost of goods available for sale	1 800 000	
Less: Closing stock	(380 000)	
Cost of goods sold		1 420 000
Gross profit		980 000

9.6.1.2 Taxation purposes

For taxation purposes, each item that forms part of the accounting calculations in example 9.2 is considered separately. In other words, even though the fact that the gross profit is calculated for accounting purposes, the gross profit of $980 000 shown is not considered assessable for income tax purposes. Instead, the assessability/deductibility of each line item has its own taxation treatment.

For taxation purposes, the gross sales arising from the sale of trading stock gives rise to ordinary income under section 6-5 of the ITAA97.

Where the taxpayer is using the periodic inventory system, the taxpayer is allowed an outright deduction under section 8-1 of the ITAA97 for the cost of purchasing trading stock as shown as the 'purchases' amount in the cost of goods sold schedule.

In terms of opening and closing stock, section 70-35 applies. In summary:
- where the value of closing stock is greater than the value of the opening stock (i.e. it has increased), the difference is assessable income to the taxpayer[7]
- conversely, where the value of closing stock is less than the value of the opening stock (i.e. it has decreased), the difference is an allowable deduction to the taxpayer.[8]

Example 9.3 applies the periodic inventory system method for tax purposes.

EXAMPLE 9.3

Periodic inventory system (taxation treatment)

Use the same facts contained in example 9.2.

What are the tax consequences of the trading stock purchased and sold?
- The gross sales of $2 400 000 are assessable income (section 6-5).
- The purchases of $1 480 000 are an allowable deduction (section 8-1).
- As the value of the closing stock (i.e. $380 000) is greater than the value of the opening stock (i.e. $320 000), the difference of $60 000 is assessable (section 70-35(2)).

---

7 ITAA97 section 70-35(2).
8 ITAA97 section 70-35(3).

In summary, the total assessable amount comes to $2 460 000 (being $2 400 000 sales + $60 000 excess of closing stock over opening stock). The net allowable deduction is $1 480 000, being the purchases.

Hence, the impact of the above is that a net amount totalling $980 000 is included in the taxpayer's assessable income (which equates to total gross profit using accounting concepts explained in example 9.2).

9.6.2 Perpetual inventory method

This section describes the perpetual inventory method for accounting purposes and for taxation purposes.

9.6.2.1 Accounting purposes

Under the **perpetual inventory system**, detailed records of inventory movements are recorded through the inventory account. Every time an item of inventory is purchased, the 'inventory' account is debited. Conversely, every time an item of inventory is sold, the 'inventory' account is credited and the 'cost of goods sold' account is debited.

As such, there is no need to prepare a cost of goods sold schedule under the perpetual inventory method. Most computerised accounting systems will perform this calculation automatically and instantaneously every time each item of inventory is sold.

This concept is illustrated in example 9.4.

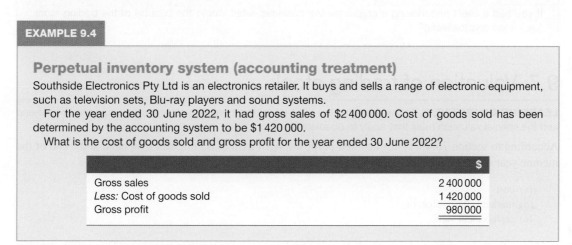

EXAMPLE 9.4

Perpetual inventory system (accounting treatment)

Southside Electronics Pty Ltd is an electronics retailer. It buys and sells a range of electronic equipment, such as television sets, Blu-ray players and sound systems.

For the year ended 30 June 2022, it had gross sales of $2 400 000. Cost of goods sold has been determined by the accounting system to be $1 420 000.

What is the cost of goods sold and gross profit for the year ended 30 June 2022?

	$
Gross sales	2 400 000
Less: Cost of goods sold	1 420 000
Gross profit	980 000

9.6.2.2 Taxation purposes

As the purchases have already been booked to the inventory account, there is no purchases account.

However, as we have been able to more precisely calculate the cost of goods sold during the reporting period using the perpetual inventory system, we are allowed to simply use the cost of goods sold value reported in the income statement as a tax deduction.

This is illustrated in example 9.5.

EXAMPLE 9.5

Perpetual inventory system (taxation treatment)

Use the same facts as in example 9.4.

What are the tax consequences of the trading stock purchased and sold?

The gross sales are assessable under section 6-5. The cost of goods sold of $1 420 000 is an allowable deduction (section 8-1).

There is no need to consider the opening and closing stock rules contained in section 70-35 as these rules only apply in the case of a periodic inventory system.

Can cryptocurrency be trading stock?

Whilst cryptocurrency is considered a CGT asset for capital gains tax purposes, it can also represent trading stock where the taxpayer is trading cryptocurrencies.

Where the taxpayer is considered a trader in cryptocurrencies, the gross sales of cryptocurrency will be regarded as assessable income pursuant to section 6-5. The purchase of cryptocurrency will be deductible under section 8-1. At year-end, the taxpayer undertakes a stocktake of the amount of cryptocurrency held. The normal provisions contained in section 70-35 will apply to determine the amount considered assessable or deductible.

Hence, in the case of a cryptomining business, the taxpayer typically acquires cryptocurrency through their regular mining (or 'striking') activities rather than purchasing cryptoassets directly for capital (or investment) purposes. This constitutes trading stock.

It is also important to note that a business that is not a crypto-business may still use cryptoassets in their business activities. For example, a business may accept cryptoassets as payment for goods and services.

In this case, the normal rules of taxation apply. Hence, despite using cryptocurrency to sell goods, the taxpayer must include the Australian dollar value of the goods or services sold or provided as ordinary income. Similarly, if goods or services are purchased using cryptoassets, the deduction is the market value of the item acquired in Australian dollars.

REFLECTION

If you had a client undertaking a crypto-mining business, what would the cost be of the trading stock (i.e. mined cryptoassets)?

9.7 Valuation of trading stock

LEARNING OBJECTIVE 9.7 Use the valuation rules permitted in valuing closing stock on hand at year-end and the special valuation rules that apply to obsolete stock.

According to section 70-45(1), for taxation purposes, *each* item of trading stock on hand at the end of the income year can be valued at:

(a) cost
(b) market selling value, or
(c) replacement value.

Hence, there is a choice of 3 methods to value trading stock for taxation purposes. This is illustrated in figure 9.3.

FIGURE 9.3 Inventory valuation methods — taxation

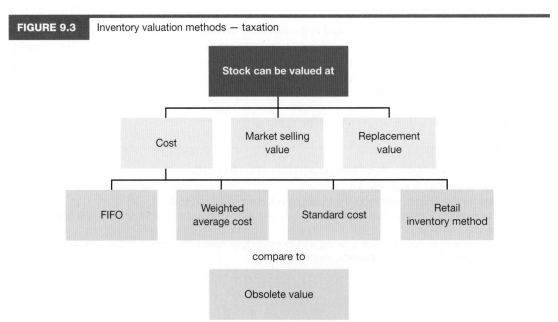

A taxpayer is required to notify the Commissioner in their tax return as to which method was the primary method used to value closing stock. They do this by way of a code on their tax return, as per table 9.3.

TABLE 9.3 Valuation method codes

Code	Valuation method
C	Cost
M	Market selling value
R	Replacement value

Source: Extract from Australian Taxation Office, 'Financial and other information' (Web Page, 2021) https://www.ato.gov.au/Forms/Company-tax-return-instructions-2021/?page=13#closingstock.

Section 70-45(1) refers to the valuation of *each* item of trading stock. In other words, a different basis may be adopted for each class of stock and even for each individual item of stock. Furthermore, a taxpayer may choose to change the valuation of each item of trading stock at the end of each income year.

The only restriction is that closing value adopted for a particular item of trading stock at the end of one income year automatically becomes its opening value at the beginning of the next income year (see section 70-40(1) of the ITAA97).

Where more than one trading stock valuation method has been used in valuing the closing stock, the ATO has indicated that the code applicable to the method which represents the highest value of closing stock should be used in the tax return (see table 9.3).

9.7.1 Cost price

The **cost price** of trading stock is not simply the invoice price. It also includes all direct and indirect costs (such as import duties and other taxes, freight inwards and handling costs and any other costs directly attributable to the cost of acquisition less trade discounts, rebates and subsidies) incurred in bringing inventories to their present location and condition.

If the entity is registered for GST, the cost price of inventory excludes the GST paid to acquire the trading stock.

In the case of manufacturers, the Commissioner of Taxation considers the **absorption costing** method as the only method appropriate in determining the cost of inventories.[9] This concept equates to the same principles for accounting purposes.

Under absorption costing principles, the 'cost price' of trading stock includes the cost of direct labour as well as a share of all fixed *and* variable overhead costs incurred in producing or manufacturing the inventory. This is to be contrasted to the concept of variable costing, which only incorporates a share of variable (and not fixed) overheads into the cost of inventory.

As illustrated in figure 9.3, for taxation purposes, the Commissioner accepts the following valuation methods under the cost method.

- *First-in, first-out (FIFO).* Based on the assumption that the first units of inventory acquired (purchased) are the first units sold. In other words, the earliest items purchased are the first ones to be sold. Hence, the amount of inventory on hand at the end of the year consists of the most recent acquisitions of inventory immediately prior to the end of the reporting period.
- *Weighted average cost.* The average cost of inventory acquired for the reporting period is calculated. Once the average cost of inventory for the reporting period has been calculated, the average cost per unit is then multiplied by the number of goods on hand at the end of the year to derive a closing stock figure.
- *Standard cost.* Primarily used by manufacturers who set a predetermined price for each inventory item. This budgeted price is used for all items of inventory acquired during the reporting period. However, this price must be reviewed regularly and updated if necessary, particularly if prices change.
- *Retail inventory method.* The cost of inventory is determined by reducing the sales value of inventory by the appropriate percentage gross margin. An average percentage for each retail department is often used. Not surprisingly, this inventory valuation method is not particularly common, but is sometimes used in the retail industry.

---

9 See IT 2350 and *Phillip Morris v FCT* 79 ATC 4352.

The Commissioner does not accept the last-in first-out (LIFO) method of inventory valuation as, in times of steadily rising prices, the Commissioner considers that it undervalues the value of closing stock.

9.7.2 Market selling value

The second method allowable for taxation purposes is the **market selling value**. Market selling value for trading stock purposes is the current *selling value* of stock in the taxpayer's own selling market. In the case of a wholesaler, this is the current wholesale value of comparable items and, in the case of a retailer, the current retail value.

The concept of 'market selling value' was explained in the case of *Australasian Jam Co Pty Ltd v FCT* (1953).

Australasian Jam Co Pty Ltd v FCT (1953) 88 CLR 23

Facts: The taxpayer was a food processing company that manufactured jams and canned fruits. Since 1924, the company valued its closing stock at standard cost. Over the years, the actual costs increased. However, the taxpayer continued to use the initial values.

Held: The High Court held that the taxpayer was only allowed to value its closing stock under one of three methods, being cost price, market selling value or replacement cost. The method adopted by the taxpayer was not one of the three prescribed methods.

The High Court went on to explain that 'market selling value' contemplates the sale of stock in the ordinary course of the taxpayer's business and not the amount realisable as the result of a forced sale or break up.

9.7.3 Replacement value

The **replacement value** of trading stock is the amount the taxpayer would have to pay in its normal buying market on the last day of the income year to replace (or re-buy) a substantially identical article in his/her stock on the last day of the income year.

Replacement value can only be used as a method of trading stock valuation if replacement items are available in the market and these are substantially identical to the replaced items.[10]

Example 9.6 demonstrates choice of valuation method for closing stock.

EXAMPLE 9.6

Valuation of closing stock

At 30 June 2022, Tennis World Pty Ltd, had the following stock on hand with the following values.

Item	Market selling value ($)	Replacement value ($)	Cost ($)
Tennis racquets	27 500	27 800	19 800
Tennis balls	1 750	1 620	1 880
Tennis clothes	6 800	7 200	7 400
Tennis bags	2 500	2 800	1 900

Assuming that Tennis World Pty Ltd wishes to minimise its tax payable for the year ended 30 June 2022, what value should the company value its closing stock at?

If Tennis World Pty Ltd wishes to minimise its taxable income for the year ended 30 June 2022, the company should value each type of trading stock on hand at 30 June 2022 at the lowest possible value.

A lower value of closing stock results in a lower taxable income. Hence, at 30 June 2022, each item of trading stock should be valued as shown in the following table, valuing closing stock in total at $30 120.

---

10 See TD 92/198.

Item	Valuation basis	Value ($)
Tennis racquets	Cost	19 800
Tennis balls	Replacement value	1 620
Tennis clothes	Market selling value	6 800
Tennis bags	Cost	1 900
Total closing stock		**30 120**

9.7.4 Special value in case of obsolescence

According to section 70-50 of the ITAA97, where the value of trading stock falls below its cost, market selling value or replacement value due to obsolescence or other special circumstances particular to the relevant trading stock (e.g. discontinuation of a product line or a fickle market), the taxpayer may elect to value the trading stock at its **obsolete value** as long as that value is considered reasonable.

The Commissioner has issued general guidelines for trading stock valuations where obsolescence or other special circumstances exist (see TR 93/23).

According to paragraph 5 of TR 93/23, the Commissioner of Taxation considers the following factors in determining whether an item of stock is obsolete:

- the age of stock on hand
- the quantity of stock on hand which, according to operating and sales budgets, is expected to be used or sold during the year and in the future
- the length of time since the last sale, exchange or use of an item of the stock
- industry benchmarks
- the price at which the last sale of the stock was made, the price of the stock on the taxpayer's price list and the price at which the taxpayer is prepared to sell the stock.

9.8 Special rules applying to trading stock

LEARNING OBJECTIVE 9.8 Describe various special rules applying to trading stock.

This final section of the chapter discusses tax rules applying to various transactions and circumstances relating to trading stock.

9.8.1 Disposals of stock outside the ordinary course of business

Normally, a business disposes of its trading stock by selling it to customers. In this case, sale proceeds are brought to account as assessable income under section 6-5 of the ITAA97.

However, sometimes trading stock may be disposed outside the ordinary course of business (e.g. a business may donate items of stock for a sporting club raffle, stock may be given away to friends or family members or disposed of in liquidation).

In these instances, section 70-90 of the ITAA97 requires the taxpayer to include in his/her assessable income the market value of that stock on the date of disposal. A person who acquires the trading stock is deemed to have acquired it at the same value (see section 70-95 of the ITAA97).

In the case where trading stock is donated to a DGR, section 30-20 of the ITAA97 provides that the entity is entitled to a tax deduction equivalent to the market value of the trading stock at the date of disposal.

Example 9.7 examines the disposal of stock outside the ordinary course of business.

Disposal of stock outside the ordinary course of business

Amy owns and operates a jewellery store. Amy gives her niece a pair of earrings (taken from her jewellery store) for her 21st birthday. The earrings cost $180 and retail for $300.

What are the tax consequences of this treatment of trading stock?

As the earrings were disposed of outside the ordinary course of business, section 70-90 of the ITAA97 requires Amy to bring to account as assessable income the market value of that stock on the date of disposal. Hence, even though Amy did not receive any proceeds from the 'sale' of the earrings, she will need to include an amount of $300 as assessable income in the business's income tax return.

It should be remembered that when the store bought the earrings, it would have claimed the $180 purchase of these earrings as a tax deduction under section 8-1 of the ITAA97.

9.8.2 Stock taken by the owner for their own personal use

Section 70-110 of the ITAA97 provides that if the taxpayer takes stock for his/her own personal use and it remains in possession of the taxpayer, the taxpayer is required to include the cost price of that stock as at the date of transfer as part of the assessable income of the business.

This is demonstrated in example 9.8.

Stock taken for personal use

Amy owns and operates a jewellery store. Amy takes a diamond ring from her jewellery store for her own personal use. The diamond ring costs $6000 and retails for $10 000.

What are the tax consequences of this treatment of trading stock?

According to section 70-110 of the ITAA97, if a taxpayer takes stock for their own personal use, the taxpayer must include the cost of trading stock in their assessable income. Hence, Amy will be required to include an amount of $6000 in the assessable income of the business's income tax return.

It should be remembered that when the store bought the diamond ring, it would have claimed the $6000 purchase of the diamond ring as a tax deduction under section 8-1 of the ITAA97. Hence, the effect of the 'deemed' assessable income of $6000 is to offset (or neutralise) the purchase of the diamond ring of $6000, resulting in an overall net effect of nil.

For certain industries, it can be difficult to ascertain the value of stock takenby the owner during the income year. Each year, the Commissioner of Taxation releases standard values for goods taken from trading stock for private use. This is done each year via the issuance of a Taxation Determination. In November 2021, the Commissioner released TD 2021/8, *Income tax: value of goods taken from stock for private use for the 2021–22 income year*, outlining the standard value of goods taken for private use for named industries. The Schedule for the value of goods taken from trading stock for private use in the 2021–22 income year is shown in table 9.4.

TABLE 9.4   Schedule for the value of goods taken from trading stock for 2022

Type of business	Amount for adult/child over 16 years of age $	Amount for child 4 to 16 years of age $
Bakery	1 350	675
Butcher	920	460
Restaurant/cafe (licensed)	4 640	1 830
Restaurant/cafe (unlicensed)	3 660	1 830

Caterer	3 870	1 935
Delicatessen	3 660	1 830
Fruiters/greengrocer	960	480
Takeaway food shop	3 790	1 895
Mixed business (includes milk bar, general store and convenience store)	4 590	2 295

Source: Australian Taxation Office, *Income tax: value of goods taken from stock for private use for the 2021–22 income year* (TD 2021/8, 2021) https://www.ato.gov.au/law/view/pdf/pbr/td2021-008.pdf.

9.8.3 Stock lost or destroyed

Trading stock lost through events such as fire, flooding, theft or spoilage is not specifically covered in the income tax legislation. However, as a result of the loss, the amount of closing stock will be lower as this lost or destroyed stock will not be included in the value of closing stock. As the initial purchase of the stock would have been deductible under section 8-1, the loss of stock effectively results in a deduction being allowed.

Compensation received for the loss of trading stock (e.g. insurance proceeds) is regarded as assessable income under section 70-115 of the ITAA97.

9.8.4 Items that become or cease to be trading stock

There are instances where an asset previously held by the taxpayer becomes trading stock, and other instances where an item of trading stock no longer is held for resale and becomes a CGT or depreciable asset of the taxpayer. The taxation consequences of these two scenarios is considered next.

9.8.4.1 Property that becomes trading stock

According to section 70-30 of the ITAA97, where an item of property owned by a taxpayer but not held as trading stock (such as a capital asset) subsequently becomes or is held as trading stock, the taxpayer can elect that the trading stock be valued at:

- cost, or
- market value.

In other words, a taxpayer can elect whether the notional disposal (from a capital asset to trading stock) and subsequent re-acquisition takes place at cost or market value.

This concept is demonstrated in example 9.9.

EXAMPLE 9.9

Property that becomes trading stock

Katie owns and operates her own bottle shop. At a recently charity gala ball that she attended, Katie wins a raffle conducted by the charity and wins $4000 worth of wine. Instead of consuming the wine herself, she places the wine into her bottle shop to be sold to customers in the ordinary course of business.

In this situation, property has become trading stock to Katie. As per section 70-30, Katie can elect to value the new trading stock at either cost or market value. As she did not purchase the wine, there is no cost to Katie, and she can elect to use market value (i.e. $4000). In this instance, Katie can claim a tax deduction for this amount pursuant to section 8-1.

At year-end, Katie can elect that any unsold wine in this batch be valued at either cost: replacement value or market selling value. In this instance, if the cost valuation method is chosen, the deemed cost will be the market value at the time that Katie added the wine to her trading stock.

9.8.4.2 Property that ceases to be trading stock

Section 70-110 deals with property that stops being trading stock of a taxpayer but continues to be held by the taxpayer. This might occur where a taxpayer takes an asset that has previously been classified as an asset and converts it to trading stock (e.g. a taxpayer that has bought a block of land to run their business, but now changes their business activity to be a property developer and intends to use this land for the purposes of resale).

In such a case, section 70-110 deems the item of stock to have been disposed of at cost and immediately reacquired by the taxpayer at cost. In this situation, there are generally no tax consequences. The sale of the asset at cost is recognised as assessable income under section 6-5 and the movement in stock value is recognised as an allowable deduction under section 70-35.

9.8.5 Purchase of trading stock at other than arm's length

In some situations, trading stock may be acquired for more than its market value. This may be the case where the buyer and seller are not dealing with each other at arm's length (i.e. the two parties are related to each other or are related entities).

In this situation, section 70-20 of the ITAA97 provides that if the two parties are not dealing with each other at arm's length in respect of a trading stock transaction and the transaction price is greater than its market value, the transaction price is deemed to be the market value of the trading stock (i.e. its arm's length price).

However, the arm's length rule does not apply where the amount paid is less than the market value. In this situation, section 70-20 also operates to make the sale at the arm's length value assessable for the seller.

This concept is demonstrated in example 9.10.

EXAMPLE 9.10

Purchase of trading stock at non-arm's length

Joe carries on a business as a second-hand car dealer. In May 2022, Joe bought a used car from his brother, Alf, for $25 000. However, the market value of the car at the time was $18 000. As the sale price (i.e. $25 000) is more than its market value of the car at the time (i.e. $18 000), then Joe would only be entitled to a (reduced) deduction of $18 000 in accordance with sections 8-1 and 70-20.

Conversely, if Joe paid $16 000 for the car and the market value of the car at the time was $18 000, then Joe would only be entitled to a deduction of $16 000.

9.8.6 Prepayments for trading stock

For a deduction for the purchase of trading stock to be allowed under section 8-1, the stock needs to be 'on hand', unless an amount is included in the taxpayer's assessable income in connection with the disposal of that item.

Section 70-15 denies a deduction for prepayment of trading stock that is not on hand at the end of the year of income in which the payment is made. The deduction for the purchase of the trading stock will be allowed at the time when the stock actually becomes 'on hand'.

This is demonstrated in example 9.11.

EXAMPLE 9.11

Prepayments for trading stock

Coconut Burst Pty Ltd is an Australian distributor of coconut water. It buys and imports coconut water in containers from Thailand. The goods are shipped from Thailand to Australia for sale to Australian retailers, including supermarkets, gymnasiums, independent grocers and petrol stations. Coconut Burst Pty Ltd has a year-end of 30 June.

On 2 June 2022, Coconut Burst Pty Ltd paid $54 000 for the purchase of trading stock. The goods are shipped to Australia FOB destination and arrive in Australia on 3 July 2022.

When can Coconut Burst Pty Ltd claim a deduction for the purchase of the trading stock?

Even though the trading stock was paid for on 2 June 2022, the prepayment rules contained in section 70-15 will apply, meaning that the company cannot claim a deduction for this amount until the trading stock arrives in Australia (i.e. 3 July 2022). As such, the trading stock will be deductible in the 2023 income year, and not the 2022 income year.

9.8.7 Small business entities and the simplified trading stock provisions

Optional simplified trading stock rules apply to small business entities.

According to section 328-285, where the difference between the value of opening stock and closing stock of a small business entity is less than $5000 (determined by a reasonable estimate), the small business taxpayer may choose not to value their closing stock, but leave the value of their closing stock at the same amount as their opening stock.

In the ATO's view (see PS LA 2008/4), an estimate will be reasonable where it:

- takes into account all relevant factors and considerations likely to affect the number and value of the particular entity's items of trading stock on hand
- has been undertaken in good faith
- results from a rational and reasoned process of estimation, and
- is capable of explanation to, and verification by, a third party.

If the small business taxpayer chooses to use this provision, then the value of their opening stock will be deemed to become the value of their closing stock for the relevant income year (see section 328-295).

The overall effect of these provisions is to defer the recognition of any stock increases or decreases until they become material (i.e. greater than $5000).

Where the difference between the value of trading stock on hand at the start of the year and the end of the year is more than $5000, the amount of the change is included in taxable income as per the ordinary rules contained in section 70-35.

This is demonstrated in example 9.12.

EXAMPLE 9.12

SBE and the simplified trading stock provisions

Perfect Vision Pty Ltd is a small optometry practice operating in Brisbane. It conducts eye tests for patients and sells a range of frames, spectacles, contact lenses, sunglasses and a range of optical accessories. For the year ended 30 June 2022, the company derived gross sales of $84 000, making it a small business entity for income tax purposes.

On 1 July 2021, the opening stock was $278 000. At 30 June 2022, the company undertook a stocktake and valued the closing stock at $282 000.

Being a small business entity taxpayer, as the difference between the opening and closing stock values was only $4000 (i.e. less than $5000), the company can elect to adopt the SBE simplified trading stock provisions. If it does so, this means that it can elect to value its closing stock at the same value as its opening stock (i.e. $278 000) and therefore not account for the change in value of $4000.

On the other hand, if the company elects not to adopt the simplified trading stock provisions, then it would account for the change between the value of its opening stock and closing stock. In this case, according to section 70-35(2) of the ITAA97, as the value of the closing stock is greater than the value of the opening stock by $4000, this amount would form part of the assessable income of Perfect Vision Pty Ltd.

ETHICS IN PRACTICE

Ethics in tax accounting and trading stock

You are the external accountant and tax agent for a bookstore. The bookstore has an annual turnover of $14 million. As they use a periodic inventory system, you have recommended to your client that they conduct a physical stocktake of books on hand in their warehouse and in their retail stores at 30 June 2022.

It is now early July 2022, and your client has advised you that they 'did not have time to conduct the stocktake' and have suggested that you simply use the opening stock value at 1 July 2021.

They said that, as the amount of stock on hand at 30 June 2022 was likely to be significantly higher than the amount of the opening stock, they were aware that if they conducted a stocktake at 30 June 2022, the difference between the closing and opening stock values would be quite significant, which would mean that they would be required to bring to account the difference between these values as assessable income

▶

in their tax return. They felt that this not doing a physical stocktake at 30 June 2022 would be a 'good tax minimisation strategy'.

What advice would you provide to your client? What would be your reaction in resolving this ethical dilemma?

Not doing the stocktake and simply using the opening stock value at 1 July 2021 would result in a significant understatement of the closing stock value, which would result in a lower taxable income. However, this overlooks the requirement contained in section 70-35(2) of the ITAA97 which requires that the taxpayer bring to account the difference between the value of the closing stock and opening stock as assessable income in its 2022 tax return.

Section 120 of APES 110 *Code of Ethics for Professional Accountants* requires the tax agent to act with objectivity, whilst section 130 also requires the tax advisor to act with professional competence and due care. This means that the tax advisor cannot simply 'turn a blind eye' to the client's request.

Furthermore, section 7 of APES 220 *Taxation Services* requires that members shall not, under any circumstances, become associated with any tax return or submission on behalf of a client if is contains incorrect or misleading information.

Finally, ignoring the issue and allowing the client to include the value of its opening stock in its 2022 tax return would constitute a breach of the Code of Conduct for professional tax advisors.

For all of these reasons, the tax agent needs to ensure that the client accurately includes the value of its closing stock on hand at 30 June 2022 in its 2022 tax return.

SUMMARY

9.1 Explain the difference between the accounting treatment and income tax treatment of revenues and expenses.

While most items of revenue are assessable for tax purposes, this is not always the case. There are some items of accounting revenue that are not assessable for income tax purposes (e.g. exempt income). Conversely, there may be some items that are assessable for taxation purposes but are not included as revenue for accounting purposes (e.g. franking credits).

In terms of deductions, several expenses recorded in the Income Statement are not tax-deductible (e.g. provisions for bad debts, annual leave, entertainment provided to clients). Conversely, there may be some items that are deductible for income tax but are not shown as an expense in the Income Statement; rather they are recorded in the Balance Sheet (e.g. prepayments).

9.2 Determine when income is derived for taxation purposes, including the various rules that apply to each type of income.

The concept of derivation is about timing — when has the income been derived? Derivation determines which income year an amount will be assessed in. For taxation purposes, a taxpayer derives income based on either the cash basis of accounting or the accruals basis.

For taxation purposes, the correct basis of accounting (i.e. cash or accruals) is dependent upon the type of income derived, not the type of taxpayer. Generally, income from personal exertion should be on a cash basis; trading (business) income should be on an accruals basis; revenue received in advance should be on an accruals basis (provided no refunds are given); income from small professional practices should be on a cash basis; income from large professional practices should be on an accruals basis; and income from property should be on a cash basis.

The derivation rules based on the type of income derived and not the type of taxpayer.

9.3 Determine when losses and outgoings are incurred for taxation purposes, including the various rules that apply to each type of loss and outgoing.

Section 8-1 requires that the loss or outgoing be 'incurred' before it will qualify for deduction. The word 'incurred' is not defined in either the ITAA36 or ITAA97 and we therefore need to look at case law to determine the meaning of this word.

'Incurred' is not synonymous with 'paid'. As long as the taxpayer is totally committed to making the payment (even though it may remain unpaid at the end of the year of income) and the amount can at least be reliably estimated (i.e. if the invoice has not been received), the loss or outgoing is incurred for taxation purposes. Discretionary payments are incurred only when paid.

The timing of when a deduction is incurred applies regardless of whether the taxpayer is an individual, a small business entity, or a large business taxpayer. Furthermore, the Commissioner accepts that these principles apply regardless of whether the taxpayer uses the cash or accruals basis of accounting.

9.4 Describe the trading stock provisions of the ITAA97.

Trading stock is defined in section 70-10 of the ITAA97 as including anything produced, manufactured or acquired that is held for purposes of manufacture, sale or exchange in the ordinary course of a business and livestock.

Trading stock refers to goods that are purchased by a business with the intention of resale. Accountants refer to trading stock as inventory. The taxation rules relating to trading stock are contained in Division 70 of the ITAA97.

9.5 Explain when trading stock becomes on hand.

From a taxation perspective, the Commissioner considers trading stock to be 'on hand' when the taxpayer has dispositive power (i.e. the power to deal with it as if it were his or her own).

In other words, stock on hand is not a question of physical possession. The crux lies with whether the taxpayer has the legal power to dispose of the goods. This depends on the terms of shipping rather than who physically has possession of the goods at year end. The freight concept of free on board (FOB) is important in determining who is the legal owner of goods being shipped. This principle was confirmed by the court in *All States Frozen Foods Pty Ltd v FCT* (1990) 90 ATC 4175.

Where the terms of the shipment are FOB shipping point, the legal title to the goods passes to the buyer at the point of shipping. Conversely, if the terms of the shipment are FOB destination, the legal title to the goods remains with the seller until the goods are received by the buyer at the point of destination. These principles are the same for accounting purposes.

9.6 Apply the rules for determining the assessability/deductibility of trading stock under both the periodic and perpetual inventory systems.

Under the peiodic inventory system, detailed records of inventory movements are not maintained. The only way that the amount of inventory on hand can be ascertained is by performing a physical stocktake (i.e. counting the inventory on hand).

For taxation purposes, under a periodic inventory system, the gross sales are assessable income under section 6-5. Purchases of trading stock is deductible under section 8-1.

In terms of opening and closing stock, according to section 70-35(2), where the value of closing stock is greater than the value of the opening stock, the difference is assessable income to the taxpayer. Conversely, according to section 70-35(3) of the ITAA97, where the value of closing stock is less than the value of the opening stock, the difference is an allowable deduction to the taxpayer.

Under the perpetual inventory system, detailed records of inventory movements are recorded through the inventory account. As inventory is able to be more precisely calculated, the cost of goods sold amount reported in the Income Statement is able to be claimed as a tax deduction under section 8-1. The gross sales are assessable income under section 6-5.

There is no need to consider the opening and closing stock rules contained in section 70-35 as these rules only apply in the case of a periodic inventory system.

9.7 Use the valuation rules permitted in valuing closing stock on hand at year-end and the special valuation rules that apply to obsolete stock.

Trading stock on hand at the end of the income year can be valued at cost, market selling value, or replacement value. A different basis may be adopted for each class of stock and even for each individual item of stock.

The cost price of trading stock is the invoice price plus all direct and indirect costs incurred in bringing inventories to their present location and condition. The Commissioner accepts first-in, first-out (FIFO), weighted average cost, standard cost and the retail inventory method.

Market selling value for trading stock purposes is the current selling value of stock in the taxpayer's own selling market.

The replacement value of trading stock is the amount the taxpayer would have to pay in its normal buying market on the last day of the income year to replace (or re-buy) a substantially identical article in his/her stock on the last day of the income year.

Where trading stock falls below its cost, market selling value or replacement value due to obsolescence or other special circumstances, the taxpayer may reasonably value the trading stock at its obsolete value.

9.8 Describe various special rules applying to trading stock.

Special taxation rules apply where trading stock is disposed of outside the ordinary course of business (section 70-90) and where the owner of the business takes stock for their own personal use (section 70-110).

There are also specific tax issues where items become or cease to be trading stock (section 70-30) and where trading stock is acquired at an amount other than arm's length (section 70-20). Optional simplified trading stock rules contained in section 328-285 are available to small business entities.

KEY TERMS

accrual basis of accounting The basis whereby revenues are recorded in the period in which the business sells the goods or performs the services, not in the period where the cash is received. Similarly, expenses are recognised in the period when the expenses have been incurred or consumed, not in the period that the cash is paid.

absorption costing Includes the cost of direct labour as well as a share of all fixed and variable overhead costs incurred in producing or manufacturing the inventory. For taxation purposes, the Commissioner considers the absorption costing method to be the only method appropriate in determining the cost of inventories.

cash basis of accounting The basis whereby revenues are recorded in the period in which the cash is received, not the period in which the goods have been sold or services have been provided. Similarly, expenses are recorded in the period in which the cash is paid, not the period in which the expenses have been incurred.

cost price The cost price of trading stock includes not only the purchase price but all incidental costs (such as import duties and other taxes, freight inwards and handling costs and any other costs directly attributable to the cost of acquisition less trade discounts, rebates and subsidies) incurred in bringing inventories to their present location and condition. If the entity is registered for GST, the cost price of inventories excludes the GST paid to acquire the trading stock.

doctrine of constructive receipt You are taken to have received an amount of income as soon as it is applied or dealt with in any way on your behalf as you direct.

free on board (FOB) This is freight terminology which helps indicate who is responsible for paying the cost of transportation and who is the appropriate legal owner while the goods are in transit. This is important for legal disputes and for year-end accounting purposes.

FOB destination Where the terms of the shipment are FOB destination, the legal title to the goods remains with the seller until the goods are received by the buyer at the point of destination. Typically, in this instance, the seller pays the freight and any related insurance costs.

FOB shipping point Where the terms of the shipment are FOB shipping point, the legal title to the goods passes to the buyer at the point of shipping. In this case, the buyer usually pays the freight and any related insurance costs.

inventory Goods or property acquired by an entity carrying on business for the purposes of resale within the ordinary course of business. Referred to as 'trading stock' for taxation purposes.

market selling value The current selling value of stock in the ordinary course of business in the taxpayer's own selling market. In the case of a wholesaler, this is the current wholesale value of comparable items and, in the case of a retailer, the current retail value.

obsolete value Where the value of trading stock falls below its cost, market selling value of replacement value, due to obsolescence or other special circumstances particular to the relevant trading stock. For taxation purposes, the taxpayer may elect to value the trading stock at its obsolete value if that value is considered reasonable.

periodic inventory system Under a periodic inventory system, every time an entity buys inventory, it records that purchase in the profit and loss statement as an expense. There is no continuous record of how much inventory is on hand at any particular time. The amount of inventory can only be ascertained by performing a physical stocktake (i.e. by counting the inventory).

perpetual inventory system Under a perpetual inventory system, an inventory account is maintained to record increases and decreases in inventory from sale and purchase transactions.

replacement value The amount that the taxpayer would have to pay in its normal buying market on the last day of the income year to replace (or re-buy) a substantially identical item of stock on the last day of the income year.

small business entity (SBE) Also known as an SBE. A term defined in Division 328 of the ITAA97. A small business entity is defined as one that carries on business during the income year and has an aggregated turnover of less than the 'annual SBE turnover' threshold. For the year ended 30 June 2022, the relevant SBE threshold is $10 million. This means that an SBE is defined as any entity with an annual turnover of $10 million or less. A small business entity has the option to adopt a simplified depreciation regime instead of using the depreciation rules applicable for large business entities.

tax accounting A concept that reconciles the differences between the accounting rules set out in AASB Accounting Standards and the taxation rules and principles contained in the ITAA36 and ITAA97.

tax reconciliation A statement is prepared to reconcile the net profit for accounting purposes to the taxable income.

trading stock For taxation purposes, trading stock is defined as including anything produced, manufactured or acquired that is held for the purposes of manufacture, sale or exchange in the ordinary course of a business and livestock. Referred to as 'inventory' for accounting purposes.

QUESTIONS

9.1 What do you understand by the term 'tax accounting'?

9.2 When does a taxpayer 'derive' income? Is this the same rule for all taxpayers?

9.3 When does a taxpayer 'incur' a deduction? Is this the same rule for all types of expenses?

9.4 Briefly explain the prepayment rules? Are these the same rules for all taxpayers?

9.5 What is trading stock? When is trading stock on hand for taxation purposes?

9.6 How is trading stock assessed for taxation purposes?

9.7 How is trading stock valued at year-end for taxation purposes? Can a taxpayer choose a different value for each item of trading stock on hand at year-end?

9.8 When can a taxpayer choose to value their stock on hand at year-end at obsolete value? What guidelines exist to assist taxpayers in determining the obsolete value of stock?

9.9 What are the taxation consequences should the owner of a business take an item of trading stock from their business for their own personal use?

9.10 What are the taxation consequences should the owner of a business donate an item of trading stock from their business to a deductible gift recipient (DGR)?

9.11 What are the taxation rules relating to stock purchased where the parties (i.e. the buyer and seller) are not dealing at arm's length?

9.12 In what circumstances can a taxpayer claim a tax deduction for the prepayment of trading stock?

9.13 Briefly explain the small business entity trading stock provisions. Why would a small business enterprise wish to adopt the optional simplified trading stock rules?

PROBLEMS

9.14 A Sydney jewellery store recorded the following transactions on 30 June 2022.
  (a) Cash sales of $4000 (not including a $200 gift voucher in part (d)).
  (b) Credit card sales of $6500. However, the store did not receive payment until 3 July 2022.
  (c) A lay-by sale of $550. The customer paid the first instalment of $50 on 30 June 2022 and has 60 days to pay the final instalment of $500.
  (d) A gift voucher of $200 sold to a customer on 30 June 2022. The customer paid cash for the voucher. The gift voucher is valid for 12 months and can be redeemed towards the purchase of any item in the store. The gift voucher cannot be refunded. The customer redeems the gift voucher to buy a watch on 4 August 2022.

Required

For each of the mentioned transactions, determine what amount of income, if any, has been derived by the jewellery store during the income year ended 30 June 2022?

9.15 Dr Richardson runs a medical practice in the suburb of Geelong. Dr Richardson is a sole practitioner with Melissa, his medical receptionist, attending to a variety of administration tasks.

The following items relate to Dr Richardson's medical practice for the year ending 30 June 2022.

	$
Cash received from patients in 2022	180 000
Opening accounts receivable at 30 June 2021 (cash received during 2022)	16 000
Closing accounts receivable at 30 June 2022 (cash received during 2023)	12 000
Salary paid to Melissa during the 2022 income year	50 000

Required

Based on this information, what is Dr Richardson's taxable income for the year ended 30 June 2022 from his medical practice?

9.16 (a) Amelia receives her monthly Telstra mobile phone bill on 27 June 2022. Assume that Amelia uses the phone 75 per cent for business purposes. The amount of $100 is due for payment on 27 July 2022. Amelia pays her phone bill on 14 July 2022.
  (b) On what date has Amelia incurred the phone expense?
  (c) Frances works as a practising solicitor in her own practice in Geelong. On 30 June 2022, she receives tax invoices for a number of business-related expenses, including:
    – telephone expenses of $740
    – stationery expenses of $160
    – motor vehicle costs (consisting of fuel and oil) of $375
    – professional indemnity insurance premium renewal of $3800.

All these expenses were paid by Frances on 17 July 2022.

Required

On what date has Frances incurred each of the expenses?

9.17 Gigantor Ltd, a large business taxpayer, made the following payments during the 2022 income year.

(a) On 1 June 2022, the company paid its WorkCover insurance policy of $8000. This compulsory insurance, which protects employees in the event of a work-related injury, is an annual insurance policy and this renewal was for the period 1 July 2022 to 30 June 2023.

(b) On 21 June 2022, an employee is paid $22 000 in advance of taking three months maternity leave on half-pay. Their leave is to scheduled to start on 21 July 2022.

(c) On 30 June 2022, payment of a two-year subscription to a business magazine that costs $780.

(d) On 1 April 2022, interest of $144 000 was prepaid for a period of fifteen years in respect of a loan used to acquire business premises.

Required

What amounts are deductible (if any) in respect of each of the expenditure items for the 2022 income year? Please quote appropriate references to the ITAA36 and ITAA97 in your answer.

9.18 Discuss whether the following constitute trading stock for the purposes of Division 70 of the ITAA97.

(a) Unmined coal.

(b) Buses belonging to the Launceston City Council.

(c) Petroleum sold by a petrol station.

(d) Chocolate, drinks, magazines, newspapers and cigarettes sold by the same petrol station.

(e) Hotel rooms of a 5-star hotel.

(f) Wood used by a furniture manufacturer in making desks.

(g) A motor vehicle sold by a dentist that was used for business purposes in his dental surgery.

9.19 What are the taxation implications for the following trading stock transactions?

(a) A convenience store purchases soft drinks to be sold to customers.

(b) A convenience store sells chocolates to customers.

(c) A convenience store donates chocolates to the Salvation Army.

(d) The owner takes stock costing $800 for their own use. The market value of this stock at the time was $1100.

9.20 Computer Works Ltd is a computer retailer. It buys and sells personal computers and laptops. The company provides you with the following information for the year ended 30 June 2022.

	$
Sales	1 125 000
Purchases	880 000
Opening stock (at 1 July 2021)	65 000
Closing stock (at 30 June 2022)	46 000

Included in the $46 000 closing stock amount are laptop computers (costing $12 500) that were purchased from a supplier in China. At 30 June 2022, these computers are currently on board a ship from China. The terms of the shipment are FOB destination.

Required

Based on this information, calculate Computer Works Ltd's taxable income for the year ended 30 June 2022. Assume that Computer Works Ltd uses the periodic inventory system.

9.21 Charlotte runs her own computer retail business. A stocktake at 30 June 2022 revealed that she had the following closing stock on hand.

(a) Assuming that Charlotte wishes to minimise the taxable income of her business for the year ended 30 June 2022 (and she does not want to claim the small business concessions), calculate the value of her closing trading stock.

(b) Given an opening stock value of $225 600 at 1 July 2021, what amount is assessable/deductible to Charlotte's business in respect of the year ended 30 June 2022?

(c) Assume that during the 2022 income year Charlotte took a laptop computer costing $660 for her own personal use. The market value of the computer at that time was $1040. What amount (if any) is assessable to Charlotte's business?

(d) Assume that Charlotte donated an Apple iPad costing $500 to Lifeline, a deductible gift recipient (DGR) under Division 30 of the ITAA97. At the time of making the donation, the iPad had a market value of $730. What amount (if any) is assessable to Charlotte's business?

(e) Charlotte has just informed you that 8 of the 55 desktop computers on hand at 30 June 2022 are extremely out-dated due to technological advances. She estimates that these eight desktop computers will sell for only $800 each. Is there any relief available to Charlotte's business in determining the value of closing stock for these eight desktop computers? What will then be the revised value of the closing stock for the 55 desktop computers?

Item	Quantity	Cost ($)	Market selling value ($)	Replacement value ($)
Desktop computers	55	1 220	1 040	1 310
Laptop computers	120	740	1 190	960
Apple iPads	68	520	750	480
Computer accessories	176	150	200	185

ACKNOWLEDGMENTS

Tables 9.1, 9.3: © Australian Taxation Office
Extracts: © Federal Register of Legislation. Licensed under CC BY 4.0.
Extracts: © High Court of Australia

CHAPTER 10

Taxation of individuals

LEARNING OBJECTIVES

After studying this chapter, you should be able to:

10.1 analyse the tax implications of different types of income receipts of individual taxpayers

10.2 describe the basic types of deductions an individual taxpayer may receive

10.3 apply the basic tax offsets (rebates and credits) an individual may be entitled to in a given scenario

10.4 determine taxable income and calculate tax payable/refundable for an individual taxpayer.

Overview

This chapter consolidates some of the information outlined in previous chapters and specifically focuses on the tax implications of an individual receiving various types of income and deductions. In particular, it focuses on the taxation of employment income, dividend income, interest income, business income, property income, cryptoassets, trust income, royalties, and annuities. This chapter also covers the taxation of personal services income (PSI) received by individuals and employment termination payments (ETPs).

We then discuss the typical types of deductions available to individual taxpayers. Finally, the chapter outlines the main tax offsets (rebates/credits) that an individual taxpayer may be entitled to and how to determine taxable income and calculate tax payable/refundable on that income. Ethical issues in the taxation of individuals are also raised at the end of the chapter.

10.1 Income

LEARNING OBJECTIVE 10.1 Analyse the tax implications of different types of income receipts of individual taxpayers.

Individual taxation raises the most revenue for the tax authority in Australia.[1] Consequently, the taxation of various forms of income and the entitlement to tax deductions and/or tax offsets is critical for tax policy reasons. In an earlier chapter, we introduced the **income tax formula** and tax rates, levies and offsets. This chapter builds on that premise from the individual's perspective, incorporating all the various income types an individual might receive as part of their **assessable income**. From this figure, various **deductions** are subtracted to arrive at **taxable income**. The taxable income is then multiplied by the applicable **tax rate**, less any **tax offsets** to arrive **at tax payable/refundable**. To this figure is added any **charges** or **levies** (e.g. Medicare levy) to arrive at **net tax payable**. Within this fundamental tax framework, the balance of this part will deal with tax treatment of various possible types of taxable income receipts of individuals.

10.1.1 Employment income

When an employment or services relationship is established, payments/remuneration by way of cash or in kind (non-cash) can be made in return for services rendered. The critical factor is the connection or **nexus** between the payment and the service provided by the taxpayer. An example of judicial consideration of the concept of nexus between payment and service provided is the United Kingdom case of *Moorhouse v Dooland*.

Moorhouse v Dooland [1955] I All ER 93

Facts: A professional cricketer collected donations from the crowd for a meritorious performance in a game. The legal issue was whether there was a sufficient nexus between the payments and the service provided by the cricketer for the 'donations' to constitute assessable income. The taxpayer argued the donations were mere personal gifts, whereas the UK Tax Commissioners classified the donations as employment-related income.

Held: The Court held that the reason for the taxpayer receiving the payments was because of his profession as a cricketer, not because of his personal qualities. The collections were in truth and substance part of the earnings of the taxpayer's profession and could not fairly be called 'mere personal presents'. There was a strong nexus between the payment and the taxpayer's profession — particularly in light of the fact that the entitlement to the donations was recorded in the employment contract of the taxpayer.

Comment: The character of the sums received in these types of cases is to be judged in relation to the recipient rather than the giver. However, not every voluntary payment to an employee will be taxable and each case will be fact dependent.

This nexus between the payment and the professional service provided by the taxpayer is easier to establish in cases where the payment is by way of salary or wages or where the payment is made voluntarily and constitutes **ordinary income** and taxed under section 6-5 of the ITAA97. Clearly, in the case of a mere gift, there is a lack of nexus to employment and the gift would not be considered ordinary income. However, it is in between these two extremes, where many cases (like *Moorhouse v Dooland*) are uncertain.

---

1 Australian Taxation Office, *Commissioner of Taxation Annual Report 2018–2019* (Report, 2019) 48–49.

The employee may also be in receipt of statutory income for services rendered. Statutory income, as indicated previously, includes allowances, bonuses and gratuities which are received in the course of employment. Specifically, section 15-2 of the ITAA97 encompasses gains from employment and services that are not classified as ordinary income or fringe benefits. There are three requirements for amounts to be assessable under section 15-2.

1. Applies to cash or non-cash benefits.
2. Benefit must be 'provided' to the taxpayer.
3. Benefit must be 'in respect of, or for or in relation directly or indirectly to any employment or services rendered by the taxpayer'.

These three requirements mean that section 15-2 only applies in very specific situations. Example 10.1 demonstrates the application of sections 6-5 and 15-2.

EXAMPLE 10.1

Application of sections 6-5 and 15-2 — employment income

Paul Smith is an Australian resident and works as a sales representative for IPI Kitchen Appliances. Paul had a highly successful year where, in addition to his salary of $70 000, he received a car allowance of $8000 and a bonus for achieving the highest sales of the firm of a further $10 000.

What is Paul's employment income?

In this case, Paul's employment income would comprise his salary $70 000 (section 6-5 ITAA97), car allowance $8000 and the bonus of $10 000 (section 15-2 ITAA97) = total $88 000. Note that the bonus would not be subject to Fringe Benefits Tax as it is cash.

Practical tip: Make sure you understand the interaction between sections 6-5 and 15-2 and the fringe benefits tax when dealing with individual's receipts from their employer.

10.1.2 Business/contract/sharing economy income

Apart from taxpayers deriving income through traditional employment channels, the increase in various small businesses and sharing economy contractual arrangements involving services provided by individuals in recent years has created new and non-traditional income streams for self-employed individuals. This part briefly discusses the tax implications and treatment of payments made for these types of contractual and business arrangements.

10.1.2.1 Business/contract income/franchising

Individuals who are not salaried employees may also register for an Australian Business Number (ABN) and conduct a business enterprise. In order to successfully register for an ABN, the individual must demonstrate that they are in fact conducting a business as opposed to a hobby.[2] As discussed at length in an earlier chapter, there a number of indicators that the courts have used over the years that assist in deciding whether an individual is conducting a business activity. Each case must be determined on its own facts (see TR 2019/1) but there are a number of factors that have been referred to in various cases, which include:

- profit-making intention
- the size and scale of the activities including the nature and type of capital and level of turnover
- systematic and organised
- commercial or non-commercial approach
- sustained and frequent activity
- type of activity and type of taxpayer.

See *Ferguson v FCT* (1979) 9 ATR 873 and *FCT v JR Walker* (1985) 19 ATR 331.

There have been numerous cases (see *Trautwein v FCT* (1936) 56 CLR 196; *Stone v FCT* (2005) 59 ATR 50; *AGC Investments Ltd v FCT* (1992) 23 ATR 287; and *FCT v St Hubert's Island Pty Ltd* (1978) 8 ATR 452) which have looked at issues such as gambling, sportspeople, investment activities and land

---

2 There are some excellent tools and aids to assist in determining whether you are operating a business or merely a hobby. For example, see the tool at the Business.gov.au website: www.start.business.gov.au. The ATO also has a video discussing the differences, which is available online here: https://www.ato.gov.au/Business/Starting-your-own-business/In-detail/Tax-basics-for-small-business-video-series/?page=2#Are_you_in_business_.

sales respectively when deciding whether a business has been conducted. In all cases, it is a question of fact and degree and no one factor is determinative. A balancing of factors is required to work out the stronger case for either a business or a hobby. If this balancing exercise results in a business being in existence, the income generated is assessable and the expenses are deductible for tax purposes. In contrast, where a hobby is involved, the income will not be assessable and no expenses are deductible.

It should be noted that, where individuals are conducting contract work and have an ABN, they will need to be registered for goods and services tax (GST) where their turnover exceeds $75 000. Businesses with a turnover under the $75 000 threshold can still choose to be registered if they desire.

Another business venture that individuals may get involved in is franchising. Franchising is a business model where the franchisor controls the name, brand and business system that the individual franchisee can use. The franchisor grants the franchisee the right to run a particular type of business according to its system. A franchising Code of Conduct regulates the franchisors and franchisees to a 'franchise agreement', and stipulates the parties' behaviour and action under the agreement to act in good faith (see the *Competition and Consumer Act 2010* (Cth) (CCA)). There are pecuniary penalties and infringement notices for breaches of the Code and action can be taken by the ACCC where warranted. An example of a system franchise would be where a franchisor develops a unique manner of doing business and grants the right to the franchisee to use the system which may or may not include any trademarks, such as McDonald's, KFC and Pizza Hut franchises.

10.1.2.2 Sharing economy/crowd funding

In recent years, the world has seen an increase in casual labour and also the rise of the gig economy. In this regard, the general public connect with others via a digital platform (the internet or social media) to enter into various transactions, share resources and assets, and generally provide services and crowd funding (i.e. raising funds for a project or venture via members of the public).

Common examples of the sharing economy include renting accommodation through sites like Airbnb and Booking.com, and ride sourcing through Uber and GoCatch. Consequently, those individuals providing services through the sharing economy need to be mindful of their tax obligations, just as those who run more traditional businesses. The implications extend to GST and income tax. There may also be CGT implications for main residence concessions if private homes are being made available to the public — for example, in Airbnb-type arrangements (see later in this chapter).

The ATO's Black Economy Taskforce is monitoring those operators in the sharing economy that may not be declaring all their income which would be normally assessable. One of the key recommendations from the final report of the Black Economy Taskforce in 2017 was the introduction of a sharing economy reporting regime:

> Recommendation 6.2: A sharing economy reporting regime
>
> Operators of designated sharing ('gig') economy websites should be required to report payments made to their users to the ATO, DSS and other government agencies as appropriate. The Government should also continue to raise users' awareness about the potential tax obligations from participation in sharing economy activities.[3]

An important issue to note with regards to the sharing economy is the distinction between an employee and an independent contractor. This is not always easy to determine and will largely be a question of fact. A couple of tests that have been established over the years include the *integration test* — determining how much the individual is part of a business — and the *control test* — the degree of control a person has over the worker. The ATO has also released TR 2005/16 and established an employee/contractor decision tool[4] to assist taxpayers.

Some recent cases which also demonstrate the difficulty in deciding if a worker is an employee or contractor include delivery drivers who used motorcycles to deliver food and drinks as part of work in the gig economy (*Franco v Deliveroo Australia Pty Ltd* (2001) 73 AILR 103-313) and Uber drivers in the gig economy (*Kaseris v Rasier Pacific* (2017) FWC 6610; *Suliman Pacific Pty Ltd* (2019) FWC 4807).

Insofar as GST and tax implications are concerned, consider the following example of an Uber or similar ride-sharing arrangement driver.

---

3 Australian Government, *Black Economy Taskforce — Final Report* (Report, October 2017) 136. The full report is available at: www.treasury.gov.au/review/black-economy-taskforce/final-report.

4 The link to the employee/contractor decision tool is at: https://www.ato.gov.au/Calculators-and-tools/Host/?anchor=ECDTSGET& anchor=ECDTSGET/questions/ECDT#ECDTSGET/questions/ECDT.

EXAMPLE 10.2

Ride-sharing driver

Joel's main occupation is as a trainee accountant. In addition, on Friday evenings, Joel drives for Uber for some extra cash for his family. Uber is a 'ride-sourcing' provider. This is sometimes referred to as 'ride-sharing' — an ongoing arrangement where (a driver) makes a car available for public hire for passengers, and passengers use a third-party digital platform, such as a website or an app, to request a ride. The car is then used to transport the passenger for payment (a fare).

As a recipient of ride-sourcing income, Joel will need to pay income tax on this income. Ride-sourcing is also subject to goods and services tax (GST). Joel will need to have an Australian business number (ABN) and be registered for GST. He will need to add GST to the full fare charged to passengers as well as lodge business activity statements (BAS) monthly or quarterly and issue a tax invoice. He will also need to include the income he earns in his income tax return. Joel will only be able to claim deductions related to transporting passengers for a fare. This means he will have to apportion his expenses (e.g. fuel, car servicing and cleaning) to ensure that he only claims a deduction for the proportion of these expenses related to the time they are providing ride-sourcing services. He will need to keep records of all his expenses and income to substantiate his claimed deductions and declared income.[5]

Crowd funding also involves using the internet, social media and other platforms to find supporters to raise funds for a specific project or venture. These crowd funding arrangements can be conducted in a variety of ways, including donation-based, reward-based, equity-based or debt-based. Where payments are donation-based, no repayment is expected in return by the donor. However, supporters who receive merchandise, advertising rights, or goods and services in return for their payments (these are examples of different types of consideration received) thereby constitute the supply a taxable supply for GST purposes. Consequently, a donor will be entitled to an input tax credit if they are registered for GST to the extent the supply or payment was acquired for a creditable purpose. From an accounting perspective, it should be noted that under a crowd funding arrangement income may not be derived until a fundraising target is met or until goods or services are provided to the supporters.

10.1.3 Personal services income (PSI)

Personal services income (PSI) is income gained mainly as a reward for the personal skill and effort of an individual. Income that is derived by an entity (a company, trust or partnership) that is attributable to the personal efforts or skills of an individual will constitute PSI (see section 84-5(1) of the ITAA97). Divisions 84–87 of the ITAA97 expressly deal with the issue of individuals attempting to redirect PSI. The specific aims of this legislation are captured in sections 85-5 and 85-10. The former specifies that the aim of the legislation is to stop individuals (and, more particularly, employees) alienating their PSI (where that income is gained mainly as a reward for the personal efforts or skills of an individual) to an associated company, partnership trust or individual. Section 85-10 adds an additional objective of denying certain business deductions not normally available to employees.[6]

Where an individual has attempted to redirect PSI but is unable to establish they are operating a 'personal services business', they will be personally assessable on that income at their applicable tax rate, and they will be denied certain deductions normally not available to employees; for example, certain travel expenses, rent, mortgage interest, rates or land tax in relation to your premises (see sections 85-15, 85-20 and 85-25).[7]

The PSI provisions do not apply if:
- the income is not 'personal service income'
- the income is derived as part of a 'personal service business'.

The balance of this part discusses both of these requirements.

10.1.3.1 Is the income personal services income?

PSI is income gained mainly as a reward for the personal efforts or skills of an individual, rather than other business assets. For example, a company, XYZ Ltd, provides computer programming services through Mike, the individual who provides the service and who uses the client's equipment and software to do the

---

5 Australian Taxation Office, 'Ride-sourcing — what you need to know' (Web Page, 12 November 2019) www.ato.gov.au/General/The-sharing-economy-and-tax/In-detail/Ride-sourcing---what-you-need-to-know.

6 See also Draft TR 2021/D2 at: https://www.ato.gov.au/law/view/document?DocID=DTR/TR2021D2/NAT/ATO/00001#H79.

7 The ATO has issued a Taxation Ruling dealing with deductions that relate to personal service income and personal service business: Australian Taxation Office, *Income tax: personal services income and personal services business* (TR 2021/D2, 11 March 2021) www.ato.gov.au/law/view/document?DocID=DTR/TR2021D2/NAT/ATO/00001&PiT=99991231235958. See TR 2001/7 for the Commissioner's views on the application of the PSI rules generally.

work. The ordinary income of XYZ Ltd comprises Mike's personal efforts and skills. This income is PSI. On the other hand, where a trucking company provides a semi-trailer that transports goods, and John drives the truck, the ordinary income of the trucking company is derived from the use of the asset (semi-trailer), not from John's personal efforts and skills. The distinguishing difference is the greater use of the business assets in the trucking company case (see the examples in section 84-5.)

Key principle: Income that arises mainly from the supply or sale of goods, for granting a right to use property, or that is generated by an asset is not mainly a reward for personal efforts or skills, and as such is not PSI. Income that is gained by an entity (a company, trust or partnership) also referred to as a personal services entity (PSE) for the personal efforts or skills of an individual will be PSI.

The case of *Fowler v FC of T* (2008) ATC 2476 provides an example of judicial consideration of the distinction.

Fowler v FC of T (2008) ATC 2476

Facts: The taxpayer, a computer consultant, was the sole director and shareholder of DK Consulting Pty Ltd and its only employee. The company derived income from contracts entered into with labour hire firms. The contracts provided for the company to supply the taxpayer's services to end users in return for payment at an hourly rate. The taxpayer did all the work involved in providing the computer consultancy services to the end users and received a wage from the company. He normally carried out the work at the end users' premises, using their equipment and software.

The taxpayer returned less than the company income in his tax return and neither the company nor the taxpayer obtained a personal services business determination from the Commissioner during the relevant years. The Commissioner assessed the taxpayer on the PSI derived by the company (with some adjustments for deductions). The taxpayer appealed the Commissioner's decision.

Held: It was held that the amounts were PSI of the taxpayer, the amounts were ordinary income of the company, the company was a personal services entity, and the amounts were not income from the company conducting a personal services business.

Comment: The present case was a simple example of circumstances to which the PSI provisions apply. It should also be noted that contractors who operate through interposed entities where there is little if any business infrastructure or plant and equipment used to derive income of the entity could also be caught by the general anti-avoidance rule under Part IVA of the ITAA36.

10.1.3.2 Is there a personal services business?

As noted, the PSI rules do not apply to PSI that is income that is derived from conducting a personal services business (PSB).

An individual or personal services entity (PSE) conducts a personal services business (PSB) if:
- the individual or PSE has a **PSB determination** from the Commissioner of Taxation in force, or
- the individual or PSE satisfies the 'results test', or
- less than 80 per cent of the PSI is derived from a single source and the individual or PSE satisfies *one* of the other three PSB tests.

As alluded to previously, there are four personal services business tests. The results test requires:
- at least 75 per cent of the individual's PSI to be in return for producing a result (as opposed to working certain hours)
- the individual to supply their own equipment
- the individual to be liable for rectifying faults in their work.

If an individual or PSE satisfies the results test, they will be conducting a PSB.[8]
- The unrelated clients test requires the individual to derive income from two or more entities not related to each other.[9]

In *FC of T v Fortunatow & Anor*, the taxpayer failed to satisfy the unrelated clients test even though he maintained a LinkedIn profile which, he argued, was an advertisement of his services to the public. However, none of the taxpayer's clients made their decision to engage the taxpayer's services as a direct result of an offer or invitation constituted by the taxpayer's LinkedIn profile.
- The employment test requires the individual to employ one or more entities to perform at least 20 per cent (by market value) of the principal work on their behalf.[10]

---

8 See section 87-18; *Re Prasad Business Centres Pty Ltd and FC of T* (2015) ATC 10-396.
9 See section 87-20; *Yalos Engineering Pty Ltd v FC of T* (2010) ATC 10-139.
10 See section 87-25.

- The business premises test requires the individual to have business premises used *exclusively* to gain or produce PSI.[11]

The individual can only rely on the unrelated clients test, employment test, and business premises test if no one source provides more than 80 per cent of their income. Where more than 80 per cent of the PSI is received from one source, the individual must either satisfy the results test or obtain a determination from the Commissioner of Taxation in order to be a PSB. The operation of the PSI rules is summarised in figure 10.1.

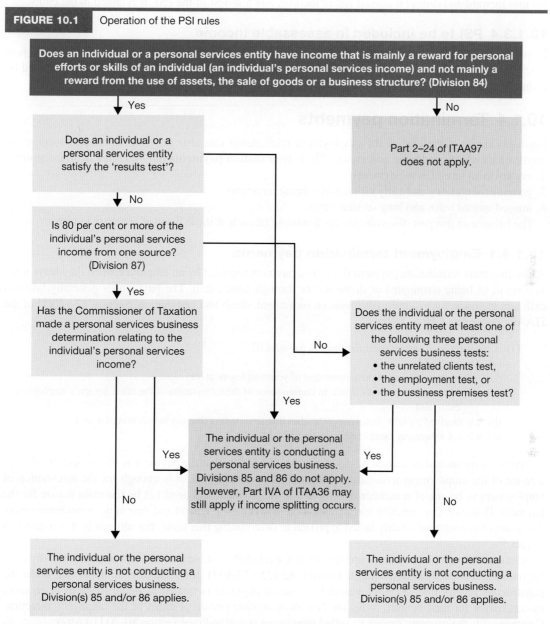

FIGURE 10.1 Operation of the PSI rules

Source: Australian Taxation Office, *Income tax: what is a personal services business* (TR 2001/8 31 August 2001) www.ato.gov.au/law/view/document?DocID=TXR/TR20018/NAT/ATO/00001.

10.1.3.3 Application of the PSI rules

As noted earlier, if an individual or PSE is not conducting a PSB, an individual's deductions against the PSI are limited. Any PSI of the PSE that is not paid as wages or salary to the individual who provides the service within 14 days after the end of the PAYG payment period will be attributed to and included in the assessable income of the individual. This amount may be reduced by the following.

---

11 See section 87-30; *Dixon Consulting Pty Ltd v FC of T* (2007) ATC 2550.

- *Personal service income deductions* — generally employee-like deductions such as the expenses of one car used exclusively for business purposes and one car with some private usage and superannuation (section 86-75).
- *Entity maintenance deductions* — such as bank and government charges, statutory fees and tax-related expenses, where these expenses have not first been offset against any non-PSI income derived by the PSE.

The individual (not the PSE) is entitled to deduct any net PSI loss that arises. The individual can carry the loss forward and deduct it against future income. Net non-PSI of the PSE is retained in the entity.

10.1.3.4 PSI to be included in assessable income

Figure 10.2 outlines the steps in the method statements set out in section 86-20(2) to work out by how much, if at all, the amount of PSI included in assessable income under section 86-15 can be reduced by deductions to which the PSE is entitled.

10.1.4 Termination payments

Payments made at the end of the employment relationship can also generate significant income tax implications which need to be understood. These **termination payments** fall into three main categories:
1. employment termination payments
2. genuine redundancy and early retirement scheme payments
3. unused annual leave and long service leave.

The balance of this part discusses the tax treatment of each of these types of payment in turn.

10.1.4.1 Employment termination payments

An employment termination payment (ETP) is a payment received by an employee when they leave a job as a result of being terminated or dismissed or through resignation. The payment is generally taken in cash and includes, for example, payments on retirement, death and resignation. Section 82-130(1) of the ITAA97 defines an ETP as follows.

> (1) A payment is an employment termination payment if:
>   (a) it is received by you:
>   (i) in consequence of the termination of your employment, or
>   (ii) after another person's death, in consequence of the termination of the other person's employment, and
>   (b) it is received no later than 12 months after that termination (but see subsection (4)), and
>   (c) it is not a payment mentioned in section 82-135.

The key requirement of section 82-130(1) of the ITAA97 is that the payment is 'in consequence' or as a result of the employment termination. To satisfy this requirement, it is enough for the termination of employment to be one of a number of reasons for the payment and need not be the main reason for the payment. However, there must be some connection between the payment and the employment termination. The courts have adopted a fairly broad approach to determining this issue, but ultimately it is a question of fact.[12]

A number of types of payments are specifically excluded — these include capital payments, dividend payments and superannuation benefits (section 82-135 ITAA97). It should also be noted that under the constructive receipt rule, an employment termination payment is treated as being made to or received by a taxpayer for their benefit, or for the benefit of another person or entity at the taxpayer's direction. Consequently, the payment cannot be rolled over into a superfund (see section 80-20 ITAA97).

From this definition in section 82-130(1) of the ITAA97 it is clear that there are two types of ETP.
1. **Life benefit termination payments**. Payments to an individual former employee who is still alive.
2. **Death benefit termination payments**. Payments to a relative of the former employee who has died. Each has its own tax rules.

---

12 See *Reseck v FCT* (1975); *McIntosh v FCT* (1979).

FIGURE 10.2 Calculating PSI

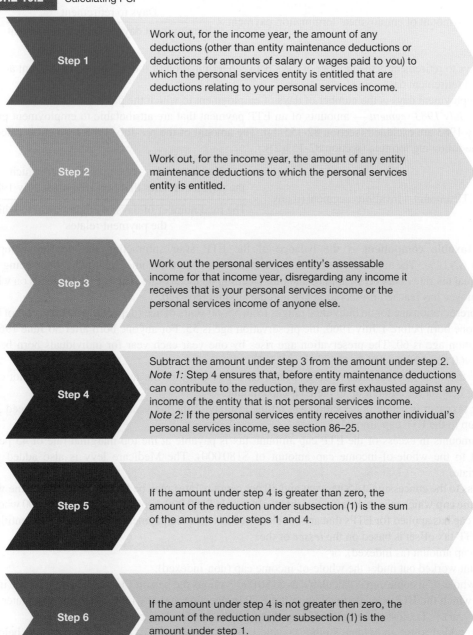

Step 1 Work out, for the income year, the amount of any deductions (other than entity maintenance deductions or deductions for amounts of salary or wages paid to you) to which the personal services entity is entitled that are deductions relating to your personal services income.

Step 2 Work out, for the income year, the amount of any entity maintenance deductions to which the personal services entity is entitled.

Step 3 Work out the personal services entity's assessable income for that income year, disregarding any income it receives that is your personal services income or the personal services income of anyone else.

Step 4 Subtract the amount under step 3 from the amount under step 2.
Note 1: Step 4 ensures that, before entity maintenance deductions can contribute to the reduction, they are first exhausted against any income of the entity that is not personal services income.
Note 2: If the personal services entity receives another individual's personal services income, see section 86–25.

Step 5 If the amount under step 4 is greater than zero, the amount of the reduction under subsection (1) is the sum of the amunts under steps 1 and 4.

Step 6 If the amount under step 4 is not greater then zero, the amount of the reduction under subsection (1) is the amount under step 1.

Note 1: Step 4 ensures that, before entity maintenance deductions can contribute to the reduction, they are first exhausted against any income of the entity that is not personal services income.
Note 2: If the personal services entity receives another individual's personal services income, see section 86-25.

Source: Federal Register of Legislation, *Income Tax Assessment Act 1997*: Section 86-20(2) (Web Page, 12 November 2021) https://www.legislation.gov.au/Details/C2021C00534.

10.1.4.2 Life benefit termination payment

A life benefit termination payment consists of both tax-free and taxable components (section 82-10).

The **tax-free component** comprises:

1. *An **invalidity segment*** — amounts related to a person's ill health or permanent disability as a result of a work injury are excluded (section 82-150(1)). Only that part of the ETP that compensates a person for the years of gainful employment that are lost due to ill health are included in the invalidity segment.

This is calculated by the following formula (section 82-150(2)):

$$\text{Amount of employment termination payment} \times \frac{\text{Days to retirement}}{\text{Employment days} + \text{Days to retirement}}$$

where:
- days to retirement is the number of days between termination of the person's employment and their last retirement day
- employment days is the number of days of employment to which the payment relates.

2. *A pre-July 1983 segment* — amounts of an ETP payment that are attributable to employment prior to 1 July 1983 are excluded (section 82-155(1)). The amount of the pre-July 1983 segment is calculated by the following formula (section 82-155(2)):

$$\big[\text{ETP amount} - \text{Invalidity segment (if any)}\big] \times \frac{\text{Number of days of employment to which the payment relates that occurred pre-1 July 1983}}{\text{The total number of days of employment to which the payment relates}}$$

The **taxable component** is the balance of the ETP after subtracting the tax-free component (section 82-145). The taxable component constitutes assessable income, but rather than being taxed at marginal tax rates a tax offset applies and puts a ceiling on the tax rate. The tax rate depends on whether the employee has reached preservation age and the amount received.[13]

The preservation age for an individual ranges from 55–60 years of age (depending on their year of birth). For anyone born before 1 July 1960, the preservation age is 55. For anyone born after 30 June 1964, the preservation age is 60. The preservation age rises by one year each year for individuals born between 1 July 1960 and 30 June 1964.

- If the taxpayer has reached preservation age on the last day of the tax year — tax does not exceed 15 per cent on the amount up to the ETP cap amount.[14]
- If the taxpayer is below preservation age on the last day of the tax year — tax does not exceed 30 per cent up to the ETP cap amount.

For amounts in excess of the ETP cap amount, tax is payable at the top marginal rate of 45 per cent (subject to the whole-of-income cap amount of $180 000). The Medicare levy is also added where appropriate.

Access to the concessional 15 per cent and 30 per cent tax rates may be further restricted by the **whole-of-income cap** which means the effective threshold is only $180 000. From 2012–13, a $180 000 whole-of-income cap has applied for ETPs that are not classified as excluded payments. For these ETPs, entitlement to the ETP tax offset is based on the *lesser* of the:

- ETP cap amount (as indexed), or
- amount worked out under the whole-of-income cap (non-indexed).

The whole-of-income cap is calculated as $180 000[15] minus the person's taxable income for the income year in which the ETP is made (excluding the ETP in question and any other ETPs received later in the income year).[16] Tax losses are ignored in working out the whole-of-income cap.

When added to the individual's other taxable income, the amount of the ETP equal to or below the whole-of-income cap is eligible for the ETP tax offset, while any amount over is taxed at 45 per cent.

Example 10.3 demonstrates calculation of the amount of tax payable on an ETP.

EXAMPLE 10.3

Tax payable on an ETP

Tony Chappell was employed by the same employer for 40 years. He retired on 30 June 2022 at age 69 and received an ETP of $500 000.

What is the tax payable on the ETP?

---

13 ITAA97 sections 82-10(2)–(4).
14 $225 000 for the 2021–22 tax year indexed annually — see section 82-160.
15 This amount is not indexed.
16 Sections 82-10(4)–(5).

There is no invalidity segment, so the tax-free component will include only a pre-July 1983 segment. The tax payable is calculated as follows.

The Pre-July 1983 segment = Pre-July 83 days/Total number of days of employment

730 days/14 610 days = 0.05 × $500 000 = $25 000 Pre-July 83 component

The taxable component, therefore, is $500 000 – $12 500 = $487 500. The whole-of-income ETP cap of $180 000 will apply. Tony pays tax at 15 per cent on the first $180 000 (i.e. $27 000) and at 45 per cent on the balance $307 500 ($487 500 – $180 000) = $138 375. Therefore, Tony's total tax liability is $165 375 + Medicare levy.

The whole-of-income cap does not apply to any life benefit termination payment that qualifies as an excluded payment, such as a genuine redundancy, an early retirement scheme or an invalidity segment (section 82-10(6)). This includes a genuine redundancy payment received by a taxpayer over the age of 65, even though they are not entitled to the specific genuine redundancy tax concessions. For example, if a taxpayer, aged 64 years, received a genuine redundancy payment (excluded payment) of $250 000 and had no other income in the 2021–22 tax year, in these circumstances the redundancy payment would be subject to the ETP cap. Consequently, the first $225 000 for the 2021–22 tax year would be concessionally taxed at 15 per cent, with the balance of $25 000 taxed at 45 per cent.

10.1.4.3 Death benefit termination payment

A death benefit termination payment (section 82-130(1)(a)(ii) of the ITAA97) must be received within 12 months of termination unless the Commissioner of Taxation determines otherwise.

The death benefit termination payment is made up of a tax-free component and taxable component. The tax-free component comprises the invalidity segment, and the pre-July 1983 segment which is non-assessable, non-exempt income.

Where a death benefit termination payment is paid to a dependant of the person who has died,[17] the taxable component is included in the recipient's assessable income (excluding the amount below the ETP cap amount, which is non-assessable, non-exempt income (see section 82-65(2)(a)). Above the cap, the payment is taxed at 45 per cent (plus Medicare levy). Where a death benefit termination payment is paid to a non-dependant, the taxable component of the payment is included in the recipient's assessable income and taxed at a maximum rate of 30 per cent up to the ETP cap amount and at 45 per cent for the amount exceeding the cap (plus Medicare levy).

10.1.4.4 Genuine redundancy and early retirement scheme payments

A genuine **redundancy payment** occurs where the:[18]
- employee has genuinely been made redundant
- employee has received a payment after being dismissed
- payment exceeds the amount that could reasonably be expected to be received if the employee had voluntarily terminated their employment.

An **early retirement scheme payment** is payment for termination of employment as part of a Commissioner-approved scheme to rationalise or re-organise the employer's operations (section 83-180).

Additional conditions attached to both these types of payments are:
- the employee must be dismissed before they reach 65 years of age
- the payment represents what would be payable under a normal commercial arrangement, and
- there is no arrangement or agreement at the time of dismissal that the employee be re-employed by the employer (see TR 2009/2).

Genuine redundancy and early retirement scheme payments are not ETPs themselves but rather consist of a tax-free amount up to a certain threshold that is non-assessable non-exempt income.

This is calculated as:[19]

Base amount + (Service amount × Years of service)

---

17 ITAA97 section 302-195.
18 Section 83-175(1); see *Weeks v Commissioner of Taxation* [2013] FCAFC 2.
19 Section 83-170(3).

The base amount and service amount are indexed annually.[20] For the 2021–22 tax year, the base amount is $11 341 and the service amount is $5672. The years of service is the number of whole years of employment.

Any amount above the threshold may constitute an ETP and be broken up into its pre and post components and taxed accordingly. If not an ETP, the balance will be taxed at marginal rates.

Calculation of the tax-free and taxable amounts of a redundancy payment is demonstrated in example 10.4.

EXAMPLE 10.4

Tax-free and taxable amounts of a redundancy payment

Sally White worked for her employer for 22 years. On 30 June 2022, her employer closed down Sally's department and she was dismissed, receiving a $175 000 genuine redundancy payment.

What is the tax-free amount and the taxable amount of the redundancy payment?

The tax-free amount is $11 341 + ($5672 × 22) = $136 125.

If the conditions in section 82-130 of the ITAA97 are satisfied, the excess amount of $38 875 ($175 000 – $136 125) is assessable as an ETP. Otherwise, $38 875 would be included in assessable income and taxed at marginal rates without any ETP concessions.

10.1.4.5 Unused leave payments

Upon termination of employment, the employee will also usually receive a lump sum payment for any annual leave or long service leave (LSL) that is still owing to them. The tax treatment of paid out unused leave varies depending on the type of leave.

10.1.4.5.1 Unused annual leave

Generally, unused annual leave payments are included in the taxpayer's assessable income in the year it is received and taxed at marginal rates (section 83-10(2) of the ITAA97).

However, if one of the following exceptions applies, the maximum rate of tax that can apply is 30 per cent (plus Medicare levy):

- where the payment is made in connection with the invalidity segment of an ETP or superannuation benefit, a genuine redundancy payment or an early retirement scheme payment (section 83-15)
- where the payment is in respect of employment before 18 August 1993.
  This amount is calculated as:

$$\text{Payment} \times \frac{\text{Number of days in accural period that occured before 18 August 1993}}{\text{Number of days in the accrual period}^{\dagger}}$$

† Number of days over which annual leave accrued: TD 94/8.

10.1.4.5.2 Unused long service leave

Unused long service leave payment accrued since 15 August 1978 is included in the taxpayer's assessable income. Any of this leave accumulated on or before that date is included only to the extent of 5 per cent of the amount of the payment (see section 83-80).

A tax offset ensures a maximum rate of tax of 30 per cent (plus Medicare levy) applies to unused long service leave payments when the payment[21] relates to employment between 16 August 1978 and 17 August 1993, is the invalidity segment of an ETP or superannuation benefit, or is a genuine redundancy or early retirement scheme payment.

Unused long service for the pre-18 August 1993 period or the post-17 August 1993 period is calculated as:[22]

$$\text{Amount of payment} \times \frac{\text{Unused long service leave days in the relevant period}}{\text{Total unused long service leave days}}$$

Example 10.5 demonstrates the principle of how this is applied.

---

20 Subdivision 960-M. In 2021–22, the base amount was $11 341 and the service amount was $5672 in 2021–22.
21 Section 83-85.
22 Section 83-95(2).

Unused annual leave and LSL

On 30 June 2022, after 35 years service with his employer, Ross Davis leaves his employment and is paid an amount of $40 000 annual leave relating to the period post 1993 and a sum of $23 000 for LSL relating to the period 1985 to 1993.

How will the payments be assessed?

In these circumstances, the annual leave of $40 000 is fully assessable and will be taxed at marginal tax rates, while the LSL accrued to 1993 will be fully assessable but capped at a tax rate of 30 per cent plus Medicare levy.

10.1.5 Dividend income

Dividend income basically comprises distributions made by a company to its shareholders in either cash or kind (generally ordinary shares) (section 6(1) of the ITAA36). Importantly, dividends paid out of company profits are assessable income (section 44 of the ITAA36) and not a return of capital to shareholders. Primarily, the taxation of dividends will depend on whether the taxpayer is a resident or non-resident and whether the dividend is franked, partly franked or unfranked. The word 'franked' basically means the dividend has been subject to taxation; that is, the company profits from which the dividend came have already been taxed once.

10.1.5.1 Resident taxpayers

Consequently, where a resident taxpayer receives a franked dividend from a resident Australian company, they must include both the dividend and a grossed-up franking credit (the tax paid by the company is imputed to the shareholders) in their assessable income. To alleviate the situation of double taxation (i.e. both the company and the shareholder paying tax on the same dividend) the resident taxpayer will receive a franking credit/tax offset for the tax already paid by the company which will directly reduce the taxpayer's tax payable/refundable. If the dividend received is only partly franked, then the resident taxpayer will receive only a partial franking credit. If the dividend is unfranked, there will be no entitlement to a franking credit.

It should be noted that in the situation where a resident individual taxpayer has received a dividend from a non-resident company, the individual will need to include in their tax return both the amount of the dividend and the amount of any foreign/withholding tax paid. To prevent double taxation, the taxpayer will receive a credit for the *lower* of foreign tax paid or Australian tax payable on that dividend. For example, if you have received $1000 in dividends and paid $100 in foreign tax on those dividends while the Australian tax payable was $150, then your credit will only be $100.

Example 10.6 demonstrates the tax treatment of dividend income.

Dividend income of a resident taxpayer

During the 2021–22 tax year, an Australian resident individual receives the following dividends.

Australian resident companies		$
TAB Bank	Fully franked dividend	4 000
Franking credit	($4000 × 1/70%/30%)	1 714
Akon Ltd	Unfranked	6 000

Foreign company		$
PQ Ltd	Net amount received ($5000 × 85%)	4 250
	Foreign tax withheld ($5000 × 15%)	750

What is the tax treatment of this income?

Assessable income		$	$
TAB Bank	Dividend received	4 000	
	Gross-up for franking credit	1 714	5 714.00
Akon Ltd	Unfranked dividend		6 000.00
PQ Ltd	Amount received	4 250	
	Gross-up for foreign tax	750	5 000.00
Assessable income from dividends			16 714.00
Tax on dividend income (assume a marginal tax rate of 45%)			7 521.30
Less: Tax offsets			
	Franking credit ($4000 × 1/70%/30%)	1 714	
	Foreign tax paid	750	2 464.00
Tax payable on dividend income (excluding Medicare levy)			5 057.30

Note: The gross-up rate is based on the standard corporate tax rate of 30 per cent.

10.1.5.2 Non-resident taxpayers

Non-resident taxpayers who receive fully franked dividends will just need to include the actual dividend in their assessable income with no franking credit and no witholding tax obligations (sections 128B(3)(ga) and 128D of the ITAA36)). Where the dividend is partly franked or unfranked, withholding tax will be paid on the unfranked portion only at the rate of 30 per cent or 15 per cent, depending on whether the country involved is a treaty country with Australia. There is no further tax payable on the dividend (section 128D). This is demonstrated in example 10.7.

EXAMPLE 10.7

Dividend income of a non-resident taxpayer

Claire Owens, a resident of the United Kingdom, received the following distributions from Australian companies during the 2021–22 tax year:
- $2700 distribution on 1 August 2021 from Tintin Ltd, on which 15 per cent withholding tax had been paid
- $2000 fully franked distribution on 1 September 2021 from XYZ Pty Ltd
- $1000 unfranked distribution on 1 February 2022 from RST Ltd
- $1500 fully franked distribution on 1 March 2022 from TOLL Ltd.

Describe the assessability of these distributions for Claire for the 2021–22 tax year.

As a non-resident of Australia, Claire is subject to section 128D of the ITAA36, and so is only assessed on distributions paid out of Australian-source profits (section 44(1)(b)). Unfranked distributions are subject to withholding tax and then excluded from assessable income by the operation of section 128D. Franked distributions are not subject to withholding tax (section 128B(3)(ga)) and are excluded from assessable income as if they had been subject to withholding tax (section 128D). Consequently, Claire would not be assessed on any of the distributions she received as a non-resident other than the unfranked distribution of $1000 from RST Ltd which would be subject to 15 per cent withholding tax of $150 as the UK is a tax treaty country with Australia. Claire would receive the balance of $850 which is excluded from assessable income. (Withholding tax calculation: $850 dividend/1 – w/tax rate of 15% = $850/85% = $1000 original dividend.)

10.1.6 Interest income

Most people think of interest income as interest paid on a bank account, but the nature of 'interest' is that it is considered to be the cost of borrowing money. If interest is incurred in the course of borrowing money for a business purpose, then it is generally considered to be deductible. Conversely, if interest is generated in the course of doing business or an individual had earned interest upon an investment, then that interest is generally considered ordinary income and assessable under section 6-5 of the ITAA97. In *Ritches v Westminster Bank* (1947), interest is described as 'a payment which becomes due because the creditor has not had his money at the due date'.[23]

---

23 *Ritches v Westminster Bank* (1947) AC 390, 400.

The taxation of interest will depend on specific timing issues and the possibility that, in some cases, it could be treated as capital and not assessable.

Interest includes the familiar interest paid by banks and other financial institutions on customers' deposits, but also includes a range of less-familiar payments. These include interest credited to the taxpayer by the ATO, interest on compensation payments, interest paid after receiving a favourable court judgement, and interest earned from overseas sources.

Lomax v Peter Dixon & Son Ltd [1943] 1 KB 671 examined the distinction between interest as ordinary income and capital return.

Lomax v Peter Dixon & Son Ltd [1943] 1 KB 671

Facts: An English taxpayer lent money to an associated Finnish company prior to World War II. Despite a high level of risk associated with the loan, the interest rate charged was comparable to commercial rates. However, the borrower had to pay both a premium and discount on the debt.

The Commissioner contended that the discount and premium were income in the hands of the taxpayer lender. The taxpayer contended they were capital receipts.

Held: The Court agreed with the taxpayer and held that the discount and premium were capital in nature and not interest. Key reasons for this decision were that a commercial rate of interest was charged on the loan and that the taxpayer was not in the business of money lending. The Court also highlighted the distinction between interest as ordinary income as opposed to a capital return which reflects a premium or discount for risk.

Comment: From the judgement, it should be noted that a reasonable commercial rate of interest on the loan is sound security and there is no presumption that a 'discount' or a premium at which it is payable is in the nature of interest. It will ultimately depend on all the circumstances (including the contractual relations) and be largely a question of fact.

The outcome may have been different if the taxpayer in *Lomax* had been in the business of money lending rather than an individual. Consider an investment company that had realised some of its investments and, in doing so, purchased some investments where no actual interest was paid but instead, on maturity, received a payment equal to the value of the investment — comprising 10 per cent more than the original amount invested. In this situation, the 10 per cent increase in value is a notional return on the original amount invested. This gain would be assessed as ordinary income, and treated as a substitute for interest rather than an increase in capital value.

10.1.7 Royalties income

Royalties are a type of property income in which a person receives payments for granting another the right to use their patents or other intellectual property. For example, the authors of a book receive royalties for the use of their intellectual property based on sales and usage of the book. This is a common arrangement. Essentially, the authors agree to sell their intellectual property in return for an amount based on its usage.

Another common situation where royalty payments are made is where someone is paid to produce items using a registered patent or design (e.g. payments to the Coca-Cola company in return for the licence to make and distribute the distinctively shaped Coca-Cola bottles in Australia), or for the supply of scientific, technical, industrial or commercial knowledge or information, or film and video recordings (see Taxation Ruling IT 2660).

A further common example arises where a taxpayer is paid for their physical resources based on the quantity of resources taken. A typical example of the latter is where oil rich land is owned by the taxpayer and a mining company pays a certain amount for every barrel of oil that is extracted from the land.

Royalty payments generally constitute ordinary income. They can be periodic, irregular or one-off payments and, under section 6-5 of the ITAA97, are generally only assessable when actually received. Royalties that are a product of exploiting intellectual property arguably constitute ordinary income.

However, royalties can also be assessable under section 15-20 as statutory income. For instance, payments for physical resources may constitute capital royalties. See *Stanton v FCT* for a good example of the tax treatment of royalties in this context.[24] If a royalty is of a capital nature, the CGT provisions also need to be considered.

---

24 *Stanton v FCT* (1955) 92 CLR 630.

> **Stanton v FCT (1955) 92 CLR 630**
>
> **Facts:** The taxpayer was a farmer who granted a sawmiller a right to income from his land and to remove timber in exchange for a predetermined sum paid quarterly. An agreement that a prescribed maximum amount of the timber to be removed was also noted where only a percentage was paid depending on the quantity removed.
>
> **Held:** It was held that the payments received by the farmer were of a capital nature and not assessable as royalties. The rationale was based on the fact that the agreement expressed the payment as a set lump sum amount despite being connected to the timber removed.
>
> **Comment:** Based on the judgement, the critical point is the definition of a 'royalty' which, in this context, describes payments made by a person for the right to enter upon land for the purpose of cutting timber of which he becomes the owner, where those payments are made in relation to the quantity of timber cut or removed. The point of the definition appears to lie in a requirement that the payments should be made to the landowner in relation to the quantity of timber cut or removed in pursuance of a right to do so. The right is an asset which is of a capital nature.

By way of contrast with the *Stanton* case, consider the following example.

Anne is a dairy farmer. Jack runs a sawmill and lumber business. Part of Anne's farm comprises heavy wooded land with trees suitable for milling for timber on it. Anne enters into an agreement with Jack, permitting him to cut down and take the trees from her land. The agreement indicates that Jack would pay Anne an amount based on the quantity of the timber cut and removed from the land. The payment received by Anne in this case would constitute a royalty, as the payment is directly related to the quantity of timber removed. See *McCauley v FCT* (1944) 69 CLR 235 for a broadly similar case example. This situation can be distinguished from the *Stanton* case where the amount of the payment was not variable dependent on the amount of timber removed.

It should be noted that while royalties received by residents are assessable under sections 6-5 or 15-20, for non-residents, any royalties derived from Australian sources will be subject to withholding tax at a rate of 30 per cent but depending on the tax treaty with other countries, the rate can be reduced to either 10 per cent or 5 per cent. After the payment of withholding tax, the non-resident has no further tax liability.

10.1.8 Trust investment income

Trusts can take many forms and the trust property can comprise both income and capital elements. As we shall see in a later chapter, the trustee is responsible for managing the trust estate on behalf of the beneficiaries and as the trust is not a separate legal entity, it is the trustee and/or the beneficiaries who will be liable to pay tax on the trust income whether they received the income or not.

Assessable income and credits received from any trust investment products must be declared in the individual's tax return including:

- cash management trust
- money market trust
- mortgage trust
- unit trust
- managed fund, such as a property trust, share trust, equity trust, growth trust, imputation trust or balanced trust.[25]

Managed investment trusts (MIT) are a common investment vehicle for individuals — see Division 275 and section 275-100 of the ITAA97. Individuals will receive a distribution advice or statement from an MIT in which they have invested which indicates the information required to complete their tax return. This information includes income and capital gains from the trust and any capital gain or loss upon disposal of any trust units by them during the relevant tax year.

Individuals can also claim credits for tax paid on or withheld from trust income distributed to them (including any foreign resident withholding tax if applicable). Taxpayers can also claim deductions for an interest in a trust that made a loss from primary production activities.[26]

---

25 Australian Taxation Office, 'Managed investment trusts' (Web Page, 1 July 2021) https://www.ato.gov.au/Individuals/Investments-and-assets/Managed-investment-trusts.

26 Australian Taxation Office, 'Trust capital gains and losses' (Web Page, 1 July 2021) https://www.ato.gov.au/Individuals/Investments-and-assets/Managed-investment-trusts/#Trustincomeandcredits.

Example 10.8 illustrates the tax treatment of income distributed by a trust to individual taxpayers — for similar and further examples and explanations of key concepts, such as present entitlement and legal disability in a trust context, see the chapter on the taxation of partnerships, joint ventures, trusts and superannuation entities.

EXAMPLE 10.8

Income distributed by a trust

The Rich family trust received the following income from investments for the year ended 30 June 2022: rental income, interest income, and both franked and unfranked dividends. Assume the trustee resolved to distribute the income equally to the following beneficiaries:

- Anne Rich, aged 40 (no other income)
- Tony Rich, aged 21 (no other income)
- Mark Rich, aged 15 (at school, no other income).

What is the taxation of each of the beneficiaries for the 2021–22 tax year?

After determining net trust income: Anne Rich, as a beneficiary presently entitled and not under any legal disability, would be assessed on her share of this amount under section 97 including her share of any imputation credits from the franked dividends. This would also be the case for Tony Rich. Mark Rich, being under 18 years, is under a legal disability, meaning the trustee will be assessed on his share of the income on his behalf.

10.1.9 Real property income

There are various forms of property from which income is derived. These include royalties, interest and dividends, discussed earlier, and income derived from real property which includes rental and lease income. The tax treatment of rent and lease income is the focus of this section.

Rent is a payment or the cost of having exclusive use of another person's property. The payment of rent from a lessee to a lessor constitutes ordinary income from property in the hands of the lessor.

In addition to the rent itself, related payments may include booking fees, payments for short-stay accommodation organised via a sharing economy platform (e.g. Airbnb), insurance pay-outs to the lessor as compensation for unpaid rent, and reimbursement of otherwise deductible expenditure such as repairs.

In some cases, property receipts may take a non-cash form (e.g. accommodation provided in return for live-in housekeeping services). In these cases, a taxpayer must include the cash equivalent of any of these 'in-kind' payments. For example, in the case of accommodation in return for live-in housekeeping services, the taxpayer must declare the value of the housekeeping services as assessable income.

Where a taxpayer has an interest in the ownership of a rental property business (either on their own or jointly with others), their share of the income generated is assessable income. A residential tenancy bond (essentially a security deposit commonly payable by renters and reimbursable at the end of the lease if the property is returned in acceptable condition and there are not rental arrears owing) is not regarded as income and its refund is not a deduction. However, if bond money is used for repairs then it becomes income and the cost of the repairs becomes a deduction.

Note that, while properties are rented, the interest on any loan to fund the purchase or improvement of the property can be claimed as a deduction. Where there is an excess of the interest deduction over the actual rental income, the property is 'negatively geared'. Likewise, when a rented property is sold there are potential capital gains tax implications.

Example 10.9 demonstrates the tax treatment of rental income.

EXAMPLE 10.9

Rental income

Russell Tate rents out two properties in inner-city Melbourne and charges a monthly rent of $3000 on each property. Russell's rental property expenses included repairs of $5000, leasing fees paid to the real estate agent of $1500 and loan interest on both properties of $12 000.

What is the tax treatment of these amounts?

The net property income Russell should declare in the 2021–22 tax year would be calculated as follows.

	$	$
Rental income [2 × ($3000 × 12)]		72 000
Less: Expenses		
Repairs	5 000	
Leasing fees	1 500	
Loan interest	12 000	18 500
Net property income		53 500

10.1.10 Cryptoassets

Following the taxation of real property income as distinct from the taxation implications of disposing of the property itself (see the chapter on capital gains tax), consideration needs to be given to cryptoassets as an area of increasing popularity amongst individual taxpayers in recent years.

TECHNOLOGY IN ACTION

Taxation implications of 'airdrops'

Taxpayers may acquire cryptoassets through what is referred to as an 'airdrop'. These occur when cryptoassets are deposited into a wallet address, generally without requiring any payment.[27] Airdrops may be announced or unannounced and often reflect a marketing technique (e.g. to create awareness, reward users, balance ownership, attract investment etc.).[28] Recipients may be required to hold a certain level of, or undertake a particular action, to be eligible.[29]

An example of an airdrop is the UNI token airdrop in September 2020 by Uniswap. Uniswap is a popular decentralised exchange (DEX) for cryptoassets. At the time the token was launched, 400 UNI tokens were airdropped to recipients who had used the Uniswap platform.[30]

The tax consequences, according to the Commissioner's guidance, are as follows (assuming this is a non-business taxpayer).

1. The recipient derives the value of the airdropped cryptoassets as ordinary income; and,
2. The recipient acquires a CGT asset, being the airdropped cryptoassets, with a cost base equating to the market value of the airdropped asset.[31]

The value of the UNI token at the time of the drop was approximately $28 per unit and, by November 2021, its value had risen to approximately AUS $30 per unit.[32] As such, applying the Commissioner's guidance: (1) a taxpayer in receipt of the UNI token airdrop derived income of AUS $800 (2 × 400); and (2) had acquired a CGT asset with a cost base of $800. At the time the taxpayer is airdropped the cryptoassets, there is no CGT event. Rather, a CGT event and potential capital gain/loss is crystalised on disposal of the CGT assets (the airdropped cryptoassets). If the taxpayer sold the UNI tokens in November 2021 for $1500, what would the taxpayer include in their 2021–22 income tax return?

A tax practitioner needs to ensure they clarify all crypto-related activities with their clients, including any airdropped cryptoassets, and clearly document their respective treatment. The pre-filled tax return is unlikely to provide a complete picture of a taxpayer's crypto-economic activity. A taxpayer may not even be aware they are recipients of airdrops! Taxpayers and practitioners need to also be wary of airdrop scams. Airdrops may be dropped to a broad number of wallets, with the aim to carry out phishing or cyberattacks.[33]

---

27 Morton and Curran, 'Crypto-donations and tax deductibility' (2021) 25(2) *The Tax Specialist*, 54, 55.
28 Ibid.
29 Ibid.
30 Werner Vermaak, 'What are crypto airdrops?', Coinmarketcap.com (Web Page) https://coinmarketcap.com/alexandria/article/what-are-crypto-airdrops.
31 Australian Taxation Office, 'Staking rewards and airdrops' (Web Page, 30 March 2020) https://www.ato.gov.au/general/gen/tax-treatment-of-crypto-currencies-in-australia—specifically-bitcoin/?anchor=Transactingwithcryptocurrency#Stakingrewardsand airdrops.
32 'Uniswap', Coinmarketcap.com (Web Page) https://coinmarketcap.com/currencies/uniswap.
33 Dan Finlay, 'Phisher Watch: Airdrop Scams' *Medium* (Web Page, 27 September) https://medium.com/metamask/phisher-watch-airdrop-scams-82eea95d9b2a.

REFLECTION

On what principles of tax law does the Commissioner conclude that the receipt of an airdropped cryptoasset will be deriving ordinary income?

10.1.11 Annuities

An annuity is a regular, periodic (not necessarily annual) payment of money for a fixed period or until the death of the recipient (the annuitant). Non-superannuation annuities are included in the assessable income of a taxpayer under section 27H of the ITAA36.

A non-superannuation annuity is:
- an annuity
- a pension paid from a foreign superannuation fund, or
- a pension paid from a scheme that is not:
  - a qualifying security under Division 16E and is not
  - a superannuation income stream (section 27H(4) ITAA36).

Any amount of the taxpayer's own capital that is included in the annuity payments is excluded from the taxpayer's assessable income using the 'recovery of capital exclusion' formula.

A deduction is available for the undeducted purchase price (UPP); that is, the proportion of each annuity payment that represents a return of capital for which the annuitant has not previously obtained a tax deduction. Note that upon the taxpayer's death the annuity becomes payable to the taxpayer's **spouse**, and they are able to claim a deduction in respect of the UPP.

The calculation of the deductible amount is determined by the formula given in section 27H(2) of the ITAA36:

… the deductible amount in relation to an annuity derived by a taxpayer during a year of income is the amount (if any) ascertained in accordance with the formula, $\dfrac{A \times (B - C)}{D}$, where:

A is the relevant share in relation to the annuity in relation to the taxpayer in relation to the year of income.
B is the amount of the undeducted purchase price of the annuity.
C is:
    (a) if there is a residual capital value in relation to the annuity and that residual capital value is specified in the agreement by virtue of which the annuity is payable or is capable of being ascertained from the terms of that agreement at the time when the annuity is first derived — that residual capital value; or
    (b) in any other case — nil; and
    D is the relevant number in relation to the annuity.

Note that D will be one of the following.
- The number of years the annuity is payable (e.g. 10 years).
- The life expectancy in years of the annuitant.
- The number that the Commissioner considers appropriate, having regard to the number of years during which the annuity may reasonably be expected to be payable.

Example 10.10 demonstrates the use of the recovery of capital exclusion formula.

EXAMPLE 10.10

Recovery of capital exclusion formula

Michael Jones, aged 71, purchased an annuity on 1 January 2022 with the following features.
- The annuity will pay Michael $22 000 a year until his death.
- Upon Michael's death, the $22 000 a year annuity will be paid to his wife Elizabeth until her death.
- Upon Elizabeth's death a lump sum of $30 000 (capital amount) will be paid to their son.

Michael paid an undeducted purchase price of $75 000 for the annuity. Michael's life expectancy is 9 years and Elizabeth's is 15 years on the date the annuity first becomes payable.

What amount should be included in Michael's assessable income?

▶

The deductible amount is calculated using the recovery of capital exclusion formula.

$$A \times \frac{(B - C)}{D}$$

$$1 \times \frac{(\$75\,000 - \$30\,000)}{15} = \$3000$$

Consequently, $19 000 (Annuity $22 000 – Deductible amount $3000) should be included in Michael's assessable income each year under section 27H(1).

10.2 Individual deductions

LEARNING OBJECTIVE 10.2 Describe the basic types of deductions an individual taxpayer may receive.

Up to now, this chapter has covered issues of assessable income of an individual. Earlier chapters provided for a thorough discussion of both general and specific deductions, non-deductibles and substantiation requirements. Consequently, the focus of this section of the chapter is upon the more *common deduction issues* faced by individual taxpayers as a result of their employment. In this regard, the first part of this section will focus upon the critical distinction between employees and independent contractors. This will be followed by a brief overview of the deductibility of the main employment-related expenditure. The deductibility of income protection/insurance and personal superannuation contributions will also be briefly covered.

10.2.1 Distinction between employees and independent contractors

When examining the deductibility of expenditure under section 8-1 of the ITAA97, it is noted that the first positive limb requires that the '*expenditure be incurred in gaining or producing assessable income*', while the second positive limb requires the '*expenditure to be necessarily incurred in carrying on a business for the purpose of gaining or producing your assessable income*'. Consequently, while the first positive limb applies to individual taxpayers (employees are generally not carrying on a business), the second positive limb does apply to business taxpayers which includes those individuals who are operating as independent contractors. Therefore, it is critical to distinguish whether the taxpayer is an employee or independent contractor as the entitlement to particular deductions will be entirely different.

An employer–employee relationship will generally only exist where there is a master–servant relationship between the payer and the payee. The **integration test** and the **control test** can be used to determine whether this relationship exists.

10.2.1.1 The integration test

The integration test examines whether the:
- individual is an integral part of the principal's business organisation
- individual is restricted to providing service to one principal
- benefits arising from the work flow to the principal.

    If any of these are satisfied, then an employer–employee relationship likely exists.

10.2.1.2 The control test

It is commonly suggested that a *contract of service* points to an employment relationship whereas a *contract for services* points to an independent contractor relationship. The control test examines whether an individual's work[34] is substantially subject to the control and direction of the person for whom the contract is being performed. The right to control how, where, when and who is to carry out particular work is usually strong evidence of an employer–employee relationship.

---

34 *World Book (Australia) PTY LTD v FC of T* 92 ATC 4327.

10.2.1.3 Other relevant factors

Nevertheless, it is necessary to examine all relevant factors defining the relationship between the parties. Mason J, in the High Court decision in *Stevens v Brodribb Sawmilling Co. Pty Ltd*,[35] said:

> Other relevant matters include, but are not limited to, the mode of remuneration, the provision and maintenance of equipment, the obligation to work, the hours of work and provision for holidays, the deduction of income tax and the delegation of work by the putative employee.

Other relevant cases which assist in deciding whether an individual is an employee or contractor include: *World Book Australia* (1992); *Roy Morgan Research Centre Pty Ltd v Commr of State Revenue (Vic)* (1997)[36]; and *Hollis v Vabu* (2001)[37]. Ultimately it is a question of fact and degree and no one factor is conclusive, but rather it is See TR 2005/16 for further discussion of the ATO's views on the factors to consider. Note the Commissioner of Taxation has released a Decision Impact Statement regarding the implications of the High Court decision in *Construction, Forestry, Maritime, Mining and Energy Union v Personal Contracting Pty Ltd* [2022] HCA 1.

EXAMPLE 10.11

Employee or independent contractor?

Joan Maiden is contracted by use of her own resources and the resources of others to sell books on behalf of a bookseller, World Book Pty Ltd. The terms of the contract specify that Joan is authorised to act by herself or through her approved employees as a selling agent for the bookseller and she is entirely free to choose the areas in which, and the times at which, she solicits purchasers for the product. She is also free to employ whatever legal style or method of selling she deems suitable. The bookseller has no right to direct or control Joan in any respect whatsoever.

Is Joan an employee or an independent contractor?

Joan is an independent contractor, as the contract is not wholly or principally for the agent's labour but rather for achieving a result, being the sale of books. This situation highlights the important distinction between a contract of services (employee) and a contract for services (independent contractor).

10.2.2 Employment-related expenditure

This section discusses the deductions available in situations where the taxpayer is an employee rather than an independent contractor. Table 10.1 presents some typical employment-related expenditure and its deductibility under the tax legislation.

TABLE 10.1   Typical employment-related expenditure deductions

Expenditure	Deductibility
Car expenses (ITAA97 Division 28)	Deductible — if used for employment purposes.
Entertainment (ITAA97 Division 32)	Not deductible, except in limited circumstances. An entertainment expense incurred in providing a fringe benefit is deductible.
Occupational clothing (ITAA97 Division 34)	Not deductible unless the clothing is a uniform or protective. In limited circumstances, deductible if extra expense is incurred necessary for the occupation of the taxpayer.
Gifts (ITAA97 Division 30)	Generally deductible provided the donation is made to a deductible gift recipient (DGR) and made voluntarily and without an expectation of something in return.

---

35 *Stevens v Brodribb Sawmilling Co. Pty Ltd* (1986) ATR 160 CLR 16.
36 *Roy Morgan Research Centre Pty Ltd v Commr of State Revenue (Vic)* (1997) ATC 5070.
37 *Hollis v Vabu Pty Ltd* (2001) ATC 4508.

10.2.3 Income protection/insurance

Individual employees are usually covered by workers compensation if they are injured at work. As the lost salary would have normally been assessable as ordinary income under section 6-5, the compensation payment that replaces this salary is also income. This is consistent with the replacement principle which was introduced and discussed in the chapter on assessable income tax (see *FC of T v DP Smith*[38] and *Somers Bay Investment Pty Ltd v FC of T*).[39]

Likewise, where an employee takes out income protection insurance, the nexus test indicates that the insurance premium paid would be a deductible expense under section 8-1 as it is revenue, not capital, in nature. If the insurance benefit includes a capital component, then the premium related to the capital component will not be deductible.

To be deductible, the employee must pay the premium themselves (income protection insurance premiums deducted from superannuation contributions are not deductible).

Other types of insurance premiums, such as life insurance and trauma insurance, do not directly replace income and are not deductible.

10.2.4 Personal superannuation contributions

The deductibility of personal superannuation contributions under section 290-150 of the ITAA97 for both employees and the self-employed is discussed in detail in the taxation of partnerships chapter. For individuals, it is noted that the concessional contributions capped amount is $27 500 in 2021–22.

10.3 Individual tax offsets

LEARNING OBJECTIVE 10.3 Apply the basic tax offsets (rebates and credits) an individual may be entitled to in a given scenario.

Once deductions are subtracted from assessable income to arrive at the taxable income, an individual taxpayer may be entitled to certain tax offsets which can reduce their potential tax payable. While tax offsets can take the form of both rebates and credits, they are generally available to recognise tax already paid (relief from double taxation), to provide subsidies or incentives, or as a concession to cap income tax rates. Most tax offsets while reducing tax payable will not result in a refund. It should also be noted that the term 'offset' and 'rebates or credits' are used interchangeably and mean the same thing. The term 'rebates or credits' is used in particular parts of the *Income Tax Assessment Act 1936* that has not been rewritten by the *Income Tax Assessment Act 1997* which uses the term 'offset'.

An earlier chapter briefly looked at the tax formula of which tax offsets were part. In this chapter, the focus is upon those tax offsets that are commonly available and used by individual taxpayers. Specifically, this section discusses the dividend tax offset, the superannuation tax offset, and the foreign income tax offset. This is then followed by a discussion of the main concessional tax offsets including: dependant (invalid carer) (DICTO), private health insurance, low (LITO) and low and middle-income tax offset (LMITO) and the zone rebate.

10.3.1 Dividend tax offsets

The dividend imputation system is discussed in a later chapter. Following the premise that distributions of dividends out of post-taxed profits from companies to its shareholders effectively means that both the company and the individual shareholder pay tax on the same income. To relieve the situation of double taxation, a tax offset is allowed to the individual taxpayer equal to the tax paid by the company on its profits (section 207-20 ITAA97). The dividend tax offset is a refundable tax offset (section 67-25).

The operation of the dividend tax offset is demonstrated in example 10.12.

---

[38] *FC of T v DP Smith* (1981) ATC 4114.
[39] *Somers Bay Investment Pty Ltd v FC of T* (1980) ATC 4411.

Dividend tax offset

Rex Dowling is a shareholder in RIP Pty Ltd. During the 2021–22 tax year, RIP made substantial profits and was subject to company tax of 30 per cent upon the profits. RIP made a distribution of a fully-franked dividend from after-tax profits to Rex of $4000.

What franking credit is Rex entitled to on the dividend received?

The tax offset (franking credit) is calculated as ($4000 × 1/70%/30% × 100% = $1714).

10.3.2 Superannuation tax offsets

Note from the chapter on superannuation that super contributions are taxed in the super fund prior to the benefits being paid to individual members. When the benefits are paid to members, they are either concessionally taxed or tax-free depending on the age of the recipient and whether it comes from a taxed or untaxed source. The concessional tax treatment of the superannuation payments arises as a result of the availability of superannuation tax offsets, that effectively prevent double taxation of the income that was already taxed in the super fund.

In particular, section 301-20 of the ITAA97 for superannuation lump sums ensures that the taxable component is taxed at 0 per cent up to the low rate cap amount and the remainder above the cap is taxed at only 15 per cent. Likewise, section 301-115 of the ITAA97 for a superannuation lump sum for untaxed elements in the fund, amounts are taxed at only 30 per cent up to the untaxed plan cap amount with the remainder taxed at the top marginal rate of 45 per cent.

10.3.3 Foreign income tax offsets (FITO)

Recall from an earlier chapter, that Australian residents are taxed on world-wide income; that is, sources both inside and outside Australia. Where the resident taxpayer has been subject to tax on income both in Australia and overseas, the taxpayer will generally receive a foreign income tax offset (FITO) which is limited or capped to the amount of Australian tax payable on the relevant income (section 770-75 ITAA97). According to section 770-15(1), *foreign income tax* is defined as tax that 'is imposed by law other than an Australian law' and is a tax on income, profits or gains, whether of an income or a capital nature, or any other tax that is subject to a tax agreement.

It should be noted that any unused foreign income tax offset is not refundable, or transferrable, and cannot be carried forward to future years. To determine the amount of the tax offset initially involves calculating the amount of foreign income tax paid on the foreign income amount included in assessable income (section 770-75). If the amount of the foreign tax paid *is $1000 or less*, the taxpayer can simply claim the amount of the tax paid as a tax offset without having to work out the Australian tax payable in respect of the foreign income or work out the offset cap. However, if the foreign tax paid exceeds $1000, the taxpayer can either claim a $1000 tax offset with any excess being wasted or calculate the offset cap.

The offset cap is calculated as follows.

- The amount of (Australian) income tax payable by the taxpayer for the income year less the amount of tax that would have been payable if the assumptions in section 770-75(4) were made. The assumptions are that the assessable income excluded amounts that were subject to foreign income tax and any other ordinary or statutory income from a non-Australian source and that the taxpayer was not entitled to any debt deductions or other deductions that relate to the excluded income.
- The offset limit would then be the difference between the amount of Australian tax payable and the amount of the offset cap.

Foreign Income tax offset

Jessie Hogan, an Australian resident for tax purposes, was working as a travel agent in Singapore for his employer Flight Centre, for a period of 3 months during the 2021–22 tax year, deriving $20 000 which was subject to $6500 in foreign tax. For the remaining 9 months of the 2021–22 tax year, Jessie derived a further $60 000 in salary on which $16 000 PAYG tax was paid, $4000 in rental income, and earned $2000 of bank interest. Assuming Jessie claimed $800 of work-related deductions and was not entitled to any other deductions or tax offsets, what is his entitlement to a FITO?

Asessable income	$
Foreign income	20 000
Australian salary	60 000
Rental	4 000
Interest	2 000
Total assessable income	86 000
Less: Deductions	800
Taxable income	**85 200**

Tax payable on $85 200 at the 2021–22 tax rates is $18 157 + $1700 Medicare levy = $19 857.

The Australian tax payable (excluding the $20 000 foreign income) plus Medicare is $12 961 which is the cap. Consequently, the difference is $19 857 less the $12 961. Jessie gets a FITO for the difference of $6896 or in the case the maximum credit is the actual foreign tax paid of $6500.

10.3.4 Common concessional tax offsets

While it is not possible to discuss all the tax offsets potentially available to a taxpayer, the following tax offsets are the ones that are commonly available to resident individual taxpayers in the 2021–22 tax year.

10.3.4.1 Dependant invalid carer tax offset (DICTO)

The dependant tax offset is non-refundable and is specifically referred to as the dependant (invalid and carer) tax offset (DICTO) in Subdivision 61-A, section 61-1 of the ITAA97. The offset is available to taxpayers who are maintaining certain types of **dependants** who are genuinely unable to work due to invalidity or carer obligations and who are in receipt of specified disability support, special needs disability support, or invalidity service pensions (section 61-10). These dependants include the taxpayer's spouse, parent or spouse's parent, and children over 16 years who are Australian residents (section 61-10).

There is an income test that limits the adjusted taxable income (ATI) of the taxpayer and the taxpayer's spouse to $100 900 in 2021–22 (section 61-20). No tax offset is available where their income exceeds this amount. Adjusted taxable income is different to taxable income and specifically comprises the *total* of the following:

- taxable income
- reportable employer superannuation contributions (RESC)
- deductible personal superannuation contributions
- total net investment loss from financial investments (e.g. shares) and rental properties
- adjusted fringe benefits (i.e. generally the grossed-up value of reportable fringe benefits)
- income from certain tax-free pensions and benefits from Department of Human Services or Veterans' Affairs
- income from a foreign source that is exempt in Australia *less* the annual amount of any child support paid by the taxpayer.[40]

The maximum amount of the DICTO for 2021–22 is $2833 and this amount is indexed in line with the CPI each year (section 61-30). Uniquely, this maximum tax offset reduces according to the income of the dependant who is being supported by the taxpayer. Specifically, the maximum offset reduces by $1 for every $4 for which the dependant's ATI exceeds $282 (excluding any disability support or service pensions received by the dependant (section 61-45)). Consequently, the tax offset cuts out where the ATI of the dependant is $11 614. Note that a taxpayer will not be entitled to the offset where either they or their spouse is in receipt of the Family Tax Benefit (Part B) (section 61-25).

---

40 CPA Australia, *Module 6 Semester 2* (CPA, 1st ed, 2019) 46.

Example 10.14 demonstrates application of the DICTO.

DICTO

Katie Mason and her spouse Paul have lived together for the entire 2021–22 tax year. Katie's adjusted taxable income for the year was $80 000 in salary. Paul had an adjusted taxable income of $7800, made up of interest income and a disability pension. The Masons are not eligible for Family Tax Benefit Part B.
  What is Katie's DICTO entitlement?
  Katie is entitled to a DICTO of $954, calculated as follows.

	$
Maximum DICTO available for 2021–22	2 833
Less: Reduction for Paul's ATI (¼ × ($7800 – $282))	1 879
Offset	954

10.3.4.2 Low-income tax offset (LITO)

Resident individual taxpayers whose taxable income is below $37 500 in the 2021–22 tax year are entitled to a maximum of $700 non-refundable tax offset (rebate) (section 61-110 ITAA97). The rebate is reduced by 5 cents in the $1 for taxable incomes between $37 500 and $45 000 and then reduced by 1.5 cents in every $1 where taxable income is between $45 000 and $66 667. Eventually, the offset cuts out when taxable income reaches $66 667. Note that minors with unearned income are ineligible for the rebate but the offset can be used in respect of employment income (section 159N(3)). The offset cannot be used to reduce the Medicare levy.
  Example 10.15 demonstrates the application of LITO.

LITO

Tim Jenkins has a taxable income of $41 000 for the 2021–22 tax year.
  What is Tim's LITO entitlement?
  His entitlement to a LITO is calculated as follows.

	$
Low-income rebate before reduction	700
Less: Reduction in rebate based on TI ($41 000 – $37 500 × 0.05)	175
LITO entitlement	525

The amount of LITO from 2021–22 is presented in table 10.2.

TABLE 10.2 LITO rebate

Taxable income	Rebate
<$37 500	$700 rebate
$37 500–$45 000	$700 less 5% of the excess over $37 500
$45 000–$66 667	$325 less 1.5% of the excess over $45 000

Source: Federal Register of Legislation, 'Income Tax Assessment Act 1997: Subdivision 61D, section 61-115', https://www.legislation.gov.au/Details/C2021C00534.

10.3.4.3 Cost of living tax offset

In the 2022 Federal Budget delivered on 29 March 2022, the government announced that, with effect from the 2021–22 tax year, a new $420 cost of living tax offset has been introduced. This cost of living tax offset has been incorporated into the low and middle-income tax offset and will work in the same way as the low and middle-income tax offset.

Taxpayers with taxable incomes between $48 000 and $90 000 will receive the full $420 cost of living tax offset.

Taxpayers with taxable income above $90 000 will lose entitlement to the full $1500 low and middle-income tax offset, including the cost of living tax offset, by 3% for each $1 of taxable income above $90 000. For example, a taxpayer with a taxable income of $95 000 will be entitled to the new low and middle-income tax offset, including the new cost of living tax offset of $1500 less ($5000 × 0.03) = $1500 − $150 = $1350.

Taxpayers with taxable incomes of $125 999 will be eligible for the $420 cost of living tax offset but $0 low and middle-income tax offset. Taxpayers with taxable incomes of $126 000 and above will not be eligible for any entitlement to the cost of living tax offset nor the low and middle-income tax offset.

Taxpayers with taxable incomes between $37 001 and $48 000 will be entitled to a portion of the low and middle-income tax offset and cost of living tax offset of $1500 based on the following formula: $675 + 7.5 cents for each $1 > $37 000.

Taxpayers with taxable incomes of up to $37 000, will be eligible for the low and middle-income tax offset plus the cost of living tax offset of $655. This new cost of living tax offset has already been legislated.

10.3.4.4 Low and middle-income tax offset (LMITO)

The low and middle-income tax offset was introduced in 2018–19 (Subdivision 61-D, section 61-105) and is set to apply for 4 years, including the 2021–22 tax year. The tax offset is available to resident taxpayers (and certain trustees), is not automatically indexed, and is not refundable. Entitlement to the LMITO is in addition to the existing LITO. The amount of the rebate is presented in table 10.3. The rebate cuts out where taxable income exceeds $126 000. Note that the Treasury Laws Amendment (Cost of Living Support and Other Measures) Bill 2022 increased the LMITO for the 2021–22 tax year.

TABLE 10.3   **LMITO rebate**

Taxable income	Rebate
<$37 000	$675 rebate
$37 000–$48 000	$255 rebate + 7.5 cents for each $ > $37 000
$48 000–$90 000	$1500 rebate
$90 000–$126 000	$1500 rebate less 3% of the amount of the income that exceeds $90 000
>$126 000	Nil

Source: Federal Register of Legislation, 'Income Tax Assessment Act 1997: Subdivision 61D, section 61-107(1)' (Web Page, 12 November 2021) https://www.legislation.gov.au/Details/C2021C00534. See also Commonwealth of Australia, *Budget 2022–23: Budget Paper No 2* (29 March 2022), 24–25; The Treasury, 'Treasury Laws Amendment (Cost of Living Support and Other Measures) Bill 2022' (Media Release, 29 March 2022).

Example 10.16 demonstrates application of the LMITO.

EXAMPLE 10.16

LMITO

Sandra Treloar has a taxable income of $91 000 for the 2021–22 tax year.
   What is Sandra's LMITO?
   Her entitlement to a LMITO is calculated as follows.

	$
Low-middle income rebate before reduction	1 500
Less: Reduction in rebate based on TI ($91 000 – $90 000 × 0.03)	30
LITO entitlement	1 470

For the 2022–23 and later years, it is proposed that both the LITO and LMITO will be replaced with a new low-income tax offset. Also note that in the Treasury Laws Amendment (Cost of Living Support and Other Measures) Bill 2022 a one-off payment of $250 became available for eligible pensioners, welfare recipients, veterans and concession cardholders who are Australian citizens. The payment is tax exempt and will not count as income support.

10.3.4.5 Private health insurance tax offset

To assist taxpayers with the cost of rising private health insurance premiums, a tax offset is available via direct payment or a taxpayer can apply for reduced health insurance premiums (Subdivision 61-G and section 61-205 ITAA97). Where more than one person is covered by the policy, the rate of rebate will be based on the age of the oldest person. Generally, two conditions must be satisfied for an individual to be eligible for the tax offset. First, the individual (or the individual's employer if providing a fringe benefit) must pay a premium in respect of a 'complying health insurance policy'. Second, the premium must be paid in the same income year that it is claimed as an offset, although premiums may in some cases be paid in advance.

The rebate is means tested and will depend on an individual's income for surcharge purposes and is equal to the sum of:
- taxable income (excluding any assessable first home super saver released amount)
- reportable fringe benefits
- reportable superannuation contributions
- net investment losses
- _less_ any taxed superannuation benefit that qualifies for a tax offset under section 301-20(2) of the ITAA97.

The private health insurance tax offset is means tested and is based on a three-tiered level, summarised in table 10.4.

TABLE 10.4   **Private health insurance tax offset means test**

Income thresholds for 2021–22				
	Base ($)	Tier 1 ($)	Tier 2 ($)	Tier 3 ($)
Singles	0–90 000	90 001–105 000	105 001–140 000	Over 140 000
Families	0–180 000	180 001–210 000	210 001–280 000	Over 280 000
Rebate available for 1 July 2021 to 31 March 2022				
	Base	Tier 1	Tier 2	Tier 3
Aged under 65 years	25.059%	16.706%	8.352%	0%
Aged 65–69 years	29.236%	20.883%	12.529%	0%
Aged 70 years or over	33.413%	25.059%	16.706%	0%

(continued)

TABLE 10.4 *(continued)*

Rebates available for 1 April 2022 to 30 June 2022				
	Base	Tier 1	Tier 2	Tier 3
Aged under 65 years	24.608%	16.405%	8.202%	0%
Aged 65–69 years	28.710%	20.507%	12.303%	0%
Aged 70 years or over	32.812%	24.608%	16.405%	0%

Source: Australian Taxation Office, 'Income thresholds and rates for the private health insurance rebate' (Web Page, 1 April 2022) https://www.ato.gov.au/Individuals/Medicare-and-private-health-insurance/Private-health-insurance-rebate/Income-thresholds-and-rates-for-the-private-health-insurance-rebate

Example 10.17 demonstrates application of the private health insurance offset.

EXAMPLE 10.17

Private health insurance offset

Paul Couch, aged 54, paid a health insurance premium of $2500 to a private health fund on 1 October 2021 for one year's family hospital and ancillary cover in advance. Paul is married with two children, and his family's adjusted taxable income for 2021–22 tax year was $123 000. Paul's wife is aged 52.

Under what circumstances would Paul be entitled to a private health insurance tax offset for the year ended 30 June 2022 and what would the offset be?

Paul will be entitled to the offset in accordance with section 61-205 of the ITAA97, subject to Subdivision 61-G conditions being met. These include the requirement that the premium be paid in respect of a 'complying health insurance policy', such as one that provides hospital cover and/or ancillary cover, and also that the premium be paid in the same income year that it is claimed as an offset.

As Paul is under 65 years and family adjusted taxable income is less than $180 000, the calculation would be the base tier of $2500 premium × 273 days/365 days × 29.236% = $546.67.

10.3.4.6 Zone rebate

A zone rebate is available to individuals who are residents of specified remote areas of Australia (section 79A of the ITAA36). Remote areas in both Zone A and Zone B include west and north of mainland Australia and Tasmania and central Australia. Zone A includes areas that are isolated, have harsh climates and a high cost of living, as compared to Zone B areas. Consequently, the rebate is higher for Zone A residents, but each zone also comprises special categories for residents in isolated areas. The ATO website has extensive lists of the various remote locations in each State and Territory.[41]

To qualify for the rebate, the taxpayer must have lived or worked within a zone for 183 days or more in an income year not necessarily continuously, although some exceptions can apply. Where a taxpayer satisfies the residency tests for more than one area, the taxpayer is entitled to the greater rebate for which he/she qualifies.

The rebate is calculated as the sum of a 'basic amount', plus a percentage of the 'relevant rebate amount', being the total of the rebates for the income year for DICTO ($2833) and certain other notional tax offsets (e.g. sole parent $1607, student offsets $376) to which the taxpayer is entitled.

Each other non-student child after the first non-student child under the age of 21 and living with the taxpayer adds $282 to the relevant rebate amount.

Table 10.5 shows the zone rebate levels for 2021–22.

---

41 The ATO provides an Australian Zone list: https://www.ato.gov.au/calculators-and-tools/australian-zone-list.

TABLE 10.5 Zone rebate levels for 2021–22

Ordinary Zone A	$338 + 50% of relevant rebate amount*
Special Zone A	$1173 + 50% of relevant rebate amount*
Ordinary Zone B	$57 + 20% of relevant rebate amount*
Special Zone B	$1173 + 50% of relevant rebate amount*

* The relevant rebate amount for 2021–22 includes the following:

- amounts for dependents who are unable to work as a result of invalidity or carer obligations, who are entitled to the DICTO of $2833 (subject to a maximum ATI of $11 614)
- any notional child or student rebate of $376 (subject to a dependent's maximum ATI of $1786) (section 79A(2)).

Source: Federal Register of Legislation, 'Income Tax Assessment Act 1936: Section 79A(2)' (Web Page, 2 November 2021) https://www.legislation.gov.au/Details/C2021C00470.

Example 10.18 demonstrates application of the zone rebate.

EXAMPLE 10.18

Zone rebate

Myers, his wife Jenny, aged 38, and his children Jack, aged 4, and Melissa, 8, resided in ordinary Zone A for the whole of the 2021–22 tax year. Myers maintains Jenny, Jack and Melissa. Melissa attends school. Jenny's ATI was $5400 for the year.

What is Myer's zone rebate?

	$
Notional dependent spouse rebate ($2833 – (¼ × ($5400 – $282)) (ignore cents)	1 553
Notional dependant rebate — one student	376
Notional child rebate — first child, not being a student	376
Relevant rebate amount	2 305

Myer's ordinary zone A rebate is, thus, $338 + 50% of $2305 = $1490.

10.4 Individual tax rates, levies and charges

LEARNING OBJECTIVE 10.4 Determine taxable income and calculate tax payable/refundable for an individual taxpayer.

An earlier chapter introduced the income tax formula and this has been specifically examined in this chapter from the individual's point of view. After determining assessable income less deductions and arriving at taxable income, prior to the application of any tax offsets, the amount of tax payable and exposure to any additional levies/charges needs to be determined. In this regard, the final section of the chapter outlines the current tax rates for the 2021–22 tax year, the Medicare levy and other potential charges for individual taxpayers.

Figure 10.3 expands on this outlining the sequence to be followed. After deriving assessable income and subtracting allowable deductions, the taxpayer has their taxable income. From that, they need to apply the correct marginal tax rate, which is presented in the following section, to determine gross tax payable. From this, non-refundable tax offsets (most offsets) are applied and then the Medicare levy and Medicare levy surcharge if any, as well as any other debts are added. Then the remaining refundable offsets (the franking credit and the private health insurance offset) are applied. The last step is to deduct any tax already paid by, or amounts credited to, the individual taxpayer from the resulting sum to determine the *total amount of tax payable or tax refund due.*

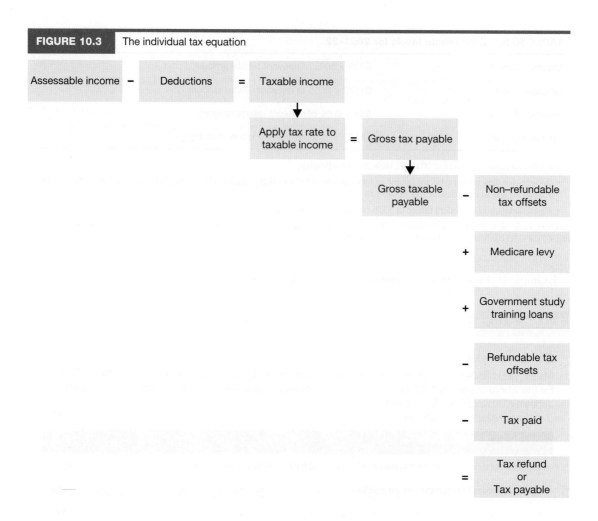

FIGURE 10.3 The individual tax equation

10.4.1 Tax rates

Individual income tax is charged at a progressive rate according to the level of taxable income.

Table 10.6 presents the rates for Australian resident individuals for the 2021–22 tax year, exclusive of the Medicare levy.

TABLE 10.6 Resident tax rates 2021–22

Taxable income	Tax on this income
$0–$18 200	Nil
$18 201–$45 000	19c for each $1 over $18 200
$45 001–$120 000	$5092 plus 32.5c for each $1 over $45 000
$120 001–$180 000	$29 467 plus 37c for each $1 over $120 000
$180 001 and over	$51 667 plus 45c for each $1 over $180 000

Source: Australian Taxation Office, *Individual income tax rates* (Web Page) www.ato.gov.au/rates/individual-income-tax-rates.

Table 10.7 presents the rates for individuals who are foreign residents for tax purposes for the 2021–22 tax year. Foreign residents do not pay the Medicare levy.

TABLE 10.7	Foreign resident tax rates 2021–22
Taxable income	**Tax on this income**
$0–$120 000	32.5c for each $1
$120 001–$180 000	$39 000 plus 37c for each $1 over $120 000
$180 001 and over	$61 200 plus 45c for each $1 over $180 000

Note: The tax rates for working holiday-makers are 15% from zeo to $45 000, 32.5% for $45 000 to $120 000, 37% for $120 000 to $180 000, and 45% for incomes greater than $180 000.

10.4.1.1 Tax-free threshold

A tax-free threshold applies to all Australian adult resident taxpayers. In 2021–22, this was $18 200 for taxpayers who were resident for the entire tax year. The threshold is pro-rated for taxpayers who are residents for only part of the tax year. The formula to pro rate the threshold for the 2021–22 tax year is:[42]

$$\$13\,464 + \left(\frac{\$4736 \times \text{Number of months in the year the individual is a resident}}{12\,\text{months}} \right)$$

10.4.2 Medicare levy

To fund Australia's universal health care system, a **Medicare levy** is imposed upon Australian resident individual taxpayers whose income exceeds a certain threshold as per the *Medicare Levy Act (1986)* (Cth). The rate of the Medicare levy is 2 per cent on the whole of an individual's taxable income. Generally, all taxpayers are liable for the levy, but there are exemptions in some cases. Likewise, a reduced levy applies to low-income earners and an increased levy (Medicare levy surcharge) applies to high-income earners who do not have adequate private patient hospital insurance. These specific areas are discussed in the following sections.

10.4.2.1 Low-income earners

A Medicare levy reduction applies for low-income earners, seniors and pensioners. No Medicare levy is payable for:
- individual taxpayers with taxable income equal to or less than $23 365[43]
- seniors and pensioners entitled to the seniors and pensioners tax offset with taxable income equal to or less than $36 925.[44]

Only part of the Medicare levy is payable by:
- individual taxpayers with a taxable income from $23 365 to $39 402[45]
- seniors and pensioners entitled to the seniors and pensioners tax offset with taxable income from $36 925 to $51 401.[46]

For the amount of income between these threshold levels, the levy is charged at a rate of 10 cents per $1. This is demonstrated in example 10.19.

EXAMPLE 10.19

Reduction of Medicare levy for low-income earners

Max is single and has a taxable income of $24 000 for the 2021–22 tax year.

What is Max's liability for the Medicare levy?

Max's income exceeds the threshold at which no Medicare levy is payable. It falls between the thresholds in which only part of the Medicare levy is payable.

Max's liability is reduced as he is a low-income earner to 10% × ($24 000 – $23 365) = $63.50

---

42 *Income Tax Rates Act 1986* (Cth) section 20.
43 For the 2021–22 tax year. See also Commonwealth of Australia, *Budget 2022–23: Budget Paper No 2* (29 March 2022), 24–25; Treasury Laws Amendment (Cost of Living Support and Other Measures) Bill 2022.
44 For the 2021–22 tax year.
45 As of the 2021–22 income year.
46 As of the 2021–22 income year.

10.4.2.2 Family taxable income

Resident taxpayers with an income exceeding the thresholds for a low-income Medicare levy reduction[47] may qualify for a reduction based on family taxable income[48] if they meet the family taxable income thresholds ($39 402 plus $3619 for each child)[49] and they:

- had a spouse
- had a spouse who died during the year, and did not have another spouse that year
- were entitled to an invalid and invalid carer tax offset in respect of a child, or
- had full responsibility for the upbringing, welfare and maintenance of one or more dependent children or students.

10.4.2.3 Medicare levy exemption

In accordance with sections 251T and 251U of the ITAA36, taxpayers are exempt from the Medicare levy if one of the following applies.

- They met certain medical requirements (e.g. they received a sickness allowance from Centrelink).
- They were entitled to free health care under defence force arrangements or the *Veteran's Entitlement Act 1986* (Cth).
- They were members of diplomatic missions or consulate posts in Australia and members of their families are not Australian citizens or residents.
- They were non-residents.
- They were not entitled to Medicare benefits.

10.4.2.4 Medicare levy surcharge

Taxpayers with income exceeding a certain level who do not have the required level of private patient hospital insurance must pay the **Medicare levy surcharge (MLS)**. The surcharge is calculated on the taxpayer's (and spouse's) *sum* of:

- taxable income (excluding any assessable first home super saver released amount)
- reportable fringe benefits
- reportable superannuation contributions
- net investment losses, and
- any amount on which family trust distribution tax has been paid
- exempt foreign employment income
- *less* any taxed superannuation benefit that qualifies for a tax offset under section 301-20(2) of the ITAA97.

The actual calculation of the surcharge is based on the relevant surcharge percentage multiplied by the sum of taxable income and reportable fringe benefits. The rate of the MLS increases as income increases, as shown in table 10.8.

TABLE 10.8	MLS income thresholds for 2014–15 to 2022–23			
	Base tier	**Tier 1**	**Tier 2**	**Tier 3**
Single threshold	$90 000 or less	$90 001–$105 000	$105 001–$140 000	$140 001 or more
Family threshold	$180 000 or less	$180 001–$210 000	$210 001–$280 000	$280 001 or more
Medicare levy surcharge	0%	1%	1.25%	1.5%

Note: The family threshold increases by $1500 for each Medicare levy surcharge dependant child after the first child.

Source: Australian Taxation Office, *Income thresholds and rates for the Medicare levy surcharge* (Web Page, 5 July 2021) https://www.ato.gov.au/Individuals/Medicare-and-private-health-insurance/Medicare-levy-surcharge/income-thresholds-and-rates-for-the-medicare-levy-surcharge.

The application of the MLS is shown in example 10.20.

---

47 As of the 2021–22 income year: Commonwealth of Australia, *Budget 2022–23: Budget Paper No 2* (29 March 2022), 24–25; Treasury Laws Amendment (Cost of Living Support and Other Measures) Bill 2022.

48 Being the sum of the income of an individual and their spouse.

49 As of the 2021–22 income year.

Medicare levy surcharge

Charlie is a 40-year-old single woman. For the 2021–22 tax year, Charlie's taxable income was $95 000, and she had reportable fringe benefits of $15 000. Charlie did not have private patient hospital cover at any time throughout the year.

What is Charlie's Medicare levy surcharge liability?

Charlie's income for surcharge purposes is $95 000 + $15 000 = $110 000.

This places Charlie in Tier 2 of the MLS rates (see table 10.8).

MLS is charged on taxable income plus reportable fringe benefits (in this case, $110 000). In Tier 2, the MLS rate is 1.25 per cent. Therefore, Charlie's MLS is $110 000 × 1.25% = $1375.

10.4.3 Government study and training loans

In addition to the Medicare levy, those individual taxpayers who are undertaking higher education, trade apprenticeships and other training programs, such as the higher education loan program, are entitled to financial assistance by way of government study and training loans but they create a repayment debt.

The loans must be repaid once an individual's repayment income exceeds a particular threshold. Repayment income is the sum of taxable income and reportable fringe benefits, adjusted for net investment losses, reportable superannuation contributions plus exempt foreign employment income in 2021–22. Also, from 1 July 2019, repayment thresholds including minimum repayment income have been indexed using the CPI rather than average weekly earnings. Since 1 July 2017, Australians living overseas with outstanding education loans have also been required to make repayments.

Recovery of the study and training debt is through the PAYG withholding system. The repayment rates and income thresholds for 2021–22 are shown in table 10.9.

TABLE 10.9   Repayment rates and income thresholds for 2021–22

Repayment income thresholds	Rate of repayment
Below $47 014	Nil
$47 014–$54 282	1%
$54 283–$57 538	2%
$57 539–$60 991	2.5%
$60 992–$64 651	3%
$64 652–$68 529	3.5%
$68 530–$72 641	4.0%
$72 642–$77 001	4.5%
$77 002–$81 620	5%
$81 621–$86 518	5.5%
$86 519–$91 709	6%
$91 710–$97 212	6.5%
$97 213–$103 045	7%
$103 046–$109 227	7.5%
$109 228–$115 781	8%
$115 782–$122 728	8.5%

(continued)

TABLE 10.9 *(continued)*

Repayment income thresholds	Rate of repayment
$122 729–$130 092	9%
$130 093–$137 897	9.5%
$137 898 and above	10%

Source: Australian Taxation Office, 'Study and training loan repayment thresholds and rates 2021–22' (Web Page, 30 June 2021) www.ato.gov.au/Rates/HELP,-TSL-and-SFSS-repayment-thresholds-and-rates/#HELPandTSLrepaymentthresholdsandrates.

10.4.4 Determining taxable income and calculating tax payable

Given the information presented throughout this chapter, the taxpayer is in a position to determine final taxable income and tax payable/refundable.

A comprehensive example is provided in example 10.21.

EXAMPLE 10.21

Comprehensive example

Jill Jones worked as a sales rep for an electronics wholesaler in 2021–22. Jill's assessable income included:
- salary (including $11 000 PAYG tax withheld): $57 000
- entertainment allowance: $5000
- telephone allowance: $3000
- fully-maintained company car: $17 000.
  Jill's expenses included:
- mobile phone business use: $1200
- entertainment of business clients: $3200.
  What is Jill's tax liability for the year ended 30 June 2022?

We follow the process shown in figure 10.3. The first step is to calculate Jill's taxable income. Jill would not be assessed on the fully-maintained company car as fringe benefits tax on this benefit is payable by her employer.

Assessable income	$
Salary	57 000
Allowances	8 000
	65 000

No tax deduction is allowable for the entertainment of business clients (see Division 32). Only the business use of the mobile phone is deductible.

	$
Assessable income	65 000
Less: Allowable deductions	
Mobile phone — business use	1 200
Taxable income	**63 800**

The next step is to calculate the gross tax payable by applying the tax rates.

	$
Gross tax payable on $63 800	11 202

Next, we subtract non-refundable tax offsets.

	$
Gross tax payable on $63 800	11 202
Less: Low-income rebate	
Maximum low-income rebate	325
Less: ($63 800 − $45 000) × 0.015	43
Less: Low and middle-income tax rebate	1 500
	9 659

Then we add the Medicare levy.

		$
		9 659
Medicare levy	2% of taxable income (2% × $63 800)	1 276
		10 935

Jill is below the MLS threshold. She has no government study training loans or refundable tax offsets. We therefore now look at the tax already paid.

	$
	10 935
Less: PAYG withholding tax	11 000
Tax refund	**65**

Thus, Jill will get a refund of $65 from the ATO.

ETHICS IN PRACTICE

Determining the taxable income and tax payable for a taxpayer

In preparing the tax return for Jill Jones as her tax agent, the client insists that the entertainment and both private and business telephone expenses are fully deductible and that she has documentation to support this. She has indicated that she will go to another accountant if this claim is not made.

What would be your reaction in resolving this ethical dilemma?

(a) Claiming the expenses would make her happy and keep the client.

(b) Claiming the expenses would jeopardise my job and I would breach the Code of Conduct for professional tax advisors.

(c) Claiming the expenses would increase my fee or prevent me losing money.

(d) I couldn't defend myself for making the claim as the expenses are not legally deductible and I need to inform her of this.

SUMMARY

10.1 Analyse the tax implications of different types of income receipts of individual taxpayers.

Individual taxpayers can receive assessable income from employment, employment termination payments, business, contracts, personal services, dividends, interest, royalties, trusts and real property. Statute and case law have established under what circumstances income from each source is considered assessable.

10.2 Describe the basic types of deductions an individual taxpayer may receive.

The deductions a taxpayer may claim in order to reduce their taxable income depends on whether they are an employee or an independent contractor, determined generally by applying the control and integration tests. The deductions are limited if the income is personal services income (generally to those available to an employee) unless the taxpayer is running a personal services business (PSB). Income protection, insurances and personal superannuation contributions can be deducted under specific circumstances.

10.3 Apply the basic tax offsets (rebates and credits) an individual may be entitled to in a given scenario.

Offsets are amounts that directly reduce the income tax payable. They are generally available to recognise tax already paid, to provide subsidies or incentives or as a concession to cap income tax rates. Some examples of tax offsets that assist in preventing double taxation include: the dividend tax offset, the superannuation tax offset and the foreign income tax offset. Other common tax offsets include: the dependant invalid carer tax offset, low-income tax offset, low and middle-income tax offset, private health insurance tax offset and the zone rebate.

10.4 Determine taxable income and calculate tax payable/refundable for an individual taxpayer.

Taxable income is derived from assessable income less allowable deductions. The correct marginal tax rate is applied to taxable income to determine gross tax payable. From this, non-refundable tax offsets are applied, then the Medicare levy and Medicare levy surcharge if any, as well as any other debts are added. Refundable offsets are then applied. Finally, any tax or amounts credited to the individual taxpayer are subtracted from the resulting sum to determine the total tax payable or tax refund due.

KEY TERMS

assessable income Gross income including salary and wages, dividends, interest and rent before any deductions are allowed. Assessable income also includes net capital gains, eligible termination payments and other amounts that are not ordinarily classed as income.

charges The amount of tax paid on each dollar of taxable income in each income tax bracket.

control test An employer–employee relationship generally exists where one person contracts to perform work for another and the performance of that work is substantially subject to the control and direction of the person for whom the contract is being performed.

death benefit termination payment A termination payment paid to a relative of a former employee who has died.

deductions Expenses that are subtracted from assessable income to determine taxable income.

dependant Includes an Australian resident who is a brother/sister of the taxpayer or their spouse, child of the taxpayer or their spouse, parent of the taxpayer or their spouse.

early retirement scheme payment A scheme approved by the Commissioner of Taxation to rationalise or reorganise the employer's operations.

income tax formula Income Tax Payable = (Taxable Income × Tax Rate) – Tax Offsets.

integration test An employer–employee relationship generally exists where an individual is part and parcel of the principal's business organisation, or an individual's activities are restricted to providing service to one principal, or if the benefits arising from the work flow to the principal.

invalidity segment The portion of an employment termination payment that compensates a person for the loss of years of gainful employment because of ill health.

levies Amounts payable on taxable income in addition to the tax paid on the taxable income.

net tax payable Tax payable plus any charges or levies.

life benefit termination payment A termination payment generally paid to a former employee.

Medicare levy A levy intended to contribute towards funding of Australia's public health care system.

Medicare levy surcharge (MLS) An additional levy charged on those who earn above a threshold income level and do not have the required level of private health insurance.

nexus Can be defined as an important connection between the parts of a system or a group of things.

ordinary income Income according to ordinary concepts — reflecting common usage and common, everyday meaning.

personal services business (PSB) An individual or personal services entity (PSE) is a PSB where the individual or PSE has a PSB determination from the Commissioner of Taxation in force, or the individual or PSE satisfies the results test, or less than 80 per cent of the PSI is derived from a single source and the individual or PSE satisfies one of the other three PSB tests.

personal services entity (PSE) A company, partnership or trust whose ordinary income or statutory income includes the personal services income (PSI) of one or more individuals

personal services income (PSI) Income gained mainly as a reward for the personal skill and effort of an individual.

PSB determination A determination from the Commissioner of Taxation that an individual or PSE is conducting a personal services business (PSB).

redundancy payment A payment upon the termination of an employee for redundancy reasons where the payment exceeds what the employee would have reasonably received had they voluntarily terminated their employment.

royalties Payments made by one person for the use of rights or patents owned by another person.

spouse Person in a registered relationship with another individual (including same sex relationship) and a person who, although not married, is in a relationship with another individual where the couple live together on a genuine domestic basis.

tax-free component A part of a payment that is not subject to tax.

taxable income Assessable income less deductions.

taxable component A part of a payment that is subject to tax.

tax offsets Direct reductions in the amount of tax payable.

tax payable/refundable The amount of (taxable income × tax rate) – tax offsets.

tax rate The amount of tax payable in every dollar for each income tax bracket depending on your circumstances.

termination payments Payments upon termination of employment, including employment termination payments, genuine redundancy and early retirement scheme payments and unused annual leave and long service leave.

whole-of-income cap The reduction of the amount of an ETP that qualifies for a concessional rate of tax by the amount of any other taxable income received in the relevant income year.

QUESTIONS

10.1 John Tate started work in 1982 with Try Ltd and consequently has no pre-16 August 1978 eligible service. John retired on 30 June 2022 and received a pay-out of $28 000 for his unused long service leave. Assume that the:
- total number of days of unused long service leave is 90
- number of days long service leave unused prior to 18 August 1993 is 15
- number of days long service leave unused after 17 August 1993 is 75.

What is the tax payable in respect of the long service leave?

10.2 Reece and Sally Morrison have been renting their house out to overseas visitors and backpackers for short stays while the travellers are in Melbourne and they are away overseas themselves during the 2021–22 tax year. The Morrisons do not have an ABN and receive only cash from the travellers which is not declared in their income tax returns. In addition, the Morrisons employ a friend, Rob, who keeps an eye on the premises while it is being rented and Rob is also paid in cash by the Morrisons.

What are the tax obligations and implications for the Morrisons in regard to the rental of their property in these circumstances?

10.3 On 1 July 2021, a local council department entered into a contract with Computer Co Pty Ltd for the provision of services by Diane Walker, a computer analyst, who is nominated in the contract.

The contract specifies that Diane is required to develop computer programs for use in the department's financial centre in accordance with functional specifications provided by the department.

The contract specifies a fixed amount by way of payment to Computer Co for the development of the programs, which is required to be produced within 15 months of commencement of the contract. The contract is for the performance of a specific task that produces an outcome or result, with Diane maintaining a high level of discretion and flexibility as to how the work ought to be carried out. Final payment is not made until the work is performed, although instalments are payable upon the achievement of particular milestones.

Discuss whether or not the personal services income (PSI) legislation applies to the arrangement.

10.4 On 1 November 2021, Paul Sergent, an Australian resident, received a cheque for $6800 from US Ltd, an American company listed on the New York Stock Exchange. Withholding tax of $1200 had been deducted from the distribution. On 1 April 2022, Paul received a distribution cheque from an Australian company ISI Ltd for $4000. The distribution was 60 per cent franked. On 30 April, he received a further distribution from the Australian company Miners Ltd for $2000, which was unfranked.

Assuming that the Australian entities pay tax at the standard corporate tax rate of 30 per cent, advise Paul of his assessable distribution income for the 2021–22 tax year.

10.5 For the tax year ended 30 June 2022, Kane Rodgers, a self-employed masseur, rented a property and generated a rental income of $45 000. Kane also incurred the following expenses in relation to the property.

		$
01.08.2021	Repairs to leaking roof	1 400
10.09.2021	Painting the outside of the property	2 800
01.03.2022	Replacement of vinyl flooring in kitchen (assume a 20-year life)	4 500
10.04.2022	Repairs paid for by the tenants	4 100
15.06.2022	Gardening: removal of dead tree	500

Advise Kane Rodgers of his net rental income for the year ended 30 June 2022.

10.6 On 1 March 2022, Bert Hudson, aged 60, sold his farm for $300 000. In order to secure his retirement, he immediately purchased an annuity of $30 000 per annuma, which was to be paid until his death. There is no lump sum payable on death. The annuity cost $280 000. The annuity tables indicate that Bert at age 60 has a life expectancy of 23.37 years.

Advise Bert Hudson as to the assessability of the annuity.

10.7 John McKenzie and his family have resided for the whole of the 2021–22 tax year in ordinary Zone A. John maintains a wife, aged 39 who is disabled, and two children, one aged 4 and the other aged 7. The 7-year-old attends school. John's wife had an adjusted taxable income for rebates from investments of $4111 for the year.

Calculate John's entitlement to a zone rebate for the 2021–22 tax year.

10.8 Upon graduating from University, Kathy Freebaorn left Australia to live and work in the UK for six months. Kathy obtained part-time cash jobs while she was travelling around Europe. Upon her return to Australia, Kathy obtained full-time employment in an office role. When lodging her tax return, Kathy failed to declare the overseas income as she thought it was not subject to tax.

What are the relevant ethical and legal issues at play here and what should Kathy do?

10.9 Determine the amount of tax payable/refundable to Wayne Wilson for the year ended 30 June 2022 based on the following information.

Wayne, aged 48, is living with June, aged 41, his invalid partner, who is in receipt of a disability support pension of $2500, which constitutes June's adjusted taxable income. Wayne has lived with June since 1 April 2021 and receives a carer allowance. Peter, Wayne's 14-year-old son from his marriage to Kim, lives with his mother. Peter has an income of $350. Wayne paid $2000 for a laptop computer used for Peter's secondary studies. Kim and Wayne separated in March 2021, although they are not yet divorced. Wayne's 21-year-old daughter, Claire, has an adjusted taxable income of $28 000. Kim's net income of $13 000 consists of maintenance paid by Wayne. Wayne's gross salary was $51 000, from which $8122 tax was withheld. Wayne has adequate private health insurance cover and is not entitled to any family tax benefits.

Other information is as follows.

	$
Receipts	
Salary	51 000
Dividend received from an Australian public company (only 40% of the dividend is franked)	1 000
Payments	
Premium for personal sickness and accident disability insurance policy	450
Self-education expenses	5 680
Maintenance to Kim	13 000

10.10 Dina Martin is an individual resident taxpayer for the 2021–22 full income tax year. She is aged 42, is single, and has no dependants.

Dina holds private hospital health insurance which meets the requirements of the private health insurance tax offset. Her annual premium for the 2021–22 income tax year was $4200, which has not been reduced to take any offset available into account. Dina also paid $20 500 in tax instalment deductions during the 2021–22 tax year.

Dina has the following transactions.

	$
Income from wages	90 000
Rental income received	25 000
Interest received	3 500
Expenses	
Substantiated car expenses*	
Entertainment of clients	5 000
Landlord fees, rates, interest on rental property	18 000
Other	
Reportable fringe benefits amount	15 000

*Dina has travelled 1500 km for work. Calculate using the cents per km method, 72c per km in 2021–22, applied to an estimate of the number of business kilometres travelled.

Determine Dina's taxable income and tax payable for the 2021–22 income tax year.

PROBLEMS

10.11 Phillip Mansell, since his early retirement as an accountant, now has excess time on his hands and is becoming bored. He has therefore decided to start a project involving his great love — cooking — and wants to start a catering business providing services to the public. Initially, he anticipates he will operate by himself and work directly with the public, obtaining work through advertising and word-of-mouth.

However, a local caterer has made an offer whereby the caterer will offer Phillip work where the caterer would not otherwise have sufficient staff to accept the job, subject to the following conditions.

1. If work is offered by the caterer, Phillip must accept it. However, Phillip has insisted that he be given at least one week's notice and can refuse if the notice is any shorter.

2. While performing the work, Phillip must wear the caterer's uniform.
3. The menu and the timing of delivery of the courses are determined by the customer. It is Phillip's responsibility to ensure that timing of the courses can be achieved and if they cannot, he must advise the client. Additionally, he is responsible for the purchase of all ingredients and the preparation of the food.
4. There will be a member of the caterer's staff supervising all functions to ensure that they go smoothly. They can advise Phillip of potential changes needed on the night (e.g. if some of the guests are late) but they cannot interfere with Phillip in the preparation of the food.

Phillip expects that if he accepts the caterer's offer, he will continue to offer his services to the public and each will represent approximately 50 per cent of his catering income.

If Phillip accepts the offer, which will commence in the 2021–22 tax year, advise Phillip as to whether he would be treated as an employee or independent contractor for tax purposes. *Cite relevant authorities to support your answer*. (Note: you can assume that the income is *not* subject to the personal services income provisions.)

10.12 George Simmons is an IT professional who, for a number of years, has worked as an employee or contractor in the IT departments of various large corporations. George recently married and he and his spouse set up a private company, 'IT Ahead Pty Ltd' of which George and his spouse are the shareholders and directors. The use of the company would allow protection of private assets and allow income to be split between George and his spouse.

IT Ahead employs George as its consultant and employs his spouse to undertake part-time administrative duties. IT Ahead registers with a number of IT Agencies and George contacted a number of firms for which he has worked offering the services of IT Ahead to provide software analysis and design. Through an Agency IT Ahead signed a contract to provide 100 per cent of its IT services to a multinational corporation.

The standard terms of the contract include:
- IT Ahead to perform services assigned by the client
- the client will give directions to the IT contractors employed by IT Ahead
- IT Ahead will be paid for work done at a specified hourly rate on submission of invoices detailing the hours worked as recorded on time sheets
- the clients will nominate the hours to be worked to meet deadlines
- the clients would reimburse expenses of IT Ahead that are outside the scope of the contract
- to ensure security, IP security standardisation software, and protection against viruses, work would be done at the client's premises on computers provided by the clients
- unsatisfactory work would be rectified at the expense of IT Ahead
- only qualified IT staff could be used by IT Ahead.

For the 2021–22 tax year, IT Ahead received $180 000 in fees from the multinational corporation client under the contract and paid the following expenses:
- $550 annual IT registration fees
- $640 bank account fees
- $75 000 for George's salary.

Advise George and IT Ahead of the possible application of the PSI regime and the assessability of the amounts received from the client. *Cite relevant authorities to support your answer.*

10.13 On 10 July 2022, Sharon Jones requested her accountant to calculate her tax liability for the year ended 30 June 2022. Sharon retired from Cleo Constructions Ltd on 31 October 2021, her 70th birthday, after 40 years of service with the company. The superannuation fund membership commenced on the date of commencement of employment — 1 November 1981.

Sharon provides the following information.

	$
Salary from Cleo Constructions Ltd 1 July 2021 to 31 October 2021[1]	30 000
Lump sum received on retirement[2]	39 500
Superannuation income stream paid out of the Cleo Constructions Ltd Superannuation Fund for the period 1 November 2021 to 30 June 2022[3]	25 000

Note 1: Payment summaries show that tax totalling $12 800 had been with held.
Note 2:

- $4500 unused annual leave (this payment is in lieu of 20 days annual leave accrued from 1 January 2021 until retirement on 31 October 2021)
- $15 000 in lieu of 80 days long service leave (Sharon's eligible service period was 40 years (i.e. 14 610 days) of which 50 days long service leave refers to post-1993)
- $20 000 as a retirement gratuity not paid from a taxed source.

Note 3: The superannuation fund is a complying taxed superannuation fund.

Assuming that Sharon's tax deductions totaled $1200 and she is not entitled to any tax offset or family tax benefit, calculate the tax payable/refund for her in the 2021–22 tax year.

10.14 On 11 February 2022, Outboard Marine Australia Co Ltd entered into a contract with NY Marine Co Ltd, a New York-based company, whereby NY Marine would provide technical expertise to Outboard Marine on the development and installation of a fuel injection system for Outboard's new range of outboard motors. In return, NY Marine received $75 000 to cover the initial expenses and a fee of $65 for every outboard motor sold by Outboard Marine for a period of two years.

Advise NY Marine of the tax consequences in Australia of such an arrangement.

10.15 The following information is provided by Kerry Smith for the purposes of preparing her income tax return for the year ended 30 June 2022.

	$	$
Income		
Salary		45 000
Rent received from a shop		16 550
Drawings for year from partnership		6 000
Directors' fees from Company Ltd		7 500
Annuity from uncle's estate		2 300
Dividend from UK resident company (after deduction of UK withholding tax at 15% — $60) (ignoring protocol to UK/Australia Double Tax Agreement)		340
Dividend from a resident Australian company (the dividend statement shows a franked amount of $140 and an unfranked amount of $60)		200
Expenses		
Premium on sickness and accident policy for herself		450
Rates on shop		1 500
Insurance for shop		1 100
Repairs to shop:		
Painting of shop—internally	1 500	
Painting of shop—externally	1 200	
At the request of the local council, trimmed back shop awning which was protruding over a driveway	850	
Replaced part of a rotten wooden floor with a cheaper concrete floor on 1 July 2021	1 800	5 350
Interest on shop mortgage		5 700

Kerry also advises the following.

- David, Kerry's husband aged 50, does not work and was in receipt of an invalid pension constituting his adjusted taxable income of $11 000. The couple did not receive any family tax benefits, but Kerry received a carer allowance on behalf of David.
- Kerry's son is aged 16 and her daughter is aged 12. Both are still at school and neither has any income.
- An entertainment allowance of $1000 was received from Kerry's employer — the actual cost of entertaining clients on behalf of her employer was $1200.
- Payment summaries showed that $12 500 tax had been withheld.
- The partnership of which Kerry is a partner revealed that her share of the net partnership income is $10 500.

Prepare a statement of Kerry's taxation position and determine the tax payable/refundable for the year ended 30 June 2022.

ACKNOWLEDGEMENTS

Figure 10.1: © Australian Taxation Office
Figure 10.2: © Federal Register of Legislation. Licensed under CC BY 4.0.
Tables 10.2, 10.3, 10.5: © Federal Register of Legislation. Licensed under CC BY 4.0.
Tables 10.4, 10.6, 10.7, 10.8, 10.9: © Australian Taxation Office
Extract: © Australian Government. Licensed under CC BY 3.0.
Extracts: © Federal Register of Legislation. Licensed under CC BY 4.0.
Extract: © Australian Taxation Office

CHAPTER 11

Taxation of companies

LEARNING OBJECTIVES

After studying this chapter, you should be able to:

11.1 describe what a company is and how it is taxed

11.2 explain how a company's taxable income is calculated

11.3 explain the tax treatment of company losses

11.4 explain the research and development concessions available to companies

11.5 explain how dividends are taxed

11.6 apply the concepts of Division 7A to the tax treatment of a loan by a private company to a shareholder

11.7 describe the operation of a company franking account

11.8 describe anti-avoidance and integrity measures applicable to company distributions.

Overview

Companies are separate legal entities and have a taxable income. As such, they are taxed. In Australia, companies pay tax at a flat rate of tax, dependent on the company's annual turnover and classification.

Companies are taxed differently to other taxpayers. This chapter outlines how companies are taxed, including the tax differences between a public and private company and the special rules relating to tax losses contained in Division 165 of the ITAA97. The chapter also considers the special research and development tax incentives that are only available to corporate taxpayers.

The concept of dividends is also discussed, including an overview of the dividend imputation system, and the difference between a **frankable distribution** and an **unfrankable distribution**. All companies are required to maintain a franking account, which keeps track of the **franking credits** that it can pass on to its shareholders.

The chapter concludes by discussing the concept of underfranking, overfranking, excessive overfranking and the implications of a **franking deficit tax**.

11.1 What is a company?

LEARNING OBJECTIVE 11.1 Describe what a company is and how it is taxed.

Section 9 of the *Corporations Act 2001* (Cth) ('the Corporations Act') defines a **company** as one that is registered, or taken to be registered, under the Corporations Law. The tax law draws on this but extends it for tax purposes.

A company is defined in section 995-1 of the ITAA97 as:

(a) a body corporate (i.e. a company incorporated in Australia); or
(b) any unincorporated association or body of persons but does not include a partnership.

For taxation purposes, a company also includes a club, an incorporated association or a society.

A company is a separate legal entity. Hence, like an individual, it has a taxable income. As such, it pays income tax in its own right on its taxable income. A company is considered a taxpayer for the purposes of the ITAA36 because it derives income. Accordingly, a company is required to lodge a **company income tax return** (C form).

In the company income tax return, the company includes its assessable income and deducts its allowable deductions on the basis that it is a resident taxpayer. Hence, a company tax return includes both Australian and foreign-sourced income and deductions.

11.1.1 How is a company taxed?

As stated, a company's taxable income is determined by including its assessable income and deducting its allowable deductions on the basis that it is a resident taxpayer.

Although a company's taxable income is calculated in the same manner as an individual taxpayer's taxable income, the ITAA36 and ITAA97 treat companies differently from individuals in many respects.

For example:

- In Australia, companies with an annual turnover of $50 million or more pay tax at a flat rate of 30 per cent. Companies with an annual turnover of less than $50 million in 2020–21 and are classified as a base rate entity (BRE) pay income tax at the rate of 26 per cent. In 2021–22 the rate applicable is 25 per cent (base rate entities as defined in section 23AA).[1]
- Unlike resident individuals, companies do not receive a tax-free threshold.
- Companies do not pay the 2 per cent Medicare levy or the Medicare levy surcharge.
- Companies do not get many of the rebates and tax offsets that individuals do (e.g. private health insurance rebate, invalid carer tax offset, low income tax offset).
- A company is subject to specific rules restricting its ability to carry forward tax losses (Division 165 of the ITAA97).
- The debt/equity rules contained in Division 974 of the ITAA97 specifically apply to companies.
- The substantiation rules for car, travel and other expenses do not apply to companies.
- A company must appoint a public officer under section 252 of the ITAA36 to sign income tax returns and deal with the Australian Taxation Office on behalf of the company.

---

1 *Income Tax Rates Act 1986* (Cth) section 23(2); Australian Taxation Office, 'Changes to company tax rates' (Web Page, 2020) www.ato.gov.au/Rates/Changes-to-company-tax-rates.

- Companies are subject to the thin capitalisation rules contained in Division 820 of the ITAA97.
- Companies are required to maintain a franking account.
- Companies are *not* eligible for the CGT discount method but are eligible to use the indexation method (where applicable).
- Only companies are eligible for the special research and development tax concessions contained in Division 355 of the ITAA97.

11.1.2 Classification of companies — public or private?

A company's status for income tax purposes does not depend upon its status for company law purposes.

According to section 9 of the Corporations Act, a public company is defined as a company incorporated in Australia other than a proprietary company. A public company must have at least one shareholder (section 114 of the Corporations Act). There is no maximum number of shareholders.

According to section 114 of the Corporations Act, a proprietary company must have at least one shareholder. Section 113(1) prescribes that it cannot have more than 50 shareholders.

Under taxation law, companies are classified as either:
- public, or
- private.

Section 103A(1) of the ITAA36 states that a **private company** is one that is *not* a public company in relation to the year of income.

Section 103A(2) deems a company to be a **public company** for taxation purposes if:
- its shares were listed on a stock exchange (anywhere in the world) on the last day of the income year
- despite being listed on a stock exchange, a company will *not* be considered to be a public company for taxation purposes where, at any time during the income year, 20 or fewer persons held 75 per cent or more of the company's capital, voting or dividend rights
- it is a subsidiary of a listed public company (section 103A(4))
- it is a non-profit company
- it is a mutual life assurance company
- it is a friendly society
- it is a registered organisation
- it is a statutory body or a company in which a government body established for public purposes had a controlling interest on the last day of the year of income.

11.1.2.1 Why is the distinction important?

For taxation purposes, the distinction between a public company and a private company is important for the following reasons.
- Excessive payments made by private companies to their shareholders, directors or associates may be treated as unfranked dividends and disallowed as a deduction to the company (sections 109 and 26–35). This is designed to stop private companies from paying salaries and wages well above market rates to family members who are employed by the company.
- The Commissioner applies more stringent rules to a private company in respect of other benefits (e.g. loans, debts forgiven, etc.) for shareholders and associates (Division 7A). Division 7A is discussed in more detail in section 11.6 of this chapter.
- The continuity of ownership tests is not as strict for public companies (section 165–165(7)). This issue is discussed in more detail in section 11.3 of this chapter.
- The benchmark franking rules differ for private companies because a private company only has one **franking period** compared to two in the case of a public company. This issue of franking periods is discussed in more detail in section 11.7 of this chapter.
- The timing for issuing dividend (or distribution) statements is discussed in more detail in section 11.7 of this chapter.
- Private companies can access certain SBE capital gains tax (CGT) concessions if the requirements for these concessions are met, you should refer back an earlier chapter for a more detailed discussion on this.

11.1.3 Company tax rates

Companies pay tax at a flat rate on their taxable income. The company tax rate for large corporate entities is 30 per cent. However, a reduced rate of tax applies to companies that are classified as a BRE and have an aggregated turnover below a certain threshold.

A BRE is one which:
- has annual turnover less than $50 million and,
- base rate passive income, which is not more than 80 per cent of the assessable income of the company. BREs are taxed at 25 per cent for the 2021–22 financial year.

Examples of passive income include:
- interest
- rent
- royalties
- capital gains.

Note: The comparison must be made with assessable income, not taxable income.

EXAMPLE 11.1

Base rate entity (BRE)

Happy Feet Pty Ltd is a company that sells socks online. Its owner, Lloyd Chan, wants to expand the business into running shoes as well. The capital he needs to expand the business is put into a term deposit while he negotiates with suppliers.

In the 2021–22 income year, Happy Feet Pty Ltd has an aggregated turnover under the $50 million aggregated turnover threshold. Its assessable income is $104 000, comprising:
- $100 000 trading income from running the business
- $4000 of interest income.

The interest income is BRE passive income. Because this income is only 3.8 per cent of its assessable income, Happy Feet Pty Ltd is a BRE for the 2021–22 income year and the 25 per cent company tax rate applies.

Source: Australian Taxation Office, 'Changes to company tax rates' (Web Page, 28 October 2021) https://www.ato.gov.au/Rates/Changes-to-company-tax-rates.

EXAMPLE 11.2

Not a BRE because passive income is too high

Best Equity Ltd is a listed investment company which invests in Australian shares.

In the 2021–22 income year, Best Equity Pty Ltd has an aggregated turnover under the $50 million aggregated turnover threshold. Its assessable income is $5 million, comprising:
- $1 million of interest income
- $4 million in dividends.

100 per cent of Best Equity Ltd's assessable income is BRE passive income. As a result, they are not a BRE for the 2021–22 income year and the 30 per cent company tax rate applies.

Source: Australian Taxation Office, 'Changes to company tax rates' (28 October 2021) https://www.ato.gov.au/Rates/Changes-to-company-tax-rates.

TABLE 11.1 **Comparison of the various entities for taxation purposes**

Financial year	Aggregated turnover less than	Tax rate for BREs under threshold	Tax rate for all other companies
2015–16	$2 million	28.5%	30%
2016–17	$10 million	27.5%	30%
2017–18	$25 million	27.5%	30%
2018–19	$50 million	27.5%	30%
2019–20	$50 million	27.5%	30%
2020–21	$50 million	26%	30%
2021–22 and future years	$50 million	25%	30%

11.2 Calculation of a company's taxable income

LEARNING OBJECTIVE 11.2 Explain how a company's taxable income is calculated.

For accounting purposes, a company's net profit is calculated as the difference between income and expenses, calculated in accordance with the AASB Accounting Standards. In other words:

$$\text{Net profit} = \left[\text{Revenue} - \text{Expenses}\right]$$

For taxation purposes, a company's taxable income is determined by the principles set out in both the ITAA36 and ITAA97. According to section 4-15 of the ITAA97:

$$\text{Taxable income} = \left[\text{Assessable income} - \text{Deductions}\right]$$

While the two figures may produce similar results, they are not necessarily the same. The differences between the net profit for accounting purposes and the taxable income may be:

(a) permanent differences — those items of revenues and expenses that never reverse over time
(b) the **temporary differences** — those differences where the accounting and taxation treatments are the same but occur in differing periods.

Temporary differences result in either:

- **deferred tax assets** — which give rise to adjustments that result in a decrease in income tax payable in a future tax period. This occurs because the entity is entitled to a tax deduction in the future, or
- **deferred tax liabilities** — which give rise to adjustments that result in an increase in income tax payable in a future tax period. This may occur in one of two ways: the entity will be liable to pay more tax in the future, or the entity receives a tax deduction now, and not in the future (e.g. prepayments), which results in additional tax to pay in future periods.

Table 11.2 outlines the difference treatment for accounting and taxation purposes.

TABLE 11.2   **Accounting treatment versus taxation treatment**

Accounting treatment	Taxation treatment
Profit on sale of CGT assets — accounting income	Capital gains tax — for tax purposes
	Pre-CGT (no resale intention at purchase — exempt from tax
Franking credits — not accounting income	Franking credits — assessable for tax purposes
Accounting depreciation	Tax depreciation
	Low-value pool
	General business pool
	Outright deduction or temporary full expensing
Provision annual leave, sick leave — accounting deduction	Provision annual leave, sick leave — deductible when taken and paid
Provision for bad debts — accounting deduction	Provision for bad debts — deductible when written off
Purchase of capital assets (e.g. buildings) — accounting deduction	Purchase of capital assets (e.g. buildings) — Division 43 capital works write-off
Repairs on purchase — accounting deduction	Repairs on purchase — not deductible incurred too soon
Fees on borrowings — accounting deduction	Fees on borrowings — borrowing costs — capital but written off using s 25-25
Payments to directors/associated persons — accounting deduction	Payments to directors/associated persons — reasonable amount deductible only
Prepaid expenses — accounting deduction	Prepaid expenses — apportioned or outright if SBE or eligible entity and taxpayer has met conditions
Non-deductible items — accounting deduction	Non-deductible items — no deduction allowed

(continued)

TABLE 11.2   *(continued)*

Accounting treatment	Taxation treatment
Exempt income — accounting income	Exempt income — not assessable for tax purposes
Prepaid income — accounting income	Prepaid income — review refund policy
Losses — deductible	Losses — subject to being offset against exempt income and rules for companies

In practice, a statement is prepared in order to reconcile the net profit for accounting purposes to the taxable income. The statement is typically referred to as a **tax reconciliation**.

The tax reconciliation is generally set out as shown in figure 11.1.

FIGURE 11.1   Example of a tax reconciliation format

	$
Accounting net profit	xxx
Add: Amounts assessable for tax purposes (e.g. gross-up of franking credits in respect of franked dividends and foreign withholding tax deducted)	xxx
Add: Non-tax-deductible expenses (e.g. client entertainment)	xxx
Less: Non-assessable income (e.g. exempt income)	(xxx)
Less: Amounts deductible for tax purposes (e.g. lease payments)	(xxx)
Taxable income	xxx
Multiplied by tax rate (@ a flat 25% or 30%)	xxx
Less: PAYG instalments paid during the income year	(xxx)
Less: Tax offsets (franking credits)	(xxx)
Less: Tax offsets (foreign withholding tax)	(xxx)
Income tax payable	xxx

11.2.1 Treatment of foreign income

Recall that a resident of Australia for taxation purposes (including a company) is assessed on their worldwide income (section 6-5(2)), while a non-resident is assessed only on income derived from Australian sources (section 6-5(3)).

Hence, where a resident Australian company receives foreign income (e.g. interest or dividend income), it must include the gross amount received of that interest or dividend in its assessable income.

When an Australian company receives this payment in their bank account, the payer (whether a foreign bank or foreign share registry) has already deducted the foreign withholding tax, meaning that the amount received by the resident Australian company is the net amount, not the gross amount.

As the Australian resident company must include the gross amount of the interest or dividend received, it needs to gross-up the amount received by the amount of foreign withholding tax deducted by the overseas payer (section 128D). A company can then claim a foreign income tax offset against its tax payable. However, the amount of the foreign income tax offset is calculated as the *lesser* of the foreign tax paid and the amount of the Australian tax payable (sections 770-75(2)–(4)).

11.2.1.1 Foreign interest

To illustrate how withholding tax applies, assume that a resident Australian company receives interest from a Malaysian bank of AU$900 (net of foreign withholding tax deducted at the source of AU$100).

The Australian resident company will be required to include a gross amount of AU$1000 in its assessable income. It would then pay tax at the company tax rate (either 25 per cent or 30 per cent depending on whether it is a BRE). It would then receive a tax offset for the amount of foreign tax deducted of AU$100.

11.2.1.2 Foreign dividend

Take a similar example relating to foreign dividends. Assume that an Australian resident company receives a dividend from a US company of AU$1700 (net of foreign withholding tax deducted at the source of AU$300).

The Australian resident company will be required to include a gross amount of AU$2000 in its assessable income. After paying tax at the company tax rate (either 25 per cent or 30 per cent depending on whether it is a BRE), it would then receive a tax offset for the amount of foreign tax deducted of AU$300.

11.3 Company losses

LEARNING OBJECTIVE 11.3 Explain the tax treatment of company losses.

There may be instances where a company's allowable deductions exceed its assessable income. In this instance, the company has a negative taxable income. This is referred to as a **tax loss** and comes within the provisions of Division 36 of the ITAA97.

A tax loss incurred in one income year may be carried forward and deducted in arriving at the taxpayer's taxable income of succeeding income years. According to Division 36 of the ITAA97, a tax loss may be carried forward indefinitely until it is exhausted (*Case W52* 89 ATC 486).

According to section 165-10 of the ITAA97, a company cannot carry forward prior year losses for offset against future years' income unless it satisfies either:
(a) the 'continuity of ownership test' (section 165-12), or
(b) the '**similar business test**' (section 165-13).

The tests must be applied in this order. If the continuity of ownership test is satisfied, then there is no need to consider the similar business test. However, if the continuity of ownership test is failed, then the similar business test can be considered.

These same tests are also used to determine whether net capital losses and bad debts may be claimed for tax purposes.

As part of the 2020–21 Federal Budget, the Government announced that companies with an aggregated turnover of less than $5 billion will be entitled to choose to carry-back tax losses incurred in the 2020, 2021 and 2022 income years to offset the company's taxable income in the 2019 or later income years. This is known as the 'loss carry-back tax offset'.

11.3.1 Continuity of ownership test

The **continuity of ownership test** requires that the same persons collectively own exactly the same shares that gave them more than 50 per cent of the voting power, rights to dividends, and rights to capital distributions at all times during the 'ownership test period time' (section 165-12).

The ownership test period time is the entire period from the start of the loss year to the end of the income year. Where the company has derived losses over several income years, the continuity of ownership test is applied to each year. This may result in the company recouping some of its prior year losses, but not all.

Example 11.3 demonstrates application of the continuity of ownership test.

EXAMPLE 11.3

Continuity of ownership test

For the year ended 30 June 2021, Capricorn Holdings Pty Ltd incurred a tax loss of $54 000. The company has three shareholders. As at 1 July 2020 (i.e. at the start of the loss year), the three shareholders were as follows:
1. A holds 40 per cent of the shares
2. B holds 40 per cent of the shares
3. C holds 20 per cent of the shares.

For the year ended 30 June 2022, the company derived a taxable income of $72 000 and wishes to use the $54 000 tax loss that was incurred in 2021.

In 2022, the shareholding of the company has changed. As at 30 June 2022 (i.e. the end of the income year), the shareholding is:
- A holds 40 per cent of the shares
- B holds 12 per cent of the shares

- C is no longer a shareholder of Capricorn Holdings Pty Ltd, and
- D holds 48 per cent of the shares.
  Is the continuity of ownership test satisfied?
  In this case, the continuity of ownership test is satisfied because together both A and B hold 52 per cent of the shares in Capricorn Pty Ltd from the start of the loss year to the end of the income year.

11.3.1.1 Change of ownership rules for widely held companies under Division 166

Division 166 provides for a simplified continuity of ownership test for all widely held companies and a range of subsidiary companies. In short, Division 166 makes it less onerous for widely held entities to satisfy the continuity of ownership test.

A company is a **widely held company** if it is listed on an approved stock exchange. A company is also widely held if it has more than 50 members where more than 20 of those members hold 75 per cent or more of the voting, dividend or capital distribution rights.

The main concessions that are available to widely held companies (such as public companies) include:
- maintenance of the same owners between certain points of time is required, rather than proof of maintenance of the same owners throughout the periods in between
- direct shareholdings of less than 10 per cent in the company are treated as if they were held by a single notional entity, so that it is unnecessary to trace through to the persons who beneficially own those shareholdings
- direct and indirect shareholdings of between 10 and 50 per cent in the company held by a widely held company are treated as having been held by that widely held company, so that it is not necessary to trace beyond those companies.

This concession applies to public companies and not private companies as tracing shareholding in public companies is much more problematic.

11.3.2 Similar business test

If a company fails the continuity of ownership test (because of a change in ownership), it may still be able to deduct a tax loss from an earlier income year if it satisfies the similar business test contained in section 165-13.

The similar business test replaced the former same business test on 1 March 2019. The similar business test is intended to make it easier for companies to deduct losses. The law applies retrospectively from 1 July 2015.

Under the similar business test, following a change in ownership or control, a company can deduct its tax losses if the business carried on at the time of deduction is 'similar' to the business carried on at the time of the loss.

The rationale for the change was that the former 'same business test' was considered very narrow, meaning that if a business changed its operations, it was unable to use carried-forward losses. Under the former same business test, a company could only offset the loss if it carried on the same business throughout a year of income as it carried on immediately before the change in ownership.

To satisfy the same business test, the company could not derive assessable income during the income year from a business or transaction of a kind in which it did not engage in immediately prior to the change in ownership of the shares (section 165-210(2)). Furthermore, a company could not commence a new business or initiate a transaction in order to meet the same business test (section 165-210(3)).

Over the years, the Commissioner and the courts have taken a restrictive approach, meaning that it proved very difficult for the new owners to use the losses incurred by the owners of the former business. If they changed functions of the old business, then they would be denied the ability to use the tax losses. Essentially, the courts had interpreted 'same business' to mean 'identical business'.

As a result, the view was that the same business test was considered too restrictive, making it very difficult for companies to satisfy this test as well as restricting innovation. This, in turn, discouraged companies that had losses from seeking new investors or exploring new profit-making activities because they may have lost access to prior year tax losses when acquiring the company.

The new relaxed test applies to losses made in income years commencing from 1 July 2015.

In simple terms, a company can carry forward and use prior year losses if it carries on a business (the current business) which is 'similar' to the business (former business) carried on immediately before the failure of the 'continuity of ownership' test.

In working out whether a business is 'similar', regard must be had to the following factors:

- the extent to which the assets used in the current business to generate assessable income (including goodwill) were used in the former business
- the extent to which the activities from the current business to generate assessable income were also activities in the former business
- the identity of the current business and the identity of the former business
- the extent to which changes to the former business resulted from development or commercialisation of assets, products, processes, services, or marketing or organisational methods, of the former business.

Examples provided in the explanatory memorandum include the following.

- The similar business test is passed where an online furniture reseller starts manufacturing and selling mattresses or a plastics manufacturer discovers that the same process makes teeth whitener.
- The similar business test is failed where a homewares shop becomes a stationery retailer or where a drinks manufacturer becomes a bottling company.

The ATO has already indicated that in their opinion, it will not be enough if a business is of a similar type to a previous business. It says a business is similar where there is an element of continuity, and that it has grown over time without changing its core identity or core source of income.

11.3.3 Tax loss carry-back for companies

As part of the 2020–21 Federal Budget, the Government announced that companies with an aggregated turnover of less than $5 billion will be entitled to choose to carry-back tax losses incurred in the 2020, 2021 and 2022 income years to offset the company's taxable income in the 2019 or later income years (Division 160 of the ITAA97). When tax losses are carried back, the company will generate a refundable tax offset when the company lodges its tax return for the income year in which the tax loss is made.

The refundable tax offset will be limited to the amount of taxable income in the earlier years and will not be available where the carry-back generates a franking account deficit. Thus, carry-back tax refunds may not be available where a company has distributed its earlier year after-tax profits as franked dividends. Companies that do not choose to carry-back tax losses can still carry forward tax losses in accordance with the existing rules.

Refundable tax offsets can result in a cash refund if the eligible entity is still not in a taxable position. A company can claim the tax offset if it:

- is an eligible entity which is defined as a corporate tax entity throughout the income year for which it elects to claim the carry back and throughout the period it is seeking to carry back the loss. It must also satisfy one of the following:
  - be a small business entity (SBE) for the income year as defined in Subdivision 328-C, or
  - would be an SBE for the income year if the SBE annual aggregated turnover threshold was $5 billion instead of $10 million
- made tax losses the 2019–20, 2020–21 or 2021–22 income years
- had an income tax liability for the 2018–19, 2019–20 or 2020–21 income years; use table 11.3 to check eligibly to claim the offset
- had a surplus in its franking account at the end of the income year for which it is claiming the tax offset
- has met its tax return lodgement. It is a requirement that the company has satisfied its lodgement requirements or assessments have been made for the current year and each of the five income years before the current year (unless the entity was not required to lodge an income tax return for the year).

TABLE 11.3

Tax liability in the income year	Tax loss made in 2018–19 or prior income years	Tax loss made in 2019–20 income year	Tax loss made in 2020–21 income year	Tax loss made in 2021–22 income year
2018–19	N/A	Can carry the 2019–20 loss back to the 2018–19 income year	Can carry the 2020–21 loss back to the 2018–19 income year	Can carry the 2021–22 loss back to the 2018–19 income year
2019–20	Not eligible	N/A	Can carry the 2020–21 loss back to the 2019–20 income year	Can carry the 2021–22 loss back to the 2019–20 income year
2020–21	Not eligible	Not eligible	N/A	Can carry the 2021–22 loss back to the 2020–21 income year

Source: Adapted from Australian Taxation Office, 'Claiming the loss carry back tax offset' (Web Page) https://www.ato.gov.au/General/Gen/Claiming-the-loss-carry-back-tax-offset.

A flowchart outlining loss carry-back tax offset eligibility is provided in figure 11.2.

11.3.3.1 The method statement

The following steps outline how to calculate the tax offset amount for an income year.
- *Step 1* — Start with the amount of the tax loss the company has chosen to carry back to the income year.
- *Step 2* — Reduce the step 1 amount by the company's net exempt income for the year.
- *Step 3* — Multiply the step 2 amount by the corporate tax rate for the loss year.
- *Step 4* — If the amount calculated under step 3 is greater than the franking account surplus at the end of the income year in which the tax offset is being claimed, the offset is limited to the franking account surplus. Otherwise, the amount of the tax offset is the amount calculated under step 3.

Example 11.4 uses these steps to calculate tax offset.

EXAMPLE 11.4

Carry-back losses

In the current year, a company made a tax loss of $400 000. It is not a BRE. It had a taxable income in the 2020–21 year of $8 million and the balance in its franking account at 30 June 2021 was $1.3 million.

It decides to make the choice to carry back the tax loss of $400 000 to the 2021 tax year.

The amount of the offset is $400 000 × 30% = $120 000. As this is less than the balance in the franking account, the tax offset is $120 000.

When the company lodges its 2022 tax return, it will be entitled to a refundable tax offset of $120 000. Using the step method, the calculations are as follows.
- Step 1: $400 000 loss.
- Step 2: No exempt income (therefore still $400 000).
- Step 3: $400 000 × 30% = $120 000.
- Step 4: $1 300 000 versus $120 000. Offset is the lessor of the 2 amounts, being $120 000.

The Explanatory Memorandum to the Act states that ordinarily a change of control that arises from generational change or as a result of the breakdown of marital and personal relationships within family-owned CTEs would not indicate that there was a purpose of obtaining a tax offset.

FIGURE 11.2   Claiming the loss carry-back tax offset: your eligibility

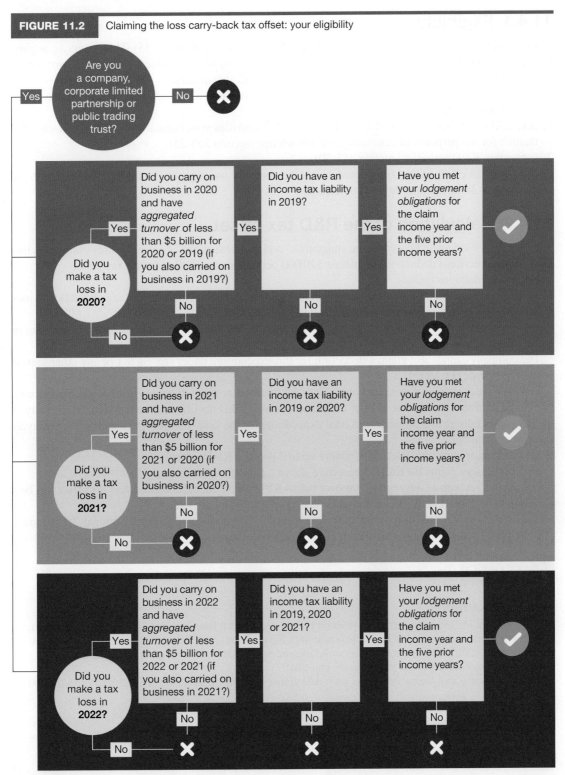

Source: Australian Taxation Office, 'Loss carry back tax offset flow chart', https://www.ato.gov.au/uploadedFiles/Content/SME/downloads/Loss_carry_back_tax_offset_factsheet.pdf.

11.4 Research and development tax concessions

LEARNING OBJECTIVE 11.4   Explain the research and development concessions available to companies.

Under Division 355 of the ITAA97, companies are provided with special research and development (R&D) tax incentives to undertake research and development activities in Australia and particularly, to provide incentives for smaller companies to engage in R&D activities.

The incentives are based on a company's aggregated turnover and their relevant company tax rate.

11.4.1 Eligibility

To claim an R&D tax offset, a company must be an 'R&D entity' (section 355-35). This covers a company incorporated, or otherwise resident, in Australia. However, certain non-resident companies carrying on business in Australia through a permanent establishment will also qualify.

Generally, a company can only claim the tax offset where R&D activities are conducted in Australia. The activities must fall within the definition of either:

1. core R&D activities, which are basically experimental activities systematically conducted in a scientific manner for the purposes of generating new knowledge (section 355-25)
2. supporting R&D activities (section 355-30).

The R&D tax offset cannot be claimed unless the company has registered its R&D activities with the Department of Industry, Innovation and Science.

11.4.2 Calculation of the R&D tax offset

The tax offset is calculated based on the company's 'notional deductions'. Generally, only companies that have incurred notional deductions of at least $20 000 per annum are eligible for the tax offset.

Notional deductions include:

- expenditure incurred on R&D activities including salaries and wages of staff working on R&D activities
- depreciation on depreciating assets used in R&D activities.

However, it does not include interest paid or expenditure included in acquiring a depreciating asset or constructing a building.

The company cannot also claim a deduction for this expenditure under section 8-1 or any other section of the ITAA36 or ITAA97.

For companies with an aggregated turnover of $20 million or more, the Government has introduced a two-tiered premium that ties the rates of the non-refundable R&D tax offset to the incremental intensity of the R&D expenditure as a proportion of total expenditure for the year. The new rates will be the taxpayers company tax rate plus:

- 8.5 percentage points for R&D expenditure up to 2 per cent R&D intensity
- 16.5 percentage points for R&D expenditure above 2 per cent R&D intensity.

For companies with an aggregated turnover below $20 million, the refundable R&D tax offset will be a premium of 18.5 percentage points above the taxpayer's company tax rate.

The offset is calculated by applying the relevant rate of the company to the total notional deductions.

Example 11.5 demonstrates calculation of the R&D tax offset.

EXAMPLE 11.5

R&D tax offset

Totalconcept Pty Ltd is an Australian resident private company. It has an annual turnover of $7.5 million, and has registered for the R&D tax concession with the Department of Industry, Innovation and Science.

During the 2021–22 income year, it incurred expenditure of $350 000 on eligible R&D activities.

What is the R&D tax offset the company can claim?

The company can claim a 43.5 per cent refundable tax offset equivalent to $152 259 (i.e. $350 000 × 43.5%).

The 43.5% is worked out as follows BRE company tax rate of 25% + 18.5% = 43.5%

If the company was a non BRE then the offset rate would be 30% + 18.5% = 48.5%

No deduction is available for the expenditure of $350 000 in calculating Totalconcept Pty Ltd's 2022 taxable income.

11.4.3 Early-stage innovation companies (ESIC)

Division 360 of the ITAA97 provides certain tax concessions to encourage new investment in small Australian innovation companies with high growth potential.

From 1 July 2016, investors in early-stage innovation companies (ESIC) are entitled to:

- a 20 per cent non-refundable tax offset on the amount paid for the investment (capped at a maximum of $200 000 per investor per year). For example, if an ESIC company issues $100 000 in shares to an investor, the investor can claim a $20 000 non-refundable tax offset that reduces their tax payable, and
- a CGT exemption on the sale of ESIC shares that have been held for between 1 and 10 years.

To meet the early stage test, the company must meet four requirements, namely:
- the company must have been incorporated or registered in the Australian Business Register
- the company must have total expenses of $1 million or less in the previous income year
- the company must have assessable income of $200 000 or less in the previous income year, and
- the company must not be listed on any stock exchange.

The offset is generally equal to 20 per cent of the total amount paid for the ESIC shares. However, the maximum offset an investor and their affiliates can claim in a tax year is capped at $200 000.

Where the offset exceeds the tax payable by the investor, the excess can be carried forward to offset taxable income in future years (subject to the $200 000 cap).

11.5 The taxation of dividends

LEARNING OBJECTIVE 11.5 Explain how dividends are taxed.

A **dividend** is defined widely in section 6(1) of the ITAA36 to include:

    (a) any distribution made by a company to any of its shareholders, whether in money or other property, or

    (b) any amount credited by a company to its shareholders.

Essentially, a dividend represents any distribution of a company's profit to its shareholders. The dividend may include payments of:
- cash
- dividends reinvested in further shares (under a dividend reinvestment plan)
- bonus shares (in certain limited circumstances).

According to section 44(1)(a) of the ITAA36, a resident individual taxpayer must include in their assessable income, all dividends paid by a company (regardless of whether they are based in Australia or not) out of profits derived by it from any source.

Section 44(1)(b) provides that a non-resident taxpayer is assessable on only those dividends paid by a company out of profits derived by it from an Australian source.

A dividend is paid out of net profit after income tax. The directors of the company determine the amount of dividend paid to the shareholders.

11.5.1 The dividend imputation system

Prior to the introduction of the **dividend imputation system** on 1 July 1987, the payment of dividends to an individual shareholder involved double taxation.

On 1 July 1987, the Commonwealth Government introduced the dividend imputation system. The dividend imputation system removes the effect of double taxation on company dividends in the hands of the individual shareholder. Since this date, there are two types of distributions (or dividends) that shareholders can receive:
- an unfrankable distribution (or unfranked dividend)
- a frankable distribution (or franked dividend).

An unfrankable distribution (or unfranked dividend) means that the company has not paid tax on the dividend distributed to shareholders.

Conversely, a frankable distribution (or franked dividend) means that the company has paid tax on the dividend distributed to shareholders. A dividend can be franked from 1 to 100 per cent, but cannot be franked more than 100 per cent.

Resident individual shareholders who receive either franked or unfranked dividends must include them as assessable income by virtue of section 44(1)(a).

Furthermore, where a shareholder (including a company) receives a franked dividend, it must not only include the amount of the dividend received in its assessable income (section 44(1)(a) of the ITAA36), but also the franking credit in accordance with section 207-20(1) of the ITAA97).

The amount of franking credits is ascertained by reference to the following formula.

$$\text{Amount of franked dividend} \times \frac{\text{Company tax rate}}{(1 - \text{Company tax rate})} \times \% \text{ franked}$$

For companies with an annual turnover of *less than* $50 million, for the year ended 30 June 2022, the company tax rate is 25 per cent. Applying the formula results in the following calculation of franking credits.

$$\text{Amount of franked dividend} \times \frac{25}{75} \times \% \text{ franked}$$

For all companies with an annual turnover of *more than* $50 million, for the year ended 30 June 2022, the company tax rate is 30 per cent. Applying the formula results in the following calculation of franking credits.

$$\text{Amount off ranked dividend} \times \frac{25}{75} \times \% \text{ franked}$$

The calculation of franking credits is demonstrated in example 11.6.

EXAMPLE 11.6

Calculation of franking credits

In April 2022, Charlotte, an Australian resident taxpayer, receives a franked dividend of $1500 from a family company, Blue Star Training Pty Ltd. The dividend was franked to 60 per cent.

Assume that the annual turnover of Blue Star Training Pty Ltd is $2.2 million per annum. Hence, as it is a BRE, the appropriate tax rate is 25 per cent.

The amount of the franking credit attached to this franking credit is calculated as:

$$\$1500 \times \frac{27.5}{72.5} \times 60\% \text{ Franked} = \$341 \text{ (rounded)}$$

11.5.1.1 Inclusion of the franking credit as assessable income

The inclusion of the franking credit as assessable income seemingly increases the shareholder's taxable income. However, according to section 207-20(2) of the ITAA97), a resident shareholder is also entitled to a credit or tax offset (being the amount of the 'franking credit') in respect of the tax paid by the company on the dividend. This effectively provides the shareholder with a rebate for the amount of tax which the company has paid on the dividends received.

Where the franking credit exceeds the net tax payable, the excess is a refundable tax-offset to individual shareholders (see section 67-25 of the ITAA97).

The inclusion of franking credit as assessable income is demonstrated in example 11.7.

EXAMPLE 11.7

Inclusion of franking credit as assessable income

In October 2021, Michael, an Australian resident taxpayer, receives an unfranked dividend of $1200 from Oz Minerals Limited. In March 2022, he receives a $1400 franked dividend from CSR Limited, franked to 60 per cent. Assume that the company tax rate of 30 per cent applies.

In June 2022, Michael receives a dividend from a US company of AU$1700 (net of foreign withholding tax deducted at the source of AU$300).

What amounts are reflected in Michael's assessable income?

Michael's assessable income is calculated as:

	$
Unfranked dividend (s 44(1)(a))	1 200
Franked dividend (s 44(1)(a))	1 400
Franking credit (s 207-20(1))	360*
Net US dividend (s 44(1)(a))	1 700

Add: Withholding tax gross-up (s 128D)	300
Total assessable income	**4 960**

*The franking credit of $360 is calculated as: $1400 × 30/70 × 60% franked = $360.

Figure 11.3 is an extract of the individual tax return showing where unfranked dividends, franked dividends and the franking credit associated with franked dividends are included.

FIGURE 11.3	Dividends section of an individual tax return

11 Dividends

Unfranked amount **S** [.00]

Franked amount **T** [.00]

Tax file number amounts withheld from dividends **V** [ ]

Franking credit **U** [.00]

26%	Unfranked	Franked	Franking credit	TFN amount	Business?

Source: Extract of individual tax return taken from HandiTax.

11.5.1.2 Impact of a fully franked dividend to individual shareholders

Table 11.4 illustrates the tax consequences to resident individual shareholders on various marginal tax rates of receiving a $7000 fully franked dividend (franked to 100 per cent from a resident Australian company).

TABLE 11.4	**Impact to individual shareholder of receiving a fully franked dividend**

Marginal tax rate (excluding Medicare levy)	45%	37%	32.5%	19%	0%
Fully franked dividend	$ 7 000	$ 7 000	$ 7 000	$ 7 000	$ 7 000
Franking credit gross-up	3 000	3 000	3 000	3 000	3 000
Taxable income	**$ 10 000**	**$ 10 000**	**$ 10 000**	**$ 10 000**	**$ 10 000**
Tax payable	$ 4 500	$ 3 700	$ 3 250	$ 1 900	$ 0
Less: Franking credit	(3 000)	(3 000)	(3 000)	(3 000)	(3 000)
Tax payable/(refund)	**$ 1 500**	**$ 700**	**$ 250**	**$ (1 100)**	**$ (3 000)**

To be entitled to a franking credit in relation to a particular dividend, a taxpayer must be a 'qualified person' in relation to the dividend.

A taxpayer is a qualified person in relation to a dividend if he/she satisfies one of the following four tests.

1. The taxpayer satisfies the holding period rule. This rule requires the person to hold shares for at least 45 days for ordinary shares (or 90 days for preference shares) excluding the day of acquisition and disposal.
2. The taxpayer is a particular kind of taxpayer who elects to have a franking credit or franking rebate ceiling applied, calculated according to a prescribed formula.
3. The taxpayer is a natural person whose franking rebate entitlement for the year is less than $5000.
4. The dividend is paid on certain shares issued in connection with winding up a company.

11.5.1.3 Special rules for companies — converting excess franking credits into tax losses

While a company is entitled to a credit in respect of the franking credits under section 207-20(2), unlike other shareholders (such as individuals, partnerships, trusts and superannuation funds), excess franking credits are *not* refundable to companies (section 67-25 of the ITAA97).

Instead, companies are able to convert the amount of excess (or unused) franking credits to the equivalent amount of tax loss, which can be carried forward to be offset against future taxable income of the company in a later year of income (section 36-55). This is done by dividing the excess franking credit by 0.25 or 0.30.

The conversion of excess franking credits into tax losses is demonstrated in example 11.8.

EXAMPLE 11.8

Conversion of excess franking credits into tax losses

For the year ended 30 June 2022, Thunderbird Ltd derived a tax loss of $1250. The company's assessable income totalled $10 000 and its allowable deductions totalled $11 250.

Included in the $10 000 assessable income was a fully franked dividend of $700 received from Wesfarmers Ltd. Franking credits of $300 are attached to the franked dividend and have been included in the calculation of taxable income.

As the company is already in a tax loss position of $1250, the franking credits of $300 are effectively 'lost' as the company has no tax payable to offset the franking credit against. Companies are not entitled to a refund of excess franking credits (section 67-25).

To provide relief, the excess franking credit can be converted into an equivalent amount of tax loss. How is this done?

The excess franking credit can be converted into an equivalent amount of tax loss by dividing the amount of the franking credit by the company tax rate of 30 per cent.

In other words, the $300 franking credit is converted into a tax loss of $1000 (being $300/0.30). This $1000 can be added to the $1250 tax loss to give a total tax loss of $2250 which the company can carry forward to a future income year to offset against future assessable income.

11.5.2 Deemed dividends

The definition of dividends catches most company distributions or payments. In addition, some distributions or payments are specifically deemed to be dividends paid to shareholders. However, most of the deemed dividend provisions only apply to private companies for taxation purposes.

The following represent the most common instances where company distributions or payments will be deemed to be dividends:

- distributions made under a liquidator (section 47)
- off-market share buy-backs (section 159GZZZP)
- profits distributed or credited by a private company to a shareholder or an associate as an advance, payment, loan or debt forgiven (Division 7A)
- excessive remuneration paid or credited by a private company to a shareholder, director or associate (section 109)
- bonus shares issued where there is a choice between dividends and shares where section 6BA(5) applies and section 6BA(6) does not, and
- a distribution to a shareholder from a 'tainted share capital account' (Division 197).

The most significant of these deemed dividends is Division 7A. This concept is explained in further detail in the next section of this chapter.

11.6 Division 7A

LEARNING OBJECTIVE 11.6 Apply the concepts of Division 7A to the tax treatment of a loan by a private company to a shareholder.

From 4 December 1997, **Division 7A** (comprising sections 109B to 109ZE of the ITAA36) operates to automatically deem certain loans made by private companies to a shareholder or a shareholder's associate as dividends.

If the loan is not repaid by the date of lodgement of the company's income tax return, the amount of the loan is deemed to constitute an unfranked dividend in the hands of the shareholder receiving the money.

Figure 11.4 summarises the application of Division 7A.

FIGURE 11.4 A sample distribution statement for a private company

Did one of the following transactions occur on or after 4 December 1997?
- The company paid an amount to a shareholder (or associate) (s 109C)
- An existing loan was significantly altered (s 109D(5))
- The company lent an amount to a shareholder or associate that was not fully repaid by the end of the current year (s 109D–109E)
- A debt owed by a shareholder or associate to the company was forgiven (s 109F)

→ No → **Has one of these transactions occurred through an interposed entry?**

↓ Yes

Is the transaction excluded?
- Payments of genuine debt (s 109J)
- Payments or loans to other companies (s 109K)
- Payments or loans that are otherwise assessable (s 109L)
- Loans made in the ordinary course of business (s 109M)
- Loans that meet the criteria for minimum interest rate and maximum term (s 109N)

Yes (from interposed entry question) →

No (from interposed entry question) → **Rules do *not* apply**

Yes → **Rules do *not* apply**

↓ No

Is the amount of the loan greater than the company's distributable surplus? → Yes → **The division 7A deemed dividend is equal to the company's distributable surplus (s 109Y)**

↓ No

A deemed dividend arises under Division 7A for the amount of the loan advanced to the shareholder

For the provisions of Division 7A to apply, the criteria in table 11.5 must be met.

TABLE 11.5 When Division 7A applies

Criteria for Division 7A to apply	Applies
The company is a private company for taxation purposes	✓
The person receiving the loan is a shareholder or an associate of the shareholder	✓
The loan has not been repaid by date of lodgement of the company's tax return	✓
The loan has not been put on a commercial footing (i.e. no written loan agreement exists)	✓

11.6.1 Division 7A: Consequences of a deemed dividend

If Division 7A applies, payments, loans and forgiven amounts provided to a shareholder (or associate) of a private company that are not repaid by the due date for lodgement of the company's income tax return, nor put on a commercial footing, are deemed to constitute an unfranked dividend in the hands of the shareholder.

As such, the shareholder will be required to include the amount received as assessable income as an unfranked dividend (section 202-45(g)).

Where a shareholder is also an employee, both Division 7A and fringe benefits tax (FBT) could apply. However, Division 7A overrides FBT in relation to such payments (refer to the definition of a 'fringe benefit' contained in section 136(1)(r) of the FBTAA86). As such, the FBT rules do not apply to loans that are deemed to be a dividend under Division 7A.

Example 11.9 demonstrates the consequences of a deemed dividend.

EXAMPLE 11.9

Consequences of a deemed dividend

On 14 September 2021, Fluffy Duck Pty Ltd (a private company for tax purposes) lends $60 000 to a shareholder (Fred).

Assume that by the date of lodgement of the company's 2022 income tax return, the loan has not been repaid by Fred, nor has it been put on a commercial footing. In other words, no loan agreement has been drafted in relation to the $60 000 lent to Fred.

How is this loan treated under Division 7A?

This loan meets all the requirements as a Division 7A loan. It is deemed to constitute an unfranked dividend to Fred and, as such, he is required to include it as an unfranked dividend in his 2022 income tax return.

11.6.2 Deemed dividend limited to the amount of the company's distributable surplus

A Division 7A deemed dividend is taken to have been paid out of the company's profits up to the extent of the company's 'distributable surplus' at the end of the income year in which the loan was made (section 109Y).

According to section 109Y(2), a company's distributable surplus is broadly calculated as follows:

$$\text{Distributable surplus} = \text{Net assets} - \text{Non-commercial loans} -$$
$$\text{Paid-up capital} - \text{Repayment of non-commercial loans}$$

Non-commercial loans are essentially loans that have been treated as Division 7A deemed dividends in a previous income year. Repayment of non-commercial loans means any repayment of loans previously deemed as Division 7A dividends.

In essence, a company's distributable surplus is its total shareholders' equity minus share capital. Therefore, it basically includes retained profits and other reserves.

Assets and liabilities included in the calculation of net assets are brought to account at their book value. Book value is the amount shown in the company's accounting records unless the Commissioner considers that the company's accounting records significantly undervalue its assets or overvalue its liabilities (section 109Y(2)). In this instance, the Commissioner can substitute a different value if the assets are significantly understated or the liabilities significantly overstated.

If a private company has no distributable surplus, then no amount will be deemed to be an unfranked dividend.

Furthermore, if, in a later income year the company has a higher distributable surplus, it will *not* affect the amount of the deemed dividend paid in the prior year.

This is demonstrated in example 11.10.

EXAMPLE 11.10

Distributable surplus

Refer to the facts of example 11.9. On 14 September 2021, Fluffy Duck Pty Ltd (a private company for tax purposes) lent $60 000 to a shareholder (Fred), which remained unpaid at the time of lodgement of the company's 2022 income tax return.

In example 11.9, the amount of the Division 7A dividend was $60 000 (being the amount of the loan). However, under section 109Y, the amount of the deemed Division 7A dividend is limited to the extent of the company's 'distributable surplus' at the end of the company's income year in which the loan was made.

Assume, as at 30 June 2022, that Fluffy Duck Pty Ltd has total assets of $120 000 (including the $60 000 loan owing by Fred) and total liabilities of $80 000, meaning that it has net assets of $40 000. Shareholders equity comprises paid-up capital of $5000 and retained profits of $35 000.

What is the distributable surplus?

The distributable surplus of Fluffy Duck Pty Ltd is calculated at $35 000. This amount is determined by taking away the paid-up capital of $5000 from the net assets of $40 000. The amount of the Division 7A deemed dividend is therefore $35 000, *not* $60 000.

Fred will only need to include an amount of $35 000 as an unfranked dividend in his 2022 income tax return.

If the company generates a higher distributable surplus in a subsequent income year (e.g. $75 000 in respect of the year ended 30 June 2023), this will *not* affect any deemed dividends paid in a prior year.

In effect, the amount of the unfranked dividend is the *lesser of* the loan made to the shareholder and the company's distributable surplus at the end of the income year in which the loan was made.

11.6.3 Forgiveness of a Division 7A loan

If a private company forgives (wholly or partly), a debt owed to it by a shareholder or associate, the amount forgiven is automatically treated as an unfranked dividend at the end of the private company's year of income (section 109F).

11.6.4 Exclusions from Division 7A

Not all payments, loans or debts forgiven by private companies will be treated as dividends. Table 11.6 summarises those payments and loans which are excluded from the operation of Division 7A.

TABLE 11.6   Exclusions from Division 7A

Payments not treated as dividends	Loans not treated as dividends
Payments of genuine debts (s 109J)	Loans to other companies (s 109K)
Payments to other companies (s 109K)	Loans that are otherwise assessable (s 109L)
Payments that are otherwise assessable (s 109L)	Loans made in the ordinary course of business on commercial terms (s 109M)
Certain liquidator's distributions (s 109NA)	Loans that meet criteria for minimum rate and maximum term (s 109N)
	Certain liquidator's distributions (s 109NA)
	Loans to purchase qualifying shares or rights under an employee share scheme (s 109NB)
	Amalgamated loans in the year they are made (s 109P)
	Where undue hardship is caused (s 109Q)

11.6.5 Loans that meet the minimum interest rate and maximum criteria

A Division 7A loan does *not* apply where the loan is put on a commercial footing by the due date of the company's income tax return (section 109N).

For loans to fall under section 109N they must satisfy the following criteria before the earlier of the lodgement date or the due date for lodgement of the company's income tax return:

- the loan must be made under a written agreement
- the rate of interest payable on the loan for years of income after the year in which the loan was made must equal or exceed the **benchmark interest rate** for the relevant year (see table 11.7)
- the term of the loan must not exceed the maximum term of the loan as defined in section 109N(3), that is 25 years where there is a registered mortgage over real property of not more than 91 per cent of the value of the property, otherwise, the maximum term of the loan is 7 years
- minimum yearly repayments calculated in accordance with section 109E must be made.

Table 11.7 summarises the benchmark interest rate over the past 5 years.

TABLE 11.7 Benchmark Division 7A interest rates[2]

Income year	Benchmark interest rate	Reference
2021, 2022	4.52%	Reserve Bank of Australia
2020	5.37%	Reserve Bank of Australia
2019	5.20%	TD 2018/14
2018	5.30%	TD 2017/17
2017	5.40%	TD 2016/11

11.6.5.1 No interest or repayments need to be made in the year of the loan

In the case of a Division 7A loan, interest does not need to be calculated or charged for the income year in which the loan is made. Interest is only payable in respect of the second and subsequent income years. Furthermore, no loan repayments need to be made in the income year in which the loan is made.

For example, if a $100 000 Division 7A loan was made to a shareholder on 14 August 2021, no loan repayments are required to be made for the year ended 30 June 2022. Interest does not need to be calculated until the first day of the income year following the year in which the loan was made (i.e. from 1 July 2023).

11.6.5.2 Minimum yearly repayments

In order to avoid the application of Division 7A, minimum yearly repayments must be made. Section 109E(6) sets out the formula for determining minimum yearly repayments.

The formula is:

$$\frac{\text{Amount of the loan not repaid by the end of the previous year of income} \times \text{Current year's benchmark interest rate}}{1 - \left(\dfrac{1}{1 + \text{Current year's benchmark interest rate}}\right)^{\text{Remaining term}}}$$

The application of the formula is demonstrated in examples 11.11 and 11.12.

EXAMPLE 11.11

Determining minimum yearly repayments to avoid application of Division 7A Part 1

Assume that Adrian is the sole shareholder of Capricorn Holdings Pty Ltd. On 17 October 2020, the company lent Adrian an amount of $100 000 under a written loan agreement. The loan is unsecured and has a term of 5 years.

---

2 These benchmark interest rates are based on the 'Loans; Banks; Variable; Standard; Owner-occupier' lending rate published by the RBA.

Under the terms of the loan agreement, no interest is charged in the first year of the loan (i.e. 2021 income year). Furthermore, no loan repayment is required to be made in the first year of the loan.

Interest is required to be charged during the subsequent income year (i.e. 2022 income year). The benchmark Division 7A interest rate for the 2022 income year is 4.52 per cent (see table 11.7).

The first repayment is made on 30 June 2022.

What is the minimum yearly repayment required?

The minimum yearly repayment required is calculated as:

$$\frac{\$100\,000 \times 4.52\%}{1 - 1/(1.0452)^5} = \$22\,756$$

EXAMPLE 11.12

Determining minimum yearly repayments to avoid application of Division 7A Part 2

Carrying on from example 11.11, assume that no other payment or loans were taken out. Assume that the minimum yearly repayment of $23 334 is made on 30 June 2022 (as per the written loan agreement).

What is the outstanding loan balance?

The outstanding loan balance is calculated as follows.

	$
Loan — original amount advanced (on 17 October 2020)	100 000
Add: Interest charged for the period 1 July 2021 to 30 June 2022	—
Less: Repayments made during 2022 financial year	
Loan balance at 30 June 2022	**100 000**
Loan balance at 30 June 2022	100 000
Add: Interest at 4.52% for period 1 July 2021 to 30 June 2022	4 520
Less: Minimum loan repayment made on 30 June 2022	(22 756)
Loan balance at 30 June 2022	**81 764**

The minimum repayment for the 2023 income year will be based on the loan outstanding of $81 764.

The ATO has published a Division 7A calculator and decision tool on its website. The calculator will:
- calculate the minimum yearly repayment required on a loan to avoid a deemed dividend arising under Division 7A, and
- calculate the amount of the loan not repaid by the end of the income year.

The Division 7A calculator and decision tool can be accessed on the ATO website.

11.6.5.3 Proposed changes to Division 7A

Following a review by the Board of Taxation concluding that the Division 7A rules are 'complex, inflexible and impose significant compliance costs on taxpayers, including many small businesses', in the 2016–17 Federal Budget the Commonwealth Government announced that it would make improvements to Division 7A.

These changes were scheduled to come into effect from 1 July 2019 but were deferred in the 2020–21 Federal Budget to on or after the income year when the legislation receives Royal Assent. The main changes are summarised as follows:
- the benchmark interest rate that will be applied to Division 7A loans will be changed to the Reserve Bank of Australia's Small Business Variable Overdraft rate, which is currently 7.74 per cent (compared to the current rate of 4.52 per cent)
- there will be no requirement for a formal written loan agreement; however, written or electronic evidence showing that the loan was entered into must exist by the lodgement day of the private company's income tax return

- interest will be calculated for the full income year, regardless of any loan repayments made during the income year (except Year 1)
- there will be one '10-year loan model' for all loans made by private companies. The existing 7- and 25-year loan options will be discontinued. Any existing loans will be transitioned to the new 10-year loan model
- the minimum yearly repayment amount consists of equal annual payments (both principal and interest) over the term of the loan
- the interest component is the interest calculated on the opening balance of the loan each year using the benchmark interest rate
- the removal of the concept of 'distributable surplus'.

11.6.6 Distribution statements

According to section 202-75 of the ITAA97, companies are required to provide shareholders with a distribution (or dividend) statement in an approved form. The timing of when a distribution statement must be provided to a shareholder depends on whether the company is a private company or not.

- Public company — the company must provide the shareholder with a distribution statement on or before the day on which the distribution is made (section 202-75(2)(a)).
- Private company — the company must provide the shareholder with a distribution statement no later than 4 months after the end of the income year (section 202-75(3)(a)). In the case of a company with an income year-end of 30 June, this means that the distribution statement must be provided to the shareholder no later than 31 October.

11.6.6.1 What is included in a distribution statement?

The **distribution statement** must be in the approved form and must contain the following information (section 202-80(3)):

(a) the name of the entity making the distribution
(b) the date on which the distribution is made
(c) the name of the shareholder
(d) the amount of the distribution
(e) the amount of the frankable distribution
(f) the amount of franking credits allocated to the frankable distribution
(g) the franking percentage of the frankable distribution
(h) the amount of the unfrankable distribution.

A sample distribution statement for a private company is shown in figure 11.5.

FIGURE 11.5   A sample distribution statement for a private company

SHAREHOLDER DISTRIBUTION STATEMENT

FOR THE YEAR ENDED 30 JUNE 2022

Name of company:	Maximus Ltd
ABN:	88 054 096 874
Date of distribution:	3 April 2022
Company tax rate:	30%
Name of shareholder:	Ms Elizabeth Jones

Franked/unfranked	Distribution	Franking credit
Franked amount	$7000.00	$3000.00
Franking percentage		100%
Unfranked amount	$1000.00	-

Note: You should retain this statement to assist you in preparing your 2022 income tax return.

Example 11.13 shows how to calculate assessable income from the information in a distribution statement.

EXAMPLE 11.13

Calculating assessable income from a distribution statement

Refer to the distribution statement in figure 11.5 and determine Elizabeth's assessable income. Elizabeth's assessable income is calculated as follows.

	$
Unfranked dividend (s 44(1)(a))	1 000
Franked dividend (s 44(1)(a))	7 000
Franking credit (s 207-20(1))	3 000*
Total assessable income	**11 000**

*The franking credit of $3000 is calculated as: $7000 × 30/70 × 100% franked = $3000

An extract of Elizabeth's 2022 income tax return is shown in figure 11.6.

FIGURE 11.6   Extract of income tax return — dividends

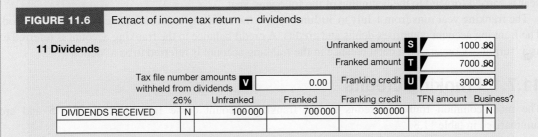

Source: Extract of individual tax return taken from HandiTax.

As outlined, the franking percentage is a measure of the extent to which a frankable distribution has been franked. A franked dividend can be franked anywhere from 1 to 100 per cent but cannot be franked to more than 100 per cent.

It is expressed as a percentage of the frankable distribution, rather than the whole of the distribution. The formula to calculate the franking percentage is outlined in section 203-35:

$$\frac{\text{Franking credit allocated to the frankable distribution (in dollars)}}{\text{Maximum franking credit in dollars as if franked to 100\%}} \times 100\%$$

The first step is to calculate the **maximum franking credit** (i.e. the denominator). The maximum franking credit (in dollars) is calculated as if the frankable distribution was franked to 100 per cent. The numerator is the actual amount of the franking credit. The denominator is the amount of the franking credit as if the franked dividend was franked to 100 per cent. This concept is illustrated in example 11.14.

EXAMPLE 11.14

Franking percentage

On 18 September 2021, Pivot Point Ltd paid a dividend of $120 000 to its shareholders, made up of $70 000 frankable and $50 000 unfrankable components. The relevant corporate tax rate is 30 per cent.

The maximum franking credit (i.e. 100 per cent) that Pivot Point Pty Ltd could allocate to the $70 000 frankable distribution is:

$$\$70\,000 \times \frac{30}{70} \times 100\% = \$30\,000$$

Assume that the directors of Pivot Point Ltd allocated franking credits of $24 000 to the distribution.

What is the franking percentage for the $70 000 frankable distribution?
The franking percentage is calculated as:

actual franking credit $\longrightarrow$ $\dfrac{\$24\,000}{\$30\,000}$ $=$ 80% $\longleftarrow$ as if franked to 100%

11.7 Franking account

LEARNING OBJECTIVE 11.7 Describe the operation of a company franking account.

Each resident Australian company is required to maintain a **franking account** (section 205-10). A franking account is an account that a company maintains to keep track of the franking credits that it can pass onto its shareholders.

Franking accounts are kept on an annual basis. The franking account does not form part of a company's financial statements. It is usually a schedule that accompanies the company's income tax return. The franking year aligns to the company's income year.

From 1 July 2002, entries in the franking account are recorded on a tax-paid basis. The franking account is a rolling balance that removes the need for franking entries to affect the transfer of a credit balance to the following income year. In other words, the balance in the franking account at the end of the franking year is carried forward to the beginning of the following year.

The franking year runs from 1 July to 30 June, unless the company has a substituted accounting period. The franking account comprises debits and credits. A credit balance in the franking account is referred to as a 'surplus'. Conversely, a debit balance in the franking account is referred to as a 'deficit'.

11.7.1 Franking credits

The most common franking credits to the franking account come from section 205-15 and are summarised in table 11.8.

TABLE 11.8 Credits in the franking account

Situation	A credit of ...	arises ...
If the company pays a PAYG instalment	the amount of the instalment	on the day on which the payment is made
If the company pays income tax	the amount of the payment	on the day on which the payment is made
If the company receives a franked distribution from another Australian resident company	the franking credit as per the distribution statement	on the day that the distribution is made
If the company receives a franked distribution that has flowed indirectly to it through a partnership or trust	the entity's share of the franking credit as per the distribution statement	at the end of the income year of the last partnership or trust interposed between the entity and the company that made the distribution
The entity incurs a liability to pay franking deficit tax under ss 205-45 or 205-50	the amount of the liability	immediately after the liability has been incurred (i.e. 30 June)

11.7.2 Franking debits

The most common **franking debits** to the franking account come from section 205-130 and are summarised in table 11.9.

TABLE 11.9   Debits in the franking account

Situation	A debit of ...	arises ...
If the company makes a franked distribution	the amount of franking credits allocated to the distribution	on the day on which the frankable distribution is made
If the company receives a refund of income tax	the amount of the refund	when the company receives the refund, or the Commissioner applies it against another tax liability
If the company underfranks a distribution	franking percentage differential × amount of frankable distribution × rate tax corporate 100% rate tax corporate (s 203-50(2)(b))	on the day that the distribution is made
If the company ceases to be a franking entity	the amount of the franking surplus	on the day specified in s 204-15(4)
If the company makes a linked distribution of issues tax-exempt bonus shares instead of making a frankable distribution	the amount equal to the franking debit if the company had made a frankable distribution with franking credits equal to its benchmark franking percentage	the day the determination is made
If the Commissioner determines that dividend streaming has occurred	the amount of the Commissioner's determination	the day the determination is made
On market share buy-back	the amount equal to the debit that would have arisen if the company had purchased the interest off-market	on the day the interest is purchased

11.7.3 Franking periods

A private company has one franking period in its income year (from 1 July to 30 June) and it is the same as its income year.

Conversely, according to section 203-40(2), a public company has two franking periods in its income year (from 1 July to 31 December and from 1 January to 30 June).

11.7.4 The benchmark rule

The **benchmark rule** contained in section 203-25 provides that all frankable distributions made by a company during a franking period must be franked to the same extent as the **benchmark franking percentage** (section 203-10). This ensures that franking credits representing tax paid on behalf of all shareholders of the company are not allocated (i.e. streamed) to only some shareholders.

The franking percentage for the first frankable distribution made in the franking period establishes the benchmark franking percentage to be used in respect of all frankable distributions for that franking period (section 203-30).

If no frankable distributions are made in the franking period, the entity does not have a benchmark franking percentage for the franking period.

Furthermore, the declaration and payment of an unfranked dividend does not establish the benchmark franking percentage for the period.

Example 11.15 demonstrates the calculation of a benchmark franking percentage.

EXAMPLE 11.15

Benchmark franking percentage

Knight Rider Ltd is a private company for tax purposes. On 18 July 2021, the directors declare and pay an unfranked dividend of $20 000 to its shareholders.

▷

On 11 August 2021, the directors declare and pay a franked dividend of $30 000 to its shareholders, franked to 80 per cent.

What is the company's benchmark franking percentage?

First, we are told that Knight Rider Pty Ltd is a private company for income tax purposes. Hence, it has one franking period (from 1 July to 30 June). This means that, once the benchmark franking percentage has been determined, that franking percentage must be used throughout the entire franking period (i.e. the full income tax year).

The payment of the unfranked dividend on 18 July 2021 does not establish the benchmark franking percentage for the period. Instead, the first franked dividend paid on 11 August 2021 of $30 000, which the directors franked to 80 per cent establishes the benchmark franking percentage for the rest of the income year in accordance with section 203-30.

Hence, if the directors declared and paid a second or subsequent franked dividend until 30 June 2022 (i.e. the rest of the franking period), these franked dividends must also be franked to 80 per cent.

11.7.4.1 Consequences of breaching the benchmark rule

A penalty will be imposed on the company for breaching the benchmark rule. A company may underfrank or overfrank its second and subsequent franking percentages from the first frankable distribution.

11.7.5 Underfranking

Underfranking occurs where the company franks its second (and subsequent) frankable distributions at an amount less than the benchmark franking percentage.

For example, if the benchmark franking percentage is 100 per cent and the company franks its second frankable distribution within the same franking period to 80 per cent, then it has underfranked the second distribution by 20 per cent.

The penalty for underfranking is that the company is required to debit its franking account on the same date on which the frankable distribution is made for the amount of the franking shortfall.

The franking shortfall is defined in section 203-50. It is essentially the difference between the benchmark franking percentage for the franking period in which the frankable distribution is made and the franking percentage for the second and subsequent distributions.

Shareholders do not receive the benefit of any additional franking credits as a consequence of the debit to the franking account (section 203-50).

Underfranking is demonstrated in example 11.16.

EXAMPLE 11.16

Underfranking

On 5 July 2021, Genesis Ltd makes a frankable distribution of $1400. It allocates franking credits of $600 (at 30%) to the frankable distribution. Hence, its benchmark franking percentage is set at 100 per cent. The franking credit is calculated at:

$$\$1400 \times \frac{30}{70} \times 100\% = \$600$$

On 16 December 2021, Genesis Ltd makes a second frankable distribution of $10 500. It allocates franking credits of $3600 to the frankable distribution. This equates to a franking percentage of 80 per cent. This is calculated as:

$$\frac{\$3600}{\$4500} = 80\%$$

The $4500 shown in the denominator is based on the maximum amount of franking credits able to be allocated to the frankable distribution, being 100 per cent. The $4500 is calculated as: $10 500 × 30/70 × 100%. Consequently, the company has underfranked this distribution by 20 per cent and an underfranking penalty debit arises (being 100% – 80%).

What is the penalty for the underfranking?

The amount of the underfranking tax is equivalent to the franking debit that should have been allocated to the distribution in accordance with the benchmark franking percentage. It is calculated as:

$$(100\% - 80\%) \times \$10\,500 \times \frac{30}{70} = \$900$$

The underfranking penalty debit of $900 that arises in the franking account results in lost franking credits. This is because the beneficiary of the distribution only receives a franking credit based on the 80 per cent franking level, even though the franking account reflects the higher benchmark franking rate of 100 per cent.

This effectively constitutes a permanent loss of franking credits to the entity. The penalty debit arises on the same day as the underfranked distribution was made.

11.7.6 Overfranking

Overfranking occurs where the company franks its second (and subsequent) frankable distributions at an amount more than the benchmark franking percentage.

For example, if the benchmark franking percentage is 80 per cent and the company franks its second frankable distribution within the same franking period to 100 per cent, then it has overfranked the second distribution by 20 per cent.

The penalty for overfranking is that the company is liable for 'overfranking tax' which is determined based on the 'franking percentage differential' as per section 203-50. This is essentially the difference between the franking percentage for the second and subsequent distributions and the benchmark franking percentage for the franking period in which the frankable distribution is made.

The company is required to remit the overfranking tax to the ATO by the last day of the month following the end of the income tax year (section 214-150(1)). In other words, overfranking tax is payable to the ATO by 31 July.

Overfranking tax is a penalty, meaning that when the company pays this to the ATO, it does not result in a franking credit to the franking account and therefore represents lost franking credits.

Example 11.17 demonstrates overfranking.

Overfranking

On 11 August 2021, Eaglehawk Pty Ltd makes a frankable distribution of $14 000. It allocates franking credits of $4800 (at 30%) to the frankable distribution. Hence, its benchmark franking percentage is set at 80 per cent. The franking credit is calculated at:

$$\$14\,000 \times \frac{30}{70} \times 80\% = \$4800$$

On 9 March 2022, Eaglehawk Pty Ltd makes a second frankable distribution of $7000. It allocates franking credits of $3000 to the frankable distribution. This equates to a franking percentage of 100 per cent. The franking credit is calculated at:

$$\$7000 \times \frac{30}{70} \times 100\% = \$3000$$

The company has therefore overfranked this distribution by 20 per cent and is liable for overfranking tax. What is the penalty for the overfranking?

The amount of the overfranking tax is equivalent to the franking credit allocated in excess of the benchmark. It is calculated as:

$$(100\% - 80\%) \times \$7000 \times \frac{30}{70} = \$600$$

Overfranking tax is payable by the last day of the month following the end of the income year (section 214-150). A company that overfranks will be required to prepare and lodge a franking account tax return with the ATO no later than 31 July.

When the company pays overfranking tax to the ATO, it does not result in a credit to the franking account as overfranking tax is regarded as a penalty. Hence, it results in lost franking credits.

11.7.7 Franking deficit tax

The franking account is never closed off. Instead, it is a rolling balance account, which means that the balance of the franking account rolls from one franking year to another. However, at the end of the income year, if a company has a deficit in its franking account (i.e. the total of the franking debits exceeds the total of the franking credits), it has imputed to its members more tax than it has paid.

As a result, it is liable to pay franking deficit tax (FDT) to account for the over-imputation of tax. The amount of the franking deficit tax is equal to the franking deficit.

Franking deficit tax is payable by the last day of the month following the end of the income tax year (section 214-150(1)). In other words, franking deficit tax is payable by 31 July. Franking deficit tax is not a penalty, but merely a payment that is required to be made to make good the amount imputed to shareholders that exceeds the amount of tax actually paid.

Hence, the entity can credit its franking account for the amount of FDT payable to the ATO. Unlike the timing of all other franking debits and credits that are entered into the franking account on a cash paid basis, the credit to the franking account for the amount of the FDT is made on the last day of the income year in which the deficit arises (i.e. 30 June).

Furthermore, payment of FDT to the ATO represents a refundable tax offset (called the 'franking deficit tax offset') which is deducted from the company's income tax liability at the end of the relevant income year. In effect the FDT is regarded as a 'deemed' PAYG instalment.

Example 11.18 demonstrates the application of franking deficit tax.

EXAMPLE 11.18

Franking deficit tax

Trans Pacific Ltd (a large business taxpayer) has a taxable income for the year ended 30 June 2022 of $10 000 000 and it has made PAYG instalments during the year totalling $2 400 000.

Assume that at 30 June 2022, the balance of the company's franking account is in deficit by $100 000. Accordingly, the company is liable to pay franking deficit tax of $100 000 to the ATO no later than 31 July 2022.

What is the company's income tax payable?

The company can offset the $100 000 franking deficit tax against its 2022 income tax liability as follows.

	$
2022 taxable income	10 000 000
Tax payable on taxable income @ 30%	3 000 000
Less: PAYG instalments paid during 2021	(2 400 000)
Less: Franking deficit tax (able to be offset against income tax liability)	(100 000)
2022 income tax payable	**500 000**

The franking rules described in sections 11.7.5, 11.7.6 and 11.7.7 are summarised in table 11.10.

TABLE 11.10 Summary of franking rules

Item	Debit/credit in franking account	Cheque to ATO?
Underfranking	Debit (on same day)	x
Overfranking (when tax paid)	x	✓ (payable by 31 July)
Franking deficit tax	Credit (on 30 June)	✓ (payable by 31 July)

11.7.8 Excessive overfranking

As explained, if a company pays a franking deficit tax, it is entitled to a tax offset (franking deficit tax offset) equal to the amount of the franking deficit tax paid.

However, situations may arise where a company has excessively overfranked. **Excessive overfranking** occurs where a company had a franking deficit at the end of the income year and the amount of that deficit (in absolute terms) was more than 10 per cent of all of the franking credits that arose during the year (excluding the payment of the franking deficit tax to the ATO, which is credited to the franking account on 30 June).

The penalty for excessive overfranking is a reduction of an entity's franking deficit tax offset by 30 per cent (or 25 per cent in the case of a SBE in the 2021 income year) against future income tax liability (section 205-70). In other words, the entity will only be allowed a tax offset against its current tax liability equivalent to only 70 per cent (or 75 per cent in the case of a SBE in the 2021 income year) of the franking deficit tax paid to the ATO. The reduction in the amount of the offset is to discourage companies from excessively overfranking.

Excessive overfranking is demonstrated in examples 11.19 and 11.20.

EXAMPLE 11.19

Excessive overfranking: Part 1

Trans Pacific Ltd (a large business taxpayer) has a taxable income for the year ended 30 June 2022 of $10 million and it has made PAYG instalments during the year totalling $2 400 000. Hence, the applicable tax rate is 30 per cent.

Assume that at 30 June 2022, the balance of the company's franking account is in deficit by $100 000. Accordingly, the company is liable to pay franking deficit tax of $100 000 to the Australian Taxation Office no later than 31 July 2022.

Determine the company's income tax payable.

The company can offset the $100 000 franking deficit tax against its 2022 income tax liability as follows.

	$
2022 taxable income	10 000 000
Tax payable on taxable income @ 30%	3 000 000
Less: PAYG instalments paid during 2022	(2 400 000)
Less: Franking deficit tax (able to be offset against income tax liability)	(100 000)
2022 income tax payable	**500 000**

EXAMPLE 11.20

Excessive overfranking: Part 2

Refer to the facts contained in example 11.19. Assume that Trans Pacific Ltd has a franking account deficit of $100 000.

During the 2022 income year, Trans Pacific Pty Ltd's franking account has $600 000 of franking credits posted to the franking account.

What is the company's income tax liability for 2022?

As the franking deficit of $100 000 exceeds 10 per cent of the total of the franking credits (i.e. $60 000), Trans Pacific Ltd has excessively overfranked during the 2022 income year.

Accordingly, the company's franking deficit tax offset entitlement is reduced by 30 per cent. Hence, instead of offsetting FDT of $100 000 against its 2022 tax liability (as per example 11.19), it can only offset $70 000 against its 2022 tax liability (being $100 000 × 70%).

Hence, the company's 2022 income tax liability is calculated as follows.

▶

	$
2022 taxable income	10 000 000
Tax payable on taxable income @ 30%	3 000 000
Less: PAYG instalments paid during 2022	(2 400 000)
Less: Franking deficit tax (net of 30% penalty for excessive overfranking)	(70 000)
2022 income tax payable	**530 000**

11.7.8.1 Relief from 30 per cent tax offset reduction for private companies

A concession is provided to private companies under section 205-70(5). This section allows private companies to claim the full franking deficit tax (and not have the 30 per cent penalty for excessive overfranking apply) where the company has franked dividends in its first profitable year of operation in anticipation of franking credits arising after the year end when the company pays its final tax liability.

Furthermore, the franking deficit tax offset reduction will not occur if the franking debit(s) that caused the franking account to go into deficit arose because of the imposition of a penalty.

Lastly, the Commissioner has discretion to disregard the franking deficit tax reduction if it arose because of events outside the entity's control (see section 205-70(6)).

11.7.9 Comprehensive example

Example 11.21 brings together various aspects of preparation of a franking account.

EXAMPLE 11.21

Preparing the franking account

Assume that Phoenix Consulting Pty Ltd (a private company for tax law purposes) has an opening franking account surplus of $150 000.

During the 2021–22 income year the company entered into the following transactions.

1. On 28 July 2021, paid a PAYG instalment of $42 000 in respect of 2021–22.
2. On 1 August 2021, paid a dividend of $100 000 with a franking percentage of 80 per cent.
3. On 10 September 2021, received a dividend from JB Hi-Fi Ltd of $7000, fully franked carrying franking credits of $3000.
4. On 28 October 2021, paid a PAYG instalment for 2021–22 income year of $25 000.
5. On 9 December 2021, paid a dividend of $62 000 with a franking percentage of 100 per cent.
6. On 28 February 2022, paid a PAYG instalment of $25 000.
7. On 31 March 2022, paid a dividend of $140 000 with a franking percentage of 60 per cent.
8. On 1 April 2022, received a dividend from Telstra Ltd of $8500, fully franked carrying franking credits of $3643.
9. On 29 April 2022, paid a PAYG instalment of $25 000.
10. On 15 May 2022, paid FBT owing of $24 700.

Assume that the company has a company tax rate of 30 per cent.

Prepare the dividend franking account for Phoenix Consulting Pty Ltd for the year ended 30 June 2022. Show all workings. Round all transactions to the nearest whole dollar.

PHOENIX CONSULTING PTY LTD Dividend franking account for the year ended 30 June 2022		Debit $	Credit $	Balance $
2021				
1 July	Opening balance of dividend franking account (surplus)		150 000	150 000
28 July	PAYG instalment paid		42 000	192 000
1 August	Payment of a dividend of $100 000 with a franking percentage of 80% ($100 000 × 80% × 30/70) (2)	34 286		157 714
10 September	Receipt of franked dividend from JB Hi-Fi Ltd carrying $3000 franking credits		3 000	160 714
28 October	PAYG instalment paid		25 000	185 714
9 December	Payment of a fully franked dividend of $62 000 with a franking percentage of 100% ($62 000 × 100% × 30/70) (3)	26 571		159 143
2022				
28 February	PAYG instalment paid		25 000	184 143
31 March	Payment of a dividend of $140 000 with a franking percentage of 60%	36 000		148 143
31 March	Underfranking penalty debit ($140 000 × 20% × 30/70) (4)	12 000		136 143
1 April	Receipt of franked dividend from Telstra Ltd carrying $3643 franking credits		3 643	139 786
28 April	PAYG instalment paid		25 000	164 786
30 June	Closing balance			**164 786**

Notes:

1. The franking credit attached to a franked distribution received by the franking entity is the amount of the credit posted to the franking account.
2. The first frankable distribution establishes the benchmark rate for all distributions in a franking period. For a private company, its franking period is generally the same as its income year (i.e. 12 months).
3. A company is liable for overfranking tax if it overfranks a distribution greater than the benchmark rate. The overfranking penalty tax does not result in a credit to the franking account and therefore the imputation benefit is lost. The formula for calculating the overfranking tax is:

$$\text{Franking \% differential} \times \text{Amount of the frankable distribution} \times \frac{\text{Corporate tax rate}}{100\% - \text{Corporate tax rate}}$$

   Phoenix Consulting Pty Ltd is liable to pay overfranking tax of $5314 ($62 000 × 20% × 30/70).
4. Underfranking penalty debit is calculated using the following formula:

$$\text{Franking \% differential} \times \text{Amount of the frankable distribution} \times \frac{\text{Corporate tax rate}}{100\% - \text{Corporate tax rate}}$$

   Phoenix Consulting Pty Ltd's franking debit is calculated as: $140 000 × 20% × 30/70 = $12 000.
5. Payment of an FBT instalment has no effect on the dividend franking account, as it is not a payment of income tax.

11.8 Anti-avoidance and integrity measures

LEARNING OBJECTIVE 11.8 Describe anti-avoidance and integrity measures applicable to company distributions.

A range of anti-avoidance and integrity measures apply to company distributions. This section briefly analyses two such rules, namely:

- the disclosure rule, and
- the dividend streaming rules.

11.8.1 The disclosure rule

The **disclosure rule** operates in conjunction with the benchmarking rule and requires a company to notify the Commissioner in writing if there is a 'significant variation' in the benchmark franking percentage from the last franking period in which a frankable distribution was made.

A 'significant variation' is one where the current benchmark franking percentage has changed from the last franking period by an amount greater than the amount worked out under the following formula:

$$\text{Number of franking periods starting immediately after the last relevant franking period* and ending at the end of the current franking period} \times 20\%$$

*The last relevant franking period is the last franking period in which a frankable distribution was made.

An extract of the company's franking account (from the company's tax return) is shown in figure 11.7.

FIGURE 11.7 Company tax return — franking section

Section C significant variation in benchmark franking percentage

Was there a significant variation in benchmark franking percentage between franking periods? ☐ Print Y for yes or N for no.

Benchmark franking period	Day Month Year		Day Month Year	Benchmark franking percentage
Franking period A		to		**G**
Franking period B		to		**H**
Franking period C		to		**I**
Franking period D		to		**J**

Source: Extract of company tax return taken from HandiTax.

Example 11.22 demonstrates the operation of the disclosure rule.

EXAMPLE 11.22

The disclosure rule

Grand Ltd has a benchmark percentage of 30 per cent in the current franking period and a benchmark percentage of 0 per cent in the immediately preceding franking period.

Does Grand Ltd have a disclosure requirement?

Grand Ltd's benchmark franking percentage has increased by 30 per cent, greater than a 20-percentage point increase (1 × 20 percentage points). As the benchmark franking percentage for the current franking period has varied significantly it has a disclosure requirement for the current franking period.

If a company's benchmark franking percentage varies significantly between franking periods, the entity must notify the Commissioner in an approved form of the following information (section 204-75):

- the benchmark franking percentage for the current franking period, and
- the benchmark franking percentage for the last franking period in which a frankable distribution was made.

11.8.2 Streaming distributions

This rule, found in section 204-30 of the ITAA97, applies where an entity streams distributions in such a way as to give those shareholders who benefit most from franking credits (e.g. resident taxpayers) a greater imputation benefit than those who benefit less (e.g. non-resident taxpayers).

When this rule applies, the Commissioner may determine that a franking debit arises in the franking account of the entity, or that no imputation benefit arises in the hands of the 'favoured member'.

ETHICS IN PRACTICE

Ethics in companies

You have taken on a new company client within your accounting/taxation practice. When you commence their work, you notice on the previous year's accounts provided by the previous accountant that there is a loan account showing on the balance sheet to the director of the company. You realise this is a Division 7A issue and bring it up with the client as it seems the previous accountant has not been treating it correctly and the loan has been increasing over several years. At the meeting with the client, you explain the concept of Division 7A and how it will affect them personally as there is the potential that they will receive unfranked dividends from the company and you will need to amend the company financial statements and tax return as well as the director's personal returns. The client is obviously not happy to receive this news and suggests that if the previous accountant has not worried about it then you should not worry about it either and just let it be.

What should you do in a situation like this? Can you ignore the Division 7A issue and plead ignorance or do you have a duty to fix the area of concern you have discovered?

Things to consider are as follows.

- Are you meeting your requirements under the TPB Code of Conduct as a registered tax agent?
- Would your behaviour, if you followed the client's wishes, be ethical and in line with your professional body's standards?
- If you choose to ignore it and the client was subsequently audited by the ATO and subsequently received penalties, the client may take action against you under safe harbour provisions.

TECHNOLOGY IN ACTION

The next generation of the firm?

Blockchain technology has seen the growth of decentralised governance structures that enable community-led projects and investment activities to flourish without central management or authority. There is an expectation that through 2022 there will be an explosion of DAO activity, potentially reflecting the beginning of disrupting traditional legal structures.[3] DAOs can be described as:

> ... a new category of organisation that operates on decentralised blockchain infrastructure, whose operations are pre-determined in open source code and enforced through smart contracts.[4]

---

3 See, eg, 'Crypto Theses for 2022' *Messari* (Web Page, 2021) 10 https://messari.io/pdf/messari-report-crypto-theses-for-2022.pdf

4 Select Committee on Australia as a Technology and Financial Centre, 'The Senate Select Committee on Australia as a Technology and Financial Centre' (Final Report, October 2021) 75 https://www.aph.gov.au/Parliamentary_Business/Committees/Senate/Financial_Technology_and_Regulatory_Technology/AusTechFinCentre/Final_report ('Bragg Report').

More simply, we can describe DAOs as a new type of firm relying on blockchain's technology to make decisions, coordinated by a community for a particular purpose.[5] Decisions made by token-holders are enforced through the DAO smart contracts and protocols. There is no need for a central authority; instead, the DAO relies on the participants: thus, it is decentralised governance. Importantly though, not all DAOs are the same and open-source platforms and DAO tools enable a dynamic set of capabilities when launching and governing DAOs.[6]

This raises questions as to what a DAO is for legal and tax purposes. For tax purposes, a company excludes partnerships but includes unincorporated association or body of persons. Is a DAO a partnership or unincorporated association? Are participants liable for actions and debts of the DAO (as is the case for partnerships)? What about when a DAO hires a worker, pays wages? There are numerous questions over taxation, property, contracting, liabilities and so on. The legal and taxing outcomes will differ substantially and raise several serious concerns.[7] This was highlighted by the Senate Select Committee on Australia as a Technology and Financial Centre ('The Committee'):

> Currently, most Australian lawyers interpret DAOs as partnerships. These interpretations each lead to concerns that, amongst an organisation of potentially infinite parties, each individual party could be held personally liable for the debts of the organisation.
>
> The current legal status of DAOs is analogous to the legal status of corporations prior to limited liability companies. Prior to limited liability companies, it was untenable for individual shareholders to have 'moral culpability' for the actions of corporations, as they lacked the power and control mechanisms to discipline errant management.
>
> It is equally untenable for individual stakeholders of decentralised systems, such as decentralised financial applications, to have moral culpability for the actions of those decentralised systems, because the individuals lack the power and control mechanisms to discipline errant decision-making.[8]

The Committee recommended that the Australian Government establish a new legal DAO structure and suggests that the Coalition of Automated Legal Applications (COALA)'s DAO Model Law could be a 'starting point' for its development.[9] In response, the Australian Government confirmed it agrees in principle and would consult on a new corporate structure in 2022.[10] Note that if this occurs, it will not be the first instance of a DAO legal entity. In Wyoming, United States, for example, a new legal structure was established in 2021 allowing for a DAO to be a form of Limited Liability Company (LLC), when it meets their DAO Law.[11] This was a major development for blockchain in 2021.[12]

....

REFLECTION

Reflecting on your understanding of the taxation of companies and other entities, how will the taxing method differ for a DAO when interpreted as a partnership as opposed to an unincorporated association? You may need to contemplate the next chapter in this text to consider your response.

---

5 See, eg, investment, charitable and fundraising activities, buying and lending activities and many other projects.

6 See, eg, *The DAOist*, 'DAO Tool Observatory' (Web Page, 12 November 2021) https://thedaoist.mirror.xyz/FfzZ8NnWdb5ygJu1 3mLi9PdWoGqaoKSm8mJoRIi3GJI.

7 See ITAA97 section 995-1.

8 Mycelium, cited in Bragg Report, 76.

9 Bragg Report, 77–78 and 138. See also Coala, *Coala Blog* (Web Page) https://coala.global.

10 The Australian Government (The Treasury), 'Transforming Australia's Payments System' (Report, December 2021) 12 https://treasury.gov.au/sites/default/files/2021-12/p2021-231824_1.pdf.

11 Bragg Report, 77.

12 See, eg, Andrew Bull, 'Regulators everywhere should follow Wyoming's DAO Law' *CoinDesk* (Web Page, 9 July 2021) https://www.coindesk.com/markets/2021/07/08/regulators-everywhere-should-follow-wyomings-dao-law.

SUMMARY

11.1 Describe what a company is and how it is taxed.

For tax purposes, a company is a body corporate or any unincorporated association or body of persons, but not a partnership. A company is a separate legal entity, has a taxable income, must lodge a company tax return and must pay income tax on its taxable income. A company includes assessable income and deducts allowable deductions on the basis that it is a resident taxpayer, and thus a company tax return includes both Australian and foreign-sourced income and deductions.

Many rules apply to companies that are different from tax rules for individual taxpayers. Public and private companies are each subject to different tax rules.

Companies pay a flat rate of tax, equal to 30 per cent for companies with annual turnover of $50 million or more and those that do not fit the BRE conditions and 25 per cent for BRE companies with lower turnover

11.2 Explain how a company's taxable income is calculated.

A company's taxable income is determined by the principles set out in the ITAA36 and ITAA37 and differs from the accounting profit determined in accordance with accounting standards. Differences between tax income and accounting profit may be permanent differences that never reverse or temporary differences where the accounting and tax treatment are the same but occur in different periods. Temporary differences give rise to deferred tax assets and deferred tax liabilities.

Resident Australian companies that receive foreign income must include the gross amount in its assessable income but can then claim a foreign income tax offset.

11.3 Explain the tax treatment of company losses.

A tax loss occurs when a company's allowable deductions exceed its assessable income. A tax loss may be carried forward to be deducted against assessable income in a future year provided the company satisfies either the continuity of ownership test or the similar business test. If the continuity of ownership test is satisfied, then there is no need to consider the similar business test. However, if the continuity of ownership test is failed, then the similar business test can be considered. These same tests are also used to determine whether net capital losses and bad debts may be claimed for tax purposes.

11.4 Explain the research and development concessions available to companies.

Division 355 of the ITAA97 provides companies with special tax incentives for research and development activities undertaken in Australia: a refundable tax offset for companies with less than $20 million turnover and a non-refundable tax offset for other eligible companies.

11.5 Explain how dividends are taxed.

A dividend is a distribution of a company's profits to its shareholders. In 1987, the dividend imputation system was introduced to remove the effects of double taxation on company dividends. An unfranked dividend is one on which the company has not paid tax. A franked dividend is one on which the company has paid tax. Resident shareholders must include dividends and any franking credit in assessable income but can claim a credit or tax offset in respect of the tax already paid by the company. Certain transactions between private companies and shareholders are deemed to be dividends.

11.6 Apply the concepts of Division 7A to the tax treatment of a loan by a private company to a shareholder.

Division 7A of the ITAA36 operates to automatically deem certain loans made by private companies to a shareholder or a shareholder's associate as dividends. If the loan is not repaid by the date of lodgement of the company's income tax return, the amount of the loan is deemed to constitute an unfranked dividend in the hands of the shareholder receiving the money.

11.7 Describe the operation of a company franking account.

Each resident Australian company is required to maintain a franking account to keep track of the franking credits that it can pass on to shareholders. The benchmark rule provides that all frankable distributions made by a company during a franking period must be franked to the same extent as the benchmark franking percentage. Underfranking occurs when the company franks its second and subsequent frankable distributions at an amount less than the benchmark franking percentage.

Overfranking occurs when the company franks its second and subsequent frankable distributions at an amount more than the benchmark franking percentage. Penalties apply for both. If a company imputes to its members more tax than it has paid then it becomes liable for franking deficit tax. This is deducted from the company's income tax liability. However, excessive overfranking results in a reduction of this offset.

A discussion followed as to the impact of franking credits and debits in the franking account. Finally, the chapter discussed the concept of underfranking, overfranking, excessive overfranking and the implications of franking deficit tax.

11.8 Describe anti-avoidance and integrity measures applicable to company distributions.
There is a range of anti-avoidance and integrity measures applying to company distributions. The disclosure rule requires a company to notify the Commissioner of Taxation if there is a significant variation in the benchmark franking percentage from the last franking period in which a frankable distribution was made. Dividend streaming rules are intended to prevent the company from streaming distributions in such a way as to provide greater imputation benefits to those who benefit most from franking credits.

KEY TERMS

base rate entity A company that has an aggregated turnover less than the aggregated turnover threshold — which is $50 million for the 2021–22 income year. For the 2021–22 income year, companies that are BREss are taxed at 25 per cent. All other companies are taxed at 30 per cent. BREs have less than 80 per cent of their income derived from passive sources (e.g. dividends, captail gains and rent).

benchmark franking percentage The franking percentage for the first frankable distribution made in the franking period establishes the benchmark franking percentage to be used in respect of all frankable distributions for that franking period. Penalties apply if a company overfranks or underfranks subsequent dividends.

benchmark interest rate The interest rate that must be charged on a Division 7A loan for the relevant interest rate. Each year, the Commissioner of Taxation publishes this rate in a Taxation Determination. For the year ended 30 June 2022, the benchmark interest rate was 4.52 per cent.

benchmark rule The rule that requires that all frankable distributions made by a company during a franking period must be franked to the same extent as the benchmark franking percentage.

company A body corporate (i.e. company incorporated in Australia) or any unincorporated association or body of persons but does not include a partnership. For taxation purposes, a company also includes a club, incorporated association or society.

company income tax return The tax return lodged by a company. Also referred to as the 'C' form.

continuity of ownership test One of the two tests a company must pass in order to offset its carry forward tax losses against income in a subsequent year. The continuity of ownership test requires that the same persons collectively own exactly the same shares that gave them more than 50 per cent of the voting power, rights to dividends, and rights to capital distributions at all times during the 'ownership test period time'.

deferred tax assets Those temporary differences that give rise to adjustments which result in a decrease in income tax payable in a future tax period. This occurs because the entity is entitled to a tax deduction in the future.

deferred tax liabilities Those temporary differences that give rise to adjustments which result in an increase in income tax payable in a future tax period. This may occur in one of two ways. First, the entity will be liable to pay more tax in the future or, second, the entity receives a tax deduction now, and not in the future (e.g. prepayments). This results in additional tax to pay in future periods.

disclosure rule A rule operates in conjunction with the benchmarking rule and requires a company to notify the Commissioner in writing if there is a 'significant variation' in the benchmark franking percentage from the last franking period in which a frankable distribution was made. A 'significant variation' is one where the current benchmark franking percentage has changed from the benchmark franking percentage for the last franking period by an amount greater than 20 per cent.

distribution statement Also called a dividend statement. This is a statement that the company must give to its shareholders when paying a dividend. The distribution statement must contain prescribed information. A public company must provide the shareholder with a distribution statement on or before the day on which the distribution is made. A private company must provide the shareholder with a distribution statement no later than 4 months after the end of the income year.

distributable surplus The maximum amount that a Division 7A loan can be treated as a dividend. The distributable surplus is defined as net assets less non-commercial loans less paid-up capital less the repayment of non-commercial loans). In essence, a company's distributable surplus is its total shareholder's equity minus share capital. Therefore, it basically includes retained profits and other reserves.

dividend Defined to include any distribution made by a company to any of its shareholders, whether in money or other property, or any amount credited by a company to its shareholders. Essentially, a dividend represents any distribution of a company's profit to its shareholders.

dividend imputation system The system introduced by the Commonwealth Government on 1 July 1987 to remove the effect of double taxation on company dividends in the hands of the individual shareholder.

Division 7A A provision that deems that certain loans made by private companies to a shareholder or a shareholder's associate after 4 December 1997 to be an unfranked dividend in the hands of the shareholder receiving the money.

excessive overfranking A situation that occurs where a company has a franking deficit at the end of the income year and the amount of that deficit (in absolute terms) is more than 10 per cent of all of the franking credits that arose during the year. The penalty for excessive overfranking is a reduction of an entity's franking deficit tax offset against its future income tax liability.

frankable distribution Also called a franked dividend. A dividend from which the company has paid tax on the dividend distributed to shareholders. A dividend can be franked from 1 to 100 per cent. It cannot be franked more than 100 per cent.

franking account An account that a company maintains to keep track of the franking credits that it can pass onto its shareholders. Each resident Australian company is required to maintain a franking account. The franking account is usually a schedule that accompanies the company's income tax return. The franking year aligns to the company's income year.

franking credits Amounts that result in a credit to the franking account. The most common franking credits are PAYG instalments paid, company tax paid and the franking credits in respect of franked dividends received by the company.

franking debits Amounts that result in a debit to the franking account. The most common franking debits are the amount of the imputation credits attached to franked dividends paid by the company to its shareholders, refunds of income tax received by the company and underfranking tax.

franking deficit tax A situation where a company has a deficit in its franking account at the end of the income year. As a result, it is liable to pay franking deficit tax to account for the over-imputation of tax. The amount of the franking deficit tax is equal to the franking deficit. Franking deficit tax is payable by the last day of the month following the end of the income tax year (i.e. by 31 July). Franking deficit tax is not a penalty. It is a payment to make good the amount imputed to shareholders that exceeded the amount of tax actually paid.

franking period The period covered by the franking account. A private company has one franking period in its income year. Conversely, a public company has two franking periods in its income year (one for the first six-month period and the other for the second six-month period).

maximum franking credit The maximum franking credit is calculated as the maximum amount of franking credits that can be allocated to a frankable distribution as if that distribution was franked to 100 per cent.

overfranking A situation that occurs where the company franks its second (and subsequent) frankable distributions at an amount more than the benchmark franking percentage. The penalty for overfranking is that the company is liable for 'overfranking tax', which must be remitted to the ATO by the last day of the month following the end of the income tax year (i.e. by 31 July). Overfranking tax is a penalty that does not result in a franking credit to the franking account and therefore represents lost franking credits.

permanent differences A term used in tax-effect accounting to describe the situation for those items of revenues and expenses that are never tax-deductible.

private company A company that is not a public company in relation to the year of income.

public company A company whose shares were listed on a stock exchange on the last day of the income year. However, it will not be considered a public company for taxation purposes where, at any time during the income year, 20 or fewer persons held 75 per cent or more of the company's capital, voting or dividend rights; a subsidiary of a listed public company; a non-profit company; a mutual life assurance company; a friendly society; a registered organisation; or is a statutory body or a company in which a government body established for public purposes had a controlling interest on the last day of the year of income.

similar business test One of the two tests a company must pass in order to offset its carry forward tax losses against income in a subsequent year. The test requires that following a change in ownership or control, companies can deduct its tax losses if the business carried on at the time of deduction is 'similar' to the business carried on at the time of the loss.

tax loss A situation where the taxpayer has a negative taxable income. A tax loss is defined as the situation where allowable deductions exceed assessable and net exempt income. A tax loss can be carried forward indefinitely by the taxpayer and in the case of a company can be used to offset future taxable income provided one of two tests are met.

tax loss carry back offset Companies with an aggregated turnover of less than $1 billion will be entitled to choose to carry-back tax losses incurred in the 2020, 2021 and 2022 income years to offset the company's taxable income in the 2019 or later income years (Division 160).

tax reconciliation A statement is prepared to reconcile the net profit for accounting purposes to the taxable income.

temporary differences A term used in tax-effect accounting to describe the situation for those items of revenues and expenses that have tax consequences in a future income period. Temporary differences result in either deferred tax assets or deferred tax liabilities.

underfranking A situation that occurs where the company franks its second (and subsequent) frankable distributions at an amount less than the benchmark franking percentage. The penalty for underfranking is that the company is required to debit its franking account on the same date on which the frankable distribution is made for the amount of the franking shortfall.

unfrankable distribution Also called an unfranked dividend. A dividend from which the company has not paid tax on the dividend distributed to shareholders.

widely held company A company listed on an approved stock exchange. A company is also widely held if it has more than 50 members where more than 20 of those members hold 75 per cent or more of the voting, dividend or capital distribution rights.

QUESTIONS

11.1 What is a company for taxation law purposes and how are companies taxed?

11.2 What are the two types of companies for taxation law purposes? Why is this distinction important?

11.3 What is a dividend for taxation purposes? What is the difference between a franked and an unfranked dividend? What are the taxation consequences to an individual shareholder who receives a franked and unfranked dividend?

11.4 Explain the two tests required for a company to offset carry-forward tax losses. Is a company required to satisfy one or both tests?

11.5 What special concessions are available to companies who conduct research and development activities under the ITAA97?

11.6 What is Division 7A? Who does it apply to and what are the consequences to a shareholder if Division 7A applies?

11.7 Explain the benchmark rule and how it differs in the case of a public and private company for taxation law purposes?

11.8 What does underfranking mean? What are the implications for companies should a company underfrank its dividends?

11.9 What does overfranking mean? What are the implications for companies should a company overfrank its dividends?

11.10 What is franking deficit tax? What are the implications for companies should a company's franking account balance at the end of the income year be in deficit?

PROBLEMS

11.11 For the year ended 30 June 2022, Green Acres Pty Ltd, a SBE taxpayer, derived a taxable income of $120 000, excluding the following transactions.

	$
Dividend received from UK company (net of $300 withholding tax)	1 700
Unfranked dividend from Minatour Pty Ltd, a resident Australian company	10 000
Fully franked dividend received from Xero Ltd ($1500 franking credits)	3 500

The taxable income of $120 000 was arrived at after deducting the following items.

	$
Bad debts expense	5 400
Accounting depreciation expense on plant and equipment	16 800
Entertainment – clients	4 200
Fines and penalties	660

Notes:

(a) The opening balance of provision for doubtful debts was $14 200. The closing balance of provision for doubtful debts was $12 800. Bad debts can only be claimed as an income tax deduction when the bad debt is written off. The company uses the provisioning method in providing for doubtful debts.

(b) Client entertainment is not allowable as an income tax deduction.

(c) Fines and penalties are not allowable as an income tax deduction.

(d) There was no tax depreciation for the 2022 income year as the company adopted the simplified depreciation regime and claimed all of its SBE tax depreciation relating to depreciable assets owned in a previous income year.

Required

Calculate Green Acres Pty Ltd's taxable income and tax payable for the year ended 30 June 2022.

Assume that Green Acres Pty Ltd paid PAYG instalments during the 2022 income year to the ATO totalling $28 000. Assume that the company has a BRE tax rate of 25 per cent. Round all calculations to the nearest whole dollar.

11.12 Flavours of Italy Pty Ltd is a resident Australian private company. It was incorporated on 1 July 2019. At that time, it had two shareholders, namely:

- Mario: 100 shares
- Luciano: 100 shares.

From 1 July 2019 to 30 June 2020, the company operated an Italian restaurant in Melbourne.

For the year ended 30 June 2020, the company incurred a trading loss of $40 000.

For the year ended 30 June 2021, the company incurred a trading loss of $60 000.

For the year ended 30 June 2022, the company derived a taxable income of $75 000.

On 1 July 2021, the company sold its Italian restaurant business and acquired a travel agency. The company's shareholding of ordinary shares at 30 June each year is shown as follows.

Shareholder	30 June 2020	30 June 2021	30 June 2022
Mario	100 shares	100 shares	100 shares
Luciano	100 shares	100 shares	100 shares
Emily		300 shares*	300 shares
Charlotte			400 shares**
Total	**200 shares**	**500 shares**	**900 shares**
Taxable income/(loss)	($40 000)	($60 000)	$75 000

* Assume that Emily acquired her 300 shares in the company on 1 July 2020.
** Assume that Charlotte acquired her 400 shares in the company on 1 July 2021.

Required

Is the company able to use its tax losses incurred in the 2020 and 2021 income years when calculating its taxable income for the year ended 30 June 2022?

11.13 Jane Harris is getting married. Harris Holdings Pty Ltd want to give Jane $50 000 towards the cost of the wedding.

Harris Holdings Pty Ltd is a private company for tax purposes and is owned by Andrew and Melissa Harris equally.

The balance sheet of Harris Holdings Pty Ltd for the year ended 30 June 2022 is as follows.

	$
Assets	
Cash at bank	$25 000
Amounts owing by Jane Harris	50 000
Property, plant and equipment (net of depreciation)	190 000
Total assets	265 000
Liabilities	
Accounts payable	12 000
Bank loan	100 000
Total liabilities	112 000
Net assets	**$153 000**
Shareholder's equity	
Share capital	5 000
Retained profits	148 000
Total shareholder's equity	**$153 000**

On 1 January 2021, Harris Holdings Pty Ltd lent Jane $50 000. A written loan agreement was drafted stating that the loan was required to be repaid within 5 years. The loan is interest-free. This loan is shown as a receivable (under current assets) in the balance sheet.

Jane does not hold any shares in the company. Furthermore, she is not employed by the company in any capacity whatsoever.

The retained profits of Harris Holdings Pty Ltd on the date the loan was made (i.e. 1 January 2021) was $36 000.

The retained profits of the company as at 30 June 2021 was $42 000.

Required

(i) What are the income tax consequences in respect of the loan made by Harris Holdings Pty Ltd to Jane for the years ended 30 June 2021 and 30 June 2022?

(ii) How would your answer change if, instead of an interest-free loan, the interest payable on the loan was equal to the benchmark interest rate published by the Reserve Bank of Australia?

11.14 Titan Holdings Ltd (a public company for tax law purposes) has an opening franking account surplus of $40 000 at 1 July 2021.

During the 2022 income year the company entered into the following transactions.

1. On 21 July 2021, the company paid its fourth and final PAYG instalment of $30 000 in respect of the 2021 income year.
2. On 18 August 2021, the company paid a dividend of $98 000 franked to 70 per cent.
3. On 25 September 2021, the company received a fully franked dividend from JB Hi-Fi Ltd of $12 000.
4. On 12 October 2021, the company paid its first PAYG instalment for the 2022 income year of $25 000.
5. On 9 January 2022, the company paid a franked dividend of $112 000, franked to 100 per cent.
6. On 28 February 2022, the company paid its second PAYG instalment for the 2022 income year of $25 000.

7. On 14 April 2022, the company received a fully franked dividend from Qantas Ltd of $9600.
8. On 28 April 2022, the company paid its third quarter PAYG instalment for the 2022 income year of $25 000.
9. On 4 May 2022, the company paid a franked dividend of $212 000, franked to 80 per cent.
Assume a company tax rate of 30 per cent. Round all calculations to the nearest whole dollar.

Required

Prepare a dividend franking account for Titan Holdings Ltd for the year ended 30 June 2022. Show all workings. Round all transactions to the nearest whole dollar.

11.15 Vision Eyewear Pty Ltd (a private company for tax law purposes) has an opening franking account surplus of $30 000 at 1 July 2021.

During the 2022 income year the company entered into the following transactions.
1. On 17 July 2021, the company paid an unfranked dividend of $5000 to its shareholders.
2. On 28 July 2021, the company paid its fourth and final PAYG instalment of $7500 in respect of the 2021 income year.
3. On 11 August 2021, the company paid a dividend of $18 000 franked to 80 per cent.
4. On 17 September 2021, the company received a fully franked dividend from Coles Ltd of $1500.
5. On 28 October 2021, the company paid its first PAYG instalment for the 2022 income year of $5000.
6. On 19 December 2021, the company paid a franked dividend of $12 000, franked to 100 per cent.
7. On 28 February 2022, the company paid its second PAYG instalment for the 2022 income year of $5000.
8. On 23 March 2022, the company paid a franked dividend of $6000, franked to 60 per cent.
9. On 7 April 2022, the company received a fully franked dividend from Telstra Ltd of $1200.
10. On 28 April 2022, the company paid its third quarter PAYG instalment for the 2022 income year of $5000.
11. On 6 June 2022, the company paid a franked dividend of $150 000, franked to 80 per cent.
Assume a company tax rate of 25 per cent. Round all calculations to the nearest whole dollar.

Required

Prepare a dividend franking account for Vision Eyewear Pty Ltd for the year ended 30 June 2022. Show all workings. Round all transactions to the nearest whole dollar.

11.16 Show in the following table the accounting amount and the assessable or deductible amount for taxation purposes. Show in the final column the effect on the net or taxable income of the business.

This exercise is designed to help students understand the concept of reconciling. It is not specific to any specific entity. Assume that the 'amount' is what was recorded for accounting purposes.

Item	Amount ($)	Accounting	Taxation	Effect on income
Non-SBE trading business received cash of $160 000 but outstanding sales of $25 000 at 30 June. Assume this is the first year of business.	160 000			
Dividend of $70 000 franked to 100%. It carried franking credits of $30 000.	70 000			
Sale of goodwill cost $10 000, sold for $50 000. Held for 14 months and sold in current year. This is an SBE business.	40 000			
Provision for bad debts	30 000			
Entertainment expenses – 40% on staff, 60% on clients	71 000			

(continued)

(continued)

Item	Amount ($)	Accounting	Taxation	Effect on income
Borrowing expenses $2000. Loan taken out on 1 July for 4 years.	2 000			
Accounting depreciation of $200 on asset bought for $999 on 1 July. This is an SBE business.	200			
Excessive salary to spouse of business owner. The Commissioner considered that $50 000 was reasonable.	60 000			
Pre-paid expense in prior year. Actual expense last year $13 000 prepaid for 13 months on 1 June PY.	Nil			

11.17 The accounts of Bettertrap Ltd, a company incorporated in 1983 and engaged in the manufacture of mousetraps, disclose the following for the current income year. The company did not wish to use any SBE elections.

		$
Gross profit from trading (before depreciation charges)		217 950
Net rental from factory premises		1 000
Dividend from subsidiary company		12 900
		231 850
Interest on debentures	600	
Administration and selling expenses	144 800	
Depreciation on existing fixed assets — calculated at tax rates	18 000	
Provision for holiday pay	2 500	
Provision for doubtful debts	3 000	168 900
Net profit		**62 950**

The following information is supplied.
- The debentures on which interest was paid during the year were issued to enable the company to acquire shares in its subsidiary, from which dividends of $12 900 were received. Franking credits of $5400 were attached to the dividends.
- The following legal expenses were included in administration expenses.

	$
Costs of registering petty patent in Australia (1 July 2021)	1200
Costs of registering trade mark in Australia	7 000
Costs associated with income tax objection	850
Debt collection expenses	300
Costs of preparing lease of store	2 500

- Holiday pay amounting to $2900 was paid to employees during the year and debited to the provision account by transfer from the profit and loss appropriation account.
- Bad debts amounting to $2600 were written off against the provision account during the year.

Required

Prepare a reconciliation statement of net profit to taxable income for inclusion in the company's income tax return for the year and calculate the tax payable for the company who is a BRE.

ACKNOWLEDGEMENT

Figure 11.2: © Australian Taxation Office
Figures 11.3, 11.6, 11.7: © Creative Commons
Examples 11.1, 11.2: © Australian Taxation Office
Extracts: © Federal Register of Legislation. Licensed under CC BY 4.0.
Extracts: © The Senate

CHAPTER 12

Taxation of partnerships, joint ventures, trusts and superannuation entities

LEARNING OBJECTIVES

After studying this chapter, you should be able to:

12.1 explain the taxation of partnership income

12.2 describe the tax consequences of various transactions between the partnership and the partners

12.3 describe the taxation consequences of a joint venture

12.4 describe the basic principles of how trusts operate and how they are taxed

12.5 calculate the tax liability of various types of beneficiaries and the trustee of a trust

12.6 describe the basic principles of how superannuation funds operate and how they are taxed

12.7 explain the taxation treatment of superannuation contributions

12.8 explain the taxation treatment of superannuation funds during the investment phase

12.9 calculate the tax liability of recipients of superannuation distributions.

Overview

This chapter covers the tax treatment of several types of business entities — partnerships, joint ventures, trusts and superannuation funds — as well as explaining the tax treatment of transactions related to these entities.

Many taxpayers operate their business in the form of a partnership. This chapter outlines the taxation definition of partnerships and how they are taxed, including the calculation of the net income of the partnership as well as the taxation treatment of partners' salaries, drawings and interest on capital contributions. The capital gains tax implications of partnerships are also briefly considered.

Joint ventures are very common in the mining, primary production and infrastructure industries. This chapter explains the difference between a partnership and a joint venture, and briefly outlines the taxation considerations of a joint venture.

The discussion of trusts in this chapter focuses on the income tax treatment of Australian resident trusts and, in particular, when the trustee is liable to pay tax on trust net income and when the beneficiaries are liable to pay tax on their share of the trust net income. In addition, tax planning is introduced and tax avoidance controversies relevant in trust contexts are discussed.

The final section of the chapter introduces the basics of the taxation of superannuation funds (which are also a type of trust), in particular how superannuation fund trustees are taxed and how superannuation fund beneficiaries are taxed. The analysis extends to taxation of contributions and withdrawals from superannuation funds.

Types of business structures

Figure 12.1 outlines the most common business structures used by taxpayers to run their businesses.

Complex business structures are combinations of these basis structures in figure 12.1. Some complex structures that are widely used include:

- business entity plus a service trust
- licensing of goodwill or intellectual property
- business property held by a trust
- unit trust owned by discretionary trusts
- partnership of discretionary trust
- spouse owing assets
- superannuation fund and unit trust
- superannuation fund as joint owner of property.

12.1 Partnerships

LEARNING OBJECTIVE 12.1 Explain the taxation of partnership income.

All States and Territories in Australia have a Partnership Act[1] that contains a virtually identical definition to the one contained in section 5(1) of the *Partnership Act (1891)* (Qld), where a partnership is defined as:

- two or more persons
- carrying on a business
- with a view to profit.

However, for taxation purposes, a partnership is more broadly defined. According to section 995-1 of the ITAA97, a **partnership** is defined as:

(a) an association of persons (other than a company or a limited partnership) carrying on business as partners or in receipt of ordinary income or statutory income jointly, or
(b) a limited partnership.

Most Australian states and territories allow limited partnerships. Limited partnerships offer partners limited liability to the extent of the amount of capital contributed.

---

1 *Partnership Act 1963* (ACT); *Partnership Act 1892* (NSW); *Partnership Act 1997* (NT); *Partnership Act 1891* (Qld); *Partnership Act 1891* (SA); *Partnership Act 1891* (Tas); *Partnership Act 1958* (Vic); *Partnership (Limited Partnerships) Act 1992* (Vic); *Partnership Act 1895* (WA).

FIGURE 12.1 Types of business structures

Sole traders

- A sole trader is an individual who is trading in his or her own name. That person controls and manages the business. The income of the business is treated as the person's individual income and he or she is solely responsible for any tax payable by the business.

Partnerships

- For tax purposes a partnership is an association of persons or entities that carry on business as partners or receive income jointly. A partnership does not pay income tax — each partner includes the share of the profit or loss in his or her own individual tax return.

Trusts

- A trust is an obligation on a person to hold property for the benefit of others (beneficiaries). The beneficiary includes the share of the trust income in his or her personal income tax return. The trustee is liable for tax on income distributed to minors, non-residents or if it accumulates income. Trusts can either be fixed or *inter vivos* and the beneficiaries can be individuals or entities.

Companies

- A company is a legal entity separate from its shareholders. Companies are regulated by the Australian Securities and Investments Commission. A company pays tax on its income at the rate of 30% or 25%.

Superannuation funds

- A superannuation fund is a trust fund that is set up for the ultimate purposes of providing retirement funds for its members. The current tax rate is 15% and therefore it is the best vehicle to accumulate wealth. A self-managed superannuation fund is a fund set up by small businesses and other taxpayers who wish to participate in managing their own superannuation funds. Small businesses can also use their superannuation funds to purchase business premises.

From 19 August 1992, sections 94A to 94X of the ITAA36 treat limited partnerships (referred to as 'corporate limited partnerships') formed after that date as companies.

In Taxation Determination TD 2008/15, the Commissioner of Taxation takes the view that limited partners in a limited partnership have to be carrying on business in order to be limited partnerships. This effectively means that tax law partnerships (i.e. where partners are in receipt of joint income) are not considered limited partnerships for tax purposes. They must be carrying on a business.

As can be seen, the taxation law definition of a partnership is much broader than it is under the various state partnerships legislation. Not only does a taxation partnership exist if the partners are carrying on a business; it also exists where two people earn income jointly.

Hence, if two people derive interest from a joint bank account or derive rental income from a rental property owned in joint names, a taxation partnership exists (see *FCT v McDonald*).[2]

---

2 (1987) 87 ATC 4541.

Facts: The taxpayer and his wife entered into a partnership arrangement where they jointly purchased two units from which they derived rental income. The oral partnership agreement provided that the taxpayer's share of the net profit of the partnership was 25 per cent and his wife's share was 75 per cent. The agreement also provided that the taxpayer would absorb all of the partnership losses. For the year ended 30 June 1978, the partnership derived a net loss of $1941. Based on the partnership agreement, the taxpayer claimed the full amount of the loss in his tax return.

In doing so, the taxpayer argued that the partnership was a partnership under both general law and under the ITAA36 and that the two units constituted partnership property.

The Commissioner denied the loss as a deduction in the taxpayer's tax return and argued that no partnership existed between the taxpayer and his wife, and that the only relevant relationship between them was that of 'co-ownership' of property.

Held: The Court held that the taxpayer was only a 'notional' partner for tax purposes, as opposed to a 'true' partner at general law. As such, the taxpayer and his wife were considered partners for tax purposes, but not general law partners. The taxpayer could only claim half of the loss for the current income year.

From a practical perspective, the Commissioner of Taxation has advised that a partnership only needs to lodge a partnership tax return if it is carrying on a business.

Therefore, where two or more persons are simply in receipt of joint income, instead of lodging a partnership tax return, the income is usually split between the two parties with each person declaring their share of the income in their individual tax returns.

The amount of income each person will include depends on his or her ownership interest in the property. For example, Alex and Emily own a rental property. Alex owns 70 per cent and Emily owns 30 per cent. If the tax profit from the rental property was $10 000, Alex will include $7000 in his income tax return and Emily will include $3000 in her income tax return.

12.1.1 Does a partnership exist?

Whether or not a partnership exists is a question of fact. Taxation Ruling TR 94/8 outlines the factors the Commissioner of Taxation considers relevant to determining whether a partnership exists. These factors include:

- whether or not there is a formal partnership agreement
- the intention of the parties to the partnership
- sharing of profits and losses
- whether a partnership bank account exists
- whether or not partners have contributed capital, services and labour and/or expertise
- participation of partners in control and management of the business
- whether business records are maintained
- whether a business name has been registered
- whether there is joint ownership of assets
- who has authority to act on behalf of the partnership.

While none of the factors in themselves are determinative, a conclusion on whether a partnership exists may be drawn from an examination of the noted factors.

EXAMPLE 12.1

Common law partnership

Chris and Gloria allegedly run a plumbing business under a common law partnership.

Business income is paid into a joint account and can be accessed by both parties who have shared profits equally as set out in their partnership accounts, although all investment decisions are implemented by Chris.

No partnership agreement was executed before the business commenced and the minor amount of capital invested to start the business was wholly provided by Chris.

Chris provides the plumbing services for clients but all the related management, client liaison and bookkeeping is done by Gloria who typically invoices clients in the name of the partnership.

In these circumstances, a common law partnership would arise as the parties have demonstrated the mutual intention to carry on a business in partnership as reflected in their actions, especially their sharing of profits as shown in the partnership accounts. This is despite the fact that no written partnership agreement was entered into and there was no capital contribution by Gloria.

Generally speaking, as discussed, the Commissioner only requires that a partnership tax return be lodged where the partners are carrying on a business, and not simply where two or more persons jointly earn income from investments.

12.1.2 Taxation of partnership income

A partnership is *not* a separate legal entity. Hence, it cannot have a taxable income. As such, it cannot pay income tax in its own right. However, a partnership is considered a taxpayer for the purposes of the ITAA36 because it derives income. Accordingly, under section 91 of the ITAA36, a partnership is required to lodge a **partnership income tax return** (P form) but will not be liable to pay any tax.

In the partnership tax return, the partnership includes its assessable income and deducts its allowable deductions on the basis that it is a resident taxpayer. Hence, a partnership tax return includes both Australian and foreign-sourced income and deductions.

However, as the partnership does not pay tax, the partnership profit is distributed to each partner who includes it in their own tax return and pays tax at their marginal tax rate. This concept is explained in further detail next.

Since a partnership cannot have a taxable income, the difference between the partnership's assessable income and its allowable deductions is called the **net income of the partnership** rather than 'taxable income'.

In other words:

$$\text{Net income of the partnership} = [\text{Assessable income} - \text{Allowable deductions}]$$

This figure is essentially the tax profit of the partnership.

In determining the net income of the partnership, the following deductions are not able to be claimed in the name of the partnership. Instead, these items are included in the tax return of each partner rather than in the partnership's tax return:

- prior year losses under Division 36 of the ITAA36
- personal superannuation contributions made by the partners under section 290-150 of the ITAA97
- capital gains and losses (ITAA97 section 106-5).

Once the net income of the partnership has been ascertained, this tax profit is distributed to each partner in accordance with their profit-sharing ratio as per the partnership agreement. This is the case, regardless of whether there has been a cash distribution of the profit or not (see *Rowe v FCT*).[3]

Each partner consequently includes their share of the partnership distribution in their respective income tax returns and pays tax on this partnership distribution at their respective marginal tax rates (section 92(1)). This is shown in figure 12.2.

12.1.2.1 What happens if the partnership makes a loss?

If the partnership derives a tax loss, unlike a company or trust (discussed later in this chapter), the loss is distributed in that income year to each of the partners and is recorded as an allowable deduction (in accordance with section 92(2)). This has the effect of reducing the taxable income in the partner's individual tax return.

In other words, unlike a company or trust, partnership losses are not quarantined within the partnership.

---

3 *J Rowe and Son Pty Ltd v FCT* (1971) 71 ATC 4157.

Supplementary section
Income

Refer to the supplement instruction before you complete item 13. If you are required to complete item 13 include deferred non-commercial business losses from a prior year at either X or Y as appropriate. Refer to the supplement instructions for the relevant code.

13   Partnerships and trusts

Primary production

Distribution from partnerships	**N**	.00	/	
Share of net income from trusts	**L**	.00	/	
Landcare operations and deduction for decline in value of water facility, fencing asset and fodder storage asset	**I**	.00		
Other deductions relating to amounts shown at N and L	**X**	.00	/	TYPE
Net primary production amount		.00	/	LOSS

Note: If you have a net loss from a partnership business activity, complete item P3 and P9 in the Business and professional item section of this tax return in addition to item 13.

TFN		Name of partnership / Trust		
486 255 899	P	THE BATMAN AND ROBIN PARTNERSHIP		

NPP income	Investments	.00	**Credits:**	ABN	
	Net rental	.00	Franking	
	Other	40,000.00	TFN	
PP income		.00	Closely held trusts	
			Tax paid by trusts	
Franked distributions	Investments	.00	Foreign Resident Withholding	
	Other	.00	Rental Affordability Scheme	
Net small business inc	Partnership	.00		
	Trust	.00		

Source: Australian Taxation Office, 'Tax return for individuals (supplementary section) 2019' (Web Page, 2019) www.ato.gov.au/uploadedFiles/Content/IND/Downloads/Tax-return-for-individuals-(supplement)-2019.pdf.

12.1.3 Determining each partner's share of the net income of the partnership

The net income or loss of a partnership is calculated on the basis that the partnership is a resident taxpayer. The assessable income of the partnership therefore includes income from all sources both within and outside Australia.

Each partner is then subsequently assessed on their share of the net income or loss of the partnership. If a loss is distributed to the partners ,then they must review the loss provisions in Division 36 of the ITAA36 in their own income tax returns — for example, if they have exempt income, this must be reduced from the loss prior to being offset against other assessable income.

12.1.3.1 Resident partner

Where a partner in the partnership is a resident, the partner includes their share of the net partnership income as assessable income in their tax return (section 92(1)(a)). This situation is demonstrated in example 12.2.

EXAMPLE 12.2

Resident partner

Tim and Irena are partners in a business. Both are residents of Australia. The partnership carries on business in both Australia and Denmark.

The net income of the partnership for the year ended 30 June 2022 has been calculated as $120 000. The Australian-sourced net income of the partnership came to $100 000. The Danish-sourced income was $20 000.

According to the partnership agreement, Tim is entitled to 75 per cent of the partnership profits and Irena 25 per cent.

What is each partner's share of the net income of the partnership?

The share of the net income of the partnership for the year ended 30 June 2022 in accordance with section 92(1)(a) is as follows.

	$
Tim: Resident ($120 000 × 75%)	90 000
Irena: Resident ($120 000 × 25%)	30 000
Total	**120 000**

12.1.3.2 Non-resident partner

Where a partner in the partnership is a *non-resident*, the partner is only assessed on their share of the net partnership income attributable to Australian sources, and is entitled to a deduction for their share of partnership losses attributable to Australian sources (section 92(1)(b)). This is demonstrated in example 12.3.

Non-resident partner

Assume the same facts as in example 12.2. However, this time assume that Tim is a resident and Irena is a non-resident for Australian tax purposes.

What is each partner's share of the net income of the partnership?

Their share of the net income of the partnership for the year ended 30 June 2022 in accordance with sections 92(1)(a) and 92 (1)(b) is as follows.

	$
Tim: Resident ($120 000 × 75%)	90 000
Irena: Non-resident ($100 000 Australian-sourced income × 25%)	25 000
Total	**115 000**

The remaining $5000 (being Irena's 25% share of the Danish-sourced income of $20 000) is not subject to Australian income tax, as this is foreign-sourced income derived by a non-resident.

However, Irena will need to include this $5000 in her Danish tax return and pay tax on it under Danish tax law.

12.1.3.3 Assignment of a partner's interest in a partnership

The Full High Court in *FCT v Everett* 80 ATC 4076 established that a partner may assign his or her share (or part of his or her share) in a partnership under a deed of assignment with the consequence that the net income of the partnership attributed to the assigned share is derived beneficially by the assignee. Such assignments were effective for taxation purposes but, due to the fact the ATO have, in recent times, suspended the application of its guidelines in relation to *Everett*-type assignments, they may no longer be effective for tax purposes.

Facts: The taxpayer, a partner in a Sydney law firm, assigned to his wife, by deed of assignment and for valuable consideration, 6/13ths of his share in the partnership (including the right to partnership distributions).

Under the terms of the assignment, Everett's wife was not entitled to become a partner in the partnership, nor was she able to vote or interfere in the running of the law practice.

Held: The Court held that a partner's interest in a partnership is a chose in action (right to sue) that may be assigned in whole or part.

> A majority of the High Court held that the assignment was effective for tax purposes on the basis that the taxpayer had disposed of a capital asset to his wife (being a share in the partnership and the right to receive a future income stream of profits from the law practice).
>
> As such, the taxpayer's wife was assessed on the full amount of the share of income attributable to her, while the husband escaped tax liability on that income.

However, the practice of '*Everett*' assignments largely ended with the introduction of capital gains tax in 1985 and the case has limited continuing relevance. If the facts in *Everett* were to take place today, the assignment would result in the disposal of a CGT asset (i.e. the partner's interest, or part-interest, in a partnership) and would trigger CGT event A1. As such, a capital gain would be recognised under section 104-10 of the ITAA97.

The ATO suspended the application of the guidelines and *Everett* assignment web material as of 14 December 2017. The ATO have advised that those who entered into arrangements before 14 December 2017 that comply with the guidelines and do not exhibit high risk factors can rely on those guidelines. However, those arrangements demonstrating high-risk factors may be subject to review. During 2018, the ATO began consulting with stakeholders with a view to publishing draft guidance on this issue. As at the date of writing, no guidance has been issued on this matter. However, the ATO has provided certainty for the years ended 30 June 2019, 30 June 2020 and 30 June 2021, noting that taxpayers who have entered into arrangements prior to 14 December 2017 can continue to rely on the suspended guidelines as long as their arrangement:

- complies with the suspended guidelines
- is commercially driven
- does not exhibit high risk factors.

12.1.4 CGT issues for partnerships

For capital gains tax purposes, a partnership is not a separate legal entity. Consequently, any capital gain is derived in the name of each partner, not the partnership as for CGT purposes, each partner is regarded as owning an interest in relation to each partnership asset (sections 108-5(2) and 106-5).

As such, any capital gain is shown in the individual tax returns of each partner, not the partnership tax return.

To enable any capital gain or capital loss to be determined, each partner has a separate cost base and reduced cost base for their interest in each CGT asset of the partnership (section 106-5(2)).

On admission of a new partner, a new partnership is created. As such, the existing partners each dispose of a part of their interest in each of the assets of the partnership for their share of consideration paid by the incoming partner. Where an existing partner's share of the capital proceeds exceeds that partner's cost base, an assessable capital gain will arise.

Similarly, if a partner retires, disposing of their interest in the partnership assets, an assessable capital gain will arise if the capital proceeds received by the retiring partner are greater than the cost base of the retiring partner's interest in each partnership CGT asset, a capital loss could also arise if the capital proceeds are less than the cost base.

This is demonstrated in example 12.4.

EXAMPLE 12.4

CGT — admitting a new partner

Isaac and Emily are equal partners in a business. The partnership acquired business premises to run its business on 19 September 2010 for $1 200 000. The current market value of the premises is $1 800 000.

Isaac and Emily are considering admitting a third and equal partner, Stephanie, into the partnership. Stephanie will contribute $600 000 into the partnership for a 1/3 interest.

What are the CGT consequences of admitting Stephanie into the partnership?

Isaac and Emily each acquire a 1/3 interest in the asset (i.e. $600 000 contributed by Stephanie). The cost base of that interest is based on the market value of the interest disposed of by each of Isaac and Emily in the asset previously contributed by them (section 110-25(2)).

Isaac and Emily each dispose of 1/6 of the total interest in the asset of the old partnership which has a market value of $1 800 000. It follows that Isaac and Emily each have a cost base of $300 000 in respect of the interest acquired in Stephanie's asset.

The CGT consequences for Isaac and Emily from disposing of their 1/6 interest in the business premises are as follows.

	$
Capital proceeds for giving up one-third of the CGT asset ($1 800 000 × 1/6)	300 000
Less: Cost base ($1 200 000 × ½ interest each × 1/3)	(200 000)
Capital gain	100 000
Less: 50% CGT discount (as held for more than 12 months)	(50 000)
Net capital gain	**50 000**

The capital gains tax provisions for small business entities can apply to partnerships if they meet the necessary conditions.

12.1.5 Taxation consequences of a partnership receiving a franked dividend

There may be instances where a partnership receives a franked dividend from an Australian company. In this instance, the partnership is required to not only include the amount of the franked dividend as part of its assessable income, but also the franking credit.

Both of these figures are included in determining the net income of the partnership under section 90 of the ITAA36.

This amount is distributed to each partner. As a result, not only is the franked dividend included in each partner's tax return, but the franking credit is also distributed. The franking credit is then used as a tax offset to reduce the tax payable of the respective partners. This is demonstrated in example 12.5.

EXAMPLE 12.5

Partnership receiving a dividend

Stephen and Joanne are in partnership. Under the partnership agreement, they share profits and losses equally. For the year ended 30 June 2022, the partnership derived assessable income from trading of $500 000. It has allowable deductions of $360 000.

However, the partnership received a fully franked dividend of $7000 from Woolworths Ltd. Franking credits of $3000 were attached to these franked dividends.

What is the partnership's income and how is it distributed?

The partnership's assessable income comes to $510 000 (being $500 000 + $7000 + $3000). Its allowable deductions totalled $360 000 resulting in a net income (or tax profit) of $150 000. This amount is distributed 50 per cent each to Stephen and Joanne.

Stephen and Joanne will each include an amount of $75 000 in their respective income tax returns. It will be noted that the distribution not only includes the amount of the franked dividend, but also the franking credit.

Both Stephen and Joanne will receive a franking credit of $1500, which they can use to offset their tax payable.

12.2 Transactions between the partnership and partners

LEARNING OBJECTIVE 12.2 Describe the tax consequences of various transactions between the partnership and the partners.

Besides the basic distribution of partnership income to the partners, other transactions between partnerships and partners have various tax consequences. These are described in the following subsections.

12.2.1 Partners' salaries

The partnership agreement may provide for the payment of a salary to a working partner.

The Commissioner confirms that an agreement to pay a partner a salary must be documented in an agreement and signed by the partners before the end of the relevant income year. The amount of the partner's salary must also be reasonable and commensurate with the amount of work performed by the partner.

For such an agreement to be effective for tax purposes in an income year, the agreement must be entered into before the end of that income year (see *FCT v Galland*).[4]

A sample clause in the partnership agreement providing for the payment of a partner's salary is shown in figure 12.3.

| **FIGURE 12.3** | Sample partnership agreement clause providing for a partner's salary |

> **9   Salary**
>
> Each partner or such of them as may be agreed from time to time shall be entitled to such sum per week as salary as shall be mutually agreed from time to time and such salary shall be deemed to be a partnership outgoing and not on account of the partner's share of the profits.

For accounting purposes, a salary paid to a partner is considered an expense, which is recorded in the profit and loss statement, like any other expense of the business.

A partner is not considered to be an employee of the partnership. (This concept only applies to partners, and not to other employees.)

Hence, for taxation purposes (even if the partnership pays a salary to a partner and calls it a salary in its management accounts), a partner's salary is not deductible to the partnership under section 8-1 of the ITAA97. Instead, a salary paid to a partner is regarded as a distribution of profit. This principle is confirmed by the Commissioner in TR 2005/7.[5]

Paragraph 7 states:

> A partnership salary is *not* truly a salary, nor is it an expense of the partnership, but instead is an additional distribution of partnership profits to the recipient partner.

Therefore, if the partner's salary has been expensed to the profit and loss statement, then the amount of the partner's salary must be added back in determining the 'net income of the partnership' for taxation purposes.

When the net income of the partnership is distributed to each partner, any partnership salaries must firstly be attributed to each relevant partner, and then the remaining amount of profit needs to be distributed among the partners in accordance with their profit sharing ratio as per the partnership agreement (see paragraph 21).

However, where a partnership has made a loss, any salary paid to a partner is disregarded and is not considered in determining the partnership's net income. In other words, where the partnership derives a tax loss, the salary paid to the partner is disregarded and considered to be drawings.

For example, assume that a partnership derives a tax loss of ($40 000) for the year ended 30 June 2022, and the partnership agreement provides for all profits and losses to be shared 50 per cent each. If one of the partners has been paid a salary of $10 000, the tax loss is still considered to be $40 000 and each partner will receive a distribution of the tax loss of $20 000 each. The $10 000 salary paid to the partner is disregarded and treated as drawings for that year. This is demonstrated in example 12.6.

EXAMPLE 12.6

Losses

Assume that Jason and Charlotte are equal partners in a partnership. In other words, they share all partnership profits and losses on a 50/50 basis.

---

4 (1986) 86 ATC 4885.

5 The link to the Ruling is at: https://www.ato.gov.au/law/view/document?src=as&pit=20200728000000&arc=false&start=1&pagesize=10&total=19&num=3&docid=txr/tr20057/nat/ato/00001&dc=false&stype=find&tm=and-basic-tr%202005/7.

Both are residents for taxation law purposes. According to the partnership agreement, Jason is to receive a predetermined salary of $60 000 per annum for managing the business. Charlotte is not entitled to any partner's salary.

A summary of the profit and loss statement for the partnership for the year ended 30 June 2022 is shown.

	$
Revenue	600 000
Less: Expenses (all tax-deductible)	(460 000)
Less: Partner's salary — Jason	(60 000)
Net profit of the partnership (i.e. accounting profit)	**80 000**

Calculate each partner's share of the net income of the partnership for the year ended 30 June 2022.

Each partner's share of the net income of the partnership for the year ended 30 June 2022 is calculated as follows.

	$
Accounting partnership profit	80 000
Add: Jason's salary (non-tax deductible)	60 000
Net income of the partnership (i.e. tax profit)	**140 000**
DISTRIBUTION	
Jason	
Jason — salary (comes off first)	60 000
Jason — 50% share of balance ($80 000 × 50%)	40 000
	100 000
Charlotte	
Charlotte — 50% share of balance ($80 000 × 50%)	40 000
Net income of the partnership (i.e. tax profit)	**140 000**

The $60 000 salary paid to Jason is not an allowable deduction to the partnership for tax purposes as per TR 2005/7. Instead, it is regarded as a distribution of partnership profit.

12.2.2 Interest on partner's capital contributions

In order to become a partner, the incoming partner is usually required to make an initial (and/or ongoing) capital contribution. Given the large amounts of contributions that may be made, in some instances, the partners may agree that the partnership will pay each partner interest on their capital contribution.

Where interest is paid by the partnership on the capital contributed by a partner, TR 2005/7 confirms that the interest is not deductible to the partnership. It is not an expense of the partnership as one cannot incur an expense to oneself (the partnership is not a separate legal entity).

Instead, like a salary, the interest paid to a partner is regarded as a distribution of partnership profit.

12.2.3 Interest on loans made to the partnership by the partners

In some instances, a partner may lend money to the partnership. This is referred to as a 'partnership loan' or a 'partnership advance'. The partnership agreement usually provides for this and specifies the interest rate that may be charged on loans made to the partnership.

A sample clause from a partnership agreement is shown in figure 12.4.

FIGURE 12.4	Sample partnership agreement clause on loans made by a partner

6 Advances to partnership

Any partner with the consent of the other partner may make advances to the partnership but such advances shall not increase the capital of the partner making the same nor entitle him or her to any additional share in the profits but shall be a debt due by the partnership to the partner making the same and shall not carry interest unless so agreed by all the partners.

The relevant journal entry if a partner were to lend (or advance) $100 000 to the partnership is as shown in figure 12.5.

FIGURE 12.5 Journal entry to record partner's loan to partnership

Date	Particulars	Post Ref	Debit	Credit
July 1	Cash at bank	1–1000	100 000	
	Loan made by partner A	2–4000		100 000
	(Loan of $100 000 advanced to the partnership by partner A)			

If interest is paid monthly on the $100 000, the relevant journal entry to record the interest expense is as shown in figure 12.6.

FIGURE 12.6 Journal entry to record interest paid on partner's loan to partnership

Date	Particulars	Post Ref	Debit	Credit
Aug 1	Interest expense	6–1380	400	
	Cash at bank	1–1000		400
	(To record interest on the loan of $100 000 advanced by partner A)			

In this instance, the partner lends that money not in his or her capacity as a partner, but in the capacity of a lender (see *Leonard v FCT*).[6] Thus, interest is assessable income to the partner and a deductible expense to the partnership.

Interest on borrowings to fund the partnership's business activities is generally allowable as a deduction and, where there is a partnership at general law, interest on borrowings by the partnership to refinance contributed capital is allowable as a deduction. Refer to *FCT v Roberts*; *FCT v Smith* (1992) 23 ATR 494; TR 95/25.

In *Roberts* and *Smith*, money was borrowed by a partnership (a firm of solicitors) to allow each partner to withdraw $25 000 (amounts they had previously contributed to the partnership as part of the working capital) which in turn reduced the net worth of each partner's interest in the partnership, as a result new partners could buy into the partnership at a reduced cost. This case established the re-financing principal.

12.2.4 Partner's drawings

Partners drawings are not taken into account in determining the net income of the partnership. They are neither assessable to the individual partners nor deductible to the partnership for taxation purposes.

As in the case of accounting, a partner's drawing is considered a reduction in equity, not an expense. Hence, it is not reflected in the Profit and Loss Statement but rather as a debit to drawings. The accounting journal entry is as shown in figure 12.7.

Table 12.1 summarises the taxation implications of the transactions to both the partnership and the individual partner.

---

6 *Leonard v FCT* (1919) 26 CLR 175.

FIGURE 12.7   Journal entry for partners' drawings

Date	Particulars	Post Ref	Debit	Credit
Feb 26	Partner A drawings	3–3000	25 000	
	Partner B drawings	3–4000	25 000	
	Cash at bank	1–1000		50 000
	(Drawings of $25 000 taken by each partner)			

TABLE 12.1   Taxation implications to partners and partnership

Transaction	Tax implication to partnership	Tax implication to partner
Partner salaries	Not tax deductible to the partnership. Regarded as a distribution of profit to the partner	Included in the assessable income of the partner
Interest on partner's capital contributions	Not tax deductible to the partnership. Regarded as a distribution of profit to the partner	Included in the assessable income of the partner
Interest on partner's advances (i.e. loan or advance made by a partner to the partnership)	Interest paid is deductible to the partnership	Interest received by the partner is included in the assessable income of the partner
Partner drawings	Not deductible to the partnership	Not assessable and not deductible to the partners

Table 12.2 can be used to assist in working out the partnership distributions.

TABLE 12.2   Calculating partnership distributions

	Partner A	Partner B	Total
Salary received			
Add: Interest on capital			
Less: Interest on drawings			
Add: % of distribution			
Total			Net income of partnership

12.2.5 Changes to partnership structures

Where there are changes in the members of the partnership (such as when a partner dies or a new partner is admitted), the partnership is dissolved and a new partnership comes into existence. The ATO requires that a taxation return be lodged for the old partnership until it ceases to exist and the new partnership from the time of creation until the end of the income year. If the partnership has at least 20 partners, there is no need for this requirement to be undertaken as no new partnership exists (this mainly occurs in large legal and accounting firms).

A change in the identity of the partners of a partnership will mean that there is a new GST entity. There could be GST problems (particularly under the increasing adjustment provisions of Division 138 of the *A New Tax System (Goods and Servies Tax) Act 1999* (Cth) (GST Act) if the existing partnership is terminated. Depending on the nature of the partnership assets, there may be transfer duty implications.

12.3 Joint ventures

LEARNING OBJECTIVE 12.3 Describe the taxation consequences of a joint venture.

A partnership for taxation purposes is to be distinguished from a joint venture. A partnership is usually carried on as a business by two or more persons with a view to profit. In contrast, a **joint venture** is usually carried on by the venturers for a specific project (as distinct to carrying on business) and the participants usually receive a share of the final product (or output), rather than profit. Whereas a partnership can have many partners, a joint venture usually has only two or three venturers.

Where assets are contributed to the joint venture, each venture typically has a share in the individual assets rather than a share in the joint venture itself. The joint venture itself is not considered to be a separate legal entity. The resources contributed to a joint venture are typically predetermined by an agreed contractual arrangement.

Furthermore, unlike a partnership where each partner is responsible for the actions and liabilities of the other partners, each venture is usually responsible for their own liabilities, and is not contractually bound by the actions and liabilities of their co-venturer.

Ultimately, the most important distinction between a joint venture and a partnership depends upon whether or not the participants have entered into the project 'with a view to profit'. It is usually accepted that the project must generate a profit centre for it to be considered a partnership. If all that is shared is output, then a joint venture exists. This concept was explored in *United Dominions Corporation Ltd v Brian Pty Ltd*.

United Dominions Corporation Ltd v Brian Pty Ltd (1985) 157 CLR 1

Facts: There was a joint venture agreement for the development of land between United Dominions Corporation (UDC), Security Projects Ltd (SPL) and Brian Pty Ltd (Brian).

The land in question was owned by SPL. The joint venture was largely financed by funds from UDC, secured by a mortgage signed by SPL. The joint venturers provided the balance of funds for the development.

The development realised a significant profit. However, UDC retained the profit and no distribution of profit was made to Brian.

UDC's claim to what would otherwise have been Brian's share of profits was based upon a provision in the mortgage to SPL, referred to as the 'collateralisation clause' to the effect that the mortgage was security for any money that had been advanced to SPL. Brian claimed that the clause breached fiduciary obligations owed to it by UDC and SPL.

The issue was whether the relationship of joint venture had given rise to fiduciary obligations.

Held: The Court held that a fiduciary relationship existed. Even though the term 'partnership' was not explicitly used in the agreements between the parties, it did not preclude a finding that the agreement exhibited all the criteria of a partnership. Even though the agreement was drafted as a joint venture, for all intents and purposes, the agreement was more akin to a partnership.

As put by Dawson J at [7]:

> Perhaps, in this country, the important distinction between a partnership and a joint venture is, for practical purposes, the distinction between an association of persons who engage in a common undertaking for profit and an association of those who do so in order to generate a product to be shared among the participants. Enterprises of the latter kind are common enough in the exploration for and exportation of minerals resources and the feature which is most likely to distinguish them from partnerships is the sharing of product rather than profit.

A typical joint venture operation is where two or more venturers contribute their operations, resources and expertise for a specific project and each venture bears its own costs and takes a share of the output, rather than sale proceeds or profits.

Under the joint venture agreement, each venture has joint control, rather than being bound by the actions of their fellow participants. This is primarily to avoid the imposition of fiduciary obligations, restrictions and liabilities located under the relevant State Partnership Acts.

Joint ventures are very common in the mining, primary production and infrastructure industries.

A joint venture does not lodge a tax return. As output from the joint venture is distributed to each venture, rather than sale proceeds or profits, each venture is responsible for determining how the product or output is disposed of.

This means that each venture is required to lodge their own tax return and include the relevant income from the sale of the product/output, claim their own deductions and make their own elections, such as trading stock, depreciation etc.

From a GST perspective, separate joint venturers may be allowed to form a single group and become participants in a GST joint venture if they meet the requirements of Subdivision 51-A of the GST Act.

The nominated joint venture operator is responsible for the GST payable and can claim the GST credits on transactions undertaken by group members (except transactions between group members). This arrangement helps to reduce administrative cost in relation to GST compliance. In effect, the nominated joint venture operator manages the group's GST affairs.

On 7 April 2004, the Commissioner of Taxation issued GST Ruling GSTR 2004/2 dealing with a range of administrative matters that the joint venture must comply with in order to form a GST group.

12.4 Introduction to trusts

LEARNING OBJECTIVE 12.4 Describe the basic principles of how trusts operate and how they are taxed.

The legal owner of an asset usually has the exclusive legal right to the asset itself and manages the asset for their own personal enjoyment and benefit. However, if an asset is held in a **trust**, the legal ownership and benefits of the trust property are divided between the trustee of the trust and the beneficiaries of the trust.

The **trustee** is the legal owner of the **trust property**; however, the trustee holds the property for the exclusive benefit of the **beneficiaries**, who are regarded as the 'beneficial owners'. This includes the value of the property itself as well as any income derived from that property. Understanding this separation of legal and beneficial interest is essential to understanding how trusts work and how they are taxed.

Table 12.3 presents some basic terminology to describe how trusts are structured and operated.

TABLE 12.3 Simple trust terminology

Term	Definition
Trust property	The capital assets of the trust — sometimes also known as the 'corpus' (body) of the trust. Can be any asset, including real property, personal property or intellectual property such as a trademark or licence.
Trustee	Legal owner of the trust property. Holds the property 'on trust' for the exclusive benefit of the beneficiaries. Trustees will usually have a wide discretion as to how they manage the assets of the trust as long as what they decide is in the best interests of the beneficiaries and nobody else. This obligation — to put the interests of the beneficiaries ahead of their own or those of anybody else — is the fundamental 'fiduciary duty' of a trustee. A trustee can be one or more people. Companies can also be trustees. A trustee can also be one of the beneficiaries of the trust (but they cannot be the sole beneficiary). The trustee is usually personally liable for the debts of the trust.
Beneficiaries	Those who get all the benefits from trust property. This includes the trust income. It also includes the trust capital when the trust ends (known as 'vesting' of the trust). Their entitlement will vary from a 'mere expectancy' which can vary over the life of the trust to a fixed entitlement, depending on the type of trust. Beneficiaries can be one or more individuals, companies and other entities, including other trusts. Beneficiaries can also include unborn children and entities not in existence at the time the trust is established.
Trust Deed	The Trust Deed (sometimes called a 'Deed of Settlement') sets out the contractual terms of the trust. In the Trust Deed, you will find the powers and rights of the trustee and the beneficiaries. There are also laws that govern trusts. These are contained in state Trustee Acts. Trusts do not have to be created in writing, but in a business context they usually are.
Settlor	This is the person who contributes the initial assets to the trust to set it up (often a nominal sum of money). The settlor cannot be the initial trustee or a beneficiary of the trust. Usually, the settlor will have little or no further involvement in the trust after it is established.
Controller	Trusts will often also have a nominated 'controller' or 'appointor'. This is the person who has the power to appoint new trustees and, in the family setting, is usually the head of the family who decided to set up the trust and contribute the main trust assets.

Figure 12.8 illustrates the basic features of a trust.

Trusts are a popular form of investment and business structure due to the asset protection and tax planning benefits potentially capable of being derived using a trust structure. From an asset protection point of view, the assets in a trust can be shielded from creditors and others who might otherwise have a claim over those assets if they were held by an individual (because the individual is no longer the legal owner) without the individual having to give up the beneficial use of those assets. This is one of the reasons professional service businesses often set up 'service trusts' which own the valuable assets of the business, and provide the use of those assets under contract to the business operating entity which often then conducts potentially high risk activities that might give rise to claims against those assets.

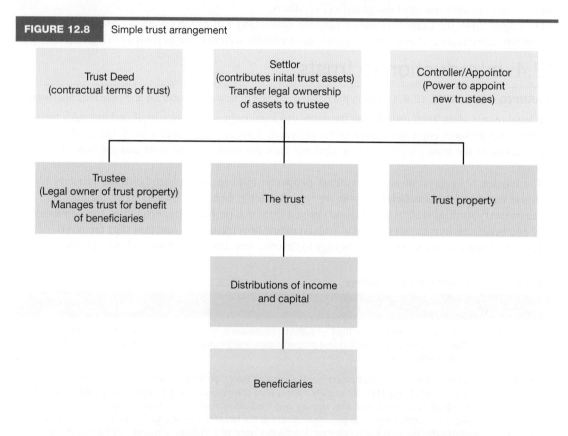

FIGURE 12.8   Simple trust arrangement

Trusts can also be used to help preserve testamentary assets (assets gifted in a Will) rather than gifting them to beneficiaries outright. This is useful in situations where young children incapable of managing their own affairs are involved or where there might be concerns that the beneficiary might not use those assets wisely or may subject those assets to risk of depletion or attack from third parties if they were to become the legal owner of those assets.

Trusts can also enable income to be distributed to specific beneficiaries in accordance with their individual needs and tax position from year to year. These benefits are also a source of public debate and controversy through what some see as unfair benefits and opportunities for tax avoidance stemming from the use of trusts. The tax planning benefits of trusts and the controversies they raise will be discussed further in a later section.

Notwithstanding these controversies, trusts continue to increase in popularity (see table 12.4).

12.4.1 Types of trusts

There are many different kinds of trust. The most common are described, but trusts also include superannuation funds, charitable trusts and special disability trusts. As flagged, trusts are also sometimes established in wills to gift and preserve assets — these are known as 'testamentary trusts'.

The two main types of trusts that are used in business and by individuals (which we introduced in an earlier chapter in the context of discussing residency of trusts) are discretionary trusts and fixed trusts.

TABLE 12.4   Trust total business income

Trust size (see definition)	2016–17 Trusts (no.)	2016–17 TBI ($m)	2017–18 Trusts (no.)	2017–18 TBI ($m)	2018–19 Trusts (no.)	2018–19 TBI ($m)
Loss	511	–638	500	–58	526	–60
Nil	515 444	0	535 943	0	544 893	0
Micro	327 750	112 633	333 852	115 100	331 051	113 678
Small	26 333	104 157	27 103	107 287	26 647	105 403
Medium	4 597	109 532	4 638	109 617	4 551	105 947
Large	184	27 605	195	29 623	186	27 196
Very large	55	32 377	55	33 163	60	38 486
Total	**874 874**	**385 667**	**902 286**	**394 732**	**907 914**	**390 650**

Source: Australian Taxation Office, 'Trusts' (Web Page, 2019) https://www.ato.gov.au/About-ATO/Research-and-statistics/In-detail/Taxation-statistics/Taxation-statistics-2018-19/?page=10#Trust_statistics.

12.4.1.1 Discretionary trusts

A **discretionary trust** (sometimes also called a 'family trust') is the most common form of trust used in family and small business settings. The beneficiaries of the trust have no defined entitlement to the income of the trust — they have a 'mere expectancy'. This means each year the trustee decides which beneficiaries are entitled to receive a share of the net income of the trust and how big a share they should get. This makes discretionary trusts an attractive tax planning tool (see the next section). An example of a discretionary trust structure is described in example 12.7.

EXAMPLE 12.7

Discretionary trust arrangement

Mr and Mrs Khan wish to establish a small business. They have three adult children who will help in the business and a large extended family. They seek to operate the business through a trust structure.

How might the trust be structured in these circumstances?

The Khan Family Trust could be structured as follows.

Settlor: A non-family member — for example, their financial or legal advisor or a friend.

Trustee: Mr and Mrs Khan or a company set up with Mr and Mrs Khan as the Directors and Shareholders.

Beneficiaries: Mr and Mrs Khan, their parents and siblings, their children and the children of their siblings, any grandchildren or great grandchildren, and any entities owned or controlled by any of those people

Initial trust property: $50 contributed by the settlor and used to open the trust bank account.

12.4.1.2 Fixed trusts

Unlike a discretionary trust, the beneficiaries of a **fixed trust** have a defined entitlement under the trust, similar to a shareholder in a company. Beneficiaries are usually issued with 'units' in the trust in the same way as shareholders of a company are issued shares (fixed trusts are often called 'unit trusts' — although unit trusts are simply a common type of fixed trust). The units have certain rights attached to them in the same way as shares have rights attached to them. These usually include entitlements to a fixed share in the income and capital of the trust.

Unlike the trustee of a discretionary trust, the trustee of a fixed trust does not have any discretion as to how they distribute the trust's capital and net income. A fixed trust is often used for joint venture business arrangements which involve bringing together different groups of unrelated people to complete a project (e.g. a property development project). A fixed trust arrangement is described in example 12.8.

EXAMPLE 12.8

Fixed trust arrangement

Mr Chen has just retired and is looking to invest some money. His neighbour, Mr Gabrielatos, is a builder. One night they discuss the possibility of collaborating on a property development project. Mr Chen would contribute the funds to purchase the land and Mr Gabrielatos would contribute the labour and materials to build a block of units on the land. They consider this to be an equal contribution to the project.

How might a trust be used for this project?

The Chen-Gabrielatos Property Trust could be structured as follows.

Settlor: A financial or legal advisor or a friend.

Trustee: Mr Chen and Mr Gabrielatos or a company set up with Mr Chen and Mr Gabrielatos as the Directors and Shareholders.

Beneficiaries: Mr and Mrs Chen and Mr and Mrs Gabrielatos — each are issued with 25 Units of a total of 100 issued units in the trust. Each unit represents a 1 per cent interest in the trust.

Initial trust property: $100 contributed by the settlor, used to open the trust bank account and representing an initial value of $1 per issued unit in the trust.

The discussion of fixed trusts in this chapter centres on private fixed trusts like the one described in example 12.8. However, there are also large publicly listed unit trusts (managed funds usually holding large property portfolios and portfolios of assets in other asset classes). Units in these trusts are traded on the Australian Securities Exchange.

12.5 Trust taxation regime

LEARNING OBJECTIVE 12.5 Calculate the tax liability of various types of beneficiaries and the trustee of a trust.

The main provisions setting out the tax treatment of trusts are contained in Division 6 of the ITAA36 in sections 95 to 102. These provisions contain three fundamental principles.

1. The trustee must calculate its annual 'trust net income' and lodge an annual income tax return but is not a separate taxable entity (i.e. it is not treated as a separate taxpayer as is the case, for instance, with a company).
2. Beneficiaries are liable to pay tax on their share of 'trust net income' (i.e. it is not essential that income is actually distributed to them).
3. The trustee will pay tax on the share of the 'trust net income' where there is no 'presently entitled' beneficiary, the beneficiary is under a legal disability, or non-resident beneficiaries are present.

The rest of this section will explain and apply these three key principles.

12.5.1 Calculation of trust net income

The first step for working out the tax liability of a trust is to work out the net income of the trust. **Trust net income** is defined in section 95 of the ITAA36. It says the trust net income is the total assessable income of the trust estate calculated as if the trustee was a resident taxpayer less allowable deductions (see example 12.9). Note that net losses cannot be distributed to beneficiaries — losses are effectively 'trapped' in the trust, although they can be carried forward to offset future trust income. Further, the character of an item of income retains its character when it is distributed to a beneficiary — for example, a dividend received by the trust and distributed to a beneficiary is treated as a dividend receipt in the hands of the beneficiary.

EXAMPLE 12.9

Trust net income

A trust derives $15 000 rental income and deductible expenses were $5000.

What is the trust net income?

Under section 95(1), net income of the trust estate is calculated as if the trustee were a resident taxpayer as follows.

	$
Assessable income	15 000
Less: Allowable deductions	5 000
Net income of trust estate	**10 000**

Once trust net income is worked out, it is necessary to work out whether the beneficiaries or the trustee will be liable to pay tax on the trust net income. This will determine how much tax is payable.

Figure 12.9 summarises who will be liable to pay tax on net income of a trust and the discussion which follows will explain this further.

FIGURE 12.9	Who pays tax on the net income of a trust?

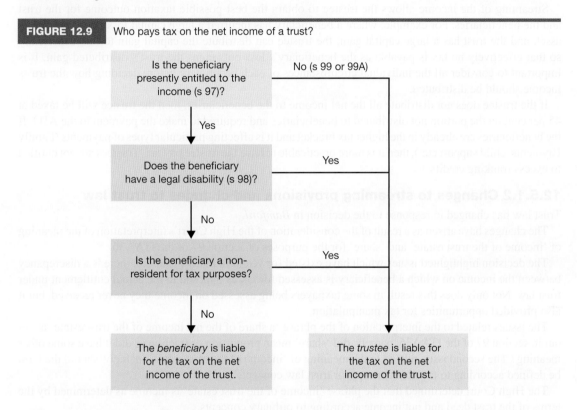

The tax treatment (including who pays and how much tax is payable) will not necessarily be the same for all of the net trust income. For example, the share of the income of a non-resident beneficiary will be taxed differently to the share of net trust income of a legally incapable beneficiary and so too will the share of net trust income of legally capable resident beneficiaries.

Where the amount distributed is less than the net income under section 95, there is a problem determining how the excess of net income is to be taxed. The two approaches which have been applied are as follows.

1. The proportionate approach is that the net income for tax purposes is distributed to beneficiaries based on their proportional entitlement to net income for trust law purposes.
2. The quantum approach is to tax trust income in the year in which it is derived by the trust and to apportion liability between the beneficiaries and the trust according to weather and to what extent the beneficiaries have an indefeasible interest in that income.

Since the outcome of the *Bamford* case discussed later, the proportionate approach is required to be used at all times.

12.5.1.1 Streaming of trust income

Income 'streaming' or the 'attribution' of income refers to the ability of a trustee to direct certain types of income to particular beneficiaries. Income, which flows through a trust to beneficiaries, will retain its identity. For example, exempt income received by a trustee will retain its exempt status when distributed to a beneficiary. Similarly, imputation credits attaching to franked dividends can also be passed on.

The following list provides suggestions for streaming of income.

- Distribute capital gains to beneficiaries with capital losses.
- Distribute franked dividend income to beneficiaries who can use the credits.
- Distribute foreign sourced income to non-resident beneficiaries so that no tax is payable.
- Distribute income to beneficiaries with low tax rates or carry forward tax losses.

The Commissioner accepts the practice of income streaming, subject to the terms of the trust deed, and to certain bookkeeping requirements. These requirements are outlined in TR 92/13. It is important that the trust deed gives the trustee the power to distribute income from different classes to different beneficiaries. The trustee's resolution as to how the income is to be distributed must also refer to the distribution by classes.

The trustee is required to minute two months after the end of the financial year the way in which the trust's income is to be distributed and to whom.

Streaming of the income allows the trustee to obtain the best possible taxation outcome for the trust and the beneficiaries. For example, where a beneficiary has incurred a large capital loss on the sale of an asset, and the trust has a large capital gain, the trustee can distribute the capital gain to that beneficiary so that effectively no tax is payable as the beneficiary's loss outweighs the trust's distributed gain. It is important to consider all the individual circumstances of each beneficiary before deciding how the trusts income should be distributed.

If the trustee does not distribute all the net income to the beneficiaries, then the trustee will be taxed at 45 per cent on the portion not distributed to beneficiaries and required to make the payment to the ATO. If the beneficiaries are already in the higher tax bracket and it is affecting particular types of payments (Family Payments, child support etc.), then it is more practicable to have the trustee pay tax. Trustees are not entitled to excess franking credits.

12.5.1.2 Changes to streaming provisions and changes to trust law

Trust law has changed in response to the decision in *Bamford*.

The changes have arisen as a result of the consideration of the High Court's interpretation of the meaning of 'income of the trust estate' and 'share' for the purposes of section 97 of the ITAA36.

The decision highlighted issues which have existed for years. In many instances, there is a discrepancy between the income on which a beneficiary is assessed for tax as opposed to the actual entitlement under trust law. Not only does this result in some taxpayers being assessed on income they never received, but it also provided opportunities for tax manipulation.

The issues related to the interpretation of the phrase 'a share of the net income of the trust estate' as set out in section 97 of the ITAA36: namely, did 'share' mean proportion or fraction or did it have some other meaning? The second issue related to the meaning of 'income of the trust estate': namely, should the term be defined according to taxation concepts or trust law concepts?

The High Court determined that the phrase 'income of the trust estate' is income as determined by the terms of the trust deed and not income according to ordinary concepts.

Trust deeds today provide trustees with considerable flexibility in determining how to calculate and categorise income of the trust. These deeds allow trustees to allocate expenses from either capital or from current year profits. This ensures that modern-day trustees have maximum flexibility in determining what is trust law income, who is entitled to that income, and who will be liable to tax on that income.

As an example, while the sale of an asset is a capital receipt if the trust deed gives the trustee the power to categorise this as income, it can be included in the 'income of the trust estate'.

As a result of this decision, the Commissioner has incorporated a number of changes into the legislation. The changes have tried to better align the concept of 'income of the trust estate' with 'net income of the trust estate'. In addition, the changes allow the 'streaming' of dividends and capital gains.

In order to achieve this, capital gains and franked dividends are excised from the income of the trust and are included in the income of the beneficiary or assessed to the trustee on behalf of the beneficiary under Subdivisions 115-C or 207-B.

12.5.2 Tax payable by the beneficiaries

A beneficiary will pay tax on their share of the trust income where they are 'presently entitled' to that income. A beneficiary is presently entitled to a share in the trust net income when the income is legally available for distribution and the beneficiary has a present or immediate right to demand payment of the share of the net income.

The High Court described the concept of **present entitlement** in *Whiting v FCT* in the following terms:

> The words 'presently entitled to a share of the income' refer to a right to income 'presently' existing i.e., a right of such a kind that a beneficiary may demand payment from the trustee … A beneficiary who has a vested right to income … but who may never receive any payment by reason of such a right, is entitled to income but cannot be said to be 'presently entitled' as distinct from merely 'entitled'.[7]

12.5.2.1 Deemed present entitlement

'Present entitlement' for tax purposes does not mean the beneficiary has to actually have received the income. In fact, where the trustee has discretion to pay or apply trust income for the benefit of specific beneficiaries, section 101 of the ITAA36 will deem beneficiaries to be presently entitled to an amount paid or applied for their benefit by the trustee in exercise of their discretion. Consider example 12.10.

EXAMPLE 12.10

Deemed present entitlement

Anastacia is a beneficiary of her family's discretionary family trust. Her parents are the trustees and they distribute income of the trust among the beneficiaries of the trust according to their discretion from year to year. In the 2021–22 tax year Anastacia does not receive any money from the trust. However, her parents paid $10 000 in university fees for her accounting degree from the trust net income for the year.

Will Anastacia be deemed to be presently entitled to any net income from the trust?

Yes. Anastacia will be deemed to be presently entitled to $10 000 in net income of the trust. She will need to pay tax at her applicable marginal tax rate. This is because even though she did not physically receive the money, the $10 000 was applied for her benefit by the trustees.

Section 95A(2) of the ITAA36 also extends the concept of deemed present entitlement to situations ' … where a beneficiary has a vested and indefeasible interest in any of the income of a trust estate but is not presently entitled to that income … '.

If the beneficiary derives income from other sources as well as the trust, the beneficiary must lodge an individual tax return (otherwise they may not need to do so) and include their share of the trust net income in that tax return. Any tax paid by the trustee on that income will reduce the amount of tax payable by the beneficiary (rebate under section 100(2) of the ITAA36).

12.5.3 Tax payable by the trustee

As noted in figure 12.9, the trustee will be liable to pay tax on the amount of trust net income for which:
- no beneficiary is presently entitled: where the trust derives net income to which none of the beneficiaries are presently entitled
- a legally disabled beneficiary is entitled: where a beneficiary would be presently entitled, but they have a legal disability, or
- a non-resident beneficiary is presently entitled: where the presently entitled beneficiary is a non-resident at the end of the income year.

The income will be taxed either under section 99 (net trust income taxed at ordinary individual marginal tax rates) or section 99A (net trust income taxed at maximum marginal rate). The rate of tax payable will depend on whether the Commissioner will exercise his or her discretion under section 99A(2) to assess the trustee under section 99 or section 99A.

The Commissioner will exercise his or her discretion in favour of the trustee taxpayer only when it would be unreasonable for section 99A to apply. This includes situations resulting from wills or estates, bankruptcy, compensation claims, family breakdowns or insurance or superannuation pay-outs resulting from death.

---

7 *Whiting v FCT* (1943) 68 CLR 199.

12.5.3.1 No beneficiary presently entitled

If no beneficiary is presently entitled to a share of the trust net income, the trustee will need to pay tax on that share of the trust net income. The income will be taxed at the maximum marginal tax rate under section 99A unless the Commissioner exercises his or her discretion under section 99A(2) to apply the ordinary marginal tax rate (section 99).

12.5.3.2 Legal disability

A legal disability means a person who the law views as lacking legal capacity to enter into certain legal transactions on their own behalf. Examples include people under the age of 18 ('minors'), people who are bankrupt or people who are severely mentally incapacitated. Trusts often have beneficiaries who lack legal capacity. In fact, where a person lacks legal capacity, it is often necessary for a trustee to be appointed to manage their affairs on their behalf. Hence, understanding the tax implications where there are legally incapable beneficiaries is very important.

Where there is a legally incapable beneficiary, section 98 applies in the same way as it does where there is a legally capable beneficiary with a present entitlement to the relevant share of the trust income. Section 98 says the trustee will be liable to pay tax on the share of the net income of the trust as if it were the income of an individual. In effect, this means the trustee pays tax at the rate of tax the beneficiary would have paid if they did not have a legal disability. Consider example 12.11.

EXAMPLE 12.11

Tax on net trust income where beneficiary has a legal disability

For the year ending 30 June 2022, the trustee of the Howard Family Trust exercised their discretion to distribute $18 000 of net trust income to Ron, who is a resident, aged 25 and is under a 'legal disability' ('being of unsound mind').

Who is liable for the tax on the income distributed to Ron?

The trustee will pay tax on Ron's behalf at individual resident rates. Assuming that Ron has no other income for the 2022 tax year then no tax would be payable on the $18 000 share of net trust income distributed to Ron as it is below the tax-free threshold for individual resident taxpayers.

Where the beneficiary is a minor, the same rules as for other legally incapacitated beneficiaries apply only if the minor is an 'excepted person'.

If the beneficiary is a minor and the beneficiary is not an 'excepted person' or the income is not 'excepted income' under section 102AC(2), the trustee will pay tax at the rates set out in Division 6AA of the ITAA36. If a minor is not an 'excepted person', they are a 'prescribed person'. Section 102AC(1) defines a 'prescribed person' as a person who is under 18 at the end of the year of income and who is not engaged in full-time occupation.

Distributions of income which is not 'excepted income' to minors who are 'prescribed persons' are taxed at the following rates:
- first $416: tax-free
- between $417 and $1307: taxed at 66 per cent
- if amount exceeds $1307: the entire amount of the distribution (including the first $1307) is taxed at 45 per cent, plus the applicable Medicare levy.

Minors who are prescribed persons also cannot apply any low-income rebate to effectively increase their tax-free threshold. Excepted persons under Division 6AA include:[8]
- minors in full-time employment, and
- minors suffering from some incapacity or disability and eligible for child disability allowance.
  Excepted income under Division 6AA includes:[9]
- employment or business income, and
- distributions to minors of income from deceased estates.

---

8 ITAA36 section 102AC.
9 ITAA36 section 102AE.

12.5.3.3 Non-resident beneficiaries

The trustee is liable for tax payable by a non-resident beneficiary at the rates payable by non-residents (sections 98(2A) and 98(3) of the ITAA36). A reason for this rule is that it can be difficult to trace and collect tax from non-resident beneficiaries. The non-resident beneficiary is also assessable on the income under section 98A and is entitled to claim a tax credit for any tax already paid by the trustee on the Australian source income distributed to them. The tax residency and source rules (explained in an earlier chapter) also apply — non-residents are only taxable on Australian source income.

12.5.4 Calculating tax payable on trust net income

Example 12.12 illustrates how the rules and concepts discussed apply in a practical setting.

EXAMPLE 12.12

Calculating tax payable on trust net income

The Adams Family Trust is a discretionary family trust and the trustee, Adams Pty Ltd, has prepared trustee minutes for the year ended 30 June 2022 to distribute the net income of the trust ($120 000) in the following way:
 (i) $40 000 to Douglas, an adult resident beneficiary
 (ii) $40 000 to Simon, a non-resident adult beneficiary
 (iii) $10 000 to Jack, a 10-year-old resident beneficiary, and has not made any other beneficiary presently entitled to the remainder.
 What tax consequences arise from these distributions?
 As a result of the trustee exercising its discretion in this way, the following tax consequences will result.
 (i) The $40 000 distributed to Douglas will be taxable to Douglas as an adult resident beneficiary under section 97 of the ITAA36 at individual resident marginal tax rates.
 (ii) The $40 000 distributed to Simon, who is a non-resident, will be taxable to the trustee, Adams Pty Ltd on behalf of the beneficiary under section 98(2A) and section 98(3) of the *ITAA36* at non-resident individual tax rates.
 (iii) The $10 000 distributed to Jack, who is a minor, will be taxable to the trustee at the Division 6AA penalty rates of 45 per cent.
 The $30 000 net trust income, to which no beneficiary is presently entitled, will be taxable to the trustee under section 99A at penalty tax rates (presently 45 per cent).

12.5.5 Capital gains tax

Creating a trust over a CGT asset is CGT event E1 which is dealt with under section 104-55. Therefore, when the settlor transfers property to the trustee to establish the trust, the settlor may incur a liability for capital gains tax. Although there is no disposal of the legal interest in the property, the beneficial title has passed.

12.5.5.1 Net capital gain derived by a trust

The application of capital gains tax must be considered from the point of view of both the trustee and the beneficiary. A capital gain arising from disposal of trust assets will be included in the net income of the trust. Section 95 of the ITAA36 defines the net income of a trust as being calculated as if the trustee was a resident taxpayer. Therefore, capital gains must be included in the net income of the trust. However, the beneficiary may also be liable in respect of dealings in an interest in the trust as capital gains can be distributed to beneficiaries.

Capital gains are derived when the capital proceeds received on disposal of an asset acquired on or after 20 September 1985 exceed the cost base of that asset or the indexed cost base. The indexed cost base is the consideration paid for the asset, adjusted for inflation according to the consumer price index.

Individuals and trusts are able to exclude one-half of certain capital gains made on CGT assets from their assessable income. This concession applies only to assets acquired after 21 September 1999 and held for at least 12 months before disposal. Refer to the earlier chapter on CGT for a fuller explanation of how the rules regarding indexation and discounting work.

The calculation of the net tax payable where an individual has derived a net capital gain ensures that the gain is taxed with reference to the individual's marginal rate of tax on other income. Where a beneficiary is

---

presently entitled to income from a trust, that income may contain a share of the net capital gain. The capital gain, that was discounted or received any other concessions, has to be grossed up by the beneficiary. This amount is treated as a capital gain of the beneficiary for the purposes of calculating the net capital gain for the year. This is to allow the beneficiary to apply the capital losses against the trust capital gain before applying the appropriate discount percentage and other reductions where applicable.

Many of the capital gains tax provisions refer to the beneficiary as being absolutely entitled to an asset. This is in contrast to the use of the term 'present entitlement' in relation to trust income. It appears that the legislation looks through the trust to determine the ownership of trust assets in terms of equitable ownership rather than legal ownership. Where the beneficial ownership of an asset does not change, generally no capital gains tax liability will arise.

12.5.5.2 Interests in a trust

A beneficiary is liable to capital gains tax on the disposal of an interest in a unit trust. The capital gains tax provisions apply to:
• bonus issue of units
• rights to acquire units
• options to acquire unissued units
• convertible notes able to be converted to units.

Beneficiaries in a discretionary trust do not have an interest in a trust as they only have the right to be considered by the trustee. Therefore, any distribution of capital will be tax free.

12.5.5.3 Distributions of capital from a trust: CGT event E4

Where the trustee of a unit trust pays an amount to a beneficiary that is not in respect of a disposal of the unit-holder's interest in the trust, that amount will not be included in the unit-holder's assessable income. The amount not included in the beneficiary's assessable income is called the 'non-assessable part'.

The non-assessable amounts consist of:
• CGT general discount
• CGT indexation
• CGT small business concessions
• depreciation
• building allowances.

The way CGT event E4 operates is to apply the non-assessable part of the payment in reduction of the cost base and reduced cost base of the unit or trust interest and to treat any excess over the cost base as a capital gain.

A payment or distribution of property that is made from certain events is excluded from the operation of CGT event E4. These include CGT event A1 (disposal of a CGT asset) and CGT event C2 (cancellation, surrender and similar endings).

The receipt of the CGT general discount amount is not caught under this provision.

EXAMPLE 12.13

CGT event E4

Hannah acquired a unit in a unit trust for $1000 in May 2018. During the 2021–22 tax year, the trustee paid Hannah a non-assessable amount of $2000. This payment will reduce Hannah's cost base below 0 and a capital gain of $1000 ($2000 – $1000 cost base) will arise as a result of E4. If Hannah receives any further non assessable amounts, it will result in a further capital gain as her cost base is 0.

12.5.5.4 Small business concessions

The small business concessions can be utilised by a trust in relation to the active assets or by a beneficiary or unit-holder if certain conditions in addition to the standard conditions are met.

The major issue previously was the ability of the trust to pass the $6 million net asset test, as all the assets of the beneficiaries needed to be included. This included potential beneficiaries as well as those who actually received distributions. As most trusts deeds included charities in their list of potential beneficiaries, the test would never have been able to be passed. To overcome these shortfalls in the legislation, the

Government introduced changes so that any distributions to charities will be ignored for the purposes of working out the net assets test limit (via connected entities) and introduced a control test.

The control test in relation to discretionary trusts is based on the level of actual distributions made by the trust. An entity controls a discretionary trust only if the distributions made by the trust to the entity and or its small business CGT affiliates are at least 20 per cent of the total distributions of the trust in any of the 4 income years before the year for which access to the concessions are sought. If a trust makes a tax loss and no distributions are made by the trustee, the trustee can nominate up to 4 beneficiaries to be controllers of the trust for that income year (this must be in writing and signed by both the trustee and the nominated beneficiary). From 1 July 2007, those persons who control the trustee will also be connected with the trust regardless of whether they or their affiliates receive distributions from the trust.

In order for trusts to access the concessions, they must have a 'significant individual'. An individual is a significant individual of a fixed trust if they have entitlements to at least 20 per cent of the income and capital of the trust. An individual is a significant individual of a non-fixed trust at a time if, during the income year in which the time occurs, the trust made a distribution of income or capital and the individual was beneficially entitled to at least 20 per cent of the total distribution of income and of capital made by the trust during the income year.

See the discussion in relation to CGT small business concessions in an earlier chapter.

12.5.5.5 Capital gains on vesting of trust

The capital gains tax provisions relating to vesting a trust other than a unit trust are found in sections 104-75 to 104-100. CGT event E5 deals with a beneficiary becoming entitled to a trust asset. This may be through the distribution of corpus on winding up, or through the operation of law — for example, when a minor reaches the age of 18, section 104-75 deems the trustee to have disposed of the asset to the beneficiary at the time the beneficiary became entitled to that asset for a consideration equal to the market value of the asset. Simultaneously, the beneficiary is deemed to have disposed of his interest in the corpus, to the extent to which that asset formed part of corpus, for consideration equal to the market value. Where the beneficiary paid no consideration to acquire the interest in the estate, and did not acquire it by way of an assignment, then the indexed cost base of that interest is deemed to be an amount equal to the market value at the time of disposal.

The effect is that if the trustee makes a distribution in specie of assets with unrealised capital gains attached, the trustee will be deemed to have disposed of those assets for market value, thus realising the capital gain which becomes a part of the net income of the trust. The beneficiary has no liability on the disposal of the interest in the trust as the consideration and the indexed cost base of the interest are both deemed to be market value. Having acquired the asset for market value the beneficiary may derive a capital gain on the eventual sale of that asset.

EXAMPLE 12.14

CGT event E5

On 21 October 2000, the AM Family Trust was established by Mrs AM. As part of the settlement, Mrs AM transferred a house with a market value of $170 000. The beneficiaries of the AM Family Trust include HM. On 27 June 2022, HM is 25 years old and becomes absolutely entitled to the house which at that time has a market value of $470 000. The capital gains to the trustee on HM become absolutely entitled to the house is as follows.

	$
Market value of house	470 000
Less: Cost base	170 000
Capital gain	300 000
As asset held for more than 12 months 50% general discount will apply	150 000
Net capital gain	**150 000**

Note: Any capital gain or capital loss made by HM with respect to her interest in the trust will be disregarded because she incurred no expenditure to acquire it. Her cost base for the house is $470 000.

Event E6 deals with the disposal to the beneficiary to end an income right. Where the trustee transfers assets to a beneficiary in satisfaction of a right to receive income from a trust, section 104-80 applies. It deems there to be a disposal of the asset from the trustee to the beneficiary, and a corresponding disposal from the beneficiary to the trustee of the right to receive income. The deemed consideration for each disposal is the market value of the asset that has been transferred to the beneficiary.

The note attached to section 104-80(5) ensures that, where a person acquires a right to receive income only from a trust estate without paying any consideration for that interest, the cost base is nil. On disposal of such a right, the total consideration will be assessable, whereas if the consideration on acquisition had been deemed to be market value, the capital gain on disposal would be restricted to any increase in value. As the section applies to a right to receive income, it appears that it cannot be applied to discretionary trusts as the beneficiary does not have any right to the income, but merely a right to be considered in the exercise of the trustee's discretion.

Event E7 deals with the disposal to the beneficiary to end capital interests. Where the trustee disposes of an asset of the trust to a beneficiary in satisfaction of the beneficiary's interest in the trust capital, section 104-85 applies.

Event E8 deals with the disposal by the beneficiary of capital interest. Section 104-90 requires the capital gain or capital loss to be calculated by reference to section 104-95. It provides method statements and examples on how to work out the capital gain where there is one or more than one beneficiary. Section 104-100 deals with the capital loss situation.

12.5.6 Tax planning and trust controversies

As flagged earlier, trusts provide a number of tax advantages in certain circumstances. In particular, there can be significant tax savings in circumstances where it is possible to distribute net income of the trust to beneficiaries on a low marginal tax rate. These benefits can be further maximised through the trustee exercising their discretion to direct the greatest proportion of the trust net income from year to year to those beneficiaries on the lowest marginal tax rates. This is illustrated in example 12.15.

EXAMPLE 12.15

Using trusts for tax advantage

The trustee of a discretionary trust has $40 000 trust net income to distribute for the year ending 30 June 2022 and has a choice to exercise its discretion in favour of the following beneficiaries:
(a) Joseph, a 47-year-old resident individual whose other taxable income is likely to be $300 000+
(b) James, a 20-year-old university student resident individual with no other taxable income for the year
(c) Peter, a 25-year-old unemployed resident individual.

How should the trustee exercise its discretion to distribute the trust net income in the most tax efficient way?

It would not be tax efficient to distribute any of the trust net income to Joseph, as he has other taxable income and his marginal tax rate is 47 per cent (including the Medicare Levy). However, it would be tax efficient to distribute $20 000 each to James and Peter, who are both resident individuals with no other or very little other taxable income, as in so doing this may result in each having a $0 tax liability for the year, as together with the low-income rebate they are unlikely to pay any tax on a $20 000 taxable income.

In *FCT v Bamford* [2010] HCA 10, the High Court ruled that a trustee could treat capital amounts as income for the purposes of making distributions to beneficiaries under section 97 of the ITAA36 if the trust deed empowers the trustee to make such characterisations.[10] This stems from trust law concepts of capital and income which are not the same as tax concepts of income and capital.

These types of flexibilities, not available to other entities such as companies, attract controversy and lead trusts to be viewed by some as vehicles for secrecy, tax avoidance and evasion. For example, the Australian Council of Social Services proposed the following tax reforms to restrict the tax advantages of trusts:
- tax private trusts as companies
- attribute trust income back to the controller (who is generally also the source of the funds settled in the trust) so that it is taxed in their hands

---

10 For the ATO response to this decision, see its Decision Impact Statement at: www.ato.gov.au/law/view/document?docid=%22L IT/ICD/S310/2009/00001%22.

- raise tax rates on distributions from discretionary trusts to their beneficiaries
- improve transparency by requiring trustees to disclose the controller and ultimate beneficiaries of private trusts, and setting up a public register of trusts.[11]

Although none of these proposals have been adopted by the Government, there are provisions designed to minimise opportunities for trusts to be used to gain unfair tax advantages and to minimise opportunities for trusts to be used to avoid or evade tax. We have already discussed one such measure concerning limiting the tax benefits possible through distributing net trust income to beneficiaries who are minors. In addition, other tax avoidance rules such as limitations on diverting or splitting personal service income except in circumstances where a personal service income business is in operation also limit the opportunities for trusts to be used to gain unfair tax advantages. Others, specifically aimed at trusts, are discussed in the following section.

12.5.6.1 Anti-avoidance measures

There are a range of measures in place aimed at limiting the ability of trusts to be misused to obtain undesirable tax advantages. These include limitations on the transfer of trust losses, and certain distributions made for the purposes of avoiding tax.

12.5.6.1.1 Tax loss distribution limitations

As flagged, trustees cannot distribute income losses to beneficiaries. They are 'trapped' within the trust. However, they can be carried forward and used to reduce the net income of the trust in later income years provided there has been no majority change in ownership or control of the trust. The relevant tests for working out when income losses can be carried forward in situations where there has been a change in ownership or control of a trust are contained in Schedule 2F of the ITAA36.

These are the:
- 50 per cent stake test
- control test
- business continuity test
- pattern of distributions test.

The first three tests apply to fixed trusts and the fourth applies to discretionary trusts.

The reason for the limitations on the ability to carry forward trust losses and claim them as tax deductions in a future year is to discourage trading of trust losses by ensuring that, broadly speaking, tax benefits arising from income losses cannot be passed on to those who did not incur those losses.

12.5.6.1.2 Trust stripping

Rules exist to prevent complex 'reimbursement agreement' arrangements where, rather than paying trust income direct to an intended beneficiary, the income is distributed to another beneficiary who is a tax exempt entity or an entity with tax losses who then via a contractual arrangement such as a loan, effectively directs the income to the intended beneficiary in a tax free or reduced tax form. These rules are contained in section 100A of the ITAA36. Sections 100AA and 100AB deal specifically with situations involving distributions of trust income to tax-exempt beneficiaries.

12.5.6.1.3 Closely held trusts

There are rules preventing closely held trusts making distributions to trust beneficiaries in order to avoid paying tax. A closely held trust is either a:
- fixed trust in which fewer than 20 beneficiaries are entitled to at least 75 per cent of the trust income, or
- a discretionary trust.

In some circumstances, trustees of closely held trusts must include a 'trustee beneficiary statement' detailing the beneficiaries of the trust who are trustees of another trust. The ATO uses this information to check whether these trustee beneficiaries correctly declare their share of the trust net income or capital. If these rules are not complied with, the trustee must pay 'trustee beneficiary non-disclosure tax' on the distribution, which is equal to the top marginal tax rate.[12]

---

11 Australian Council of Social Services, 'Ending tax avoidance, evasion and money laundering through private trusts' (Web Page, November 2017) www.acoss.org.au/wp-content/uploads/2017/11/Tax-treatment-of-private-trusts_November-2017_final.pdf.

12 For more detail about the rules relating to closely held trusts, see Australian Taxation Office, 'Rules for closely held trusts' (Web Page, 20 November 2019) www.ato.gov.au/General/Trusts/In-detail/Closely-held-trusts/Rules-for-closely-held-trusts.

In addition to these measures, since 2014 there has also been an ongoing 'Tax Avoidance Taskforce' involving a number of agencies including the ATO and the Australian Federal Police aimed at identifying and taking action against taxpayers involved in tax avoidance or evasion using trusts.[13]

12.5.6.2 Loans to beneficiaries

In the previous chapter, it was discussed that when a shareholder of a company owes the company money the loan will be caught under the Division 7A rules. Subdivision EA is the provision that relates to trusts.

Usually what happens is that a discretionary trust will distribute to a corporate beneficiary for the tax effective rate of 30 per cent but will not actually pay the money across — it still sits within the trust's own bank account. The trust will pay the tax for the company but the balance of the beneficiary account will be withdrawn by the other family members who will also be shareholders of the company. Effectively, the withdrawals are loans to the shareholders of the corporate beneficiary and this is what triggers the Division 7A issue in the same manner we discussed in the previous chapter. Therefore, unless the shareholder enters into a commercial loan agreement with the company or repays the amount, it will be treated as a deemed dividend. It should be also noted that if the trust actually pays the corporate beneficiary its entitlement, then the provisions of Division 7A do not apply.

The loan will be taken to have been fully repaid at the end of a year of income if the loan has been fully repaid by the earlier of the due date for lodgement and the date of lodgement of the trust's tax return for the year in which the loan was made.

EXAMPLE 12.16

Division 7A — Trusts: Subdivision EA

Ellie is a shareholder of Moo Pty Ltd, a private company. On 29 July 2020, Ellie received a $10 000 loan from the C Trust. At the time of the loan, Moo Pty Ltd has an unpaid present entitlement to net income due from the C Trust of $60 000.

The loan received by Ellie is treated as an unfranked dividend of $10 000, subject to the distributable surplus of Moo Pty Ltd.

Any monies owing to a company but not paid across to the corporate beneficiary are known as unpaid present entitlements (UPE).

The amounts unpaid must be treated as a commercial loan with the benchmark interest rate being charged and a yearly repayment made against the loan. Other ways to ensure that the payment is not treated as a deemed dividend is to hold the monies on trust for the company (known as a 'sub-trust arrangement') but the income generated from the monies held on trust belong to the company. The money can either be invested in new assets held on trust for the company (see example 12.17) or be intermingled with the trusts other assets. If the funds are intermingled, then the trust must pay the company an agreed rate of return (benchmark interest rate) each year as well as return the capital within 7 years, the proportionate return method could also be used in this instance (see example 12.17).

EXAMPLE 12.17

Sub-trust

Investment in specific assets

Trust earns income of $100. Trustee confers entitlement to that on corporate beneficiary, but retains the funds on a sub-trust for the benefit of the corporate beneficiary.

The Trustee invests that $100 in a specific asset — for example, in an interest-bearing account or income-producing asset.

All income and capital gains from the investment must be paid to the corporate beneficiary each year. The $100 base UPE amount must ultimately be paid to the corporate beneficiary.

---

13 For further information about the Taskforce, see Australian Taxation Office, 'Tax Avoidance Taskforce' (Web Page, 23 February 2022) www.ato.gov.au/general/trusts/in-detail/compliance/tax-avoidance-taskforce---trusts.

Trust earns income of $100. Trustee confers entitlement to that $100 on corporate beneficiary, but retains the funds on a sub-trust for the benefit of the corporate beneficiary.

The $100 UPE is intermingled with the remainder of the main trust (e.g. used for working capital). Benchmark interest rate arrangements put in place.

Each year, the main trust pays the sub-trust that year's benchmark interest rate on $100. This amount must be paid to the corporate beneficiary.

After 7 years, the $100 must be paid to the sub-trust and to the corporate beneficiary.

ETHICS IN PRACTICE

Choice of business structures

When deciding what type of business entity is best suited for a taxpayer, there are a number of factors that must be considered, but the four most important are:
1. asset protection
2. income tax minimisation
3. capital gains tax minimisation
4. ease of administration and costs.

If a client's ultimate aim is just to pay the least amount of tax possible and wants you to set up an entity based on that criteria only, do you also owe them a duty of care to consider the other factors and would you be in breach of any of the Tax Practitioners Boards Code of Conduct?

Provide a detailed analysis of how the four factors work with the basic tax structures we have discussed in this chapter.

1. *Asset protection:* involves protecting the assets of both the owner and the assets used in the business. It can be achieved by using the correct entity and ensuring adequate insurance is in place.
2. *Income tax minimisation:* involves ensuring that the entity and any associated persons taxes are taxed at the lowest possible rate. For example, where a company is the chosen business entity for its tax rate of 25 per cent, it can pays the directors a salary that does not exceed the personal income tax rate of 32.5 per cent, thereby keeping the average rate of tax at approximately 30 per cent. When considering income minimisation, taxpayers need to be mindful of the ATO's view especially in relation to Personal Services Income and Part IVA.
3. *Capital gains tax minimisation:* if a future capital gain is going to be achieved by the entity, then consideration must be given to ensure that the capital gains is minimised to reduce the overall tax position. Concessions given for capital gains tax reductions include small business concessions and a 50 per cent general discount. The discount is not applicable to companies. Taxpayers will require the CGT on the ultimate sale of the business or rollovers to other entities to be minimal. Since the introduction of the small business concession, the choice of structure is important, as a capital gain can effectively be reduced to nil for certain taxpayers. When using trusts or companies it is of upmost importance to have a significant individual.
4. *Costs and ease of administration:* any of the five mentioned business entities will be subject to costs and these include: (a) the cost of purchasing an entity; (b) the cost of initial registrations; (c) the costs of ongoing renewals; (d) the cost of accounting and tax requirements. It is generally understood that the more complex a structure is, the harder it will be to administer, but then again a complex structure may be applicable for the taxpayer's individual needs. Therefore, before setting up a structure the taxpayer needs to weigh up the benefits achieved compared to the administration burden and costs.

12.6 Introduction to superannuation

LEARNING OBJECTIVE 12.6 Describe the basic principles of how superannuation funds operate and how they are taxed.

Superannuation funds are funds set up to aid in funding the retirement of individuals at the end of their working lives. The rules relating to superannuation funds are notoriously complex and this complexity is not helped by regular legislative changes. In the rest of this chapter, you will learn about the general operation of the tax regime governing superannuation funds and their members. Superannuation funds are types of trusts — hence, the terminology is similar with superannuation fund managers being 'trustees' and superannuation fund members being 'beneficiaries'.

The structure of the balance of this chapter will be to cover the basic types of superannuation funds and the basic tax framework. We will then examine in turn how superannuation is taxed at each of the three phases of the superannuation cycle: the contribution phase, the investment phase and the distribution phase.

12.6.1 Types of superannuation funds

There are a number of different types of superannuation funds. It is important to understand this from the outset because the taxation rules which apply can vary depending on the type of fund involved. There are three main ways superannuation funds can be classified and these are discussed in the following section.

12.6.1.1 Employer-sponsored or self-managed

Employer-sponsored funds are those into which regular contributions are made by employers on behalf of their employees. There are compulsory contribution rates that must be observed. Employees can also make personal contributions to these funds. Some of these funds are public funds — these invest in a range of investment asset classes. Some of these are specifically set up as 'industry superannuation funds' to benefit members of particular industries. There are presently 15 industry superannuation funds in Australia covering industries ranging from the health industry (HESTA), building and construction (CBUS) and even the legal sector (LegalSuper).[14]

A **self-managed superannuation fund (SMSF)**, as the name suggests, is managed by the employees themselves. Employers can contribute to these funds, but they do not manage them. These funds can be set up as single member funds and there are particular rules regulating these types of funds. Key rules include:

- they are limited to a maximum of six members
- each trustee of these funds must be a member or, if a company is the trustee, all of the directors of that company must be members of the fund
- payments to the trustees of the fund are prohibited.

Self-managed superannuation funds are regulated by the Australian Taxation Office.[15]

12.6.1.2 Defined benefit or accumulation

Most superannuation funds are **accumulation funds**. These funds invest contributions to the fund. The return ultimately payable to the beneficiaries depends on the accumulated returns on those investments. Hence, these returns are not guaranteed and can vary depending on investment performance over time.

In contrast, **defined benefit funds** effectively guarantee a particular return to their members. This is usually calculated as a particular multiple of the annual salary of the member. Defined benefit funds have historically been more common in public service settings than in private sector settings and are becoming less common.

12.6.1.3 Complying or non-complying

One of the most significant classifications for determining the correct tax treatment of a superannuation fund is determining whether the fund is a **non-complying fund** or **complying fund**. This is because there are certain significant tax concessions and different (lower) tax rates that apply to 'complying' funds and do not apply to non-complying funds. The taxable income of non-complying superannuation funds is taxed at 45 per cent. In contrast, the taxable income of complying superannuation funds is taxed at a rate of 15 per cent. Thus, the distinction is very important.

To qualify as a 'complying superannuation fund', a fund must meet the following criteria.

- Comply with regulatory provisions under the *Superannuation Industry Supervision Act 1993* (SISA)
- Be an Australian resident fund.
- Satisfy the 'sole purpose' test contained in section 62 of the SISA. The fund must be established and run for the 'core purpose' of providing superannuation benefits to its members for retirement or the members' dependants if a member dies before retiring. Limited 'ancillary purposes' are allowed, such as provision of benefits to members in the event of physical or mental ill-health, financial hardship or on compassionate grounds. To satisfy the test, the fund also must NOT provide any pre-retirement benefits to members (for example, allowing personal use of a fund asset).
- Not borrow or mortgage assets except in very limited circumstances. A complying fund can only borrow money:
  - provided the borrowing does not exceed 10 per cent of the value of the fund's total assets, and

---

14 See Industry Super Funds (Web Page) www.industrysuper.com.
15 See Australian Taxation Office, 'Self-managed super funds' (Web Page, 16 July 2021) www.ato.gov.au/Super/Self-managed-su per-funds.

- the borrowing is:
  - (i) for a maximum of 90 days to meet benefit payment obligations to members, or
  - (ii) to meet outstanding superannuation tax surcharge liabilities, or
  - (iii) for a maximum of 7 days to cover the settlement of security transactions if at the time the security transaction was entered into it was likely that the borrowing would not be needed.

In addition:

- Transactions of SMSFs involving related parties or relatives of members are generally prohibited. The underlying principle is that the fund must not provide personal benefits to members or relatives that are not retirement or death benefits.
- All transactions including investment decisions must be done on an arm's length commercial basis.
- SMSFs can carry on a business but that business must be operated solely for the purpose of providing retirement benefits for the members of the fund.

12.6.2 Preservation standards

Unlike other trusts, there are strict regulations restricting the ability of trustees to pay out benefits to members to ensure that members are 'preserved' to fund the retirement of members. These **preservation standards** include a restriction on benefits being paid out to members unless they have reached the 'preservation age' and have retired, have died or become personally incapacitated or are suffering severe financial hardship.[16]

A member's preservation age varies depending on when they were born. For any person born after June 1964, their preservation age is 60 years old. Table 12.5 sets out the current preservation ages.

TABLE 12.5 Preservation ages

For a person born	Preservation age
Before 1 July 1960	55
1.7.60–30.6.61	56
1.7.61–30.6.62	57
1.7.62–30.6.63	58
1.7.63–30.6.64	59
After 30 June 1964	60

12.6.3 Superannuation guarantee scheme

In 1992, the Commonwealth Government introduced the **superannuation guarantee scheme (SGS)**. This scheme effectively requires employers to contribute prescribed levels of superannuation support to benefit their employees. If they do not do so, the employer must pay a non-deductible charge. Over the years, the percentage of an employee's earnings that the employer must pay to their employees' superannuation fund has increased. For the 2019–20 and 2020–21 financial year, the rate is 9.5 per cent and this increased to 10 per cent from 1 July 2021. Table 12.6 shows the relevant historical rates and the rates going forward.

Example 12.18 demonstrates the application of the SGS.

EXAMPLE 12.18

The SGS

Suburban Motors Pty Ltd has two employees and for the quarter ending 31 March 2022, the company paid wages of $18 000 to each of them.

▶

---

16 The financial hardship rules for accessing superannuation were relaxed as part of the suite of measures introduced by the Commonwealth Government to address the COVID-19 pandemic. The relaxation allowed for those financially affected by COVID-19 to apply to access up to $10 000 from their superannuation funds in 2019–20 and up to a further $10 000 in 2020–21. See Australian Taxation Office, 'COVID-19 early release of super' (Web Page, 2019) www.ato.gov.au/Individuals/Super/In-det ail/Withdrawing-and-using-your-super/COVID-19-early-release-of-super.

What is the SGS contribution that Suburban Motors Pty Ltd must provide?

The company must pay an SGS rate of 10 per cent, which equates to a $1800 superannuation contribution per employee into the respective superannuation funds of each employee.

TABLE 12.6	Superannuation guarantee scheme contribution rates
Year	SGS contribution rate
1 July 2013–30 June 2014	9.25%
1 July 2014–30 June 2021	9.50%
1 July 2021–30 June 2022	10.00%
1 July 2022–30 June 2023	10.50%
1 July 2023–30 June 2024	11.00%
1 July 2024–30 June 2025	11.50%
1 July 2025–30 June 2026	12.00%

The aim of the SGS is to ensure, as much as possible that employees have adequate savings to fund their retirement and to ease the future burden on the pension and social welfare system. The scheme has added considerably to the national savings. According to the Australian Prudential Regulatory Authority (APRA), as at 31 December 2019, total superannuation assets in Australia were $2951 billion.[17] APRA is the independent statutory authority which oversees the regulation of superannuation funds other than self-managed superannuation funds. Self-managed superannuation funds are overseen by the Australian Taxation Office.

12.6.4 Phases in tax treatment of superannuation

There are three main taxing points or 'phases' involved in superannuation, represented in figure 12.10.

FIGURE 12.10	Phases in the lifecycle of a superannuation fund

Contributions phase → Investment phase → Distribution phase

The first point which raises tax consequences for contributors of funds is the 'contributions' phase. Contributors could mean the fund members themselves, their employers and other persons who make contributions.

Once funds are contributed to a superannuation fund, the trustee invests those contributions and the earnings from those contributions. This is the second point in which these 'investment phase' activities raise a further set of tax considerations for the trustee.

Eventually, members will receive their superannuation investment — when they become eligible through retirement or other circumstance in which the law permits distributions to members. These distributions then trigger the third point, raising tax consequences. However, the consequences will differ depending on the age of the member, the type of distribution (lump sum or income stream), the amount of the distribution and the event that triggered the payment (e.g. death, disablement or retirement).

17 APRA, 'APRA releases superannuation statistics for December 2019' (Web Page, 2019) www.apra.gov.au/news-and-publications/apra-releases-superannuation-statistics-for-december-2019.

12.7 The contributions phase — taxation of contributions

LEARNING OBJECTIVE 12.7 Explain the taxation treatment of superannuation contributions.

The tax paid on contributions to superannuation funds depends on three factors:
* whether the contribution was made from before or after-tax income
* whether the contribution exceeds the relevant 'superannuation contributions cap', and
* whether or not the taxpayer is a high-income earner.

12.7.1 Before-tax ('concessional') and after-tax ('non-concessional') contributions

Before-tax contributions are taxed at a concessional rate of 15 per cent. The typical example is the compulsory superannuation guarantee contributions made by an employer on behalf of an employee out of the gross (pre-tax) earnings of the employee. This is the main source of superannuation contributions for most people.

After-tax contributions are tax-free. The most common examples are personal contributions made by employees out of their post-tax income which they have NOT claimed as a tax deduction. If they are claimed as a tax deduction, they attract 15 per cent tax (in other words, they treated the same as before-tax contributions).

12.7.2 Superannuation contributions cap

There are caps on the maximum amounts that can be contributed to superannuation funds in a financial year. Amounts in excess of these caps are subject to additional tax.
* Before-tax (concessional) contributions cap: $27 500 for the 2021–22 income tax year. This reduces to nil if the taxpayer has a total superannuation balance of $1.7 million or more.
* After-tax (non-concessional) contributions cap: $110 000 per year for the 2021–22 income tax year. This reduces to nil if the taxpayer has a total superannuation balance of $1.7 million or more.

If the before-tax contributions cap is exceeded, the excess is taxed at the member's marginal tax rate plus an 'excess concessional contributions charge'. The formula for calculating this charge uses a base interest rate for the day plus an uplift factor of 3 per cent.[18]

If the after-tax contributions cap is exceeded, the excess is taxed at 47 per cent which represents the top marginal tax rate of 45 per cent plus the 2 per cent Medicare levy.

These caps and how they are calculated have changed many times over the years. The caps are indexed annually. The same cap applies irrespective of age (this was not the case prior to the 2017–18 financial year).

In addition, changes introduced from 1 July 2018 allow those with a total superannuation balance of under $500 000 to contribute more than the general concessional contributions caps in certain circumstances and to carry forward unused concessional cap amounts for a maximum of five years (after which the unused amounts expire).

The changes also allow for taxpayers who are under 65 years old and with a fund balance below $1.4 million to make up to $300 000 in non-concessional contributions in a particular year provided they do not exceed their aggregate non-concessional contributions cap over a three-year period.

12.7.3 High-income earners

For individuals whose annual income exceeds $250 000, the tax concession on superannuation contributions is reduced. These individuals are subject to an additional 15 per cent tax (Division 293 of the ITAA97). The amount of tax payable is calculated by adding the individual's income and superannuation contributions together. If these exceed $250 000, the 15 per cent tax is payable on the excess over $250 000 or on the superannuation contributions of the individual (whichever is the lesser amount). This is demonstrated in example 12.19.

---

18 The base interest rate is the monthly average yield of 90-day Bank Accepted Bills published by the Reserve Bank of Australia.

Effect of high income on contributions tax concessions

Matteo's taxable income for the year ended 30 June 2022 was $300 000 and for that year his employer contributed $28 500 into Matteo's superannuation fund.

How will the tax on the contribution be assessed?

As Matteo's annual income exceeds $250 000, then an additional tax of 15 per cent applies on these employer contributions (15% × $28 500 = $4275). This additional tax will be assessed to Matteo personally and be payable on issue of his 2022 Notice of Assessment.

12.7.4 Deductibility of superannuation contributions and superannuation contribution tax offsets

The deductibility of contributions to superannuation depends on a number of factors, including whether the contribution is made by the employer, or by the employee. Deductibility of employee contributions also depends on the amount of the contribution and whether the contribution falls within certain statutory 'contributions cap' limits.

There are also offsets available to low-income taxpayers and in some cases where contributions are made by taxpayers on behalf of their spouse.

12.7.4.1 Employer contributions

Employers can claim a deduction for contributions made on behalf of their employees to complying superannuation funds (Subdivision 290-B and section 290-60 of the ITAA97).

12.7.4.2 Employee contributions

Section 290-150 allows employees to claim a tax deduction for amounts they contribute to their own superannuation. The contributions caps apply — personal contributions may attract additional tax if they exceed the relevant cap.

Any contribution claimed as a tax deduction below the relevant contributions cap is treated as a 'concessional contribution' and taxed at 15 per cent (as noted in the previous section). So, if the marginal tax rate is above 15 per cent, tax savings are possible through making deductible personal superannuation contributions. This is demonstrated in example 12.20.

Employee contributions

Jasmina's taxable income for 2022 is expected to be $200 000 and her employer is expected to contribute $19 000 to her superannuation fund.

What contribution can Jasmina make?

Jasmina will be permitted to contribute a further $8500 (up to the $27 500 concessional contributions cap) and will be able to claim a tax deduction for this amount. If she does contribute this additional $8500 to her superannuation fund, then she will save $3995 in tax and Medicare levy (at the effective tax rate of 47 per cent); however, 15 per cent tax will be paid by the super fund on these additional contributions of $8500. Despite this, Jasmina would save a net amount of tax by making those deductible contributions of $2720.

Interest on borrowings to pay for personal superannuation contributions are not deductible (section 26-80 of the ITAA97).

12.7.4.3 Low-income employees

Low-income employees might also be entitled to government co-contributions. These government co-contributions (matching personal contributions of eligible low-income employees) are capped at $500 per financial year.[19]

In addition, low-income employees may be able to claim the 'low-income superannuation tax offset' equal to 15 per cent of concessional contributions they or their employers make to their superannuation fund to a maximum of $500. This offset is available to low-income employees earning less than $37 000 per annum.

12.7.4.4 Offset for spouse contribution

A tax offset may be available for contributions made by persons to their low-income earning spouse's superannuation fund. To be eligible, your spouse must have assessable income of under $40 000. The maximum amount of the offset is equal to 50 per cent of the after-tax contribution up to a maximum of $540. The offset phases out from $37 000 reducing to nil when the assessable income of the spouse is $40 000 or more (Subdivision 290-D and section 290-235 of the ITAA97). Example 12.21 illustrates how the offset is calculated.[20]

EXAMPLE 12.21

Offset for spouse contribution

Patrice and Suzel are spouses. Patrice earns $19 000 in 2021–22. Suzel contributes $3500 to Patrice's superannuation fund.

How does the offset for spouse contribution apply to these circumstances?

Patrice and Suzel meet the eligibility requirements, so Suzel can claim a tax offset in her 2021–22 tax return for the contributions she paid into Patrice's fund. The tax offset is calculated as 18 per cent of the lesser of:

- $3000 minus the amount over $37 000 that Patrice earned ($0)
- the value of the spouse contributions ($3500).

Suzel is thus entitled to a tax offset of $540, being 18 per cent of $3000.

Source: Based on Australian Taxation Office, 'Super-related tax offsets' (Web Page, 24 June 2021) https://www.ato.gov.au/Individuals/Income-and-deductions/Offsets-and-rebates/Super-related-tax-offsets.

12.8 The investment phase — taxation of superannuation funds

LEARNING OBJECTIVE 12.8 Explain the taxation treatment of superannuation funds during the investment phase.

This section will examine the tax treatment of the superannuation fund during the period in which contributions are invested. This includes considering what constitutes the assessable income of a superannuation fund and the tax deductions available to a superannuation fund.

Generally speaking, superannuation funds are taxed according to the usual principles that apply under the ITAA36 and the ITAA97. However, there are some modifications of the usual rules and special rules that also apply. These are set out in Division 295 of the ITAA97. There are also particular rules relating to capital gains which are touched on in the following section.

12.8.1 Assessable income

The assessable income of superannuation funds includes the following.

1. Taxable contributions from members — this includes employer contributions made on behalf of employees and contributions made by members for which the members have received a tax deduction (section 295-190).

---

19 For further information on the eligibility rules for the co-contribution see the information on the ATO website at: www.ato.gov.au/Individuals/Super/In-detail/Growing-your-super/Super-co-contribution.

20 This example and more information about the offset can be found at: www.ato.gov.au/Individuals/Income-and-deductions/Offsets-and-rebates/Super-related-tax-offsets.

---

2. Investment income — this includes interest, rent and dividends.
3. Capital gains on disposals of CGT assets (e.g. shares or property).

Non-assessable income of superannuation funds includes the following.

- Contributions made by members for which the member has not claimed a tax deduction (section 295-195).
- Government co-contribution payments or payments on behalf of persons under 18 by someone other than an employer (section 295-170).
- Contributions made on behalf of a spouse (section 295-175).
- Items listed in Subdivision 295-E.

Exempt income items are listed in Subdivision 295-F. They include an exemption for income from assets set aside to meet current pension liabilities (section 295-385).

12.8.2 Capital gains tax (CGT)

The CGT treatment of capital gains of a superannuation fund depends on how long the superannuation fund held the CGT asset which generated the gain.

If an asset has been held for more than 12 months, the superannuation fund is liable to pay tax on 2/3 of the gain at a rate of 15 per cent. Effectively, this gives a 1/3 discount. This gain is called a 'discount capital gain' (section 115-100).

If the capital gain relates to disposal of a CGT asset held for less than 12 months, the superannuation fund is taxable on the entire gain and the applicable tax rate is 15 per cent. This is called a 'non-discount capital gain'.

Other modifications to the CGT rules are contained in Subdivision 295-B.

Example 12.22 demonstrates the application of tax to the investment phase of a superannuation fund.

EXAMPLE 12.22

Tax and the investment phase

For the year ended 30 June 2022, the ZYW Self-Managed Superannuation Fund entered into the following transactions.
(a) $50 000 in deductible concessional contributions were received (for two eligible members).
(b) $9000 in interest income was earned on investments held by the Fund.
(c) Fully franked dividends of $14 000 were received.
(d) All 1000 shares in Brambles Ltd were sold for $10 a share. These shares had been purchased by the Fund in 2008 for $4 a share.
(e) One member contributed $80 000 in non-concessional contributions to the Fund.
(f) The Fund paid $2000 in accounting fees and $800 in auditing fees.

What will be the taxable income of this Fund for the year ended 30 June 2022 and what will the CGT treatment be?

The assessable income of the Fund will be made up of $50 000 in deductible concessional contributions plus $9000 in interest income plus $14 000 in fully franked dividends plus $6000 in imputation credits. This totals $79 000.

There will also be a capital gain of $6000 on the sale of the Brambles shares and this will be eligible for the CGT discount of 33.33 per cent. This means the net capital gain will be $4000. Therefore, the total assessable income of the Fund will be $83 000.

The allowable deductions of the Fund will be $2800. This means that the taxable income of the fund will be $80 200. The tax payable on $80 200 will be $12 030. The imputation tax credit of $6000 will be allowed a tax offset, resulting in a tax liability to the Fund of $6030.

12.8.3 Tax deductible expenses

Deductions available to superannuation funds are listed in Subdivision 295-G. Typical tax deductions available to superannuation funds include:

- actuarial costs
- accountancy fees and audit fees
- compliance costs
- life insurance policy investment costs (section 295-100)
- investment advice

- tax agent fees and legal costs
- death and disability premiums (section 295-460)
- amounts incurred in obtaining contributions (even if the contributions aren't assessable (section 295-95)).

12.9 The distribution phase — taxation of distributions

LEARNING OBJECTIVE 12.9 Calculate the tax liability of recipients of superannuation distributions.

Distributions from superannuation funds will often comprise a 'taxable component' and a 'non-taxable' component. The majority of the discussion in this final section is focused on the 'taxable component'. However, the relevance of a non-taxable component must be understood. Figure 12.11 visually represents the position.

| FIGURE 12.11 | Overview of tax on superannuation distributions |

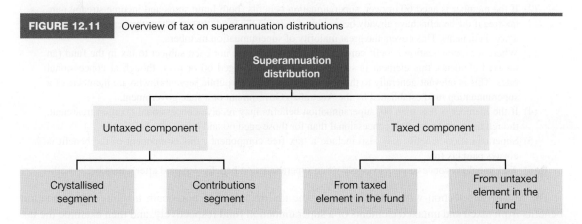

As figure 12.11 illustrates, the untaxed component of a superannuation distribution comprises a 'crystallised' segment and a 'contributions' segment (section 307-210 of the ITAA97).

The contributions segment comprises all contributions from 1 July 2007 that have not been included in the assessable income of the fund (section 307-220 of the ITAA97). In effect, this captures post-1 July 2007 after-tax (non-concessional) contributions to the fund. The logic is that these contributions have already been taxed and, therefore, should not be taxed again coming out of the fund.

The crystallised segment (defined in section 307-225 of the ITAA97) includes 5 different tax-free components relating to contributions made prior to 1 July 2007.

Before 1 July 2007, superannuation distributions consisted of up to 7 different components — each of which attracted a different tax treatment. From 1 July 2007, the system was simplified to effectively include only 2 components — tax-free or taxable. Hence, the 'crystallised component' is essentially a way of translating tax treatment under the pre-1 July 2007 system into today's simpler tax-free/taxable system.

So, to calculate the crystallised amount, the value of the superannuation interest as at 30 June 2007 is worked out and the value of each component (and the taxable status of each) is determined as if the distribution had occurred at that date.

For example, the crystallised segment includes all contributions to superannuation made prior to 1 July 1983 ('the pre-July 1983 component') as superannuation distributions only became taxable from this date. The ATO has an online calculator to assist in determining the crystallised amount.[21]

A 'proportioning rule' applies (section 307-125 of the ITAA97) to ensure that any lump sum withdrawals from superannuation funds comprise taxable and non-taxable components in the same proportions as the overall percentage of those components in the entire superannuation account of the recipient (i.e. if 80 per cent of the total superannuation balance of the recipient is taxable; 80 per cent of any withdrawal of a lump sum which is less than the entire balance will also be taxable).

Note that, as most superannuation distributions to individuals aged 60 or over are completely tax free, in these cases, working out the taxable and non-taxable component is a moot point. It is much more significant for those in other age groups, where working out both components is essential to working out the amount of tax that will ultimately be payable on their superannuation distribution.

---

21 The calculator can be found at: www.ato.gov.au/Calculators-and-tools/Superannuation-crystallisation-calculator.

In the case of the taxable component of superannuation benefits paid to members, the amount of tax payable will vary depending on 4 factors:

- the age of the member
- whether the payment is paid as a lump sum or as an income stream
- whether or not the payment is a 'death benefit' (i.e. a benefit paid because the member has died)
- whether the payment comes from a 'taxed element' or 'untaxed element' within the superannuation fund (i.e. whether contributions tax has already been paid on the amount in the fund).

Note that 'taxable' does not necessarily mean that the whole of the amount is taxed. In fact, as the following discussion shows, whether tax is ultimately payable (and how much is payable) depends on the relevant combination of the four factors listed.

Section 280-30 of the ITAA97 sets out some general principles of the taxation of benefits:

(1) The taxation of superannuation benefits depends primarily on the age of the member.

(2) If the member is aged 60 or over, superannuation benefits (both lump sums and income streams) are tax free if the benefits have already been subject to tax in the fund (that is, where the benefits comprise a taxed element). This covers the great majority of superannuation members.

(3) Where a superannuation benefit contains an amount that has not been subject to tax in the fund (an untaxed element), this element is subject to tax for those aged 60 or over, though at concessional rates. This is relevant generally to those people (for example, public servants), who are members of a superannuation fund established by the Australian Government or a state government.

(4) If the member is less than 60, superannuation benefits may receive concessional taxation treatment, though the treatment is less concessional than for those aged 60 and over.

(5) Superannuation benefits may also include a 'tax free component'; this component of the benefit is always paid tax free.

(6) Additional tax concessions may apply when superannuation benefits are paid after a member's death.

The rest of this section will address, in turn, the tax treatment of non-death taxable superannuation benefits from taxed and untaxed elements of a superannuation fund respectively, and then examine the tax treatment of death benefits.

12.9.1 Tax treatment of non-death benefits

12.9.1.1 Superannuation distributions from taxed elements in the fund

Taxable distributions from taxed elements in the fund (i.e. contributions which were taxed in the fund) are generally tax free for anybody 60 years or older. This is the case, irrespective of whether the distributions are made as an income stream (e.g. a pension or annuity) or as a lump sum.

Everybody else will pay some tax on their distributions from a taxed element in the fund. However, the amount of tax paid will vary depending on the age of the recipient and whether they have reached the preservation age and whether the payment is made as an income stream or as a lump sum.

In the case of a person who is 59 or under but who has reached their preservation age (see table 12.5), the tax treatment is different depending on whether they receive a lump sum or an income stream. In the case of a lump sum, they pay no tax on the first $225 000 (for the 2021–22 financial year). This is known as the 'low rate cap amount'. This amount is adjusted annually. The amount in excess of this 'low rate cap amount' attracts tax at 15 per cent plus the applicable Medicare levy. For the 2021–22 financial year, the low cap amount is $225 000. In the 2020–21 financial year, it was $215 000, and in the 2019–20 financial year, it was $215 000. Note that this is a lifetime cap — not $225 000 per year.

If the payment is made to a person who is 59 years old or younger but has reached the preservation age as an income stream, the whole amount attracts tax at the relevant marginal tax rate of the individual plus the applicable Medicare levy. However, the recipient can claim a tax offset of 15 per cent. Example 12.23 shows the tax treatment of a lump sum and income stream respectively.

EXAMPLE 12.23

Lump sum and income stream tax treatments from a taxed element

Boris is 58 and born in April 1963. He was paid a lump sum of $260 000 from his superannuation fund. What is the tax treatment of this lump sum?

If instead Boris chose to receive his superannuation benefits as an income stream payment of $40 000 a year instead of a lump sum payment, how would the tax treatment differ?

As Boris has reached his preservation age, but is under age 60, he is eligible for the low rate cap amount of $225 000. Therefore, there would be no tax payable on this $225 000. On the amount in excess of this low rate cap amount, the remaining $35 000, this would be taxed to Boris at the tax rate of 15 per cent plus the 2 per cent Medicare levy. This would result in a tax bill of $5950 on the $260 000 paid to him.

If Boris chose to receive his superannuation benefits as an income stream payment of $40 000 a year instead of a lump sum payment, then he would be subject to tax on the $40 000 benefit received at his marginal rate and the Medicare levy would also be payable. He would be eligible for a 15 per cent tax offset. Therefore, in this example, the tax payable on the $40 000 income stream payment would be $4142 (assuming a marginal tax rate of 19 per cent) less the 15 per cent tax offset of $6000, resulting in a net tax payable amount of $0 (the tax offset is not refundable).

For individuals who are 59 years old or younger and who have *not* reached the preservation age, any lump sum will attract tax of 20 per cent on the entire amount (plus the applicable Medicare levy). Income streams will attract tax at the recipient's applicable marginal tax rate. However, the recipient will usually not be able to claim any tax offset. An offset of 15 per cent is only available if the income stream is paid as a result of disability or death.

Table 12.7 summarises the tax treatment of non-death benefits from a taxed element in a fund.

TABLE 12.7   Tax treatment of non-death benefits from a tax element in a fund

Age of recipient	Income stream	Lump sum
60 or older	Nil — whole amount is non-assessable not exempt income	Nil — whole amount is non-assessable, non-exempt income
Under 60 but at or above preservation age	Taxed at marginal tax rates — tax offset of 15% is available	Nil up to low rate cap amount — 15% on amount above low rate cap amount
Under 60 and also under preservation age	Taxed at marginal tax rates, with no tax offset — tax offset of 15% is available if a disability super benefit	20% on whole amount

12.9.1.2 Superannuation distributions from untaxed elements in the fund

In the case of distributions to individuals from untaxed elements in a superannuation fund (i.e. contributions that were not taxed in the fund), similar distinctions on the tax treatment based on age apply as for distributions from taxed fund elements. However, the tax rates are slightly different.

In the case of individuals 60 years of age or older, the tax payable on a lump sum distribution will be 15 per cent on the first $1 615 000 (for the 2021–22 financial year). This is known as the 'untaxed plan cap amount' which limits the concessional tax treatment of benefits that have not been subject to contributions tax in a super fund. Amounts in excess of the untaxed plan cap amount are taxed at 45 per cent (plus the applicable Medicare levy). For the 2021–22 financial year, it is $1 615 000.

In the case of an income stream distribution, the whole amount is taxed at the recipient's applicable marginal tax rate. However, the recipient can claim a 10 per cent tax offset.

For individuals who are 59 years old or younger (irrespective of whether they have reached the preservation age), income stream distributions are taxed at their relevant marginal tax rate, but they are *not* entitled to any tax offset.

In the case of lump sum distributions, for individuals aged 59 years old or younger but who have reached their preservation age, tax is payable as follows (in addition to the applicable Medicare levy) for 2021–22:

- 15 per cent on the first $225 000 (the low rate cap amount)
- 30 per cent on the amount in excess of $225 000 up to $1 615 000 (the untaxed plan cap amount)
- 45 per cent on any amount in excess of $1 615 000.

In the case of lump sum distributions to individuals aged 59 years old or younger and who have NOT reached their preservation age, 30 per cent tax is payable on the first $1 615 000 (the untaxed plan cap amount) and any amount in excess attracts 45 per cent tax.

Example 12.24 shows the tax treatment of a lump sum and income stream from an untaxed element of a fund respectively.

Table 12.8 summarises the tax treatment of non-death benefits from an untaxed element in a fund.

TABLE 12.8   **Tax treatment of non-death benefits from an untaxed element in a fund**

Age of recipient	Income streams	Lump sums
60 or older	Taxed at marginal rates, with a 10% tax offset	15% up to the untaxed plan cap amount and 45% on amount above untaxed plan cap amount
Under 60 but at or above preservation age	Taxed at marginal rates, with no tax offset	15% up to the low rate cap amount and 30% on amount above the low rate cap amount and up to the untaxed plan cap amount — 45% above the untaxed plan cap amount
Under 60 and also under preservation age	Taxed at marginal rates, with no tax offset	30% up to untaxed plan cap amount and 45% on amount above cap amount

EXAMPLE 12.24

Lump sum and income stream tax treatments from an untaxed element

Assume Boris, from example 12.23, had received the same payments from an untaxed fund.

What would be the tax consequences?

On the $260 000 lump sum, the first $225 000 is now taxed at 15 per cent (resulting in $33 750 tax payable) and the remaining $35 000 is taxed at 30 per cent (resulting in $10 500 tax payable), with a total tax payable amount of $44 250.

On the $40 000 income stream payment, the full $40 000 is taxed at marginal rates with no 15 per cent tax offset. Assuming a 19 per cent marginal tax rate plus 2 per cent Medicare Levy, this would result in a tax bill of $8400.

12.9.2 Tax treatment of death benefits

The main issue determining the tax treatment of death benefits is the relationship of the recipients of the death benefits to the deceased. In particular, concessional tax treatment applies to distributions to 'dependants' of the deceased which does not apply to other recipients. So, the first issue to determine is whether or not the recipients are dependants of the deceased.

A dependant is anybody who falls into one or more of the following categories:
- the deceased's spouse, former spouse or de facto
- the deceased's child aged less than 18 years
- any other person with whom the deceased had an interdependency relationship with just prior to death
- any other person who was financially dependent on the deceased just prior to death.

12.9.2.1 Lump sums

Death benefit lump sums paid to dependants (irrespective of their age) are tax free. They are treated as non-assessable, non-exempt income.

Death benefit lump sums paid from a taxed element in a superannuation fund to anybody else attracts the lower of the recipient's applicable marginal tax rate or 15 per cent tax.

Death benefit lump sums to non-dependants from an untaxed element in a superannuation fund are taxable at the lower of the recipient's marginal tax rate or 30 per cent tax.

Table 12.9 summarises these rules and example 12.25 applies these rules.

TABLE 12.9   Tax treatment of lump sum death benefits

Benefit recipients	Age of recipient	Tax payable
Death benefit lump sum benefit paid to non-dependants	Any age	15% on whole taxable amount unless from untaxed element in the fund in which case the rate is 30%
Death benefit lump sum benefit paid to dependants of deceased or to terminally ill member	Any age	Nil — no tax payable

EXAMPLE 12.25

Lump sum death benefits

If a $500 000 death benefit lump sum is paid from a taxed element in a superannuation fund to Dana, who is not a financial dependant, what tax is payable?

What if the benefit is paid from an untaxed element in a superannuation fund?

What if the amount was paid to a financial dependant?

On the death benefit lump sum, the rate payable would be 15 per cent, resulting in $75 000 tax payable.

If the same amount is paid from an untaxed element in a superannuation fund, then the tax rate payable would be 30 per cent, resulting in $150 000 tax payable.

If this same amount is paid from either a taxed or untaxed element in a fund to a financial dependant, then no tax is payable.

12.9.2.2 Income streams

Death benefit income streams are slightly more complicated. In part, this is due to legal limitations on who can receive a superannuation death benefit as an income stream. First, non-dependants cannot be paid a death benefit as an income stream. In addition, adult children can only receive an income stream if they are under 25 years old and financially dependent on the deceased or have a permanent disability. Once the recipient turns 25 (unless they have a permanent disability), the income stream must be converted to a lump sum.

The tax treatment of superannuation income stream payments depends on the age of the recipient AND the deceased. Generally speaking:

- a super income stream to a dependent is non-assessable, non-exempt income if deceased and recipient are both over 60 years old
- if both the recipient and the deceased are under 60, only the tax-free component of the income stream is non-assessable, non-exempt income. The taxable component is assessable at the marginal rates of the recipient, but a 15 per cent tax offset can be claimed by the recipient if the payment is from a taxed element in the fund.[22]

---

22 Different rules apply if the deceased is over 60, but the recipient is under 60 or if the deceased is under 60 but the recipient is over 60, respectively. For further information explaining the applicable rules in these situations see the ATO website: www.ato.gov.au/Individuals/Super/In-detail/Withdrawing-and-using-your-super/Withdrawing-your-super-and-paying-tax/?page=6#Ifyouareadependantofthedeceased.

Superannuation and crypto-remuneration

As table 12.6 indicates, the SGS contribution rate has been slowly increasing to 12 per cent. This rate is applied to the employee's ordinary time earnings (OTE), which includes salary or wages. A recent article by Craig Cameron explored how the SGS may apply where cryptoassets are provided as part of the employee's remuneration package.[23]

In short, reflecting on the ATO's guidance that crypto-remuneration can be salary or wages for PAYG withholding purposes, Cameron concluded that cryptoassets can form part of the employee's OTE and, as such, result in superannuation being payable.[24] Note, however, this would not be the case if the cryptoassets provided to the employee fell within the FBT regime:

> It appears that if cryptocurrency is not a fringe benefit, but is salary or wages for which PAYG tax must be withheld, then as a matter of interpretation, cryptocurrency may also be considered salary or wages under the SGAA [*Superannuation Guarantee Assessment (Administration) Act 1992* (Cth)]. Consequently, superannuation is payable on crypto-remuneration that forms part of the employee's OTE.[25]

As such, this characterisation will impact salary package structuring negotiations, due to the additional super annuation liability created when cryptoassets are salary and wages.[26] With this in mind, Cameron outlined the need for legislative change and clarification in the characterisation of cryptoassets as salary and wages, due to the legal uncertainty and inconsistency currently present:

> The ATO's present position, which is published online as general information only and not legally binding, is that crypto-remuneration, other than as part of a salary sacrifice arrangement, is the equivalent of salary or wages and subject to personal income tax. This position appears to be inconsistent with labour regulation of crypto-remuneration, which is unlikely to treat any part of crypto-remuneration as a salary or wage, as well as ATO Taxation Determination 2014/28 which provides that the provision of all Bitcoin by an employer is a fringe benefit and subject to FBT.[27]

Moreover, Cameron highlighted the issues that cryptoasset volatility can create.[28] In particular, both employer and employee risks were noted:

- the time that lapses between the employer acquiring cryptoassets, providing these to the employee and calculating/paying obligations such as PAYG and superannuation (employer risk), as well as,
- the time that lapses between the employee receiving the cryptoassets, when the employee uses these for goods and services and calculating/paying obligations such as income tax and CGT (employee risk).[29]

What about the superannuation funds themselves? Cryptoasset investments have generally been seen as too risky for the superannuation industry; however, in 2021, Rest Super announced it was making cryptoassets part of their diversified portfolio.[30] This has been reported to be the first in Australia to do so.[31]

REFLECTION

What issues may arise if an employee requests that their employer pay their wages in cryptoassets instead of Australian dollars?

---

23 Craig Cameron, 'The Regulation of Cryptocurrency to Remunerate Employees in Australia' (2020) 33 *Australian Journal of Labour Law* 157 ('Cameron').

24 Cameron, 176. See also Australian Taxation Office, 'Cryptocurrency used in business' (Web Page, 30 March 2020) https://www.ato.gov.au/general/gen/tax-treatment-of-crypto-currencies-in-australia—specifically-bitcoin/?page=3#Cryptocurrency_used_in_business.

25 Ibid. Recall the discussion in an earlier chapter on crypto-remuneration.

26 Ibid.

27 Ibid, 178. See also can earlier chapter on crypto-remuneration.

28 Cameron, 179.

29 Ibid, 179–180.

30 See, eg, Brian Quarmby, 'Australia's Rest Super retirement fund to invest in crypto for its 1.8M members' *Cointelegraph* (Web Page, 24 November 2021) https://cointelegraph.com/news/australia-s-rest-super-retirement-fund-to-invest-in-crypto-for-its-1-8m-members.

31 Ibid.

SUMMARY

12.1 Explain the taxation of partnership income.

A partnership is regarded as a taxpayer for the purposes of the ITAA36 and must lodge an annual income tax return. However, as a partnership is not a separate legal entity, it cannot have a taxable income. Instead, the difference between the assessable income and allowable deductions is called the 'net income of the partnership'. The net income of the partnership is distributed to the partners, who include this distribution as assessable income in their own tax returns and pay tax at their marginal tax rate. Partnership losses are also able to be distributed to partners who can offset this loss against their assessable income to reduce their overall taxable income.

12.2 Describe the tax consequences of various transactions between the partnership and the partners.

Salary paid by a partnership to a partner is considered a distribution of profit (not an expense) for tax purposes and thus is not deductible. Interest paid by a partnership on a partner's capital contribution is, similarly, considered a distribution of profit for tax purposes and is not deductible.

When a partner lends money to a partnership it is in the capacity of a lender, not as a partner. Thus, interest is assessable income to the partner and a deductible expense to the partnership.

Partners' drawings are considered a reduction in equity and thus are not assessable to the individual partners and are not deductible by the partnership.

12.3 Describe the taxation consequences of a joint venture.

A joint venture is an arrangement between two or more parties, characterised by the following features:
- a contractual agreement between the participants
- sharing of product or output, rather than sale proceeds or profits
- joint control
- a specific economic project
- cost sharing.

Unlike a partnership, a joint venture does not lodge a tax return. Instead, each venturer lodges their own tax return and includes the sale of the respective product or output (not profit) as assessable income and claims deductions in their own names.

12.4 Describe the basic principles of how trusts operate and how they are taxed.

In a trust arrangement, a trustee is the legal owner of the trust property, but the beneficiaries are entitled to all benefits flowing from the trust property (including income and the value of the property itself). Trusts provide asset protection and tax planning benefits. In terms of tax planning, trusts enable income to be distributed to beneficiaries according to their various tax positions from year to year.

12.5 Calculate the tax liability of various types of beneficiaries and the trustee of a trust.

Trust net income is the total assessable income of the trust estate calculated as if the trustee was a resident taxpayer less allowable deductions. Losses can be carried forward in the trust, but not distributed to beneficiaries.

A beneficiary pays tax on their share of the trust income where they are 'presently entitled' to that income. The trustee is liable to pay tax on the amount of trust income for which no beneficiary is presently entitled, a legally disabled beneficiary is entitled or a non-resident beneficiary is presently entitled.

A range of anti-avoidance measures are in place to limit the use of trusts for the purposes of gaining undesirable tax advantages.

12.6 Describe the basic principles of how superannuation funds operate and how they are taxed.

Superannuation funds are funds set up to aid in funding the retirement of individuals at the end of their working lives and are subject to restrictions on the distribution of benefits until members reach preservation age. They are a type of trust. Superannuation funds may be employer-sponsored or self-managed; defined benefit of accumulation; and complying or non-complying. Complying funds have significant tax advantages over non-complying funds.

The superannuation guarantee scheme obliges employers to contribute to their employees' superannuation funds.

12.7 Explain the taxation treatment of superannuation contributions.

Contributions made from before-tax income are taxed at a concessional rate of 15 per cent. Contributions made from after-tax income are tax-free (unless a deduction is claimed, in which case 15 per cent tax applies). Contributions are subject to caps. Where contributions exceed these caps in a financial year, additional tax is applied. Taxpayers with annual income in excess of $250 000 are subject to an additional 15 per cent tax on superannuation contributions.

Employers can claim a tax deduction for contributions made on behalf of employees to complying superannuation funds. Employees can claim a tax deduction for contributions they make up to a cap. Low-income employees who contribute to their superannuation may be eligible for a matching contribution from the government and may also be able to claim an offset. An offset is also available for contributions to a low-income spouse's superannuation fund.

12.8 Explain the taxation treatment of superannuation funds during the investment phase.

The assessable income of superannuation funds includes taxable contributions from members, investment income and capital gains on disposals of CGT assets. Typical tax deductions available to superannuation funds include actuarial costs, accountancy and audit fees, compliance costs, life insurance policy investment costs, investment advice, tax agent fees and legal costs, death and disability premiums and amounts incurred in obtaining contributions.

12.9 Calculate the tax liability of recipients of superannuation distributions.

Distributions from superannuation funds will often comprise a 'taxable component' and a 'non-taxable' component.

Taxable distributions from contributions which were taxed in the fund are generally tax free for anybody 60 years or older. Everybody else will pay some tax on their distributions from a taxed element in the fund, depending on age and whether an income stream or lump sum is taken.

Similarly, distributions to individuals from untaxed elements in a superannuation fund are taxed differently based on age.

The tax treatment of death benefits depends mainly on the relationship of the recipients of the death benefits to the deceased. Concessional tax treatment applies to distributions to 'dependants' of the deceased.

KEY TERMS

accumulation funds Superannuation funds in which the return is ultimately payable to the beneficiaries depends on the investments contributed to the fund and the returns on those investments.

beneficiaries In the case of a trust, the parties in a trust relationship that are entitled to benefits, including income, arising from trust property.

complying fund A superannuation fund that complies with regulatory. provisions, is an Australian resident, satisfies the sole purpose test, and does not borrow or mortgage assets except in limited circumstances.

defined benefit funds Superannuation funds that guarantee a particular return to their members, usually calculated as a particular multiple of the annual salary of the member.

discretionary trust A trust in which the beneficiaries have a 'mere expectancy' in the trust — their entitlement to share in the income of the trust is subject to the exercise of discretion of the trustee which can vary from year to year.

employer-sponsored funds Superannuation funds into which regular contributions are made by employers on behalf of their employees.

fixed trust A trust in which the beneficiaries have a defined entitlement to income and capital under the trust.

joint venture An arrangement between venturers for a specific project in which the participants usually receive a share of the final product (or output), rather than profit. A joint venture is not a separate legal entity. In contrast with a partnership, the arrangement is for the sharing of products or outputs, not the sharing of profits.

net income of the partnership The difference between the partnership's assessable income and its allowable deductions.

non-complying fund A superannuation fund that is not a complying fund.

partnership An association of persons (other than a company or a limited partnership) carrying on business as partners or in receipt of ordinary income or statutory income jointly; or a limited partnership.

partnership income tax return A tax return lodged by a partnership, showing its assessable income and deducts its allowable deductions on the basis that it is a resident taxpayer. A partnership tax return includes both Australian and foreign-sourced income and deductions. The partnership does not pay income tax.

present entitlement In relation to a share of trust income, a right to income 'presently' existing (i.e. a right of such a kind that a beneficiary may demand payment from the trustee).

preservation standards Regulations restricting the ability of superannuation fund trustees to pay out benefits to members to ensure that members are 'preserved' to fund the retirement of members.

self-managed superannuation fund (SMSF) A superannuation fund managed by the employee themselves.

superannuation funds Funds (in the form of a trust) set up to aid in funding the retirement of individuals at the end of their working lives.

superannuation guarantee scheme A government-imposed requirement that employers contribute prescribed levels of superannuation support to benefit their employees.

trust An obligation imposed on a person or other entity to hold property for the benefit of beneficiaries. A trust is a relationship rather than a legal entity, but trusts are treated as entities for tax purposes.

trustee The party in a trust relationship that holds the trust property for the benefit of the beneficiaries.

trust net income The total assessable income of the trust estate calculated as if the trustee was a resident taxpayer less allowable deductions.

trust property Assets held in trust.

QUESTIONS

12.1 How is a partnership taxed?

12.2 What are the tax consequences if:
  (a) a partnership derives a tax loss?
  (b) a trust derives a tax loss?

12.3 What are the taxation implications of partners' salaries and partners' drawings both to the partnership itself and to the individual partners?

12.4 How is a joint venture taxed?

12.5 What are some uses of trusts in Australia? What particular benefits are likely to arise from the use of a trust to run a business?

12.6 How does a trust calculate its 'net income'?

12.7 In what circumstances will tax be payable by a trustee of a trust?

12.8 Explain the concept of how Division 7A works in relation to a trust.

12.9 How does CGT event E4 work?

12.10 What are the requirements for a fund to be a complying superannuation fund? What tax rate applies to income of a complying superannuation fund?

12.11 (a) What rate of tax would apply to benefits withdrawn from a self-managed superannuation fund if the fund was a taxed fund and the taxpayer is aged 62?
  (b) What amount of tax would apply if the same facts as in (a) apply except that the taxpayer is aged 56 but has nevertheless reached the required preservation age in the fund?

12.12 Who is a 'dependant' for the purposes of the payment of death benefits out of a superannuation fund?

PROBLEMS

12.13 Damien and Linda are residents of Australia for tax purposes. They carry on business as a partnership together in Sydney. According to the partnership agreement, Damien and Linda share profits and losses on the basis of:
  • Damien: 60 per cent
  • Linda: 40 per cent.

During the year ended 30 June 2022, their trial balance showed the following.

	$	$
Gross sales		978 000
Interest income		140
Purchase of trading stock	414 200	
Wages to employees (other than Damien and Linda)	116 000	
Salary paid to Damien	32 000	
Drawings by Damien	14 000	
Drawings by Linda		
Other tax-deductible expenses	284 500	

Stock on hand at 1 July 2021 was $68 000. Stock on hand at 30 June 2022 was $97 000.

For the year ended 30 June 2021, the partnership made a tax loss of $26 000.

Required

(a) Calculate the net income of the partnership for the year ended 30 June 2022.

(b) Calculate the amount to be included in the assessable income of each partner's personal income tax return for the year ended 30 June 2022.

12.14 The Zimmer Unit Trust is a fixed trust which has a residential rental property as its major type of trust property and during the year ended 30 June 2022 the trust entered into the following transactions.

- The trust received fully franked cash dividends of $2100 from ABC Bank.
- The trust received gross rental income of $26 000.
- The trust paid $2000 in council rates on the rental property.
- The trust paid $1800 in insurance on the rental property.
- The trust paid $14 000 in bank interest.
- Depreciation as per taxation rules of $4300.
- The trust paid $2400 in management fees to a real estate firm.

Calculate the trust net income of the Zimmer Unit Trust for the year ended 30 June 2022.

12.15 Holly and Jack (both 44 years old) are two of the beneficiaries in their family trust which operates a business selling shoes. They have two children, Brett and Fiona, both 16 years old. The following data reflects the income and expenses of the family trust during the current financial year.

Income	$
Sale of shoes	380 000
Dividends — with attached credits of $2143	5 000
Capital gain on sale of goodwill of former champagne business	
The capital proceeds on the sale of the business was $100 000, and they paid $30 000 to buy the business —both the general and active discounts apply	17 500
Sale of shares — after general discount applied	45 000

Expenses	$
Purchase of shoes	125 000
Motor vehicle expenses for Jack — 80% work-related	15 000
Salaries — staff (this includes $10 000 to their nephew, Oscar who works part-time and is actually paid $3000 more than a non-family member who works the same hours)	40 000
Salary — Holly	65 000

Salary — Jack	30 000
Superannuation for both Jack and Holly, paid equally	50 000
Telephone expenses for salesman — 85% work-related, 15% private	2 800

The trust made a loss of $20 000 in the previous year. It was not to be met from corpus.

Notes:

- Holly: in addition to her salary, she was made specifically entitled to the net capital gain of the trust. She had a capital loss from the sale of assets last year of $95 000.
- Jack: in addition to his salary, he was made specifically entitled to the dividends from the trust.
- Fiona received $10 000 from the trust. She also worked full-time and had a salary of $15 000.
- Brett has some shares. The shares had been left to him in the estate of his late grandfather and have been transferred into Brett's name. This financial year, Brett received a dividend of $10 000 with franking credits of $2400 attached for these shares.
- Any remaining income was to be accumulated for Brett until he turned 21 years of age. If he were to die before turning 21, then his accumulated funds would be given to Fiona. The trustee could, however, pay for specified expenses, and in the current year bought Brett a new car for $11 000.

Required

Calculate the net income of the trust and the taxable income and net tax payable including Medicare levy by the beneficiaries and/or the trustee assuming the trust is an SBE taxpayer.

12.16 The Ball Family Trust was set up in 2014 as a discretionary family trust.

Roger Ball is the head of the Ball family and arranged for a Trust Deed setting up the Ball Family Trust appointing him as sole trustee of this Trust. The beneficiaries of the Ball Family Trust are Roger and Dina Ball and their children, grandchildren and other descendants.

For the 2022 year, the Ball Family Trust had a net income of $100 000. Roger produced written Trustee Minutes in which he, as trustee, exercised his discretion to distribute $20 000 of that net income to himself; $20 000 to Dina (his wife); $20 000 to Nick (his adult resident son, aged 23 who was recently declared bankrupt); $20 000 to James (his adult non-resident son, who now lives in Singapore) and $10 000 to AXZ Pty Ltd (a private company that has only two shareholders, Roger and Dina Ball). Roger miscalculated and forgot to distribute the remaining $10 000 to anyone.

Please advise Roger Ball as to the tax consequences of these intended distributions, indicating which party has the responsibility to pay the relevant tax and which tax rates would apply to each distribution.

12.17 Paula, aged 34, is a self-employed plumber. During the 2022 year (before 30 June 2022) she deposited $60 000 into her complying superannuation fund. Paula wishes to meet her tax obligations and not claim anything more than she is entitled. Explain to Paula how much of the contribution of $60 000 she is able to claim as a tax deduction for the year ended 30 June 2022 under income tax law. If Paula only claims up to the limit of what she is entitled to, how will any excess contributions be taxed?

12.18 Bob is 43 years old and a self-employed builder and 2022 was a good year for his business. He tells you he has $300 000 in excess funds which he decides to put into his self-managed super fund (SMSF) before 30 June 2022. Bob also tells you that he has not contributed anything to this SMSF in the previous three years.

He had been told by a friend that you could claim $100 000 in a tax deduction (without any further taxes) for superannuation contributions and he wants to do this in his 2022 tax return.

Bob's taxable income for 2022 (before this superannuation contribution) was $180 000.

Advise Bob what the tax consequences are of his putting $300 000 into his SMSF for the year ended 30 June 2022.

ACKNOWLEDGEMENTS

Figure 12.2: © Australian Taxation Office
Table 12.4: © Australian Taxation Office
Example 12.21: © Australian Taxation Office
Extracts: © Federal Register of Legislation. Licensed under CC BY 4.0.
Extract: © Australian Taxation Office
Extracts: © High Court of Australia
Extract: © Cameron (2020)

CHAPTER 13

Goods and services tax

LEARNING OBJECTIVES

After studying this chapter, you should be able to:

13.1 explain how the GST works

13.2 explain the concept of taxable supplies

13.3 explain the concept of taxable importations

13.4 explain the concept of GST-free supplies

13.5 explain the concept of input-taxed supplies

13.6 explain the concept of out-of-scope supplies

13.7 explain the concept of creditable acquisitions

13.8 explain the concept of creditable importations

13.9 describe administrative issues associated with the GST

13.10 describe a range of special GST rules

13.11 describe the GST general anti-avoidance rule and relevant ethical issues.

Overview

This chapter provides an overview of Australia's goods and services tax (GST), which commenced on 1 July 2000. The GST is a flat 10 per cent broad-based indirect tax on the private consumption of most goods and services provided in Australia as well as imports.

The chapter provides an overview of the concept of a taxable supply, including the six components that are necessary before GST can be charged to the consumer. GST is also payable on taxable importations.

GST is not payable on non-taxable supplies, which consist of GST-free supplies, input-taxed supplies and out-of-scope supplies. A GST-registered entity can still claim back input tax credits on the inputs used to produce a GST-free supply. This effectively results in no GST being collected on the supply of GST-free goods and services. If a supply is input-taxed, the registered entity (i.e. the supplier) is not required to charge the 10 per cent GST to the consumer, but is also not able to claim an input tax credit on the inputs used to produce the input-taxed supply.

Entities that are registered for GST can claim back the GST they have paid on 'creditable acquisitions'. This credit is known as an 'input tax credit'. A creditable acquisition is essentially the purchase or acquisition of something that is used in carrying on a business or enterprise.

The chapter concludes with an overview of a range of administrative matters, the general anti-avoidance rules, as well as a discussion of a range of special GST rules.

13.1 Basic operation of GST

LEARNING OBJECTIVE 13.1 Explain how the GST works.

The **goods and services tax (GST)** commenced in Australia on 1 July 2000. The principle Act governing the operation of the GST is the *A New Tax System (Goods and Services Tax) Act 1999* (Cth) as amended (the GST Act). The GST replaced several indirect taxes, including wholesale sales tax and a wide range of indirect state taxes.

In addition to the Act, the Commissioner has issued a number of GST Rulings and GST Determinations outlining the Australian Taxation Office's (ATO) interpretation of the legislation.

According to the most recently published ATO annual report, in 2020–21, the GST raised $73.1 billion for the Commonwealth Government (representing 16.20 per cent of total net tax collections of $451.4 billion).[1] The GST is collected by the Commonwealth Government but is distributed to the States and Territories.

The main GST collections come from the wholesale sector and the property, personal and other services sector.

The major features of the GST are that the:

- GST is a flat 10 per cent broad-based indirect tax on the private consumption of most goods and services in Australia and importations into Australia
- price of all goods and services are required to be shown inclusive of GST — in order to calculate the amount of GST included in the price of goods or services, simply divide by 11
- tax is charged and collected by registered entities at each stage in the production chain
- at the same time, the supplier of the goods or services is entitled to claim a credit for any GST paid — this credit is known as an 'input tax credit'
- 'net amount' of GST (i.e. GST collected minus GST paid) is remitted by the registered entity to the ATO each month or quarterly or annually on a form called the **business activity statement (BAS)**
- tax is ultimately borne by the end consumer, not by producers or suppliers
- entities need to be registered for GST to be able to charge GST and claim back input tax credits
- accounting basis for GST is either cash or accruals
- GST has a number of exemptions including transactions that fall outside its scope
- GST has a number of special GST rules that apply to a wide variety of items.

Figure 13.1 illustrates taxable supplies where each registered business in the chain charges and collects GST, the ultimate GST liability is borne (and paid for) by the consumer. This is why the GST is also referred to as a 'consumption tax'. It is also referred to as a 'value added tax' (or VAT) in some overseas jurisdictions.

---

1 Australian Taxation Office, *Annual Report 2020–21* https://www.transparency.gov.au/annual-reports/australian-taxation-office/reporting-year/2020-21-68.

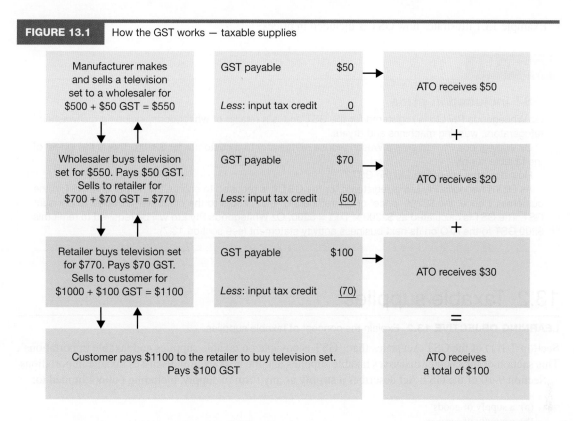

FIGURE 13.1 How the GST works — taxable supplies

Figure 13.2 outlines the different GST treatment of various types of supplies. GST is only payable on taxable supplies and taxable importations. Non-taxable supplies are excluded from the definition of 'taxable supply'. Non-taxable supplies include GST-free supplies, input-taxed supplies and out-of-scope supplies.

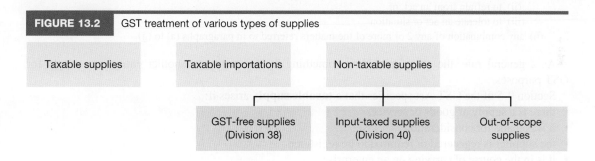

FIGURE 13.2 GST treatment of various types of supplies

13.1.1 Rate of GST in Australia

The rate of GST in Australia is 10 per cent. In Australia, according to the *Competition and Consumer Act 2010* (Cth), all prices of goods and services are required to be shown inclusive of all taxes and charges. Hence, the price of the goods or services must include the 10 per cent GST.

According to section 9-70 of the GST Act, the amount of GST on a taxable supply is 10 per cent of the **value** of the taxable supply. Value is defined in section 9-75 to be 10/11 of the **price**. Hence, if the price of goods or services is $110, the value is calculated at $100 (i.e. $110 × 10/11). Put simply:

$$\text{Price} = (\text{Value} + 10\%\,\text{GST})$$

In order to calculate the amount of GST that has been included in the price, simply divide by 11. The GST is therefore $10 (being 1/11 of the GST-inclusive price).

Example 13.1 illustrates how GST is included in prices.

EXAMPLE 13.1

GST included in price

Oz Whitegoods Pty Ltd is registered for the GST and is a retailer of whitegoods, including dishwashers, refrigerators, washing machines and dryers.

Oz Whitegoods Pty Ltd sells a Westinghouse refrigerator to a customer for $2200. This is the 'price' of the taxable supply.

How does the price relate to the GST?

As Oz Whitegoods Pty Ltd is registered for the GST, it is required to charge the 10 per cent GST to the customer. Hence, the $2200 'price' of the refrigerator that is sold to the customer includes 10 per cent GST. The GST is calculated as $2200 \times 1/11 = $200. Oz Whitegoods Pty Ltd will be required to remit this $200 GST to the ATO on its next business activity statement (see section 13.7).

13.2 Taxable supplies

LEARNING OBJECTIVE 13.2 Explain the concept of taxable supplies.

Section 7-1(1) of the GST Act states that: 'GST is payable on taxable supplies and taxable importations'. This section of the chapter discusses taxable supplies and the next section discusses taxable importations.

Section 9-10 of the GST Act describes a **supply** as any form of supply, including but not limited to:

(a) a supply of goods
(b) a supply of services
(c) a provision of advice or information
(d) a grant, assignment or surrender of real property
(e) a creation, grant, transfer, assignment or surrender of any right
(f) a financial supply
(g) an entry into, or release from, an obligation:
    (i) to do anything, or
    (ii) to refrain from an act, or
    (iii) to tolerate an act or situation
(h) any combination of any 2 or more of the matters referred to in paragraphs (a) to (g).

As a general rule, the act of providing something by one entity to another entity is a supply for GST purposes.

Section 9-5 of the GST Act specifies that a **taxable supply** arises if:

- there is a supply of goods or services
- it was made for consideration
- the supplier is registered or required to be registered
- it is in the course of carrying on an enterprise
- it is connected with an indirect tax zone (i.e. Australia)
- it is not GST-free, input-taxed or out of scope.

All six of these components of a taxable supply must be present before a liability for GST arises. In other words, if all six components are not satisfied, the supply is *not* a taxable supply, and then no GST arises. The very wide interpretation of a taxable supply was illustrated in *FCT v Qantas Airways Limited* [2012] HCA 41.

Facts: The taxpayer had regularly offered extremely low airfares for flights within Australia, which must be paid for in full at the time of booking. However, as the prices were so low the company found that customers regularly cancelled the bookings and never appeared for the flights. Under no circumstances were customers entitled to a refund. The issue was whether Qantas had made a taxable supply on the non-refundable bookings.

Held: The High Court found that Qantas was liable for the GST on the flight cancellations and 'no shows'. The High Court indicated that it was necessary to identify the supply for which the consideration is paid and determine whether that supply was provided. It indicated that it is also not necessary to extract from the transaction the essence and sole purpose of the transaction for there to be a GST liability. The airline's contractual conditions did not mean that it had made an unconditional promise to carry the passenger and baggage on a particular flight. In fact, the taxpayer supplied something less: merely the promise to carry the passenger and baggage, having regard to the circumstances and business operations of the airline. This was clearly a taxable supply where the fare was the consideration received.

Comment: Consequently, the making of a supply does not always involve the taking of some action on the part of the supplier. As long as a commitment or obligation is present that will be sufficient. The ATO considers a supply is normally something that will pass from one entity to another. See GSTR 2001/4 and GSTR 2006/9.

The other contentious component in the definition of taxable supply is the definition of an 'enterprise'. For GST purposes, 'enterprise' is a very broad concept. The GST Act section 9-20(1)(e) includes an activity or series of activities done 'by a charitable institution or by a trustee of a charitable fund'. Any supply made in connection with an enterprise is deemed to be 'in the course of or furtherance of' including a one-off commercial transaction with a profit-making intention.

This is not always clear cut, as illustrated by the following cases.

The Administrative Appeals Tribunal (the AAT) held that the activities of a taxpayer which consisted of acquiring artworks amounted to carrying on an enterprise (*FC of T v Swansea Services Pty Ltd* (2009) ATC 20-100), while those of a taxpayer who carried on part-time horse breeding were not (*D'Arcy v FC of T* (2008) ATC 10-041). Also, in the case of *Rendyl Properties Pty Ltd v FC of T* (2009) ATC 10-082, the AAT held that the taxpayer's boating activities did not amount to the carrying on of an enterprise as it was entered into, and then carried on, in a haphazard and unbusinesslike manner. Likewise, any activities undertaken to establish an entity or preparatory activities would be insufficient in qualifying as an enterprise (see *Clayton & Anor v FCT of T* (2013) ATC 10321).

Consequently, a weighing up of a number of factors will be required in determining whether an enterprise is being carried on.

Generally, GST is charged by a supplier who is registered for the GST in respect of the sale of goods and services that will be consumed within Australia. The liability for payment of the GST rests with the entity that made the taxable supply (section 9-40).

The concept of a taxable supply, incorporating the 6 components outlined, is illustrated in figure 13.3.

Example 13.2 works through the assessment of whether a taxable supply has been made.

When determining the final amount of GST charged and collected on taxable supplies reference needs to be made to the relevant labels on the business activity statement (BAS). In particular, the total amount owed to the ATO at Item 8A includes the sum of:

- Item 1A GST on sales or GST instalment
- Item 4 PAYG tax withheld
- Item 5A PAYG income tax instalment
- Item 7 Deferred company fund instalment.

See figure 13.4 and BAS in appendix at end of chapter.

FIGURE 13.3 The 6 steps needed for a taxable supply

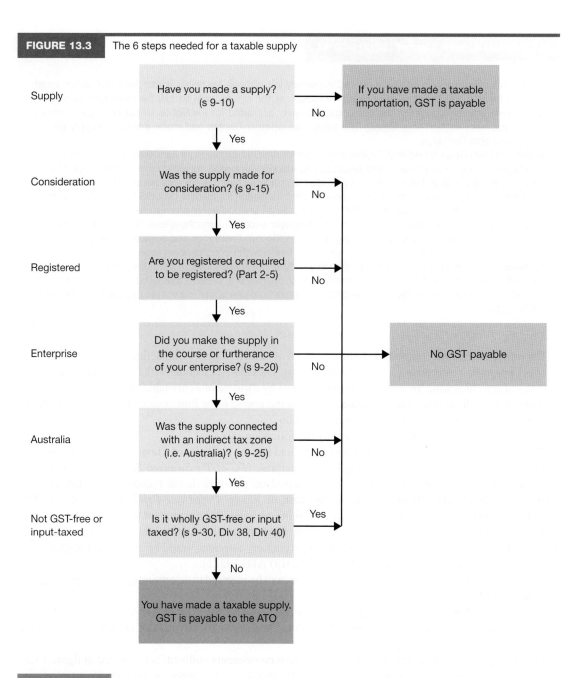

EXAMPLE 13.2

Has a taxable supply been made?

Ace Jewellers Pty Ltd owns and operates several jewellery stores throughout Australia. It is registered for the GST. It sells a diamond ring to a customer for $22 000.

Will Ace Jewellers need to remit GST on the sale to the ATO?

If the sale of the diamond ring satisfies the requirements of a taxable supply, it will be liable for GST in respect of the sale of the diamond ring.

The following table lists all 6 criteria of a taxable supply.

Step	Criteria	Yes/No
1	Has a supply been made?	Yes
2	Was the supply made for consideration?	Yes

3	Is the entity registered for GST?	Yes
4	Was the supply made in the course of furtherance of its enterprise?	Yes
5	Was the supply connected with an indirect tax zone (i.e. Australia)?	Yes
6	Is the supply GST-free or input-taxed?	No

As all 6 criteria are satisfied (remember that the sixth component requires a 'no'), Ace Jewellers Pty Ltd will be required to remit the GST to the ATO on its next business activity statement.

Based on a GST-inclusive amount of $22 000, the amount of GST included in the sale price is $2000 (i.e. $22 000 × 1/11).

FIGURE 13.4   Amounts owed to the ATO reported on the BAS

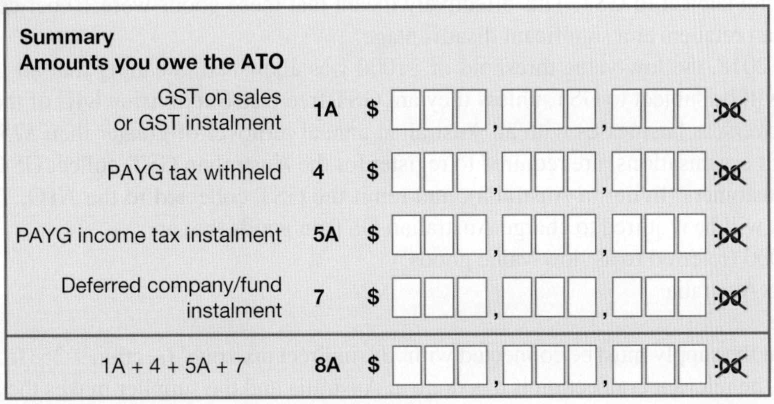

Summary
Amounts you owe the ATO

GST on sales or GST instalment	**1A**	$	
PAYG tax withheld	**4**	$	
PAYG income tax instalment	**5A**	$	
Deferred company/fund instalment	**7**	$	
1A + 4 + 5A + 7	**8A**	$	

Source: Australian Taxation Office, 'Business activity statement' https://www.ato.gov.au/uploadedFiles/Content/CAS/downloads/BUS25199Nat4189s.pdf.

13.3 Taxable importations

LEARNING OBJECTIVE 13.3 Explain the concept of taxable importations.

In addition to taxable supplies, GST is also payable on goods imported into Australia. These are termed taxable importations. In this case, according to section 13-15 of the GST Act, the liability to pay the GST falls on the receiver/importer and not the overseas supplier.

According to section 13-5(1) of the GST Act, an entity makes a taxable importation where goods are:
- imported, and
- entered into Australia for home consumption.

The GST is calculated as 10 per cent of the value of the taxable importation, which is defined in section 13-20(2) of the GST Act as the sum of:
- the 'customs value' of the goods (this is the free-on-board (FOB) value)[2]
- any additional costs incurred in transporting the goods to Australia, including lading or handling the goods, freight, insurance and transportation
- any customs duty payable in respect of the importation of the goods, and
- any wine equalisation tax (WET)[3] payable.

Example 13.3 provides a simple illustration of the application of GST to a taxable import.

---

2 The value at the point at which the seller provides the goods to the freight carrier.
3 WET tax is 29 per cent of the wholesale value of the wine and is paid on the last wholesale sale of the wine (usually between the wholesaler and the retailer) and on wine imports.

GST on taxable importation

Everything Electronic Pty Ltd is an Australian electronics retailer. It imports goods costing $400 000 from Hong Kong. Freight and insurance totalled $15 000 and customs duty was assessed at $50 000.

What GST is payable?

The value of taxable importation is $465 000 (i.e. $400 000 + $15 000 + $50 000). The GST payable would be 10 per cent of $465 000, or $46 500. If the importer is registered for GST, an input tax credit of $46 500 may then be claimed.

13.3.1 Low-value imported goods

Prior to 1 July 2018, goods imported into Australia (often by consumers online) which cost less than $1000 were not subject to GST. This meant that goods bought in Australia from Australian retailers costing less than $1000 attracted GST, whereas low-value goods costing less than $1000 bought online from overseas suppliers were not subject to GST. This effectively meant that these goods were 10 per cent cheaper and placed Australian retailers at a significant disadvantage.

From 1 July 2018, the low-value threshold of $1000 was abolished, meaning that all goods imported into Australia will be subject to GST, unless they are GST-free (see Subdivision 84C of the GST Act).

As a result, overseas businesses with an Australian annual turnover of greater than $75 000 ($150 000 for not-for-profit organisations) are required to register for the Australian GST, collect GST on sales made to Australian customers (living in Australia), and remit the GST collected to the ATO. This means that overseas sellers will be required to charge Australian GST on goods that are:

- less than $1000 (referred to as 'low-value goods')
- imported into Australia
- not GST-free.

It is noted that the supply must be connected with 'the indirect tax zone' (section 9-25) from 1 July 2015. The supply has the relevant connection if it is done in Australia and the supplier makes the supply through an enterprise which is a permanent establishment in Australia. As such, GST is charged at the point of sale (see Subdivision 84C). The effect is that an offshore supplier will normally be required to register, collect and remit GST where certain conditions are satisfied.

Briefly, the conditions are:

- there is an offshore supply of goods (section 84-77)
- the goods are low value (Customs value of <$1000) (section 84-79)
- the supplier has an Australian GST turnover of $75 000 or more ($150 000 for not-for-profit bodies) including the GST turnover from the relevant supply
- the supply is connected with Australia (section 84-75).

Also from 1 July 2017, supplies of things other than goods or real property (i.e. services or rights) are treated as having a connection with Australia if they are made to an 'Australian consumer' (see GST Act section 9-25(5); GSTR 2018/1). An Australian consumer is an Australian resident who is either not registered or is registered but does not acquire the supply solely or partly for purpose of carrying on an enterprise.

13.4 GST-free supplies (Division 38)

LEARNING OBJECTIVE 13.4 Explain the concept of GST-free supplies.

A supply is GST-free if it is specifically listed in Division 38 of the GST Act (1999). If a supply is GST-free, it means that the registered entity (i.e. the supplier) is not required to charge the 10 per cent GST. However, the registered entity can still claim back input tax credits on the inputs used to produce the **GST-free supply**. This effectively results in no GST being collected on the supply of GST-free goods and services (see figure 13.5).

GST-free supplies are listed in Division 38 of the GST Act. Examples of GST-free supplies include:

- basic food (Subdivision 38-A, Schedules 1 and 2)
- health (Subdivision 38-B, Schedule 3)
- education (Subdivision 38-C)
- child care (Subdivision 38-D)

- exports and other supplies for consumption outside Australia (Subdivision 38-E)
- religious services (Subdivision 38-F)
- non-commercial activities by charitable institutions etc. (Subdivision 38-G)
- raffles and bingo conducted by charitable institutions (Subdivision 38-H)
- water and sewerage facilities (Subdivision 38-I)
- supplies of going concerns (Subdivision 38-J)
- transport and related matters (Subdivision 38-K)
- precious metals (Subdivision 38-L)
- supplies through inward duty-free shops (Subdivision 38-M)
- grants of freehold and similar interests by governments (Subdivision 38-N)
- farmland (Subdivision 38-O)
- cars used by disabled persons (Subdivision 38-P)
- international mail (Subdivision 38-Q)
- telecommunication supplies made under arrangements for global roaming in the indirect tax zone (Subdivision 38-R)
- eligible emissions units (Subdivision 38-S), and
- inbound intangible consumer supplies (Subdivision 38-T).

Each of these categories have particular definitions, hence, care should be taken to ensure that all of the requirements relating to that section have been satisfied before making the decision that a supply is GST-free.

The most common GST-free categories are discussed in the sections that follow.

FIGURE 13.5 GST-free supplies

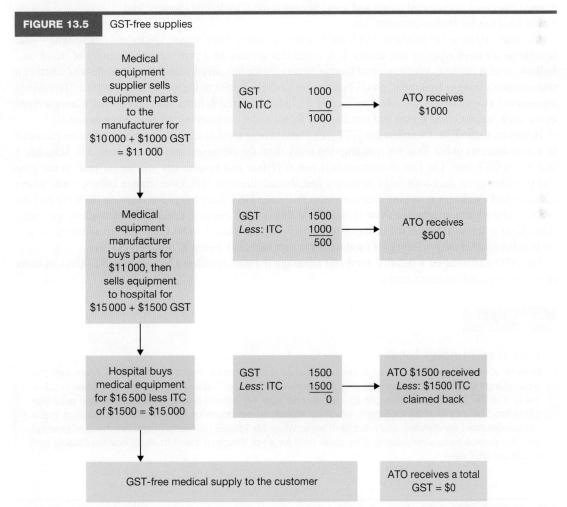

Note: The medical equipment supplier and manufacturer are making normal taxable supplies that are not GST free. The GST is collected on the supply of the equipment parts to the manufacturer and the GST is charged on the sale of the equipment to the hospital. As the hospital uses the equipment in making GST-free supplies of medical services, a full ITC can be claimed by the hospital refunding all the previous GST collected earlier.

13.4.1 Basic food (Subdivision 38-A, Schedules 1 and 2)

Most basic food for human consumption is GST-free (section 38-2). The definition of 'food' not only includes food but also beverages.

Food that is considered GST-free includes:

- fruit, vegetables, fish and soup (fresh, frozen, dried, canned or packaged)
- all meats for human consumption (except prepared meals or savoury snacks)
- cooking ingredients, such as flour, sugar, pre-mixes and cake mixes
- bread and bread rolls
- cheese and eggs
- unflavoured milk
- bottled drinking water, fruit, orange juice or vegetable juice (of at least 90% by volume)
- baby food and infant formula
- sugar, tea and coffee (unless ready-to-drink), and
- breakfast cereals.

Conversely, the following foods are taxable:

- bakery products such as cakes, pastries, pies, sausage rolls
- biscuits, crispbreads, crackers, cookies, pretzels, cones and wafers
- savoury snacks, popcorn, potato chips, chocolates, ice-cream, cookies and donuts
- carbonated and flavoured beverages (including flavoured milk, flavoured water and sports drinks)
- all food and beverages sold for consumption in restaurants and food courts
- hot food (takeaway) such as hot dogs, hamburgers and pizzas
- food marketed as prepared meals and some prepared food, including platters, and
- any food not for human consumption.

All other drinks — for example, alcoholic beverages, such as beer, wines, spirits and champagne — are taxable as are most types of soft drinks. It is noted that section 38-4 provides the meaning of 'food' and indicates that it can be a combination of food or beverages for human consumption, regardless of whether it requires processing or treatment, goods that can be mixed or added to these forms of food (i.e. flavourings and spices), as well as fats and oils. Specifically excluded from the definition are live animals, unprocessed cows' milk, unprocessed grains and cereals, and plants under cultivation that can be consumed.

However, section 38-3 restricts the GST-free status where food is supplied and consumed on premises (e.g. a restaurant) or hot food for consumption away from the premises, and food specified in Schedule 1 that is not GST-free. The fine distinction between GST-free and taxable can still be difficult to navigate and previous court decisions from Australia and abroad illustrate this. One strange instance was where an uncooked chicken was sold to a customer (at this point GST-free) but before leaving the store had the chicken placed in a microwave oven to heat it (at this point it became taxable). Nevertheless, generally when food is fresh, unprocessed or untreated in any way, it is likely to be GST-free. In addition, section 38-6 indicates that the packaging of food which is supplied GST free will also be GST-free.

The ATO has released a detailed food and beverage list that contains a list of the GST status of more than 500 food and beverage items.[4]

EXAMPLE 13.4

GST-free supply: food

Andrew Johnston operates a hotel in Brisbane catering for overseas travellers. The hotel offers free bus pick-up from the airport for guests staying at the hotel. Mr Toshinori Takano arrives from Tokyo and catches the bus to the hotel for an overnight stay. During his stay, Mr Takano purchases breakfast and asks that some food be prepared for his lunch, which he intends to eat down by the river. Mr Takano asks that it contain gourmet sandwiches and a bottle of wine. When Mr Takano comes to check out, he is so pleased with the service he has received that he gives Andrew a tip. Which of these transactions are taxable and which are GST-free?

---

4 This list is updated on a regular basis. A person merely has to type in the name of the food or drink item in the 'search' box and the decision tool will automatically determine whether the item is subject to GST or is regarded as GST-free. This online GST food and beverage decision tool can be accessed via the ATO website. The food and beverage checklist is also available to download in pdf format from the ATO website. The document lists each food and beverage in alphabetical order and spans a total of 88 pages.

The free bus pick-up is a supply ('supply' is very broadly defined to mean 'any form of supply whatsoever' (GST Act section 9-10(1)). However, it is not a taxable supply, as it is not made for consideration but supplied free of charge (GST Act section 9-5). It is not necessarily GST-free; this depends on whether the operator can claim input tax credits. The supply of breakfast at the hotel and the accommodation are taxable supplies. Andrew would need to account for GST on these supplies as all elements of a taxable supply under section 9-5 are satisfied.

Goods and services consumed by tourists in Australia, such as meals and hotel accommodation, are generally subject to GST. Andrew is also liable for the GST on the supply of wine and the sandwiches. The sandwiches are covered by the GST Act Schedule 1, Item 2, while wine is not named in Schedule 2 as a GST-free beverage, so GST applies. It should also be noted that food for consumption on the premises from which it was supplied is subject to GST. The definition of 'premises' as set out in section 38-5 and GSTD 2000/4 includes the grounds surrounding a café or public house. The river would probably qualify in this case as an area designed for use in connection with the supplies of food from an outlet. GST would arguably be accountable on the tips as Andrew has made a supply for consideration in return for hotel services.

13.4.2 Health (Subdivision 38-B, Schedule 3)

The supply of most health and medical services is GST-free (GST Act section 38-7). This includes:
- services provided by approved medical practitioners and pathologists
- services provided by allied health professionals, such as physiotherapists naturopaths, nurses and opticians
- hospital treatment
- medical aids and appliances
- prescribed drugs, medicines and health goods, and
- health insurance.

Laser vision correction surgery, HIV detection screening and check-ups are GST-free, as are pap smear tests and specified organ transplants. Psychotherapy and psychoanalysis may be GST-free if provided by a medical practitioner such as a psychiatrist.

Treatments that are carried out for cosmetic purposes are not GST-free, unless they qualify for Medicare benefits. For example, the government considers that a nose reconstruction for purely cosmetic reasons is not GST-free, but a reconstruction that alleviates breathing difficulty or is performed following an accident would be GST-free.

Certain other prescribed services are also not GST-free — for example, removal of tattoos.

Goods supplied to a person in the course of providing any of the GST-free health services to that person are also GST-free if they are supplied at the same premises. On this basis, the exemption extends to the application of bandages to the patient by a physiotherapist at the time of treatment. However, this does not apply to optometry and pharmacy services.

Medical appliances and aids for use by people with severe medical conditions or disabilities (e.g. wheelchairs, crutches, artificial limbs and modifications to cars) are GST-free. Supplies of cars to disabled veterans and other disabled people may be GST-free in certain circumstances. Schedule 3 of the GST Act lists medical aids and appliances which are designated GST-free.

Drugs and medicines are GST-free only if they:
- are supplied on prescription (supply without prescription is restricted)
- qualify as pharmaceutical benefits and are sold on prescription, or
- can only be supplied by a medical practitioner, dental practitioner or pharmacist, or other legally permitted people (e.g. optometrists or chiropodists).

13.4.3 Education (Subdivision 38-C)

Most educational courses are GST-free (GST Act section 38-35). These cover:
- a pre-school course
- a primary school course
- a secondary school course
- a tertiary course
- a Master or Doctoral course
- special education courses for children or students with disabilities

- an adult and community education course
- an English language course for overseas students
- a first aid or lifesaving course
- a professional or trade course, and
- a tertiary residential college course.

Figure 13.6 provides a visual illustration of Subdivisions 38A and 38B.

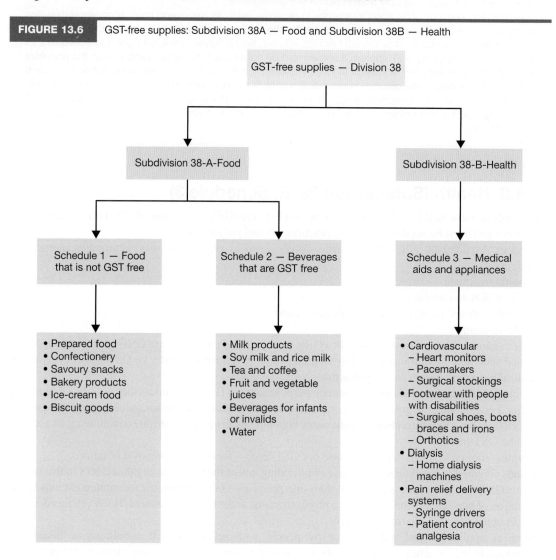

FIGURE 13.6   GST-free supplies: Subdivision 38A — Food and Subdivision 38B — Health

It does not matter whether the educational body is public or private. However, an education course normally does not include private tutoring.

The ATO considers that the GST-free supply of an educational course includes the provision of tuition fees, as well as course materials, such as pre-printed educational materials, course notes and workbooks. Excursions or field trips are generally GST-free, provided they are directly related to the curriculum of the course and not predominately recreational (section 38-90(1)). However, while course materials are GST-free, the supply of any accommodation or food as part of an excursion or field trip is not GST free (sections 38-90 and 38-95).

However, the following education-related supplies are subject to GST:

- school bus services and uniforms
- textbooks, lecture tapes, musical instruments and other materials sold by the educational institution
- hire charges associated with textbooks, lecture tapes, musical instruments and other materials leased by the educational institution
- recreational, leisure and personal enrichment courses
- hobby courses
- courses undertaken to maintain an individual's professional or trade qualification

- the supply of membership to a student organisation
- fees charged by a registered tutor
- accommodation provided to students undertaking a tertiary education course, and
- hiring out of lecture halls, theatres, sporting grounds, etc. to external parties.

13.4.4 Child care (Subdivision 38-D)

Child care is GST-free if it is supplied by a registered carer approved under Commonwealth family assistance laws (section 38-140). This includes long-day care centres, family day care centres, outside-school-hours care services and some occasional care services. A supply of child care is also GST-free if it is subject to a determination made by the Child Care Minister, and the supplier of that child care is eligible for Commonwealth funding under section 38-150(2) and any other supplies of child care that are directly related to the provision of this care (section 38-155).

EXAMPLE 13.5

GST-free education and child care

Barwick TAFE College offers a number of courses, including professional qualification courses that enable students to practice in that profession, other certificate courses that enable students to operate a particular type of machinery or equipment, and continuing professional development courses that are needed to retain membership of a professional body. The College also offers a child-care service during class times for students who have children.

What are the GST implications for these types of supplies?

Professional or trade qualification courses are GST-free (GST Act Subdivision 38-C). This covers courses leading to qualifications that are 'essential prerequisites' for entering into a particular profession or trade in Australia (GST Act section 195-1). To be an essential prerequisite, the qualification must be imposed by:

- a law, award, order or industrial agreement, or
- a professional or trade association that has uniform national requirements for entry.

The qualification course conducted by Barwick TAFE College would be GST-free under GST Act section 38-85. Courses enabling students to operate a particular type of machinery or equipment would also be GST-free. Continuing professional development (CPD) courses that are taken to retain membership of a professional body are not GST-free; it would only be GST-free to obtain membership (see GSTR 2000/27 and GSTR 2001/1).

Whether the child-care facility for the students is GST-free depends on whether Barwick TAFE is a registered carer under the family assistance law (i.e. section 3 of the of the *New Tax System (Family Assistance) (Administration) Act 1999* (Cth); GST Act section 38-140). Alternatively, it may qualify as approved child care services (i.e. section 3 of the *New Tax System (Family Assistance) (Administration) Act 1999* (Cth); section 38-145 of the GST Act), or be eligible for funding from the Commonwealth under guidelines made by the Child Care Minister (section 38-150).

13.4.5 Exports (Subdivision 38-E)

As GST is primarily a tax on consumption in Australia, it is not intended to apply to things that are not consumed in Australia, such as exports. Exports are thus GST-free. The export exemption applies to the export of goods.

A supply of goods is GST-free if the supplier exports them from Australia within 60 days after the earlier of the day the consideration is received or the day the supplier provides the tax invoice for them (section 38-185(1); GSTR 2002/6). Note also that the export of services used to repair, renovate or modify goods from outside Australia will remain GST-free if the final destination of the goods when the alterations were undertaken is still outside Australia (section 38-190(1) Item 5).

13.5 Input-taxed supplies (Division 40)

LEARNING OBJECTIVE 13.5 Explain the concept of input-taxed supplies.

A supply is input-taxed if it is listed in Division 40 of the GST Act. If a supply is input-taxed, it means that the registered entity (i.e. the supplier) is not required to charge the 10 per cent GST to the consumer.

However, unlike a GST-free supply, the supplier is not able to claim an input tax credit on the inputs used to produce the **input-taxed supply** (see figure 13.7).

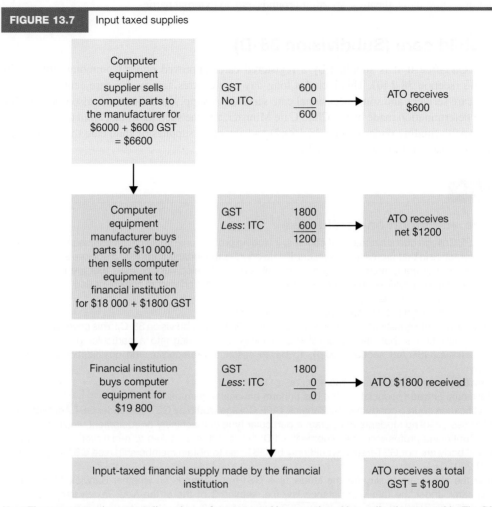

| FIGURE 13.7 | Input taxed supplies |

Note: The computer equipment supplier and manufacturer are making normal taxable supplies that are taxable. The GST is collected on the supply of the computer equipment parts to the manufacturer and the GST is charged on the sale of the computer equipment to the financial institution. As the financial institution uses the computer equipment in making input-taxed supplies of financial services no ITC can be claimed by the financial institution thereby making it bear the total cost of the GST included in the cost of the computer.

Input-taxed supplies are listed in Division 40 of the GST Act. Examples of input-taxed supplies include:
- financial supplies, such as loans, bank charges, interest, dividends etc. (Subdivision 40-A)
- residential rent (Subdivision 40-B)
- residential premises (Subdivision 40-C)
- precious metals (Subdivision 40-D)
- school tuckshops and canteens (Subdivision 40-E)
- fund raising events conducted by charitable institutions (Subdivision 40-F), and
- inbound intangible consumer supplies (Subdivision 40-G).

Figure 13.8 provides a visual illustration of Subdivisions 40A–40E.

13.5.1 Financial supplies (Subdivision 40-A)

Under section 40-5 of the GST Act, financial services (or supplies) made by a registered entity are input-taxed. Financial services (or supplies) cover most services provided by banks and other financial institutions. They include bank charges, interest charged on credit cards and loans, loan facility fee charges and account-keeping fees. A simple example is given in example 13.6. 'Financial supplies' does not include general insurance, debt collection services, actuarial advice and merchant fees charged by banks and financial institutions for EFTPOS and credit card transactions. These charges are not considered financial supplies and are therefore subject to GST.

FIGURE 13.8 Main input-taxed supplies — Subdivisions 40A–40E

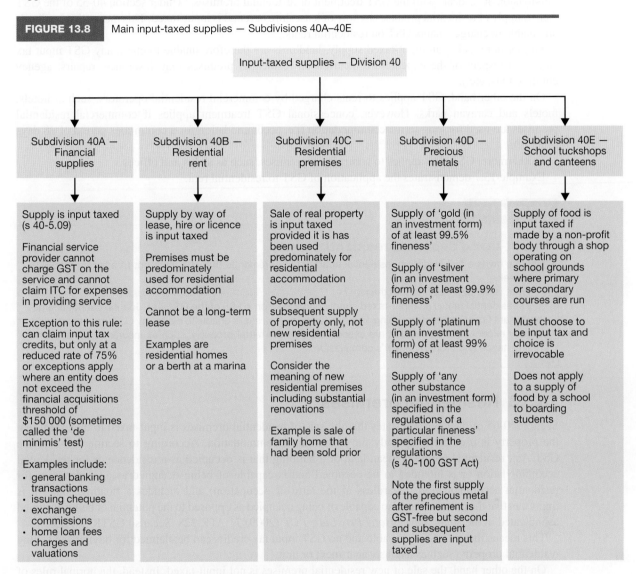

Input-taxed supplies — Division 40

Subdivision 40A — Financial supplies	Subdivision 40B — Residential rent	Subdivision 40C — Residential premises	Subdivision 40D — Precious metals	Subdivision 40E — School tuckshops and canteens
Supply is input taxed (s 40-5.09)

Financial service provider cannot charge GST on the service and cannot claim ITC for expenses in providing service

Exception to this rule: can claim input tax credits, but only at a reduced rate of 75% or exceptions apply where an entity does not exceed the financial acquisitions threshold of $150 000 (sometimes called the 'de minimis' test)

Examples include:
• general banking transactions
• issuing cheques
• exchange commissions
• home loan fees charges and valuations | Supply by way of lease, hire or licence is input taxed

Premises must be predominately used for residential accommodation

Cannot be a long-term lease

Examples are residential homes or a berth at a marina | Sale of real property is input taxed provided it is has been used predominately for residential accommodation

Second and subsequent supply of property only, not new residential premises

Consider the meaning of new residential premises including substantial renovations

Example is sale of family home that had been sold prior | Supply of 'gold (in an investment form) of at least 99.5% fineness'

Supply of 'silver (in an investment form) of at least 99.9% fineness'

Supply of 'platinum (in an investment form) of at least 99% fineness'

Supply of 'any other substance (in an investment form) specified in the regulations of a particular fineness' specified in the regulations (s 40-100 GST Act)

Note the first supply of the precious metal after refinement is GST-free but second and subsequent supplies are input taxed | Supply of food is input taxed if made by a non-profit body through a shop operating on school grounds where primary or secondary courses are run

Must choose to be input tax and choice is irrevocable

Does not apply to a supply of food by a school to boarding students |

The provision of home loans and the fee charges which accompany the mortgage are also input taxed, while the valuations of the homes are input taxed, as the valuation is incidental to the loan. That is, the valuations are supplied at about the same time as the mortgages, not for separate consideration and supplied as part of the ordinary course of business (see GST Regulations reg 40-5.10). According to reg 40-5.12, the provision of various advisory services relating to finance, investments and other financial supplies and in-house legal and accounting services are not treated as financial services, and these are therefore subject to GST (see GSTR 2006/3 regarding the Commissioner of Taxation's preferred methods of how to apportion when supplies are both input taxed and taxable, and GSTR 2002/2).

EXAMPLE 13.6

Input-taxed supplies: financial supplies

Leighton borrows $500 000 from an Australian bank to buy a rental property in his own name. In the first year of the loan, interest of $18 000 is charged by the bank.
  What is the GST treatment of the interest component of the loan?
  No GST applies as interest is a financial supply under section 40-5 of the GST Act.

13.5.2 Residential rent

Subdivision 40-C deals with the GST treatment of residential premises.[5] Under section 40-35 of the GST Act, a supply of residential premises by way of lease, hire or rental is input-taxed. This means that landlords are unable to charge tenants GST on residential rents.

Furthermore, being an input-taxed supply, landlords are therefore unable to claim any GST input tax credits in respect of the expenditure incurred on residential premises (e.g. insurance, repairs, agency commissions, etc.).

On the other hand, GST applies to rents charged by commercial residential operators, such as hotels, motels and caravan parks. However, concessional GST treatment applies if commercial residential premises are used for long-term accommodation (i.e. accommodation for a continuous period of 28 days or more).

Furthermore, GST also applies to commercial premises, such as shops and offices.

Example 13.7 demonstrates the application of GST to residential rent.

EXAMPLE 13.7

Input-taxed supplies: residential rent

Joanne owns a two-bedroom residential apartment in Fremantle that she rents out to a tenant for $600 per week.

What is the GST treatment of the rent?

As residential rent is an input-taxed supply under section 40-35 of the GST Act, Joanne cannot charge her tenant GST. Furthermore, being an input-taxed supply, she is unable to claim any GST input tax credits on any expenses she pays that are associated with the rental property, such as insurance, repairs and maintenance and property agent's commission.

13.5.3 Residential premises

Section 40-65 of the GST Act states that the sale of residential premises is input-taxed to the extent that the property is used predominantly for residential accommodation. According to section 195-1 of the GST Act, residential premises mean land or a building that is occupied as a residence or for residential accommodation or is intended to be occupied and is capable of being occupied as a residence or for residential accommodation (regardless of the term of occupation) and includes a floating home. It is important that the premises are also capable of being occupied as opposed to the potential of being occupied as indicated in the *South Steyne Hotel Prty Ltd v FCT* (2009) 71 ATR 228. See also GSTR 2012/5.

This means that no GST is payable and no GST input tax credits can be claimed for buying and selling residential property, such as a house, apartment or unit.

On the other hand, the sale of new residential premises is not input-taxed. Instead, the normal rules of GST apply to the sale of new residential premises (section 40-70(2)(b) of the GST Act). This will typically apply to builders and developers. Section 40-75(1) defines new residential premises as those that have not been previously sold as residential premises, nor have been subject to a long-term lease, have been created through substantial renovations, or have been built or contain a building that has been built to replace demolished premises on the same land. For clarification as to what constitutes substantial renovations, see GSTR 2003/3.

Similarly, the sale of commercial residential premises is subject to GST. This includes the situation where a hotel, motel and caravan park or camping ground is sold. Section 195-1 extends the definition of commercial residential premises to mean a hostel or boarding house, premises which are used to provide accommodation in connection with a school, or a ship that is let or hired in the ordinary course of business which includes for entertainment or transport. For further clarification, see GSTR 2012/6.

---

5 The ATO has released an online GST property decision tool designed to assist taxpayers to understand their GST obligations in respect of property transactions and determine whether GST is payable or not. The topics covered within the tool include:
- GST implications involving the sale, lease and purchase of residential premises, commercial residential premises, commercial premises and vacant land
- claiming input tax credits
- margin scheme eligibility
- GST-free supplies of real property.
  The GST property tool can be accessed via the ATO website.

The sale of non-residential premises, such as shops and offices, is also subject to GST (section 40-65 of the GST Act).

Example 13.8 illustrates the application of the GST to residential premises.

EXAMPLE 13.8

Input-taxed supplies: residential premises

In 2022, Tim and Irena sell their family home (which had been purchased in 2004) in the Sydney suburb of Balmoral Beach for $4 500 000.

What is the GST treatment of this sale?

As this is a sale of residential premises, the sale is input-taxed. No GST is payable and no GST input tax credits can be claimed.

13.5.3.1 GST withholding measures

From 1 July 2018, purchasers of new residential premises and potential residential land (i.e. residential zoned vacant land) are required to withhold the GST on the purchase price at settlement and remit this directly to the ATO.[6] Previously, purchasers paid it to the vendor as part of the price, and the vendor would then remit it to the ATO with their post-settlement business activity statement.

13.5.4 Precious metals

Section 40-100 indicates that the first supply of the precious metal after refinement is GST-free but second and subsequent supplies are input taxed.

'precious metal' means:
(a) gold (in an investment form) of at least 99.5% fineness; or
(b) silver (in an investment form) of at least 99.9% fineness; or
(c) platinum (in an investment form) of at least 99% fineness; or
(d) any other substance (in an investment form) specified in the regulations of a particular fineness specified in the regulations.

In a recent case of *STNK v FCT* (2021) AATA 3399, the taxpayer was unsuccessful in proving that one group of supplies were GST-free under the precious metal refining rules in section 38-385 of the GST Act. It was found there was a lack of evidence that the requisite refining had taken place and the taxpayer was unable to show that it qualified as a dealer in precious metals. Accordingly, the taxpayer was liable for the GST on the supplies in addition to penalties; however, Division 165 anti-avoidance rules did not apply.

13.5.5 School tuckshops and canteens

Section 40-130 indicates a supply of food is input taxed if made by a non-profit body through a shop operating on school grounds where primary or secondary courses are run and the non-profit body chooses to be input tax and this choice is irrevocable . Note this does not apply to a supply of food by a school to boarding students (see section 40-130(3)).

13.6 Out-of-scope supplies

LEARNING OBJECTIVE 13.6 Explain the concept of out-of-scope supplies.

Some supplies are not covered by the GST Act. These are referred to as 'out-of-scope' supplies. An **out-of-scope supply** is one which falls outside the scope of the GST Act and hence has no GST consequences at all. Examples of out-of-scope supplies include:
- salaries and wages
- superannuation contributions
- annual leave, sick leave and long service leave expenses
- donations made

---

6 *Treasury Laws Amendment (2018 Measures No. 1) Act 2018* (Cth).

- depreciation expense
- fringe benefits tax paid
- government fees and charges
- gain and loss on sale of non-current assets
- JobKeeper payments
- transfer of monies between bank accounts
- owner's contributions
- owner's drawings/dividends paid, and
- payroll tax.

These items are typically coded to 'no tax' in management accounts and are not reported in the BAS. A summary of the four types of GST supplies for a business is shown in table 13.1.

TABLE 13.1 Summary of the four types of GST supplies for a business

Type of supply	Charge the 10% GST? (i.e. GST collected)	Claim back input tax credits? (i.e. GST paid)
Taxable (Division 7)	✓	✓
GST-free (Division 38)	x	✓
Input-taxed (Division 40)	x	x
Out-of-scope	N/A	N/A

13.7 Creditable acquisitions

LEARNING OBJECTIVE 13.7 Explain the concept of creditable acquisitions.

Section 11-20 of the GST Act states: 'You are entitled to the input tax credit for any creditable acquisitions that you make'.

Entities that are registered for GST can claim back the GST they have paid on **creditable acquisitions**. This credit is known as an **input tax credit**. A creditable acquisition is essentially the purchase or acquisition of something that is used in carrying on a business or enterprise.

According to section 11-5 of the GST Act, an entity can claim back the GST paid (termed an input tax credit) for a creditable (business) acquisition if:
- the entity provides, or is liable to provide, consideration for the supply
- the entity is registered or required to be registered
- the entity acquires goods or services
- the acquisition was solely or partly for a creditable purpose, and
- the thing supplied was a taxable supply (i.e. GST was charged).

All 5 components listed are needed in order for the entity to claim an input tax credit.

This concept of a creditable acquisition, incorporating the 5 components outlined is illustrated in figure 13.9.

In order to claim back any GST input tax credits, the acquisition must be for a 'creditable purpose'. According to section 11-15 of the GST Act, a 'creditable purpose' means that:
(a) it is acquired in carrying on an enterprise
(b) the acquisition must not be of a private or domestic nature, and
(c) the acquisition cannot relate to making supplies that would be input-taxed (e.g. financial supplies, residential rent etc.).

Something acquired for the purpose of generating input-taxed supplies or something used exclusively for private or domestic purposes does not constitute a creditable purpose (section 11-15(2)(a)(b) GST Act).

According to section 69-5(3) of the GST Act, an input tax credit cannot be claimed if the expense is not deductible under the ITAA36 or ITAA97. This includes:
- penalties and fines
- relatives' travel expenses
- family maintenance
- recreational club expenses
- expenses for a leisure facility or boat

- entertainment expenses
- non-compulsory uniforms, and
- agreements for the provision of non-deductible, non-cash business benefits.

Where an entity is entitled to claim a GST input tax credit in respect of a creditable acquisition, section 11-25 of the GST Act states that the amount of the input tax credit is the amount of the GST paid for the acquisition. This will generally be 1/11 of the price paid to acquire the good or service.

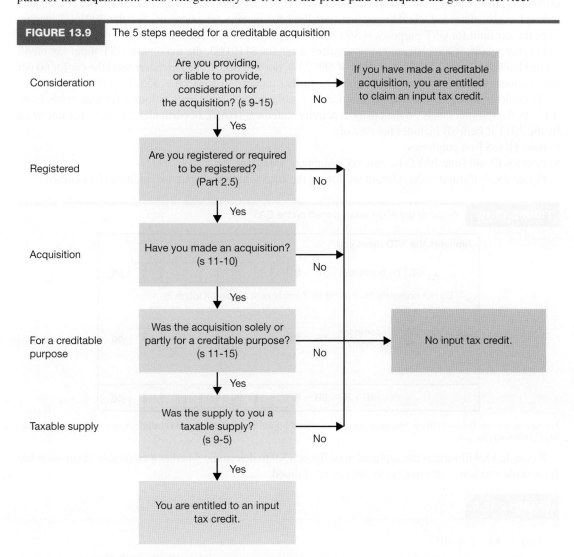

FIGURE 13.9 The 5 steps needed for a creditable acquisition

Consideration — Are you providing, or liable to provide, consideration for the acquisition? (s 9-15) — No → If you have made a creditable acquisition, you are entitled to claim an input tax credit.

Yes ↓

Registered — Are you registered or required to be registered? (Part 2.5) — No →

Yes ↓

Acquisition — Have you made an acquisition? (s 11-10) — No →

Yes ↓

For a creditable purpose — Was the acquisition solely or partly for a creditable purpose? (s 11-15) — No → No input tax credit.

Yes ↓

Taxable supply — Was the supply to you a taxable supply? (s 9-5) — No →

Yes ↓

You are entitled to an input tax credit.

13.7.1 Partly creditable purposes

An acquisition may be made only partly for a creditable purpose. For example, in the case of a mobile telephone bill, 60 per cent may be for a creditable (business) purpose and 40 per cent for a non-creditable (private) purpose.

In this case, according to section 11-30 of the GST Act, an apportionment is appropriate and the entity would only be able to claim 60 per cent of the input tax credits. The Commissioner expects the apportionment to be done on a fair and reasonable basis.

The actual amount that is apportioned for a partly creditable purpose is calculated according to the following formula in section 11-30(3).

$$\text{Full input tax credit} \times \text{Extent of creditable purpose} \times \text{Extent of consideration}$$

For example if a bank made $15 000 worth of purchases which included $5 000 for computer services from a IT provider and a further $10 000 which were spent on general banking operations the creditable acquisition would be apportioned as the $10 000 banking services are classified as input taxed financial supplies.

Therefore the input tax credit in this case is only available to the extent of $5000/$15 000 × 33.3% = $454.55.

13.7.2 The GST 'car cost limit' and claiming input tax credits

If a registered entity purchases a car for use in its business, it can only claim back an input tax credit based on 1/11 up to the luxury car threshold (section 69-10 of the GST Act). This **car cost limit** is the same concept as the motor vehicle depreciation cost limit for income tax purposes. For the 2021–22 income year, the car limit for GST purposes is $60 733.

In other words, if a registered entity acquires a car for $110 000, the maximum GST input tax credit allowed to be claimed is $5521 (i.e. 1/11 of $60 733), not $10 000. If the purchaser used the car for 60 per cent business use, the input tax credit would be further reduced to $3313 (i.e. $5521 × 60%).

When determining the final amount of GST payable on creditable acquisitions reference needs to be made to the relevant labels on the business activity statement (BAS). In particular, the total amount owed by the ATO at Item 8B includes the sum of:

- Item 1B GST on purchases
- Item 5B Credit from PAYG income tax instalment variation.

Figure 13.10 illustrates the relevant section on the BAS where the input tax credit can be claimed.

| **FIGURE 13.10** | Amounts the ATO owes reported on the BAS |

Amounts the ATO owes you

GST on purchases **1B** $ ▢▢▢,▢▢▢,▢▢▢ ⋈

Do not complete 1B if using GST instalment amount (Option 3)

Credit from PAYG income tax instalment variation **5B** $ ▢▢▢,▢▢▢,▢▢▢ ⋈

1B + 5B **8B** $ ▢▢▢,▢▢▢,▢▢▢ ⋈

Source: Australian Taxation Office, 'Business activity statement' https://www.ato.gov.au/uploadedFiles/Content/CAS/downloads/BUS25199Nat4189s.pdf.

Example 13.9 illustrates the application of figure 13.9 to determine whether a creditable acquisition has been made and hence an input tax credit can be claimed.

| **EXAMPLE 13.9** |

Input tax credits

Alexia owns and operates her own graphic design business and is registered for the GST. Alexia purchases some graphic design equipment for $4400 GST-inclusive for her business.
  Can Alexia claim the GST paid on the equipment purchase?
  Alexia is able to claim back the GST of $400 in respect of the purchase of the graphic design equipment as all five criteria of a creditable acquisition have been met as follows.

Step	Criteria	Yes/No
1	Was consideration provided for the acquisition?	Yes
2	Is the entity registered for the GST?	Yes
3	Has an acquisition of goods or services been made?	Yes
4	Was the acquisition solely or partly for a creditable purpose?	Yes
5	Was the supply made to the entity a taxable supply?	Yes

As Alexia satisfies all of the requirements of a creditable acquisition, she is able to claim the input tax credits associated with the purchase of the graphic design equipment, being $400 (i.e. $4400 × 1/11).

13.8 Creditable importations

LEARNING OBJECTIVE 13.8 Explain the concept of creditable importations.

As well as creditable acquisitions, an input tax credit can be claimed for goods that have been imported into Australia (s 15-15 of the GST Act). These are termed **creditable importations**.

An entity makes a creditable importation if:

- the entity imports goods solely or partly for a creditable purpose
- the importation is a taxable importation, and
- the entity is registered or required to be registered.

The amount of input tax credit is equal to the amount of GST that the importer paid on importation (section 15-20 of the GST Act).

The GST on a taxable importation is usually payable at the time of customs clearance (section 33-15 of the GST Act). The input tax credit is able to be claimed in the tax period in which GST is paid on the importation (section 29-15 of the GST Act).

However, to avoid cash flow difficulties, some importers that are registered for GST may be able to defer the payment of GST by participating in the deferred GST scheme. The scheme allows an importer to defer paying the GST on taxable importations until the first BAS lodged after the goods were imported. In other words, the importer pays the GST on the imported goods on the same BAS in which they claim the input tax credit. These two amounts will usually offset each other.

Goods that are purchased from overseas should enter Australia for home consumption via the purchasers agent not necessarily via the owner themselves. Otherwise, neither party may be able to claim the input tax credit as the entity that brings the goods into Australia may not be the one that completes the customs formalities and pays the GST.

EXAMPLE 13.10

Credible importations

Jill from Coolac in New South Wales purchases a horse from Ireland. Jill engages a specialist horse transporter to move the horse from Ireland to Australia, to complete customs and quarantine formalities, and to pay GST on the taxable importation. The horse transporter enters the goods for home consumption as 'the owner' of the horse, and delivers the horse to Jill's stables in Coolac.

Jill is registered for GST. She is bringing the horse to Australia to race. The horse transporter does not cause the horse to be brought to Australia to apply for its own purposes after importation. Therefore, the horse transporter does not import the horse within the meaning of section 15-5, and is not entitled to an input tax credit. Jill imports the horse for a creditable purpose as she will race it in the course of her enterprise. Only if the horse transporter enters the goods for home consumption on behalf of Jill as her agent is Jill entitled to an input tax credit on importation of the horse.

Source: Australian Taxation Office, *Goods and services tax: importation of goods into Australia* (GSTR 2003/15, 2003) https://www.ato.gov.au/law/view.htm?docid=GST/GSTR200315/NAT/ATO/00001.

13.9 GST administration

LEARNING OBJECTIVE 13.9 Describe administrative issues associated with the GST.

This section discusses various administrative tasks required of entities that are registered for the GST, beginning with registration itself.

13.9.1 Registration

According to section 23-5, an entity is required to register for the GST if:

    (a) it carries on an enterprise, and
    (b) its annual turnover meets the registration turnover threshold.

Section 184-1 of the GST Act defines an entity as any one of the following:

    (a) an individual
    (b) a body corporate
    (c) a corporation sole

(d) a body politic

(e) a partnership

(f) any other unincorporated association or body of persons

(g) a trust

(h) a superannuation fund.

The term 'enterprise' is defined in section 9-20 of the GST Act as an activity or series of activities, done in the form of a business or in the nature of trade. Excluded from the meaning of enterprise are the activities of:

- an employee
- a hobby
- not-for-profit activities of an individual or partnership
- as a member of a local government body (State or Territory).

According to section 23-15, an entity is required to register for the GST if its annual turnover exceeds $75 000 per annum. In the case of not-for-profit organisations, the registration threshold is set at $150 000 per year. An entity above these thresholds *must* register for the GST. Registration must be made within 21 days of becoming required to register.[7]

An entity below the registration thresholds may voluntarily register for the GST.[8]

Entities may register by completing the appropriate form or registering on-line at www.business.gov.au.

An entity with a turnover of less than $75 000 is not required to register for the GST. However, they must still register for an **Australian Business Number (ABN)** from the ATO. The ABN is a unique 11-digit number. Their ABN must be displayed on all invoices issued, but they are not permitted to charge the customer the 10 per cent GST (as only businesses registered for the GST can do so).

If a taxpayer provides goods or services to a customer and does not quote their ABN, the payer is required to withhold 47 per cent from the gross payment and remit this to the ATO. This is referred to as **ABN withholding tax**. The provider of the goods or services receives the net amount of 53 per cent of the invoiced amount. In order to get back this tax, the supplier of the goods or services is required to include the gross amount in their tax return and the amount of ABN withholding tax. By doing so, they have effectively quoted their tax file number, and in doing so, the ATO refunds the ABN withholding tax to the supplier.

13.9.2 Attribution basis

According to Division 29, there are two **attribution** methods of accounting for GST. These two methods are the:

1. cash basis
2. accruals (or non-cash) basis.

13.9.2.1 Cash basis

Under the cash basis of accounting, GST is payable on a taxable supply in the tax period when the cash is received from the customer in respect of a taxable supply and not necessarily the period in which the service was provided or the tax invoice issued.

Similarly, an input tax credit for a creditable acquisition can only be claimed in the tax period when the entity makes the payment and not necessarily the period in which the expense occurred or when the tax invoice was issued (sections 29-5(2) and 29-10(2)).

According to section 29-40 of the GST Act, an entity may elect to use the cash basis if it meets at least one of the following conditions:

- the entity is a small business entity within the meaning of section 328-110(1) of the ITAA97
- the entity does not carry on a business and has a turnover of $10 million or less
- the cash basis is used for income tax purposes, or
- the entity is a charitable, gift-deductible entity or government school.

If an entity meets any one of the conditions, it has a choice as to whether to adopt the cash or non-cash (or accruals) basis of accounting for GST.

If an entity is not eligible to use the cash basis, it must use the non-cash (or accruals) basis of accounting for GST.

---

7 GST Act section 25-1.

8 GST Act section 23-10.

13.9.2.2 Accruals (or non-cash) basis

According to section 29-5(1), under the non-cash basis of accounting for the GST, the GST payable on a supply that is made is attributed to the tax period in which:

- the taxpayer received payment in relation to the supply
- the date the invoice was issued, or
- whichever is the earliest.

Similarly, according to section 29-10(1), under the non-cash basis of accounting for the GST, the GST input tax credit is able to be claimed in the tax period in which the:

- taxpayer paid for the goods or services, or
- date of the invoice, whichever is the earliest.

However, it is important to note that an entity cannot claim an input tax credit unless it holds a valid tax invoice for the purchase at the time of lodging the BAS.

The non-cash method is often referred to as the 'accruals method' by the accounting profession but this is rather misleading as it is not connected with accrual accounting. It is better to consider this non-cash method as the 'invoice' method.

An entity should adopt the GST accounting method which is most reflective of how their business operates, bearing in mind the requirements of the legislation, which method they adopt for income tax purposes, and what is best for their business cash flow. The following example assists in illustrating these considerations.

EXAMPLE 13.11

Accounting for GST

Jones Pty Ltd has a GST turnover of less than $5 000 000. Given the following information regarding three months of trading under the GST regime, what accounting method should Jones Pty Ltd adopt? Assume a monthly return is lodged and tax invoices are issued at the time of sales and purchases.

- In July 2021, sales including GST were $11 000, while purchases including GST were $5500. No moneys were received or paid.
- In August 2021, sales including GST were $11 500, while purchases including GST were $6050. No other money was received, but $5500 was paid.
- In September 2021, sales including GST were $13 200, while purchases including GST were $7150. $11 000 was received, while $6050 was paid in the month.

Using the cash basis of accounting:

- the July GST payable (nil), less input tax credit (ITC) (nil), equals nil amount due to the ATO
- the August GST payable (nil), ITC $500, equals a refund of $500 from the ATO
- the September GST payable ($1000), ITC $550, equals a net amount of $450 owing to the ATO.

Using the accruals basis of accounting:

- the July GST payable ($1000), less ITC $500, equals $500 payable to the ATO
- the August GST payable ($1045), less ITC $550, equals $495 owing to the ATO
- the September GST payable ($1200), less ITC $650, equals $550 owing to the ATO.

Jones Pty Ltd should adopt a cash basis of accounting for the GST, as this produces a more favourable cash flow. If Jones Pty Ltd carries on an enterprise that does not constitute a business given that it operates under the $10 000 000 cash accounting threshold, it is entitled to account for GST on a cash basis. Should the company exceed this threshold, it will be required to account on an accruals basis unless permission has been granted to remain on a cash basis (see Subdivision 29-B of the GST Act). It should be noted that Jones Pty Ltd cannot change its attribution basis (i.e. from cash basis to accruals or vice versa) until a minimum of 12 months has elapsed from the start of using a particular basis.

13.9.3 Tax periods

A **tax period** is a period for which an entity calculates its GST and lodges its business activity statement (BAS). According to Division 27, there are two tax periods for GST purposes:

1. monthly
2. quarterly.

An entity has a choice of either quarterly or monthly tax periods. However, according to section 27-15, an entity must use a monthly tax period if the:

- entity's annual turnover is $20 million or more
- entity is only carrying on an enterprise for less than 3 months, or
- entity has a history of failing to comply with tax obligations.

13.9.3.1 Monthly tax periods

Section 31-10 of the GST Act provides that entities with monthly tax periods are required to lodge their BAS with the ATO no later than the 21st day of the month following the end of a tax period.

The due dates for lodgement of the BAS are shown in table 13.2.

TABLE 13.2   Monthly GST taxpayers

Month	Lodgement date of BAS	Time to complete
31 July	21 August	3 weeks
31 August	21 September	3 weeks
30 September	21 October	3 weeks
31 October	21 November	3 weeks
30 November	21 December	3 weeks
31 December	21 January	3 weeks
31 January	21 February	3 weeks
28 February	21 March	3 weeks
31 March	21 April	3 weeks
30 April	21 May	3 weeks
31 May	21 June	3 weeks
30 June	21 July	3 weeks

13.9.3.2 Quarterly tax periods

Section 31-8 of the GST Act sets out a table showing when entities with quarterly tax periods are required to lodge their BAS with the ATO. This table is reproduced in table 13.3.

TABLE 13.3   Quarterly GST taxpayers

Quarter	Lodgement date of BAS	Time to complete
30 September	28 October	4 weeks
31 December	28 February	8 weeks
31 March	28 April	4 weeks
30 June	28 July	4 weeks

Example 13.12 illustrates both the attribution methods of accounting and the use of tax periods.

EXAMPLE 13.12

Tax periods and attributing GST

Paul Smith runs an old book shop and chooses to register for GST. On 10 October 2021, Paul makes a taxable supply of several books for a total price of $220 and issues a tax invoice to the customer for this amount. The customer pays half the amount at the time of purchase, and the remaining half three months later. What factors need to be considered in determining which tax periods Paul is to account for GST on the sale? Having regard to these factors, when might Paul have to account for GST?

As Paul Smith is registered and the supply is a taxable supply, attention now needs to be given to:

- whether or not Paul is operating on cash or accruals basis, and
- what tax periods he has chosen (quarterly or monthly).

If Paul is operating on an accruals basis, he is required to account for the GST in the tax period in which he receives any of the consideration or issues a tax invoice, whichever comes first. In this case, GST is payable on the total price of $220, and if he uses quarterly tax periods he will need to include the GST of $20 in the tax period ending on 31 December 2021 (or 31 October 2021 if he is using monthly tax periods). If, on the other hand, Paul is operating on a cash basis, he only accounts for any GST to the extent that he receives any consideration. Assuming quarterly tax periods, he would account for GST of $10 (1/11 of $110) in the tax period ending 31 December 2021, and account for the remaining $10 of the GST in the tax period ending 31 March 2022. See also GSTR Ruling 2000/13.

13.9.4 Net amount

When lodging its business activity statement, an entity is required to remit to the ATO the 'net amount'. The 'net amount' is Item 9 on the BAS.

According to section 17-5 of the GST Act, the net amount is defined as:

$$\text{Net amount} = [\text{GST payable} - \text{GST receivable}]$$

If the net amount (Item 9) is positive (Item 8A is more than Item 8B on the BAS), the registered entity must remit the GST owing to the ATO when the business activity statement (BAS) is lodged.

Conversely, if the net amount (Item 9) is negative (Item 8A is less than Item 8B on the BAS), this means that the registered entity is entitled to a refund. The ATO must process the refund within 14 days of receipt of the BAS. Figure 11.5 shows an extract of the payment or refund section of the BAS (which is also shown in full in the chapter appendix).

FIGURE 13.11	Net amount reported on the BAS

Source: Australian Taxation Office, 'Business activity statement' https://www.ato.gov.au/uploadedFiles/Content/CAS/downloads/BUS25189Nat4235s.pdf.

13.9.5 GST adjustments

Situations inevitably arise when the amount of GST reported in a previous BAS period may need to be adjusted. In other words, a taxpayer may have paid too much or too little GST or claimed too many or too few input tax credits. This gives rise to the concept of adjustments which are addressed in Division 19 of the GST Act.

Adjustments can arise as a result of:
- adjustment events (Division 19)
- bad debts (Divisions 21 and 136)
- settlement of insurance claims (Division 78)
- changes in creditable purpose (Division 129)
- goods applied solely for private use (Division 130)
- supplies acquired without full input tax credit (Division 132)
- supplies of a going concern (Division 135)
- newly registered entities (Division 137)
- cessation of registration (Division 138), or
- deceased estates (Division 139).

Generally, if an adjustment happens in the same tax period, there is no need to amend a previous amount. The change is simply reflected in the final amount for that period. Hence, adjustments generally affect the amounts of GST reported in a previous tax period.

13.9.5.1 Adjustment events

Section 19-10 of the GST Act provides that an adjustment event is any event that has the effect of:
- cancelling a supply or acquisition
- changing the consideration for a supply or acquisition, or
- causing a supply or acquisition to become, or stop being, a taxable supply or creditable acquisition. There are two types of adjustment events.

1. An *increasing adjustment event*, which is an event that has the effect of increasing the taxpayer's net GST liability, by either increasing the GST liability or reducing the input tax credit entitlement (GST Act sections 19-50 and 19-80).
2. A *decreasing adjustment event*, which is an event that has the effect of decreasing the taxpayer's net GST liability, by either decreasing the GST liability or increasing the input tax credit entitlement (GST Act sections 19-55 and 19-85). In the case of a decreasing adjustment event, the entity must hold an adjustment note from the supplier before making the adjustment (GST Act section 29-20).

The amount of adjustment is the difference between the input tax credit that the entity actually received and the input tax credit that the entity would have been entitled to receive if the original claim had been based on its actual subsequent use. Figure 13.12 outlines how an adjustment event for a supply or acquisition can give rise to an increasing adjustment or a decreasing adjustment (GST Act section 19-5).

FIGURE 13.12 The effect of adjustment events

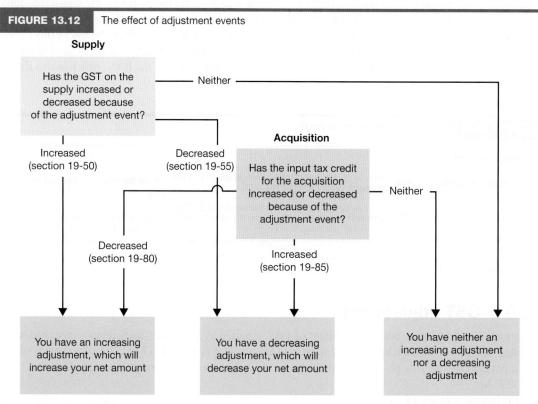

Source: GST Act section 19-5.

13.9.5.2 Adjustment periods

An adjustment for changes in planned use is made annually, usually in the tax period that ends on 30 June or the closest to 30 June. This is designed to fit in as closely as possible with the income tax year (section 129-20). This period is called the **adjustment period**.

The period of time after the acquisition during which an adjustment is required depends on the GST-exclusive value of the acquisition. In the case where the supply is not a financial supply, the maximum number of adjustment periods that may apply to a purchase or importation are shown in table 13.4.

It should also be noted that if a change of use adjustment is required, it is not made immediately.

The adjustment is correctly made in the next adjustment period. Adjustment periods under Division 129 always occur in the month or quarter ending 30 June, commencing at least 12 months after the acquisition was made.

TABLE 13.4   **Annual adjustment periods**

Value of the purchase or importation (GST-exclusive)	Number of annual adjustment periods
< $1000	0*
$1001–$5000	2
$5001–$499 999	5
$500 000 or more	10

*There is no need to adjust for a value of less than $1000.

Hence, if an asset was acquired on 15 February 2021, the first annual adjustment period is the tax period ending 30 June 2022. The second annual adjustment period is 30 June 2023, and so on.

Example 13.13 demonstrates how adjustments are made.

EXAMPLE 13.13

Adjustments

Eric is a carpenter and is registered for the GST. He lodges a quarterly BAS with the ATO. In March 2021, Eric buys a Toyota Hi-Lux for $55 000 GST-inclusive for his business to carry his tools and materials to and from client premises where he undertakes work.

At the time he acquires the motor vehicle, Eric estimates that he will use the vehicle 80 per cent for business purposes. Accordingly, Eric claims GST of $4000 in his March 2021 BAS (being $55 000 × 1/11 × 80%).

As the GST-exclusive value of the motor vehicle was between $5001 and $499 999, Eric has *five adjustment periods* during which an adjustment may be made. The *first adjustment period* is the tax period from 1 April 2022 to 30 June 2022.

At the end of the *first annual adjustment period (i.e. 30 June 2022)*, Eric has actually used the motor vehicle 90 per cent for business purposes, instead of the expected 80 per cent. This results in an *increasing GST adjustment of $500* (i.e. $5000 GST × 10%).

At the end of the *second annual adjustment period (i.e. 30 June 2023)*, Eric has actually used the motor vehicle 85 per cent for business, purposes, which is 5 per cent lower than the previous period. This results in a *decreasing GST adjustment* of $250 (i.e. $5000 × 5%).

This process continues for the remaining three adjustment periods (i.e. 30 June 2024, 2025 and 2026), after which no further adjustments are required for this item.

13.9.5.3 Goods applied solely for private use

Division 130 of the GST Act also requires an adjustment to the net amount where an input tax credit has been claimed but later the acquisition is used solely for private or domestic purposes. An increasing adjustment is necessary because no input tax credit can be claimed on supplies used for private or domestic purposes.

A Division 130 adjustment is always 100 per cent of the previous input tax credit that has been claimed. This applies regardless of the length of time the item has been used for a creditable purpose. Note that section 130-5 does not apply if the taxpayer had previously had an adjustment under Division 129 for the acquisition or importation.

13.9.6 Tax invoices

A registered entity who makes a taxable supply and charges the GST is required to issue a tax invoice (section 29-70).

Section 29-70(2) of the GST Act specifies that a supplier must issue a tax invoice within 28 days of the date of sale for all supplies with a total GST exclusive price exceeding $75 (i.e. $82.50 inclusive of GST).

According to section 29-70(1), a **tax invoice** must be in the approved form and is required to contain the following information:

- that the document is intended as a tax invoice (usually with the words 'tax invoice' clearly displayed)
- the supplier's identity (e.g. its legal name, business name or trading name) and its ABN

- the date the tax invoice was issued
- a brief description of what is sold, including the quantity (if applicable) and the price of what is sold
- the GST amount (if any) payable in relation to the sale — this can be shown separately or, if the GST to be paid is exactly 1/11 of the total price, as a statement such as 'total price includes GST', and
- the extent that each sale to which the document relates is a taxable sale.

Where the price of the supply is $1000 or more (including GST), the tax invoice must also include the buyer's identity or ABN.

The GST included in the price can either be shown separately or must contain a statement stating that the amount payable is inclusive of GST.

A sample tax invoice for goods and services that consists exclusively of taxable supplies is shown in figure 13.13.

FIGURE 13.13 Sample tax invoice (registered for GST)

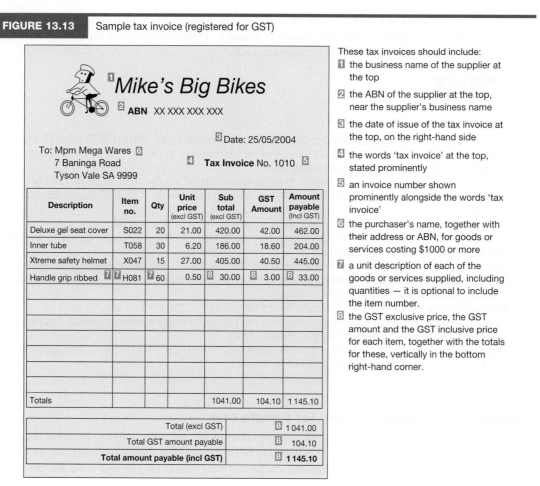

Source: Australian Taxation Office, 'Tax invoices' www.ato.gov.au/Business/GST/Tax-invoices.

Where the amount of the GST is not exactly 1/11 of the tax invoice amount (i.e. where the supply consists of a taxable supply and a GST-free supply), the amount of GST payable must be separately disclosed. This is referred to as a **mixed supply**. While a mixed supply can be broken up into its separate parts, such as taxable, GST free or input taxed and taxed accordingly, they should be distinguished from **composite supplies**. A composite supply is a single supply which has one main or dominant part with attached ancillary or incidental parts. The ATO suggests a number of methods in which to perform this allocation and apportion the total cost. See GSTR 2001/8.

Generally, this Ruling indicates that a reasonable method of apportionment will be acceptable provided it is supportable and that the appropriate records are kept. However, the direct method of apportionment is preferred where, for instance, a mixed supply is apportioned on the basis of relevant variables such as price, time to perform a service, or an area of property.

It is important to remember that an entity must also hold valid tax invoices for all creditable acquisitions to be able to claim input tax credits.

If an entity is not registered for GST, it should not issue a 'tax invoice'. Instead, it should simply issue an **invoice**. An invoice should still contain the 11-digit ABN, but it should not contain GST.

A sample invoice for goods and services that does not include GST is shown in figure 13.14.

FIGURE 13.14 Sample invoice (not registered for GST)

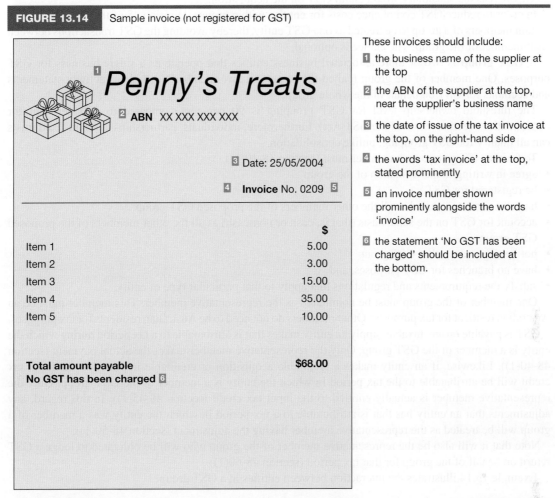

These invoices should include:

1 the business name of the supplier at the top

2 the ABN of the supplier at the top, near the supplier's business name

3 the date of issue of the tax invoice at the top, on the right-hand side

4 the words 'tax invoice' at the top, stated prominently

5 an invoice number shown prominently alongside the words 'invoice'

6 the statement 'No GST has been charged' should be included at the bottom.

Source: Australian Taxation Office, 'Tax invoices' www.ato.gov.au/Business/GST/Tax-invoices.

A summary of the differences between a taxpayer that is registered for the GST and one that is not, including whether a tax invoice or invoice is required to be supplied, is summarised in table 13.5.

TABLE 13.5 Difference between an invoice and a tax invoice

Document	Registered for the GST?	Quote ABN?	Charge GST?
Invoice	x	✓	x
Tax invoice	✓	✓	✓

13.10 Special GST rules

LEARNING OBJECTIVE 13.10 Describe a range of special GST rules.

This last section of the chapter will examine a number of special rules that apply to particular GST-registered entities and the impact of technology.

13.10.1 GST grouping

Special GST grouping rules apply to entities that operate as one group. This is the case of a parent–subsidiary relationship where there may be several transactions between group members.

Under the normal GST rules, a taxable supply and a creditable acquisition occurs where one member of the group (for example, the parent entity) sells goods to one of its subsidiaries. This means that the parent entity would charge GST to the subsidiary. This results in the parent entity having to remit GST to the ATO, whereas the subsidiary would claim GST on the acquisition.

In order to reduce GST compliance costs for entities within groups, Division 48 of the GST Act allows certain members of a group to be treated as one GST entity, thereby avoiding the GST transactions between each member of the group. The choice is optional.

A **GST group** is two or more associated business entities that operate as a single business for GST purposes. One member of the group (called the 'representative member') completes activity statements and accounts for GST on behalf of the whole group.

The threshold ownership level for GST grouping is 90 per cent compared to 100 per cent for consolidation (section 190-1 of the GST Act). Furthermore, individuals, partnerships and non-fixed trusts can all qualify for GST grouping, unlike consolidation.

To form a GST group, each member must (section 48-10(1)):
- agree in writing to the formation of the group
- be registered for GST
- have the same tax period as all the other members of the proposed GST group
- account for GST on the same basis (that is, cash or non-cash) as all the other members of the proposed GST group
- not belong to any other GST group
- have no branches for GST purposes, and
- satisfy the requirements and regulations that apply to that particular type of entity.

One member of the group must be nominated as the representative member. This member must be an Australian resident for tax purposes. Other members do not need to be Australian residents for tax purposes.

GST is payable on any taxable supply an entity makes that is attributable to a tax period during which the entity is a member of the GST group. Only the representative member makes the actual payment (section 48-40(1)). Likewise, if an entity makes a creditable acquisition or creditable importation the input tax credit will be attributable to the tax period in which the entity is a member of the GST group. Only the representative member is actually entitled to the input tax credit (section 48-45(1)). In this regard, any adjustments that an entity has that is attributable to a tax period in which the entity was a member of a group will be treated as the representative member having the adjustment (section 48-50(1)).

Note that it will also be the representative member of the group who will be obligated to lodge a GST return on behalf of the group for that tax period (section 48-60(1)).

Example 13.14 illustrates the interaction between entities in a GST group.

EXAMPLE 13.14

GST groups

A Ltd, B Ltd and C Ltd have GST turnovers of $6 000 000, $8 000 000 and $8 000 000 respectively and have formed a group. Each company is registered; each previously accounted for GST on a cash basis. A Ltd recently made a purchase of some equipment from outside the group, which it intended to use to make taxable supplies to an outsider. However, some of the equipment was eventually supplied to B Ltd, who itself makes input-taxed supplies. C Ltd also made a sale to an outsider in return for two instalment payments. C Ltd later decided to leave the group before the second instalment had been paid. What are the GST implications for the group?

Subject to section 48-5 of the GST Act, the entities may form a GST group. The entities can self-assess their eligibility to form, change and dissolve a GST group. To form a GST group, certain requirements need to be met. In this case, first, that the companies must be members of the same 90 per cent owned group. This is achieved where one company has at least a 90 per cent stake in the other, or the third company has at least a 90 per cent stake in the other two (section 190-1 of the GST Act). Second, the companies must be registered, have the same tax periods, and account on the same basis as other members of the group, and must not be a member of any other GST group.

Once the conditions have been satisfied and the group formed, their turnover now exceeds $10 000 000, which means the representative member must now account on the accruals basis. If this is unsatisfactory, it may be appropriate to apply for permission to continue using the cash basis (section 29-45 of the GST Act). On the establishment of the group, it will be treated as a single body. The representative member will be responsible for the GST on all supplies and claim ITCs on all acquisitions outside the group. In addition, all income tax liabilities will be actually paid by the representative member. Note that an adjustment must be made for the input tax credit which would have been claimed by A Ltd on the purchase of the equipment outside the group, as there has been a change in creditable purpose (section 11-5 of the GST Act; GSTR 2008/1). Likewise, the sale to an outsider by C Ltd would require the representative member to account for GST on the first instalment while C Ltd would have to account for GST on the second instalment under the accounting rules that apply to it. This would be on the cash basis.

13.10.2 GST branch

By law, a branch is merely an extension to the parent entity, not a separate legal entity; however, Division 54 of the GST Act allows a branch of a registered entity to be treated as a separate GST entity. This means:

- GST is payable on taxable sales between GST branches and the parent entity
- GST is payable on taxable sales between GST branches, and
- **GST credits** can be claimed on both of these transaction types.

Generally, a registered entity is able to register its branch as a GST branch if the (section 54-5 of the GST Act):

- branch has an independent system of accounting
- branch can be separately identified (either because of its distinctive activities or location)
- entity carries on (or intends to carry on) an enterprise through the branch, and
- entity is not a member of a GST group.

An 'independent system of accounting' is one that can produce the results of each branch without relying on the accounts of the parent entity, another branch or any other entity. It is not simply a cost centre in the parent entity's accounts, but rather, where the branches have their own accounting staff and maintain separate accounting hardware and software, this is more conclusive.

Entities can register as many of their branches as they wish, provided they satisfy the mentioned requirements.

When an entity registers a branch for GST purposes, the entity is called the 'parent entity'. The parent entity is liable for any GST amounts that the branches owe to the ATO. In other words, the parent entity is responsible for lodgement of the BAS; however, it can be prepared and lodged by either the parent entity or the GST branch.

The parent entity must lodge a separate activity statement for any transactions not included in the activity statements of the GST branches.

13.10.3 GST and second-hand goods

Special rules apply to the purchase of second-hand goods, particularly those by second-hand dealers because these goods are often acquired from persons who are not registered for GST. Second-hand goods are defined as goods that have been previously owned but do not include precious metals or livestock (see GST Determination GSTD 2013/2). It is important that dealers keep accurate identity records of the supplier and that the goods are acquired for the purposes of sale or exchange in the ordinary course of business (section 66-5; see *Lease Plan Australia Ltd v DFC of Tax* 2009 ATC ¶20-144.)

Hence, when the second-hand dealer acquires these goods, they are not able to claim any input tax credits. However, when they sell those goods, typically, the second-hand dealer is registered for the GST, which means that they are required to charge the 10 per cent GST to the final customer.

Special rules relating to second-hand goods are contained in Division 66 of the GST Act. Section 66-5 indicates that the acquisition of second-hand goods can be a creditable acquisition provided that they are for resale or exchange and not:

- for manufacture
- a GST-free supply
- goods that are divided for re-supply
- imported goods
- hired, or
- used to make a non-taxable supply.

Section 66-10 of the GST Act allows a notional GST input tax credit in certain circumstances. Generally speaking, if the goods were purchased for $300 or less, the second-hand dealer is deemed to have purchased the goods from an unregistered entity GST-inclusive.

This means that the second-hand dealer is entitled to a notional input tax credit equivalent to 1/11 of the amount paid to acquire the goods in the tax period in which they received an invoice, or when the payment was made, whichever is the earlier. This is referred to as the 'direct method'.

However, if the second-hand goods were acquired for more than $300, the second-hand dealer is entitled to a notional input tax credit equivalent to 1/11 of the amount paid to acquire the goods if the dealer is on the accruals basis, the credit normally cannot be claimed until the dealer subsequently sells the goods as part of its business. The credit will be attributed to the tax period in which the dealer receives any payment for the sale, or the period when an invoice it issued, whichever comes first, or if the dealer is on a cash basis, the credit can be claimed only to the extent that payment is actually received for the dealer's subsequent sale of the goods (section 66-15 of the GST Act).

However, the amount of the notional input tax credit that can be claimed exceed the amount of GST payable in respect of the subsequent sale of the second-hand goods.

If the second-hand goods are acquired from an entity that is already registered for GST, the normal provisions of the GST Act override Division 66.

For guidelines on when second-hand goods are acquired for the purposes of sale or exchange see GSTD 2013/2.

The GST treatment of second-hand goods handled by a dealer is demonstrated in example 13.15.

EXAMPLE 13.15

GST on second-hand goods acquired and sold by a dealer

Max operates a second-hand store in Adelaide. The business is registered for GST and adopts a quarterly tax period. On 19 February 2022, Max buys a second-hand bicycle from John for $110. John is not registered for GST.

On 2 June 2022, Max sells the bicycle to a customer for $275 (GST-inclusive).

How will GST apply from Max's perspective?

As the amount for which the bicycle was acquired is less than $300, Max is entitled to claim a notional input tax credit of $10 (being $110 × 1/11) in his March 2022 BAS (section 66-10(1A)).

Arising from the sale of the bicycle to a customer, in his June 2022 BAS, Max must remit GST of $25 (being $275 × 1/11) to the ATO.

If Max bought the bicycle from John for $330, instead of $110, then the notional input tax credit of $30 (i.e. $330 × 1/11) will be claimed in the June 2022 BAS (being the same tax period in which the bicycle was sold) in accordance with the special rules contained in section 66-15(1)(a) of the GST Act.

13.10.4 Vouchers

Special GST rules apply to vouchers, tokens, coupons and prepaid phone cards or similar articles that can be redeemed for other supplies up to a monetary value stated on the voucher (Division 100, section 100-25 of the GST Act).

A typical example is a voucher purchased from a retail store (e.g. Myer, David Jones, etc.) that entitles the holder to any goods from that store up to a stated value (e.g. $100).

Section 100-5 of the GST Act provides that the initial sale of a voucher is not considered taxable, provided the monetary value of the voucher is stated and the voucher entitles the holder to buy goods or services up to the stated monetary value. In other words, no GST applies when the voucher is sold to the customer. Instead, GST applies when the voucher is redeemed by the holder and the relevant goods or services are sold to the customer.

Example 13.16 illustrates the GST treatment of a voucher with a stated monetary value.

EXAMPLE 13.16

Vouchers with stated monetary value

Amelia buys her grandmother a $50 gift voucher from a large department store for her birthday. The voucher entitles her grandmother to buy any goods in the store up to the dollar value of $50. Four weeks later, her grandmother buys her favourite perfume in the store to the value of $50 and uses her voucher.

How does the GST apply to the voucher?

Under Division 100 of the GST Act, no GST applies on the initial provision of the gift voucher.

> However, the sale of goods constitutes a taxable supply under section 9-5 of the GST Act. The store is liable to remit the GST of $4.54 (i.e. $50 × 1/11) to the ATO in its next BAS in respect of the sale of the perfume.

This situation is to be contrasted to a situation in which the voucher does not state a monetary value, but instead entitles the holder to receive specified goods or services (e.g. a voucher that states that the holder is entitled to a facial).

In these instances, the voucher is considered to constitute a taxable supply. GST is therefore charged when the voucher is issued, not when the voucher is redeemed and the goods or services are provided.

It should be noted that the redemption of a voucher is not a supply (section 100-10 of the GST Act). However, the actual consideration on the redemption of vouchers is taken to be the sum of:

(a) the stated monetary value of the voucher, reduced by any amount of that value refunded to the holder of the voucher in respect of the supply, and

(b) any additional consideration provided for the supply (section 100-12(1) of the GST Act).

In this regard, an increasing adjustment for unredeemed vouchers may be required if:

(a) a voucher was supplied for consideration

(b) on redemption of the voucher, the holder of the voucher was entitled to supplies up to the stated monetary value of the voucher

(c) the voucher has not been fully redeemed, and

(d) any reserves for the redemption of the voucher have been written back to current income (section 100-15(1) of the GST Act).

For further clarification on how the GST operates with respect to vouchers, see GSTR 2003/5. The legislative references are sourced directly from the legislation.

Example 13.17 illustrates the GST treatment of a voucher without a stated monetary value.

EXAMPLE 13.17

Vouchers without stated monetary value

David buys his wife, Melissa, a gold class movie ticket, which entitles her to a movie of her choice plus food and drinks. The voucher cost $100.

How does the GST apply to the voucher?

As the service is specified on the voucher, the supply of the voucher constitutes a taxable supply and Division 100 of the GST Act does not apply. Hence, the cinema is required to remit $9.09 (i.e. $100 × 1/11) to the ATO on its next BAS after selling the voucher.

TECHNOLOGY IN ACTION

Digital currency and GST

After the emergence of cryptoassets and the ATO release of guidelines in 2014, the ATO shifted its position on digital currency and GST in order to remove the incidence of double taxation (i.e. GST).[9] Since 1 July 2017, sales and purchases of digital currency are not subject to GST and are treated somewhat equivalently to money.[10] For the purposes of the GST system, **digital currency** refers to digital units of value that:

(a) are designed to be fungible

(b) can be provided as consideration for a supply

(c) are generally available to members of the public without any substantial restrictions on their use as consideration

▶

---

9 In particular the *A New Tax System (Goods and Services Tax) Act 1999* (Cth) ('GST Act') and New Tax System (Goods and Services Tax) Regulations 1999 (Cth) were amended, as well as GSTR 2014/3 withdrawn.

10 The inconsistency of treating cryptoassets as 'money' for GST purposes but not for the CGT regime has created some controversy: see, eg, Nathan De Zilva, 'The evolving treatment of cryptocurrencies' (2018) 52 *Taxation in Australia* 372, 374.

(d) are not denominated in any country's currency
(e) do not have a value that depends on, or is derived from, the value of anything else
(f) do not give an entitlement to receive, or to direct the supply of, a particular thing or things, unless the entitlement is incidental to:
  (i) holding the digital units of value; or
  (ii) using the digital units of value as consideration.[11]

The ATO suggest that this definition encompasses, for example, 'Bitcoin, Ethereum, Litecoin, Dash, Monero, ZCash, Ripple, and YbCoin'.[12] The ATO also excludes such things as:
(a) loyalty points
(b) 'currencies' used in online gaming not able to be used outside of the game, and,
(c) digital currencies that have a value based on something else or give holders some form of entitlement or privilege.[13]

Murray and Pirovich argue that the definition therefore may not capture cryptoassets such as collateralised stable coins and utility tokens. For these, there may continue to be a double taxation issue.[14]

The ATO advises that, although no GST consequences arise when digital currency is used to pay for goods and services, if digital currency is received as payment for the sale of goods and services, the normal GST rules apply to the sale itself.[15] Here, 1/11 of the GST-inclusive price received[16] reflects the GST liability on the taxable supply made by the business. There is not an additional GST consequence for the transfer of digital currency (i.e. no double taxation). In contrast, the ATO advises that where the business is selling the digital currency itself, the sales are generally treated as financial supplies (i.e. input taxed supplies).[17] As such, even if the business taxpayer is registered for GST, they generally cannot claim input tax credits for inputs used to produce or acquire the digital currency.[18] On this point, it may be a good idea to reflect on the capital allowances and tax accounting and trading stock chapters, where we discussed blockchain-related business activities.

However, this gets complicated if we consider the global reach of blockchain-related activities. The ATO advises that where the digital currency sales are to non-residents, the sale is GST-free rather than input taxed.[19] What does this mean for charging GST and claiming input tax credits on inputs relating to the supply?[20]

REFLECTION

What does the ATO advise when it comes to complying with the standard tax invoice requirements for supply of digital currency? What additional information is considered sufficient?

13.11 GST anti-avoidance rule and ethical issues

LEARNING OBJECTIVE 13.11 Describe the GST general anti-avoidance rule and relevant ethical issues.

13.11.1 GST general anti-avoidance rule

This next section of the chapter will examine the GST **general anti-avoidance rule** found in Division 165 of the GST Act and some related ethical issues.

The aim of this anti-avoidance legislation is to deter schemes which give entities benefits, such as reducing GST, increasing refunds, or altering the timing of payment of GST or refunds. If the *dominant purpose* or *principal effect* of a scheme is to give an entity such a benefit, the Commissioner may negate

---

11 Section 195-1 GST Act.

12 Australian Taxation Office, 'GST and digital currency' (Online, 16 March 2018) https://www.ato.gov.au/business/gst/in-detail/your-industry/financial-services-and-insurance/gst-and-digital-currency.

13 Ibid.

14 Peter Murray and Joni Pirovich, 'The taxation of cryptocurrencies' (NSW Annual Tax Forum, 25 May 2018).

15 Australian Taxation Office, 'GST and digital currency' (Online, 16 March 2018) https://www.ato.gov.au/business/gst/in-detail/your-industry/financial-services-and-insurance/gst-and-digital-currency.

16 The GST-inclusive price is expected to reflect the digital currency received, converted to Australian dollars at the time of sale.

17 Ibid.

18 Ibid. Note that there are instances where business taxpayers can claim GST credits or reduced GST credits. This is generally when the entity makes a relatively small amount of financial supplies in contrast to their taxable or GST-free supplies: Ibid. See also for example: Australian Taxation Office, Goods and services tax: reduced credit acquisitions (GSTR 2004/1).

19 Australian Taxation Office, 'GST and digital currency' (Online, 16 March 2018) https://www.ato.gov.au/business/gst/in-detail/your-industry/financial-services-and-insurance/gst-and-digital-currency.

20 Hint! Take a look at the GST-free supplies section of this chapter.

the benefit an entity gets from the scheme by declaring how much GST or refund would have been payable, and when it would have been payable, apart from the scheme (section 165-1 of the GST Act).

Section 165-5 applies when:

(a) an entity (*the avoider*) gets or got a *GST benefit* from a *scheme*, and
(b) the GST benefit is not attributable to the making, by any entity, of a choice, election, application or agreement that is expressly provided for by the GST law, the wine tax law or the luxury car tax law; and
(c) taking account of the matters described in s 165-15 it is reasonable to conclude that either:
    (i) an entity that (whether alone or with others) entered into or carried out the scheme, or part of the scheme, did so with the *sole or dominant purpose* of that entity or another entity getting a GST benefit from the scheme; or
    (ii) the principal effect of the scheme, or of part of the scheme, is that the *avoider gets the GST benefit* from the *scheme* directly or indirectly; and
(d) the scheme:
    (i) is a scheme that has been or is entered into on or *after 2 December 1998*; or
    (ii) is a scheme that has been or is carried out or commenced on or after that day.

The scheme can also be entered into or carried out both inside and outside Australia.

Clearly, the key elements of the provision require the Commissioner to establish what is the *GST benefit* and the *scheme* involved.

The *GST benefit* has been described in section 165-10(1) as:

(a) an amount that is payable by the entity under this Act apart from this Division is, or could reasonably be expected to be, smaller than it would be apart from the scheme or a part of the scheme; or
(b) an amount that is payable to the entity under this Act apart from this Division is, or could reasonably be expected to be, larger than it would be apart from the scheme or a part of the scheme; or
(c) all or part of an amount that is payable by the entity under this Act apart from this Division is, or could reasonably be expected to be, payable later than it would have been apart from the scheme or a part of the scheme; or
(d) all or part of an amount that is payable to the entity under this Act apart from this Division is, or could reasonably be expected to be, payable earlier than it would have been apart from the scheme or a part of the scheme; or
(e) in other specific cases.

A *scheme* has been described in section 165-10(2) as:

(a) any arrangement, agreement, understanding, promise or undertaking:
    (i) whether it is express or implied; and
    (ii) whether or not it is, or is intended to be, enforceable by legal proceedings; or
(b) any scheme, plan, proposal, action, course of action or course of conduct, whether unilateral or otherwise.

A GST benefit can arise even if there is no economic alternative (section 165-10(3)).

The other critical element of the provision is the *dominant purpose* or *principal effect* of a scheme which gives an entity such a benefit. Under section 165-15(1), the matters that must be taken into account in determining purpose or effect include:

(a) the manner in which the scheme was entered into or carried out;
(b) the form and substance of the scheme, including:
    (i) the legal rights and obligations involved in the scheme; and
    (ii) the economic and commercial substance of the scheme;
(c) the purpose or object of this Act, the *Customs Act 1901* (so far as it is relevant to this Act) and any relevant provision of this Act or that Act (whether the purpose or object is stated expressly or not);
(d) the timing of the scheme;
(e) the period over which the scheme was entered into and carried out;
(f) the effect that this Act would have in relation to the scheme apart from this Division;
(g) any change in the avoider's financial position that has resulted, or may reasonably be expected to result, from the scheme;
(h) any change that has resulted, or may reasonably be expected to result, from the scheme in the financial position of an entity (a connected entity) that has or had a connection or dealing with the avoider, whether the connection or dealing is or was of a family, business or other nature;

(i) any other consequence for the avoider or a connected entity of the scheme having been entered into or carried out;

(j) the nature of the connection between the avoider and a connected entity, including the question whether the dealing is or was at arm's length;

(k) the circumstances surrounding the scheme;

(l) any other relevant circumstances.

While it is important for the Commissioner to identify the scheme involved, a misinterpretation of the scheme will not be fatal. What is more important is the timing of the scheme, as it must be judged against the law in force at the time and a reconstruction of a situation that would have applied if the scheme had not been entered into.

If the Commissioner has established these key elements, he may make a declaration and negate the effects of the scheme for GST benefits (section 165-40), or he may reduce an entity's net amount or GST to compensate the loser who was disadvantaged as result of the scheme The disadvantage is either that the amount or timing of the GST is not fair or reasonable (section 165-45(2)).

Penalties for failing to comply with various GST obligations are contained in the *Taxation Administration Act 1953* (Cth). The Commissioner may impose substantial penalties under Division 165. See the case of *FC of T v Unit Trend Services Pty Ltd* 2013 ATC ¶ (Full High Court) where Division 165 applied to arrangements involving the margin scheme and going concern provisions, as the GST benefit derived was not due to choices provided by the GST Act. Guidelines regarding the remission of penalties with respect to false and misleading statements are contained in *Practice Statement PS LA 2006/2.*

For an illustration of when the general anti-avoidance rule may apply see example 13.18.

EXAMPLE 13.18

GST general anti-avoidance rule

A furniture shop, Franco Cuzo, is run by a company which commenced business on 10 July 2020. The main shareholder/manager, Francesco, visits a second-hand goods shop, Furniture and Things, and realises that an old table that is being sold for $500 plus GST is in fact worth $10 000 plus GST. Francesco purchases the table in his own name, and he is not registered for GST. He pays $550 including GST for the table, with no entitlement to an input tax credit. Francesco then sells the table to Franco Cuzo for its true market value of $11 000. Franco Cuzo then claims a second-hand goods input tax credit of $1000 when the table is resold. The GST consequences of these transactions and potential application of the general anti-avoidance provisions (GAAP) need to be considered.

Francesco is not registered for the GST, and therefore he is not entitled to any credit for the $50 GST paid on the purchase of the table. When selling the table back to his business for $11 000, Francesco has not made a taxable supply, as he is not registered for GST. Franco Cuzo has acquired second-hand goods and is therefore entitled to credit for imputed GST even though none was paid by Franco Cuzo on the sale and there is no tax invoice (GST Act section 66-5). The credit would be $1000 (1/11 × $11 000). If Franco Cuzo had purchased the table directly for $550, it would only have received an input tax credit of $50, not $1000. As such, these arrangements may be subject to Division 165 of the GST Act if it can be shown that there was a scheme that resulted in a GST benefit and the dominant purpose or dominant effect of the scheme was to obtain a tax benefit. The scheme is clearly the transactions of Francesco to purchase the table himself and then resell it to his company, and the benefit is the added credit received by Franco Cuzo (i.e. an additional $950). For Division 165 to apply, it is not necessary for the benefit to be received by the person carrying out the scheme. See Practice Statement PS LA 2005/24 with respect to the application of Division 165.

To establish Francesco's dominant purpose, it is necessary to consider the factors listed in section 165-15(1). If it can be shown that the dominant purpose and effect of the scheme was to obtain the benefit, then it can be concluded that Division 165 applies. However, this may be difficult, as Francesco could argue that he was not aware of the true value of the table at the time of purchase and he truly acquired it originally for his own private use. The subsequent sale to Franco Cuzo may then have been for the purpose of obtaining the best resale value for the table once its true value was realised. Proving a dominant purpose or effect is a subjective test of the taxpayer's intentions and is often difficult to establish. Where Division 165 applies, the Commissioner will negate the avoider's advantage; namely, the transaction between Francesco and Furniture and Things would be negated, and the transaction would effectively become a transaction between Franco Cuzo and Furniture and Things. Franco Cuzo would then return the GST of $1000 on selling the table and claim the input tax credit of $50. This would require an increasing adjustment of $950 ($1000 credit claimed – $50 credit entitled).

13.11.2 Ethical considerations

Just like for income tax purposes, taxpayers obligations under the GST system also raise various ethical considerations. In particular, if taxpayers meet the conditions of carrying on an enterprise, they must then apply for an ABN and, depending on their turnover and operations, register for the GST. This is particularly so for workers in the sharing economy and, for ride-sharing drivers, GST registration is compulsory. However, sometimes there is a fine line between some business and private transactions which make it difficult to navigate.

An example of the seriousness of manipulating the GST system was highlighted in the recent case of a Western Australian man who had made false GST claims. A Perth court sentenced Joseph Popic to 3 years jail for dishonestly obtaining a financial advantage by deception. An analysis of the bank accounts of Joseph Popic Real Estate', which had claimed fraudulent GST refunds, showed no receipt of business income and insufficient cashflow to support the reported acquisitions made. In addition, it was established that Mr Popic was not carrying on a business but rather had been employed in various roles throughout the offending period.[21]

Example 13.18 illustrates a situation of deliberate evasion and deception which is a crime, but in many other cases the morals and ethics of taxpayers are also tested. See the following ethics box.

ETHICS IN PRACTICE

Possible manipulation of the GST system

In advising your client Francesco with regards to the tax implications on purchasing the table, you note that he is not forthcoming with any additional information. In trying to provide creditable evidence to support the reason behind the purchase, Francesco insists that the table was for his own private use. Francesco is very pleased with the outcome in that he obtained the best resale value for the table once its true value was realised. However, you have your doubts and want to establish Francesco's true motives.

What would be your reaction in solving this ethical dilemma? Consider the following options.

(a) You would direct Francesco to the matters the Commissioner will consider under section 165-15 and gather that information.

(b) As Francesco has a very sound argument, and due to your time pressures, you are prepared to take his word.

(c) You would be able to charge Francesco an additional fee if you were to accept his position.

(d) You can advise Francesco of the possible outcomes of accepting his position and if incorrect, the possible tax and penalties that may apply.

---

21 'False GST claims land WA man in jail' (Web Page, 28 January 2022) https://www.ato.gov.au/Media-centre/Media-releases/False-GST-claims-land-WA-man-in-jail.

SUMMARY

13.1 Explain how the GST works.

The GST is a flat 10 per cent broad-based indirect tax on the private consumption of most goods and services in Australia and importations into Australia. The tax is charged and collected by registered entities at each stage in the production chain. GST-registered suppliers are entitled to claim an input tax credit for any GST paid. Suppliers report and remit the difference between GST collected and GST paid to the ATO each month or quarter on a form called the business activity statement (BAS). The tax is ultimately borne by the end consumer, not by producers or suppliers.

13.2 Explain the concept of taxable supplies.

GST is charged on taxable supplies. A taxable supply arises if goods or services are provided from one entity to another, the supply was made for consideration, the supplier is required to be registered for GST, the supply is made in the course of carrying on an enterprise, the supply is made in connection with Australia and the supply is not a GST-free, input-taxed or out-of-scope supply.

13.3 Explain the concept of taxable importations.

Taxable importations are goods imported into Australia for home consumption. The liability to pay the GST on taxable importations lies with the importer, not the overseas supplier. The GST on taxable importations is the sum of the customs value of the goods, any additional costs incurred in importing the goods, customs duty payable and wine equalisation tax payable. For low-value goods (under $1000), the supplier is required to register for GST if their turnover exceeds the GST thresholds and remit GST to the ATO.

13.4 Explain the concept of GST-free supplies.

GST-free supplies are those on which the supplier is not required to charge GST under Division 38 of the GST Act. GST-free supplies are listed in Division 38 of the GST Act and include basic foods, health and medical services, education, child care, exports and a range of other goods and services.

13.5 Explain the concept of input-taxed supplies.

Input-taxed supplies are those on which the supplier is not required to charge GST under Division 40 of the GST Act. Input-taxed supplies are differentiated from GST-free supplies in that the supplier cannot claim an input tax credit on the inputs used to produce the input-taxed supply. Input-taxed supplies are listed in Division 40 of the GST Act and include financial supplies, residential rent, residential premises, precious metals and school tuckshops and canteens.

13.6 Explain the concept of out-of-scope supplies.

An out-of-scope supply is one that falls outside the scope of the GST Act and hence has no GST consequences at all. Out-of-scope supplies include salaries, wages, superannuation contributions, annual leave, sick leave, long service leave expenses, donations, depreciation expenses, fringe benefits tax paid, government fees and charges, gain and loss on sale of non-current assets, Jobkeeper payments, transfers between bank accounts, owner's contributions, owner's drawings, dividends paid and payroll tax.

13.7 Explain the concept of creditable acquisitions.

A creditable acquisition is the purchase or acquisition of something that is used in carrying on a business or enterprise. GST-registered entities are entitled to claim the GST back on creditable acquisitions — the credit is known as an input tax credit. A creditable acquisition arises if the entity provides, or is liable to provide, consideration for the supply; the entity is registered or required to be registered; the entity acquires goods or services; the acquisition was solely or partly for a creditable purpose; and the thing supplied was a taxable supply (i.e. GST was charged).

13.8 Explain the concept of creditable importations.

A creditable importation arises if an entity imports goods solely or partly for a creditable purpose, the importation is a taxable importation and the entity is registered or required to be registered. A GST-registered entity is entitled to claim an input tax credit equal to the amount of GST they paid on the importation.

13.9 Describe administrative issues associated with the GST.

The main administrative issues for GST-registered entities are the initial registration, accounting and reporting GST on either the cash basis or the non-cash basis on a monthly or quarterly basis, remitting the net amount of GST to the tax office with lodgement of a business activity statement, reporting adjusting amounts in later activity statements and issuing tax invoices in a specified format. Tax invoices can also reflect the case of both mixed and composite supplies where necessary.

13.10 Describe a range of special GST rules.

Members of a group may choose to report as a single business for GST purposes to reduce compliance costs. Nominating as a GST group avoids the need to make GST transactions between the members of the group.

A branch of a registered GST entity can register as a separate GST entity provided it maintains an independent system of accounting and meets certain other requirements.

Special rules apply to second-hand goods. When a second-hand dealer acquires second-hand goods from an entity not registered for GST they are not generally able to claim input-tax credits (reflecting the fact that most private sellers of second-hand goods are not registered for GST), but they are required to charge GST when they sell the goods to customers. There is an allowance for dealers to claim a notional input tax credit on goods acquired for less than $300. Acquisitions from GST-registered entities are subject to the usual GST rules.

Vouchers with a stated monetary value are not taxable when purchased, but GST applies when the voucher is redeemed for goods or services. Vouchers without a stated monetary value are a taxable supply and GST is charged when the voucher is issued, not when it is redeemed.

Note that, since 1 July 2017, sales and purchases of digital currency are not subject to GST and are treated somewhat equivalently to money.

13.11 Explain the GST general anti-avoidance rule and relevant ethical issues.

The aim of the GST anti-avoidance legislation is to deter schemes which have a dominant purpose or principal effect of producing benefits, such as reducing GST, increasing refunds, or altering the timing of payment of GST or refunds. A number of ethical issues are raised as a result of these schemes and transactions which need to be carefully considered by prudent taxpayers and tax practitioners.

KEY TERMS

ABN withholding tax   The amount withheld from a supplier who provides either an invoice or tax invoice where the eleven-digit Australian Business Number (ABN) has not been quoted. Where a supplier does not quote their ABN, the payer is required to deduct and remit 47 per cent of the gross amount of the invoice to the ATO on the next business activity statement (BAS).

adjustment period   The period of time after acquisition during which an adjustment to the GST payable or refundable is made. An adjustment for changes in planned use is made annually, usually in the tax period that ends on 30 June or the closest to 30 June. This is designed to fit in as closely as possible with the income tax year.

attribution   Attribution rules determine the attribution of GST payable and GST receivable to tax periods. An entity can choose one of two attribution methods of accounting for the GST: the cash method and the non-cash (or accruals) method.

Australian Business Number (ABN)   Abbreviated to ABN. A unique eleven-digit number assigned to each entity that is carrying on an enterprise.

business activity statement (BAS)   Abbreviated to BAS. A document issued to entities that are registered for GST. A pre-printed document issued by the ATO either monthly or quarterly which reports the business's entitlements and obligations to the ATO. The BAS allows businesses to report the following: GST, luxury car tax, wine equalisation tax, fuel tax credits, pay-as-you-go withholding and instalments, FBT instalments and deferred company instalments. The ATO sends out personalised, pre-printed activity statements either via the internet or to the nominated postal address on the Australian Business Register.

car cost limit   The GST Act allows an entity that is registered for GST to claim an input tax credit based on 1/11 of the purchase price up to the 'car limit'. The 'car limit' for GST purposes is the same as the depreciation car cost limit for income tax purposes. For the 2022 income year, the 'car limit' for GST purposes is $60 733. This means that for GST purposes, the maximum GST input tax credit that can be claimed is $5521 (i.e. $60 733 × 1/11). Any input tax credit in excess of this amount cannot be claimed.

composite supplies is a single supply which has one main or dominant part with attached ancillary or incidental parts.

creditable acquisition The purchase or acquisition of something that is used in carrying on a business or enterprise.

creditable importation A taxable good imported by a GST-registered entity for a creditable purpose.

digital currency Refers to digital units of value that: (a) are designed to be fungible; (b) can be provided as consideration for a supply; (c) are generally available to members of the public without any substantial restrictions on their use as consideration; (d) are not denominated in any country's currency; (e) do not have a value that depends on, or is derived from, the value of anything else; and (f) do not give an entitlement to receive, or to direct the supply of, a particular thing or things, unless the entitlement is incidental to: (i) holding the digital units of value; or (ii) using the digital units of value as consideration.

general anti-avoidance rule Aims to deter schemes which have a dominant purpose or principle effect of deriving benefits such as, reducing GST, increasing refunds or altering the timing of payment of GST or refunds.

goods and services tax (GST) GST is a broad-based tax of 10 per cent on the supply of most goods, services and anything else consumed in Australia, and the importation of goods into Australia.

GST credits See 'input tax credit'.

GST-free supply A GST-free supply is one in which the supplier is not required to charge the 10 per cent GST to the customer. However, the supplier can claim back the GST paid on any purchases made in making the supply.

GST group A GST group is two or more associated business entities that operate as a single business for GST purposes. One member of the group (called the 'representative member') completes activity statements and accounts for GST on behalf of the whole group.

input tax credit The credit claimed for the GST component of the price of goods or services acquired in carrying on an enterprise. A tax invoice is required to claim an input tax credit (except for purchases of $75 or less).

input-taxed supply An input-taxed supply is one in which the supplier is not required to charge the 10 per cent GST to the customer. However, unlike a GST-free supply, the supplier is not able to claim an input tax credit on the inputs used to produce the input-taxed supply.

invoice A document issued by a supplier who is not registered for GST. This document must still have an ABN, otherwise the payer is required to withhold 47 per cent of the gross amount and remit it to the ATO on the next BAS. See also *tax invoice.*

mixed supply Can be broken up into its separate parts, such as taxable, GST free or input taxed and taxed accordingly.

out-of-scope supply Out-of-scope supplies are those supplies that fall outside the scope of the GST Act. GST cannot be charged in respect of revenue and cannot be claimed back in respect of expenses. These expenses are not reported in the BAS.

price For GST purposes, the value of goods and services plus 10 per cent.

supply For GST purposes, the term 'supply' is very broad and includes the supply of services, provision of advice or information, a grant, assignment or surrender of real property, a creation, grant, transfer, assignment, a financial supply and an entry into or release from an obligation to do anything, to refrain from an act, or to tolerate an act or situation. Not all supplies are taxable.

taxable importation A good imported and entered into Australia for home consumption.

taxable supply A taxable supply is one for which the supplier is required to charge the 10 per cent GST to the customer. However, the supplier can claim the GST paid on any purchases incurred in making the supply.

tax invoice A document issued by a supplier who is registered for GST. This document should have the supplier's ABN and the amount of GST included in the supply. See also *invoice.*

tax period A tax period is a period for which an entity calculates its GST and lodges its BAS. A tax period is either quarterly or monthly depending on the entity's annual turnover. Quarterly tax periods end on 30 September, 31 December, 31 March and 30 June. Monthly tax periods end on the last day of each calendar month.

value For GST purposes, 10/11 of the price of the goods or services.

QUESTIONS

13.1 What is the GST? Who charges the GST and who ultimately pays the GST? Why is the GST commonly referred to as a 'consumption tax'?

13.2 What is a taxable supply? What are the criteria that must be met before an entity can charge GST?

13.3 What is a GST-free supply? Please provide three examples of GST-free supplies.

13.4 What is an input-taxed supply? Please provide three examples of input-taxed supplies.

13.5 What is a creditable acquisition? What are the criteria that must be met before an entity can claim back input tax credits?

13.6 What are the main features of the GST general anti-avoidance rule?

13.7 What are the two attribution methods for GST? Does an entity have a choice as to which methods it adopts?

13.8 What are the two tax periods for GST purposes? Does an entity have a choice as to which methods it adopts?

13.9 What is the difference between an 'invoice' and a 'tax invoice'?

13.10 What is the difference between the GST rules for vouchers with a stated monetary value and those without a stated monetary value?

PROBLEMS

13.11 Dodgy Deals provides spare parts to Earnest Enterprises for $11 000, including $1000 GST. Six months later, Earnest Enterprises discovers that 25 per cent of the spare parts are defective, and receives a refund from Dodgy Deals of $2750, including $250 GST.

What accounting treatment is required, and what documentation must be kept?

13.12 Styx Pty Ltd is an Australian furniture manufacturer that makes furniture and sells it directly to retailers. One of their major retailers is Southern Cross Furniture Ltd. (SCF).

Both Styx Pty Ltd and Southern Cross Furniture Ltd (SCF) are registered for GST.

Consider the following diagram.

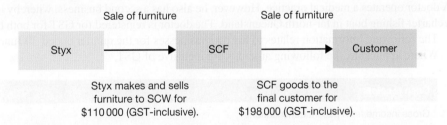

Calculate the net GST payable/(refundable) to SCF in the following circumstances. Assume that SCF is registered for the GST.

(a) SCF sells the furniture to a customer in Australia.

(b) SCF exports the furniture to a customer in China.

13.13 Kiwi, a New Zealand business, regularly imports goods into Australia, and is registered for GST. Under a contract for the sale of goods to Emu, an Australian business, Kiwi imports the goods and installs them at Emu's premises. Emu pays a GST-inclusive price of $110 000. The customs value plus transport, insurance and duty is $70 000.

Platypus, which deals in exports, is a related Australian company of Emu. Platypus currently has a contract to build and export a machine. Payments are to be made in two instalments. The first instalment is invoiced on 1 March 2022 and paid on 30 March 2022. The second instalment is invoiced on 1 May 2022 and payable on 30 May 2022. The machine is actually exported on 15 June 2022. What are the GST implications?

13.14 Jonathan Davies is a lawyer who operates as a sole practitioner in Brisbane. He also owns several residential rental properties, which he rents out to tenants.

Jonathan is registered for GST and uses the GST cash basis. He has elected to lodge his business activity statements on a quarterly basis with the ATO.

The following information relates to his two businesses for the quarter ended 30 June 2022.

Where applicable, the following amounts are inclusive of GST.

Cash receipts	$
Gross income from legal services	165 000
Gross income from residential rent	15 000
Interest income (arising from the maturity of a term deposit with the bank)	180
Gross proceeds from sale of a laptop computer used in the legal practice	300

Cash payments	$
Purchase of new motor vehicle used in the legal practice	82 000
Commercial rent paid for the legal practice	16 500
Wages paid to legal receptionist	15 000
Depreciation expense on plant and equipment used in the legal practice	2 750
Bank charges on legal practice's bank account	100
Superannuation for legal receptionist @ 10%	1 500
Purchase of a new dishwasher for one of his rental properties	1 250
University tuition fee for undertaking a Master of Law at QUT	3 600

Additional information
- Jonathan maintained a log book for 12 weeks. According to this log book, the vehicle was used 60 per cent of the time for business purposes and 40 per cent of the time for private purposes.
- Calculate the net GST payable/(refundable) to the ATO for the quarter ended 30 June 2022.
- You can assume that Jonathan holds valid tax invoices for all relevant payments.

13.15 A doctor operates a medical practice. However, he also has a second business, whereby he operates a charter fishing boat in far-north Queensland. The doctor is registered for GST for both businesses. The following information relates to his two businesses for the quarter ended 30 June 2022. Where applicable, the following amounts are inclusive of GST.

Cash receipts	$
Gross income from patient consultations	88 000
Gross income from charter boat business	33 000
Franked dividends	1 100
Income from managed fund	440
Gross proceeds from sale of medical equipment used in the business	3 520

Cash payments	$
Purchase of new computer for doctor's surgery	3 300
Wages and superannuation paid to nurse and receptionist	28 000
Depreciation expense on medical equipment	2 750
Rent, electricity and telephone expenses relating to medical surgery	11 000
Bank charges on business bank account	330
Fresh fruit, salad and vegetables for catering on the charter boat	1 650

Cold chicken and fresh bread for catering on the charter boat	880
Fuel and repairs and maintenance relating to charter boat	4 400
Management fee charged by financial planner for managed fund investment	2 200

Calculate the net GST payable/(refundable) to the ATO for the quarter ended 30 June 2022. You can assume that the taxpayer holds valid tax invoices for all relevant payments.

ACKNOWLEDGEMENTS

Figures 13.4, 13.10, 13.11, 13.13, 13.14: © Australian Taxation Office
Figure 13.12: © Federal Register of Legislation. Licensed under CC BY 4.0.
Example 13.10: © Australian Taxation Office
Appendix: © Australian Taxation Office
Extracts: © Federal Register of Legislation. Licensed under CC BY 4.0.

APPENDIX
Business activity statement

A

Office use only

41891119

Business activity statement

Document ID

ABN

Form due on

Payment due on

GST accounting method

Contact phone number

Authorised contact person who completed the form

HOW TO LODGE

This form can be lodged online. Visit ato.gov.au/general/online-services
- Individuals and sole traders can lodge online via their myGov account.
- Businesses can use the secure portal or Standard Business Reporting (SBR) enabled software.

If lodging by paper:
- print clearly using a black pen
- use whole dollars or '0' (zero)
- do not use n/a, nil, negative figures or symbols.

Goods and services tax (GST)

Complete Option 1 OR 2 OR 3 (indicate one choice with an X)

Option 1: Calculate GST and report quarterly

Total sales
(G1 requires 1A completed) **G1** $ .00

Does the amount shown at G1 include GST? (indicate with **X**)   Yes   No

Export sales **G2** $ .00

Other GST-free sales **G3** $ .00

Capital purchases **G10** $ .00

Non-capital purchases **G11** $ .00

Report GST on sales at 1A and GST on purchases at 1B in the Summary section over the page

OR

Option 2: Calculate GST quarterly and report annually

Total sales
(G1 requires 1A completed) **G1** $ .00

Does the amount shown at G1 include GST? (indicate with **X**)   Yes   No

Report GST on sales at 1A and GST on purchases at 1B in the Summary section over the page

OR

Option 3: Pay GST instalment amount quarterly

G21 $

Write the G21 amount at 1A in the Summary section over the page (leave 1B blank)

OR if varying this amount, complete G22, G23, G24

Estimated net GST for the year **G22** $ .00

Varied amount payable for the quarter **G23** $ .00

Write the G23 amount at 1A in the Summary section over the page (leave 1B blank)

Reason code for variation **G24**

NAT 4189-11.2019 [DE-9137]

PAYG tax withheld

Total salary, wages and other payments	**W1**	$ ▢▢▢▢▢▢▢ . ▢▢
Amount withheld from payments shown at W1	**W2**	$ ▢▢▢▢▢▢▢ . ▢▢
Amount withheld where no ABN is quoted	**W4**	$ ▢▢▢▢▢▢▢ . ▢▢
Other amounts withheld (excluding any amount shown at W2 or W4)	**W3**	$ ▢▢▢▢▢▢▢ . ▢▢
Total amounts withheld (W2 + W4 + W3)	**W5**	$ ▢▢▢▢▢▢▢ . ▢▢

Write the W5 amount at 4 in the Summary section below

Reason for varying (G24 & T4)	Code	Obligation
Change in investments	21	PAYG only
Current business structure not continuing	22	GST & PAYG
Significant change in trading conditions	23	GST & PAYG
Internal business restructure	24	GST & PAYG
Change in legislation or product mix	25	GST & PAYG
Financial market changes	26	GST & PAYG
Use of income tax losses	27	PAYG only

PAYG income tax instalment

Complete Option 1 OR 2 (indicate one choice with **X**)

☐ **Option 1: Pay a PAYG instalment amount quarterly**

T7 $ ▢▢▢▢▢▢▢

Write the T7 amount at 5A in the Summary section below
OR if varying this amount, complete T8, T9, T4

Estimated tax for the year	**T8**	$ ▢▢▢▢▢▢▢ . ▢▢
Varied amount payable for the quarter	**T9**	$ ▢▢▢▢▢▢▢ . ▢▢

Write the T9 amount at 5A in the Summary section below

Reason code for variation	**T4**	▢▢

OR

☐ **Option 2: Calculate PAYG instalment using income times rate**

PAYG instalment income	**T1**	$ ▢▢▢▢▢▢▢ . ▢▢
	T2	▢▢▢ %
OR New varied rate	**T3**	▢▢▢ . ▢▢ %
T1 x T2 (or x T3)	**T11**	$ ▢▢▢▢▢▢▢ . ▢▢

Write the T11 amount at 5A in the Summary section below

Reason code for variation	**T4**	▢▢

Summary

Amounts you owe the ATO

GST on sales or GST instalment	**1A**	$ ▢▢▢▢▢▢▢ . ▢▢
PAYG tax withheld	**4**	$ ▢▢▢▢▢▢▢ . ▢▢
PAYG income tax instalment	**5A**	$ ▢▢▢▢▢▢▢ . ▢▢
Deferred company/fund instalment	**7**	$ ▢▢▢▢▢▢▢ . ▢▢
1A + 4 + 5A + 7	**8A**	$ ▢▢▢▢▢▢▢ . ▢▢

Amounts the ATO owes you

GST on purchases	**1B**	$ ▢▢▢▢▢▢▢ . ▢▢

Do not complete 1B if using GST instalment amount (Option 3)

Credit from PAYG income tax instalment variation	**5B**	$ ▢▢▢▢▢▢▢ . ▢▢
1B + 5B	**8B**	$ ▢▢▢▢▢▢▢ . ▢▢

Payment or refund?

Is 8A more than 8B?
(indicate with **X**)

☐ Yes, then write the result of **8A minus 8B** at 9. **This amount is payable to the ATO.**

☐ No, then write the result of **8B minus 8A** at 9. **This amount is refundable to you** (or offset against any other tax debt you have).

Your payment or refund amount

9 $ ▢▢▢▢▢▢▢ . ▢▢

🛈 Do not use symbols such as +, −, /, $

Declaration I declare that the information given on this form is true and correct, and that I am authorised to make this declaration. The tax invoice requirements have been met.

Signature _____ Date __ / __ / __

Return this completed form to

🛈 Taxation laws authorise the ATO to collect information including personal information about individuals who may complete this form. For information about privacy and personal information go to **ato.gov.au/privacy**. Activity statement instructions are available from **ato.gov.au** or can be ordered by phoning **13 28 66**.

Australian Government
Australian Taxation Office

Source: Australian Taxation Office, 'Business activity statement' https://www.ato.gov.au/uploadedFiles/Content/CAS/downloads/BUS25189Nat4235s.pdf.

Note: In the summary section of the BAS (calculating your PAYG and GST instalments), the Treasurer announced in the 2022 Federal Budget that a 2 per cent uplift rate would apply to small to medium enterprises who are eligible to use the relevant instalment method (i.e. those with $10 million annual aggregated turnover for GST instalments and $50 million for PAYG instalments) in respect of instalments that relate to the 2022–23 tax year and fall due after legislation has been passed.[22]

---

22 Australian Government, *Budget 2022–23 Budget Measures* (Budget Paper No 2, 29 March 2022) 29.

CHAPTER 14

Tax administration, tax avoidance and tax evasion

LEARNING OBJECTIVES

After studying this chapter, you should be able to:

14.1 describe key aspects of our tax administration system

14.2 explain the difference between tax avoidance and tax evasion

14.3 describe the nature of shams and explain the action that should be taken against them

14.4 explain the operation of Australia's specific anti-avoidance rules

14.5 explain the operation of Australia's general anti-avoidance rule

14.6 explain the operation of Australia's multinational anti-avoidance rule and diverted profits tax

14.7 understand the ethical consequences of tax avoidance and evasion, particularly for tax advisers.

Overview

The first section of this chapter describes the key aspects of our tax administration system, with a particular focus on the increasing use of technology in tax administration. Attention in the next part of the chapter shifts to describing the difference between tax avoidance and tax evasion. The chapter then discusses shams — schemes intended to avoid tax, but that fail to do so.

The fourth, fifth and sixth sections of the chapter discuss those aspects of the Australian income tax legislation that are designed to prevent taxpayers engaging in tax avoidance. First, we briefly review specific anti-avoidance provisions intended to prevent certain types of tax avoidance and that target only one type of scheme. Then we examine the general anti-avoidance rule intended to prevent tax avoidance that is not covered by specific anti-avoidance rules — it is designed to operate on numerous tax avoidance schemes (even ones that have not been invented yet). We will discuss what constitutes a tax avoidance scheme under Australia's income tax legislation and what the consequences are for taxpayers who engage in those types of schemes. We will also discuss the multinational anti-avoidance rule and the diverted profits tax rules, which are both designed to prevent large multinationals from avoiding paying Australian income tax on income earned through their activities in Australia.

In the final section of the chapter, we will briefly touch on the possible ethical and legal implications for tax advisers when faced with situations involving possible tax evasion or avoidance.

14.1 Tax administration

LEARNING OBJECTIVE 14.1 Outline the basics of the Australian tax administration system.

14.1.1 Overview of our self-assessment system

The Australian income tax system is a 'self-assessment' system.[1] This means that the onus is on the taxpayer to calculate their tax liability and lodge an accurate and complete annual tax return containing all the information supporting that assessment of tax liability. The ATO will usually accept this information as accurate and issue a Notice of Assessment confirming the taxpayer's tax liability for that particular period. This is consistent with section 169A(1) of the ITAA36:

> Where a return of income of a taxpayer of a year of income is furnished to the Commissioner (whether or not by the taxpayer), the Commissioner may, for the purposes of making an assessment in relation to the taxpayer under this Act, accept, either in whole or in part, a statement in the return of the assessable income derived by the taxpayer and of any allowable deductions or rebates to which it is claimed that the taxpayer is entitled and any other statement in the return or otherwise made by or on behalf of the taxpayer.

An *assessment* is defined in section 6(1)(a) of the ITAA36 as the ascertainment by the Commissioner of the amount of taxable income and the tax payable on that income and any applicable tax offsets for a taxpayer. The Commissioner is empowered to make assessments by section 166 of the ITAA36. Section 166 states:

> From the returns, and from any other information in the Commissioner's possession, or from any one or more of these sources, the Commissioner must make an assessment of:
>
> (a) the amount of the taxable income (or that there is no taxable income) of any taxpayer; and
> (b) the amount of the tax payable thereon (or that no tax is payable); and
> (c) the total of the taxpayer's tax offset refunds (or that the taxpayer can get no such refunds).

The majority of taxpayers must lodge an annual income tax return. Returns can be lodged as paper returns or e-returns. The 2020–21 ATO Annual Report shows that in 2020–21, 98.2 per cent of tax returns were lodged electronically.[2] Returns take a particular form and the ATO produces different forms for different taxpayers: individuals, companies, trusts, partnerships and superannuation funds.[3]

Returns must be lodged by 31 October following the end of the financial year. For example, for the financial year ending 30 June 2021, the taxpayer must have lodged their tax return by 31 October 2021. These time limits are contained in section 170 of the ITAA36.

---

1 Self-assessment was introduced in Australia in 1986.

2 Australian Taxation Office, *Annual Report 2021–21* (Web Page, 2021) 201 https://www.ato.gov.au/uploadedFiles/Content/CR/downloads/ATO_annual_report_2020-21.pdf.

3 The link to individual tax return forms is at: www.ato.gov.au/Forms.

It will be recalled from the discussion in earlier chapters that different deadlines and reporting periods apply to different taxpayers and also with respect to different taxes. For example, in the case of FBT, the reporting period is 1 April to 31 March. In the case of the goods and serivces tax (GST), most businesses are required to report on a quarterly basis within 28 days after the end of the relevant quarter (e.g. the September quarter return must be lodged by the 28 October).

Penalties and interest can apply to late lodgments. The applicable penalty varies depending on a number of factors, including the turnover of the relevant taxpayer.[4] However, the base penalty for failing to lodge a return on time is 1 penalty unit for each period of 28 days or part of a period of 28 days starting on the day when the document is due and ending when the document is lodged (up to a maximum of 5 penalty units).[5]

Taxpayers using e-filing have pre-filled information in their tax returns (e.g. information received by the ATO from health funds, banks, employers and other government agencies).[6] This information may relate to interest income earned, company dividends, and welfare payments received during the financial year.

Many taxpayers use the services of a tax agent to prepare and lodge their tax return. Tax agents use lodgement programs which allow for a spreading of their workload throughout the year and effectively extend the deadline for lodging tax returns for taxpayers using their services.[7] However, it should be noted that even when using a tax agent, the responsibility for accuracy and completeness of the tax information lodged remains with the taxpayers who must sign and declare as to the truth and correctness of the return prior to lodgment.

14.1.2 Amending assessments

The ATO has power to amend the tax assessment of the taxpayer. Different timeframes for amending a tax assessment apply in different circumstances as follows.

- *Individuals and 'small business entities':* 2 years. Note that prior to 1 July 2021, the two year time limit applied to 'small business entities' with an annual turnover of under $10 million. However for income years starting on or after 1 July 2021, the 2 year time limit will also apply to businesses with an annual turnover of between $10 million and $50 million. As a result, the time limit for amending a tax assessment will be two years for most taxpayers.
- *Other taxpayers:* 4 years. This includes taxpayers who are running a business in excess of the small business entity threshold turnover, and trustees of trusts (unless the trust is a small business entity). The 4 year time limit also applies in situations where it is reasonable for the Commissioner to conclude that there has been tax avoidance in accordance with Part IVA of the ITAA36 (discussed in detail later in this chapter).
- *In cases of fraud or evasion:* No time limit. This means that where the Commissioner is of the opinion that there has been fraud or evasion, the Commissioner can amend the assessment at any time in future if fraud or evasion is detected.[8]

Amendments are often the consequence of an audit or other compliance monitoring activity that has found errors, omissions or other inaccuracies in a taxpayer's return. Audits can take the form of limited requests for clarification or further information right through to lengthy physical audits by tax officers. The ATO are also conducting e-audits to analyse electronic records of taxpayers.[9]

14.1.3 Record-keeping and substantiation

The integrity of the tax assessment system depends on taxpayers keeping complete financial records and being able to substantiate their calculation of their tax liability, including records of their income and the expenses incurred in earning that income. The general record-keeping requirements are contained in section 262A of the ITAA36 and section 382-5 of Schedule 1 of the TAA53.[10]

---

4 Administrative penalties in Division 286, Schedule 1 of the TAA53. The penalty unit rate since 1 July 2020 is $222.

5 Section 286-80(2) Schedule 1 of the TAA53.

6 Information about pre-filling is available at: https://www.ato.gov.au/individuals/Your-tax-return/in-detail/pre-fill-availability.

7 A link to a list of various lodgement deadlines for tax professionals is at: www.ato.gov.au/Tax-professionals/Prepare-and-lodge/Due-dates.

8 These time limits are contained in section 170 of the ITAA36.

9 Further information about the audit process can be found at: https://www.ato.gov.au/Business/Privately-owned-and-wealthy-groups/What-you-should-know/Tailored-engagement/Audits.

10 Further information about substantiation requirements is available at: https://www.ato.gov.au/individuals/income-and-deductions/records-you-need-to-keep.

Written records must be kept for 5 years from the date of lodging a tax return. Records in digital form are acceptable provided they are readily accessible and in English, or convertible into English. Failures to keep records required by the law can result in an administrative penalty under section 288-25 of Schedule 1 of the TAA53.[11] Section 298-20 of Schedule 1 to the TAA53 allows the Commissioner to remit all or part of the penalty imposed under section 288-25.

Records substantiating income include payment summaries or income tax statements from employers, bank records showing payments of interest, company statements recording payments of dividends, and statements from property agents recording rental income. As we have seen in earlier chapters, different forms of expenses have special substantiation requirements. Examples include special rules for substantiating car expenses such as log book records and special rules for substantiating travel expenses such as travel diaries.

If you accidentally lose your records or have them destroyed (e.g. in a flood or fire) the ATO may accept copies or may permit claiming relevant expenses if you can satisfy them you took reasonable precautions to prevent the loss or destruction of the records and it is not reasonably possible to obtain a copy of the records.

14.1.4 Tax rulings and determinations

The Commissioner of Taxation can issue **rulings** setting out the Commissioner's interpretation and position on the meaning and application of particular tax laws. The aim is:

> ... to provide a way for you to find out the Commissioner's view about how certain laws administered by the Commissioner apply to you so that the risks to you of uncertainty when you are self-assessing or working out your tax obligations or entitlements are reduced.[12]

There are two main categories of rulings: 'public rulings' and 'private rulings'. Public rulings are general in nature and do not apply to a specific taxpayer.

Private rulings are rulings provided on request by a taxpayer seeking the view of the ATO on a particular tax issue being contemplated by the taxpayer. A taxpayer must use a specific form for their application. Care must be taken to ensure full disclosure of all relevant facts and information to enable the Commissioner to make an accurate ruling and one which can subsequently be relied upon by the taxpayer. A taxpayer has a right to object against a private ruling decision they are unhappy about. Rulings are typically in writing, although taxpayers can seek oral rulings; however, oral rulings cannot be objected against.

There are also class rulings which apply to particular classes of taxpayer (e.g. a particular public company's shareholders concerning a company proposal) and product rulings (e.g. rulings concerning particular investment schemes or products). Most of the rulings you have encountered in this book are public rulings. Rulings are 'binding' on the Commissioner.[13] This means that if a taxpayer relies on a ruling and correctly follows the interpretation of the law set out in the ruling, they will be protected against having to pay penalties if the ruling turns out to be incorrect or the Commissioner subsequently changes their opinion. The Commissioner can also issue **tax determinations** which operate in a similar way to rulings except they usually relate to more confined or specific matters. These can be identified because their names usually start with the letters 'TD' whereas tax rulings start with the letters 'TR'. The names of rulings also usually include the year the ruling was made; for instance, the ruling recording the Commissioner's interpretation of the operation of the rulings system is 'TR 2006/10' — this tells you it was the 10th public ruling issued in 2006.

14.1.5 The Commissioner's information-gathering powers

The Commissioner of Taxation has a range of significant powers to effectively carry out their important tax administration functions. It is important to have a basic awareness of the nature and scope of these powers. Some of the most significant are the information-gathering powers of the Commissioner.

Section 353-15 of the TAA53 authorises the ATO to enter any land or building in order to access taxpayer books, documents or other property to make tax enquiries. These powers extend to computerised records.

---

11 The penalty under section 288-25 is 20 penalty units. The penalty unit rate since 1 July 2020 is $222.
12 TAA53 section 357-5 Schedule 1.
13 TAA53 section 257-60 Schedule 1.

The ATO can take copies of documents while they are there. Limits on the powers of the ATO to access information include limits on the ability to seize information without consent. In addition, the ATO will usually give notice of their intentions unless there is a real risk that information will be destroyed if advance notice is provided.

Information-recording correspondence with legal advisors is protected by 'legal professional privilege' which means the ATO is not permitted access to this correspondence. There is a similar privilege applying to correspondence with accounting advisors containing tax advice, known as the 'accountants' concession'.

It should be noted that the accountants' concession is an administrative concession made by the ATO (not a legal requirement). In other words, the Commissioner has the legal power to request access to documents relating to a taxpayer's affairs prepared by a professional accounting advisor. However, the Commissioner accepts that there are some documents which should, in all but exceptional circumstances, remain confidential between a taxpayer and their professional accounting advisers. The reasoning is that taxpayers should be able to consult with their professional accounting advisers on a confidential basis in respect of their rights and obligations under taxation laws to enable full and frank discussion and for advice to be communicated freely and without reservation.[14]

It should be noted that the accountants' concession only applies to advice received from independent professional accounting advisers external to the taxpayer (i.e. not to 'in-house' accountants). The concession also does not extend to most 'source documents' — documents which record a transaction or arrangement entered into by a taxpayer. The concession is not automatic and must be applied for.[15]

Further evidence and information gathering powers are contained in section 353-10 of the *TAA53*. This provision empowers the ATO to compel production of information or provision of evidence they require to carry out their statutory duties. This includes information both concerning the individual from which the information is sought or information concerning others (i.e. taxpayers to whom the individual has provided advice).

Effectively, these powers override the duty of confidentiality owed to third parties by those from whom information is sought. They also override the 'privilege against self-incrimination' — the right that applies in most cases (e.g. in criminal matters) that allows an individual to refuse to answer questions on the basis that the answers might incriminate her or him. The justification for this broad power was explained in *Commissioner of Taxation v De Vonk*:

> If the argument were to prevail that the privilege against self-incrimination was intended to be retained in tax matters, it would be impossible for the Commissioner to interrogate a taxpayer about sources of income since any question put on that subject might tend to incriminate the taxpayer by showing that the taxpayer had not complied with the initial obligation to return all sources of income. Such an argument would totally stultify the collection of income tax.[16]

14.1.6 Taxpayer rights and obligations

Taxpayers have a set of rights and obligations that establish basic principles for how the ATO will deal with them and how they must deal with the ATO. These are described in some detail in the following sections.

14.1.6.1 Objections and appeals

Taxpayers dissatisfied with a tax assessment or private tax ruling decision can lodge an objection. A taxation objection is a statutory right to dispute certain assessments, determinations, notices or decisions of the Commissioner. Most objections under Part IVC of the TAA53 involve assessments.[17] Subsection 175A(1) of the ITAA36 states: 'A taxpayer who is dissatisfied with an assessment made in relation to the taxpayer may object against it in the manner set out in Part IVC of the *Taxation Administration Act 1953*.'

---

14 The Commissioner's guidelines on the application of the Accountants' Concession can be found here: Australian Taxation Office, *Guidelines to accessing professional accounting advisers' papers* (Web Page) https://www.ato.gov.au/General/Gen/Guidelines-to-accessing-professional-accounting-advisers--papers.

15 The relevant application form can be found here: https://www.ato.gov.au/uploadedFiles/Content/CR/downloads/ATOC_37615_AC1form.pdf.

16 *Commissioner of Taxation v De Vonk* (1995) 61 FCR 564, 583.

17 Note that objections under Part IVC are not limited to assessments. Section 14ZL of Part IVC of the TAA53 states: '(1) This Part applies if a provision of an Act … provides that a person who is dissatisfied with an assessment, determination, notice or *decision*, or with a failure to make a private ruling, may object against it in the manner set out in this Part. (2) Such an objection is in this Part called a *taxation objection*' [emphasis added]. The ATO also lists on their website the various types of decisions against which taxpayers can object: https://www.ato.gov.au/General/dispute-or-object-to-an-ato-decision/object-to-an-ato-decision/decisions-you-can-object-to-and-time-limits.

Note that there are some decisions of the Commissioner that cannot be objected to (e.g. decision to commence an audit) as the right to object only arises in relation to decisions set out in Part IVC of the TAA53.

Insofar as objections to income tax assessments are concerned, the time frame in which a taxpayer must object generally corresponds with the relevant period of amendment of tax assessments by the ATO applicable under section 170 of the ITAA36 (i.e. generally either 2 years or 4 years from the date of service of the relevant notice of assessment, depending on the taxpayer and circumstances as discussed earlier in this chapter).

A variety of different timeframes apply for different types of objections and to objections concerning different taxes. Insofar as many other taxation decisions are concerned, a 60-day time limit usually applies. For example, a taxpayer wishing to object to an amended assessment generally has only 60 days from the date of service of the amended notice of assessment to lodge any objection to particulars of the amendment. Table 14.1 provides a general outline of the various time frames.[18]

TABLE 14.1

If the taxpayer is objecting against:	Then the objection must be lodged with ATO within:	Legislation
an original income tax assessment	A period effectively corresponding with the period during which the taxpayer can amend the assessment in situations not involving fraud or evasion (i.e. 2 years or 4 years from the date of service of the assessment, depending on the taxpayer and circumstances)	Section 14ZW(1)(aa) TAA53 Section 170(1) ITAA36
an amended taxation decision — limited to the particulars of alteration or addition*	The later of: 60 days after the amended decision served OR applicable 2 or 4 years after original decision served	Sections 14ZW(1B) and 14ZW(1BA) TAA53 Section 14ZV TAA53
other determinations, notices or decisions	60 days after notice of decision served	Section 14ZW(1)(c) TAA53
an income tax private ruling	The later of: 60 days after the private ruling was made OR applicable 2 or 4 years from last day to lodge tax return	Section 14ZW(1A) TAA53
the Commissioner's failure to make a private ruling	60 days after the end of the 30-day period referred to in that subsection	Subsection 359-50(3) Schedule 1 TAA53 Section 14ZW(1)(ba) TAA53

* If an objection is made against an amended assessment, the taxpayer can only object to those alterations or additions of the amended Notice of Assessment. However, the taxpayer retains their objection rights to the unamended assessment, subject to their original period of review (2 or 4 years).

Objections must include full and detailed information to enable a decision on the objection to be made. This means it is not sufficient to simply complain that the tax assessed was too high; there must be sufficient facts and reasons provided to support that proposition.

The objection must also be made in the manner prescribed in section 14ZU of the TAA53.[19] In essence, the objection must be in the approved form, to be lodged within the prescribed timeframe, and clearly detail the grounds for the objection.

Pursuant to section 14ZY of the TAA53, the Commissioner, having received a valid objection can decide to either allow the objection in full or in part or to disallow the objection. The objection decision must be made within 60 days and communicated to the taxpayer (section 14ZY(3) TAA53). If the Commissioner fails to make a decision within 60 days, the taxpayer can request in writing that the Commissioner make a

---

18 For an expanded version of the table incorporating timeframes for objecting to decisions relating to taxes other than income tax see: https://www.ato.gov.au/General/dispute-or-object-to-an-ato-decision/object-to-an-ato-decision/decisions-you-can-object-to-and-time-limits.
19 A link to the Objection Form is here: https://www.ato.gov.au/forms/objection-form---for-taxpayers.

decision (section 14ZYA(2) TAA53). If the Commissioner still does not make a decision within the next 60 days, the Commissioner is deemed to have disallowed the objection in full.

If the taxpayer is dissatisfied with an objection decision they may seek redress in accordance with section 14ZZ of the TAA53. This provision essentially provides that a taxpayer dissatisfied with the objection outcome can appeal to the Administrative Appeals Tribunal seeking a complete review of the decision (both the facts and the law) or appeal to the Federal Court on a question of error of law by the ATO. Appeal options were outlined in the opening chapter.

14.1.6.2 The Taxpayers' Charter

Australia has a **Taxpayers' Charter** setting out the basic rights and obligations of taxpayers and the service commitments of the ATO when dealing with taxpayers. Key rights recorded in the Charter include rights to privacy and confidentiality, rights to fair and reasonable treatment, and rights to complain and seek a review of ATO decisions. Key taxpayer obligations recorded in the Charter include the obligation to keep records, be truthful, take reasonable care, and lodge and pay taxes by due dates. Table 14.2 summarises the Charter rights and obligations.

TABLE 14.2   Taxpayers' Charter: summary of rights and obligations

Your rights — what you can expect from us	
Fair and reasonable	We will treat you with courtesy and respect and take your personal circumstances into account where relevant.
Honest	We treat you as being honest and give you an opportunity to explain any discrepancies.
Professional service and assistance	We will: • provide advice that meets your needs • explain our responses to your enquiries and requests • get back to you when we say we will and at a time that suits you • make sure you are dealing with someone who can help.
Representation	You can get help with your affairs and someone to deal with us on your behalf, but you must tell us who it's going to be. You are still responsible for ensuring the information given to us is accurate.
Privacy	We will respect your privacy and keep your personal information confidential.
Confidentiality	We take security and confidentiality of your information seriously. We ensure your data and online transactions are secure and safe.
Information access	We will: • update your personal information when you ask us to • give you access to information about you, if lawful • give you access to information that helps us make decisions.
Help	We aim to help you understand your rights and obligations. Contact us, or a professional adviser, if you are unsure.
Decisions	When making decisions about you we will: • inform you of your rights or obligations • keep you informed of our progress.
Your right to question	We will outline your options if you want a decision or action reviewed including, legal review rights and the formal complaint process. We will: • try to resolve problems quickly and fairly • keep you informed of progress.
Easy for you to comply	We will: • make your obligations and how to meet them easy to understand • develop products and services that fit with everyday use • design products and services with the community.
Accountability	We will inform you of any rights or obligations and keep you informed of our progress to resolve issues.

(continued)

TABLE 14.2 *(continued)*

Your obligations — what we expect of you	
Be truthful	We expect you to: • give us correct information and act within the law • give us all the relevant facts and circumstances • answer questions accurately, completely and honestly.
Keep records	We expect you to: • keep good records in English as required by law • keep records for five years.
Take reasonable care	We expect you to: • meet your obligations • be responsible for correct information, even if someone is representing you.
Lodge by the due date	We expect you to: • lodge all information on time • contact us before the due date if you cannot lodge on time.
Pay by the due date	We expect you to: • pay due amounts on time • contact us before the due date if you cannot pay on time.
Be cooperative	We expect you to treat us with the same courtesy, consideration and respect we are expected to give you.

Source: Australian Taxation Office, 'Taxpayers' Charter Essentials' https://www.ato.gov.au/About-ATO/Commitments-and-reporting/Taxpayers–Charter/Taxpayers–Charter—essentials.

14.1.7 Penalties for tax shortfalls

Errors and reckless or deliberate omissions leading to paying less than the amount of tax that should have been paid ('tax shortfall') can result in heavy penalties. Table 14.3 shows the various penalties which apply depending on the behaviour which led to the tax shortfall. These penalties are in addition to the amount of the shortfall and any interest that might be payable on the shortfall.

TABLE 14.3   Penalties for tax shortfalls

Behaviour	Base penalty
Failure to take reasonable care	25% of tax shortfall
Recklessness	50% of tax shortfall
Intentional disregard of the law	75% of tax shortfall

Failure to take reasonable care means not taking the degree of care expected of a taxpayer in similar circumstances. Recklessness is when a reasonable person in the same situation would have known there was a risk of a tax shortfall, but the taxpayer disregarded or was indifferent to that risk. Intentional disregard arises when the taxpayer is fully aware of a tax obligation but deliberately ignores that obligation.

The base penalties (percentage of the shortfall amount) are adjusted up or down depending on whether the taxpayer has hindered the ATO (or is a repeat offender) or has voluntarily disclosed any tax shortfall (with a greater downward adjustment if the voluntary disclosure was made before any audit of the taxpayer was commenced).

In addition to any possible penalties, a general interest charge (GIC) is payable on unpaid tax liabilities from the date the liability was due for payment until it and any accrued interest charge is paid. The GIC rate is adjusted quarterly. Table 14.4 shows the GIC rates for the 2020–21 financial year and for the first three quarters of the 2021–22 financial year available at the time of writing.

TABLE 14.4   General interest charge rates, 2020–21, 2021–22

Quarter	GIC annual rate	GIC daily rate
January–March 2022	7.04%	0.01928767%
October–December 2021	7.01%	0.01920548%
July–September 2021	7.04%	0.01928767%
April–June 2021	7.01%	0.01920548%
January–March 2021	7.02%	0.01923288%
October–December 2020	7.10%	0.01939891%
July–September 2020	7.10%	0.01939891%

Source: Australian Taxation Office, 'General interest charge (GIC) rates' www.ato.gov.au/Rates/General-interest-charge-(GIC)-rates.

A shortfall interest charge (SIC) is payable on any tax shortfall assessed as owing because of an amendment to an assessment. The SIC rate is adjusted quarterly. Table 14.5 shows the SIC rates for the 2020–21 financial year and for the first three quarters of the 2021–22 financial year available at the time of writing.

TABLE 14.5   Shortfall interest charge, 2020–21, 2021–22

Quarter	SIC annual rate	SIC daily rate
January–March 2022	3.04%	0.00832877%
October–December 2021	3.01%	0.00824657%
July–September 2021	3.04%	0.00832877%
April–June 2021	3.01%	0.00824657%
January–March 2021	3.02%	0.00827397%
October–December 2020	3.10%	0.00846994%
July–September 2020	3.10%	0.00846994%

Source: Australian Taxation Office, 'Shortfall interest charge (SIC) rates' www.ato.gov.au/Rates/Shortfall-interest-charge-(SIC)-rates.

Taxpayers can apply for remission from penalties or interest charges. The ATO will consider whether it is fair or reasonable for the interest or penalty to be reduced or completely cancelled. Factors which the ATO will consider include the taxpayer's compliance history, whether any tax shortfall was voluntarily disclosed by the taxpayer or discovered by the ATO, the reasons for the tax shortfall, whether the shortfall involved a deferral or complete avoidance of the shortfall amount, and the taxpayer's attitude to complying with tax laws.

14.1.8 Technology and tax administration

As noted in the first chapter of this book, technology is playing an increasingly important role in tax administration and interactions with the ATO. In particular, in the opening chapter, we outlined the digital forms of taxpayer and tax adviser interaction with the ATO. In this part we detail some of the main tools the ATO uses to administer the tax laws and ensure taxpayer compliance:

14.1.8.1 Benchmarking

The ATO uses industry benchmarks[20] to identify individuals and businesses that might be under-reporting their income. Industry benchmarks are particularly effective in aiding detection of individuals and businesses who may be accepting income in the form of cash and not reporting that cash income.

---

20 Australian Taxation Office, *Benchmarks by Industry* www.ato.gov.au/Business/Small-business-benchmarks/In-detail/Benchmarks-by-industry.

Information provided by small business taxpayers is compared to benchmarks for income and expenditure for the industry in which the taxpayer's business operates. The benchmarks are also used to calculate tax liability where inadequate (or no) records have been kept by the taxpayer. Example 14.1 demonstrates the use of benchmarking by the ATO.

EXAMPLE 14.1

Applying a benchmark ratio where there is a lack of records

We identified a computer retail business that was outside of the small business benchmarks along with other risks identified, using our data analysis modelling. The 'cost of sales to turnover' benchmark for a business in the computer retailing industry with a turnover of $200 001 to $600 000 per annum was 46 per cent to 59 per cent for the year being looked at. This business was reporting at 88 per cent to 96 per cent over a 3-year period. When asked, the business owner couldn't explain why they were reporting so far outside the benchmarks and had few reliable business records to substantiate amounts lodged. As the business didn't have evidence of their sales, purchases and other records, we decided to apply the benchmark ratio in line with our findings. This resulted in the business having to pay just under $110 000 in tax and more than $27 000 in penalties.

Source: Australian Taxation Office, 'How we use benchmarks' www.ato.gov.au/Business/Small-business-benchmarks/How-we-use-benchmarks.

14.1.8.2 Pre-filling

Pre-filling is the automatic population of labels in electronically prepared income tax returns. The ATO pre-fills a range of information in individual tax returns using data it accesses from other government agencies, financial institutions and employers. According to the ATO: 'In 2020–21, we used our data and analytics technology to pre-fill over 85 million pieces of data, including information relating to COVID-19 support measures for employees'.[21]

Typical pre-filled data in tax returns includes dividend income, salary and wage earnings, social welfare payments and bank interest. The ATO take the view that 'pre-filling makes it easier for our clients to meet their obligations and increases trust and confidence in the accuracy of final tax outcomes'.[22]

14.1.8.3 Nudging

Technology is increasingly being used in a proactive manner to prompt taxpayers to ensure they are complying with their tax obligations. One such tool is the use of 'nudges'. For example, in 2020–21, the ATO sent over 140 000 nudge messages to clients to consider the tax consequences of their cryptocurrency sales. In addition, it also provided over 360 000 real-time prompts to taxpayers to check amounts in their 2019–20 income tax returns.[23] A typical example of these real-time prompts might be a pop-up message while a taxpayer is completing their tax return letting them know that their work-related expense claims might be out of step with their peers.

14.1.8.4 Data matching

Increasingly, the ATO uses data matching to identify possible taxpayer reporting errors or omissions. This includes electronic cross-referencing of information reported from taxpayers with information from third parties such as other government departments, banks and financial institutions and employers. Many of these third parties (e.g. banks, employers and health funds) have legal obligations to report information to the ATO. According to the ATO, over 600 million transactions are reported annually. The ATO lists the following as examples of third-party sources and the information they provide.

- *Banks, financial institutions and investment bodies:* investment income
- *Employers:* payments to employees and contractors
- *State and Territory motor vehicle registering bodies:* motor vehicles sold, transferred or newly registered
- *State and Territory title offices and revenue agencies:* sales and other transfers of real property
- *Government bodies:* pensions, benefits, rebates, taxable grants and other payments

---

21 Australian Taxation Office, *Annual Report 2020/21* (Report, 2021) 29 https://www.ato.gov.au/uploadedFiles/Content/CR/downloads/ATO_annual_report_2020-21.pdf.
22 Ibid 44.
23 Ibid 29.

- *Australian Transaction Reports and Analysis Centre (AUSTRAC) and international treaty partners:* foreign source income
- *Online selling platforms:* quantity and value of online sales
- *Sharing economy facilitators:* payments to participants
- *Financial institutions providing merchant facilities and administrators of specialised payment systems:* electronic payments processed for business including total credit and debit card payments received
- *Stock exchanges and share registries:* share transactions
- *Businesses in the building and construction industry:* payments made for building and construction services
- *Health insurers:* confirmation of health insurance cover and premiums paid
- *Cryptocurrency designated service providers:* purchase and sale information.[24]

This information can also be used for risk profiling to ensure that any audit attention is directed to taxpayers with the highest risk of having underreported their tax liability.[25] Data matching is particularly useful in detecting undeclared interest and income in tax returns, and to ensure government payment receipts are recorded. It is also used to capture distributions from partnerships and trusts, capital gains from sales of shares and other property, and some foreign source income and contractor payments.

The ATO also conducts specific data matching programming targeting particular types of transactions and industries, to identify underreporting of income, black market activities and businesses that might not be lodging returns as required. The ATO is currently examining credit and debit card activities, specialised payment systems, online selling activities, ride-sourcing, motor vehicle registry transactions and cryptocurrency.

Insofar as cryptocurrency is concerned, the ATO explain why they have chosen to focus on crypto-transactions:

> The innovative and complex nature of cryptocurrencies can lead to a genuine lack of awareness of the tax obligations associated with these activities. Also, the pseudonymous nature of cryptocurrencies may make it attractive to those seeking to avoid their taxation obligations.
>
> As interest in cryptocurrency has increased, the ATO has worked with partners to:
>
> - understand the tax implications
> - plan an appropriate regulatory response.
>
> This ensures our approach is consistent with government policy and aligned to that of our partner agencies.
>
> The tax consequences for taxpayers acquiring or disposing of cryptocurrency vary depending on the nature and circumstances of the transaction.
>
> The cryptocurrency data-matching program will allow us to identify and address multiple taxation risks.
>
> - Capital gains tax (CGT) — If you acquire cryptocurrency as an investment, you may have to pay tax on any capital gain you make on disposal of the cryptocurrency. Disposal occurs when:
>   - selling cryptocurrency for fiat currency
>   - exchanging one cryptocurrency for another
>   - gifting cryptocurrency
>   - trading cryptocurrency
>   - using cryptocurrency to pay for goods or services.
> - Omitted or incorrect reporting of income — In some situations cryptocurrency transactions can also give rise to ordinary income. Taxpayers who trade cryptocurrency or businesses that accept cryptocurrency as payment have obligations to report the income generated in their tax returns.
> - Fringe benefits tax (FBT) — When employees receive cryptocurrency as remuneration under a salary sacrifice arrangement, the payment of the cryptocurrency is a fringe benefit.[26]

---

24 Australian Taxation Office, *How we use data* https://www.ato.gov.au/About-ATO/Commitments-and-reporting/In-detail/Privacy-and-information-gathering/How-we-use-data-matching/?anchor=Sources_of_thirdparty_information#Sources_of_third party_information.

25 Further information on the ATO's data matching activities is available here: https://www.ato.gov.au/About-ATO/Commitments-and-reporting/Information-and-privacy/Data-matching.

26 Australian Taxation Office, *Why we look at cryptocurrency* https://www.ato.gov.au/General/Gen/Cryptocurrency-2014-15-to-20 22-23-data-matching-program-protocol/?anchor=Programobjectives#Programobjectives.

14.1.8.5 Data analytics and artificial intelligence

All of the activities outlined prior utilise increasingly sophisticated uses of data analytics and artificial intelligence (AI)[27] by the ATO. A good illustration of these sophisticated uses of data analytics and AI is in the use of nudges to prompt compliance as previously outlined. Insofar as nudging is concerned, the ATO uses real-time analytics in prompting taxpayers while they are completing their electronic tax return. The ATO systems compare amounts entered into the tax return by the taxpayer with people in similar circumstances and industries as the data is being entered by the taxpayer. If a significant discrepancy is found, an automated message pops up, prompting the taxpayer to check their figures.

The process of issuing Notices of Assessment is also largely automated. Increasingly, this process is also being used proactively. For example, in 2020, the ATO automatically provided assessments and refunds to individual taxpayers over the age of 60 eliminating the need for those taxpayers to lodge a request for a tax refund.[28]

Data analytics and AI are also being extensively deployed by the ATO to improve its customer services. For example, speech recognition technology is used to transcribe call centre calls for quality assurance and to detect call patterns and trends. This information is then used be the ATO to better deploy resources and information to assist taxpayers. Machine learning algorithms are also used to monitor call volumes. This can assist in predicting call volume trends and, again, ensure efficient and effective use of ATO resources to deal with taxpayer queries. Intelligent machines are also being used by the ATO to assist in process and analyse data to inform and speed-up ATO decision making.

The ATO have also deployed an online AI-powered virtual assistant to deal with online queries from taxpayers and their advisers, known as 'Alex'. Alex is accessible via an 'Ask Alex' pop-up on the ATO website. Figure 14.1 is a screen shot of the 'Ask Alex' interface.

FIGURE 14.1   Ask Alex interface

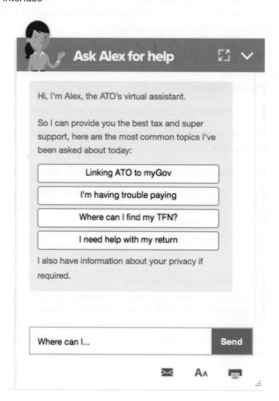

Source: Australian Taxation Office, *Ask Alex interface* https://www.ato.gov.au.

---

27 The concept of artificially intelligent or 'thinking' machines is not new — they were mooted by Turing in the 1950s: see Alan Turing, 'Computing Machinery and Intelligence' (1950) 49 *Mind* 433. Over time, however, artificial intelligence has become an ubiquitous and flexible umbrella term capturing a range of data analytics techniques of various levels of sophistication. These various techniques endow machines with capabilities for independent problem-solving and decision-making which, to varying degrees, enhance or replicate human intelligence.

28 Australian Taxation Office, *How we use data and analytics* https://www.ato.gov.au/About-ATO/Commitments-and-reporting/ Information-and-privacy/How-we-use-data-and-analytics/#Deliveringgreaterautomationanddigitalser.

ATO data gathering of blockchain activity

Since 2019, the ATO has undertaken data matching on cryptocurrency transactions occurring from the 2014–15 income year.[29] In particular, purchase and sale information is obtained from cryptocurrency designated service providers (DSPs) and then matched against ATO records to assess whether taxpayers are meeting their compliance obligations.[30]

Depending on the DSP, all or a selection of the following information is obtained.

Client identification details		Cryptocurrency transaction details
Individuals	**Non-individuals**	**Cryptocurrency transaction details**
• Given and surname(s) (if more than one name on the account) • Date(s) of birth • Addresses (residential, postal, other) • Australian business number (if applicable) • Email address • Contact phone numbers • Social media account	• Business name • Addresses (business, postal, registered, other) • Australian business number • Contact name • Contact phone number • Email address	• Status of account (open, closed, suspended, lost etc.) • Linked bank accounts • Wallet address associated with the account • Lost or stolen (crypto)currency amounts linked to accounts • Unique identifier • Transaction date • Transaction time • Type of (crypto)currency • Amount (in fiat and cryptocurrency) • Type of transfer • Transfer description • Total account balance

Source: Australian Taxation Office, *How we use the data* (Web Page, 9 June 2021) https://www.ato.gov.au/General/Gen/Cryptocurrency-2014-15-to-2022-23-data-matching-program-protocol/?page=4#Clientidentificationdetailsindividuals.

The data-matching results in relevant taxpayers being contacted by the ATO. In 2021, the ATO sent letters to approximately 100 000 taxpayers regarding their cryptoassets and tax obligations and 'prompted' almost 300 000 to lodge their 2021 tax returns to report gains or losses from cryptoassets.[31] As Assistant Commissioner Tim Loh stated:

> We are alarmed that some taxpayers think that the anonymity of cryptocurrencies provides a licence to ignore their tax obligations … While it appears that cryptocurrency operates in an anonymous digital world, we closely track where it interacts with the real world through data from banks, financial institutions, and cryptocurrency online exchanges to follow the money back to the taxpayer.[32]

More generally, the ATO works with regulators, including the Australian Transaction Reports and Analysis Centre (AUSTRAC) and the Australian Securities and Investment Commission (ASIC).[33] In 2018, the Joint Chiefs of Global Tax Enforcement (J5) was established to fight international tax crime and money laundering, including cryptocurrency threats.[34] The J5 is made up of the ATO (Australia), Her Majesty's Revenue and Customs (UK), Internal Revenue Service Criminal Investigations (US), Canadian Revenue Agency (Canada) and the Dutch Fiscal Information and Investigation Service (Netherlands).[35]

▶

---

29 Australian Taxation Office, *Cryptocurrency 2014–15 to 2022–23 data-matching program protocol* (Web Page, 9 June 2021) https://www.ato.gov.au/General/Gen/Cryptocurrency-2014-15-to-2022-23-data-matching-program-protocol.

30 Ibid.

31 Australian Taxation Office, *Cryptocurrency under the microscope this time* (Web Page, 28 May 2021) https://www.ato.gov.au/Media-centre/Media-releases/Cryptocurrency-under-the-microscope-this-tax-time.

32 Ibid.

33 Australian Taxation Office, *ATO receives cryptocurrency data to assist tax compliance* (Web Page, 30 April 2019) https://www.ato.gov.au/Media-centre/Media-releases/ATO-receives-cryptocurrency-data-to-assist-tax-compliance.

34 Australian Taxation Office, *Joint Chiefs of Global Tax Enforcement* (Web Page, 1 November 2021) https://www.ato.gov.au/General/The-fight-against-tax-crime/Our-focus/Joint-Chiefs-of-Global-Tax-Enforcement.

35 Ibid.

14.2 The concepts of tax avoidance and tax evasion

LEARNING OBJECTIVE 14.2 Explain the difference between tax avoidance and tax evasion.

For as long as rulers and governments have been charging taxes, subjects and citizens have been working out ways of escaping them. Methods of doing so may be categorised as follows.

- Tax evasion — where a person reduces their tax liability fraudulently by being dishonest about their tax affairs.
- Tax avoidance — where a person reduces their tax liability in unacceptable ways by taking advantage of an error, omission or some ambiguity within the Income Tax Acts.
- Tax planning — where a person reduces their tax liability in generally acceptable ways by complying within the purpose of the law and making choices that the law allows.

These three approaches are plotted against a 'sliding scale' axis in figure 14.2.

FIGURE 14.2 Tax planning, avoidance and evasion

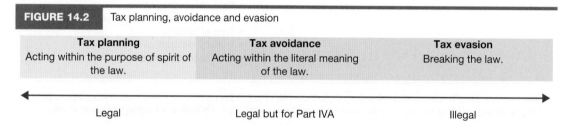

Tax evasion is the deliberate misstatement by a taxpayer of their tax status. For example, a taxpayer might seek to evade tax by underreporting their income. In contrast, tax avoidance and tax planning involve reducing one's tax through the operation of the tax laws themselves.

Since tax evasion involves deliberate fraud to a greater or lesser extent, it is an illegal activity and can result in criminal charges against the taxpayer under section 135 of the *Criminal Code Act 1995* (Cth). Examples include cash income not being reported to the ATO), deductions claimed when the taxpayer has not and will not spend the money, or a property sold where the capital gain should have been reported but was not.

The ATO attempts to detect tax evasion by matching statements that taxpayers have made to data gathered from elsewhere. With respect to cash income that goes unreported, the ATO may attempt to access the taxpayer's bank statements and search for cash deposits. With respect to a property disposal, the ATO can check with each State's Land Titles Office and match sales of property against statements made. Increasingly, data matching via technology is used to automatically flag apparent mismatches of information. The Commissioner of Taxation is given broad power to obtain information and evidence of this nature via Division 353 of Schedule 1 of the *Tax Administration Act 1953* (Cth). We discussed data matching earlier in the context of tax administration as discussed earlier in this chapter.

The most obvious form of tax evasion occurs through the cash economy. Here, taxpayers, typically in small business, receive cash for goods and services they provide without declaring it to the ATO. Documentary evidence of the transaction in the form of invoices and the like is absent. This is tax evasion since it represents blatant dishonesty about the income received. The ATO can attempt to gauge the level of a person's receipts by inspecting cash deposits in bank accounts. Alternatively, it can estimate likely levels of income from other aspects of the business which would line up with sales and services provided. For example, the ATO might estimate the amount of fish purchased by a fish and chip shop to estimate a dollar value for fish and chips sold. We discussed such activities in the context of our discussion of the use of benchmarking as a tax administration tool earlier in this chapter. Despite these courses of action, tracking down cash transfers is very difficult, and the cash economy continues to be a drain on tax revenues.

A notable example of tax evasion in Australia was the Bottom of the Harbour schemes of the 1970s. These schemes were notorious for allowing companies to evade significant amounts of tax on profits derived during the year, but before any tax liability had been created. Just before the end of the income tax year, the company would be stripped of all assets which were transferred to a new company where the business would continue. Shares in the old company would be owned for a short period by a promoter who facilitated this transfer, earning a fee in the process. After a short time, the company's shares would be sold to a financially vulnerable person who would then be made a scapegoat for the old company. The feature that makes this tax evasion is that the company is stripped of its ability to pay tax. The operation of a bottom of the harbour scheme is illustrated in figure 14.3.

FIGURE 14.3   The operation of a Bottom of the Harbour tax scheme

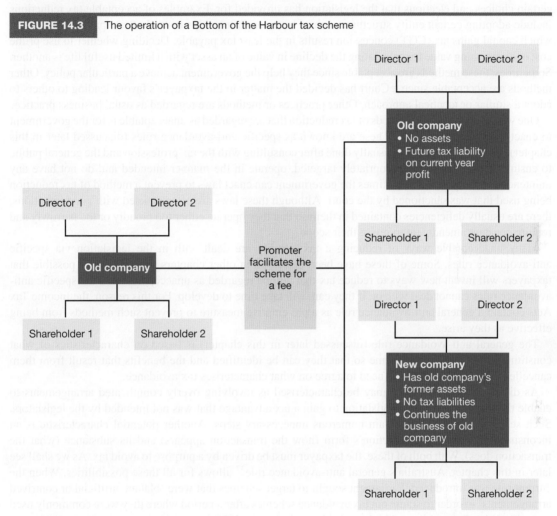

Note: Director 1 and Shareholder 1 can be the same person. Similarly, for the rest. Director 2 and shareholder 2 are people of limited means.

It is often said that **tax avoidance** involves compliance with the letter of the law rather than the spirit of the law (i.e. the intention of the law). In this way, the law is technically complied with, but not for the purposes for which it was enacted. To comply with tax laws outside its purpose to gain an advantage requires specific intent on the part of the taxpayer to arrange his or her affairs in an overly complicated manner to come within the operation of tax law that gives them some advantage. Sometimes, this involves making transactions appear to be something that they are not or labelling them superficially in a tax advantageous manner only becoming exposed by looking beneath the surface at the detail. Some examples of tax avoidance are discussed in the case excerpts in this chapter.

Even though tax avoidance and tax evasion are separate and distinct ways of reducing one's tax liability, the line between them can be blurred. Consider the Bottom of the Harbour schemes previously discussed. Schemes that involved the stripping of accumulated profits from earlier financial years, as opposed to stripping profits from the current year only, were not regarded as tax evasion since they did not amount to fraudulent conduct. Indeed, stripping of accumulated profits was regarded by the High

Court in cases like *Slutzkin v FCT*[36] as merely resulting in a realisation of profits associated with the shareholdings on which tax had already been paid. This contrasted with the stripping of current year profits on which tax had not yet been paid which successfully led to evasion of tax through having no assets to pay it. This subtle difference has led to the Bottom of the Harbour schemes being referred to as either tax evasion or avoidance, either correctly or incorrectly. Although the High Court in *Slutzkin* held that tax avoidance had not taken place, the case was decided under the predecessor of Part IVA, section 260, and criticism of the High Court in this case, among others, as well as the issues with the Bottom of the Harbour schemes, led to section 260 being replaced by Part IVA a few years later.

Tax planning, by contrast, involves reducing one's tax in generally acceptable ways through making certain choices and elections that the legislation has provided for. Examples of acceptable tax reductions include adopting certain entity structures such as trusts or partnerships instead of companies or selecting which capital gains tax (CGT) concession results in the least tax payable. Deciding whether to use prime cost or diminishing value for calculating the decline in value of an asset with a limited useful life is another. Sometimes, these methods are acceptable since they help the government achieve a particular policy. Other methods are acceptable since a Court has decided the matter in the taxpayer's favour leading to others to adopt a similar or identical approach. Other practices or methods are regarded as usual business practice.

One way of dealing with methods of tax reduction that are regarded as unacceptable is for the government to enact laws that target them. These are known as specific anti-avoidance rules (discussed later in this chapter). Enacting these laws is usually done after consulting with the tax profession and the general public to ensure that the laws are appropriately targeted, operate in the manner intended and do not have any unintended consequences. Sometimes the government can enact laws to prevent a method of tax reduction being used that was sanctioned by the court. Although these laws are often enacted with good intentions, there are usually deficiencies contained in them so that they operate either too broadly or too narrowly and require constant amendment to revise their scope.

Many unacceptable ways of reducing a tax liability are dealt with in the legislation via specific anti-avoidance rules. Some of these have been discussed in other chapters. However, it is possible that taxpayers will invent new ways to reduce tax that will be regarded as unacceptable that the specific anti-avoidance rules cannot deal with or, if they can, will take time to develop. For this reason, the Income Tax Acts contain a general anti-avoidance rule as a pre-emptive measure to prevent such methods from being effective as they arise.

The general anti-avoidance rule (discussed later in this chapter) is based on characteristics of what constitutes a tax avoidance scheme so that they can be identified and the benefits that result from them cancelled. To do this, legislators need to agree on what characterises tax avoidance.

As discussed, tax avoidance may be characterised as involving overly complicated arrangements to enable the taxpayer to use the legislation to gain a tax advantage that was not intended by the legislators. Such schemes will usually contain numerous unnecessary steps. Another potential characteristic is an inconsistency between a transaction's form (how the transaction appears) and its substance (what the transaction does). With both of these, the taxpayer must be driven by a purpose to avoid tax. As we shall see later in this chapter, Australia's general anti-avoidance rule[37] allows for all these possibilities. When the current rule was introduced, Parliament sought to target schemes that were 'blatant, artificial or contrived arrangements' in order to stamp out tax avoidance schemes after a period where they were commonly used to avoid tax by the wealthy and by large business during the 1970s.

Before using a specific or general anti-avoidance rule against a tax avoidance scheme, it is worthwhile considering whether the transaction achieves its desired or intended legal effect. If it does not, the transaction is a sham and an anti-avoidance rule is not required to defeat it. Shams are discussed in the next section.

14.3 Shams

LEARNING OBJECTIVE 14.3 Describe the nature of shams and explain the action that should be taken against them.

As mentioned earlier, before invoking an anti-avoidance rule against a tax avoidance scheme, consideration should be directed toward whether the scheme is a sham. A **sham** is a legally ineffective arrangement which

---

36 [1977] HCA 9. The link to this case is at: http://www8.austlii.edu.au/cgi-bin/viewdoc/au/cases/cth/HCA/1977/9.html.
37 Part IVA of the *Income Tax Assessment Act 1936* (Cth).

---

does not achieve what was intended due to some deficiency in acts undertaken and documents prepared. This is most obviously communicated in *Jaques v FCT*[38] (1924) 34 CLR 328 at 358, where Isaacs J said: 'A sham transaction is inherently worthless and needs no enactment to nullify it'.

The legal rights and obligations that were intended to be created and enforced did not eventuate. If the arrangement's purpose was to reduce tax, potentially making it a tax avoidance scheme, then a specific or general anti-avoidance rule is not required since these deficiencies prevent the transaction from reducing tax in the manner intended. Recognising shams is therefore important since they are inherently worthless as a tax avoidance device. In *Snook v London and West Riding Investments Ltd*,[39] Diplock J said:

> [Sham] means acts done or documents executed by the parties to the 'sham' which are intended by them to give to third parties or to the court the appearance of creating between the party's legal rights and obligations different from the actual legal rights and obligations (if any) which the parties intend to create.

The following case is a more recent example of a case involving arrangements characterised as a sham.

Case N40 81 ATC 197

Facts: The taxpayers were a husband and wife partnership that owned and managed a service station. They arranged for the creation (known as 'settlement' in legal terms) of a discretionary trust with themselves and their children as beneficiaries to take over management of the service station for a fee. This fee would be deductible to the partnership but assessable in the trust. The trust income could be distributed to the beneficiaries in a tax effective manner. While this was the intention of the arrangement, the trust did not provide any management services to the partnership and the husband and wife continued to manage the partnership as they always had. Nevertheless, funds were transferred from the partnership to the trust and accounting entries were done to record that transfer.

Held: The Board of Review held that the payment of the fees and the other transactions were a sham. Citing *Albion Hotel Pty Ltd v FCT* (1965) 13 ATD 435 as authority, a Board member said that journal entries do not make transactions, they should only record transactions that have occurred. Similarly, another member said the following (at 203): 'Nothing moved (except the accountant's pen) and nothing changed as a result of the alleged trust activities'.

Since the arrangement in *Case N40* 81 ATC 197 was a sham, no further action needed to be taken against it. The management fees that the partnership paid to the trust were not deductible to the partnership and were not assessable income to the trust. This means that the husband and wife continued to be assessed in the manner they were before the establishment of the trust. It is important to note that if the trust had provided management services to the service station partnership and was paid for those services at a commercial rate, the arrangement would not have been a sham. Such arrangements, properly effected, are quite common and are an example of effective tax planning as demonstrated by *FCT v Phillips*.[40]

Federal Commissioner of Taxation v Phillips [1978] FCA 28

Facts: The taxpayer was a partner in a national accounting firm. In 1971, the firm established a unit trust with the intention that the trust would provide administrative services to the firm (e.g. typing, secretarial and general clerical work, maintenance of share registers, photocopying and printing work, organisation of seminars and training courses, etc.). Furniture and office equipment of the firm were transferred into the trust and leased back to the firm. Administrative staff employed by the firm were terminated and then re-employed by the trust. The unit-holders were the spouses, family trusts and companies of the partners of the firm. The trust charged fees to the firm (at commercial rates) for the provision of the services and the taxpayer sought to claim a tax deduction for these expenses. The Commissioner contended that the arrangement was one intended to divert income from the firm the wives, dependents and other associates of the partners of the firm.

Held: The deductions were allowable. The Court accepted that there were good commercial reasons for the arrangement, apart from the tax savings it generated for the partners of the firm. In particular, the

---

38 The link to this case is at: http://www8.austlii.edu.au/cgi-bin/viewdoc/au/cases/cth/ArgusLawRp/1924/39.html?query=.
39 *Snook v London and West Riding Investments Ltd* [1967] 1 All ER 518, 528.
40 [1978] FCA 28.

> arrangements assisted in providing protection of the firm's assets in the event of the firm being sued for professional negligence. A key factual finding was that the service fees charged by the trust to the firm were not in excess of commercial rates.

In contrast, example 14.2 provides an illustration of a sham in a service trust situation.

EXAMPLE 14.2

Shams

Martha, a real estate developer, settled a discretionary trust with herself as trustee and herself and her spouse and children as beneficiaries. The intention of this arrangement was for the trust to derive the income from her real estate development business so that it could be distributed among her family at her discretion in accordance with their effective marginal rates of tax. Apart from settling the trust, no other documentation was prepared or actioned except for journal entries which were entered into the trust's accounts to record income and deductions against it.

Is this arrangement a sham? Why or why not? If it is a sham, what action is required to nullify the arrangement?

The arrangement is a sham since the trust did not acquire Martha's business. To be legally effective, Martha should have transferred her real estate development business into the trust. Since this did not occur, Martha continues to derive all the income from this business. Even though journal entries are made in the accounts of the trust, no action is required to be taken to negate such transactions since they do not record real events.

If the transaction is not a sham but is designed to reduce tax, then Australia's specific or general anti-avoidance rules may be used against the transaction to stop the tax reduction. These rules are discussed in detail in sections 14.4, 14.5 and 14.6.

14.4 Australia's specific anti-avoidance rules

LEARNING OBJECTIVE 14.4 Explain the operation of Australia's specific anti-avoidance rules.

As discussed earlier, Australia's tax legislation includes **specific anti-avoidance rules** that prevent various specific approaches to avoiding tax and **general anti-avoidance rules** intended to catch tax avoidance that is not covered by specific anti-avoidance rules. The specific anti-avoidance rules have priority over the general anti-avoidance rules.

Throughout the chapters, we have addressed specific anti-avoidance rules in context. Some of these include the following.

- Transfer pricing rules — Division 815 of the ITAA97 prevents multinational groups from manipulating tax liabilities across jurisdictions by taking advantage of different tax rates in those jurisdictions. These rules are elaborated in a following section.
- Thin capitalisation rules — Division 820 of the ITAA97 prevents entities from reducing tax liabilities in Australia through financing operations through too much debt. These rules are elaborated in a following section.
- Non-commercial losses — Division 35 of the ITAA97 prevents a taxpayer from using the losses of a non-commercial business to reduce tax payable on the taxpayer's assessable income from other sources. We discussed these rules in an earlier chapter.
- Personal services income — Divisions 85 to 87 of the ITAA97 prevents a taxpayer from using a business structure to alienate personal services income. Division 7A of the ITAA36 deems preventing them from making deductions for various expenses against income that is mainly a reward for their personal efforts. These rules were elaborated in an earlier chapter.
- Deemed dividends for private companies — Division 7A of the ITAA36 deems certain loans and other payments made to shareholders of private companies to be dividends to prevent attempts to disguise payments to shareholders. We discussed these provisions in detail in an earlier chapter.
- Taxation of minors — Division 6AA of the ITAA36 assesses distributions from trusts to certain minors at punitive rates in order to discourage income splitting. These rules were also discussed in an earlier chapter.

Each of these will be discussed in further detail to provide examples of how specific anti-avoidance rules work.

14.4.1 Transfer pricing

Entities within a multinational group often transact with each other for various products and services. The amounts charged for such intra-group transactions is referred to as 'transfer pricing'. If the transacting entities reside in different jurisdictions with different tax rates, there is an incentive for the entity residing in a higher taxing jurisdiction to purchase items from the other for relatively high amounts to reduce its taxable income in that jurisdiction. The combination of low taxable income in a high taxing jurisdiction and higher taxable income in a lower taxing jurisdiction reduces the tax paid by the group in total compared to the situation where the companies were dealing with each other at arm's length.

A broad solution to tackle such incentives is to force entities in the same multinational group to adopt arm's length pricing principles when dealing with each other. This principle was embodied in the former Division 13 of the ITAA36 which was enacted to deal with multinational tax avoidance as a result of transfer pricing. Two decisions revealed deficiencies in applying this principle with respect to intangible assets (*FCT v SNF (Australia) Pty Ltd* (2011) FCAFC 74) and products and services provided in closed markets (*Roche Products Pty Ltd v FCT* 2008 AATA 639). The Full Federal Court in *FCT v SNF* was also critical of the OECD's pricing methods guidelines that the Commissioner had relied upon, expressing the view that they are of limited assistance in interpreting Division 13 of the ITAA36. In response, a new transfer pricing regime was enacted to operate for income years commencing on or after 29 June 2013 so that the *OECD Transfer Pricing Guidelines for Multinational Enterprises and Tax Administrations* could be used to inform the application of the arm's length principle in Australia. This new regime consists of Subdivision 815-B, which applies to entities generally, Subdivision 815-C, which applies to permanent establishments, and Subdivision 815-D, which applies to trusts and partnerships. Subdivision 284-E Schedule 1 of the *Tax Administration Act 1953* (Cth) contains rules about documentation that need to be kept and penalties that may apply.

The new rules require that an entity operating in Australia substitutes arm's length conditions for the actual conditions when a transfer pricing benefit has been obtained (section 815-115). This means that unlike the transfer pricing rules under Division 13 and Subdivision 815-A, the entities do not need to be related, rather they only need to not be dealing at arm's length. Furthermore, the new provisions are self-executing and do not need any determination from the Commissioner to operate. A transfer pricing benefit is defined in section 815-120 to be one that arises from commercial or financial relations that differ from arm's length that, if conducted under arm's length, would have resulted in an increase in taxable income, a reduction in losses, a reduction in tax offsets, or an increase in withholding tax for an entity.

Arm's length conditions are defined in section 815-125(1) as those that might be expected to operate between independent entities dealing wholly independently with one another in comparable circumstances. Section 815-125(2) requires that in identifying the arm's length conditions, the most appropriate and reliable method, or combination of methods, must be used. A number of factors must be considered in determining the most appropriate and reliable method. Refer to section 815-125 for further details.

While Subdivision 815-B operates on companies, there are similar rules for permanent establishments (Subdivision 815-C). There are also similar rules for trusts and partnerships (Subdivision 815-D) which are treated like companies or permanent establishments where relevant as if the trust or partnership were a separate legal entity or permanent establishment.

Subdivision 284-E of Schedule 1 of the *Taxation Administration Act 1953* (Cth) (TAA1953) requires that entities keep documentation so that it can be ascertained whether the entity's transfer pricing has been conducted at arm's length. It must keep sufficient documentation to ensure that its transfer pricing position is reasonably arguable. Refer to section 284-255 of the TAA1953 for details. From this information, the ATO is able to make its own independent assessment as to whether entities, trusts and partnerships are dealing with each other at arm's length and conduct compliance action where appropriate.

14.4.2 Thin capitalisation

Entities may finance their business via equity or debt. Interest repayments on borrowings will generally be income tax deductible providing the debt is used for business purposes whereas payments out of equity will not. This creates an incentive for entities in higher taxing jurisdictions to finance their operations with high levels of debt. These entities are referred to as being thinly capitalised. The rules to dissuade financing through relatively high levels of debt are referred to as thin capitalisation rules. In Australia, these rules may be found in Division 820 of the ITAA97. They operate on companies, trusts, partnerships and individuals by disallowing debt deductions claimed against Australian income when the levels of debt exceed certain levels compared to equity. A debt deduction is defined in section 820-40 as a cost incurred in relation to a debt interest. Further details regarding what this includes are provided in that section.

The thin capitalisation rules are quite detailed and the exact manner in which they apply depends on whether the entity is outwardly investing (Subdivisions 820-B) inwardly investing (Subdivisions 820-C) or an authorised deposit-taking institution (ADI) that may be inwardly or outwardly investing (Subdivisions 820-D and 820-E). An outward investment entity is an Australian entity that either controls or is associated with a foreign entity or a business carried on through a permanent establishment. An inward investing entity, as might be expected, is essentially the reverse, an Australian entity controlled by a foreign entity or an Australian permanent establishment of a foreign entity. Entities that have debt deductions of less than $2 million for an income year including those of associated entities are excluded (section 820-35). Also exempted are outward investing entities that are not foreign controlled with foreign investments of 10 per cent or less of the entity's total assets (section 820-37). To determine whether the entity is thinly capitalised, it must calculate its adjusted average debt and compare it to its maximum allowable debt. If the adjusted average debt exceeds the maximum allowed, the debt deductions will be reduced to the extent of the excess.

The maximum allowable debt for an outward investing entity that is not an ADI is the greater of a safe harbour debt amount, an arm's length debt amount, or the worldwide gearing debt amount. Refer to Subdivision 820-B for details. For an inward investing entity that is not an ADI, the maximum allowable debt is the greater of a safe harbour debt amount and an arm's length debt amount. Refer to Subdivision 820-C for details. The maximum allowable debt for ADIs is calculated similarly but with modifications to take into account the purpose of these entities as financing and deposit-taking entities. Refer to Subdivisions 820-D and 820-E for details.

In working out adjusted average debt, average values of assets, liabilities and debt must be used. As might be expected given the discussion, the available methods to calculate these values differ depending on the type of entity. They are distinguishable by the timeframe over which the averages are calculated. Non-ADIs have the most choice available to them as they can use the following methods in accordance with section 820-630(1). The first is the opening and closing balances method which considers the opening and closing values for the period (i.e. an income year). The next is the three measurement days method which allows the average to be based on three particular days during the period. This method is only available if the last day of the first half of the income year and either the first day or the last day of that year are in the period (section 820-640(1)). The third method is the frequent measure method which, as the name suggests, allows values to be taken more frequently, generally every quarter but provision for more frequent measurement is available. ADIs are restricted to using the frequent measurement method. Refer to Subdivision 820-G for details of each of these methods.

14.4.3 Non-commercial losses

The question of whether a business is being carried on or whether an activity is merely a hobby has presented difficulties for tax practitioners, the ATO and the courts because a business cannot be defined with certainty by reference to one factor alone. Instead, numerous factors need to be evaluated and weighted. For example, an activity that is conducted in a systematic and organised way with a view to making a profit having substantial turnover through offering products to the public may be easily identifiable as a business, but a business may also constitute a disorganised, loss-making, small-scale activity with few transactions due to the nature of the industry it operates in. Furthermore, hobbies can also be substantial in size, have numerous transactions, be systematic and organised, and turn a profit.

This issue manifests itself practically when the activity makes losses since taxpayers have an incentive to argue that their loss-making activity is a business so that losses made may be offset against other income. The ATO will not have the resources to appropriately classify all the activities that taxpayers conduct into hobbies or businesses leading to many taxpayers claiming these losses inappropriately. Even though the non-commercial loss rules in Division 35 of the ITAA97 are only designed to operate on businesses rather than hobbies, from a practical point of view these rules take away the incentive to argue your hobby is a business by disallowing deductions for losses unless the activity is commercially viable. This is why the rules in Division 35 of the ITAA97 are regarded as specific anti-avoidance rules.

However, the rules act more widely than simply disallowing deductions for losses on activities that are businesses in form but are hobbies in substance. The rules also prevent deductions for losses from what might be regarded as genuine businesses but are non-commercial in the sense that they are unlikely to ever make a profit or profits are rarely made. In operating this broadly, the non-commercial loss rules in Division 35 of the ITAA97 have essentially redefined what constitutes a business and what constitutes a hobby for tax purposes. These rules only apply to individual taxpayers, including those carrying on a business as partners; they do not apply to passive income from investments.

In broad terms, losses from activities will be deferred to later income years unless the taxpayer meets one of the exceptions. These exceptions may be categorised into three groups.

1. Applies to most business and contains an income test that must be satisfied before applying the remaining four other tests of which one must be satisfied to deduct a loss in the current year.
2. For primary producers, artists and the like whose income is likely to be volatile. It is considered unfair to apply the rules of the first category to taxpayers in those industries and so there is another test that is applied relating to the amount of income generated outside of the primary production and artist business.
3. Allows the Commissioner of Taxation some discretion in allowing a taxpayer to deduct a loss in circumstances where they would likely meet the tests in the first category but have not due to some unforeseen circumstance beyond the taxpayer's control.

We covered the operation of these rules and the exceptions in detail in an earlier chapter.

14.4.4 Personal services income

The general deductions provision in section 8-1 of the ITAA97 allows deductions in two circumstances as discussed in an earlier chapter: when losses and outgoings are incurred in producing assessable income, or when losses and outgoings are incurred in carrying on business to produce assessable income provided that the expenditure is not capital, not private, not incurred in producing exempt income, and not denied by the operation of another provision of the Income Tax Acts. The second circumstance is broader than the first, providing an incentive for taxpayers to arrange their affairs to come within it. One of the most common ways to fall within the second circumstance involves employees ceasing their employment and subsequently providing the same services to their former employer as a contractor. The former employee (now contractor) would likely use the same equipment, wear the same uniform and sit at the same desk as they did previously. Furthermore, the former employee (now contractor) would generally only provide services to the former employer and work the same hours and report to the same person as they did previously.

While the form of the arrangement is a contracting one, in substance it continues to be an employment arrangement. The personal services income (PSI) rules in Division 85 to 87 of the ITAA97 are designed to assess the taxpayer according to their substance as an employee by limiting the deductions available to those that an employee might claim except for those specified in Division 85 including expenditure in gaining work, paying for income protection and liability insurance, employing staff, paying superannuation and complying with workers' compensation and goods and services tax legislation.

Since employment involves the provision of personal services, the provision of personal services is the starting point or indicator that the PSI rules ought to be applied. Personal services income is defined as income derived mainly through the effort of an individual, but the rules recognise that there are many legitimate businesses that provide personal services (including legitimate contracting arrangements) which are not attempting to take advantage of the second circumstance of section 8-1. Such legitimate businesses are excluded from the PSI rules through the operation of certain tests which, if passed, lead to the business being classified as a personal services business (PSB) which can deduct expenditure in the same manner as any other business. More specifically, to be regarded as a PSB, the taxpayer must satisfy either the results test or, alternatively, at least one of a further three tests. Refer to Division 85-87 of the ITAA97 for further detail. We also dealt with the PSI rules in an earlier chapter.

14.4.5 Deemed dividends from private companies

For many individual taxpayers, the distinction between themselves and entities they are in control over, such as companies in which they are directors and shareholders, can be confusing. Many small family businesses operate through companies where the parents are the only shareholders and the only directors, but the concept that companies are separate legal entities is poorly understood. This means that many shareholder/directors of small private companies tend to regard the assets held within the company as their own. This leads to the temptation for them to withdraw cash and other assets from the company, often for private use, as they see fit. For accounting purposes, withdrawal of cash creates a loan receivable in the company, but since those making the withdrawal are also those in control of the company, the loan is unlikely to ever be repaid.

Since a company is a separate legal entity, shareholders should receive investment returns through capital returns, dividends or distributions on liquidation. These forms of remuneration are assessable, while withdrawals of cash and assets are not. The tax system addresses this problem in Division 7A of the ITAA36 by deeming such withdrawals to be dividends to the shareholder (or relevant associate) unless it comes under one of the exceptions.

Division 7A (also discussed in an earlier chapter) applies to deem a dividend during an income year when a private company:

- pays an amount (section 109C)
- provides an asset (section 109CA)
- makes a loan that is not repaid prior to lodgement of the company tax return (section 109D)
- forgives a debt (section 109F)

to a shareholder or associate of the shareholder. The amount of the deemed dividend is the amount paid, asset provided, loan made, or debt forgiven and it will be assessable as a dividend in accordance with section 44(1) of the ITAA36.

There are numerous exceptions that prevent a deemed dividend arising outlined in Subdivisions C, D, DA and DB of Division 7A. The most common are loans made in the ordinary course of business (section 109M) or other payments made under written loan agreements at an interest rate that is equal to or greater the Division 7A interest rate (section 109N). The period of the loan must be no more than 7 years or, in the case of mortgages over real property, not more than 25 years. In keeping with the spirit of such loan agreements, minimum repayments under the agreement must be paid to the company by the shareholder or associate. If repayments do not occur but instead are capitalised, the resultant new loan (the amalgamated loan) will also be treated as a dividend in accordance with section 109E. These exceptions are discussed in further detail in an earlier chapter.

14.4.6 Taxation of minors

Trusts allow for splitting of income that is not a result of personal services (unless the trust operates a PSB), and discretionary trusts are particularly useful for this since income can be distributed to beneficiaries at the discretion of the trustee, usually up to certain marginal tax rates for each beneficiary. For example, where members of the same family are beneficiaries of a discretionary trust, the trustee can (in principle) distribute $18 200 to each individual beneficiary before any tax is paid. Many regard it as inappropriate to distribute in this manner to minors (individuals under 18 years of age) since it amounts to using children as a means of escaping tax. To remedy this, minors are subject to special rates contained in Division 6AA of the ITAA36 in certain circumstances. While these rates do not amount to a specific anti-avoidance rule, they are quite high and come into effect at low-income thresholds, thereby acting as a deterrent to effectively penalise distributions from trusts made to minors when those circumstances apply.

Not all minors are subject to these rates. Indeed, they only apply to prescribed persons who are in receipt of certain types of income. In accordance with section 102AC of the ITAA36, a prescribed person is a minor who is not an excepted person and an excepted person is a minor who is engaged in full-time employment on the last day of the relevant income year. This means that a minor who works full-time on the last day of the income year is not subject to the minors' rates in Division 6AA at all, and distributions from trusts will be assessed at normal individual rates of tax. This will allow distributions up to $18 200 to be made to the minor without penalty. These rules were discussed in further detail in an earlier chapter.

This section has discussed a few specific anti-avoidance rules including the reasons for their existence and their manner of operation. These target specific methods of reducing tax that are regarded as unacceptable, but there are potentially many other ways that taxpayers and the ATO have not thought about as yet. Australia's general anti-avoidance rule is ready to render those methods useless as and when they arise. The next section will introduce this anti-avoidance rule and discuss it in some detail.

14.5 Australia's general anti-avoidance rule

LEARNING OBJECTIVE 14.5 Explain the operation of Australia's general anti-avoidance rule.

Australia's federal income tax legislation has contained a **general anti-avoidance rule** since income tax was first legislated. It was first contained in section 53 of the *Income Tax Assessment Act 1915* (Cth) until it was replaced by section 93 of the *Income Tax Assessment Act 1922* (Cth) which existed until it was replaced by section 260 ITAA36 which remains in operation to this day, but for schemes entered into until before 27 May 1981. Due to problems with the interpretation and application of section 260, which are beyond the scope of this chapter, it was replaced by Part IVA of the ITAA36. It comprises sections 177A to 177R and operates on tax avoidance schemes entered into on or after 28 May 1981. This section will focus on the most fundamental provisions.

Under Part IVA, the three components to tax avoidance are:
1. there must be a scheme (section 177A)
2. there must be a tax benefit associated with the scheme (section 177C)
3. the taxpayer's dominant purpose in entering that scheme must have been to obtain the associated tax benefit (section 177D).

While these components are discussed separately, they are interrelated. Part IVA gives the Commissioner the power to cancel the tax benefit that arises from the scheme (section 177F). To affect this power, the Commissioner must make a Part IVA determination against a taxpayer that has benefited from this scheme. This means that the Commissioner must have knowledge of the taxpayer's conduct, usually via an audit, and must have already come to a decision that Part IVA applies to it.

Even though tax avoidance can be conceptualised in different ways, as discussed, Part IVA considers the taxpayer's purpose in obtaining a tax benefit as a key differentiator between it and tax planning. How the taxpayer's purpose is determined is discussed later.

The operation of the general anti-avoidance rule contained in Part IVA is summarised in figure 14.4.

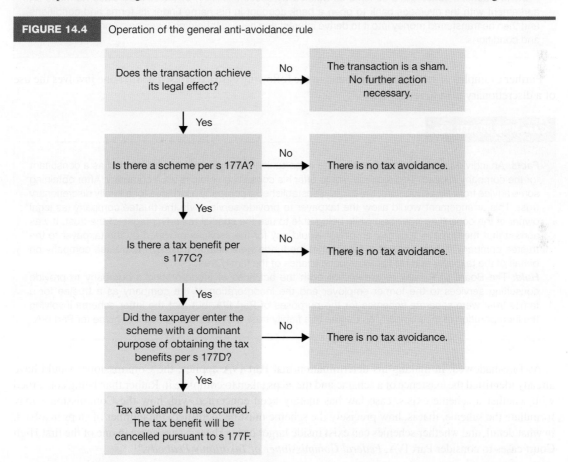

FIGURE 14.4 Operation of the general anti-avoidance rule

As mentioned, Part IVA requires a scheme that was entered into with the dominant purpose of obtaining a tax benefit. These three components will now be discussed with some emphasis on principles that have been determined by the courts. Areas of difficulty and uncertainty will also be raised.

14.5.1 Scheme

Scheme is broadly and exhaustively defined in section 177A(1) as any agreement, arrangement, understanding, promise or undertaking, whether express or implied and whether or not enforceable, or intended to be enforceable, by legal proceedings. It is additionally defined as any scheme, plan, proposal, action, course of action or course of conduct. In accordance with section 177A(3), a scheme also includes a unilateral scheme. This means that a scheme may be developed and carried out by only one person and does not require any type of agreement with another party. Furthermore, a scheme may be entered into with others (section 177A(4)). Given the very broad definition, virtually any action can be regarded as a scheme and the fact that a scheme exists will rarely be in dispute. Schemes can also be carried on for more than one purpose, in such cases if the dominant purpose is the attainment of the tax benefit then the scheme will amount to tax avoidance (section 177A(5)).

Example 14.3 demonstrates the assessment of whether a scheme is in place.

EXAMPLE 14.3

Scheme

David inherits a substantial sum of money on the death of his mother. On the advice of his financial planner, David decides to invest the inheritance in an overseas bank located in a tax haven. He obtains forms to open the bank account and completes them by signing them and agreeing to the bank's terms and conditions which include the bank paying a certain interest rate on deposited funds and withholding relevant taxes on any interest earned. He subsequently transfers the money via internet banking into the new account once he has obtained the relevant account details.

Do David's actions constitute a scheme as defined by section 177A(1) of the ITAA36?

David's actions constitute a scheme as defined by section 177A(1) of the ITAA36 since he made an agreement with the overseas bank to open a bank account in his name under its terms and conditions and then he transferred money into it to derive interest and have withholding taxes paid under those terms and conditions.

Further examples of scheme may be found in the following case excerpts. The first one involves the use of a discretionary trust to reduce tax.

Case W58 89 ATC 524

Facts: An individual taxpayer was offered the opportunity to cease employment and act as a consultant for the company instead. This required him to offer his consulting services via a company. After obtaining some advice from his accountant, the taxpayer established a company as trustee for a family discretionary trust. This arrangement would allow the taxpayer to provide services via the trustee company (as legal owner of the consulting business) while being able to use the special tax advantages of the trust. It was agreed that the taxpayer's former employer would pay for the services provided by the taxpayer to the trustee company. The arrangement meant that the funds were held in trust by the trustee company on behalf of the taxpayer and his family as beneficiaries of the family trust.

Held: The Board of Review regarded that both the activities of incorporating a company to provide consulting services to the former employer and the incorporation of the company as a trustee for a family trust were separate schemes for the purposes of Part IVA, but that the latter scheme involving the incorporation of the company as trustee of a family trust was the more relevant scheme for Part IVA.

As foreshadowed, in making his determination that Part IVA applies, the Commissioner would have already identified the existence of a scheme and the steps taken to complete it. Rather than being concerned with whether a scheme exists, case law has mainly been concerned with how the Commissioner may formulate the scheme, that is, how precisely the scheme must be identified, the number of steps involved, in what detail, and whether schemes can exist inside larger ones. These issues arose in one of the first High Court cases to consider Part IVA, *Federal Commissioner of Taxation v Peabody*.[41]

Federal Commissioner of Taxation v Peabody (1994) 181 CLR 359

Facts: The taxpayer, Mrs Peabody, was the beneficiary of a discretionary family trust. TEP Holdings Pty Ltd (TEP), in its capacity as trustee of that trust, owned 68 per cent of a group of four companies while the

---

41 [1994] HCA 43.

remaining 32 per cent were owned by an unrelated party, Mr Kleinschmidt. All these shareholdings were acquired before the introduction of capital gains tax.

Mr Peabody, a director of TEP, wanted to float 50 per cent of the group of four companies on the stock exchange, but he would lose control over the group if this were to occur with the current ownership arrangement in place. To remedy this, Mr Peabody planned to purchase Mr Kleinschmidt's shares in the group, worth $8.6m, but the purchase of Mr Kleinschmidt's shares would transform them into post capital gains tax assets resulting in capital gains tax on their future disposal. To solve this, a particular arrangement was conducted after taking legal and financial advice.

The purchase of Mr Kleinschmidt's shares was financed by issuing a bank with redeemable preference shares in a shelf company (known as Loftway) in exchange for the funds to buy out Mr Kleinschmidt's shares. This arrangement was attractive since it led to a reduction in financing costs of $1 160 952 compared to financing via a loan. Loftway, now having acquired the shares, received a dividend from the group of four which was passed on to the bank as a preference dividend. The preference shares were redeemed by the bank which had no further involvement in the arrangement.

Importantly, the shares that Loftway purchased from Mr Kleinschmidt were converted into 'Z' class preference shares with no voting rights. This reduced their value from $8.6 million to less than $500 and led to TEP holding as trustee virtually all the equity in the group of four companies and the avoidance of tax on the profits arising from the sale of property acquired within 12 months of the sale under section 26AAA of the ITAA36 which was in operation at the time. TEP then sold its interest in the group to Loftway. Now that Loftway owned all the shares in the group, it was floated on the stock exchange resulting in all the shares in Loftway being publicly owned and the owner of all the shares in the group.

The Commissioner made a Part IVA determination since it was a scheme entered into after 27 May 1981 to avoid the operation of section 26AAA. The Commissioner formulated a scheme of 10 steps which included all the actions described, but the taxpayer argued that there was no scheme or that if there was that it was a normal financing arrangement.

Held: The Federal Court (that heard the case first) was of the view that the relevant scheme ought to be confined to conversion of the preference shares to 'Z' class shares or, possibly, the issuing of the redeemable preference shares as a means of obtaining cheap finance. Despite this, the Federal Court decided in favour of the Commissioner, so the taxpayer appealed to the Full Federal Court where the taxpayer was successful. This led to the Commissioner requesting special leave to the Full High Court which was granted. There, the Commissioner relied on the narrower scheme proposed earlier by the Federal Court.

The Full High Court confirmed that courts must consider the scheme that the Commissioner identifies and that courts cannot substitute the Commissioner's scheme with a different one.

Also, how the Commissioner defines the scheme is important since the existence of a tax benefit and the purpose of the taxpayer are determined with reference to it. The Court also held that, Part IVA could apply even where the Commissioner identified the incorrect scheme because the connection between a tax benefit and a scheme is an objective fact that does not rely on any discretion exercised by the Commissioner. The Commissioner is able to re-formulate the scheme (in this case, rely on a narrower one) when it would not cause undue embarrassment or surprise to the taxpayer and if it is capable of 'standing on their own without being robbed of all practical meaning'. In essence, Part IVA 'does not provide that a scheme includes part of a scheme' in circumstances where the scheme could not 'stand on its own without being robbed of all practical meaning'.

Whether schemes could be part of schemes without standing on their own was reconsidered in *Federal Commissioner of Taxation v Hart & Anor.*[42]

Federal Commissioner of Taxation v Hart & Anor (2004) 217 CLR 216

Facts: Mr and Mrs Hart purchased a property as their primary residence via a loan. After a certain period, they moved to live in a second property and rented the first one to tenants. Since the acquisition of the second property required finance, the Harts refinanced with their bank using a loan product known as the Wealth Optimiser. This loan was a special banking product that allowed both houses to be financed by one loan which had two separately identifiable components relating to each property. Since there was only one loan, only one repayment per month was required, but since the loan was identifiably split among both properties, the interest on each property could be calculated separately and the monthly repayment could be allocated to the property of their choosing.

---

42 (2004) 217 CLR 216.

The Hart's proceeded to allocate their monthly repayment wholly to their primary residence which resulted in that component of the loan being reduced over time while the rental property component of the loan increased due to the interest to that component being capitalised. Over time, while the balance of both components combined decreased with each monthly repayment, the component corresponding to the rental property increased. The Hart's claimed income tax deductions for the interest accrued.

Following *Peabody*,[43] the Commissioner identified a wide scheme and a narrow scheme. The narrow scheme comprised the parts of the loan agreement that allowed for it to be split for each property and for repayments to be directed to one part. The wide scheme comprised all the steps up to and including the entering into and implementation of the loan arrangements between the taxpayers and their bank. Austral. The taxpayers conceded that the Commissioner's broad scheme was a scheme for Part IVA.

Held: In the Federal Court, the taxpayers conceded that the wide scheme was a scheme for Part IVA. On appeal, the Full Federal Court, following *Peabody*,[44] dismissed the narrow scheme since it was considered incapable of standing on its own. On appeal once more, the justices of the High Court disagreed on how schemes should be formulated with some agreeing with *Peabody* while others were critical of it.

The disagreement among the Justices of the High Court in *Hart*[45] has led to the issue regarding whether schemes need to stand on their own or whether schemes can be part of other schemes being unresolved. Following this decision, the Commissioner continued to define a narrow scheme and a wide scheme in Part IVA cases.

The issue as to the precise formulation of the scheme is important, since some commentators argue that the narrower the scheme, the more likely it would be concluded that there was a dominant purpose to obtain a tax benefit. This is because narrow schemes tend to focus on only the specific elements of the transaction that produced the tax benefit. In contrast, wider schemes allow for the context of the transaction to be considered. There is still disagreement, however, concerning this matter.

As can be seen from the discussion in this section, the courts and various commentators hold divergent views about some aspects regarding schemes. Thus, the debate concerning the connection between scheme and purpose remains unresolved. Later cases[46] helped matters to a certain extent by stating that schemes need to have some coherence since the identification of a scheme is a question of objective fact to be determined by the evidence.

No matter how the scheme is defined, the Commissioner must show that a tax benefit arose from one to be successful in a Part IVA case. We now turn our attention to what constitutes a tax benefit.

14.5.2 Tax benefit

A tax benefit that is obtained by a taxpayer in connection with a scheme or would be obtained if the Commissioner had not cancelled it, is defined in section 177C(1). Under section 177C(1) paragraphs (a) to (bc), a tax benefit may arise in the following ways that ought not to have arisen if it were not for the scheme:

- income not being included
- deductions being allowed
- a capital loss being incurred
- a foreign tax offset being allowable
- an innovation tax offset being allowable
- an exploration credit being issued
- the taxpayer not being liable for withholding tax on an amount.

In accordance with section 177C(1) paragraphs (c) to (g), for the purposes of Part IVA, the amount of the tax benefit shall be the following if it were not for the scheme:

- the income not included
- the deduction allowed
- the capital loss allowed
- the foreign tax credit allowed
- the innovation tax offset allowed

---

43 *Federal Commissioner of Taxation v Peabody* [1994] HCA 43.
44 Ibid.
45 *Federal Commissioner of Taxation v Hart & Anor* [2004] HCA 26.
46 See, eg, *Ashwick (QLD) No. 127 Pty Ltd & Ors v FCT* [2009] FCA 1388; *Star City Pty Ltd v FCT* (2007) 68 ATR 413.

- the exploration credit allowed
- the withholding tax not payable.

For example, a scheme that transforms income that would normally be assessed into exempt income would be regarded as producing a tax benefit since the scheme leads to income not being included that normally would be if it were not for the scheme.

As discussed, many argue that tax avoidance should not occur where a provision of the Act allows for reductions in tax due to certain choices and options that are available in the Act. This has been referred to as the **choice principle**. Section 177C(2) contains a choice principle by saying that reductions specified in section 177C(1) paragraphs (a) to (bc) arising from the making of a declaration, agreement, election, selection or choice, the giving of a notice or the exercise of an option that is expressly provided for by either the ITAA36 or the ITAA97 by any person will not be considered tax benefits.

For example, a taxpayer who operates a bookstore can value his books as trading stock in one of three ways (cost, market selling value or replacement value). This does not produce a tax benefit since this choice is expressly provided for in the Income Tax Acts.

While the choice principle sounds fair and reasonable, it has a history of exploitation in Australian tax. Indeed, this principle potentially led to the downfall of the anti-avoidance rule that existed before Part IVA, namely, section 260 of the ITAA36. Taxpayers who exploited the choice principle arranged their affairs with the intention of circumventing its usefulness as a tax avoidance measure. This modification of the choice principle occurs via the following provisions:

- section 177C(2)(a)(ii), with respect to assessable income
- section 177C(2)(b)(ii), with respect to deductions
- section 177C(2)(c)(ii), with respect to capital losses
- section 177C(2)(d)(ii), with respect to foreign income tax offsets
- section 177C(2)(e)(ii), with respect to innovation tax offsets
- section 177C(2A)(a)(i), with respect to non-inclusion of income attributable to a choice under Subdivision 126-B or an agreement under Subdivision 170-B of the ITAA97
- section 177C(2A)(b)(i), with respect to a capital loss attributable to a choice under Subdivision 126-B or an agreement under Subdivision 170-B of the ITAA97
- section 177C(2A)(c)(i), with respect to an exploration credit attributable to making a choice under Division 418 of the ITAA97.

Case W58 89 ATC 524

Facts: Recall that the taxpayer established a company as trustee for a family discretionary trust to provide consulting services to his former employer. The former employer insisted on the services being provided through a company, but the decision to establish it as a trustee company of a family discretionary trust was the taxpayer's idea based on advice from his accountant. The company, as trustee for the family trust, paid fees to the taxpayer, a salary and any remaining fees were distributed to members of his family. The taxpayer argued that the arrangement was a choice made by him under the Act so there was no tax benefit in accordance with section 177C(2).

Held: The Board of Review held that if the scheme were not entered into, the taxpayer would reasonably have derived the income that was otherwise distributed to his family. Therefore, the scheme generated a tax benefit. Furthermore, even though income tax Acts recognise the existence of trusts, the Act does not 'expressly provide for' the choice to use them to split income and reduce tax in the manner the taxpayer used them.

14.5.2.1 Alternate hypothesis

Determining whether a tax benefit has been obtained is not always as easy as it appears. This is due to the apparent requirement that in determining the existence of a tax benefit the court must consider an **alternate hypothesis**, sometimes also referred to as the 'alternate postulate' or 'counterfactual'.

The alternate hypothesis is based on the notion that determining whether there is a tax benefit requires comparing what occurred with what would reasonably have occurred (or reasonably expected to occur) if the scheme were not entered into. This is because section 177C(1) requires a connection between the tax benefit and the scheme it arose from. The taxpayer doing nothing instead of entering the scheme may be a reasonable alternative. The purpose of developing this hypothesis is to ensure that the scheme entered into actually produced the tax benefit. We have seen this already in the discussion of *Case W58* where the

Board of Review considered what would have happened if the scheme were not entered into in determining if there was a tax benefit. Rather than considering whether the tax benefit would have been obtained if the scheme had not been entered into, the alternate hypothesis test requires consideration about whether a tax benefit has been obtained from a scheme which would not have been if the taxpayer did not enter into it.

Example 14.4 demonstrates an assessment of whether a tax benefit exists.

EXAMPLE 14.4

Tax benefit

David (from example 14.3) opened the overseas bank account in a tax haven on the advice of his financial planner who told him that while the funds deposited in that account would return less interest than if he made the same investment in Australia, the investment only attracts 5 per cent withholding tax in the tax haven while simultaneously being exempt from tax in Australia. This means that David will receive a greater net after-tax return on his investment overseas than if he invested in Australia.

Has David received a tax benefit in accordance with section 177C(1) of the ITAA36 as a result of entering the scheme? Can David argue that his decision to invest in the tax haven is not a tax benefit under the choice principle in section 177C(2) of the ITAA36? Explain why or why not.

Consideration of the alternate hypothesis suggests that if David did not enter the scheme involving the steps involved in opening an overseas bank account and depositing funds in it, he would reasonably have invested in Australia instead where he would have derived assessable interest. David is not able to argue that his decision to invest in the tax haven is not a tax benefit by appealing to the choice principle in section 177C(2) of the ITAA36 since the Income Tax Acts do not expressly provide for such a choice. Consequently, he received a tax benefit in accordance with section 177C(2) of the ITAA36 equal to the amount of tax on the interest that he would have derived on such an investment if the bank account was open and interest received in Australia.

The alternate hypothesis was used by the Court in its decision that there was no tax benefit in *Peabody*.[47]

Federal Commissioner of Taxation v Peabody (1994) 181 CLR 359

Facts: Recall that Mr Peabody wanted to float shares in a group of companies owned by a trustee company on the stock exchange, but he did not want to lose control of the group so he sought to purchase Mr Kleinschmidt's shares although capital gains tax would be payable on any subsequent disposal of these shares.

The Commissioner argued that if Mr Kleinschmidt's shares had not been converted to 'Z' class preference shares, a proportion of the amount of profit which would have been derived from their sale might reasonably be expected to have been included in Mrs Peabody's assessable income for the year ended 30 June 1986. The Commissioner argued that the amount of this tax benefit was $888 005. This is based on the alternative postulate or counterfactual that TEP would have reasonably been expected to purchase the shares if it were not for the scheme and the profits would have then flowed through to Mrs Peabody as a beneficiary of the trust that TEP was a trustee.

Held: The Full Federal Court found that there was no tax benefit. This matter was reconsidered on appeal to the Full High Court. The Full High Court agreed with the Full Federal Court that there was no tax benefit. There were two reasons for this. The first is the Court disagreed with the Commissioner's alternative hypothesis that TEP would have acquired the shares. The Court was of the view that a corporation other than TEP would have reasonably been expected to acquire the shares. This is because the cost-effective financing arrangement (that saved $1 160 952) required that a corporation other than TEP acquired them.

The High Court formulated the alternative hypothesis test in the process of providing its reasoning: 'Here, the reasonable expectation requires more than a possibility. It involves a prediction as to events which would have taken place if the relevant scheme had not been entered into or carried out and the prediction must be sufficiently reliable for it to be regarded as reasonable ... '.

As a consequence, the Commissioner was unable to show that the profit from the disposal of Mr Kleinschmidt's shares had the devaluation not taken place would have flowed through to TEP and ultimately to Mrs Peabody, the taxpayer who received the Part IVA determination from the Commissioner. This would also have required Loftway to have declared a dividend to TEP as Trustee for the Peabody Family Trust which was also not reasonably expected.

---

47 *Federal Commissioner of Taxation v Peabody* [1994] HCA 43.

In contrast, determining the existence of a tax benefit was not controversial in *Federal Commissioner of Taxation v Hart & Anor.*[48] It is worthwhile completing the discussion regarding *Hart* to see how the High Court determined that there was a tax benefit in that case.

Federal Commissioner of Taxation v Hart & Anor (2004) 217 CLR 216

Facts: Recall from the discussion of the facts how Mr and Mrs Hart took out one loan for a primary residence and a rental property with a split loan facility that allowed repayments to be made against the primary residence part of the loan but not against the rental property component. As a result, interest on the rental property component was treated as if it were not paid and was capitalised or accrued leading to an increasing loan balance against the rental property. This meant that interest was being charged on accrued interest resulting in higher income tax deductions than would have occurred without the scheme. The Commissioner argued that the tax benefit was the difference between the interest on the investment portion loan and the interest on that would have been incurred on the investment loan if the monthly repayment had been allocated proportionally across both properties. Alternatively, the tax benefit was the difference between the interest the taxpayers would have incurred on the investment loan if they had a conventional interest only loan and the interest the taxpayers would have incurred on the investment loan if they had operated accounts as separate loans.

Held: The High Court found that the benefit that was cancelled by the Commissioner was of the type that was referred to in section 177C(1) as a deduction that was available to the taxpayer where it would not have been if the scheme were not entered into. The High Court agreed with the Commissioner's (and the Full Federal Court's) formulation of the tax benefit as being, in broad terms, the difference between the interest deducted being the interest charged to the investment portion of the loan and the interest that would have been charged on a loan requiring regular principle and interest repayments.

With the determination that a tax benefit exists, cases then turn to whether there was a dominant purpose of entering the scheme to obtain that tax benefit. This has been the most controversial aspect of Part IVA as we shall see in the following section.

14.5.3 Purpose

It is possible for a taxpayer to obtain a tax benefit from a scheme, but if a **dominant purpose** in entering the scheme to obtain that tax benefit is absent, the scheme will not be a tax avoidance one. Determining the taxpayer's purpose is the most important aspect of Part IVA and the majority of your application of Part IVA to an issue should be dedicated to it. In determining whether there has been the required dominant purpose, the Commissioner and the courts must consider eight factors from section 177D(2). These factors are as follows.

(a) the manner in which the scheme was entered into or carried out
(b) the form and substance of the scheme
(c) the time at which the scheme was entered into and the length of the period during which the scheme was carried out
(d) the result in relation to the operation of this Act that, but for this Part, would be achieved by the scheme
(e) any change in the financial position of the relevant taxpayer that has resulted, will result, or may reasonably be expected to result, from the scheme
(f) any change in the financial position of any person who has, or has had, any connection (whether of a business, family or other nature) with the relevant taxpayer, being a change that has resulted, will result or may reasonably be expected to result, from the scheme
(g) any other consequence for the relevant taxpayer, or for any person referred to in paragraph (f), of the scheme having been entered into or carried out
(h) the nature of any connection (whether of a business, family or other nature) between the relevant taxpayer and any person referred to in paragraph (f).

If the Commissioner is satisfied that the taxpayer had a dominant purpose of obtaining the tax benefit, he will issue a Part IVA determination to that taxpayer in accordance with section 177F. Further, if there is more than one purpose involved in entering into the scheme, then the requisite purpose for section 177D is the dominant purpose in accordance with section 177A(5).

---

48 [2004] HCA 26.

The eight factors represent an objective test. This means that the subjective or actual reasons for why the taxpayer entered the scheme are not relevant. Instead, the court considers what a third party would think of the scheme based on an assessment of those eight factors. This can make it difficult for taxpayers to self-assess whether they are engaging in tax avoidance. Furthermore, all eight factors must be considered, although they do not have to be individually referred to in a court judgement as the court is allowed to make a global assessment considering them and their application to a scheme simultaneously. Some factors may point to tax avoidance while others point away from it. Some may be neutral. There is very little judicial guidance on how the courts weigh up each factor, which are more or less important and this aspect has proved to be very controversial.

Many transactions that taxpayers engage in are tax driven to a greater or lesser extent, particularly for business taxpayers. The lack of guidance over weighting of the factors means that taxpayers do not know how commercial a transaction must be to avoid Part IVA. To put it another way, taxpayers do not know how tax effective their transactions are allowed to be before Part VIA becomes an issue. The fact that a taxpayer can point to a commercial purpose in entering a scheme is not enough to avoid Part IVA. Compounding this problem is that the taxpayer's own reasons and justifications for entering the scheme are not relevant, as mentioned.

Determining a taxpayer's dominant purpose requires a consideration of what other possible transactions the taxpayer could have engaged in. Some argue that this amounts to a kind of 'alternate hypothesis' directed at assessing the taxpayer's dominant purpose, but not everybody agrees arguing instead that a consideration as to what other possibilities existed involves amounts to a 'but for' test. This involves thinking about whether the taxpayer would have entered the scheme 'but for' the tax benefit that resulted from it. In other words, would the taxpayer have entered the scheme if the tax benefit did not arise from it. While this test sounds appropriate, it has been criticised for not actually being in section 177D and for potentially skewing the argument in the Commissioner's favour that a dominant purpose of entering the scheme to obtain the tax benefit exists.

Another method of determining the taxpayer's objective purpose is to consider whether the scheme introduced an unusual feature that can only be explained by its fiscal (including tax) consequences. This approach has also been criticised on the basis that it does not consider the entire scheme but rather the parts that produced the tax benefit, and that it places too much reliance on one of the eight criteria of section 177D(2), probably the manner in which the scheme was entered into and carried out. These disagreements illustrate that determining a taxpayer's dominant purpose in entering a scheme to obtain a tax benefit is not an easy task. Example 14.5 examines determination of a taxpayer's purpose and the following cases, which were introduced, illustrate how the courts may determine the objective purpose of the taxpayer in entering the schemes to obtain the tax benefits.

EXAMPLE 14.5

Determining the taxpayer's purpose

This example continues from examples 14.3 and 14.4 involving David. To recap, he invested a substantial amount of money in an overseas bank account. The investment returns are low compared to the returns that he would have obtained if he had invested in Australia, but since the overseas country is a tax haven, the after-tax return from the investment is higher than a similar investment in Australia. It has been established from examples 14.3 and 14.4 that David entered a scheme and obtained a tax benefit from it.

With reference to the factors in section 177D(2) of the ITAA36, has David entered the scheme with a dominant purpose of obtaining the tax benefit?

Consideration of the factors in section 177D(2) of the ITAA36 on a global level suggests that the dominant purpose of the investment is to obtain a tax benefit since the investment does not make sense without it, compared to the reasonable alternative of investing in Australia.

Case W58 89 ATC 524

Facts: Recall the facts of this case from the earlier discussion.

Held: The Board held that there was a dominant purpose to obtain a tax benefit from the scheme. The manner in which the scheme was entered into and carried out, such as establishing a trustee company and a family trust and distributing to family members in a tax effective manner, could not be explained by any other purpose other than to avoid tax. The form of the scheme was a corporate trustee and a family discretionary trust through which to run a business was in substance a means to reduce tax since the taxpayer and his wife were in complete control over the whole arrangement with distributions to beneficiaries made to minimise tax. The timing appears not to have pointed to a dominant purpose, but the result of the scheme was to reduce tax suggesting a dominant purpose to do so. The final four factors were evaluated together where the fact that the taxpayer's income decreased while his wife and children's income increased due to having received distribution from the trust as part of the scheme, was also suggestive of a dominant purpose.

Whether the taxpayer entered the scheme to obtain the tax benefit was also a key issue in *Federal Commissioner of Taxation v Hart & Anor*.[49] There were a couple of judgements given by the justices of the High Court and these were very detailed. The key elements of those judgements are summarised as follows.

Federal Commissioner of Taxation v Hart & Anor (2004) 217 CLR 216

Facts: Refer to the earlier discussion.
Held: The Court was unanimous in its decision that the scheme (whether narrow or broad) was entered into to obtain the tax benefit. Indeed, entering the scheme could only be explained by it. They compared the scheme with the alternative and concluded that if the taxpayers had not entered the scheme, they would have taken out separate loans for each property. The scheme that the taxpayers entered into was attractive and effective only due to the tax benefits that arose from it.

The way in which the scheme was entered into and carried out strongly pointed to a dominant purpose of obtaining a tax benefit and the form and substance of the scheme also pointed towards a dominant purpose. While the form of the arrangement was one loan, in substance there were two. Consideration of the third factor brought attention to the fact that the scheme was to be implemented over many years. Consideration of factors four to eight demonstrated that the taxpayers' wealth was optimised to the exclusion of others.

As can be seen from these case examples, the taxpayers entered into comparatively complex arrangements in order to specifically obtain a tax benefit. *Federal Commissioner of Taxation v Hart & Anor*[50] is potentially the most illustrative in this aspect since, as noted by the High Court, the usual way to finance the purpose of two properties is to simply take out one loan for each.

14.5.4 Cancellation of the tax benefit

If all three components of Part IVA: scheme, tax benefit and dominant purpose are demonstrably present, the Commissioner can cancel the tax benefit that arose from the scheme.

Where a tax benefit to which this Part applies has been obtained by the taxpayer, the Commissioner is empowered under section 177F(1) to cancel that benefit in one of two ways consistent with the nature of the benefit defined in section 177C(1). That is, he may include the omitted income or disallow the deduction gained. In addition, any necessary compensating adjustments arising from a section 177F(1) determination may be made in accordance with section 177F(3). The necessary amendments to give effect to these adjustments are provided for in section 177G.

Example 14.6 applies the cancellation of the tax benefit to the facts presented in examples 14.3 to 14.5.

EXAMPLE 14.6

Cancellation of the tax benefit
Recall the facts about David from examples 14.3 to 14.5. What would the Commissioner of Taxation likely do if Part IVA were to apply to that scheme?

▶

---

49 [2004] HCA 26.
50 Ibid.

Given that Part IVA likely applies to David's scheme, the Commissioner would likely make a Part IVA determination against him under section 177F(1) to cancel the tax benefit obtained from the scheme. This means that income that was not included as a result of the scheme would now be included in David's assessable income. This is likely to be an amount of interest derived from the investment that he reasonably would have made if he did not enter the scheme.

Case W58 89 ATC 524

Facts: Refer to the earlier discussion regarding facts.
Held: The whole of the tax benefits that the Board of Review referred to in its judgement were cancelled.

Similarly, the tax benefit in *Federal Commissioner of Taxation v Hart & Anor* was also cancelled.

Federal Commissioner of Taxation v Hart & Anor (2004) 217 CLR 216

Facts: Refer to the previous box for the basic facts:
Held: Since Part IVA applied in this case, the tax benefit that was described was cancelled. This means that Mr and Mrs Hart were not able to claim income tax deductions for the extra interest they incurred due to the scheme.

Example 14.7 provides a comprehensive illustration of the application of all the elements of Part IVA.

EXAMPLE 14.7

Part IVA comprehensive example

Consider a taxpayer who owns shares in two companies. The shares in Company A have increased in value substantially while the shares in Company B have fallen by the same amount. The taxpayer sells all his shares in Company B to generate a capital loss, but he immediately repurchases the same number of shares in that company. A few months later, he sells the shares in Company A, resulting in a capital gain. The taxpayer offsets the capital loss made earlier against the gain, resulting in no net capital gain and no tax payable.

Is this tax avoidance under Part IVA?

We must consider whether there is a scheme, a tax benefit and the dominant purpose.

This is a scheme since it broadly involves an agreement to sell the shares in Company B, immediately repurchase them and sell the shares in Company A. It may alternatively be defined narrowly as selling the shares in Company B and immediately repurchasing them.

A tax benefit has arisen from this scheme since a reasonable course of action would have been to not sell the Company B shares at all since the outcome is the same. This alternate hypothesis demonstrates that a tax benefit came from the scheme in the form of a capital loss.

A global assessment of the factors to determine the purpose in entering the scheme would suggest that the dominant purpose of doing so was to obtain the tax benefit since the scheme does not make sense without the tax benefit.

Hence, the general anti-avoidance rules are present and the Commissioner could decide to cancel the tax benefit that arose.

14.6 Multinational anti-avoidance

LEARNING OBJECTIVE 14.6 Explain the operation of Australia's multinational anti-avoidance rule and diverted profits tax.

Even though Part IVA is a general anti-avoidance rule, it has been amended over time to target some specific areas of tax avoidance. One amendment targets the activities of multinationals that try to exploit the meaning of 'permanent establishment' in double taxation agreements (DTA) to limit their presence in Australia thereby avoiding tax on transactions conducted here. This amendment is known as the **multinational anti-avoidance rule**. Another amendment also targets multinationals, but its focus is on those that try to divert profits away from Australia to offshore jurisdictions where the tax rates are lower. This amendment is called the **diverted profits tax (DPT)** but is more well known as the **Google tax**. Both amendments will be discussed in this section. These were legislated in the wake of the Organisation for Economic Cooperation and Development's (OECD) Base Erosion and Profit Shifting (BEPS) project which made numerous recommendations to prevent multinational entities from avoiding tax. Instead of implementing these recommendations, Australia, like many other countries, chose to implement its own laws aimed at reducing multinational tax avoidance. The multinational anti-avoidance rule and the diverted profits tax are examples of such laws.

14.6.1 Multinational anti-avoidance rule

Multinational companies operate in many jurisdictions. As discussed in the chapter on residency and source of income, companies that reside in Australia are assessed on income derived from all sources in accordance with section 6-5(2) of the ITAA97. Those that do not reside in Australia are only assessed on income derived from Australian sources in accordance with section 6-5(3) of the ITAA97. Despite the various laws surrounding residency of companies and source of income, DTAs may determine the final taxing jurisdiction. We touched on this issue in the chapter on residency and source of income. This is the case with companies that reside in one jurisdiction but wish to operate in another.

For Australia, this means that a foreign company may set up an operation here so that it can make sales or provide services to Australian customers and derives business profits in the process. A DTA that exists between Australia and the jurisdiction in which the company resides may determine which jurisdiction the profits of this operation are assessed. These DTAs usually state that, where the activities of the foreign company operating in Australia constitute a permanent establishment, the profits from that activity will be assessed in Australia.

If a multinational company can operate in Australia without those operations being regarded as a permanent establishment, it will not pay tax in Australia on any of the profits from that operation. The multinational anti-avoidance rule therefore focuses on companies that arrange their operations in ways designed to escape that definition. Let us consider that definition further.

A permanent establishment is defined in section 6(1) of the ITAA36 as 'a place where the person is carrying on any business' where the definition of 'person' in section 6(1) of the *ITAA36* includes a company. The definition of permanent establishment also includes places where the person is carrying on business through an agent, but it does not include the following in accordance with paragraphs (e) to (g) of the definition of permanent establishment.

> (e) a place where the person is engaged in business dealings through a bona fide commission agent or broker who, in relation to those dealings, acts in the ordinary course of his or her business as a commission agent or broker and does not receive remuneration otherwise than at a rate customary in relation to dealings of that kind, not being a place where the person otherwise carries on business;
> (f) a place where the person is carrying on business through an agent:
>> (i) who does not have, or does not habitually exercise, a general authority to negotiate and conclude contracts on behalf of the person, or
>> (ii) whose authority extends to filling orders on behalf of the person from a stock of goods or merchandise situated in the country where the place is located, but who does not regularly exercise that authority not being a place where the person otherwise carries on business, or
> (g) a place of business maintained by the person solely for the purpose of purchasing goods or merchandise.

The aspects of the definition of permanent establishment that relate to agents have been abused by multinational companies who arrange their affairs so that their operations in Australia are not regarded as agency arrangements for the foreign company. The OECD has recommended that the definition of permanent establishment be altered to prevent such abuse, but Australia has decided to insert section 177DA into Part IVA instead to cancel tax benefits that arise from companies limiting their taxable presence in Australia. This section is known as the multi-national anti-avoidance rule and it applies to significant global entities as defined in section 960-555 of the ITAA97 as entities that are global parent entities whose annual global income is $1 billion or more, or for whom the Commissioner determines them to be, or entities that are members of consolidated groups where one of the members of the group is a global parent entity. The multinational anti-avoidance rule applies concurrently to other aspects of Part IVA, meaning that the Commissioner could, in principle, attempt to apply those aspects first, then, if unsuccessful, apply section 177DA.

Section 177DA(1)(a) of the ITAA36 says that Part IVA will apply on schemes where:

(i) a foreign entity makes a supply to an Australian customer of the foreign entity, and
(ii) activities are undertaken in Australia directly in connection with the supply, and
(iii) some or all of those activities are undertaken by an Australian entity who, or are undertaken at or through an Australian permanent establishment of an entity who, is an associate of or is commercially dependent on the foreign entity, and
(iv) the foreign entity derives ordinary income, or statutory income, from the supply, and
(v) some or all of that income is not attributable to an Australian permanent establishment of the foreign entity.

If, according to section 177DA(1)(b) of the ITAA36, it would be concluded that the person or one of the persons who entered into or carried out the scheme or any part of the scheme, did so for a principle purpose of, or for more than one principle purpose that includes a purpose of enabling a taxpayer or taxpayers to obtain a tax benefit after having regard to the matters in section 177DA(2), the tax benefit associated with the scheme can be cancelled.

Even though section 177DA is targeted at multinationals avoiding tax through the definition of permanent establishment, its placement in Part IVA means that it can leverage off legal concepts such as scheme and tax benefit described. This means that in determining whether a tax benefit has arisen from a scheme to limit taxable presence in Australia, reference ought to be made to an alternate hypothesis in the manner discussed.

One key difference between section 177DA and the rest of Part IVA is that the purpose of entering the scheme to limit taxable presence in Australia only needs to be the principle purpose rather than the dominant purpose. This is a less strict requirement. Notwithstanding this, to determine the taxpayer's principle purpose of entering the scheme to limit taxable presence in Australia, section 177DA(2)(a) of the ITAA36 says that the same 8 factors in section 177D(2) of the ITAA36 are to be considered. Additionally, section 177DA(2)(b) of the ITAA36 says that regard must be had to the extent to which the activities that contribute to bringing about the contract for the supply are performed, and are able to be performed, by the foreign entity, or another entity referred to in section 177DA(1)(a)(iii), or any other entities. Section 177DA(2)(c) says that the result, in relation to the operation of any foreign tax law that would be achieved but for the operation of this Part IVA also needs to be considered.

Where the multinational anti-avoidance rule operates, the Commissioner may cancel the benefit in accordance with section 177F as described.

14.6.2 Diverted profits tax

The diverted profits tax (DPT) operates by virtue of sections 177J to 177R and it imposes a penalty rate of tax on profits of significant global entities (as defined in section 960-555) that are diverted offshore through contrived and artificial arrangements. This tax applies alongside the other anti-avoidance rules in Part IVA, including section 177DA, such that they may also be applied to the arrangement. This means that the Commissioner could, in principle, attempt to apply Part IVA, in the manner discussed in section 14.4, to schemes to divert profits then, if unsuccessful, apply the multinational anti-avoidance rule then, if unsuccessful, finally apply the diverted profits tax described here.

According to section 177J(1)(a), Part IVA applies to a scheme in relation to a DPT tax benefit where the principle purpose in entering the scheme was for the taxpayer or another entity to obtain the DPT tax benefit.

A DPT tax benefit is defined in section 177J(1)(b) as a tax benefit obtained from:
- enabling a taxpayer to obtain a tax benefit and/or reduce a liability under a foreign law in connection with a scheme, or
- enabling a taxpayer and another taxpayer to do the same whether or not that person who entered into or carried out the scheme or any part of it is the relevant taxpayer or another entity.

In addition to being a significant global entity, the taxpayer must also be associated with a foreign entity within the meaning of section 318 that either carried out the scheme or is connected to it in some way. Some entities are excluded through the operation of subsections 177J(f) and 177J(g). These are generally investment, pension or superannuation type organisations which meet the requirements in either sections 177K, 177L or 177M.

In a similar manner to the multinational anti-avoidance rule, the diverted profits tax relies on other concepts from Part IVA for its operation such as a scheme (section 177A) and a modified meaning of tax benefit (from section 177C) to define a DPT tax benefit pursuant to section 177J(1). In a similar manner to the multinational avoidance rule, the purpose of entering the scheme to obtain the DPT tax benefit need only be the principle purpose. Section 177J(2) says that this purpose is determined by reference to the factors in section 177D(2), as well as:

(b) without limiting subsection 177D(2), the extent to which non-tax financial benefits that are quantifiable have resulted, will result, or may reasonably be expected to result, from the scheme;

(c) the result in relation to the operation of any foreign law relating to taxation that (but for this Part) would be achieved by the scheme;

(d) the amount of the tax benefit mentioned in paragraph (1)(b).

Where there is a scheme that produces a DPT tax benefit and the relevant entity entered the scheme with the principle purpose of obtaining that DPT tax benefit, section 177N says that the Commissioner cannot make a determination under section 177F to simply cancel the DPT tax benefit. Section 177N determines that section 177P will impose a penalty instead. This penalty is a tax imposed at a rate determined by Parliament (currently 40 per cent) on the DPT base amount for one DPT tax benefit or the sum of the DPT base amounts if there is more than one DPT tax benefit. The DPT base amount in relation to a DPT tax benefit is defined in section 177P(2) as the DPT tax benefit if it is of the type mentioned in paragraphs 177C(1)(a), (b), (ba) or (bc). Otherwise, the amount of the DPT tax benefit is the DPT base amount divided by the standard corporate tax rate.

Sections 177Q and 177R are of an administrative nature and deal with a **general interest charge** or a **shortfall interest charge** payable on unpaid diverted profits tax and when a shortfall interest charge is payable respectively. We discussed these charges in general terms earlier in this chapter.

Taken in combination, the multinational anti-avoidance rule and the diverted profit tax provide a comprehensive framework to prevent multinational corporations from avoiding tax in Australia. Both rules are in their infancy with little, if any, case law associated with them. Consequently, whether either of these rules is effective in achieving its intended purpose remains to be seen. Example 14.8 discusses diverted profits tax.

EXAMPLE 14.8

Diverted profits tax

Goople Australia Pty Ltd, is an Australian resident private company that sells health products to Australian customers. It is part of the Goople group, a multinational conglomerate whose parent, Goople Inc, is a United States resident company with global income over $1 billion. Goople Australia Pty Ltd sells significant amounts of products but it pays very large amounts in royalties and licence fees to Goople Holdings Pty Ltd, a company based in Ireland that is also part of the Goople group, for the rights to the Goople name, brand and intellectual property. Ireland is a tax haven and Goople Holdings does not conduct any business, has no staff and has no identifiable business premises. As a result of paying this licence fee, Goople Australia Pty Ltd makes very little profit and pays very little tax in Australia.

Would Goople Australia Pty Ltd be subject to the diverted profits tax?

Goople Australia Pty Ltd is a significant global entity in accordance with section 960-555 since it is a member of a consolidated group with a parent company residing in the United States that has global income over $1 billion. It has entered a scheme in accordance with section 177A(1) with Goople Holdings to pay royalties on the sale of the Goople group's products and licence fees for the rights to use the Goople name etc. This scheme created a DPT tax benefit in accordance with sections 177C and 177J since Goople Australia Pty Ltd has deductions that would not be available if it were not for the scheme.

The alternate hypothesis suggests that if it were not for the scheme, Goople Australia Pty Ltd would pay royalties and fees at a substantially reduced rate to the parent company in the United States. The reduced rate would arise since the United States and Australia have similar tax laws and use similar rates, meaning that the group would pay more tax overall. Alternatively, a DPT tax benefit arises in accordance with section 177J since the tax liability of a foreign entity is reduced under the operation of a foreign law as a result of the scheme. A global examination of the factors in section 177D(2) would suggest that the scheme was entered into for the principal purpose of obtaining that DPT tax benefit. Therefore, it is arguable that Part IVA applies to the scheme so that Goople Australia Pty Ltd will have to pay tax at a rate of 40 per cent on the relevant DPT base amounts in accordance with section 177P.

14.7 Ethical consequences of evasion and avoidance

LEARNING OBJECTIVE 14.7 Understand the ethical consequences of tax avoidance and evasion, particularly for tax advisers.

There are a range of situations where scope might arise for a tax adviser to be tempted to take advantage of the grey area between tax avoidance and tax planning and encourage a client to enter a tax avoidance scheme. Tax evasion can be conducted in a similar fashion by the use of schemes and actions to hide income.

Advisers and their clients are regularly faced with identifying what constitutes an abuse of the law compared to its appropriate use. For example, taxpayers who operate in a competitive business context may be tempted to cross the line where a tax saving can be a competitive advantage. In these and other circumstances, advisors may feel pressured to promote schemes or provide advice that might constitute tax avoidance. Indeed, such conflicts are common since advisors have a duty to advise their clients about the operation of the tax system while also having a duty to act ethically and responsibly as we discussed at length in the first chapter of this text.

The codes of conduct that professionals are expected to follow without exception are an excellent guide to assist tax advisers to guide their actions and those of their clients. It will be recalled from an early chapter that APES 110 *Code of Ethics for Professional Accountants*, which is applicable for members of CPA Australia and Chartered Accountants Australia and New Zealand, contains an overarching principle that professional accountants are always to act in the public interest. This not only means not acting in their own interest, but also not acting in the sole interests of the client. This principle is also reflected in the Code of Professional Conduct contained in the *Tax Agent Services Act 2009* (Cth) which we discussed in an earlier chapter.

The range of penalties that might apply in the event of tax advisers breaching the various ethical codes which apply to their professions is broad and can include significant monetary penalties and even deregistration (revisit an earlier chapter to refresh your memory on the full breadth of the possible penalties). There are also a number of severe legal penalties that can be applied to tax practitioners implicated in tax avoidance and evasion. We outline some of these as follows.

14.7.1 Promoter penalty regime

Division 290 of Schedule 1 of the TAA53 allows the Commissioner to apply to the Federal Court for civil penalties and injunctions against promoters of *tax exploitation schemes*. Specifically, section 290-50(1) provides that 'an entity must not engage in conduct that results in that or another entity being a promoter of a tax exploitation scheme'. Breach of the provision can result in a civil penalty. The maximum amount of the penalty is set out in section 290-50(4) as the greater of:

(a) 5000 penalty units (for an individual) or 25 000 penalty units (for a body corporate); and
(b) twice the consideration received or receivable (directly or indirectly) by the entity and associates of the entity in respect of the scheme.

In essence, a *tax exploitation scheme* is a scheme entered into for the sole or dominant purpose of obtaining a tax advantage which it is not reasonably arguable is available at law. See Section 290-65.

For the purposes of these provisions a *promoter* is defined in section 290-60 as follows.

290-60 Meaning of *promoter*

(1) An entity is a *promoter* of a tax exploitation scheme if:
(2) However, an entity is not a *promoter* of a tax exploitation scheme merely because the entity provides advice about the scheme.
  (a) the entity markets the scheme or otherwise encourages the growth of the scheme or interest in it; and
  (b) the entity or an associate of the entity receives (directly or indirectly) consideration in respect of that marketing or encouragement; and
  (c) having regard to all relevant matters, it is reasonable to conclude that the entity has had a substantial role in respect of that marketing or encouragement.

For a good example of a case discussing and applying the provisions see *FCT v Ludekens* [2013] FCAFC 100. See also *Commissioner of Taxation v Bogiatto (No 2)* [2021] FCA 98 — a case in which a record penalty was imposed for breach of the promoter penalty provisions.

Ethics, tax avoidance and evasion

A client approaches you with a proposal to assist in setting up and promoting a business of supplying COVID-19 rapid antigen tests (RATs) to a charity in a poor African nation. Your advice is sought to come up with a way to obtain the maximum tax benefit for donor investors to ensure the best prospect of attracting the maximum amount of funds for buying and supplying the RATs. You feel strongly about trying to help those less fortunate during the pandemic and come up with the following plan, in which you actively encourage all your other clients to invest.

Donor investors would buy bulk lots of 20 RATs, priced at a total of $2000 per lot. However, they would only pay 5 per cent of the purchase price immediately. The balance was payable in 50 years time, with a nominal interest rate of 0.1 per cent per annum paid in advance. An invoice for the full cost of the RATs allowed the donor investors to claim a tax deduction for the full $2000 per lot of RATs, despite having paid only a fraction of that amount up front.

You also agree to accept payment for a small percentage of the profits from the business as payment for your assistance and advice.

Is there anything ethically or legally wrong with your involvement in this arrangement?

The answer is yes. Although you may have been motivated by honourable intentions, this arrangement clearly breaches your overarching ethical obligations to act in the public interest as a tax adviser. This could see penalties imposed on you by your relevant professional accounting body and/or the Tax Practitioners' Board. You have also likely breached the promoter penalty provisions by promoting what constitutes a tax exploitation scheme. This scenario is loosely based on a real example of a scheme found to be in breach of the promoter penalty provisions involving the provisions of AIDS medicine kits to a Kenyan charity. See *FCT v Arnold (No 2)* [2015] FCA 34.

14.7.2 *Crime (Taxation Offences) Act 1980* (Cth)

The *Crime (Taxation Offences) Act 1980* (Cth) (CTOA) was introduced to deal with serious evasion schemes of the 1970s known as the Bottom of the Harbour schemes. The schemes involved accountants and lawyers advising their corporate clients to strip company assets, shifting them to another entity before letting the stripped company to 'sink' (meaning, to be wound up). In so doing, the ATO and other unsecured creditors were left unable to recover debts. The scheme is arguably Australia's biggest corporate tax avoidance scandal. As such, the initial aim of the *CTOA* was to bolster the criminal penalties available in cases of similar tax avoidance schemes in which companies or trusts are stripped of their assets in order to avoid having sufficient funds available to pay tax liabilities of the relevant company or trust.

Specifically, section 5 provides that where a person enters into an arrangement or transaction with the intention of securing, either generally or for a limited period, that a company or trustee will be unable, or will be likely to be unable, having regard to other debts of the company or trustee, to pay income tax payable (or payable in future) by the company or trustee, the person commits an offence.

The maximum penalty is imprisonment for 10 years or 1000 penalty units, or both.

Tax advisers should be aware that section 6 extends the same potential penalties for aiding, abetting, counselling or procuring another person to enter into such a tax avoidance arrangement. However, to constitute an offence, the assistance must be provided 'knowing or believing' that the arrangement or transaction is being entered into by the other person with the intention of avoiding tax as defined in the Act.

SUMMARY

14.1 Describe key aspects of our tax administration system.

The Australian tax administration system supports the principle of self-assessment. Notwithstanding, the ATO has significant powers, including to amend assessments and to gather information from taxpayers and others to ensure the correct amount of tax is collected. Taxpayers also have responsibilities to ensure adequate record-keeping and substantiation of any tax calculations. Taxpayers also have rights under the Australian tax administration system to lodge objections and appeals. There are also significant penalties for tax shortfalls. Technology is increasingly playing a significant role in tax administration in Australia.

14.2 Explain the difference between tax avoidance and tax evasion.

Tax evasion is the deliberate and fraudulent misstatement of one's tax affairs and is an illegal activity. Tax avoidance involves compliance with tax laws, but in a manner not intended by the Acts due to some omission, error or ambiguity or due to a taxpayer arranging their affairs to take advantage of a provision of the Income Tax Acts.

14.3 Describe the nature of shams and explain the action that should be taken against them.

A sham is a legally ineffective arrangement which does not achieve what was intended due to some deficiency in acts undertaken and documents prepared. It is therefore an inherently worthless transaction since it does not achieve its intended purpose and it does not need any action to be taken against it.

14.4 Explain the operation of Australia's specific anti-avoidance rules.

Specific anti-avoidance rules operate to target separate and distinct forms of tax avoidance that are already in use by taxpayers. Examples include the transfer pricing rules, thin capitalisation rules, non-commercial loss rules, the personal services income rules and rules to deem certain payments and loans forgiven that a company makes to shareholders and their associates. While Division 6AA rates for minors are not a specific anti-avoidance rule, these rates create a disincentive to distribute from trusts to minors in certain circumstances.

14.5 Explain the operation of Australia's general anti-avoidance rule.

Australia's general anti-avoidance rule is contained in Part IVA of the ITAA36. It requires a scheme that is entered into for the dominant purpose of obtaining a tax benefit. The Commissioner has the power to cancel tax benefits associated with tax avoidance schemes.

14.6 Explain the operation of Australia's multinational anti-avoidance rule and diverted profits tax.

The multinational anti-avoidance rule operates to deny significant global entities tax benefits associated with schemes entered into with the principal purpose of obtaining that tax benefit by limiting the entity's presence in Australia by exploiting the definition of permanent establishment. The diverted profits tax imposes a penalty tax on significant global entities that obtain DPT tax benefits from schemes that divert profits out of Australia where the principal purpose of entering the scheme was to obtain the DPT tax benefit. Both are targeted anti-avoidance rules that lie within Part IVA of the ITAA36.

14.7 Understand the ethical consequences of tax avoidance and evasion, particularly for tax advisers.

In advising clients in situations where scope might arise for an opportunity to take advantage of the grey area between tax avoidance and tax planning and encourage a client to enter a tax avoidance scheme, tax advisers must be especially vigilant to ensure they comply with their ethical and legal obligations. Prime among these are obligations under the APESB and TASA codes of ethics and professional conduct. Advisers also need to be aware of the legal penalties that can apply if they engage in promoting tax exploitation schemes and potential criminal consequences for being involved in serious evasion schemes.

KEY TERMS

alternate hypothesis The course of action that a taxpayer would reasonably have undertaken if they did not enter the scheme. This can include doing nothing.

choice principle A legal principle embodied in section 177C(2) of the ITAA36 which states that a tax benefit has not been obtained in connection to a scheme where the reduction in tax has arisen through the operation of a choice or election etc., expressly provided for in the Income Tax Acts.

diverted profits tax (DPT) An amendment to the Part IVA general anti-avoidance rule targeting multinationals that try to divert profits away from Australia to offshore jurisdictions where the tax rates are lower. Also known as the Google tax.

dominant purpose Ascertaining whether a scheme is entered into for tax avoidance reasons.

ethics A field often attributed to philosophy that is concerned with making appropriate decisions and engaging in appropriate conduct.

general anti-avoidance rules Provisions within Part IVA of the income tax Acts that can prevent tax avoidance from schemes that have not yet been invented or considered by taxpayers or are otherwise not targeted by specific anti-avoidance rules.

general interest charge Charged by the ATO on overdue tax payments at rates significantly higher than market rates to discourage taxpayers using the tax system as a source of finance.

Google tax See diverted profits tax (DPT).

multinational anti-avoidance rule An amendment to the Part IVA general anti-avoidance rule targeting multinationals that try to exploit the meaning of 'permanent establishment' in Double Taxation Agreements to limit their presence in Australia, thereby avoiding tax on transactions conducted here.

scheme Any agreement, arrangement, understanding, promise or undertaking, whether express or implied and whether or not enforceable, or intended to be enforceable, by legal proceedings.

sham A legally ineffective arrangement that does not achieve what was intended due to some deficiency in acts undertaken and documents prepared.

shortfall interest charge Charged by the ATO when further tax is payable (i.e. a shortfall) due to an amended tax assessment issued to the taxpayer. The interest rate is lower than the rate used to calculate general interest charge since taxpayers are not attempting to use the ATO as a source of finance and are only made aware of the shortfall once they have received the amended assessment.

specific anti-avoidance rules Provisions in the income tax Acts that target specific tax avoidance schemes that are currently being entered into by taxpayers.

tax avoidance Reducing one's tax liability by being technically compliant with the law, but not in a manner that the law intended due to an error, omission or ambiguity in it. This is sometimes referred to as being compliant with the letter of the law, but not its spirit or purpose. Since it involves technical compliance with the income tax Acts (except for Part IVA), it is not criminal.

tax evasion Reducing one's tax liability by being dishonest about one's tax affairs. It is illegal behaviour and can lead to criminal prosecution.

tax planning Reducing one's tax liability by taking advantage of and making choices that the Acts provide for or that are otherwise acceptable to the courts and broader society.

QUESTIONS

14.1 What is the difference between tax avoidance, tax evasion and tax planning?

14.2 What is the difference between a specific anti-avoidance rule and a general anti-avoidance rule? Why is a general anti-avoidance rule useful in preventing tax avoidance?

14.3 What is required for Part IVA to apply?

14.4 How is scheme defined in Part IVA of the ITAA36? Cite the relevant section of the Act.

14.5 What can constitute a tax benefit? Cite the relevant section of the Act.

14.6 What factors are relevant in determining whether the taxpayer had a dominant purpose in entering the scheme to obtain the tax benefit? Cite the relevant section of the Act.

14.7 What is the overarching ethical responsibility that tax professionals should bear in mind when faced with ethical dilemmas concerning activities that might constitute tax avoidance?

14.8 What are the possible consequences for a tax professional involved in promoting a tax minimisation scheme?

14.9 What are some of the main ways the tax office uses technology to assist it in carrying out its tax administration functions?

14.10 How does the tax office use data matching to monitor tax compliance? Can you give some examples of the types of third party data the tax office can use to verify taxpayer information?

PROBLEMS

14.11 Jimmy Opaque claims that he has been advised by 'a person in the know' at his local sporting club that he should put his business into a trust and then can reduce his income by spreading it among his family, while retaining full control of the business and his income. Jimmy's advisor has told him that all he has to do is obtain a pre-printed trust deed (which the advisor can provide) and fill in the blank spaces, showing that he is the trustee of his business and providing him with discretionary power to distribute the business income to his family as beneficiaries. 'It is as easy as that,' says the excited Jimmy.

Comment on the advice that Jimmy received.

14.12 Achmad has just received an amended notice of assessment from the ATO. The amendment has increased his tax liability by disallowing certain tax deductions he had previously claimed and been allowed. Achmad is unhappy and wishes to contest the amended assessment. He comes to you for advice. Advise Achmad on his objection options. In your answer, make sure you address the requirements and process for lodging a valid objection and the time he has to lodge his objection.

14.13 Dave and Darren are directors of X Pty Ltd which operated a very profitable engineering business providing services to the mining industry. In anticipation of a considerable tax bill, Dave and Darren decided to transfer the assets of X Pty Ltd to a shelf company, Y Pty Ltd, and continue the business as usual as directors of Y Pty Ltd. They also arranged for Max and Marnie to become directors of X Pty Ltd paying them $1000 each as an inducement to do so, replacing Dave and Darren as directors. After this arrangement was entered into, X Pty Ltd was assessed for $500 000 in income tax, but Max and Marnie were not aware of this. Later, they were surprised when officers from the Australian Tax Office and the Australian Federal Police began contacting them about the company's outstanding tax bill at which time they discovered that X Pty Ltd had no assets to pay the debt.

What type of tax reduction strategy is involved in this arrangement? Explain your reasoning. Do you believe that this strategy is acceptable? Explain why or why not.

14.14 Two siblings decided to invest in the musical production of *Dogs* which was to run for several performances in Melbourne and Sydney with the expectation that it would be very successful. The proposed investment entailed each sibling contributing $300 000 to a partnership in charge of the production. $50 000 would be a cash contribution while the remaining $250 000 would be financed via a bank with the loan agreement stipulating that the bank would only receive income derived from the production as repayment. There was a total of 10 investors (including the two siblings) who contributed this way with the partnership recording $3 000 000 in total contribution, but only receiving $500 000 to pay for the production.

Each sibling claimed income tax deductions of $300 000 for their share of the partnership's loss compared to actual expenditure of $50 000 each.

Assuming the arrangement is not a sham, would the arrangement constitute tax avoidance? Explain your reasoning with reference to the elements of Part IVA showing whether or not its requirements for a scheme, tax benefit and dominant purpose have been satisfied.

14.15 Chemical Ltd is a manufacturer of fertilisers for the agricultural industry. This activity is capital intensive having required the purchase and maintenance of costly plant and equipment. To improve cash flows, Chemical Ltd sold a plant to a finance company for $100 million and immediately leased it back to continue operations for a period of 10 years. The lease agreement allowed Chemical Ltd to repurchase the plant back from the finance company for $100 million plus interest calculated at market rates over the lease period. Chemical Ltd claimed income tax deductions for the lease payments made each year.

Assuming the arrangement is not a sham, would Chemical Ltd's arrangement constitute tax avoidance? Explain your reasoning with reference to the elements of Part IVA showing whether or not its requirements for a scheme, tax benefit and dominant purpose have been satisfied.

14.16 Antonietta is a one of your tax adviser colleagues. She has just received a notice from the tax office advising that they require her to supply a long list of information concerning advice she has provided to a number of clients. She has also been advised that she will be required to attend an interview to answer a series of questions pertaining to this advice. What are Antonietta's rights in this situation? In your answer, explain to her the powers of the tax office to obtain access to information from tax advisers.

14.17 What are the record-keeping requirements for cryptocurrency transactions? Explain how you could use the 'Ask Alex' function on the ATO website to find the answer to this question.

14.18 Peter is a tax advisor. In examining the detailed wording of certain provisions of the income tax Acts, he realises that a particular provision omits a critical word enabling taxpayers to reduce their tax by deferring it indefinitely. Since Peter has many clients who could potentially take advantage of this, he begins to develop ways to promote this among his clients. He also discusses this with his close friend, James, who is a financial planner. James has many more clients who could take advantage of this. Peter and James develop a plan where James would promote the plan and charge $500 for every client that enters it with 50 per cent of that fee being paid to Peter. As knowledge of the plan becomes widespread, many clients come to Peter with the intention of engaging in it to reduce their tax.

Should Peter have promoted his new tax reduction method in the manner that he did? What ethical considerations should he have considered and how might they have impacted on his decision?

ACKNOWLEDGEMENTS

Figure 14.1: © Australian Taxation Office
Tables 14.2, 14.4, 14.5: © Australian Taxation Office
Example 14.1: © Australian Taxation Office
Extracts: © Federal Register of Legislation. Licensed under CC BY 4.0.
Extracts: © Australian Taxation Office
Extract: © UK Court of Appeal. Licensed under OGL v3.0.
Extract: © Cambridge University Press

INDEX